MARY LOU BURTON

BRIDAL RESOURCE GUIDE

THE AREA'S MOST COMPREHENSIVE GUIDE TO WEDDING-RELATED SERVICES

© Woodstock Photography • page 525

Bravo!® Publications, Inc.
P.O. Box 1647
Lake Oswego, Oregon 97035
(503) 675-1380, (800) 988-9887; Fax (503) 675-1204
E-mail: bravo7165@aol.com

Visit our Web sites:
www.bravowedding.com & www.bravoevent.com

This resource guide is comprised of paid advertisements. Although advertisers must meet a quality level of standards to be featured in this guide, Bravo! Publications, Inc. cannot and does not guarantee or take responsibility for services provided by said advertisers. No affiliation exists between Bravo! Publications, Inc. and any advertiser featured. Every reasonable effort has been made to provide the most accurate and up-to-date information.

ISBN 1-884471-24-2

TABLE OF CONTENTS

Consultants continued...

Banquet & Reception Sites continued...

TABLE OF CONTENTS

Caterers & Ice Carvings continued...

Honeymoon, Travel & Accommodations continued...

Musicians & Vocalists continued...

TABLE OF CONTENTS

ACKNOWLEDGEMENTS

This Guide would not have been possible without the hard work, dedication, and endless hours from the following people:

Account Managers
Carinne McCulloch
Anne Ryan

Public Relations & Marketing
Helen Kern
Amy Waetjen

Copy Writing & Layout Production
Amy Waetjen

Production Support
Amy Burton

Print Production
Kieley Malueg
Publications Plus

Prepress & Printing
NuWay Printing
Portland, Oregon

Page one
Photograph provided by:
© Woodstock Photography, See page 525

Cover Design
Roz Pasion, *Roz & Co.*

Cover photographs provided by:
top left: "bride with bouquet"
© James Loomis Photography, See page 499

top right: "wedding cake"
© Curtis Rhodes Wedding Photography

middle: "groom and groomsmen"
© Woodstock Photography, See page 525

lower right: "church"
© Strong Photography, See page 523

bottom: "buffet table"
Capers Cafe & Catering Co., See page 303
© Joseph Photographer, See page 501

Spine photograph provided by:
"flower girl by pew"
© Mount Burns Photography, See page 509

Back cover photographs provided by:
top: "cello"
© Eleanor Glorioso Photographer, See page 493

middle: "flower girl and ring bearer"
© Moments In Time Photography, See page 507

bottom: "bouquet"
© red door studio, See page 520

Front row: *Tracy Martin, Amy Waetjen, Anne Ryan, Quinn Ryan, Jake Ryan, Alex Burton*
Back row: *Carinne McCulloch, Hailey McCulloch, Mary Lou Burton, Will Burton, Helen Kern, Nick Burton, Amy Burton*
© 1999 Moments In Time

Mary Lou Burton

Mary Lou began Bravo! Publications, Inc. in 1989 after planning her own wedding for 550 Italian relatives. On the honeymoon, she and husband, John, realized the hundreds of hours they'd spent researching businesses could be helpful for other brides and grooms doing the same research. Mary Lou and Marion Clifton researched and created the first *Bravo! Bridal Resource Guide* in 1990. In 1994 an additional guide using the same concept and format was created specifically for meeting and event planners — *Bravo! Event Resource Guide*.

Mary Lou graduated from the University of Portland in 1985, with a bachelor's degree in communications management. She has appeared as a guest speaker for Nordstrom and Meier & Frank, as well as appearing on AM Northwest and other local broadcasts. She has written and contributed to several national and local publications. Over the last nine years as Bravo! has grown, so has her family. Mary Lou enjoys volunteering to read and being room parent at Alex and Nick's school and trys to keep up daily with 2-1/2 year old, Will. Husband John and partner for over 10 years has been a constant source of inspiration and has always supported this idea from the very beginning with enthusiasm. It would still just be an idea without his positive "can do" attitude.

Anne Ryan

Anne joined the Bravo! Team in 1994 after planning her wedding. Her excitement and professionalism have brought energy and growth to Bravo! Anne has believed in the Bravo! concept and philosophy and has helped develop several products including the Bravo! Meeting & Event Planners' Trade Show. Anne is a native Oregonian. She is a graduate of University of Portland, with a bachelor's degree in liberal arts, with a minor in psychology, business and history. She and husband Scott keep busy with their three-year-old son, Jake, and 6-month-old daughter, Quinn.

Carinne McCulloch

Carinne worked in the recreation industry for several years and was a client of Bravo! She decided to make a move and Bravo! was fortunate to be the place that she chose. No project is ever impossible with Carinne's "can-do" attitude. Her enthusiasm and easy-going personality has contributed to Bravo's growth while maintaining quality. Carinne graduated from Oregon State University in 1991 with a bachelor's degree in both business and human performance. Carinne and her husband, Derek, are enjoying their new daughter Hailey, as well as maintaining their love for recreation.

Amy Waetjen

Amy joined Bravo! last year as our production manager. With such a small office we wear many hats, and Amy has been able to combine production with Web design and maintenance, graphic design, marketing, plus a variety of other tasks. Amy graduated from Valparaiso University in Indiana with a bachelor's degree in communication. She grew up in Eugene and enjoys running, hiking, snowboarding and writing.

Amy Burton

Amy joined Bravo! this year helping out with production, office management and customer service. She grew up in Indiana and graduated with a BA degree in sports management from Indiana University. Amy and her boyfriend David resided in Portland three years ago to become more involved in the outdoor lifestyle. She loves being outside and enjoys camping, climbing, mountain biking, hiking, running, ultimate Frisbee and her dog Spire.

Tracy Martin

Tracy has worked with Bravo! for three years coordinating and planning the Bravo! Meeting & Event Planners' Trade Show. Tracy comes to us with six years experience from the planning and decorating side of Bravo! She and her husband, Darin, are expecting their first child this November. They enjoy gardening, camping, fishing and spending time with their families.

Helen Kern

Helen, Mary Lou's mother, joined Bravo! last year as well. She is in charge of human relations, always bringing some tasty treat or beautiful flowers to the office. She is our public relations ambassador and helps out with many projects around the office. Her words of wisdom inspire us each day! Helen is the mother of eight children — and her most important accomplishment of all is the faith and hope she gave to all of her children.

Kieley Malueg, Publications Plus

Kieley has worked with Bravo! Publications for four years managing publication print production. She's a Portland native and 1989 graduate of the University of Oregon. Her experience includes marketing, design and print production in the recreation and tourism industries. Her attention to detail and professional expertise has enhanced Bravo!'s efforts to continue to produce affordable, high-quality, user-friendly publications. She and husband Ken have a daughter, Katie, 2-1/2, and new son Timothy, 6 months.

BRAVO! PUBLICATIONS, INC. IS A WINNER OF THE 1999

families in good company

AWARD FOR PROVIDING A FAMILY-FRIENDLY WORK ENVIRONMENT

Spread The Word!

We need your help. To continue to supply this Guide we rely on you, the reader, to let the businesses and services in this book know that you heard about them through the *Bravo! Bridal Resource Guide*. Our featured businesses will recognize the Bravo! name.

Pass it on to a friend. Before they walk away with *your* copy, let them know they can fill out the order form on page 24 to receive their own copy.

The Bravo! Difference

- **Location... Location... Location!**
  This Guide will help you find the perfect spot for your ceremony or reception, whether at an intimate garden setting or a downtown glamorous ballroom—it's all right at your fingertips.
- **All the important details about the sites**
  From cost and terms to what's included and what's extra, the *Bravo! Bridal Resource Guide* includes descriptions of each facility for easier selection based on what you need. By the time you call a facility, you're thoroughly informed.
- **The ultimate tool for brides and grooms**
  From listings of over 450 ceremony and banquet sites to exceptional caterers, decorators, rental equipment, and entertainment. You'll find everything for your upcoming wedding in this one resource guide.
- **This is a book you will rely on**
  Everything has been thoroughly researched to ensure that you have the most current information, updated annually. Everyone we've included is outstanding!

Take A Look At Our Web Site
www.bravowedding.com

If you like our guide... you'll love our Web pages

- **Search by area, capacity, and type of service**
  You'll be able to search our site for the type of product or service you need. Find all downtown facilities that will accommodate more than 500 guests or a gift basket company that will deliver to Beaverton.
- **We're putting the Guide online**
  Every client in the book is listed on our Web site with location, phone number, contact and type of business or service. We are in the process of activating many client pages online as well, with the same easy-to-read format.
- **Links to event services and facilities**
  Many of our client pages have direct links to their home pages with more details and photos of their facility or service. You can get more detailed information or communicate with many of these services easily online or through e-mail.
- **Guest book and order form**
  We'd love to hear from you. Sign-in to our guest book and let us know what you like about the Bravo! products or services. We love suggestions of what we could do better. You can order any of our products online.

If You Love The Bravo! Bridal Resource Guide, Wait Until You Browse Our Bravo! Bridal Web Site!

Check out the Bravo! Publications Web sites at:
www.bravowedding.com ***and*** www.bravoevent.com

The Bravo! Web site is:

- **Easy to use!**
- Features all the **detailed information** you're used to seeing in your Bravo! Bridal Resource Guide!
- Has its own **"search engine"** so you can find things easily by category or location!
- Features **color photographs**!
- Has a comprehensive **Calendar of Events** that will let you know when and where the next bridal shows will be taking place.

The Bravo! Wedding and Event Web sites will be…
growing and changing weekly, so be sure to browse them often so you can see what's new!

ADD BRAVO! TO YOUR ROLODEX!

(Just cut out the card below and staple or slip it into your Rolodex.)

Bravo! Publications, Inc.
P.O. Box 1647
Lake Oswego, OR 97035
Phone: (503) 675-1380; **Toll-free:** (800) 988-9887
Fax: (503) 675-1204
E-mail: bravo7165@aol.com
Web sites: www.bravowedding.com
www.bravoevent.com

BRAVO!® RESOURCE GUIDES

When You Want Information, Not Glossy Ads—You Want Bravo!

Bravo!® Publications is proud to offer four regional resource guides for planning weddings, meetings, and events. Each of the guides featured on this and the following page is filled with important information and details about the area's finest businesses and services providers, and is presented in easy-to-read, résumé style formats, alphabetically, by category. Designed to be user-friendly, each of these guides truly are your planning *Resource*!

Portland • Vancouver • Salem
and outlying areas

Bravo!® Bridal Resource Guide

Churches, Chapels, Banquet & Reception Sites, Caterers, Florists, Photographers, Videographers, Invitations, Bridal Attire, Tuxedo Rentals, Bridal Registry, and more...

The 2000 Edition features 624 pages of easy-to-read, resumé-style write-ups on area businesses and service providers, listings of Banquet and Reception Sites, how-to's, check lists, and all the helpful hints!

Suggested Retail: $9.95

Portland • Vancouver • Salem
and outlying areas

Bravo!® Event Resource Guide

Venues, Attractions & Activities, Accommodations, Audience Participation, Gifts & Promotional Items, Food & Beverage, Rental Services, and more...

The 2000 Edition features 640 pages of easy-to-read, résumé-style write-ups on area businesses and service providers, listings of Banquet and Event Sites, how-to's, checklists, and all the helpful hints.

Suggested Retail: $8.95
Complimentary to pre-qualified Meeting and Event Planners.

Say You Saw It In Bravo!

Every business or service needs to track where their business is coming from. By letting them know you are using one of the *Bravo!® Resource Guides*, you not only ensure that Bravo!® will be available for meeting and event planners or brides in the future, but you also let the businesses or services know where their business is coming from.

TO ORDER CALL (800) 988-9887

Bravo!® *Organizers*

The step-by-step system to track every detail of your event.

Organizers feature:

- Detailed worksheets designed to double as contracts
- Time schedules, checklists and calendars
- Detailed budget worksheets and "who pays for what forms
- "To Do" forms and "Delegating Duties" lists

Bravo!*® *Wedding Organizer
Suggested Retail: $24.95

Bar/Bat Mitzvah Organizer
Suggested Retail: $22.95

Greater Puget Sound
Bravo!® *Bridal Resource Guide*

Churches, Chapels, Banquet & Reception Sites, Caterers, Florists, Photographers, Videographers, Invitations, Bridal Attire, Tuxedo Rentals, Bridal Registry, Favors, Accessories, Consultants and more...

The 2000 Edition features 544 pages of easy-to-read, resumé-style write-ups on area businesses and service providers, listings of Banquet and Reception Sites, how-to's, check lists, and all the helpful hints!

Suggested Retail: $9.95

Greater Puget Sound
Bravo!® *Event Resource Guide*

Venues, Attractions & Activities, Accommodations, Audience Participation, Corporate Gifts & Awards, Food & Beverage Services, and more...

The 2000 Edition features 608 pages of easy-to-read, résumé-style write-ups on area businesses and service providers, listings of Banquet and Event Sites, how-to's, checklists, and all the helpful hints.

Suggested Retail: $8.95
Complimentary to pre-qualified Meeting and Event Planners.

TO ORDER CALL (800) 988-9887

If you are planning a wedding, getting married or know someone who is, order what every bride needs to plan a perfect wedding!

The Bravo! Wedding Organizer & Bridal Resource Guide

❒ ***Bravo! Wedding Organizer*** $24.95

❒ ***Bravo! Bridal Resource Guide*** $9.95

Please select Bridal Guide edition:

❒ *Portland • Vancouver • Salem '00 Edition*

❒ *Puget Sound '00 Edition*

Shipping and handling additional—$3 per item $__________

TOTAL: $__________

METHOD OF PAYMENT:

❒ Check or money order enclosed ❒ Charge to: Visa or MasterCard

Name of card holder: ____________________

Account No: ____________________

Exp. Date: __________ Signature: ____________________

Please allow 7 to 10 days for delivery

Name: ____________________

Address: ____________________ **Mail Stop:** __________

City: ____________________ **State:** __________ **Zip:** __________

Phone: __________ **Fax:** __________ **E-mail:** __________

Wedding date: ____________________

Send order to: **Bravo! Publications, Inc.**
P.O. Box 1647 • Lake Oswego, OR 97035
(503) 675-1380, (800) 988-9887; Fax (503) 675-1204; E-mail: bravo7165@aol.com
Web sites: www.bravowedding.com & www.bravoevent.com

From the rehearsal to the wedding, reception, and honeymoon, these special events should be fun, memorable, and perfect. In other words, the events that people remember for years to come are the events that have been planned down to the last detail. That's exactly what this book is about.

It comes from a real-life need—and a real-life situation. In 1988 Mary Lou Burton had a wedding and a reception for 500 Italian relatives. In the months leading up to the wedding, she learned enough through experience to write a book. So the week after the honeymoon, she sat down with her friend, Marion Clifton, and planned the first *Portland–Vancouver Bridal Guide*. Now in its ninth year, this book has become a best seller—the largest, most complete bridal, event, and party resource guide in the Pacific Northwest.

The goal of the *Bravo!® Bridal Resource Guide* is to help brides and event planners like yourself find the facilities, caterers, florists, bakers, photographers, musicians, and other specialty services best able to fit their precise needs. Before any business is listed in this guide, it's screened to make sure the information is reliable, descriptive, and factual. It's then organized in clear and detailed descriptions and easy-to-read formats that allow you to quickly and easily make apple-to-apple comparisons of similar services.

This edition has grown to include over 450 ceremony, reception, and event sites in the Portland, Vancouver, and Salem areas, by location and capacity. Hundreds of additional business and service listings are at your fingertips, saving you countless hours of research time. Unlike other guides that simply compile advertisements and photographs, we have tried to create a bridal and event resource guide that's filled with truly useful information. We've even included pages of helpful hints that help you check references, protect deposits, secure dates, decorate inexpensively, and much more.

The *Bravo!® Bridal Resource Guide* is designed to fit in most handbags. It's easy to carry with you and includes spaces for notes. That's why so many brides call it their "Bridal Bible." And the free gifts and discounts offered by many of the companies will more than pay for the cost of the book as you use it in planning your big event!

HOW TO USE THIS BOOK

Congratulations! You've just purchased the most complete wedding, party, and event planning resource in the Pacific Northwest. Before you start, here are some tips on how to use it to your best advantage.

DISCOVER YOUR OPTIONS

Over 500 businesses, services, and resources are listed in this book. It provides detailed information about companies that can help you plan everything from engagement to the honeymoon. Within these pages you'll find a variety of resources with descriptions, services, and policies listed in detail. You'll appreciate the wealth of knowledge and be amazed by the talents and services our area supports, including outstanding caterers and exquisite florists as well as special services like talented seamstresses and unique gift shops.

IT'S EASY TO FIND THE SERVICES YOU NEED

Each page is designed to read like the résumé of a company. It's up to you to select the services that meet your needs and requirements.

As you explore your options, be sure to view samples, ask questions, get written estimates, and take notes. Make sure you feel absolutely comfortable that the companies you select will be able to provide the services or deliver the merchandise you're requesting. If you have any doubts, go to the next business on your list.

Remember, you're the customer. Use this book to help you create exactly the kind of wedding, party, or special event you've always dreamed of having!

IT'S EASY TO COMPARE THE SERVICES YOU FIND

As you start working your way through this book, you'll find it's filled with key information organized in a consistent format that allows you to compare and reference the various services easily.

For example, if you've invited 500 guests to your reception, you'll find only a few facilities that can accommodate that large of a group. That quickly narrows down the number of phone calls you'll need to make. In the *Bravo!® Bridal Resource Guide*'s "Rehearsal, Banquet & Reception Sites" section on pages 69 to 214, you'll find capacity listed first.

All the basic facts are listed at the top of each page, including company name, address, phone number, business hours, and contact person. The rest of the page describes the company's services, costs, deposits, reservation requirements, etc., and a special note. The Portland, Vancouver and Salem edition contains information on over 450 churches, chapels, parks, and reception sites. This puts the key facts you need right at your fingertips.

USE THE HELPFUL HINTS

Most sections start with a Helpful Hints page. They're there to save you time, money and headaches!

Professional planners with years of knowledge and experience in wedding planning and event coordination share their secrets on how to avoid the pitfalls and offer ways to make everything run smoothly. At one time or another, they've seen or tried it all! Some of the tips have come from brides who told us, "If only I had it to do over again, I would..." All the tips are worth reading. Some will apply, some won't. But by reading through the pages, you'll find creative and inspiring ideas that you can incorporate into your event—whatever the size or style!

USE IT AND ABUSE IT. THIS IS *YOUR* WORKBOOK!

This book is designed to fit in your purse or briefcase. Keep it handy so you can make phone calls on your coffee breaks, or book appointments during lunch. It lies flat for easy note-taking. Use Post-it notes as bookmarks. Tear pages out, doodle on it or scream into it! (Its special muffle-guard paper spares you any embarrassment.)

We know this book will make planning easier, leaving you more time to enter into the festivities surrounding your special event. So relax, and let the Bravo!® Bridal Resource Guide work for you!

The *Bravo!® Wedding Organizer* offers a more detailed workbook for organizing all the details of your wedding. More detailed information can be found on page 23.
The order form is located on page 24 of this guide.

Spread The Word!

We need your help. To continue to supply this Guide we rely on you, the reader, to let the businesses and services in this book know that you heard about them through the *Bravo! Bridal Resource Guide*. Our featured businesses will recognize the Bravo! name.

Pass it on to a friend. Before they walk away with *your* copy, let them know they can fill out the order form on page 24 to receive their own copy.

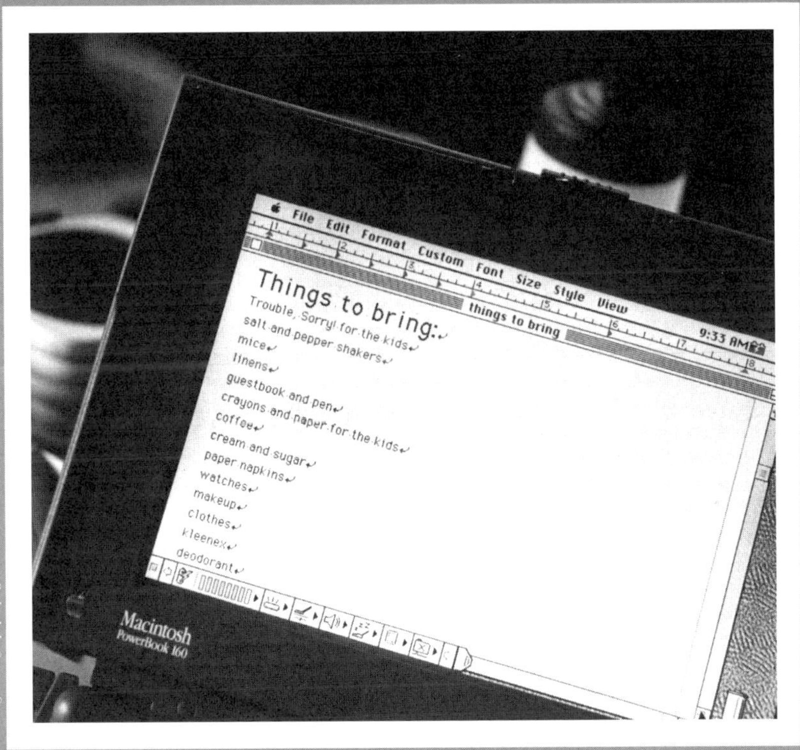

© Strong Photography • page 523

PLANNING YOUR WEDDING

Organizational Tools

•

Budgeting Tips

•

Schedules and Checklists

•

Etiquette

•

Blank Calendars

•

Start a Wedding Tradition

•

Wedding Day Survival Kit

SO NOW I'M ENGAGED—WHAT DO I DO NEXT?

He proposed—the day you've been waiting for has finally arrived! You have to tell your parents, his parents, call all your friends, call the church, get time off for the honeymoon, buy a wedding dress, find a caterer.... STOP!

First things first! Before all the hustle begins, do yourself a favor and **sit down with your fiancé and ask yourselves the following questions:**

- Are your families large or small?
- What is your budget?
- What style of wedding would you prefer to have—do you like intimate gatherings, large parties, or impromptu, unique events?
- Do you want a romantic theme or a formal affair?

Work together so that you both agree on the same things, and then commit your thoughts to paper so that you will have a plan.

ONCE YOU MAKE YOUR PLAN, STICK TO IT!

Everyone seems to become an expert on wedding planning when they find out you're engaged. You'll receive loads of unsolicited advice, and everyone will try to sway your thinking. Don't let anyone steer you away from what's important to you and your fiancé. If you do, your wedding will be a combination of everyone else's dreams but your own!

GET ORGANIZED... WITH THE *BRAVO!®* *WEDDING ORGANIZER*

Every event planner has his or her own way of getting organized. Over the years of publishing this book, we've encountered a lot of systems, both personally and professionally. From that experience and exposure, we have developed a special *Bravo!® Wedding Organizer* that incorporates the best of all the plans—along with some specially designed forms of our own. Everything you need is included:

- 40 detailed worksheets designed to double as contracts for reception site, caterer, photographer, florist, musicians, and more
- Time schedules and checklists
- "To Do" lists and forms
- Financial responsibilities guidelines
- "Delegating Duties" lists
- Guest and gift lists
- Business card holders
- Helpful Hints
- Pockets for swatches, samples, coupons, and receipts

In short, everything you need to keep you organized, on budget, and on schedule has been thought of and incorporated into the 14 tabbed sections of the *Bravo!® Wedding Organizer.* The tab headings serve as a reminder and makes it convenient to organize and store information. When it's time to deal with each element of the event, the information is there at your fingertips. Just three-hole punch and slip everything into your three-ring binder, and you're as organized as you can get.

To order your *Bravo® Wedding Organizer*
Send **$24.95** plus $3 for postage and handling to:

Bravo! Publications, Inc.
Bravo!® Wedding Organizer
P.O. Box 1647
Lake Oswego, Oregon 97035
(Please look for order form on page 24.)

A CONSULTANT CAN EASE THE STRESS

Hiring a consultant is a wise idea, especially if there is arguing between mother and daughter, between families, divorced parents and even attendants. This is an emotional time and if you can have an objective opinion of a consultant buffering between the two, it can sometimes ease the pressure. Money can be one of the biggest problems and obstacles. If a third party is involved, such as a consultant, they can collect the money without it being embarrassing. Many times these arguments result from lack of communication, emotional overload and misconceptions. The two parties just need to communicate; sometimes writing it down and having someone calm present to the other half is a good way to deal with it. They say you hurt the ones you love the most, the stresses of a wedding can truly test your relationships with family, friends and even your fiancé, remember to keep focused on what's important that day!

DELEGATE DUTIES

Every bride thinks, "If I don't do it, it won't get done the way I want it!" This may be true, but you'll soon realize you can't do it all and keep your sanity. You and your fiancé have figured out the plan, now delegate duties to family and friends. Everything can and will be done the way you want it if you give a clear description of what you need accomplished and when. Family and friends will enjoy knowing they helped contribute to making your special day a success!

RELAX AND ENJOY YOUR WEDDING DAY!

We suggest you get someone to coordinate all the details on the day of your wedding. Hire a professional or ask a trustworthy friend or family member who is not directly involved in the wedding party to oversee and coordinate delivery and setup of flowers, rental equipment, decorations, etc. Provide this person with a comprehensive list of everything he or she will need to keep an eye on, including the arrival of musicians and where they need to set up, where and when the formal photographs will be taken, phone numbers with a contact name for all the businesses providing services, etc. Your months of planning and coordination will pay off! You and your groom should be concerned and consumed only with the joy of the day and your love for each other!

If you don't read any other page from top to bottom, make sure to read this one. The following suggestions will ensure that your wedding turns out the way you want it while keeping your budget in line.

The most important advice we can offer both you AND your parents is **DO NOT GO INTO DEBT!** Weddings come in a variety of types and sizes; one is not necessarily better than the other based on the size or how much money you spend. Whatever you do, don't start your married life in debt.

BE REALISTIC WITH YOUR BUDGET

Your wedding budget should be handled like a business budget. If your boss said, "The budget for the Christmas party is $5,000," you would use only those services that would keep you within budget. The same is true for your wedding. Find the services that can accomplish what you want within the budget you've designated. Be realistic about your budget. If you have only $2,000 for your reception, it's unlikely you're going to be able to afford a full sit-down dinner for 300 guests, but a buffet with hot and cold hors d'oeuvres may work very well. Follow your budget allocations as closely as possible. This will eliminate financial stress.

SAMPLE BUDGET SHEET

Service	Budget	Actual	Deposit	Due	Balance	Due
Caterer	$2,500	$2,750	$500	5/5	$2,250	8/6
Florist						
Photos						

SETTING UP A BUDGET

It is recommended you set up a separate bank account for your wedding. This way funds can be tracked and kept separate from regular finances. Always pay businesses or services with a check or credit card for better records and tracking of expenses. Allocation of your budget depends on what is most important to the bride, groom and family contributing. Some spend more on music and entertainment or photography than others. The following is a percentage break-out of what the average dollar spent is:

- Reception—40%
- Honeymoon—15%
- Engagement rings—14%
- Photography—9%
- Miscellaneous (clergy fees, rehearsal dinner, attendants gifts, limos)—8%
- Bride's and groom's attire—5%
- Music—4%
- Flowers—3%
- Invitations—2%

WAYS TO SAVE MONEY

It's amazing how fast wedding costs can exceed the planned budget. If you find yourself in the position of needing to trim back to make everything fit within your budget, consider the following:

- **Avoid peak wedding days and seasons.** You can save money by having your wedding during the months considered to be "off-season" (January–May and late October–November) and on a Thursday or Friday evening or Sunday during the day. Because these times are in less demand, many businesses and services provide what you are looking for at reduced prices. You're also more likely to get your first choices!
- **Consider a daytime versus evening wedding.** Friday and Saturday weddings are becoming popular as well. Considering a Friday or Saturday wedding gives additional options for your wedding date. Food and alcohol costs are considerably less for daytime events than evening events. People don't drink as much if at all, and the food itself is far simpler and therefore less expensive.
- **Cut back on the guest list.** Guest lists can be the first thing to get out of control. Everyone wants to invite anybody and everybody they ever knew. Be firm with your figures of how many guests for each family. If that doesn't work, go back to the old formula of immediate family first, close personal friends second, etc., or have everyone review the list and cut back by 10%, 20%, or whatever is necessary to bring things back in line.
- **Determine what is most important to you** and put your money into that, but trim back on other areas. If fabulous flowers have always meant the most to you, spend a little less on your wedding gown or wear your mother's, sister's, or a friend's gown. If you've always wanted the most incredible dress in the world, cut back on the flower budget and have a DJ instead of a band.
- **Don't be afraid to shop around.** A little time on the phone could save you a lot of money. There can be a considerable difference in prices between different businesses for the same items or services. Just make sure that you are going to receive exactly the same item or level of service from the less-expensive company and that no short cuts are being taken at your expense.

If you're very clear about what budget you have to work with from the beginning, you'll find that the people in the wedding industry can be very helpful with all kinds of clever ideas on how to save money. Don't be afraid to ask for suggestions or ideas.

CONTRACTS

Contracts can be the most confusing and difficult part of planning a wedding. Keep in mind that this is a business arrangement. You're the customer and you are contracting with certain businesses to provide the services you request on a certain date, at a certain time, and within a certain budget. Contracts are a **MUST** when doing business with the many types of wedding-related services. Your wedding is an emotional experience, but remember—money is changing hands. A contract will spell out everything in black and white. It will also clarify any grey areas. If the business doesn't have a formal contract, write up your own and have them sign it. Estimates are a good first step, but they aren't final. Many brides have been shocked a week before their wedding when a supplier has said, "We had a price increase in the last six months; now it will cost this much for what you want." Remember, you carry a book filled with other options. **BEWARE** of contracts you feel pressured to sign! Make sure you don't sign something that you haven't thoroughly read or don't understand. Never sign a contract that makes you feel uncomfortable or that you can't afford. A contract is a legally binding document that commits you to the service or provider. Be well informed about what you are signing; ask questions, or take a copy of it home to look over if you have any hesitation at all.

CHECK OUT REFERENCES

The best way to research a business is to ask for references and then take the time to call them. This way you will rapidly discover if the services or merchandise were provided or delivered as promised. **There are state and private agencies that can provide information on a business's reputation. Don't be afraid to call them.**

DEPOSITS

In most cases a deposit is required to place an order formally or to reserve a certain date. Brides and grooms make the common mistake of assuming that the reception site is reserved based on a verbal commitment for date and time. **The agreement is not always valid, let alone recorded, until after the deposit has been received.**

YOU'RE THE CUSTOMER!

Always remember that you're the customer! Even though this can be an emotional time, **don't settle for less than what was contracted for.** Insist on the best service and accept nothing less. You may be spending more money on this one day than most people spend in a year! Make the most of your investment and do it your way.

WEDDING EXPENSES

The division of expenses depends on the financial ability of the bride, groom, and their respective families. Sit down and discuss the type of wedding you want to have and use the following list of items so each participant can choose what he or she would like to pay for. Remember that the reception can sometimes amount to 50% or more of your total expenses. If your costs need to be reduced, you may want to change to a less formal reception.

The bride and her family's expenses traditionally include:

- the wedding gown and accessories
- invitations and personal stationery
- flowers for the church, reception, and wedding attendants
- photographs
- reception, including room charge, food, servers, refreshments, and wedding cake
- music
- transportation for wedding attendants to church and reception
- gifts for bridesmaids
- accommodations for bridesmaids, if necessary

The groom and his family's expenses are normally:

- groom's wedding attire
- the clergy or judge's fees
- the marriage license
- all honeymoon expenses
- rehearsal dinner
- bride's bouquet and going-away corsage and both mothers' corsages
- boutonnieres for groomsmen
- groomsmen gifts
- accommodations for attendants

The wedding attendants' expenses are:

- wedding attire
- traveling expenses
- wedding gift

YOU'VE WAITED A LONG TIME TO GET MARRIED.

Your wedding date is a year away—it seems like an eternity! As formal weddings have become more and more popular, you should allow about one year for planning. Many reception facilities are reserved as far as a year in advance during the summer months and December. The size and formality of your wedding will play an important part in determining your date and schedule. Even if your wedding is small and less formal, allow yourself a minimum of three months. The more time you have to plan, the better your chances of reserving your first choices. On the biggest day of your life, who wants to settle for less? With all you have to do, time will fly quicker than you think!

The following schedule and checklist provide you with the basis for organizing your planning time and ensure that all the details will be handled. These are strictly recommendations; we encourage you to look on the following pages to see when the businesses themselves say they need to be reserved.

AFTER ENGAGEMENT—SIX MONTHS AND BEFORE

❒ Select a wedding date and time — be flexible.

❒ Buy a wedding notebook. *See the Bravo!® Wedding Organizer info on page 23.*

❒ Figure out your budget and write it down.

❒ Determine type of wedding and reception: formality, size, colors, and theme.

❒ Decide on the ceremony site and make an appointment with the clergy.

❒ Reserve a reception facility; if there's no in-house catering, you will need to find a caterer.

❒ Start compiling names and addresses of guests.

❒ Decide on wedding attendants — bridesmaids and groomsmen.

❒ Shop for your wedding gown and headpiece.

❒ Select a professional photographer.

❒ Start collecting favorite photographs from both of your childhoods through present that you'll want to use in your wedding video or multi-image slide program.

❒ Select dresses for your bridesmaids.

❒ Find a florist.

❒ Mail out engagement announcements.

❒ Send an announcement to your local paper.

❒ Register at the bridal registry stores of your choice — more than one is fine.

❒ Reserve a band or orchestra for your reception — if you choose.

❒ Decide on honeymoon destination; if it's a popular area, make reservations now.

FOUR TO FIVE MONTHS BEFORE

- ❒ Compile the final guest list; delete or correct as needed.
- ❒ Make sure all deposits are paid for services reserved.
- ❒ Finish planning the honeymoon.
- ❒ Order bridal attire; some manufacturers require up to six months for delivery.
- ❒ Order the wedding cake.
- ❒ Have groom, groomsmen, and ushers fitted for formal wear.
- ❒ Purchase your wedding rings.
- ❒ Order invitations, thank-you notes, imprinted napkins, and wedding programs.
- ❒ Ask people to handle certain duties like candle lighting, guest book, cake serving.
- ❒ Select musicians for ceremony

TWO TO THREE MONTHS BEFORE

- ❒ Plan ceremony rehearsal and rehearsal dinner.
- ❒ Address invitations (mail four to six weeks prior to wedding).
- ❒ Organize details with service providers: reception facility, photographer, etc.
- ❒ Check accommodations for out-of-town guests; send them information.
- ❒ Make beauty appointments: hair, nails, massage, facial, and makeup.
- ❒ Arrange for final fittings for your gown and bridesmaids dresses.
- ❒ Make your transportation arrangements for the wedding day.
- ❒ Purchase gifts for your attendants.
- ❒ Shop for your trousseau, lingerie, and going-away outfit.
- ❒ Give a bridesmaids' luncheon or bachelor party (optional).
- ❒ Send thank-yous for gifts received early.
- ❒ Get accessories: garter, unity candle, toasting goblets, ring-bearer pillow, etc.

ONE WEEK TO A MONTH BEFORE

- ❒ Change your name (if you choose) on your driver's license and Social Security card; organize which credit cards and bank accounts will be used.
- ❒ Decide where you'll be living and send change-of-address cards to post office.
- ❒ Confirm accommodations arranged for out-of-town guests.
- ❒ Get your final count of guests to caterer.
- ❒ Delegate last-minute errands and details.
- ❒ Make any necessary lists for photographer and musicians.
- ❒ Ask a responsible person to coordinate services and people on the wedding day; give them a list of who and what is supposed to be where and when.
- ❒ Get your marriage license. ***Note:** if your were married before, you'll need to know the date and place of the divorce or annulment. You may also need to have paperwork proof of divorce or annulment.
- ❒ Pick up your wedding rings; make sure they are the correct sizes.
- ❒ Pick up wedding attire; try it all on one last time to make sure it fits.
- ❒ Make sure bridesmaids have their dresses and they all fit.
- ❒ Keep up on writing thank-yous; don't let them pile up.
- ❒ Pamper yourself and make sure you eat right and get enough sleep.

THE WEDDING DAY

- ❒ Eat a good breakfast.
- ❒ Relax and enjoy getting ready for your big day.
- ❒ Go to hairdresser or start fixing your hair a few hours prior to the wedding.
- ❒ Put all the accessories you will need for dressing in one place.
- ❒ If pictures are being taken before ceremony, be ready at least two hours before.
- ❒ Just enjoy the day! All your months of planning will make your day perfect!

MONTH:

Monday	Tuesday	Wednesday	Thursday	Friday	Saturday	Sunday

Today, wedding etiquette is good manners and a blending of traditional customs with contemporary ones. When you incorporate good manners into your wedding planning, you add a special touch of caring and thoughtfulness into everything you do, because you're making others involved in your special day feel special too.

Knowing the proper things to say and do also gives you greater confidence that you can handle any unexpected or awkward situation.

Let the following helpful tips show you how to incorporate good manners and proper etiquette into every aspect of your wedding duties—from addressing envelopes properly for invitations to knowing when to send thank-you notes. Good luck!

ANNOUNCING YOUR ENGAGEMENT

Share your good news with your families as soon as possible—it's only right that they hear it from you first. If you'd also like to announce your engagement formally in both your and your fiancé's hometown papers, contact the lifestyles editor to learn the appropriate way to prepare your information. Ask if photos are also accepted. The simplest, customary form of preparing your announcement is to type it on an 8 1/2 x 11 sheet. The following sample will give you an idea of how to write your copy:

Mr. and Mrs. Dennis Brown of Dayton Avenue announce the engagement of their daughter, Ann Marie, to John Smith, the son of Mr. and Mrs. Thomas Smith of St. Louis. No date has been set for the wedding (or, The wedding will take place in December).

ORDERING INVITATIONS

Order your invitations at least three months in advance to give you plenty of time for printing, addressing, and mailing. If it's a very formal wedding, choose a rich, creamy paper. If it's semiformal, you have many options in paper stocks and colors from which to choose. It's also acceptable to include more personal touches such as a poem, a Bible verse, or other sayings.

ADDRESSING INVITATIONS

Create a master list of names in order to avoid duplications. Make sure all names and titles are spelled correctly and addresses are accurate. Below are some typical examples of different addressing styles.

When addressing invitations to married couples, use the following format:

Mr. and Mrs. John Smith
1022 Robins Court
City, California 12345

Keep in mind that many women have retained their maiden names or prefer to be called by their titles or professional names. In these cases, you may send one invitation to both husband and wife, putting her name above his on the envelope. Follow the same rule for couples with different last names or unmarried couples living together.

Ms. Jane Smith
Mr. Joseph Thomas
122 Maple Street, Apartment R-10
Dayton, Ohio 12345

Be sure to write out in full the names of streets, cities, and states as well. Don't send an invitation to a couple and "family." Instead, on the inner envelope, include the name of each child invited as:

Mr. and Mrs. Smith
Kevin, Brian, and Amy

Adult members of a family who are over age 18 should always receive separate invitations. You may, however, send one invitation to two sisters or brothers living together at one address. Generally, the rule is each invited guest should receive a personal invitation to your wedding, so avoid wordings like "and guest." Make an effort to find out the address of the guest and send a separate invitation.

MAILING INVITATIONS

Invitations are usually mailed four to six weeks before the wedding. Do send invitations to your wedding official, your fiancé's immediate family, all members of the wedding party, and a guest list made up of both your friends and his, as well as other relatives and coworkers with whom you want to share your day. Keep in mind your budget limitations and refrain from letting your list get out of control. Selection may sometimes be difficult, but it is best to stick as closely as possible to your list.

If you haven't received an RSVP by two weeks before the wedding, have a family member call and check. When each invitation is accounted for, tell your caterer how many guests to expect.

POSTAGE FOR INVITATIONS

Remember before purchasing stamps for your invitations to go to the post office and have the invitation weighed. Normally the postage will be 33 cents, but if the invitation has many inserts or is a larger size it might require more postage. Also, it is fun to have your invitations post-marked at a special location (e.g. Bridal Veil in Oregon is a popular place). You can either mail the entire finished package of invitations there or hand deliver the package with special instructions.

SAVE-THE-DATE LETTERS:

Inform out-of-town guests about the upcoming wedding date far enough in advance, so if they need to take time off work or save for the trip they will have time. This letter can also give details about hotel accommodations in different budgets, special wedding rates and who to contact at the destination and the toll-free number.

BANQUET AND RECEPTION SITES

Rehearsal Dinner: The rehearsal dinner is usually hosted by the groom's parents. This is either formal or casual and follows the ceremony rehearsal the night before the wedding, although many brides and grooms are choosing to have the rehearsal two days before the wedding. It is the beginning of the festivities and an opportunity for all wedding party attendants and family to get to know each other. Invitations should be sent or telephoned at least three weeks prior and should be extended to all those participating in the wedding: attendants and groomsmen and their spouses, the clergy, parents of any children, immediate family and out-of-town guests who have arrived. The best man begins the toasts following dessert and then the gifts are presented to the wedding party and any other special helpers. Slide shows or videos can be shown of special memories of the bride and groom as individuals and then as a couple for their family and friends. This evening usually ends early so everyone can get a good night's sleep. See "Rehearsal Dinner Sites" section on pages 69–86.

Outdoor weddings: Always play it safe with an outdoor site—make sure you either have a back-up location or rent and set up tents. In the wonderful Pacific Northwest you can never be too sure of the weather. These tents or canopies can be expensive; don't forget to figure this into your budget.

Non-traditional sites and times: Saturdays are the most popular day to get married, and most businesses and services will charge top dollar for this prime time. Consider Friday nights or Sunday weddings as an option; some services will give a considerable discount for booking this off-day. Also, sites such as restaurants, parks, historical sites and beaches can be non-traditional, but also very fun and exciting with atmosphere and unique cuisine.

ROLES MEMBERS OF THE WEDDING PARTY PLAY

Maid of Honor: Although she has no prewedding responsibilities, she is expected to assist the bride whenever she can. She lends moral support and plays a big role in making sure the other bridesmaids are dressed to perfection and they all make it to the church on time. She is responsible for her own wedding outfit and pays for everything except the flowers. She also attends all prewedding parties and may even give one herself. The maid of honor is usually one of the witnesses required by law to sign the marriage certificate. Walking down the aisle, she precedes you and your father, arranges your train and veil, carries the groom's ring if there is no ringbearer, and holds your bouquet during the ceremony. She also stands next to the groom in the receiving line and sits on his left at the bride's table.

Best Man: His duties are many and varied and carry a lot of responsibility to ensure the wedding runs smoothly. The best man serves as the personal aide and advisor to the groom, supervises the ushers, carries the bride's ring and the marriage certificate, which he also signs, tips the altar boys in a Catholic ceremony, and acts as a right-hand man to the groom on his special day. The best man sits at the right of the bride and, as official toastmaster of the reception, proposes the first toast to the new couple, usually wishing them health, happiness, and prosperity. His final duties are to ensure the new couple takes off for the honeymoon without a hitch and that all the ushers return their rented formal wear on time.

Bridesmaids: Although they don't have any prewedding responsibilities either, they often will volunteer to help with any errands or duties that need to be accomplished. They are invited to all prewedding parties and may also give one if they wish.

Ushers: Their responsibility is to seat guests at the wedding ceremony and act as escorts for the bridesmaids. To avoid seating delays, there should be at least one usher for every 50 guests. They also attend all prewedding parties the groom goes to and are required to provide their own wedding clothes, renting the proper formal attire if they do not own it. If formal wedding portraits are not being taken before the ceremony, ushers should arrive fully dressed in their formal wear 45 minutes before the ceremony and assemble near the entrance. As guests arrive, each usher should offer his right arm to each woman and escort her to her seat on the left or right of the aisle, depending on whether she is a friend of the bride or groom.

The Bride's Mother: Your mother usually helps compile the guest list and arranges the details of the ceremony and reception. It is her responsibility to keep the bride's father and future in-laws informed about wedding plans. She should also inform the groom's mother of her wedding attire so that their dresses are similar in length and style. The mother of the bride is privileged to sit in the very first pew on the bride's side. She is the last to be seated and the first to be escorted out of the church after the ceremony. She also greets all guests in the receiving line and sits in a place of honor at the bride's parents' table at the reception.

The Bride's Father: Your father rides in the limousine or car with you on the way to the church and escorts you down the aisle. He is also seated in the first pew behind the bride during the ceremony and later stands in the receiving line greeting and thanking guests. At the reception, he should dance the second dance with the bride and will usually make a short toast or welcoming speech to all the guests.

The Groom's Parents: Your fiancé's mother should be invited to all showers and both his parents should be included in the rehearsal dinner, if they don't host it themselves. They should also contribute to the guest list for the wedding and reception and may or may not offer to share expenses. The groom's parents are honored guests at the ceremony and are seated, just before your mother, in the first pew on the groom's side of the aisle.

WHEN PARENTS ARE DIVORCED

Dealing with divorced parents may add a complication to your wedding plans, but if handled well, everything can still work out just the way you planned. The key is to provide separate places of distinction at the ceremony, in the receiving line, and at the reception to ensure their happiness and enjoyment of the day.

GUIDELINES FOR DIVORCED PARENTS

- **Invitations:** Invitations are usually issued by the parent you have currently lived with. If both parents have contributed, then both names and stepparents can be mentioned.
- **Ceremony seating:** For seating at the ceremony there are two options: if parents are friends and they are not remarried, they can sit side by side in the front pew. Otherwise the parent you have lived with would sit in the front pew with his or her spouse, and the other parent sits in the second or third pew with his or her spouse.
- **Photographs:** Each set of parents will most likely want to have a photo taken with the bride and groom; it is important to spell this out to the photographers earlier. This can take longer for photographs so appropriate time needs to be allocated.
- **Down the Aisle:** Walking down the aisle can be more than just a scary walk when trying to decide whether your father or stepfather should escort you. Consider whether you have remained close to your father and if you want him to fulfill this traditional role; or if your stepfather has filled the role of your father you may decide this is more appropriate. If your father and stepfather get along, you may ask both. If the decision is impossible, choose neither and ask your mother to walk you down.
- **Receiving Line:** For the receiving line and reception, customarily the parent who is paying for the wedding greets the guests with you. The other parent can be mingling. At the reception a good solution to feuding families is to have two different parent tables.

RECEIVING LINE

Usually held at the beginning of the reception, this event allows parents and the wedding party members to greet guests and receive their good wishes. The line traditionally begins with your mother, followed by the groom's mother, the bride and groom, your maid of honor and the rest of the bridesmaids. The fathers can join in and, if so, should stand to the left of their wives. **If your parents are divorced**, your mother stands alone or with your stepfather, while your father circulates among the guests. Or, to avoid confusion, decide not to include fathers in the line. The important thing is to avoid hurt feelings or misunderstandings. Another alternative is to have your father and his new wife stand on the other side of the groom. If you feel it becomes too difficult to orchestrate, it is **perfectly acceptable to mingle and greet your guests during the reception rather than have a receiving line**. Whatever works well for your situation is fine.

SEATING ARRANGEMENTS AT THE RECEPTION

The bride's table, which should be the focus of the reception, can be of any shape and is sometimes elevated so everyone can see the wedding party. The groom usually sits to the bride's left with the maid of honor on his left. To the right of the bride is the best man, and the rest of the bridesmaids and ushers sit at the table male, female, male, female. If it's a small wedding party, the officiant and husbands and wives of the wedding party may also sit at the bride's table. Otherwise, a separate table for parents is set where your mother heads the table and the groom's father sits at her right and the wedding officiant sits at her left. The groom's mother sits on your father's right. However, if your parents are divorced, consider arranging a separate table for each set of parents.

DON'T FORGET THANK-YOU NOTES!

You and your groom must send personal, handwritten notes of appreciation thanking everyone who gave you and your new husband a gift. It is suggested you begin sending thank-you notes immediately upon receiving your gifts. Try to acknowledge each gift within two weeks of its arrival. The customary note is written in blue or black ink on a quality notepaper in white or ivory. Colored or decorated notes are also acceptable. Whatever you choose, the most important thing is that the note be timely and sincere.

If you need more information or advice, several excellent books by the editors of popular bridal magazines and by etiquette experts are available at libraries and book stores. Bridal consultants and bridal-shop personnel are also sources of lots of useful tips and information.

Weddings make us all sentimental. By including a special item or tradition in your ceremony and reception that has been used by other family members, or that you yourself may wish to pass on to future generations, you allow family and friends to share in your joy as well as the traditions of your family.

Here are some ideas that you may wish to incorporate into your wedding:

- Select a Bible that you can comfortably carry down the aisle with you. At the completion of the ceremony, you and your groom can sign your names and your wedding date in the front of the Bible as well as the location and time of your marriage. As each future bride and groom uses it, their names will be added.
- The kneeling cushions and ring-bearer's pillow used during the ceremony can be made from the wedding gown of one of the bridal couple's mothers or grandmothers or from fabric selected for the occasion, and then passed on to future generations of family brides and grooms.
- If you decide not to use your mother's wedding dress, what about using her veiling and attaching it to the headpiece you have selected? This gives you the "something old" to use with your wedding attire.
- Many brides choose to carry a family memento during their wedding. A handkerchief made from the lace of a family member's gown or veil can be easily carried with your bridal bouquet.
- Your wedding garter can be made from satin and lace used by other family members in their wedding attire. Just make sure you have a backup garter for the groom to throw at the end of the reception.
- Instruct your florist to design your bridal bouquet with two detachable flowers that you can give to your mother and mother-in-law as you return down the aisle.
- Since the first toast at the reception signifies the celebration and coming together of two families as well as the beginning of a new one, silver or pewter toasting goblets make wonderful gifts to be passed on to future family brides.
- Your cake knife and server are something you will want to save and pass on.
- The day of your wedding, plant a tree or a rose bush that you can watch grow throughout the years of your marriage.
- A perfect gift from the groom can be a charm bracelet. With each year, in celebration of your wedding anniversary, a new charm can be added.

When you've returned from your honeymoon and have packed away your dress, you'll want to get a special box in which you can carefully pack all of your wedding treasures. Someday you can share them with your daughter(s) and future daughters-in-law.

You will want to put some things together a few days before your wedding to take to the church. We call it the "Wedding Day Survival Kit." It includes all those little odds and ends that you'll need for quick repairs and to cover the things others may have forgotten.

- ❒ Scissors
- ❒ Needles and thread (in the colors of your bridal and attendant gowns)
- ❒ Safety pins
- ❒ Iron and ironing board (if none is available at church or ceremony site)
- ❒ Makeup kit (for light touchups)
- ❒ Hand mirror and makeup mirrors
- ❒ Kleenex
- ❒ Smock or towels to protect dresses from last-minute makeup touchups
- ❒ Electric curlers and curling iron
- ❒ Bobbie pins and combs to anchor veils and headpieces
- ❒ Hair spray
- ❒ Deodorant or antiperspirant
- ❒ Dress shields
- ❒ Extra nylons in the appropriate colors
- ❒ Extra socks for groomsmen and ushers (someone is bound to forget)
- ❒ Toys to keep flower girls and ring bearers busy in a quiet way
- ❒ Smocks for flower girls and ring bearers to wear over their wedding attire until it's time for the photos or ceremony (kids will get dirty!)
- ❒ Masking tape (for last-minute fix-up jobs on decorations)
- ❒ Scotch tape for taping cards to gifts so they don't fall off
- ❒ Lightweight wire (for last-minute repairs on decorations)
- ❒ Super glue
- ❒ Breath freshener
- ❒ Aspirin
- ❒ Smelling salts (just in case one of your attendants faints)
- ❒ Refreshments (pop, ice tea, juice....everyone is bound to get thirsty)
- ❒ Straws (never drink directly from a glass or can; you will undoubtedly spill)
- ❒ A hand-held fan for those hot summer months

Put all your supplies for your "Wedding Day Survival Kit" into a carryall bag and put it next to the things that are going to the church. You'll be glad you have it!

One final tip. Find out whether your church has a stool that you can use in the dressing room. If not, bring one with you. You'll get tired of standing after you've dressed in your gown. If you sit in a chair, you'll wrinkle your gown. This is where the stool comes in handy! Drape your gown skirt and train over the stool, then sit; no wrinkles!

© AJ's Photo Expressions • page 478

Giving Away The Bride

The custom of the bride being given away by her father has its origins in ancient times when women were considered to be owned by and slaves to men. The marriage was treated as a property transaction, with the right of ownership being passed from one man to another.

HELPFUL HINTS

- **You will have the opportunity to attend several excellent bridal shows throughout the year.** The advantage to these shows is that it is a perfect time to meet and talk with area businesses and services and see what they have to offer all in one place.
- **Be prepared!** It's very helpful if you have a **target list** of items and services you will need to have to make your wedding day complete. Don't wander. Have a **plan of action** and go and find the booths that have the services you are looking for.
- **Take notes.** You will receive a lot of information as you are touring the booths, and it can get confusing. Be sure to write down the names of the companies that impress you the most, so that you can come back to the booth to talk with them later. If you are collecting information as you go, **fold down the corners of the brochures or hand-outs** of the companies you like so that you can go directly to their material when you need it.
- **Keep information organized!** *The Bravo!® Wedding Organizer* is the perfect place to store all the valuable information you gather. After the show, pull out the important information and discounts and put into appropriate categories in *The Bravo!® Wedding Organizer*...it's the perfect system. For more information see page 23.
- **Dress comfortably.** Make sure you wear comfortable shoes and clothing. You'll be on your feet for a long time.
- **Take your mother or a friend to help you.** If you have an assistant, they can carry all the information you are gathering so that you can **keep your hands free** to take notes and review information.

  (**Note:** Don't take too many people with you. You'll end up spending all your time trying to find them as they wander off or start talking with other people and you won't accomplish what you set out to do.)
- **Have sticky labels or mail labels with your name and address.** You'll be signing up for a lot of door prizes. It's very quick and easy if you have a label to put on the entry forms.
- **Fashion shows.** This is always one of the biggest features of Bridal Shows. You'll see all the latest fashions for the entire wedding party, in addition to resort wear, attire for mothers of the bride and groom, and more. Most shows will provide you with a program. Keep it in-hand so that if you see something you fall in love with, you'll know where to go to find it after the fashion show is over.

For more assistance with staying organized during the wedding planning process, check out the Bravo! Wedding Organizer. Detailed question worksheets double as contracts. This step-by-step system will keep every detail of your wedding organized. To order, refer to the order form on page 24 in this Guide.

Please let this show know that you heard about them from the Bravo! Bridal Resource Guide.

the 2000 PACIFIC NORTHWEST
Wedding Showcase
for him & for Her
WINTER:
Saturday & Sunday, February 19th & 20th
SUMMER:
Sunday, July 23rd
At the Oregon Convention Center
10:00 a.m. - 5:00 p.m. Fashion Shows at Noon and 3:00 p.m.
Romance specialists from the Northwest will offer tips on how to plan your wedding. Two daily fashion shows will highlight the latest in bridal gowns, tuxedos and other wedding party attire. Mark your calendar and plan to attend our exclusive Wedding Showcases where we'll help make your wedding dreams come true…
Tickets $7 available at Fred Meyer Fastixx or at the show. Good for $1.00 off Admission with this advertisement.
MEDIA SPONSORS:
Z100
K103 fm
Soft rock for a busy world.
produced by:
CorEvents
FOR ADDITIONAL INFORMATION, PLEASE CALL (503) 295-8587

THE BEAT @ 107.5 TODAY'S MUSIC *sponsors*

The Original Portland Bridal Show

The "Bride's Bridal Show" with the Bridal Fashion Premiere of the Season

Don't Miss It!!

This is Portland's <u>*Big*</u> Bridal Show

Plan your entire wedding with over 130 "Wedding Related" exhibitors

Saturday & Sunday • January 8th & 9th, 2000

Oregon Convention Center

Win!

A Romantic Honeymoon Get-Away at the

Columbia Gorge Hotel

will be given away at <u>each show</u>!

Some Restrictions May Apply

Showtimes:

Mornings	**Afternoons**	**Evening**
Doors Open 10:30am	Doors Open 2:00pm	Doors Open 5:00pm
Fashion Show 12:30 pm	Fashion Show 3:30 pm	Fashion Show 6:30 pm
(Each Day)	*(Each Day)*	*(Saturday Only)*

Tickets:

$7 at the Door for Adults <u>*and*</u> Children

Save $1 with this ad – Advance Tickets Only

One Coupon per person - *<u>Not valid</u> for Saturday 10:30am (Morning) show.*

No Strollers or Cameras Allowed

HURRY! Shows sell out early!
Advanced tickets guarantee admission
***Advance Tickets at* FASTIXX**
Limited tickets available at the door.

For Additional Info. Call: (503) 274-6027 • www.portlandbridalshow.com

Elegance • Presentation • Selection • Answers to your Questions

Bridal Show

January 22, 2000

presented by

WeddingLink
Your Link to Wedding Professionals

Plan the wedding of your dreams with a little help from some of Portland-Vancouver's top wedding professionals. Look at the great ideas, see exciting new products and services and best of all talk directly to the experts. This is the show where you get the answers and personal help you're looking for.

We invite you to take all the time you need. Enjoy our gourmet fare, hors d'oeuvres, cakes, pastries and other delicacies. And experience one of the most elegant bridal fashion shows in the Northwest. Arrive early for best seating.

show hours 10am to 5pm
fashion shows at 11am and 2pm

DoubleTree Hotel at the Quay
Just off I-5 on the Columbia River
Vancouver, WA

Free Parking
admission $6, $5 with can food donation

Exhibitors: Call Doreen at (360) 694-9978 (doreen@teleport.com) for booth space and show information.

Weddings of Distinction

Weddings of Distinction is a nonprofit group of select professionals dedicated to excellence in bridal services.

Calendar of Events

•

6th Annual
Weddings of Distinction Bridal Tea & Fashion Show
Saturday, January 22nd • Noon
The Benson Hotel

•

9th Annual
Zell Bros Bridal Show
Saturday, April 1st
Zell Bros

•

Call to receive more information on planning the wedding of your dreams and our updated calendar of events.

•

(503) 227-8471
Zell Bros

These dates are subject to change. Please call for confirmation.

WEDDING GIFTS AND PRODUCTS

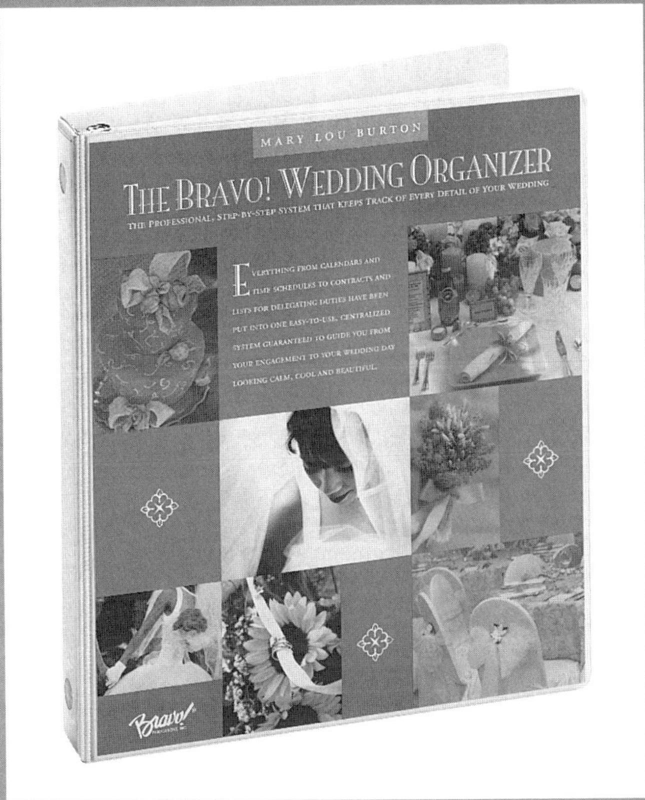

© Leo Commerical Photography • page 504

WEDDING ANNIVERSARIES

	Traditional	*Modern*
First	*Paper*	*Clocks*
Second	*Cotton*	*China*
Third	*Leather*	*Crystal, Glass*
Fourth	*Fruit, Flowers*	*Appliances*
Fifth	*Wood*	*Silverware*
Sixth	*Candy, Iron*	*Wood*
Seventh	*Wool, Copper*	*Desk Sets*
Eighth	*Bronze, Pottery*	*Linens, Laces*
Ninth	*Pottery, Willow*	*Leather*
Tenth	*Tin, Aluminum*	*Diamond Jewelry*
Eleventh	*Steel*	*Fashion Jewelry*
Twelfth	*Silk, Linen*	*Pearls*
Thirteenth	*Lace*	*Textiles, Furs*
Fourteenth	*Ivory*	*Gold Jewelry*
Fifteenth	*Crystal*	*Watches*
Twentieth	*China*	*Platinum*
Twenty-fifth	*Silver*	*Silver*
Thirtieth	*Pearls*	*Diamonds*
Thirty-fifth	*Coral*	*Jade*
Fortieth	*Rubies*	*Rubies*
Forty-fifth	*Sapphires*	*Sapphires*
Fiftieth	*Gold*	*Gold*
Fifty-fifth	*Emeralds*	*Emeralds*
Sixtieth	*Diamonds*	*Diamonds*
Seventy-fifth	*Diamonds*	*Diamonds*

The Bravo! Wedding Worry Candle

Bravo! Publications, Inc. has created a **Wedding Worry Candle.** The package includes a fragrant bag of Gardenia candle crystals in a reusable silver tin, which merge together when the wick is lit. Wrapped in a natural-fiber box and tied with a tulle bow, the box is conveniently ready for gift giving.

A poem, attached to both the can and outside of the box reads: *Planning a wedding has many a concern, So light this candle and let it burn, Your worries will rise up into the air, And your wedding is sure to be a most splendid affair.*

$16.95

For more information or to place an order
800.988.9887
E-mail: bravo7165@aol.com
Web site: www.bravowedding.com

As seen in Martha Stewart Weddings...

The Bravo! Wedding Organizer

Somewhere between "yes"... and "I do"

An expandable organizer filled with calendars, time schedules, swatch storage envelopes, and much, much more, to make your day as easy for you as it is for your guests.

Features

- Sturdy three-ring binder; it's easy to add to
- 14 easy-to-find tabbed sections
- Directs brides to answer all the right questions
- Contracts included to formalize agreements
- Worksheets to record details
- Pockets for swatches, samples and brochures
- $24.95

For more information or to place an order
800.988.9887
E-mail: bravo7165@aol.com
Web site: www.bravowedding.com

...And These Witnesses

Signature Frame

"Your Visual Guest Book"

Remember the Moment and Those Who Shared It With You

Weddings Anniversaries Showers Grandparents Day Reunions Retirement Promotions

Your picture, beautifully framed by the signatures of the friends and loved ones who helped to make your day so wonderful. Displayed in your home or given as a gift, **...And These Witnesses Signature Frames** are a wonderful reminder of a joyous occasion!

The **Signature Frame** designed by Teresa Everest is one of a number of original items she has produced for her brides and grooms. She found that there was a need for certain products specifically designed for the newly married couple and if she could not purchase the right items, being an inventor by nature, she designed them herself.

Your Survival Kit...Before, During and After the Big Event!

"Prenuptually Prepared"™

The Wedding Day Survival Kit

Specially designed as His and Hers

This very complete, very compact kit will be your life saver at the wedding, on the honeymoon, at home or in the car. Give it as a gift to yourself or a friend. Moms and Dads: give the gift that says, "We care about the little things."

Hand Mirror
Hair Spray
Deodorant
Acedminaphen
Sanitary Pads
Comb or Hair Pic
Hair Pins
Hair Elastics
Nail File
Nail Polish
Polish Remover
Hand Soap
Facial Tissue
Hand Lotions
Razor
Toothbrush and Paste

Wash/Dry Towelettes
Feminine Wash
Paper and Pencil
Sewing Needles
Thread, Five Colors
Safety Pins
Scotch Tape
String
Appropriate "I Love You" Card
First Aid Supplies for Stings
  Bites, Scratches, Bruises
  Cuts, Burns, Bleeding; Ice Pack
  Anti-Diarrhea, Anti-Acid
  Anti-Gas, Smelling Salts,
  Headache…
And More!

Made in America with Brand-Name products you know and trust!

Contact us at:
www.silvertonhillsranch.com
Teresa Everest, Certified Wedding Specialist
and Owner of Silverton Hills Ranch Weddings
Silverton, Oregon
(503) 873-2007

Something Blue™
Creators, Inc.

888.205.6606
www.bridalbox.com

Cherish memories for a lifetime…

Every bride needs a Bridal Box to store all of her delicate wedding keepsakes and treasures to be passed down through the generations. Something Blue Creators designed this hand-crafted memorabilia treasure chest to be a useful and beautiful piece of furniture. The sturdy wood frame is completely upholstered in fine designer fabric. The Bridal Box is available in eight colors/styles and features elegant closures of ribbons, tassels, buttons or tulle.

The Bridal Box is a unique gift perfect for brides (newlyweds or golden anniversary), Maids of Honor or Bridal Attendants…Anyone seeking attractive storage for keepsakes. If you have precious keepsakes or memorabilia, the Bridal Box is for you.

www.bridalbox.com
Visit our Web site or call for stores carrying the Bridal Box.

Notes

© Strong Photography • page 523

TRADITIONS

In Roman times a man gave his bride-to-be a coin or gold ring as "down payment" for the bride and to show his good intentions to wed her.

•

The bride stands to the groom's left because in Medieval times he needed to keep his sword hand free (a) to fend off attacks from those not wanting the wedding to take place and/or (b) to keep an unwilling bride at his side.

Creative Childcare Solutions, Inc.

Delivering quality childcare to you and your family

Contact: Michelle Davenport or Deanna Pulford (503) 635-1036

E-mail: michelle@munchkincare.com or deanna@munchkincare.com

Web site: www.munchkincare.com

You've reserved the hall, the speakers and the band… Now, what are you going to do with the children?

At Creative Childcare Solutions, we believe children should be allowed to be children—not act like "little adults." That's why we offer on-site childcare for your special event.

As the best man hands the ring to the groom for the vows, the children can be laughing at a clown down the hall.

When the bride and groom begin their first dance, the children can hop to the Hokey-Pokey in another room.

While your guests dine on salmon en croute and sip champagne, their children could be munching on a hotdog and slurping down rootbeer floats at their own Cowboy Hoedown!

Creative Childcare Solutions, Inc. will customize each special event to meet your unique needs and budget. Our qualified, caring CCSI staff will bring with them 25 years of childcare expertise, CPR and First Aid Certification and all the toys, games, arts and crafts the children will need to have a wonderful time!

So, for your next event, let the kids be kids and let the adults relax in the knowledge that their children are nearby in a safe, exciting, loving environment with **Creative Childcare Solutions, Inc.**

COST—Custom designed to meet your specific needs.

TERMS—One contact person required for planning of event. Retainer required for bookings.

Call or e-mail us today to book your next special occasion. Let the children come and have fun while remaining safely near the parents. No more worries about canceled babysitters—let us take care of the details so you can enjoy yourselves.

© Strong Photography • page 523

BRIDESMAIDS TEA

Traditionally, a cake that had a special ring baked into it was served to all the bridesmaids at a tea. The bridesmaid who was served the lucky slice was believed to be the next one to marry.

HELPFUL HINTS

- **A consultant can ease the stress:** Hiring a consultant is a wise idea, especially if there is arguing between mother and daughter, between families, divorced parents and even attendants. This is an emotional time, an objective opinion of a consultant can sometimes ease the pressure. Money can be one of the biggest problems and obstacles. If a third party is involved, such as a consultant, they can collect the money without it being embarrassing. Many times arguments result from lack of communication, emotional overload and misconceptions. The two parties just need to communicate; sometimes writing it down and having someone calm present to the other half, is a good way to deal with it.
- **A consultant can save money and mistakes:** Brides and grooms sometimes feel a consultant can be an additional expense that they cannot afford. In fact a consultant can be your best investment especially if you are on a strict budget. An experienced consultant can help a couple avoid common mistakes. Working with vendors can be costly if the right questions are not asked, and a bride and groom with the help of a consultant will never feel pressured into booking a service, because the consultant knows the timeline and whether a sales pitch is just that or not.
- **Services available:** Wedding consultants and event planners can arrange as little or as much of your event or wedding as you want. How they bill for their services varies. Even though you are paying them for their time, in most cases they can save you money in other areas because of their familiarity with different services and discounts that are available to them as frequent customers.
- **Why hire an event planner or consultant?** People are often under the misconception that planning your own event and preparing the food, setup, decorating and cleanup will save money. In fact it can sometimes cost more—not just in money, but in time and headaches as well. A good consultant can work with you and your budget, saving valuable time and money allowing you to enjoy the event.
- **Selecting a consultant:** Talk to different consultants before making your final decision and find out who is familiar with providing the types and level of service you're looking for. Don't be afraid to ask questions or to see portfolios and ask for references. The person or company you select should be the one you feel most comfortable with personally and professionally.
- **Finding a banquet, reception, or ceremony site:** Qualified consultants have been to and seen locations that you may never have heard of, but that are perfect for your event. Some consultants have videotapes and photographs of various sites, so you can preview a variety of locations without having to drive all over town. Once you have made your selection, your consultant can make sure your date and time are available, and arrange for you to visit the location.
- **NOTE:** Be specific about the services you want and what your budget is. From this information a consultant will be able to offer you a variety of suggestions that will work for you and your wedding plans. Be sure to read any and all contracts before signing them so that there is no confusion at a later date about who is responsible for what and how much it will cost.

For more assistance with staying organized during the wedding planning process, check out the Bravo! Wedding Organizer. Detailed question worksheets double as contracts. This step-by-step system will keep every detail of your wedding organized. To order, refer to the order form on page 24 in this Guide.

An Affair To Remember

Exceptional Event Planning, Production & Design

826 N.W. Hoyt
Portland, Oregon 97209
Office and Fax (503) 223-9267
E-mail: PXAffairs@aol.com
Web site: www.anaffairtoremember.com

As Portland's premier event planning company, we have been participants in some of the area's most creative and compelling weddings and receptions. Whether you prefer an intimate and graceful cocktail party or a grand tented affair, we can make your ideas, your dreams and your visions a reality.

Attention to Detail

Attention to detail and impeccable organization is what makes the difference between an ordinary event and an extraordinary one. Let us orchestrate the multitude of details to leave you free to enjoy your day.

A no cost–no obligation initial consultation is always provided. In the comfort of our new Pearl District design studio and showroom, we can together pour over our extensive collection of photo portfolios, client references and wedding videotapes.

Producing a Truly Memorable Event

In this same studio, we later design your wedding day from the rehearsal to the reception send off. Together we create your invitation and announcement package, sample reception menu offerings, conduct cake tastings, listen to local and national musician demo tapes, coordinate floral and fantasy decor, script the ceremony, choose photography ensemble and so on. We are there coordinating every element, every detail to plan and produce a truly remarkable event.

To view current wedding photographs and peruse some letters from past clients, simply visit our Web site at www.anaffairtoremember.com

Chérie

CHÉRIE RONNING
Special Occasion Consultant

4775 S.W. Watson Avenue • Beaverton, Oregon 97005
(360) 608.3647 or (503) 648.9730
E-Mail: ronnings@uswest.net; Web site: weloveweddings.com/cherie
By Appointment Only

Exceptional Event Planning
Your wedding is the biggest, most important event of your life, and you want it to be worry free! Cherie has the expertise you can depend on—let her share that with you. We listen to what you and your fiance want, and help you create the wedding of your dreams.

As one Bride said, (whose fairy tale wedding took place at the Lewis and Clark Chapel and the reception fit for royalty at the Portland Art Museum):
"Cherie, I cannot thank you enough for our wedding. Your help and guidance were indispensible. Our wedding was everything we wanted and more. Thank you for helping me achieve the wedding of my dreams. Much love, Tricia"

Services
We know that you are looking for something special for your wedding! You want an exceptional day that gets attention and matches the character of your group. This demands creativity, from the overall theme down to the smallest detail. We ensure that your day will create wonderful memories for you and a lasting impression on your guests.

Assisting with arranging the following services and more, are just a part of our service:

Budget development
Clergy
Invitations and Favors
Music
Decor & Florist
Cakes and Catering
Clothing
Lodging
Rental Equipment
Transportation

On location event coordinating available for: bridal luncheon, rehearsal and rehearsal dinner, ceremony and reception.

Fees
We offer a free one-hour consultation to determine your needs and explain our services. You are not a "package" so we have no package price: the price is customized to fit your event.

Experience
Cherie has over 19 years of experience and has coordinated over 800 weddings and other special occasion events. Cherie has even produced a live wedding for AM Northwest. She is a member of the Association of Catering and Event Professionals, The Wedding Link, The Greater Vancouver Chamber of Commerce and a past member of Weddings of Distinction. She twice produced the Columbian–Vancouver Bridal show.

The Wedding of Your Dreams
Cherie's goal is to help you create the Wedding of your Dreams! Her innovative and calm, professional manner will help you feel like a guest at your own wedding!

Class Act
Event Coordinators

Full-Service Event Planners

Contact: Susan Adkins, Owner

***Portland** (503) 295-7890 • **Salem** (503) 371-8904 • **Corvallis** (541) 766-2961*

Fax (503) 589-9166

Business Hours: Mon–Fri 8am–5pm

E-mail: classact@open.org • Web site: www.open.org/classact/

Class Act Event Coordinators Offers the Following Wedding Services

- ~ Budget preparation
- ~ Assistance with site selection
- ~ Vendor research and specifications
- ~ Personalized time line
- ~ Preparation of floor plans and agendas
- ~ Rehearsal direction
- ~ Complete setup and decorating
- ~ Coordination of wedding and reception
- ~ Complete tear down
- ~ Many other services available

Affordable Elegance

Class Act offers a wedding directing service package, a full-service planning package, or a customized service package, allowing you to pick and choose services to fit your needs and budget. The fee for these service packages and for the customized service is based on the details pertaining to your event plans. After an initial consultation, we will submit a service fee proposal for your approval at no cost.

We know Class Act can assist you with all that is necessary to make this exciting time of your life stress-free and enjoyable. You will have the opportunity to focus on the details you choose, while being assured that all of the other arrangements will be completed by us to your satisfaction.

About Class Act

Susan Adkins founded Class Act, Event Coordinators, in 1987. With her many years of wedding consulting and coordinating experience, Ms. Adkins possesses the skills necessary to attend thoroughly to all wedding planning details. She has been hired to coordinate weddings for as few as 50 guests and as many as 650. Her innovative style, calm approach and professional attention to detail combine to give you the highest quality of wedding planning and coordination services.

WE TAKE CARE OF DETAILS!

Class Act is committed to personalized service. Your event should match your style, your vision, and your budget. That's why we spend time just listening to you about your preferences, your goals, and your expectations. Based on your ideas, we recommend creative themes and decorating suggestions, and identify the best people and vendors to implement every aspect of your unique project.

We love to help you create the most successful event while relieving you of the responsibility of the details. We want you to enjoy the event as much as your guests will.

Interactive Innovations

Event and Wedding Consultants
(503) 620-2221

Congratulations on your engagement!

You must be ecstatic, having found that special person to share your life. Full of romance and moments to savor, the thrill is overwhelming of what will be one of the greatest celebrations of your life—your wedding! Planning your wedding can be fun and exciting, but it can also be stressful. Interactive Innovations wants to help alleviate your stress and let you fully enjoy one of the most important days of your life.

With over four years experience coordinating events and weddings and an active member of the Association of Bridal Consultants, you can be assured that we will work with you to make your wedding dreams come true. We harvest relationships with our vendors based on integrity and trust so we can ensure that we are providing you, our bride, the very best quality and price. In addition, some vendors due to their relationship with Interactive Innovations, will provide discounts which will be direct savings to your budget *(maybe that ice sculpture you've been dreaming of?)*

We are here for you. We enjoy getting to know the modern bride and her dreams for her special day. Please call for a free consultation. All decisions are yours. You can be as involved, or uninvolved, as you desire. Any budget can be worked with, any services can be rendered, and as always unlimited advice and consulting 24 hours a day. We flourish on turning your dreams into enchanted memories!

labyrinth
event consultants

3008 S.W. 1st Avenue
Portland, Oregon 97201
p 503.201.7603
f 503.916-1859
e labevents@aol.com

bringing creative solutions to parties, weddings, meetings

Labyrinth's mission is to provide our clients with elegance, quality, and a unique event experience.

"A mighty maze! But not without a plan." —Alexander Pope

Quality and Creativity

From all-inclusive planning, to event-day facilitation, Labyrinth brings expertise, professionalism, and creativity to every wedding. We plan successful events by utilizing a network of quality vendors, adding a unique creative edge, and organizing with a keen eye to detail.

Full-Service and More

- Ceremonies
- Engagement parties
- Vendor selection
- Favors
- Consultations
- Site selection
- Honeymoon plans
- Receptions
- Showers
- Vendor management
- Decorations
- Event facilitation
- Referrals
- Themes
- Rehearsals
- Luncheons
- Contract management
- Attendant gifts
- Spending plans
- Invitations
- Entertainment

Giving Back to You

Labyrinth is proud to volunteer event planning services to the 1999 American Diabetes Association's Charity Auction.

Well Connected

Labyrinth is an active member of the Portland Chamber of Commerce.

Marilyn Storch

Special Occasion Consulting
P.O. Box 219293
Portland, Oregon 97225-9293
(503) 520-9667; Fax (503) 644-5991
E-mail: mstorch@teleport.com

© Jamie Bosworth

You're engaged! Now what do you do?

You and your fiancé should look forward to the big day with the least amount of stress possible. After all, this "business" of a wedding is quite an undertaking! It involves your closest friends, your loving families, legal documents, months of planning, coordinating and deadlines, the hiring of many professionals, emotional overload...and You, the Star.

Do you really want to be the director at your own wedding? Do you really want to have your mother, aunt and friends handle the details? Wouldn't it be nicer to have your mother, aunt and friends by your side, relaxing and enjoying your day along with you?

In times gone by, the hiring of a wedding consultant was a luxury afforded a select few. Today you don't have to be a society matron with a debutante daughter to have need and access to such professional help. Today, with our lives so filled with schedules, and our time and energy sapped, it just makes good sense.

Let Marilyn relieve you from countless details, allowing you the luxury of experiencing your extraordinary day the way you should. Let her make the phone calls, do the research and the leg work; let her worry about the details. Marilyn is a problem solver by nature and not flustered by mishaps, letting you be blissfully unaware that the "photographer is lost" or the "maid of honor forgot the unity candle." She unobtrusively makes sure that everything is perfect, and that if it isn't, it's fixed before you find about it. The order of events will flow so smoothly, it will come together "effortlessly" on the day you exchange your vows.

Marilyn has gotten to know, and has good working relationships with, a vast variety of vendors, suppliers and services in the wedding business. Yet, she will act as YOUR ally. Any discounts or courtesies are ALWAYS passed on to you. Her expertise will pay off in so many ways you'll swear she's not only earned her wage, she's paid for herself!

With her very specialized knowledge and experience, her goal is to help you plan an affair that is true to your personality and is original in spirit. With her calm nature and professional demeanor, Marilyn will lift the load off of your shoulders and into her hands. Her behind-the-scenes guidance will put that extra special polish on your wedding day and allow YOU, the star, to shine.

Marilyn loves what she does and would like to help you have the wedding of your dreams. And she's only a phone call away...

careful • professional • calm

various package options **references available**

"You're a godsend!" ~ Jane H., 1998

"Thank you for all your help, advice and creative solutions to our problems. It was a pleasure to work with you." ~ Bernice S., 1999

"I can think of hundreds of things to thank you for so all I can say is thanks again and again. I don't think we could have walked down the aisle without you." ~ Anastasia S., 1999

 Please let this business know that you heard about them from the Bravo! Bridal Resource Guide.

Party Pleasers
Wedding/Event Planning Services
Keri Baird
Professional Consultant
663-0772

FULL-SERVICE PLANNING WITH PERSONALIZED SERVICE

Planning a special occasion takes time and detail, with a knowledge of available resources.

Party Pleasers specializes in planning all of the details of your special event by comparing prices, visiting facilities, making phone calls, and meeting with vendors to bring you quality services and savings, to save you time, money and stress.

Types of Events Include

- Complete wedding and event planning (You make the decisions; we will take care of all the details.)
- On-site coordinator for events, rehearsals, weddings, and receptions
- Planning and organizing the perfect location for rehearsal dinners
- Personalized bridal showers, baby showers, or luncheons
- Memorable anniversary and birthday parties (includes shopping for that special gift)
- Festive holiday parties
- Fun-filled company picnics and seminars

Experienced Business Networks

Party Pleasers recommends professional, detail-oriented vendors to provide the following services for your special event:

- Budget
- Site Selection
- Post-event Arrangements
- Catering (food and beverages)
- Bartending Services
- Florists
- Decorations and Party Supplies
- Entertainment
- Invitations, Announcements, and Programs
- Transportation
- Hotel and Travel Accommodations
- Photographers and Videographers
- Formal wear
- Makeup Artistry
- Registry and Gifts
- Rental Arrangements
- Complete Setup and Takedown

EXPECT ONLY THE BEST WITH PARTY PLEASERS!

Wedding Bells CONSULTING

Portland, Oregon
Contact: Marisol or Elissa
(503) 284-5826
E-mail: wbellsconsulting@aol.com

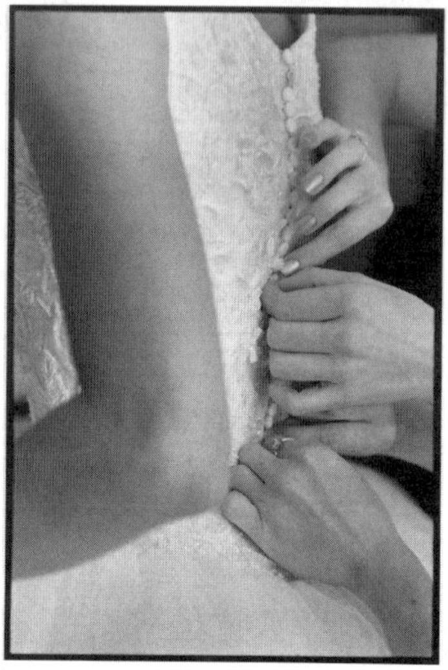

© Craig Strong

Unique Weddings and Events

Wedding Bells Consulting will work with you to develop ideas that make your wedding or event uniquely reflect your personal style.

Professional Product Management

From designing the perfect invitation to choosing the right location, Wedding Bells Consulting will help select the photographer, caterer, musician and more, all tailored to your budget and designed to bring your dream day to life.

Full Service Day or Evening Packages

Select from our full-service planning options or just take the stress out of the big day by having Wedding Bells Consulting handle the last minute details on your wedding day.

Dedicated to You

Wedding Bells consultants accept only one wedding per weekend, so your needs come first.

Experienced Event Planners

Our experienced event planners have over 10 years experience in coordinating events and weddings. Wedding Bells Consulting is available to help you plan your engagement party, bridal shower, rehearsal dinner and anniversary parties in addition to weddings.

Competitive Rates

Fees are based on services required.

Wedding Bliss

"Let Us Coordinate Your Day"
Portland, Oregon
Contact: Mary Berg
(503) 408-8315, Fax (503) 408-8342
E-mail: Weddingbliss@worldnet.att.net

© Kerry Wetzel Photography

It was a dark and snowy night. I was standing on the top deck of the Portland Spirit, freezing, while cars on either bridge around me crashed into one another. "I would be honored if you would be my wife," he said, looking up at me on bended knee. It was December 3rd, the night I became engaged…

Little did you know just what you were saying yes to when he popped the question. A wedding, so many things to look forward to, from telling your families and friends, to hiring consummate professionals, and of course, the months ahead of coordinating every little detail.

Do you really want to coordinate *every* little detail? Or would you rather give the responsibility of coordinating your wedding day to your mother or friends, taking away from their fun and enjoyment of the day?

Forget all that and let Wedding Bliss ease your mind, alleviate your stress and coordinate the details for you! By doing so, everyone, including yourself, will be able to enjoy the wedding day that you've been looking forward to ever since you were a little girl.

Whether it is an intimate gathering for 20, or a festive gala for 500, Wedding Bliss can provide as much or as little service as you need. Choose from our three different packages; vendor referral, rehearsal and wedding day service, or the full production—assistance with all the planning from the day you become engaged to the day you say "I do." Select the package that best suits your needs and spending plan.

In addition, we offer an initial consultation at no charge for you to meet with us and determine how we can assist you in the planning of this, the most memorable day of your life.

With Wedding Bliss, your wedding day will be everything you ever dreamed and one that you and your guests will remember for years to come.

◆ **Member of the Association of Catering & Event Professionals**

JEANNE LAPP

2925 Ascot Circle
West Linn, OR ❦ 97068
(503) 657-1070 ❦ Fax: 557-8825

Your Perfect Wedding

E-mail: jelapp@aol.com

You want your wedding to be perfect—each part carefully planned so that the special activities of the day flow smoothly, happen at the right time and never appear awkward. Whether you've decided on a small, intimate gathering or a grand celebration, Jeanne Lapp will help make your wedding day a dream come true.

Specialties

Weddings, and only weddings, are Jeanne's expertise. She devotes herself to helping each bride fulfill her special wedding dream. Caring, friendly and attentive to each bride's needs, she is dedicated to finding the right wedding professionals to work within a bride's vision, time frame and budget. Since producing weddings are her joy, you can rest assured that the end results will far exceed your own expectations.

Experience

Jeanne offers over ten years experience as a wedding consultant in the Portland area. Five of those years were spent as wedding coordinator at The Old Church. She has planned and carried out Bridal Faires and has given her own bridal workshops. Her customers know her as a consummate professional.

Dear Jeanne:
We want to thank you so much for all your advice and guidance in helping us plan our wedding. As newcomers to Portland, you made everything so easy and convenient for us. Your presence on the day of our wedding ensured that everything would be taken care of and allowed everyone to relax and have fun. We truly enjoyed ourselves!
Thanks again for your thoughtfulness and attention to detail.
~ Matt and Julie

From the moment you have your first conversation with Jeanne, until the final day when you prepare to walk down the aisle, you can take comfort in knowing that every detail of your special day will be handled professionally, carefully, and thoughtfully.

Fees

Call Jeanne to schedule a consultation to determine your needs. A fee will be quoted for the services you desire.

Dreams are fragile… place them in competent hands

© Strong Photography • page 523

TRADITIONS

The handkerchief carried by farmers' wives was a good luck charm. The tears cried at the wedding would bring rain for the crops. It was also said that "she who cried at her wedding wouldn't shed another tear afterwards."

•

Amongst the Romans a kiss was the bond to a legal agreement. At a wedding ceremony, however, it was the transfer of the power of the souls.

Romantic mansion located on two wooded acres overlooking the Willamette River

Amadeus at the FERNWOOD

2122 S.E. Sparrow (Off River Road Exit)
Milwaukie, Oregon 97222
Contact: Kristina (503) 659-1735, (503) 353-8948
Business Hours: Seven days a week, 5pm–midnight; Sunday Brunch 10am–2:30pm

Capacity: up to 300 people
Price Range: lunches $20; full course sit-down or buffet style dinners $30; plus gratuity
Catering: full-service in-house catering
Types of Events: bridal luncheons, rehearsal dinners, **on-location wedding ceremonies**, ceremonies and receptions, large group luncheons

Availability and Terms

We are here for your personal needs to make your rehearsal dinner celebration the most romantic and elegant. Reservations should be made as soon as possible to ensure availability. A deposit is required at the time of booking. Half the deposit is refundable if cancellations are made at least six months prior to your event. **No** cost for using the facility, bartending services, linens, flowers, and candles.

Description of Facility and Services

Seating: table and chairs provided for up to 300
Servers: provided with catering services
Bar facilities: full-service bar with bartender provided; host/no host; liquor provided according to OLCC regulations
Linens: cloth tablecloths and napkins provided in cream color
China and glassware: fine china; variety of glassware
Cleanup: provided by Amadeus at the Fernwood
Decorations: early decorating available; fresh flowers for guest tables provided by Amadeus; please discuss ideas with banquet representative
Parking: ample free parking; valet service
ADA: disabled access available

FACILITY OVERLOOKING WILLAMETTE RIVER

Amadeus at the Fernwood is the perfect setting for a romantic rehearsal dinner or wedding reception. You and your guests will enjoy fine continental dining in a wonderful old mansion on two wooded acres, filled with antiques, fireplaces, crystal chandeliers, candlelight and fresh flowers, overlooking the Willamette River. We offer a full bar with a wide variety of Oregon and international wines, and outdoor dining and wedding ceremonies on our patio is available. A classical pianist is featured nightly and during Sunday brunch.

SUNSET DINNER SPECIAL: Daily • 5–6:30pm • $9.95

Atwater's RESTAURANT & BAR

111 S.W. Fifth Avenue, 30th Floor • Portland, Oregon 97204
In-house contacts: Hollie Stafford (503) 275-3662 or Hollie@atwaters.com
Susan Lyon (503) 275-3615 or Susan@atwaters.com
Off-premise contact: Mary McKichan (503) 275-3615
Fax (503) 220-3659; Web site: www.atwaters.com

***Office Hours:** Mon–Fri 9am–6pm; **Restaurant:** Sun–Thurs 5pm–9pm; Fri–Sat 5pm–10pm*
***Bar:** Sun 5pm–9pm; Mon 4pm–9pm; Tue–Thurs 4pm–11pm; Fri 4pm–1am; Sat 5pm–1am*

Capacity: 10 to 300 people
Price Range: $30 per person and up
Catering: full-service in-house; off-premise catering up to 1,000 including food service, equipment, setup and cleanup
Types of Events: full sit-down meals, buffet, cocktails and hors d'oeuvres, theme parties

Availability and Terms

Atwater's has six separate dining rooms that can be used individually for groups of 10 to 60, or in combination to host as many as 300 guests. Atwater's requires a deposit ($100–$500) in advance to reserve space for your event. For cancellations within 180 days of the event, Atwater's will refund the deposit only if another event can be booked in your place. Deposits are credited toward your final bill. Events may be booked up to one year in advance.

Description of Facility and Services

Seating: tables and chairs for 300 available
Servers: included
Bar facilities: fine selection of wines and liquor; liquor liability, bar and bartenders provided courtesy of Atwater's
Dance floor: dance floor can be rented; large space available
Linens and napkins: cloth napkins and linens; ask about colors
China and glassware: china is white; many types of glassware
Decorations: please inquire about available table decorations; early decorating possible; decorations must conform to Portland's building and fire codes
Cleanup: we do it all
Parking: garage and street parking available; **ADA:** fully accessible

YOU SHOULD SEE OUR VIEW ON REHEARSAL DINNERS

Our 30th floor private dining suites provide an intimate and elegant setting for groups of 10 to 100. Our 11,000-square-foot banquet room on the 41st floor has a fresh, elegant new look and a breathtaking view of downtown—it can accommodate groups of up to 300 guests. In addition to our in-house catering, Atwater's offers full-service off-premise catering. Amenities include Atwater's cuisine, service staff, equipment, setup and cleanup. Whether it is a grand wedding celebration or an intimate dinner prepared in your kitchen by our chef, Atwater's will put on a flawless performance for you and your guests. Atwater's serves American cuisine featuring the bounty of the Pacific Northwest.

BUFFALO GAP SALOON & EATERY

6835 S.W. Macadam (just north of the Sellwood Bridge) • Portland, Oregon 97219
(503) 244-7111; Fax (503) 246-8848
Business Hours: Mon–Fri 7–2:30am, Sat 8–2:30am, Sun 9–2:30am
Office Hours: Mon–Fri 7am–5pm
Web site: www.buffalogap.citysearch.com

Capacity: up to 50 people
Price Range: typically $10–$15; customized menus available; room fees range from $35–100
Catering: full in-house catering exclusively
Types of Events: receptions, rehearsal dinners, parties, social events, business meetings

Availability and Terms

Early reservations strongly encouraged. The Buffalo Gap's "Attic" can be utilized as a completely private space, with full bar, private restrooms, and sundeck (weather permitting).

Description of Facility and Services

Seating: tables and chairs provided
Servers and bartenders: included in price
Bar facilities: two full-service bars; beer and wine
Linens and napkins: white or colored linens can be ordered
China and glassware: provided by Buffalo Gap
Decorations: table decorations are permissible
Cleanup: included at no extra charge
Parking: free on-site and adjacent parking available

Special Services

The Gap has one of the most beautiful and intimate (up to 24 guests) garden patios in the city, an upstairs sundeck, two full-service bars, a game and billiards room, a very accommodating staff, and live music six nights a week.

A GREAT GATHERING PLACE WITH SOMETHING FOR EVERYONE

The Buffalo Gap's building is over 100 years old, and has been used, among other things, as a private residence, rooming house, brothel and saloon. In business for over 25 years, with over 150 menu items to choose from, the gap is conveniently located and a wonderful experience for a diverse group of people.

1331 S.W. Washington
Portland, Oregon 97205
Contact: Christine, Bob or Mercedes
(503) 223-0054

A Portland Favorite since 1979!

Cassidy's Restaurant is located in a historic building in the heart of downtown Portland. Our exceptional menu features regional cuisine of delicious seafood, premium-cut meats, fresh pastas, seasonal salads and more.

Capacity: up to 70 people

Private Banquet Room

Cassidy's private banquet room is warm and inviting, and your guests will enjoy all the privileges of our restaurant service. The room is accented with beveled glass windows, natural woodwork and original art by Northwest artists. It is the perfect place for your rehearsal dinner.

Services

- **Food** From a sit-down dinner or extensive buffet to appetizers and desserts, we offer our fresh Northwest specialties. We'll help you plan a menu just right for your occasion.
- **Beverage** Cassidy's Restaurant offers a wide assortment of spirits, beers, wine and nonalcoholic beverages.
- **Staff** Cassidy's staff of experienced restaurant professionals also services our special events.
- **Cost** Cost is based on your choice of menu. There is no room charge for use of the banquet room or restaurant.
- **Linens** White tablecloths and napkins available at no additional cost.

Catering

Cassidy's offers full-service catering at the location of your choice.

RESERVE THE ENTIRE RESTAURANT
FOR AFTERNOON RECEPTIONS!

Call Bob, Mercedes or Christine for a consultation.

See page 305 under Caterers & Ice Carvings.

CHART HOUSE®

5700 S.W. Terwilliger Boulevard
Portland, Oregon 97201
(503) 246-6963
101 E. Columbia Way
Vancouver, Washington 98661
(360) 693-9211
Business Hours:
Mon–Fri 11:30am–10pm;
Sat 5–10pm; Sun 5–9pm

Capacity: 20 to 200 people
Price Range: please call for current prices
Catering: in-house
Types of Events: ceremonies, receptions, rehearsal dinners, bar mitzvahs, birthday parties and wakes

Availability and Terms

The entire facility is available for private functions on Saturdays and Sundays until 3:30pm, semi-private dining areas are available during lunch and dinner operating hours. Special event reservations are secured with a deposit. Semi-private area accommodates 60 in Vancouver, 120 in Portland.

Description of Facility and Services

Seating: we can create seating arrangements appropriate for any event
Servers: staff included in price; 19% gratuity on food and beverages
Bar facilities: full or limited bar available
Dance floor: 30-person capacity; electricity available for band or disc jockey
Linens: tablecloths and napkins available in many colors for a minimal charge
China and glassware: white china; clear glassware
Decorations: schedule early decorating; no limitations if decorations do not harm wood, plants, or paintings; flowers and candles available for arrangements; no confetti, please
Parking: complimentary valet parking
ADA: on entrance level; restroom for disabled

Special Services

Chart House offers a unique wedding and reception setting. Our banquet facility is located in a cozy room with a stone fireplace, bar and magnificent views of the city and mountains. We would be happy to offer help in arranging your event and recommending bakeries, florists and photographers. Cake cutting is complimentary.

SPECTACULAR VIEWS!

The Portland Chart House is perched high in the west hills with panoramic views of Mount Hood, Mount St. Helens, the Willamette River and the city lights below. Situated on the banks of the Columbia River, the Vancouver restaurant offers a serene view of the beautiful Northwest and ambiance of a waterfront setting. Both restaurants boast spectacular views coupled with the finest quality food and beverage, and a professionally trained staff that will ensure a memorable dining experience.

 Please let this business know that you heard about them from the Bravo! Bridal Resource Guide.

Ernesto's™

ITALIAN RESTAURANT

8544 S.W. Apple Way
Portland, Oregon 97225
Contact: Gwen Tiemeyer (503) 292-0119; Fax (503) 292-6451
Business Hours: Mon–Thu 11am–10pm; Fri 11am–11pm; Sat 4:30–11pm; Sun 4–10pm

---

Capacity: seating from 20 to 150 people, depending on requirements
Price Range: room rental and setup fees may be waived when meal minimums are met; ranges $9.95–$18.95
Catering: full service in-house and on-location catering
Types of Events: wedding receptions, rehearsal dinners, meetings, luncheons, banquets

Availability and Terms

Advance reservations of two to six months are recommended, however, we will try to accommodate last minute events when possible. A deposit is required to secure the room.

Description of Facility and Services

Seating: variety of seating options available for up to 150
Servers: provided
Bar facilities: host/no-host bars available; restaurant supplies all liquor and bartender
Dance floor: available upon request
Linens: cloth linens available in limited colors at no additional cost; special colors can be ordered for a fee
China and glassware: included in the cost of food and beverage
Decorations: standard decorations including helium balloons acceptable
Parking: ample free parking
ADA: meets all standards; all meeting rooms on ground level

CONVENIENT BEAVERTON LOCATION

Our new restaurant (between Jesuit High School and Zupans on Beaverton-Hillsdale Highway) features spacious dining rooms, a full-service lounge and gorgeous meeting/banquet rooms. Three generations of Italian recipes including fresh pasta, veal, chicken, pizza, calzone and charbroiled steaks. We feature banquet menus that include both Italian and American food, and we know you'll find the service and atmosphere first class. Accessible from both I-5 and Highway 217 and only 10 minutes from downtown Portland.

HALL STREET GRILL

3775 S.W. Hall Blvd.
Beaverton, Oregon 97005
Contact: Larry Baldwin
(503) 641-6161
Fax (503) 626-3713

Capacity: up to 100 people
Price Range: varies depending on selection
Catering: full-service in-house catering
Types of Events: rehearsal dinners, banquets, meetings

Availability and Terms

The Hall Street Grill is able to accommodate groups up to 100 for receptions or 60 for sit-down dinners on our covered patio. Reservations are taken up to one year in advance.

Description of Facility and Services

Seating: up to 60
Servers: provided by Hall Street Grill
Bar facilities: full-service bar available
Linens and napkins: provided
China and glassware: provided at no extra charge
Decorations: groups are welcome to provide decorations
Cleanup: included in price
Parking: ample free parking available
ADA: fully accessible

Special Services

Attention to detail and professionalism will ensure the success of your event.

WARM AND UNPRETENTIOUS PROFESSIONAL SERVICE

The Hall Street Grill emulates a bistro-roadhouse. With its high-beamed red ceilings, it has the feel of a French hunting lodge. Warm and unpretentious professional service provide a cozy, chic ambiance with historical Portland charcoal drawings and classic French bistro posters from the 1930s.

102 Oak Avenue
Hood River, Oregon
97031

HOOD RIVER HOTEL & Pasquale's ristorante

Reservations
(800) 386-1859

Sales
(541) 386-1900

E-mail: HRHotel@gorge.net; Web site: www.hoodriverhotel.com

A unique location for your rehearsal dinner— the Hood River Hotel

Capacity: 5 to 200 guests
Price Range: price varies according to room, time of year, and menu selection
Catering: full-service in-house catering or off-premise
Types of Events: weddings, receptions, rehearsal dinners; informal hors d'oeuvres to formal sit-down dinners; off-site catering available

Availability and Terms

Hood River Hotel's ballroom can accommodate up to 250 people. Additional areas are available for groups of 20 or fewer. We suggest that you book early to ensure availability. A deposit is required at time of booking to secure your date with the balance due the day of your event.

Description of Facility and Services

Seating: tables and chairs for up to 200 people
Servers and cleanup: included in catering cost
Bar facilities: full liquor service from Pasquale's Ristorante and Wine Cellar Bar; bartender included in price quote; extensive selection of wines and champagnes
Dance floor: accommodates up to 55 people
Linens and napkins: cloth linens available in a variety of colors
China and glassware: traditional pattern; assorted glassware
Decorations: floral supplies available upon request; early decorating by prior arrangement; some restrictions apply; in-house florist available
Parking: on-street and designated off-site parking
ADA: fully accessible

Special Services

- Baby Grand piano
- Dance floor and stage
- Wine Cellar
- Built-in sound and PA system
- Full bar
- Wood burning fireplace

ROMANTIC AMBIENCE

The Hood River Hotel offers the romantic ambience you're looking for. With our Baby Grand piano and built-in sound and PA system, you can enjoy a variety of music at your event. Use our Wine Cellar for a wine tasting party or entertain your guests by our wood burning fireplace.

Il Fornaio

115 N.W. 22nd Avenue
Portland, Oregon 97210
Contact: Faith Chhim, Event Coordinator (503) 248-4324
(503) 248-9400; Fax (503) 248-5678
Business Hours: Mon-Thu 11:30am–10pm;
Fri–Sat 11:30am–11pm; Sun 10am–10pm
E-mail: fchhim@ilfo.com; Web site: www.ilfornaio.com

Capacity: Private Dining Room up to 28 guests; Piazza (room) up to 55 guests; Piazza and the Private Dining Room combined accommodate up to 80 guests or receptions from 2–5 p.m. up to 130 people; Sala delle Luci (front window room) up to 75 guests

Price Range: varies according to menu selection; no room rental fee; minimum of $16.95 per person for lunch and $27.95 for dinner; a customized menu can be created to meet your specific needs and budget

Types of Events: full sit-down dining is available for rehearsal dinners, receptions, bridal showers, parties, and other special occasions

Availability and Terms

Il Fornaio has an intimate Private Dining Room that can accommodate up to 28 people. In addition, our indoor Piazza garden room with a fireplace and a retractable roof provides a warm setting for groups up to 55 guests. This room is available year round and can be combined with our Private Dining room to accommodate 80 guests or receptions from 2-5 p.m. up to 130 people. The Sala delle Luci area is a semi-private room filled with light that pours in from huge windows that look out onto Mount Hood. This room holds a maximum of 50 people for a sit-down dinner and 75 for cocktail parties.

The authentic Italian menu features wood fired pizzas, rotisserie meats, mesquite grilled local fish, and fresh regional pastas. Each meal includes house baked breads made fresh throughout the day. We also offer a buffet brunch on Sunday from 10am-1pm.

Description of Facility and Services

Seating: provided to accommodate group size
Servers: provided
Bar facilities: full bar, extensive Northwest and Italian wines and full service cafe-bar
Linens: white linen
Decorations: flowers, displays and decorative items are welcome
Parking: valet parking
ADA: elevator available

IL FORNAIO OFFERS AUTHENTIC ITALIAN CUISINE

Il Fornaio offers friendly and professional service in a setting that is comfortable and intimate. Bring your next special occasion to Il Fornaio with award-winning authentic Italian food and wine. Our friendly and knowledgeable staff will work with you to create a menu that is befitting to your group. We look forward to helping you plan a memorable occasion.

 Please let this business know that you heard about them from the Bravo! Bridal Resource Guide.

112 S.W. Second Avenue
Portland, Oregon 97204
Contact: Brad Yoast
(503) 227-4057; Fax (503) 227-5931

KELLS
PORTLAND'S IRISH RESTAURANT & PUB

E-mail: portland@kellsirish.com • Web site: http://www.kellsirish.com

---

Capacity: private banquet facilities located on second floor; capacities range from 15–150 and up to 300 reception-style
Price Range: varies according to room and services
Catering: full-service in-house and off-premise catering
Types of Events: buffet and formal sit-down service for receptions, rehearsal dinners, business luncheons, cocktail and hors d' oeuvre parties, holiday and surprise parties, fund raisers and gala events

Availability and Terms

The K Club is located on the second floor of the historic Kells building near the waterfront in downtown Portland. With the Irish ambiance, excellent service and outstanding food you've come to expect from Kells, the elegant K Club invites your guests to celebrate in the stately ballroom and mingle in the intimate Ulster and Cigar Rooms.

Description of Facility and Services

Seating: variety of seating customized to meet your needs from 15–150
Servers: included in service
Bar facilities: host/no host bar; largest single malt selection in the northwest, full range of micro beers, extensive wine list; fine cigars also available
Dance floor: we offer two separate locations for bands, a long list of our most popular local acts, electrical hook-ups available
Linens and napkins: included in service; inquire about our color selection
China and glassware: white china with glassware to complement
Cleanup: included with full-service catering
Decorations: discussion of your ideas and needs welcomed
Parking: parking for events may be made in advance, garages within close proximity
ADA: Kells first floor is ADA accessible; parties may be arranged for this space as well

PORTLAND'S FAVORITE IRISH RESTAURANT & PUB

Kells has become a Portland landmark since its opening in 1990. One of Portland's favorite nightspots, Kells offers a great menu of New World Irish cuisine mixing traditional favorites with fresh, northwest seafoods, produce, and all-natural ingredients. Kells also features live Irish music seven nights a week, a grand stone fireplace and comfortable cigar room. All this and the warm, friendly service and atmosphere of a genuine Irish Pub.

PARAGON

RESTAURANT · BAR

FUN DINING · PLUSH BOOTHS · GENEROUS COCKTAILS

1309 N.W. Hoyt
Portland, Oregon 97209
Contact: Joseph Moreau (503) 833-5060
Web site: www.paragonrestaurant.com
Office Hours: Tues–Sat 11am-6pm; Restaurant Hours: Open every day

---

Capacity: 20 to 150 guests
Price Range: determined by type of event
Catering: full-service in-house; off-site events
Types of Events: receptions, rehearsals, lunch and dinner parties; you may select full sit-down service, buffet or cocktail party

Availability and Terms

The entire facility is available for private functions. Upper dining room and private room available separately or together. Deposit required to secure the date. Final payment due on the date of the event.

Description of Facility and Services

Seating: indoor seating for up to 100 guests; outdoor seating for up to 25 guests
Servers: provided by Paragon
Bar facilities: full bar or limited bar
Dance floor: 20 person capacity; stage and electrical available for musicians
Linens: white linen; other colors available for minimal charge
China and glassware: white china; clear glassware
Decorations: candles provided; schedule early decorating; no nails, tacks, tape or confetti
Cleanup: provided by Paragon
Parking: ample street and pay lot parking; valet parking negotiable
ADA: fully accessible

Special Services

We are happy to assist you in all aspects of your special day including menu selection, decorations, music and any other details to make your event especially memorable. We are pleased to recommend photographers, florists and bakeries.

RUSTIC NORTHWEST CUISINE

Based upon the concept of a quintessential "neighborhood" restaurant and bar, Paragon Restaurant is a lively bistro featuring farm-fresh American cuisine, a fun, full-service bar and friendly staff. Paragon is located in the heart of the Pearl District, the home of Portland's art community, sophisticated urbanites, and vintage brick warehouse buildings—all just five minutes from downtown. Paragon's design mixes the timeless elements of a traditional grill-style restaurant with modern artistry in a converted warehouse. The unique private banquet room seats up to 22 people and features a slide-up wall to adapt to your privacy needs. The upper dining room is available for special events and can seat up to 50 people. Paragon also has ample patio seating for outdoor dining. Our chef is happy to work with you to create a menu that matches your needs. Whether it is a cocktail party, a sit-down meal, buffet or business meeting, Paragon is the perfect venue for a memorable event.

 Please let this business know that you heard about them from the Bravo! Bridal Resource Guide.

RHEINLANDER

5035 N.E. Sandy Blvd.
Portland, Oregon 97213
Contact: Banquet Staff
(503) 288-8410
Business Hours: Mon–Fri 9am–5pm

Capacity: 20 to 85 people; 100 people for stand-up
Price range: please call for current prices, customized menus available
Catering: full in-house catering; call for information regarding outside catering
Types of Events: sit-down dinners, hors d'oeuvres, rehearsal dinners, wedding receptions, anniversaries, birthdays, holiday parties, retirements, luncheons, meetings, seminars and corporate functions

Availability and Terms

Our beautiful banquet rooms can accommodate up to 100 people. We recommend reserving a room as soon as possible, but welcome you on short notice—space permitting! We require a deposit which is applied to the balance.

Description of Facility and Services

Seating: round or rectangular tables available depending on your size and needs
Servers: staff included
Bar facilities: host or no-host bars with a minimum setup fee; bartender included; cocktail service provided at no charge
Linens and napkins: linen tablecloths and napkins; color coordination available
China and glassware: beautiful, traditional china and glassware provided
Cleanup: provided by Rheinlander
Decorations: pre-approved by the banquet staff; tape only; early access for decorating. Ask about our additional decorating services!
Parking: free parking; private banquet entrance
ADA: Rheinlander is entirely handicap accessible

Special Services

We specialize in wedding rehearsal dinners, small receptions, and private dinner parties. We want your event to be perfect and exactly how you imagined it to be. Our experienced banquet staff will work with you on every detail. Please call for an appointment to view rooms, look at samples or even taste the food!

BEAUTIFUL BANQUET ROOMS ENHANCED BY DELIGHTFUL ENTERTAINMENT!

The Rheinlander is proudly celebrating 36 years in Portland. We offer authentic German cuisine and fresh continental specialties including poultry, beef, seafood and pork. Strolling accordionists and singers complement your evening with their beautiful music.

Salty's

ON THE COLUMBIA

3839 N.E. Marine Drive
Portland, Oregon 97211
Contact: Dorothy Lane
(503) 288-4444; Fax (503) 284-7397
Web site: http://www.saltys.com

Restaurant Hours:
Lunch Mon–Sat 11:15am–3pm; Dinner Mon–Thur 5–10pm, Fri–Sat 5–10:30pm; Sunday Brunch 9:30am–2pm; Sunday Dinner 4:30–9:30pm; winter hours vary

---

Capacity: up to 200 guests
Price Range: call for current prices
Catering: full-service catering; in-house or off-premise
Types of Events: rehearsal dinners, wedding receptions, bridal showers, anniversary celebrations and other events; private breakfasts, sit-down dinners and luncheons, seafood and brunch buffets, cocktails and hors d'oeuvres

Availability and Terms

We recommend reserving your space three to six months in advance. But if you need assistance with last minute planning—we can help! A deposit is required to reserve your date. Room fees are waived with a minimum purchase of food and beverage.

Description of Facility and Services

Seating: a variety of table sizes and seating options
Servers: after a specified minimum gratuity or 18%, servers provided at no additional charge
Bar facilities: full-service bar provided courtesy of Salty's; host/no-host; liquor, beer and wine
Linens: house colors available at no additional charge
China and glassware: restaurant silver, china and glassware available
Audiovisual: overhead and slide projector with screen; TV, VCR, flip charts available for rent
Cleanup: handled by Salty's staff
Parking: plenty of free parking; complimentary valet service available Mon–Sat nights
ADA: first floor accessible for handicapped; Wine Room and North Shore View Room are on second floor

Special Services

Our catering director works closely with you to ensure your event's success. We print a personalized menu for you and your guests. We are happy to refer you to florists, DJs and musicians. At Salty's, we pride ourselves on catering to your every whim.

GIVE YOUR WEDDING A BETTER POINT OF VIEW!

Salty's is located on the riverfront only 15 minutes from downtown Portland. We provide the perfect recipe for memorable occasions; rehearsal dinners, wedding receptions, or bridal showers for up to 200 guests. Salty's exceptional Northwest cuisine, warm hospitality, and spectacular views of the mighty Columbia and majestic Mount Hood will make your event a very special occasion! We're easy to get to, and ready to serve you the very best seafood, steaks, Sunday Brunch, and riverfront view in Portland.

 Please let this business know that you heard about them from the Bravo! Bridal Resource Guide.

Sayler's OLD COUNTRY KITCHEN

4655 S.W. Griffith Drive
Beaverton, Oregon 97005

10519 S.E. Stark
Portland, Oregon 97216

Contact: Sally Kanan (503) 252-4171 or (503) 644-1492

Capacity: 10 to 300 people
Price range: $7 to $20
Catering: in-house
Types of events: receptions, rehearsal dinners, meetings, banquets

Availability and Terms

West: Two private rooms available day and night. Outside patio available day and night. The entire restaurant is available Mon–Fri 7am–2pm and can be split into five separate areas.

East: Six rooms are available or the entire restaurant is available Mon–Fri 7am–4pm and Sat 7am–2:30pm.

Not available on Sunday. Reservations are on a first come, first obtained basis and should be made no later than two weeks before the event. A 50% deposit is requested with signed contract.

Description of Facility and Services

Seating: tables and chairs provided
Servers: provided by Sayler's
Bar facilities: main or portable bar available; bartenders, liquor and liability provided
Dance floor: 12′ x 12′ floor can be rented; electrical available
Linens: white available for no charge; colored linens available at extra charge
China and glassware: white china and glassware provided
Decorations: flexible; please inquire
Cleanup: provided by Sayler's staff; charge will be applied for any damage
Parking: plenty of free parking
ADA: ADA approved

Special Services

The entire restaurant is available during the day with plenty of free parking. Every function has its own host to look after any group needs.

WE SERVE A GREAT AMERICAN MEAL

The Old Country Kitchen is perfect for small daytime meetings, Monday through Friday, large daytime receptions and small banquets or rehearsal dinners in the evening. We specialize in great, affordable, American food. Try our prime beef, exceptional seafood and home-style chicken. Buffets, sit-down or food stations, are our specialty. You get all the amenities of a restaurant but lots of privacy for your meetings.

The Sweetbrier Inn

7125 S.W. Nyberg Road (Exit 289 off I-5)
Tualatin, Oregon 97062
Contact: Sales & Catering Office
(503) 692-5800, (800) 551-9167; Fax (503) 404-1950
Web site: www.Sweetbrier.com
Office Hours: Mon–Fri 7:30am–5:30pm; Sat 9am–1pm

Capacity: up to 250 for dinner; up to 300 for reception
Price Range: creative, customized menus to fit your budget
Catering: full-service in-house catering
Types of Events: cocktails and hors d'oeuvres, buffets, sit-down luncheons or dinners, rehearsal dinners, wedding receptions, anniversary, special event celebrations, holiday parties

Availability and Terms

Four separate rooms are available; we can seat 250 for dinner or 300 for a reception. You can reserve for day or night.

Description of Facility and Services

Seating: tables and chairs
Servers: staff included in catering costs
Bar facilities: full-service bar available
Dance floor: 225 square feet of dance floor; PA systems and risers available
Linens: white linen tablecloths and colored napkins; white skirting
China and glassware: white china; assorted glassware
Decorations: creative catering staff to assist you
Parking: ample free parking
ADA: all facilities ADA accessible

Hotel Features

The Sweetbrier Inn offers 131 guest rooms including 32 luxury two-room suites. Honeymoon packages are also available.

PARKLIKE SETTING

The Sweetbrier Inn is conveniently located off I-5, and offers a bistro-style restaurant, a lounge featuring live jazz music, meeting and banquet facilities, and 131 guest rooms. The banquet rooms overlook a garden setting which provides the perfect atmosphere for a rehearsal dinner, reception or wedding. The spiral staircase in the lobby, or the garden area by the pool, offer excellent ambiance for those special photographs on your memorable day.

SYLVIA'S ITALIAN RESTAURANT & CLASS ACT DINNER THEATRE

5115 N.E. Sandy Blvd. • Portland, Oregon 97213
Contact: Banquet Manager (503) 288-6828
Dinner: Sun 3–9pm; Mon–Thurs 4–10pm; Fri, Sat 4–11pm
Dinner Theatre: Thurs–Sat 6:30pm dinner, 8pm show
Sun Matinee 11:30am brunch, 1pm show;
5:30pm dinner, 7pm show

Web site:
http://www.sylvias.net

Enjoy the abundance of hospitality and generosity served up at one of Portland's foremost and popular Italian restaurants. Sylvia's has been a family tradition since 1957 offering quality Italian food and providing friendly service in an authentic and pleasant atmosphere.

Capacity: Piazza Room, 80 people; Dinner Theatre, 100 people (limited evenings)
Price Range: $9 and up (including room)
Catering: off-premise up to 5,000 people
Types of Events: rehearsal dinners, family feasts, wedding receptions, sit-down, buffet, cocktails, hors d'oeuvres, meetings

Availability and Terms

Sylvia's can be reserved on an as-available basis, with a minimum $100 nonrefundable deposit. We request a minimum of two-weeks notice for cancellations.

Description of Facility and Services

Seating: tables and chairs provided
Servers: staff included if you use in-house banquet facilities; 16% gratuity added
Bar facilities: full bar
Dance floor: available on request; extra charge
Linens and napkins: burgundy cloth linens and napkins at no charge; other colors available for extra charge
China and glassware: white dinnerware and restaurant glassware available for in-house banquets
Decorations: brass lanterns provided; table decorations provided for a charge; early decorating welcomed; please no confetti
Audiovisual: equipment available upon request for an extra charge
Equipment: podium and easel available
Cleanup: provided by Sylvia's
Parking: parking available at no additional cost
ADA: fully accessible

Sylvia's
"a place to celebrate food, a place to cherish friends."

WIDMER GASTHAUS

955 N. Russell • Portland, Oregon 97227
Contact: Gasthaus Managers (503) 281-3333; Fax (503) 331-7242
Business Hours: Mon–Thurs 11am–11pm, Fri–Sat 11am–1am, Sun noon–9pm

---

Capacity: private room, 20–46 guests; parties of 47–75 require special arrangements
Price Range: $10 to $20 per person
Catering: in-house only
Types of Events: rehearsal dinners, birthdays, retirements, holiday parties, business dinners, or any other event where great beer and delicious food will make your party complete

Availability and Terms

All parties require a nonrefundable $100 deposit to secure a date and will be considered tentative until receipt of deposit. A food and beverage minimum of $250 is required Sunday through Thursday; $350 minimum on Friday and Saturday. A 17% gratuity is applied to all food and beverage including no host bar.

Description of Facility and Services

Seating: tables and chairs for up to 46; up to 75 requires special arrangements
Servers: provided
Bar facilities: hand-crafted beers brewed on location as well as a variety of wines and soft drinks available
Dance floor: not available
Linens: white linen is provided on food and beverage tables during banquets with an array of colors available for formal dinners at a nominal fee
Decorations: no nails, tacks or confetti please
Audiovisual: large screen TV, video, DMX sound system
Equipment: overhead and slide projectors and other equipment available at a minimal charge
Cleanup: included
Parking: plenty of on-street parking as well as two parking lots
ADA: yes

FRIENDLY SETTING COUPLED WITH FINE BEER AND WINE

Widmer Gasthaus is a friendly place to enjoy fine food and our excellent handcrafted beers. The Gasthaus is housed in a turn-of-the-century brick building, adjacent to the famous Widmer Brewery. Our chef and staff are experienced in all types of events, from formal dining to Super Bowl parties, so let us make your next celebration one to remember! All information regarding the Gasthaus and its menus can be faxed to you and our managers will be happy to answer any questions you may have regarding availability or menu planning. Until then, PROST!

© red door studio • page 520

THE NOISIER THE BETTER

In order to chase away any evil spirits that

may be lurking about, rehearsal dinners were

a melee of broken glass and china,

reaffirming the belief that the more noise made

the better when it came to disposing of evil spirits.

HELPFUL HINTS

- **Begin looking for your reception, banquet, or meeting site immediately:** As soon as the engagement is announced, the first decision to be made is where to hold the event. Meet first with your clergyman to find out the days and times available at your church or synagogue.
- **Visit the location:** When you narrow down the options of sites available, view the room in person before you reserve it or send a deposit. Oftentimes the look and feel of a room or location will sway a decision one way or another. It is also easier to plan an event by keeping the room's layout and size in mind.
- **Be flexible:** If you are insistent about a certain date and time, you may spend weeks searching all over town for a place to accommodate your needs. By the time you finally discover that no options are available your first choice may also be booked on your alternate dates.
- **Be honest about your budget:** Do not be afraid to tell the facility coordinator or event planner what your budget is. This very important information can be used as a guideline and can save time and effort. Trust the person in charge to help create a successful event. They can offer time- and budget-saving recommendations based on experience.
- **Deposits are important:** Remember that when you reserve a facility, a deposit is usually required. Even though you thought your date was secure, the site is not formally reserved until a deposit is received. Many brides have lost their reception site by overlooking this fact.
- **Host or hostess for your wedding:** Ask someone to be the host or hostess for the reception. The family usually doesn't arrive at the reception until after the guests. If you have a host or hostess to greet the guests and direct them to the punch or coat rack, they will feel more comfortable.
- **Gift table:** Assign a reliable person to be in charge of gifts at the reception. He or she should have scotch tape handy to tape cards securely to packages. It is very frustrating and embarrassing to open gifts and not know who they were from. When a card is given as a gift, many times it will have cash or a check inside. These cards should be placed in a box marked "card only." Rental shops rent a wishing well with a slit in the top to slip cards through, or wrap a box and put a slit in the top. Make sure you have a vehicle to take the gifts to a safe place an hour or so after the reception begins.

For more assistance with staying organized during the wedding planning process, check out the Bravo! Wedding Organizer. Detailed question worksheets double as contracts. This step-by-step system will keep every detail of your wedding organized. To order, refer to the order form on page 24 in this Guide.

STERNWHEELER "COLUMBIA GORGE" & MARINE PARK

1200 N.W. Front Avenue, Suite 110
Portland, Oregon 97209 • (503) 223-3928
Web site: www.sternwheeler.com
E-mail: sternwheeler@inetarena.com

Owned & operated by the Port of Cascade Locks

Capacity: 200 sit-down, 350 reception
Price Range: varies depending on number of guests and length of cruise; minimum of two hours; please call
Catering: full range of catering services provided including menu selections for champagne toasts, complete dinners and hors d'oeuvres packages
Types of Events: weddings, receptions, party cruises, casino cruises—hors d'oeuvre or dinner-style

Availability and Terms

We offer a variety of accommodations for wedding parties up to 350 aboard the Sternwheeler "Columbia Gorge." Two fully enclosed heated decks provide a comfortable setting for any time of year. Marine Park and Thunder Island can accommodate up to 4,000 guests. A 25% nonrefundable deposit is required upon booking; final payment is due 60–120 days prior to scheduled event depending upon the season.

Description of Facility and Services

Seating: tables and chairs provided
Servers: provided
Bar facilities: two to three full-service bars with bartenders available
Dance floor: dance area available; full electrical hookup
Linens and napkins: cloth linens and napkins; color coordination available
China and glassware: house china available with our catering service
Decorations: elegant turn-of-the-century motif requires little decoration
Cleanup: provided courtesy of the Sternwheeler crews
Parking: *Cascade Locks Marine Park:* free parking; *Portland:* City Center and off-street parking available for a fee
ADA: disabled accessible

Special Services

With two rivers and an abundance of breathtaking views to choose from, the Sternwheeler "Columbia Gorge" and Marine Park continue to provide a unique venue for your wedding/ceremony and reception.

As a unique wedding site, we can provide catering and menu selection, music and entertainment. We can also coordinate a performance of your ceremony by one of our credited Captains. Please call our sales office to arrange a tour of either of the Sternwheeler "Columbia Gorge" or our 23-acre Marine Park and Thunder Island.

PORTLAND SPIRIT
WILLAMETTE STAR
CRYSTAL DOLPHIN

110 S.E. Caruthers • Portland, Oregon 97213
(503) 224-3900, (800) 224-3901
Web site: http://www.portlandspirit.com
E-mail: sales@portlandspirit.com

Offering spectacular views, outstanding service and first-class Northwest cuisine, prepared on board in each ship's galley. Our event planning services ensure that not one detail is overlooked, from a rehearsal dinner for 25 to an elegant sit down dinner reception for 340. A cruise on the **Portland Spirit**, **Willamette Star, or Crystal Dolphin** will guarantee the perfect place for your special day.

Availability, Price and Terms

The Portland Spirit vessels are available year round from downtown Portland. You may charter the entire **Portland Spirit** vessel or one-deck rentals are available. The **Portland Spirit** also offers public cruise schedules. The **Willamette Star** and **Crystal Dolphin** are available for private charter and offer limited public cruise schedules. Deposit and signed contract confirms cruise date. Prices depend on time of day, season of year and number of guests. NOTE: Capacity recommendations on each vessel depend on time of year, menu selected and type of wedding planned. Please call for specific recommendations.

Portland Spirit

130 foot, three level yacht, two outside decks
Available for full boat charter, one deck rental
Capacity: up to 540 guests
Seating: tables and chairs for 350, plus outside seating
Dance floor: large marble dance floor

Crystal Dolphin

130 foot, three level yacht, two outside decks
Available for private charter
Capacity: 90 guests
Seating: tables and chairs for 40, plus outside seating

Willamette Star

75 foot, two level yacht, two outside decks
Available for private charter
Capacity: up to 120 guests
Seating: tables and chairs for 80, plus outside seating
Dance floor: available

Description of Vessel Services and Facilities

Enclosed decks are temperature controlled
Linens: linen tablecloths and napkins provided
China: our house china and glassware provided
Servers: included with food and bar service
Bar facilities: full service bar, liquor, bartenders and liability insurance
Cleanup: provided
Parking: commercial and street parking available
ADA: limited with assistance

THE STERNWHEELER ROSE

PORTLAND STEAM NAVIGATION CO.

6211 N. Ensign

Portland, Oregon 97217

Contact: Judy (503) 286-ROSE (7673)

Business Hours: Mon–Fri 8am–5pm

ROMANTIC RIVER SETTING

Cruising aboard *The Sternwheeler Rose* is a unique way to make your wedding special. It's also a festive place for a rehearsal dinner, bachelor party or a bridal shower. We offer a standard wedding package that includes boat charter, ceremony by Captain, elegant hors d'oeuvre buffet, champagne, flowers, invitations, napkins and wedding cake. Of course, you are welcome to create your own package. Our experienced caterer can provide you with suggestions or create the specific menu of your choice—you're limited only by your imagination and budget! Additionally, our staff, crew and captains are available to help you plan every step and execute every detail to make your wedding a wonderful and memorable event.

Capacity: up to 130 people; you may reserve the entire boat for your private cruise
Price Range: customized wedding packages available; prices vary; please inquire
Catering: licensed, in-house catering available; flexible menus
Types of Events: wedding ceremonies, receptions, dinners, dances, rehearsal dinners, parties

Availability and Terms

The Sternwheeler Rose is Portland's finest year-round charter boat. It cruises on the Willamette river. A deposit of 50% is required. Terms are available.

Description of Facility and Services

Boarding location: OMSI; other boarding sites can be scheduled
Seating: tables and chairs provided
Servers: provided
Bar facilities: beer, wine, champagne, soft drinks and bartender standard; full-service bar available
Dance floor: floor for up to 80 people; electrical hookups available
Linens and napkins: all colors of linen tablecloths and cloth napkins available
China and glassware: glass plates, glasses and barware available
Decorations: No candles, confetti or propane allowed
Cleanup: complete cleanup courtesy of The Sternwheeler Rose with catering
Parking: free at OMSI

Special Services

Be sure to ask about decorations both for ideas and logistics

We Invite You To Celebrate On
The Sternwheeler Rose

Please call if you have any questions or would like more information.
We at The Sternwheeler Rose look forward to serving you.

Visit us at www.sternwheelerrose.com.

"WILLAMETTE QUEEN" STERNWHEELER

Located at Riverfront Park—Salem, Oregon
Contact: Irene Solomon
Message phone: (503) 371-1103, (541) 928-4090

WELCOME ABOARD THE 'WILLAMETTE QUEEN,' designed as a scaled down likeness of the former Mississippi and Yukon Territory Riverboats. Relive Oregon's historical past in an elegant dining experience as the ship leisurely glides along the Willamette River.

Capacity: **Dining room:** up to 92; during summer months an additional 15 can be accommodated on outer decks
Price Range: $10; excursions to $35 (dinner with two hour cruise)
Catering: daily lunches, Sunday brunches, dinners, hors d'oeuvres
Types of Events: birthdays, anniversaries, business meetings, banquets, weddings, class reunions, proms, fundraisers—both private and public

Availability and Terms

Reserve seating as soon as possible. Caterers require a 48 hour minimum notice for larger groups; smaller groups may be more flexible.

Description of Facility and Services

Seating: up to 115
Bar facilities: full-service bar
Dance floor: 12′ x 12′ dance floor available
Linens and napkins: available at no charge
China and glassware: available at no charge
Decorations: flowers, table decorations available, special decorations to be approved
Audiovisual: TV, VCR available at no charge
Equipment: podium, cordless microphone and punch bowels available at no charge
Cleanup: provided; fee for rearrangement of room setup
Parking: available at both Bowman and Salem Riverfront Park
ADA: ADA approved ramps at Bowman and Salem Riverfront Park

Special Services

The captain is a licensed minister and can perform weddings, renewal of vows, live music DJs, melodrama, talent nights and holiday events.

Sternwheeler Excursions, Inc.
P.O. Box 2228
Corvallis, Oregon 97339

A Night In Shining Amour

Regal Hall Ballroom

115 W. Ninth Street
Vancouver, Washington 98660
Contact: Joe and Pam Thielman
(360) 750-7891
E-mail: jthielm@pacifier.com
Web site: www.shining-amour.com

Capacity: theatre style: 120; reception: 175; meetings and other events depend on type of setup required

Price Range: varies depending on event and length of time needed; please call

Catering: full range of catering services can be provided or you can self cater your event with a deposit

Types of Events: specializing in weddings and receptions, management retreats, banquets, employee parties, meetings, seminars, and privately catered family gatherings

Availability and Terms

Call for availability. A 50% deposit is required at time of booking based on the time required at a rate of $150 per hour for the first four hours and $90 per hour after the initial four hours. Balance is due one week prior to event. Lower prices are available during the week.

Description of Facility and Services

Seating: all-white wooden chairs with padded seats, rectangular or round tables available and seating arranged as requested

Servers: provided, or as you desire

Bar facilities: arranged on request

Dance floor: beautiful hardwood flooring makes the entire ballroom area a wonderful place to dance

Linen: provided

China: available for rent or you provide

Decorations: beautiful white and gold decor accommodates a wide variety of color schemes

Cleanup: provided or extra charge, depending on package

Parking: street side and several parking lots and garages nearby

Audiovisual: available

ADA: complied

About Us

We are Pam and Joe Thielman and will serve as the host/hostess of your function, attending to every detail, if you wish. We endeavor to remain as flexible as possible regarding our service to you. We have many resources available to make your event the best it can be and will work with you to control your costs.

Built in 1910, the building has been remodeled, giving it an ambiance and charm of style and grace. You will find the ballroom a wonderful place for your special event.

THE ACADEMY CHAPEL & BALLROOM

400 East Evergreen Blvd.
Vancouver, Washington 98660
Windsor Wedding Consultants, Suite 216
(360) 696-4884
Business Hours: Tues–Fri 10am–5pm; evenings by appointment

Capacity: up to 225 guests, ceremony; up to 300 guests, reception
Price Range: beginning at $250 and up for chapel, and $700 and up for ballroom
Catering: no in-house catering; full kitchen facility available
Types of Events: sit-down, buffet, hors d'oeuvres, cake and punch

Availability and Terms

The Academy has a ballroom and a chapel. The ballroom's maximum capacity is 300 people; prices start at $700 for weekday rental. The chapel will hold a maximum of 225 people; $250 fee for weekdays. A deposit is required, and advance reservation of two to six months is recommended.

Description of Facility and Services

Seating: tables and chairs provided
Servers: provided by your caterer or yourself
Bar facilities: portable bar available in ballroom; you provide bartenders, liquor, and liability
Dance floor: 17′x26′ dance floor in ballroom
Linens and napkins: can be rented on location
China and glassware: not available from the Academy
Cleanup: included in price
Decorations: inquire about our table decorations
Parking: free parking for 400 cars
ADA: yes

Special Services

We have a variety of items and services to choose from: elegant silk-flower and candle arrangements for rent; invitations, ring pillows, cake tops and unity candles for purchase. Windsor Wedding Consultants will plan all or part of your wedding to perfection while keeping within your budget specifications.

BREATHTAKINGLY BEAUTIFUL

Located in the historic Academy building in Vancouver, Washington, the Academy Chapel features a breathtaking, three-story-high carved altar, beautiful stained-glass windows, and a lovely balcony at the rear of the chapel—perfect for a soloist. The grand ballroom is decorated with elegant wallpaper, chandeliers, and blue-gray carpet. The Academy is only 15 minutes from downtown Portland and is easy to find, with ample free parking. Give Windsor Weddings a call today to tour our facility.

© Adams & Faith

The Adrianna Hill Grand Ballroom

An Enchanting Place of Celebration

918 S.W. Yamhill • Second Floor • Portland, Oregon 97205
Philip Sword or Barbara Abalan (503) 227-6285 • Shown by appointment only
E-mail: accentevnt@aol.com

Capacity: up to 300 guests
Price Range: charge varies
Catering: and event planning provided exclusively by Accent on Events; $15.95 per person and up
Types of Events: wedding ceremonies and receptions, corporate and private celebrations, concerts, dances, fundraisers, reunions, holiday parties, proms, auctions and more

Availability and Terms

A 50% facility deposit is required to confirm your date at one of the most unique, prestigious and sought-after facilities in the Pacific Northwest. Early reservations suggested.

Description of Facility and Services

Facility rental: includes Victorian ballroom decor, all tables and chairs, dressing room for bridal party, full service bar area, Roman columns, ambiant lighting, gift and guest book tables and coat racks
Event staff: experienced managers, chefs, waitstaff, licensed bartenders and kitchen personnel provided by Accent on Events (included in catering costs)
Bar facilities: all bar services provided by Accent on Events, Inc. (full bar available)
Dance floor: hardwood floors perfect for dancing; custom stereo sound system available for cassette tapes or CDs; bands and DJs welcome
Silverware, china, glassware and linens: included in catering costs
Parking: across the street at 10th Avenue and Yamhill Street—City Center Parking

TURN-OF-THE-CENTURY GRAND BALLROOM

The Adrianna Hill Grand Ballroom is an elegant 8,000-square-foot Victorian ballroom with a beautiful restored hardwood floor, suspended "U" shaped balcony and 55 foot-long stage backed by a high cathedral-style wall. Built in 1901, this storybook setting with unique architecture is newly remodeled—complete with a 35-foot beamed and vaulted ceiling, large ornate brass chandeliers and elaborate Old World designs along the sculpted balcony. We are proud to offer you a treasured and unforgettable experience in this nonsmoking environment.

"Yes, Cinderella, You Shall Go To The Ball..."

AERO CLUB Banquet Room

9901 N.E. Seventh Avenue, Building C
Vancouver, Washington 98685
Contact: Cheryl Taylor (360) 574-7124; Fax (360) 574-2936
Business Hours: 8:30am–4:30pm

Capacity: Aero Club Banquet Room: 1,900 sq. ft.; 100 with tables, 150 classroom-style
Catering: available through three on-site restaurants or you may provide your own caterer
Price Range: varies according to event; please call for information
Types of Events: wedding receptions, anniversaries, reunions, birthdays, parties, business meetings and other group events

Availability and Terms

A 50% rental deposit and signed rental agreement reserves your date. Full payment is due three weeks prior to your reservation date.

Description of Facility and Services

Seating: 100 with tables and chairs, 150 classroom seating
Servers: not provided, self serve coffee is provided to clients
Bar facilities: user provides liquor license; $10 fee
Dance floor: 1,200 sq.ft. floating hardwood dance floor; electrical available
Linens and china: linens available upon request
Decoration limitations: little or no decoration needed; the Aero Club is tastefully decorated in nostalgic/romantic 1940s aviation theme; please discuss decoration with our staff; early decoration is usually available.
Audiovisual: overhead projector, TV/VCR, CD player and speakers
Cleanup: caterer or client to provide; must be left clean to receive deposit refund
ADA: limited; must ascent one flight of stairs to access the Aero Club
Parking: ample free parking available, one block west of I-5

Special Services

We have three on-site restaurants that cater directly to the Aero Club. Bortolami's Pizzeria offers gourmet and traditional homemade, hand-tossed pizza, soups, salads and a variety of soft drinks (360) 574-2598. Clancy's Family Restaurant offers a full service menu including burgers, fish and chips, soups, Mexican food, desserts and more (360) 573-3474. Pogy's offers a variety of sub sandwiches, party platters, salads and desserts (360) 574-0501.

WE'VE GOT THE "WRIGHT" STUFF

Conveniently located one block west of I-5 at the 99th street exit in Vancouver, the Aero Club is Vancouver's best kept secret for your wedding reception or other group event. Affordable, flexible, cozy and tastefully decorated in a nostalgic/romantic 1940s aviation theme. The Aero Club includes tables, chairs, serving counter, a floating hardwood dance floor, kitchenette and coffee. You can bring your own caterer, do it yourself or have one of our three on-site restaurants cater your event. We're only 10–15 minutes from downtown Portland. Call Cheryl for a tour or for more information (360) 574-7124.

The
ALBERTA STATION
Ballroom

"Renovated Historic Lodge"

Receptions • Events • Meetings

1829 N.E. Alberta
Portland, Oregon 97211
Contact: Patrick Goebel, Manager (503) 282-6070
Web site: www.albertastation.citysearch.com
Business Hours: Please call for an appointment

Capacity: 4,000 sq. ft., up to 570 (open floor)
Price Range: $800 per day for Ballroom rental
Catering: outside catering welcome
Types of Events: weddings, receptions, corporate and private functions, fund-raisers, holiday parties, concerts and dances

Availability and Terms

Reservations are recommended six months in advance; 60-day prior notice for cancellation. Security and cleaning deposit required.

Description of Facility and Services

Seating: available for rent
Servers: available through caterer
Bar facilities: provided through caterer
Dance floor: 4,000 sq. ft. of hardwood floors; capacity: 570 (open floor); electrical available
Linens and napkins: provided by caterer
China and glassware: provided by caterer
Decorations: please inquire
Cleanup: please inquire
Parking: free street parking available
ADA: accessible

Special Services

Our prep kitchen has ample room and provides caterers a refrigerator/freezer, stainless steel work table, and a full-size bar counter. The mezzanine level offers a private dressing room leading to a generous-sized balcony

ELEGANT BALLROOM OFFERING UNIQUE STYLE

Located on Northeast Alberta and 19th Avenue, Alberta Station was built in 1925 as the Odd Fellow Fraternal Lodge. Alberta Station features its' original wood staircase and spacious lobby. The Ballroom offers unique style—soft yellow walls, bold accented columns, and an impressive 18-foot high scalloped ceiling. Its floor boasts 4,000 square feet of maple hardwoods, and period fixtures lit with dimmers offer total control for lighting.

Albertina's

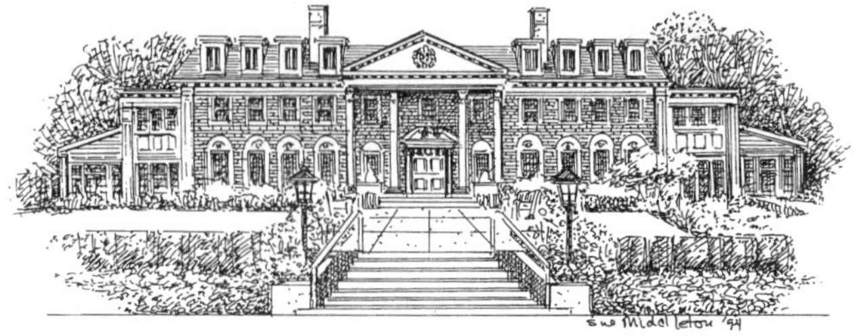

AT THE OLD KERR NURSERY

424 N.E. 22nd Avenue • Portland, Oregon 97232
Contact: Catering Coordinator (503) 231-3909
Business Hours: Mon–Fri 9am–4pm

Capacity: up to 250
Price Range: price determined by event
Catering: full-service, in-house catering
Types of Events: weddings and receptions, anniversaries, retirement parties, birthdays, family reunions, formal dinners up to 65 persons, special events

Availability and Terms

Albertina's offers four rooms to accommodate up to 250 people. Our garden patio is also available on the weekends. Reservations should be made as early as possible, six months to one year in advance is recommended. A $300 deposit will secure your date.

Description of Facility and Services

Servers: hostess and servers provided by Albertina's
Bar facilities: champagne, wine, beer; bartenders provided by Albertina's
Dance floor: dance floor available at additional cost; ample electrical hookups
Linens: cloth tablecloths for service tables and paper napkins provided by Albertina's
China, glassware and silver service: provided by Albertina's
Decorations: beautiful fresh floral arrangements in colors of your choice; please discuss your decorating ideas with the Albertina's catering coordinator
Parking: on-site parking
ADA: fully accessible

CHARMING SETTING FOR SPECIAL OCCASIONS

Barely a mile from downtown Portland stands the stately, three-story Georgian-style Old Kerr Nursery. The building was erected in 1921 with the money of canning jar magnate Alexander Kerr and over a period of 55 years provided shelter, medical care, and schooling to thousands of children. Closed as a nursery in 1967, the building reopened in 1981 after having been lovingly restored by loyal volunteers. The Old Kerr Nursery has been placed on the National Register of Historic Places and is an official Portland Historical Landmark. Equally beautiful inside and out, the intriguing Nursery is a charming setting for your most special occasion. Experience the history and unique qualities preserved within its four walls. Albertina's at The Old Kerr Nursery is operated as a nonprofit business with all proceeds donated to Albertina Kerr Centers, whose programs provide services for children and youth at risk, families in need, and individuals with disabilities.

ALFIE'S WAYSIDE COUNTRY INN
ALFIE'S LE CHARDONNAY WINE CELLARS

1111 Highway 99 West
Dundee, Oregon 97115
Contact: Alfie or Bonnie (503) 538-9407

Capacity: 400
Price Range: prices vary according to menu selection
Catering: available in-house and off-site
Types of Events: weddings, anniversaries, birthdays, reunions, holiday parties, business meetings, brunches, luncheons

Availability and Terms

Advance reservations of six months to a year recommended; however, we will accept reservations on short notice if date is open. Deposit required to hold date; 30-day cancellation policy.

Description of Facility and Services

Seating: provided for 400
Servers: full staff
Bar facilities: staffed, full-service bar
Dance floor: parquet wood; accommodates up to 50; PA and microphone available
Linens: burgundy and white; other colors available for extra cost
China: ivory china; glasses and stemware vary
Cleanup: included
Decorations: call for limitations; decorating by prior arrangement
Parking: plenty of free parking on site
ADA: yes

Special Services

Event planner on site to assist you

IN THE HEART OF OREGON'S WINE COUNTRY

Classic, elegant setting in the heart of Oregon's wine country. Beautifully decorated banquet rooms. Adjoining is the finest tasting room and wine store in the entire valley.

Romantic Mansion located on two wooded acres overlooking the Willamette River

Amadeus at the FERNWOOD

2122 S.E. Sparrow (Off River Road Exit)
Milwaukie, Oregon 97222
Contact: Kristina (503) 659-1735, (503) 353-8948
Business Hours: Seven days a week, 5pm–midnight; Sunday Brunch 10am–2:30pm

Capacity: 300 people
Price Range: lunches $20; full course sit-down or buffet style dinners $30; plus gratuity
Catering: full-service in-house catering
Types of Events: bridal luncheons, rehearsal dinners, **on-location wedding ceremonies**, ceremonies and receptions, large group luncheons

Availability and Terms

We are here for your personal needs to make your wedding the most romantic and elegant. Reservations should be made as soon as possible to ensure availability. A deposit is required at the time of booking. Half the deposit is refundable if cancellations are made at least six months prior to your event. **No** cost for using the facility, bartending services, linens, flowers, and candles.

Description of Facility and Services

Seating: table and chairs provided for up to 300
Servers: provided with catering services
Bar facilities: full-service bar with bartender provided; host/no host; liquor provided according to OLCC regulations
Dance floor: accommodates up to 50 people
Linens: cloth tablecloths and napkins provided in cream color
China and glassware: fine china; variety of glassware
Cleanup: provided by Amadeus at the Fernwood
Decorations: early decorating available; fresh flowers for guest tables provided by Amadeus; please discuss ideas with banquet representative
Parking: ample free parking; valet service
ADA: disabled access available

FACILITY OVERLOOKING WILLAMETTE RIVER

Amadeus at the Fernwood is the perfect setting for a romantic wedding reception or rehearsal dinner. You and your guests will enjoy fine continental dining in a wonderful old mansion on two wooded acres, filled with antiques, fireplaces, crystal chandeliers, candlelight and fresh flowers, overlooking the Willamette River. We offer a full bar with a wide variety of Oregon and international wines, and outdoor dining and wedding ceremonies on our patio is available. A classical pianist is featured nightly and during Sunday brunch.

SUNSET DINNER SPECIAL: Daily • 5–6:30pm • $9.95

Arnegards

Ninth and Hawthorne
1510 S.E. Ninth • Portland, Oregon 97214
Contact: Robin Andersen
(503) 236-2759; Fax (503) 231-8837
Business Hours: Tues–Fri 10am–2pm
After-hour and weekend appointments available

Capacity: our entire facility can accommodate up to 450 people; we have two ballrooms and a meeting room available
Price Range: Ballroom rental rates $800 to $1,300; discounts available Monday–Thursday
Catering: catering is supplied by renter, or you may choose from our list of caterers
Types of Events: wedding ceremonies and receptions, rehearsal dinners, private parties, cocktail parties, luncheons, dinners, banquets, dances, holiday parties, retirement parties, meetings, all-day seminars, corporate parties, and any other event imaginable

Availability and Terms

Please reserve rooms as early as possible. Short notice reservations depend on availability. A 50% deposit is due at time of booking with the balance and security deposit due one month prior to event.

Description of Facility and Services

Seating: round tables and chairs; provided up to 240; banquet tables, guest book table, and cake table included
Servers: provided by caterer
Bar facilities: provided by caterer or renter; bar located off The Winnington Ballroom
Dance floor: large dance floor available; capacity: 300+, electrical: supplied
Linens: provided by caterer or client
China: provided by caterer or client
Decoration limitations: establishment is well decorated; we are flexible to your needs; no tape, tacks, or nails on walls; no rice, birdseed or plastic confetti; please consult Event Coordinator prior to decorating
Cleanup: renter or caterer is responsible for cleanup; security deposit required
Parking: some off-street parking available; plenty of street parking

Special Services

We have a large stage available with dressing rooms.

NEWLY RESTORED 1920s BALLROOM AND CONFERENCE ROOM

Our newly renovated 1920s ballroom has been open and available to rent since December 1998. We are located conveniently in Southeast Portland. Have your next event in any of our three rooms: ***The Winnington Ballroom:*** This maple hardwood-floored ballroom has a stage, 14-foot high ceilings, lighted ceiling fans and great acoustics. It can accommodate up to 320 people. ***The Grace Ballroom:*** This maple hardwood-floored ballroom is perfect for wedding ceremonies, company functions, holiday parties, banquets or receptions and can accommodate up to 100 people. ***The Meeting Room:*** Can accommodate up to 28.

THE ATRIUM

100 S.W. Market Street
Portland, Oregon 97201
Contact: Catering Director
(503) 220-3929
Business Hours: please call for an appointment

Capacity: up to 300
Price Range: food starting at $16 per person plus room rental
Catering: The Atrium provides all catering services tailored to your special day
Types of Events: hors d'oeuvres, dinner, sit-down, and buffet

Availability and Terms

Our magnificent two-story glass building and convenient location one block from Naito Parkway in the heart of downtown Portland make The Atrium a popular facility for wedding receptions and other special events. To ensure reserving the date you want, plan to make your reservations six months to a year in advance. The $1,200 room-rental fee is required at the time of booking and is also considered the deposit for your event. A 120-day advance cancellation in writing is required for a full refund.

Description of Facility and Services

Seating: tables and chairs for 250+
Servers: full wait staff
Bar facilities: full bar service, bartenders, servers and all alcoholic beverages
Dance floor: 200-person, 1,200-square-foot dance floor with full electrical hookups
Linens and napkins: linen, cloth napkins and tablecloths in assorted colors; included in room rental
China and glassware: provided
Cleanup: included
Decorations: though our policies are fairly liberal, please call for restrictions
Parking: ample free parking
ADA: yes

GET THE FEELING OF BEING OUTDOORS YEAR-AROUND IN OUR MAGNIFICENT TWO-STORY GLASS STRUCTURE

The Atrium's unique structure offers a beautiful setting. Its two-story windows and lush greenery as well as the glass-covered roof along with the back patio and two fountains in a beautiful parklike setting will have a profound impact on all its guests. The Atrium is easily accessible on the corner of First and Market, one block from the Marriott Hotel and Front Street, and only three blocks from the RiverPlace Alexis Hotel. Please call our Catering Director at (503) 220-3929 for information or reservations.

 Please let this business know that you heard about them from the Bravo! Bridal Resource Guide.

BeckenRidge VINEYARD

300 Reuben Boise Road • Dallas, Oregon 97338
Contact: Becky Jacroux, Owner/Manager (503) 831-3652
Business Hours: Tue–Sat 10am–5pm;
evenings and weekends by appointment

Capacity: 2,100 sq. ft. event room seats 120, plus 1,600 sq. ft. covered patio
Price Range: $1,400 for the entire day; ask about midweek discounts
Catering: we have a list of preferred caterers; fully equipped kitchen
Types of Events: weddings, receptions, reunions, business meetings and team-building events

Availability and Terms

Located just west of Dallas, 18 miles from Salem. Open year-round; closed in January. A 50% deposit holds your reservation.

Description of Facility and Services

Seating: round tables and chairs for guests; rectangle accessory/serving tables
Servers: provided by caterer
Bar facilities: BeckenRidge and Airlie wines are exclusively served; bottled beer and champagne available upon request; server provided
Dance floor: hardwood floor throughout; stereo sound system available
Linens: ivory cloth tablecloths provided; quality paper napkins available in choice of color
China and glassware: fine china, silver and glassware provided to complement any function
Decorations: silk flower arrangements available at no charge; bubbles provided; please no rice, confetti, or birdseed
Cleanup: we assist with setup and cleanup
Parking: complimentary parking on site
ADA: fully equipped to accommodate ADA requirements

Special Services

BeckenRidge Vineyard produces five varieties of grapes and our custom-labeled wines are produced by Airlie Winery. Both Airlie and BeckenRidge wines are featured at our events and are also available for individual purchase by attending guests.

CELEBRATE YOUR SPECIAL OCCASION NESTLED IN THE BEAUTY OF THE VINEYARD

You will enjoy our serene, country setting and be delighted with our facility specifically designed for events. BeckenRidge has a warm, friendly lodge-like atmosphere with a commanding view of the vineyard and the Willamette Valley. Special features include a vineyard patio, rock fireplace and grand piano. Personal attention from the owner will help you create a memorable event for you and your special guests.

The Benson
HOTEL · PORTLAND

309 S.W. Broadway at Oak Street
Portland, Oregon 97205
(503) 295-4140; Fax (503) 241-3757
Office Hours: Mon–Fri 8am–6pm
Available all other times by appointment
Web site: www.bensonhotel.com

Capacity: seated dining for up to 400 guests; stand-up reception for up to 500 guests
Price Range: brunch and luncheon receptions starting at $25 per person; evening receptions starting at $30 per person
Catering: full-service in-house catering; preferred caterer for the Portland Art Museum
Types of Events: sit-down, buffet, hors d'oeuvre receptions, rehearsal dinners; brunch and luncheon receptions; French tea for bridal showers also offered

Availability and Terms

We are able to book your wedding date one year in advance. A nonrefundable deposit of 20% is required to make your booking definite. Full payment is due one week before your event. We encourage you to call as soon as possible to secure your desired date.

Description of Facility and Services

Seating: chairs provided, gold Chivari chairs available at additional charge; round tables seating 4 to 10 guests are provided
Servers: all servers and support staff included at no charge
Bar facilities: full-service bar; we provide all bartenders, servers and beverages
Dance floor: provided in a variety of sizes at no additional charge
Linens and napkins: fine linens and napkins provided at no additional charge
China and glassware: fine china, glassware and silver provided
Parking: ample free parking available, rates vary; valet available upon request
ADA: handicap accessibility and facilities in all areas

PORTLAND'S GRAND HOTEL

Begin your reception with cocktails in front of the fireplace and experience the Old World charm of our grand lobby. Then move into the Crystal Ballroom to celebrate your first dance under crystal chandeliers where your romantic wedding will be captured forever in your heart. The Mayfair Ballroom is found at the top of our grand staircase, on the mezzanine, and is the perfect setting for larger wedding groups with a built-in stage showcasing a baby grand piano. The mirror on the staircase landing came from Paris in 1883 and was designed for the Royal Palace in Honolulu; it has been with The Benson since 1958 and remains a photography favorite. For more intimate weddings and a view of Broadway, enjoy the classic Cambridge Room. Complete your event with a romantic honeymoon night with our "Champagne Kisses" package.

See page 385 under Hotel Accommodations.

BRENTWOOD-DARLINGTON COMMUNITY CENTER

7211 S.E. 62nd Avenue
Portland, Oregon 97206
Contact: Mary Davis
(503) 306-5961 ext. 223; Fax (503) 306-5946
E-mail: bdcc@hotmail.com
Center Hours: Mon–Fri 8am–5pm

Capacity: event space can be divided into three smaller spaces, plus living room. Total capacity is up to 130
Price Range: hourly base of $25 to $100
Catering: outside catering or your own arrangements
Types of Events: suitable for family reunions, receptions, anniversary parties, retirement or going-away parties, birthday parties, baby showers, workshops, classes, conferences, dinners, holiday parties, concerts and more

Availability and Terms

Call to check on available dates and times. A cleaning fee of $50 and a $100 refundable damage deposit are needed to hold the date and time.

Description of Facility and Services

Seating: 95 stackable chairs, 15 rectangular tables seating six, five round tables seating eight, 10 wooden armchairs, two bistro tables; specific equipment requirements are requested on our application form
Servers: renter or caterer provides
Bar facilities: renter or caterer to provide beer and wine only, bar, bartender, and liquor liability insurance
Dance floor: tiled floor suitable for dancing; electrical outlets available; renter must provide P.A. system
Linens and napkins: renter or caterer provides
China and glassware: renter or caterer provides
Cleanup: renter responsible for removing all decorations and sweeping floor; tables and chairs must be returned to original locations
Decorations: refer to Building Use Rules in application packet for guidelines
Parking: free parking; additional overflow parking available on weekend by prior arrangement
ADA: yes

Special Services

The Center will provide a hostess on duty during your event to assist with building operations and troubleshooting.

A PLACE FOR CELEBRATIONS!

The large windows, expansive views of play field and Brentwood Park, high ceilings, and tree-lined outdoor space provide a warm, welcoming, light-filled environment for any event. The center is an air-conditioned, nonsmoking facility. The living room has a gas fireplace and is ideal for wedding ceremonies. In addition, guests have access to a modern kitchen, a cloak room, changing area/quiet room, and accommodating restrooms.

Briarwood Inn

2752 N.E. Hogan Road
Gresham, Oregon 97030
Portland (503) 665-3894, Vancouver (360) 253-8326
Fax (503) 492-2638

Capacity: **Ballroom:** up to 200, divided into two separate rooms: **Myrtlewood Room:** up to 100, **Sandalwood Room:** up to 120; **Dogwood Room** seats up to 40 and two boardrooms are available to accommodate 20 people each

Price Range: prices vary according to size of group and selection of services

Catering: full-service catering available, provided by City Grill Catering; fresh and creative menus available for on or off-premise catering

Types of Events: sit-down, elegant dinners, cocktails and delicious hors d'oeuvres; complete reception and hotel services, seminars up to 300 people, board meetings, class reunions, weddings and trade shows—just a few of examples of the types of events that are beautifully presented at the Briarwood Inn; complete event planning available at no additional charge to ensure your event's success

Availability and Terms

We require a signed contract and a 50% deposit prior to the planned event within a reasonable time frame. We also require a guaranteed guest count three days before the event. *Remember*—City Grill Catering also provides off-site catering if our Briarwood Inn facility is booked. Please contact one of our four event planners to help you find another venue and plan your upcoming event!

Description of Facility and Services

Seating: classroom, buffet, full-service dining, or custom seating arrangements

Servers: professional servers provided and experienced banquet captains available to attend to your individual needs

Bar facilities: full-service private bars can be customized to your specific needs and feature a large list of domestic and imported beers, wines and liquors

Dance floor: available upon request

Linens and napkins: included; a large selection of custom linens and colors available

China and glassware: included in the cost of food and beverage for on-site events; available to rent for off-site events

Decorations: classic and elegant decor provided or work with our event planners to create the perfect theme for your event

Cleanup: included with full-service catering

Parking: on-site parking available at no cost

ADA: accessible

Bridal Veil Lakes

OVERLOOKING THE HISTORIC COLUMBIA RIVER GORGE

P.O. Box 5
Bridal Veil, Oregon 97010
Contact: Jennifer Miller
(503) 981-3695
Web site: www.bridalveillakes.com

Capacity: 1,000 outdoor
Price Range: price varies according to event
Catering: renter may select caterer of choice
Types of Events: picnics, reunions, anniversaries, rehearsal dinners, weddings and receptions

Availability and Terms

We suggest that you book your event one year in advance; we only schedule one event per day Fridays, Saturdays, Sundays and holidays. A $500 refundable deposit is required at booking, with full payment due 30 days before your event. Months of operation are March–October; please inquire for off-season pricing.

Description of Facility and Services

Seating: chairs available at additional charge or renter may make own arrangements; picnic tables for 100+
Servers: provided by caterer
Bar facilities: caterer or renter provides licensed bartender, liquor, and liability insurance
Linens: provided by caterer
China and glassware: provided by caterer
Dance floor: 800 sq. ft. available in pavilion for dancing
Decorations: no rice, paper or metallic confetti; nails, tacks, or staples may not be placed on building surfaces
Cleanup: renter/caterer is responsible for leaving grounds as found
Parking: ample parking available; parking attendants strongly suggested
ADA: accessible

Special Services

Bridal Veil Lakes has a number of RV spaces available.

NATURAL BEAUTY IN ITS MOST SPECTACULAR FORM

Nestled in the heart of the historic Columbia River Gorge, just 30 minutes east of Portland, natural beauty is in its' most spectacular form at Bridal Veil Lakes. Beautiful wildflowers and lush forest are the perfect backdrop for your lakeside wedding. The view of the Columbia River Gorge and the serene lakeside setting add just the hint of romance that will make your wedding memories last a lifetime. The photo opportunities are endless! Bridal Veil Lakes recreational area is protected from the Columbia Gorge east wind and our Lakeside Pavilion is wonderful for weather protection. Please call and make an appointment to visit our exclusive and private setting for the wedding of your dreams.

The Historic Broetje House

3101 S.E. Courtney
Milwaukie, Oregon 97222
Contact: Lorraine or Lois
(503) 659-8860
Business Hours: Mon–Fri 10am–4pm;
weekends by appointment

Capacity: 150 inside or outside
Price Range: $150 to $6,000; please call for specific price information
Catering: in-house catering only
Types of Events: sit-down, buffet, garden, cocktails and hors d'oeuvres, cake and punch

Availability and Terms

Rental hours are 8am to 9pm Sunday through Friday; Saturday from 9am to 2:30pm (11am ceremony), and 3:30pm to 9pm (5pm ceremony). A one-third deposit is required on booking.

Description of Facility and Services

Seating: tables and chairs for 150
Servers: provided as needed during the event
Bar facilities: bar facilities available; provide your own bartender and liquor; bottled or canned beer, wine, champagne only—no hard liquor
Dance floor: yes
Linens and napkins: linen or cloth in many colors for an added charge
China and glassware: variety of china and wine/champagne glassware
Cleanup: included in package price
Decorations: special arrangements must be made for early decorating
Parking: plenty of free parking space; valet parking also available
ADA: yes

Special Services

Our in-house catering, use of our serviceware, china, glass stemware, coffee pots, punch bowls and ladles, serving dishes, chafing dishes, and silverware are provided with the package price. You'll also find lovely honeymoon suites and rooms available for changing or an overnight stay.

ENJOY TURN-OF-THE-CENTURY ROMANTIC AMBIANCE

Enjoy the romantic ambiance offered by this magnificent, turn-of-the-century, Queen Anne–style bed and breakfast. Built in 1890 by John F. Broetje, the house features a unique four-story, 50-foot-high water tower. Over an acre of picturesque grounds with a gazebo grace this elegant estate, making it an ideal setting for your wedding and reception! Each event is specially designed to meet the needs of the bride and groom.

 Please let this business know that you heard about them from the Bravo! Bridal Resource Guide.

Canterbury Falls

P.O. Box 156 • Molalla, Oregon 97038
Contact: Judy Hall (503) 829-8821
Closed Monday and Tuesday; Shown by appointment only
Selected in 1999 for publication in Better Homes & Gardens Magazine and honored by PBS Victory Garden

---

Capacity: up to 400
Price Range: $2,495 up to 200 guests; multiple provisions; only one event per day
Catering: very large reception area includes expansive lawns, floral settings, romantic evening lighting, dance floor, plus a 28′x58′ summerhouse; 12′x20′ Catering Alcove includes a large, commercial cooler and more; may choose no food, cake only, family prepared, or professionally catered
Types of Events: weddings, receptions, theatre, concerts, poetry readings, storytelling, seminars and hot air balloon launch area; wedding rehearsal is included in the fee

Availability and Terms

Canterbury Falls offers the perfect spacious setting for a romantic English garden wedding. The gardens are available June through September. A natural setting of ferns, white flowering shrubs, and perennials nestle against the 400-square-foot Gothic Pavilion. Many colored theme gardens border the lawns and koi pond. Event is reserved upon receipt of a $500 deposit. Availability is limited; reserve early.

Description of Facility and Services

Seating: amphitheatre seating for 350; round guest tables for 200; chairs for 250
Linens: beautiful table linens and centerpiece containers; other items provided
Servers, china and glassware: caterer to provide
Cleanup: setup and cleanup included
Decorations: exquisite items provided; no decoration needed
Wedding coordinators: experienced assistance is included in fee
Florists: Victorian elegance to country; we will provide your floral and decorating needs, creatively designed to accommodate your style
Watercolorist: Judy Hall offers professionally accurate, original bridal-floral portrait paintings; this is a unique and lovely wedding gift; price range: $900 to $2,600; inquire for details
Parking: ample parking; parking attendants included; **ADA:** yes

AN ENCHANTINGLY ROMANTIC ENGLISH GARDEN

Located just 40 minutes south of Portland, or 30 minutes east of Salem, this charming setting (although easily accessible) is hidden well from the public. Canterbury Falls is approached following a 3/4 mile lane through the woods. You arrive in a secluded glade of pervading, Country-Gothic, English influence. The 80 acres include the resident's stone house, streams and waterfalls with two arched footbridges, flower gardens, forests, and meadows. The elegant pavilion boasts eight white lanterns, which enhance a Cinderella effect. In daytime hours it rests in the shade below an amphitheatre seating where your guests can experience nature's art, an unforgettable bridal entry, and your most memorable day. (Information is subject to change.)

CAPTAIN AINSWORTH HOUSE BED & BREAKFAST

19130 Lot Whitcomb Drive • Oregon City, Oregon 97045
Contact: Innkeeper (503) 655-5172
Tues–Sat 10am–4pm; evenings and weekends by appointment

Capacity: 100 stand-up reception; 70 sit-down reception May–Oct; 70 rest of year
Price Range: price varies depending on function and size of group
Catering: no in-house catering; small, fully equipped kitchen available with a large commercial refrigerator; you also may do your own catering.
Types of Events: sit-down, buffet, cake and punch receptions; reunions, teas, and other social or business functions

Availability and Terms

Open year-round. Reserve as early as possible. A one-third deposit reserves your special day.

Description of Facility and Services

Tables and chairs: round tables and chairs for 100; rectangle accessory/serving tables
Servers: provided by caterer or renter
Bar facilities: caterer or renter provides bartender, liquor, and liability insurance; canned or bottled beer, white or blush wine and champagne only
Dance floor: electrical outlets provided; stereo system available
Linens: ivory linen tablecloths; quality paper napkins available in choice of color
China, glassware and serviceware: glass plates and glassware to complement any function; china and antique silver service available at an additional charge
Cleanup: we help with setup and cleanup; catering cleanup excluded
Decorations: silk floral table centerpieces provided; inquire about limitations; no rice, birdseed, or confetti please
Parking: free on- and off-street parking
ADA: completely accessible

Special Services

Our reception facility has been elegantly decorated to complement any event. A black-and-white tiled floor, ivory silk rose garlands, and brass fixtures can easily blend into any color scheme. French doors lead to 20′x30′ covered patio area. Our two acres of picturesque grounds provide a lovely setting for photographs and outdoor weddings.

SOUTHERN HOSPITALITY WITH A NORTHWEST FLAIR

The Captain Ainsworth House Bed and Breakfast is a carefully restored 1851 Greek Revival mansion with massive two-story columns. Carefully chosen period antiques create an elegant ambiance. Two of the four bedrooms, each with a private bath, are available to be used as dressing rooms. We offer elegant overnight accommodations for your out-of-town guests. Please ask about our special B&B wedding package.

CAVANAUGHS®

HILLSBORO HOTEL

3500 N.E. Cornell Road
Hillsboro, Oregon 97124
(503) 648 3500
(800) 325-4000

Capacity: up to 150 people for receptions or dinners
Price Range: varies depending on size and length of event; please call
Catering: full range of catering services including sit-down, buffet, cocktails, hors d'oeuvres, picnics, theme or custom parties, meetings, seminars; ideal for conventions, social functions and retreats; on-premise outdoor events available

Availability and Terms

Groups up to 150 people. A six-month advance reservation is recommended; deposit is required upon booking. Deposit can be refunded with 60-90 day written cancellation notice.

Description of Facility and Services

Seating: tables and chairs provided for any set up
Servers: provided with our catering service
Bar facilities: full-service bars available with bartenders ($75 setup fee required)
Dance space: dance floor available; full electrical hookup
Linens and napkins: cloth linens and napkins available with food service
China and glassware: house china and stemmed glassware available
Decorations: we can assist you, and we allow decorations prior to event
Cleanup: provided and included in catering cost
Parking: plenty of free parking
ADA: complied

HIGH QUALITY SERVICE WITH A PERSONAL TOUCH

Nestled in the heart of the Oregon Silicon Forest, Cavanaughs Hillsboro Hotel offers the perfect location for small to mid-size weddings and receptions. Their specialty is providing high quality service with a personal touch. From cocktail and hors d'oeuvre receptions to formal sit-down buffets—every detail is checked and rechecked to assure our clients that each function becomes a success.

For the honeymoon, be sure and visit our Washington, Idaho and Montana locations.

(800) 325-4000

www.cavanaughs.com

Cedar Springs Country Estate
Romantic Wedding Park

12353 S.E. Lusted Road • Sandy, Oregon 97055
Contact: Keri, Tammy (503) 663-0772; Fax (503) 663-0772
Park is available for viewing by appointment only

Capacity: up to 200 guests
Price range: please inquire
Catering: in-house catering and bar service
Types of Events: day or evening weddings, elegant Victorian or casual country; or with dancing under the stars

Availability and Terms

Cedar Springs Country Estate is available from July 1 to September 30. A $500 nonrefundable deposit reserves your special day. We host only one wedding per day. Saturday noon–6pm or 4–10pm; Sunday noon–6pm or 2–8pm.

Description of Facility and Services

Bridal consultants: Keri Baird and Tammy Rolles are on staff to assist you in planning and coordinating all your wedding needs
Seating: tables, linens, and chairs provided for up to 200 guests; amphitheater seating is used for ceremony seating
Servers: provided by caterer
Dance floor: softly lit Victorian gazebo provides a large 350-square-foot dance floor
Linens: white linens provided for guest and banquet tables
China and glassware: disposable products included by caterer; china and glassware available to rent
Cleanup: the staff at Cedar Springs will set up and clean up
Decorations: hanging baskets, pedestals and urns for flowers, plus many other unique items
ADA: limited accessibility

A ROMANTIC COUNTRY WEDDING PARK

As if somewhere in time… At the edge of the forest, this unforgettable place is five miles north of Sandy. If you've been wanting an exiting and different outdoor wedding, this may be just the setting you've dreamed of! A picturesque white Victorian gazebo is the perfect backdrop for the wedding ceremony. A spring-fed trout lake rests placidly at the foot of towering alders and fringed cedars. With seating on the terraced hillside, your guests can view a very intimate and private ceremony. In the evening, the subdued lights, water, trees, and gardens become an enchanted setting.

 Please let this business know that you heard about them from the Bravo! Bridal Resource Guide.

CATERING AND RECEPTION FACILITY

Part of the Home Builders Association of Metro Portland

15555 S.W. Bangy Road

Lake Oswego, Oregon 97035

Contact: Barb Chirgwin

(503) 684-1880; Web site: www.hbamp.com

Business Hours: Mon–Fri 8am–5pm

Capacity: 50-200 seated; 50 to 300 reception
Price Range: room rental charge varies per event and season
Catering: in-house or at your location
Types of receptions: sit-down, buffet, theme, cocktails and hors d'oeuvres, barbecue, picnic or special requests

Availability and Terms

Spacious reception hall/auditorium featuring patio, stage, dance floor, and optional bar. Please make your reservations with as much advance notice as possible.

Description of Facility and Services

Seating: round tables and chairs for up to 200
Servers: we provide complete staff
Bar facilities: full-service bar and bartender available; host or no-host; liquor, beer, wine, and champagne
Dance floor: we have a dance floor and stage with optional media equipment
Linens and napkins: full array of tablecloths and napkins ranging from fine linen, cloth or paper
China and glassware: white china with trim; matching glassware available
Cleanup: cleanup staff provided
Decorations: rooms are accessible for early decorating
Parking: plenty of free parking, including handicapped parking
ADA: yes, handicapped accessible

CELEBRATE YOUR NEXT EVENT WITH US!
PHONE NOW FOR YOUR PRIVATE CONSULTATION
FOR MEMORIES THAT WILL LAST A LIFETIME!

We look forward to making your wedding reception a total success. Excellent facilities, friendly staff, easy freeway access and ample parking.

CENTRAL LIBRARY

801 S.W. Tenth Avenue
Portland, Oregon 97205
Contact: Events Coordinator
(503) 306-5578
Business Hours: Mon–Fri 9am–5pm
Web site:
http://www.multnomah.lib.or.us/lib/rentals/

Capacity: seated dining for up to 300; stand-up reception for up to 1,200
Price Range: $600 to $3,900 plus security; please call for specifics
Catering: choose from our list of caterers
Types of Events: ceremonies, receptions and rehearsal dinners

Availability and Terms

The reading rooms and lobbies are available at the Central Library on Friday and Saturday after 6pm. A 50% deposit is required to hold space.

Description of Facility and Services

Seating: limited number of banquet tables, round tables, and stacking chairs
Servers: provided by caterer
Bar facilities: provided by caterer; no hard alcohol or red wine
Dance floor: provided by caterer
Linens: provided by caterer
China and glassware: provided by caterer
Cleanup: provided by caterer
Decorations: no helium balloons, glitter, confetti, candles or fog/bubble machines; all decorations must be approved in advance by Central Library
Parking: available on street or in nearby lots
ADA: handicap accessibility and facilities in all areas

IMAGINE YOUR WEDDING IN OUR "GARDEN OF KNOWLEDGE"

Experience the grandeur of Central Library as never before. After a $24 million, three-year renovation, this historic 1912 building is a masterpiece and an exquisite setting for weddings, receptions, parties, rehearsal dinners, bridal teas and brunches. The building's grand lobbies and unique spaces are an elegant backdrop for any event. Enter the building and enter "The Garden of Knowledge," a theme echoed in the building's public art and unique interior detailing. Imagine your reception or rehearsal dinner in the Library's reading rooms surrounded by the works of your favorite authors. Your guests will welcome a visit to Central Library's garden paradise.

Charbonneau ON THE GREEN

32050 S.W. Charbonneau Drive
Wilsonville, Oregon 97070
Contact: Bob Russell (503) 694-5234
Fax (503) 694-6385
Web site: www.charbonneauonthegreen.citysearch.com

Capacity: 15,000 sq.ft. of banquet space available
Price Range: $5.95 to $22.95 per person
Catering: in-house catering available for up to 200 people; off-site up to 3,000
Types of Events: weddings, receptions, banquets, golf tournaments, cocktail parties, business meetings,

Availability and Terms

Deposit required to hold a room; 30 day notice required for a full refund.

Description of Facility and Services

Seating: tables and chairs provided for up to 180
Servers: provided by Charbonneau
Bar facilities: full-service bar available; portable bar
Dance floor: dance floor available; full electrical hookup
Linens and napkins: a variety of colors available at no charge
China and glassware: provided
Decorations: no limitations
Cleanup: provided by Charbonneau
Parking: 200 spaces available
ADA: handicap accessible

LOCATED ON A GOLF COURSE

Experience casual and fine dining in a country club atmosphere at Charbonneau On The Green. Featuring a view of lakes, trees and fairways, we cater to you the way that we would like to be catered to.

Cherry Hill

located in the
Columbia River Gorge National Scenic Area

1550 Carroll Road • Mosier, Oregon 97040
Contact: Elizabeth Toscano
(541) 478-4455; Fax (541) 478-4457
Business Hours: Mon–Fri 8am–5pm

Capacity: up to 80 inside; 200 in the garden
Price Range: varies according to type of event
Catering: full-service in-house catering
Types of Events: sit-down, buffets, cocktails and hors d'oeuvres, picnics

Availability and Terms

Cherry Hill is available for your private use from April 15 through October 31. A $500 deposit holds your day and is refundable if we can rebook.

Description of Facility and Services

Seating: tables and chairs for up to 200
Servers: service staff included in catering costs
Bar facilities: full-service bar provided: liquor, beer, and wine
Dance floor: available with electrical outlets
Linens and napkins: heirloom, banquet, or casual linens available
China and glassware: china and glassware provided
Cleanup: provided by Cherry Hill
Decorations: staff will decorate to your theme
Parking: on and off-street parking
ADA: limited

Special Services

The experienced coordinators at Cherry Hill look forward to helping you organize any aspect of your wedding or reception. Our on-site florist, caterer, and pastry chef work closely together to ensure that no detail is overlooked and that all is in the best of taste.

COUNTRY GARDEN SETTING

Whether you imagine an intimate wedding or a grand reception, Cherry Hill is the premiere outdoor event site in the Columbia Gorge. Our turn-of-the-century farmhouse is perched on an orchard-covered hillside with panoramic views. Ceremonies take place on the shaded lawn under the spreading limbs of towering Oregon oaks. Receptions are held beneath starry skies or in our classic American red barn. Brides and grooms often choose our Wedding Weekend, including rehearsal and dinner, ceremony and reception, with every detail thoughtfully arranged by the staff at Cherry Hill.

> "Toscano's matter-of-factness, combined with an impeccable sense of taste and organization, has helped her to become the Martha Stewart of Gorge weddings."
> —*Hood River News,* August 20, 1997

CHIEF OBIE LODGE

Boy Scouts of America
Scout Office
2145 S.W. Naito Parkway
Portland, Oregon 97201
Contact: Volunteer Services (503) 225-5759
Lodge Location
11300 S.E. 147th • Portland, OR 97236
(must contact Scout Office for viewing)
Business Hours: Mon–Fri 8:30am–5:30pm; Sat 10am–4pm

Capacity: up to 250 guests
Price Range: $850 for facility rental (10am to 11pm)
Catering: client provides outside catering service
Types of Events: any type of nonalcoholic event

Availability and Terms

We recommend that the Chief Obie Lodge be reserved at least six months in advance. A $500 refundable cleaning deposit is required to hold your reservation.

Description of Facility and Services

Seating: tables and chairs for up to 250
Servers: provided by caterer or client
Bar facilities: alcohol is prohibited
Dance floor: 250-person dance floor; electrical outlets available
Linens, china and glassware: provided by caterer or client
Cleanup: client and/or caterer is responsible for leaving Lodge as it was found
Decorations: please discuss decorating ideas with our staff; no candles
Parking: on-site parking; short walk to Lodge
ADA: limited access

Special Services

The Chief Obie Lodge offers two dormitories to accommodate up to 75 overnight guests. A new sound system will be in place by summer 1999.

PANORAMIC VIEW

A Mount Hood panorama awaits you at Chief Obie Lodge, where weddings, family reunions or corporate events will find the perfect setting. The Lodge, set on a knoll overlooking 190 acres of field and forest, is easy to find—only a five-minute hop from I-205 and Clackamas Town Center. The Great Room in the majestic building holds 250 guests under a huge cathedral ceiling. Those wishing overnight accommodations for up to 75 guests can also reserve the upstairs consisting of two large dormitories with shower facilities. Two lawn areas, fringed with fir and alder, serve well for outdoor activities.

HISTORIC PORTLAND CITY HALL

1221 S.W. Fourth Avenue
Portland, Oregon 97204
Contact: Faye Musselman,
Bureau of General Services
(503) 823-6947; Fax (503) 823-6924
E-mail: phaye@ci.portland.or.us
Business Hours: 8am–5pm

Capacity: Council Chambers (for the wedding): 200 maximum seating; **Rose Room:** up to 50 and 960 sq.ft.; **Pettygrove Room:** up to 24 and 778 sq.ft.; **Lovejoy Room:** up to 43 and 892 sq.ft.; **First Floor Public Area (for reception only):** up to 1,000 and 11,450 sq.ft.; **Full Facility:** up to 4,000

Price Range: $25 to $375/hour depending on room and type of event

Catering: select your own caterer (no on-site cooking facilities)

Types of Events: weddings, receptions, bridal luncheons, rehearsal dinners, meetings

Availability and Terms

Facility is available after 5 p.m. Monday through Friday, and anytime on weekends. Reservations are confirmed when 50% of full costs are received with reservation form. A fully refundable security deposit (between $500 and $2,500 depending upon event) is required. An information packet with reservation form, rates, policies, procedures and additional photos is provided.

Description of Facility and Services

Seating: tables and chairs are provided in meeting rooms and Council Chambers

Bar facilities: alcohol permitted; copy of OLCC license required from server

Dance floor: two marble floored light courts—1,200 sq.ft.

China, glassware and linens: not provided

Decoration limitations: no helium balloons, glitter or open flames

Audiovisual and Equipment: The Council Chambers has a state-of-the-art audiovisual system, including overhead projection screen (allowing guests front view of bride/groom vow exchanges), hearing impaired devices, etc.; all meeting rooms have 12-foot projection screens; a variety of meeting room equipment is available for rental

Cleanup: $75 per event, which includes Event Porter services

Parking: on-street parking or via Smart Park garages

ADA: City Hall is fully handicap accessible

BEAUTIFUL AND UNIQUE SETTING

Historic City Hall is a 105-year-old, four story building in the 16th Century Manneristic Renaissance architectural style. Completely renovated in 1998, red and white marble flooring throughout the structure complement the polished oak interior. Two floor-to-ceiling atriums flood the interior with natural light. Floor-to-ceiling copper-plated open staircases lends a dramatic effect. Extensive artwork (sculpture, oil paintings, wood carvings and electronic historic photo display) contribute to this extraordinary beautiful and unique setting.

 Please let this business know that you heard about them from the Bravo! Bridal Resource Guide.

Columbia Gorge Hotel

4000 Westcliff Drive • Hood River, Oregon 97031
Contact: Karen Lutz, wedding consultant
(541) 387-5403, (800) 345-0931
Business Hours: Mon–Fri 9am–5pm

Capacity: 10 to 200; 40 guest rooms; 3 function rooms
Price Range: prices vary according to wedding package
Catering: full-service catering, on- or off-premise
Types of Events: outdoor and indoor weddings, banquets, informal hors d'oeuvre receptions to formal sit-down dinners

Availability and Terms

Early reservations required, especially for summer garden weddings. Advance deposit required to secure space.

Description of Facility and Services

Seating: accommodating up to 250
Servers: included in price quote
Bar facilities: full-service bar for alcoholic and nonalcoholic beverages available; extensive selection of liquor, beer and wine
Dance floor: for 50 people; electrical hookups available
Linens and napkins: white linen tablecloths and napkins available
China and glassware: china, glassware and silverware provided
Cleanup: included in price quote
Flowers and decorations: professional in-house florist to take care of all your special needs
Parking: ample free parking

Special Services

Complete wedding services; on-site wedding consultant. Detailed wedding packages for your convenience.

ROMANCE AND ELEGANCE WITH A PERSONAL TOUCH

Experience the natural grandeur and the picturesque views from our historic country inn. Let the Columbia Gorge Hotel and your very own Professional Wedding Coordinator help plan one of the most important days of your life. Enjoy the option of four outdoor wedding lawns that are situated on five acres overlooking the mighty Columbia River. Savor our exquisite dining, voted one of Oregon's best restaurants, and stay in one of our distinctive guest rooms. Our personal style and uniqueness will ensure ever lasting memories.

COURTYARD MARRIOTT—PORTLAND NORTH HARBOUR

1231 North Anchor Way • Portland, Oregon 97217
Contact: Christine Skarphol (503) 735-1818; Fax (503) 735-0888
Business Hours: Mon–Fri 8am–5pm, or by appointment

Capacity: ***Indoor:*** **North Harbour Room:** 1,100 square feet, ideal for receptions of up to 100 people; ***Outdoor:*** our patio offers seating for up to 250 people, or up to 350 reception-style

Price Range: price will vary depending on the type of event and menu selections

Catering: full-service in-house catering

Types of Events: smaller, more intimate family weddings, rehearsal dinners and bridal showers; patio is available for larger gatherings, weather permitting; tenting available at an additional charge

Availability and Terms

Reservations must be made six months to one year in advance. There is a $50 fee to hold the date, with a minimum deposit of 50% of total charges due at the time of signing the contract, and the balance due 30 days from the date of the event.

Description of Facility and Services

Seating: tables and chairs for up to 250
Servers: staff included; a 15% service charge will be added to your bill
Bar facilities: full beverage service available; an additional charge is required for bartenders
Dance floor: available at an additional charge
Linens and napkins: all colors available
China and glassware: available upon request
Decorations: responsibility of renter; allow for time prior to the event by special arrangement
Cleanup: included in site charge
Parking: complimentary parking
ADA: fully accessible

Special Services

The Courtyard by Marriott at Portland North Harbour has 132 guestrooms decorated in a palette of colors adopted from those typically found in the French and Italian Riviera. Guestrooms feature amenities including in-room coffee and tea service, 25" televisions, hair dryers, irons and ironing boards. King Suites and a Conference Suite are available, as well as a Spa King. Book your wedding or reception with us and receive $100 off of a honeymoon trip package! Ask for details

MEDITERRANEAN STYLE ON THE COLUMBIA RIVER

The North Harbour Courtyard has an ambiance of casual elegance and sophistication both inside and out. A resort-like atmosphere is apparent throughout, but especially on our large seasonally landscaped plaza. Complete with gazebo, fountain, and peaceful scenic views, the plaza is the ideal location for summer and fall wedding receptions, rehearsal dinners, cocktail parties and celebrations.

© Julian Goble 1997

© Holland Studios

THE CROWN BALLROOM & GARDEN COURT

"The Fine Art of Weddings & Receptions"

918 S.W. Yamhill and Ninth Avenue • Portland, Oregon 97205

(diagonal from the downtown Nordstrom, on the top floor of the historic Pythian Building)

Contact: Raven David (503) 227-8440, (800) 852-1443; Fax (503) 227-2654

Business Hours: by appointment only; offering after-hours showings

---

The Crown, proudly atop the downtown Pythian Building consists of The Crown Ballroom—an elegant Victorian hall built in 1901 in the tradition of a European Grand Salon, boasting rich mahogany paneling, a beamed cathedral ceiling and full stage for beautiful wedding ceremonies. And for smaller receptions—the artful and ever romantic Garden Court.

Capacity: The Crown Ballroom: 225 guests/sit-down; Garden Court: 60 guests/sit-down; rooms may be booked together for a facility capacity of 275 sit-down or 400 cocktail-style

Price Range: $700 to $2,950, depends on room, date, type of event and number of guests

Catering: four professional in-house catering services to assist in menu/event planning for cocktail parties, buffets or formal sit-downs; can work with all budgets and themes from intimate tea parties to formal dances and concerts to black tie galas

Types of Events: elegant wedding ceremonies and receptions; corporate celebrations and banquets; famous for Casa Blanca, Titanic and masquerade/theme parties

Availability and Terms

The Crown is regularly booking 6–12 months in advance. Half the rental fee will reserve either or both rooms. Rooms are reserved for 3- to 10-hour time blocks.

Description of Facility and Services

Banquet seating: tables and double-padded black dining chairs for up to 275 guests

Bar facilities: full bar services; host/no-host with bartenders and liquor liability provided by our in-house caterers; two full-service cocktail bars; one espresso/champagne bar

Dance floors: three hardwood floors; spotlights, mirror balls, gels and accommodating two to 200 guests

Decorations: this fully decorated 10,000-ft facility is tastefully designed with Victorian architectural themes, large tropical plants, impressive chandeliers and large candelabras, while French-lace curtains on king-size windows open up to spectacular midtown city views

Convenient parking: 7-level parking structure adjacent to building with economy rates

Special Features

The Champagne Room for the Bride's party features a vanity bar, a guest phone, three sofas and city views. The in-house Black Wing Gallery for the groom's party includes a water fountain, walk-in closet and private lounge/restroom. Large gold grand piano for cake cutting ceremony; 26-foot serpentine buffet table and full-service kitchen. Full stage with raised and lighted dance floor, full-length formal velvet curtain for ceremonies, receiving lines and grand entrances! Ask for Raven David, our Director, for a private tour of this showcase venue.

Crown Vista Events

19875 N.W. Logie Trail
Portland, Oregon 97231
Contact: Wendy Daniels
(503) 240-6057

Capacity: receptions and dinners from 1 to 150; 350 with outside areas
Price Range: varies depending on type of event and catered service
Catering: full service by Party Princess Catering; guest caterers accepted
Types of Events: weddings, receptions meetings, workshops, retreats, fundraisers, corporate events, pool parties, lunches, cocktail parties, celebrations, theme parties

Availability and Terms

Please contact our sales and catering office for space availability and terms. A 50% deposit is required upon reservation; refundable security deposit.

Description of Facility and Services

Seating: provided as needed
Servers: professional staffing by Party Princess Catering
Bar facilities: full service and bartenders available
Dance floor: available for a fee; electrical outlets available
Linens and napkins: basic colors provided; specialty linens at extra cost
China and glassware: provided by caterer
Decorations: flowers and theme decorations can be arranged
Cleanup: included with site
Parking: ample free parking; valet service available
ADA: accessible

Special Services

Complete event and party planning services from concept to completion, including custom menus, flowers, decorations and entertainment. On-site staff is available to answer questions.

ABOUT CROWN VISTA

Crown Vista is a private, 47-acre estate offering a tranquil setting with a breathtaking, panoramic view of rivers and Cascade peaks. The main facility houses a unique art collection. Only 15 minutes from downtown, guests find serene ponds in the gardens and a creek running through the beautifully landscaped grounds. Lounge by the heated outdoor pool, explore the blackberry-studded forest trails, visit Sauvie Island wildlife refuge or play golf at a nearby course. Professional services and experienced staff make Crown Vista the perfect choice for your wedding reception.

CROWNE PLAZA®
HOTELS · RESORTS

14811 Kruse Oaks Boulevard
Lake Oswego, Oregon 97035
For banquet reservations:
Crystal Harrell (503) 624-8400 ext. 253
Sleeping room rates:
Kyra Olsen (503) 624-8400 ext. 251

Capacity: groups of 20 up to 300
Price Range: inquire about prices
Catering: incredible full-service custom catering
Types of Events: sit-down dinner, buffet, cocktails and hors d'oeuvres, luncheons, any custom party

Availability, Terms, and Location

One ballroom and one boardroom are available for banquets and receptions. We recommend making reservations as early as possible. The Crowne Plaza is conveniently located at the intersection of Interstate 5 and Highway 217. Its accessibility to Portland, Beaverton, Tigard, and Lake Oswego makes it ideally situated for your wedding and reception.

Description of Facility and Services

Seating: tables and chairs for up to 250 people
Servers: included
Cleanup: handled by The Crowne Plaza
Bar facilities: full-service bar facilities; bartenders available for private reception
Dance floor: space available for band; large dance floor
Linens and napkins: all colors available (some extra charge)
China and glassware: classic styles
Decorations: inquire about decorations we can provide for an extra cost
Parking: plenty of free parking; valet parking available
ADA: fully accessible

Special Services

- **Weddings:** Our six-story atrium with cascading waterfalls makes a beautiful setting for your wedding ceremony. **When booking your reception, a complimentary suite will be provided for the bride and groom.** Special rates are available for your out-of-town guests.

LUXURIOUS AND ELEGANT

The luxurious and elegant Crowne Plaza features a six-story waterfall in the atrium and 161 tastefully decorated rooms. Other amenities include an indoor-outdoor pool, spa, sauna, exercise facility, and gift shop. This hotel is ideal for rehearsal dinners, bridesmaid luncheons, and wedding receptions.

CRYSTAL BALLROOM

1332 W. Burnside
Portland, Oregon 97209
Contact: Mary Hendrickx
(503) 492-2777
Business Hours: Mon–Fri 9am–5pm; tours weekends and by appointment

Capacity: 1,000 persons reception-style; 350 seated
Price Range: please contact an event coordinator for price ranges; food and beverage minimum required to waive rental; based on day of week and time of day
Types of Events: weddings, receptions, reunions, meetings, seminars, exhibits, banquets, concerts, dances, holiday parties

Availability and Terms

We suggest that you book your event six months to one year in advance for a weekend date and three to nine months in advance for weekday functions. Function deposits are 50% of room rental cost. Deposit is due 30 days after booking.

Description of Facility and Services

Seating: 16 eight-top round tables available for assorted seating, 130 folding chairs; additional tables and chairs may be rented; fixed seating in the ballroom, including theater seats in the mezzanine and benches surrounding the ballroom, totals 180
Servers: staff included in price; 17% gratuity added to the bill
Bar facilities: full-service cocktail bar featuring McMenamins beer and wine
Dance floor: the Crystal's most remarkable feature is its maple "floating" dance floor; one of the last of its kind, it is said to have the ability to make a good dancer out of anyone
Live music: live music is welcome to complement your event; the cost is the responsibility of the renter, but recommendations will gladly be made
Linens and napkins: assorted linens included in rental fee
China and glassware: silverware and plates included; due to the nature of the "floating" dance floor, some glassware is discouraged
Decorations: responsibility of renter
Cleanup: included in price
Parking: street parking is available and several paid parking structures are in close walking distance

BEAUTIFULLY RENOVATED HISTORIC BALLROOM

The historic Crystal Ballroom boasts 7,500 square feet of floating dance floor. Its eclectic and festive decor make it an ideal setting for events ranging from an award banquet to a wedding reception. The unique Crystal has been a forum for music, dancing, and personalities that have helped define several eras. Extracting inspiration from over 80 years of history, a team of artists have added dimension to the Crystal's walls by painting murals throughout the building and the on-site brewery.

The Best Value Under The Sun.™

DAYS INN CITY CENTER

1414 S.W. Sixth Avenue • Portland, Oregon 97201
Contact: Catering Sales Manager
(503) 221-1611 or (800) 899-0248; Fax (503) 226-0447
E-mail: daysinn@transport.com
Web site: www.daysinn.com

Capacity: we offer three rooms and one suite to accommodate up to 200 people
Catering: in-house catering available
Price Range: varies depending on menu and type of event
Types of Events: breakfast meetings, brunches, lunches, business meetings, seminars, banquets

Availability and Terms

Days Inn City Center recommends that you make your reservation for space as early as possible.

Description of Facility and Services

Seating: tables and chairs provided; banquet, round and classroom tables available
Servers: staff included in catering cost
Bar facilities: full beverage service available
Linens and napkins: an extensive array of colors available at no extra charge
China and glassware: white china and stemmed glassware
Decorations: mirrored tiles, votive candles, bud vases, silk plants, themed decor available
Audiovisual: available upon request
Equipment: podiums, risers and staging available
Cleanup: provided by hotel staff
Parking: free on-site, subject to availability
ADA: accessible

Special Services

Days Inn City Center features 173 newly renovated guest rooms, including one suite. Your guests will enjoy our "heart of downtown" location and other amenities including free parking, complimentary daily newspaper delivered to your door, data ports, and pay-per-view movies and games in each room. Our heated outdoor pool is available seasonally, and Gold's Gym is available complimentary to all guests. Group rates are available for 10 or more rooms.

IN THE HEART OF DOWNTOWN PORTLAND

Plan your event in our flexible meeting space and banquet facilities. We will cater to the needs of your guests while you focus on the business at hand. *We are truly at your service!*

DOUBLETREE

HOTELS·GUEST SUITES·RESORTS™

COLUMBIA RIVER

1401 N. Hayden Island Drive • Portland, Oregon 97217
Contact: Sales Office (503) 283-2111
E-mail: crsales@teleport.com
Office Hours: Mon–Fri 8am–6pm, Sat 9am–4pm

Capacity: up to 1,200 guests
Price Range: price will vary depending on type of event and menu selection
Catering: full-service in-house catering provided by the hotel exclusively
Types of Events: from light hors d'oeuvres receptions to elegant luncheon and dinner affairs, including rehearsal dinners and bridal showers

Availability and Terms

The hotel offers many separate ballrooms to accommodate any size wedding party. Several ballrooms have floor to ceiling windows which allow for a dramatic view of the mighty Columbia River and its awesome beauty. It is suggested that reservations be made as soon as possible. A deposit is required at time of booking. Please call the Catering Office for details.

Description of Facility and Services

Seating: your choice of banquet rounds or informal cabaret style
Servers: staff included in catering costs
Bar facilities: full beverage service; hotel offers all beer, wine, and liquor
Dance floor: available for our guests
Linens and napkins: an extensive array of linen colors at no additional charge
China and glassware: white china; stemmed glassware
Cleanup: provided by hotel staff
Decorations: lattice, silk plants, mirror tiles, votive candles, and bud vases available; access for early decoration by prior arrangement
Parking: 750 complimentary parking stalls
ADA: yes

Special Services

The hotel provides complimentary deluxe accommodations for the bride and groom the night of your wedding reception, along with a complimentary bottle of champagne. In addition, we offer special group rates for your guests' sleeping needs.

BEAUTIFUL RIVERFRONT LOCATION PROFESSIONAL AND QUALITY SERVICE

By selecting this hotel on Hayden Island, you will benefit from the unique and dramatic setting on the majestic Columbia River, as well as true professional wedding coordinators who will assist with all your planning needs. From menu planning to room decor and design, our experienced and friendly staff are specially trained to ensure a memorable and worry-free event. Just north of downtown, our convenient location and ample parking make attending your special event easy for your guests. Experience the difference of the DoubleTree Hotel Columbia River, and your memories will be endless.

DoubleTree Hotel™

Portland • Downtown

310 S.W. Lincoln • Portland, Oregon 97201
Contact: Sales Office (503) 221-0450; Fax (503) 225-4303
Business Hours: Mon–Fri 8am–6pm; Sat 9am–1pm

Capacity: 250 people maximum
Price Range: $20 per person and up; customized packages available
Catering: full-service in-house catering exclusively
Types of Events: ceremonies, receptions, bridal showers, rehearsal dinners, luncheons, and dinner affairs

Availability and Terms

The DoubleTree Hotel Portland • Downtown's elegant Columbia Falls Ballroom will accommodate up to 225 people for a reception and dance. We recommend that you make your reservation as soon as possible. A $500 nonrefundable deposit is required.

Description of Facility and Services

Seating: tables and chairs provided; banquet round tables
Servers: staff included in catering costs
Bar facilities: portable bars; host/no-host; beer, wine, mixed drinks, champagne, and soft drinks
Dance floor: complimentary; electrical outlets available
Linens and napkins: linen tablecloths and napkins in a variety of colors at no additional charge
China and glassware: white china; stemmed glassware
Cleanup: provided by hotel staff
Decorations: lattice, silk plants, mirror tiles, votive candles available; access for early decorating by prior arrangement
Parking: complimentary on-site parking available
ADA: yes

A MEMORABLE OCCASION...

...Awaits you at the DoubleTree Hotel Portland • Downtown! With all the planning, choosing and coordinating, you need a hotel that can accommodate and foresee your wedding reception needs. Our Columbia Falls Ballroom combines simple elegance and versatility to reflect a variety of wedding themes. We offer creative menus to tantalize all taste buds and our professional and friendly staff will do all the work so that you will feel comfortable and confident as you visit with friends and family who have come to share your special day.

The DoubleTree Hotel Portland • Downtown is conveniently located on the southwest side of downtown directly off major interstate access. We offer complimentary parking and airport shuttle, a complimentary suite for the bride and groom on the night of the wedding, and we will arrange a discounted room rate for out-of-town guests.

Sweet dreams abound at the DoubleTree Hotel Portland • Downtown. Come see how memorable your wedding reception can be!

DoubleTree Hotel™

PORTLAND • JANTZEN BEACH

909 N. Hayden Island Drive • Portland, Oregon 97217
Contact: Sales Office (503) 283-4466
E-mail: jbsales@teleport.com
Office Hours: Mon–Fri 8am–6pm; Sat 8am–5pm

Capacity: up to 1,400 guests
Price Range: price will vary depending on type of event and menu selection
Catering: full-service in-house catering provided by the hotel exclusively
Types of Events: from light hors d'oeuvres receptions to elegant luncheon and dinner affairs, including rehearsal dinners and bridal showers

Availability and Terms

The hotel offers many separate ballrooms to accommodate any size wedding party. Several ballrooms have floor to ceiling windows which allow for a dramatic view of the mighty Columbia River and its awesome beauty. It is suggested that reservations be made as soon as possible. A deposit is required at time of booking. Please call the Catering Office for details.

Description of Facility and Services

Seating: your choice of banquet rounds or informal cabaret style
Servers: staff included in catering costs
Bar facilities: full beverage service; hotel provides all beer, wine, and liquor
Dance floor: available at no additional charge
Linens and napkins: an extensive array of linen colors at no additional charge
China and glassware: white china; stemmed glassware
Cleanup: provided by hotel staff
Decorations: lattice, silk plants, mirror tiles, and votive candles; access for early decoration by prior arrangement
Parking: complimentary parking
ADA: accessible

Special Services

The hotel provides complimentary deluxe accommodations for the bride and groom the night of your wedding reception, along with a complimentary bottle of champagne.

BEAUTIFUL RIVERFRONT LOCATION
PROFESSIONAL AND QUALITY SERVICE

By selecting this hotel on Hayden Island, you will benefit from the unique and dramatic setting on the majestic Columbia River, as well as true professional wedding coordinators who will assist with all your planning needs. From menu planning to room decor and design, our experienced and friendly staff are specially trained to ensure a memorable and worry-free event. Just north of downtown, our convenient location and ample parking make attending your special event easy for your guests. Experience the difference of the DoubleTree Hotel Jantzen Beach, and your memories will be endless.

DoubleTree Hotel™

Portland • Lloyd Center

1000 N.E. Multnomah • Portland, Oregon 97232
Contact: Catering Office (503) 249-3130
Business Hours: Mon–Fri 8am–6pm; Sat 9am–noon

Capacity: up to 1,100 guests
Price Range: price will vary depending on type of event and menu selection
Catering: full-service in-house catering provided by the hotel exclusively
Types of Events: light hors d'oeuvre receptions to elegant luncheon and dinner affairs, including rehearsal dinners and bridal showers

Availability and Terms

The DoubleTree Hotel Portland • Lloyd Center offers four separate ballrooms to accommodate any size wedding party. The Pacific Northwest Ballroom, our newest addition, offers floor to ceiling windows that overlook the pool and outside patio. Reservations are suggested six to nine months in advance with a deposit. Please call the catering office for details.

Description of Facility and Services

Seating: your choice of banquet rounds or informal cabaret style
Servers: staff included in catering costs
Bar facilities: full beverage service available; DoubleTree Hotel Portland • Lloyd Center to provide all beer, wine, and liquor
Dance floor: available at no additional charge
Linens and napkins: an extensive array of linen colors at no additional charge
China and glassware: white china; stemmed glassware
Cleanup: included in price
Parking: parking for over 750 cars; rate is discounted for all guests attending; maximum charge of $6 per car
ADA: yes

Special Services

The DoubleTree Hotel Portland • Lloyd Center provides a complimentary Bridal Suite the night of your wedding reception along with a complimentary bottle of champagne. In addition, we offer special group rates for your guests' sleeping needs.

RELAX AND ENJOY THE MOMENT

Choose the DoubleTree Hotel Portland • Lloyd Center. Our professional wedding coordinators can accommodate all your planning needs. From menu planning to room decor and design, our experienced and friendly staff are specially trained to take the stress and pressure out of planning your wedding. Our convenient location and ample parking make attending your special event easy for your guests. Our new Northwest Ballroom, with beautiful window-views of the outdoor pool and patio area, provides the perfect setting to make your wedding day memorable. Let us plan this special event while you relax and enjoy the moment.

East Fork Country Estate

9957 S.E. 222nd
Gresham, Oregon 97080
Contact: Karen Reed, owner
(503) 667-7069
or Kay Oft, manager
Closed Tues–Wed,
and December
(3.9 miles south of Gresham on Regner Road)

Capacity: up to 250 seated ceremony and reception
Price Range: please call for specific prices on wedding packages
Catering: in-house catering
Types of Events: full-service wedding receptions with sit-down buffet dinners; traditional cake, coffee, and punch receptions

Availability and Terms

Friday evening weddings are from 5 p.m. to 11 p.m. Saturday bookings are from 9 a.m. to 3 p.m. (11:30 a.m. ceremony, followed by a reception from noon to 3 p.m.) and from 4:30 p.m. to 10:30 p.m. (6 p.m. ceremony, followed by a reception from 6:30 p.m. to 10:30 p.m.). Sunday weddings are any six-hour period until 9 p.m. Closed January 2–February 28.

Description of Facility and Services

Assistance: your personal, professional wedding consultant is included in our package price
Bar facilities: beer, wine, and champagne available
Dance floor: yes, with electrical hookups
Linens and napkins: many colors to choose from
China and glassware: clear glass china with a pattern; glass coffee cups and stemware
Cleanup: included in our wedding packages
Decorations: included in our wedding package price; the gardens include hundreds of bedding plants, roses, and willow and fir trees
Parking: ample free parking is available
ADA: yes

Special Services

You may wish to reserve our horse and white vis-à-vis carriage as part of your wedding processional. Each event is given special, thoughtful, caring attention. We specialize in "stress free" weddings.

THE ESTATE FACES MOUNT HOOD AND OVERLOOKS A SERENE FARM VALLEY

Your guests will be seated under white canopies on lawn areas in front of the gazebo. The Estate includes a large, beautifully decorated indoor reception area with hardwood floors and oriental carpeting, several covered patios, four canopies on the lawn areas, and spacious bride and groom changing rooms.

Your guests will arrive to find terraced lawns and flowering gardens facing Mount Hood, horses grazing on the Estate's pastures, and a view overlooking a farm valley, the Cascade foothills, and Mount Hood. The result is a warm, relaxed country setting.

EASTMORELAND GRILL AT THE EASTMORELAND GOLF COURSE

2425 S.E. Bybee Boulevard
Portland, Oregon 97202
Contact: Jerilyn Walker
(503) 775-5910: Fax (503) 775-6349
Office Hours: 9am–5pm

Capacity: 125 for a sit-down dinner; 175 for a reception; 250 including outside area
Price Range: $350 to $700 room-rental charge, depending upon the size of the event; $13 to $30 per person; the menu will be created especially for you by our staff
Catering: full-service catering available in-house
Types of Events: cocktails, hors d'oeuvres, cake and champagne, buffet, sit-down

Availability and Terms

The Eastmoreland Grill encourages your reservations up to one year in advance. A deposit is required and is nonrefundable. Half-payment is required 30 days in advance, with the remaining half payable on the day of the event.

Description of Facility and Services

Seating: tables and chairs provided for up to 125 sit-down guests
Servers: full staff available; a gratuity will be added to food and beverage purchases
Bar facilities: full-service bar and staff bartender provided upon request; host/no-host; liquor, beer, and wine
Dance floor: we can provide a dance floor; rental fee varies according to size
Linens and napkins: cloth tablecloths and napkins available in some colors
China and glassware: white china; glassware available in plastic or glass, as required
Cleanup: cleanup provided
Decorations: our catering manager will discuss with you and help develop your decoration plans
Parking: large parking lot with overflow area
ADA: full facilities

Special Services

The Eastmoreland Grill will cater to your every need in order that your day be just as you would have it to the last detail.

GRACIOUS STYLE OVERLOOKING LUSH GREENS

The lush, beautiful greens of the Eastmoreland Golf Course are the setting for our gorgeous new Tudor-style clubhouse. The banquet room overlooks the tenth tee and has a large, gracious veranda for outdoor entertaining. Winter events are equally blessed with a handsome fireplace where guests love to gather. Our staff has extensive experience in wedding receptions, rehearsal dinners, corporate events, anniversaries, birthdays, and reunions, and we will create a personal menu exactly to your specifications. A telephone call to our staff will start you on your way to a carefree and beautiful event.

EMBASSY SUITES PORTLAND DOWNTOWN

319 S.W. Pine Street • Portland, Oregon 97204
Lisa Mattera (503) 279-9000 ext. 6169, (503) 796-3851; Fax (503) 220-0206

EMBASSY SUITES

Capacity: 220 sit down; 300 reception
Price Range: from $15 for luncheons, from $21.50 for dinners and average of $35 for receptions
Catering: complete in-house catering only
Types of Events: wedding receptions, rehearsal dinners, bridal brunches and luncheons

Availability and Terms

Two large ballrooms plus a ceremonial room and six smaller rooms, great for rehearsal dinners. Most rooms have large windows and are decorated with the elegance and style of the historic Multnomah Hotel, including all of the amenities in an Embassy Suites. Once an event is confirmed, a deposit is required.

Description of Facility and Services

Seating: all tables and chairs provided
Servers: professional service staff provided
Bar facilities: hotel provides bar facilities and professional alcoholic beverage servers
Dance floor: 15′ x 15′ floor available with electrical hookups
Linens, napkins, china and glassware: provided by hotel
Decorations: please check with catering representative
Cleanup: provided by hotel
Parking: valet and parking garage
ADA: all facilities handicapped accessible

Special Services

Let our catering representative help make your occasion one to remember. Experience the elegance and style of our restored historic hotel. You will find table decorations included with rooms and a professional staff that is flexible in helping you set up your function with confidence. Enjoy the use of a deluxe suite for the bride and her attendants as well as a complimentary suite for the bride and groom.

WHERE HISTORY MEETS HOSPITALITY

Come discover Portland's premier historic hotel where you will find contemporary amenities in a classic setting. Along with nine meeting rooms, the hotel has 276 guest suites all designed and furnished to complement the hotel's early 20th century architecture. First opened in 1912 as the Multnomah, the hotel was the hub of Portland society. The same holds true today. Plan your event at the new Embassy Suites Portland Downtown and be a part of history.

EMBASSY SUITES®

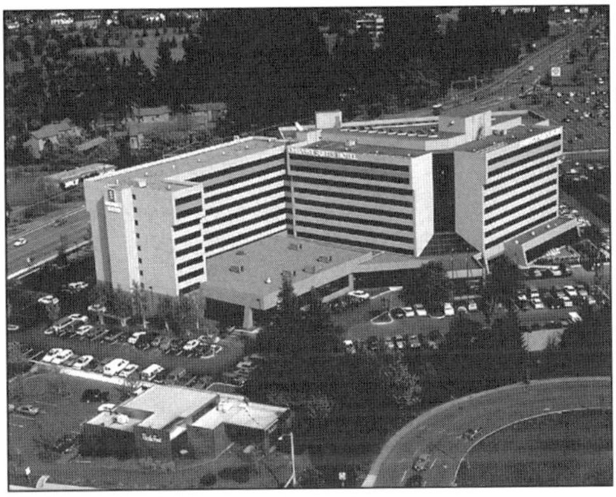

PORTLAND—WASHINGTON SQUARE

9000 S.W. Washington Square Road
Tigard, OR 97223
Contact: Lisette Crepeaux
(503) 644-4000

Capacity: up to 1,200 people
Price Range: price to be determined by event and menu selections
Catering: full service catering
Types of receptions: elegant served dinners or buffets, hors d'oeuvres receptions and special private parties

Availability and Terms

The Embassy Suites Hotel has a wide variety of banquet facilities for your special event. Our function rooms can accommodate from 10–1,200 guests.

Description of Facility and Services

Seating: provided for up to 800 guests
Servers: included in catering cost
Bar facilities: full service hosted or no host bar; beer, wine and champagne service; we provide all beverages, bartenders and servers
Dance floor: dance floor provided at no additional cost
Linens and napkins: fine linens available in colors to coordinate with banquet room decor
China and glassware: fine china, silver and glassware provided
Cleanup: included in catering charges
Decorations: limited decorations available at no additional charge
Parking: complimentary parking
ADA: fully equipped to accommodate ADA requirements

Special Services

The Embassy Suites Hotel provides a complimentary Presidential Suite ($500 value) for that special bride and groom on the night of the wedding. Special rates are available for your out-of-town guests in our luxurious suites. Contact our Catering Professionals to see why Embassy Suites is the perfect setting for your memorable occasion.

The Fairgate Inn
Bed and Breakfast

2313 N.W. 23rd Avenue
Camas, Washington 98607
Contact: Chris Foyt (360) 834-0861
Business Hours: Mon–Fri 10am–4pm

Capacity: 25 to 200; more if event is held outdoors or in tented area
Price Range: price varies according to event
Catering: caterers from the Fairgate's approved list only
Types of Events: wedding ceremonies and receptions, anniversaries, baby and bridal showers, English high tea, corporate meetings

Availability and Terms

The Georgian Ballroom can accommodate 115 seated. The spectacular formal dining room, foyer and living room provides additional space for buffet service. Finished in rich woods, the library provides a comfortable atmosphere for business conferences. A deposit is required at the time of booking with the balance due the day of your event.

Description of Facility and Services

Seating: tables and chairs provided for 115
Servers: provided by caterer
Bar facilities: champagne toast available; caterer to provide servers as well as liability insurance
Dance floor: 200 sq. ft. provided at no additional charge, located in the Georgian Ballroom; electrical outlets available
Linens and napkins: provided by caterer; table skirting available for buffet tables at no additional charge
Decoration limitations: please inquire with event coordinator
Cleanup: responsibility of caterer
Parking: ample free parking
ADA: fully accessible

Special Services

The Fairgate is conveniently located 10 minutes from the Portland Airport in Camas, Washington. The Inn is elaborately decorated, reducing the need for additional decoration. Our rental fee includes an additional hour prior to your event for caterers and floral setup. Crystal table decorations are provided at no additional cost. A bride's room is also available.

TRADITIONAL GREEK REVIVAL INN

This traditional Greek revival inn is situated on three acres atop Prune Hill. In addition to the public areas in the Georgian Ballroom and main floor, the Fairgate, with over 11,000 square feet, offers overnight accommodations in eight luxurious suites, all with private baths and fireplaces. The two bridal suites include whirlpool tubs as well; full breakfast is complimentary.

FIFTH AVENUE SUITES HOTEL
Red Star Tavern and Roast House

506 S.W. Washington • Portland, Oregon 97204
Contact: Margie Yager, Director of Catering
(503) 417-3377
E-mail: Margie.yager@redstartavern.com
Business Hours: Mon–Fri 8am–5pm

Capacity: 6,000 square feet of meeting/private dining space; intimate parties of 16; receptions up to 200
Price Range: $19 to $50 per person
Catering: enjoy "re-kindled American classics" in-house catering from Red Star Tavern and Roast House's Executive Chef Rob Pando
Types of Events: wedding ceremonies and receptions, rehearsal dinners, bridal luncheons

Availability and Terms
Space should be reserved as soon as possible—minimum of 72 hours notice. A deposit equal to one half the estimated expense is required. Cancellation terms apply.

Description of Facility and Services
Seating: tables and chairs provided
Servers: provided
Bar facilities: bartender provided; Red Star provides all beverages
Dance floor: will be rented
Linens: ivory, white and other linen colors available
China: in-house china available; other patterns will be rented
Decorations: no decorations to be attached to walls or ceilings
Cleanup: fees vary
Parking: valet parking available at Fifth Avenue Suites Hotel, 24 hours
ADA: yes

Special Services
Complimentary evening wine tasting in our fireside lobby, complimentary coffee service, fitness center, 24-hour room service, concierge, Aveda spa. Our catering consultants are available and happy to assist you in making your event successful and memorable.

THE PICTURE OF COMFORT AND SOPHISTICATION
Historic 10-story 1912 building, formerly a distinguished department store, is the picture of comfort and sophistication. Of the hotel's 221 rooms, 135 are spacious 550-square-foot suites. As part of a $25 million renovation, the hotel has the residential feel of a turn-of-the-century American country home.

Our banquet rooms are located on the main, second and third floors of the hotel. Within these rooms, you will find a decor filled with classic lines and warm ambiance.

The Fountains Ballroom

223 S.E. 122nd Avenue • Portland, Oregon 97233
(503) 261-9424; Fax (503) 261-2989 • Web site: www.fountainsballroom.com
Business Hours: Tues–Thurs 9am–9pm or by appointment

We do it all for weddings!!!

Ceremonies + Receptions + Catering + Photography + Wedding Cakes + Invitations + Flowers

And much more!

Capacity: up to 300 with beautiful outside garden patio
Price Range: $600 to $1,200 (most packages reflect a 6-hour booking); please add $300 if having a wedding ceremony and wedding reception
Catering: in-house; affordable buffet menus up to elegant plated dinners

Terms

A 50% nonrefundable deposit is requested; remaining balance due 10 days prior to event.

Description of Facility and Services

Seating: 15 round tables and 200 white wedding chairs
Servers: professional staff in formal attire
Bar facilities: full bar; formal champagne toast available (liability insurance provided)
Dance floor: three optional dance floors
Linens and napkins: linen available as well as personalized napkins; most colors
Decorations: table decorations available as well as extended decorating services
Photography: on-site professional studio (**Negatives are included** in all wedding packages)
Flowers: professional on-site florists
Parking: free parking and surrounding street parking (valet services available)

2000 SPECIAL PACKAGE

Why not call The Fountains Ballroom where most everything for your wedding can be provided in one low-cost package? We have a special offer for the 1999-2000 season that includes the following: room rental, garden patio, full catered dinner buffet, servers, custom wedding cake, complete floral package, partial bar, invitations, bride and groom food basket for the honeymoon night and ***five free gifts*** including food platter for before ceremony, special bride and groom bottle of sparkling cider, table decorations, throw bouquet, and additional 10% off invitations!!! You should not need to purchase anything extra for this package! All this plus much more is only $4,999 (menu based on 100 guests). Upgrades are available. Or you may choose the individual services you would like to use! It is all up to you.

We look forward to serving you and your family on your very special day! Please call today for a free consultation. (subject to availability)

See page 304 under Caterers & Ice Carvings and page 485 under Photographers.

GARDEN VIEW ESTATES

"The Northwest's Most Exclusive Wedding Facility"
(Only 20 minutes from downtown Portland)

Contact: Kristina Y. McMorris (503) 666-4725

Capacity: up to 500 guests
Price Range: prices vary with packages and services
Catering: in-house caterers customize your perfect menu
Type of Events: elegant wedding ceremonies, receptions, anniversaries, parties, showers

Availability and Terms

Garden View Estates takes pride in booking only one wedding per day on Saturdays and Sundays, mid-June through mid-September. A deposit is required to hold your date. Please call now for availability.

Description of Facility and Services

Seating: tables and chairs included; customize your arrangements surrounding a gazebo or waterfall
Servers: serving attendants included
Bar facilities: beer, wine, champagne; bartenders included
Dance floor: cost varies according to size desired; electrical outlets available
Linens and napkins: included in wedding packages
China and glassware: plates and silverware included; glassware available for your needs
Cleanup: cleanup and setup included; provided by Garden View Estates
Decorations: lattice gazebo, cascading waterfall, koi pond, majestic fountain, natural grotto, wisteria arbors, lush grass, towering trees and 350 rose bushes provide natural décor for your event; personal decorating touches are welcomed; canopies available in case of inclement weather
Parking: ample secured on-site parking area
Special features: Bride's Cottage and Groom's House, both equipped with full bathrooms and kitchens

THE PERFECT SETTING FOR THE WEDDING OF YOUR DREAMS…

…This 15-acre historic property is romantically hidden between the banks of a gleaming river and a rocked cliff covered with trees. Consulting and coordinating services are included, to provide you with as much or as little assistance as you would prefer. Complimentary snack trays are delivered to both houses on your wedding day, while a complimentary bottle of champagne is chilled at a reception bar for your first toast. These personalized touches are just a few examples of the special care Garden View Estates takes in helping you achieve the wedding you have always imagined. Please call for a private tour of the Estate.

TURN OF THE CENTURY CHARM

THE HISTORIC GENTLE HOUSE

855 N. Monmouth Avenue • Monmouth, Oregon 97361
Contact: Jeanette Crosby-Kruljac (503) 838-8673
E-mail: gentlehouse@wou.edu
Web site: www.wou.edu/President/University/Advancement/gentle/gentle.html

---

Capacity: Reception style: **Indoor:** up to 200; **Outdoor:** up to 500
Price Range: varies according to event; please call for information
Catering: you are welcome to bring in your own caterer or provide the food yourself; full kitchen facility on premises
Types of Events: meetings, seminars, banquets, receptions, and wedding ceremonies

Availability and Terms

Reservations should be made as early as possible. Bookings are made on a first-come, first serve basis. A $200 deposit will secure your date.

Description of Facility and Services

Seating: Meeting for 120; Banquet for 75
Servers: provided by caterer
Bar facilities: provided by caterer
Linens and napkins: table linens available for a fee
China and glassware: provided by caterer
Audiovisual: piano, pump organ, sound system and speakers available upon request
Equipment: microphone, podium, dry-erase board and projector available
Cleanup: you must remove all materials you bring in; some or all of your deposit may be kept for damage or extra labor for clean up
Parking: 22 parking spaces; additional parking available
ADA: yes

VICTORIAN CHARM AND GRACE

The Historic Gentle House is geared towards bringing people for special events, conferences, meetings, and retreats. Gentle House is a renovated Victorian country home nestled around romantic landscaped grounds. Accented by a charming gazebo and nestled in rural Monmouth (just 20 minutes from downtown Salem and adjacent to Western Oregon University). Gentle House is guaranteed to make your event special.

WESTERN OREGON
UNIVERSITY

THE GEORGIAN RESTAURANT

MEIER & FRANK

DOWNTOWN

621 S.W. Fifth Avenue
Portland, Oregon 97204
(503) 241-5162 or (503) 241-5163; Fax (503) 241-5242

Capacity: up to 175 sit-down, 250 reception; The Grill: 24' x 32', seats 48; The Party Room: 17' x 22', seats 20; The Georgian Tea Room: 54' x 62', seats 150
Price Range: price varies according to type of event
Catering: full-service in-house catering-from sandwiches to steaks, we have it all
Types of Events: banquets, receptions, rehearsal dinners, bridal teas, anniversaries, business lunches, corporate meetings, fund-raisers, class reunions, bus tour groups

Availability and Terms

Reservations recommended as early as possible. Please inquire for specific price and terms.

Description of Facility and Services

Seating: tables and chairs provided
Servers: provided by The Georgian Restaurant
Bar facilities: complete selection of Northwest wines and local microbrews
Linens and napkins: white standard; colors optional
China and glassware: provided by The Georgian Restaurant
Cleanup: provided by The Georgian Restaurant
Parking: street and parking garages nearby
ADA: fully accessible

Special Services

We are conveniently located on the 10th floor of Meier & Frank, in the center of downtown Portland along Tri-Met MAX light-rail and Fareless Square. The Georgian Restaurant's prime location makes it an easy place for all your guests to find. Our staff will be happy to assist you in any way possible.

A PORTLAND TRADITION FOR GENERATIONS

Located in the historic Meier & Frank building, built in 1909, The Georgian Restaurant has always been the restaurant where celebrations are made just a little more special. The restaurant has a quiet atmosphere with décor reminiscent of the classic colonial days.

JAKE'S CATERING
AT THE
GOVERNOR
HOTEL

611 S.W. 10th Avenue
Portland, Oregon 97205
(503) 241-2125; Fax (503) 220-1849
Web site: http://www.mccormickandschmicks.com

Capacity: 600 reception; 450 sit-down dinner
Price Range: $28 to $50
Catering: Jake's Catering is the exclusive caterer for The Governor Hotel; off-premise catering available
Types of Events: from stand-up cocktail/appetizer receptions to fabulous buffet presentations to complete sit-down dinners for groups and gatherings of all sizes

Availability and Terms

Our Italian Renaissance style rooms offer variety and flexibility for groups of 20 to 600. The majestic Ballroom, Renaissance Room, Fireside Room, Library, and five additional rooms gracefully complement the charm of The Governor Hotel. We require a 50% deposit to confirm your event and payment in full 72 hours prior to event for estimated charges.

Description of Facility and Services

Seating: tables and chairs for up to 450
Servers: all servers included as hotel service
Bar facilities: full-service bar and bartender
Linens and napkins: cloth napkins and linens provided in a variety of colors
China and glassware: fine china and glassware provided
Decorations: please inquire about specific decoration ideas and needs
Parking: ample parking available near hotel
ADA: committed to full service for guests with disabilities

Jake's Catering… A Tradition

Jake's Catering at The Governor Hotel is a division of McCormick & Schmick Management Group and "Jake's Famous Crawfish." Jake's is one of the most respected dining institutions in the Portland area, and Jake's Catering at The Governor Hotel upholds this prestigious reputation.

Known for offering extensive Pacific Northwest menu selection, including fresh seafood and fish, pasta and poultry dishes, and prime cut steaks, Jake's Catering at The Governor Hotel has the flexibility and talent to cater to your needs.

CLASSIC ELEGANCE AND SERVICE

Listed on the National Register of Historic Places, The Governor Hotel is an architectural beauty. Built in 1909 and renovated in 1992, the hotel has been completely restored to its original grandeur. The original design and ornate craftsmanship of the grand banquet space area were preserved in the original Italian Renaissance styling. The room's chandeliers, high vaulted ceilings, marble floors, and black-walnut woodwork and walls are truly unique.

Capacity: up to 299 indoors
Price Range: $650 to $1,995
Catering: open to your caterer
Types of Events: wedding ceremonies, receptions, banquets, anniversaries, birthdays, seminars, concerts, meetings and holiday parties

Availability and Terms

Available daytime or evenings, Monday through Sunday. A 50% deposit holds your date.

Descriptions of Facility and Services

Seating: all tables and chairs provided
Servers: provided by caterer
Bar facilities: allowed; call for details
Dance floor: wood floor vintage ballroom
Billiard Room: two 9-ft. Brunswick slate pool tables
Linens: available; **China and glassware:** provided by caterer
Cleanup: call for details
Decorations: candelabras, antiques, some centerpieces, silk flowers and trees available; client may decorate; some limitations
Audiovisual: upright piano, Hammond organ, 16-channel pro PA, CD player and tape deck available by arrangement; we also welcome your band or DJ
Parking: adjacent free city lots and ample street parking
ADA: Stair Glide Chairlift and ADA bathrooms

1922 WEDDING AND RECEPTION VENUE

The Grand Oregon Lodge, located in the charming Historic District of Oregon CIty, was designed, built, and operated as a private club from 1922 until 1997. Now open to the public, this grand facility has been renovated and brightened for elegant weddings, receptions, events and celebrations. Your guests will delight in the palatial room proportions, hotel height ceilings, and architectural details. Dance the night away in the Vintage Ballroom, or play one of the oak-and-leather pool tables in the Antique Billiard Room. Our beautiful Rose Room can serve as a ceremony site, additional dining, or makes an excellent food and beverage room with a convenient Caterer's Kitchen adjoining. These grand rooms flow openly into each other, keeping your party active and lively. Brides often rave that, "My friends and relatives loved having places to go, things to do, and easy ways to meet and mingle with each other…they say it is the best wedding they've ever been to!" Come see what they're talking about. **E-mail: grandoregonlodge@worldstar.com**

Gray Gables Estate

Year-round Wedding Gardens

3009 S.E. Chestnut • Milwaukie, Oregon 97267
(503) 654-0470, (877) 500-GRAY (4729)
Fax (503) 654-3929
Business Hours: 7 days a week
Web Site: www.graygables.com
Under New Management

Capacity: up to 290 in our reception center or garden park
Price Range: various wedding and reception packages
Catering: in-house catering
Types of Events: weddings, receptions, rehearsals, banquets, anniversaries

Availability and Terms

The Gray Gables takes bookings for its facility up to one year in advance, but shorter notice can be accommodated if space is available. You and your guests will have exclusive use of the estate. A $500 deposit is required to hold your reservation date.

Description of Facility and Services

Consultation: every package includes bridal consultation and event coordination
Seating: tables and chairs provided for up to 290 people
Servers: all parking and service attendants included
Bar facilities: extensive selection of beer, wine, and champagne available
Dance floor: accommodates up to 125 people; electrical outlets available
Linens and napkins: elegant linen tablecloths and skirting; quality paper napkins; specialty linens available at additional cost
China and glassware: clear crystal china, appropriate glassware; silver service available at an additional cost
Decorations: we are proud to offer a variety of decorating options
Cleanup: provided by Gray Gables staff
Parking: ample free parking

Special Services

We can provide and assist with invitations, cakes, ministers, photographers, videographers, florists, musicians, disc jockeys and live musicians. We are the Northwest's premier full-service event center. Our consultants understand the significance of your special day. We assist you in planning and executing all details, to make your event a unique and wonderful occasion.

HISTORIC, COLONIAL ESTATE: MANOR HOUSE AND NEW 6,000 SQ. FT. "TURN-OF-THE-CENTURY" WEDDING AND RECEPTION CENTER

We invite you to share the joy of having your wedding, reception, or special event at our two-acre historic estate. Enjoy the beauty of the English-style gardens accented with ponds, waterfalls and garden statuary. Gray Gables is conveniently located just a few minutes south of downtown Portland. Please call for a guided tour of our lovely facility.

404 S.W. Washington
Portland, Oregon 97204
Contact: Ted Papas (503) 224-2288
Business Hours: Mon–Thurs 7am–midnight;
Fri and Sat 7am–2:30am

Capacity: up to 500
Price Range: varies by number of persons and menu selection
Catering: in-house catering only; off-premise catering always available
Types of Events: wedding ceremonies and receptions, rehearsal dinners, banquets, holiday parties; you may choose from sit-down dinners, buffets, cocktails and hors d'oeuvres

Availability and Terms

Please make reservations as soon as possible. Short-notice reservations gladly accepted upon space availability.

Description of Facility and Services

Seating: tables and chairs for up to 500
Servers: provided
Bar facilities: provided by Greek Cusina
Dance floor: available; with electrical hookups
Linens: available upon request
China: fine china available at no extra charge
Decorations: we can decorate or client can
Cleanup: provided by Greek Cusina
Parking: available on street or in adjacent parking structure
ADA: accessible

Special Services

Music—come see what's making the Greek Cusina *the* place for entertainment. Live Greek performances at no charge!
Off-premise catering—let us cater your next event, whatever the occasion, whatever the location. Have your event Sunday through Thursday and get the band for yourself at no charge!

A TOUCH OF GREECE IN THE HEART OF PORTLAND

Our new Minoan Room is now open and awaiting you. Decorated in warm hues of gold and stunning architecture, The Minoan Room is inviting as well as elegant and romantic—the ideal place for your special day.

Let us dazzle you with our exceptional food as you enter a world of Mediterranean charm and flavor.

Our new Minoan Room
"A Must See Event Facility"
No Room Charge

The Greenwood Inn

S.W. Allen Blvd. at Hwy. 217
Beaverton, Oregon
Contact: Catering
(503) 643-7444 ext 726 or 727
Office Hours: Mon–Fri 8am–5pm
Web site: www.greenwoodinn.com

Capacity: 10 to 500 people
Price Range: Room rentals may be waived depending on food order. We make every effort to work within your budget and offer great flexibility in meeting your special needs. We're happy to custom design a menu for you.
Catering: full-service in-house catering
Types of Events: elegant sit-down or handsome buffet meals, hors d'oeuvres or simple cake-and-punch receptions, bridal luncheons, and rehearsal dinners

Availability and Terms

The Greenwood Inn has nine private rooms accommodating a variety of group sizes. Advance reservations of two to six months are recommended. A deposit is required at the time of confirmation, with the full amount applied to your bill.

Description of Facility and Services

Seating: tables and chairs provided at no additional charge
Servers: included in the cost of food or room rental
Bar facilities: host or no-host bars available; hotel supplies all liquor and bartender
Dance floor: spacious dance floor available at no additional charge
Linens and napkins: cloth linens provided in limited colors at no additional cost; special colors can be ordered for a fee
China and glassware: included in the cost of food, beverage, or room rental
Cleanup: handled by The Greenwood Inn at no additional cost, assuming normal usage
Decorations: limited supply of decorative items available for your use at no additional charge. Elaborate themed events can also be arranged by our staff of professionals.
Parking: 1,000 free spaces available for your use
ADA: all private rooms are on main level and have easy access

Special Services

Access to your room is at least one hour prior to the start of your function. In most cases we will set up your table decorations for you. Please ask about special room rates for your out-of-town guests. Complimentary guest room for bride and groom, based on availability.

OVER 20 YEARS OF EXCELLENT SERVICE

The Greenwood Inn offers a resort-like atmosphere with a convenient location for you, your family and guests. From rooms for your out-of-town guests to complete reception planning and services, we're here for you. It's our pleasure to be a part of your special day—a day to remember.

A Heathman Management Group Property

 Please let this business know that you heard about them from the Bravo! Bridal Resource Guide.

HALLMARK INNS & RESORTS, INC.

Cannon Beach
1400 S. Hemlock
Cannon Beach, Oregon 97110
Contact: Jenny Brown, Director of Sales
(503) 436-1566, (888) 448-4449

Newport
744 S.W. Elizabeth
Newport, Oregon 97365
Contact: TC Caldwell, Director of Sales
(541) 265-2600, (888) 448-4449

Web site: www.hallmarkinns.com

Capacity: *Cannon Beach:* up to 150 reception; *Newport:* up to 200 reception
Price Range: varies depending on size and length of event; please call
Catering: full range of catering services on premise; outdoor events available with tent
Types of Events: business meetings, company retreats, seminars, banquets

Availability and Terms

A six-month advance reservation is recommended; deposit is required upon booking. Deposit can be refunded with 30-day written cancellation notice.

Description of Facility and Services

Seating: tables and chairs provided
Servers: provided with our catering service
Bar facilities: full-service bars available with bartenders ($30 setup fee required)
Dance floor: dance floor available, full electrical hookup
Linens and napkins: cloth linens and napkins available with food service
Decorations: we can assist you, and we allow decorations prior to event with special arrangement
Cleanup: provided and included in catering cost
Parking: ample free parking available

OCEAN BREEZES AND BEAUTIFUL VIEWS

Cannon Beach, Oregon

This oceanfront Hallmark Resort offers 128 of the most beautifully located guest rooms on the Northern Oregon Coast. Just outside your room is the famous Haystack Rock, and the resort is within walking distance of Cannon Beach attractions and shops. Accommodations range from cozy rooms for two to family-designed two-bedroom suites for six. In addition to guest rooms, there are four oceanfront homes available for beachside retreats and group getaways.

Newport, Oregon

Hallmark Resort at Newport offers 158 of the most beautifully appointed oceanfront guest rooms and luxury suites on the Central Oregon Coast. Close to Newport's attractions, golf courses and shops. All guest rooms and suites overlook the Pacific Ocean. Accommodations range from cozy rooms for two to spacious guest rooms with in-room two-person spa, fireplace and oceanfront balcony.

HEATHMAN PRIVATE DINING

THE HEATHMAN RESTAURANT

1001 S.W. Broadway at Salmon Street • Portland, Oregon 97205
Contact: Catering (503) 790-7126

Capacity: 200 people reception; 120 people seated
Price Range: varies depending on type of event and menu selection
Catering: full-service in-house and off-premise catering available
Types of Events: sit-down meals, buffets, receptions

Availability and Terms

Please contact the catering office for details. Advance deposits are required.

Description of Facility and Services

Seating: tables and chairs provided
Servers: provided, with 19% service charge
Bar facilities: full-service bar with bartenders available for your event; The Heathman supplies the liquor, beer, and wine
Dance floor: available with electrical outlets
Linens and napkins: variety of linen selections available
China and glassware: fine china, silver, and crystal supplied
Decorations: candles available; no nails, tacks or tape permitted
Cleanup: included in price
Parking: parking available; price varies
ADA: fully accessible

Accommodations

Walk through the doors into the most elegant and enchanting atmosphere in Portland. Located in the heart of the arts and culture district of downtown Portland, the historic Heathman Hotel will exceed your highest expectations. Enjoy the stylish, warm ambiance of one of our eight private dining rooms. Adorned with silk wall coverings, classic wood shutters, topiary plants or even a fire-lit room adjacent to the Heathman Library, each room has its' own distinct character. The ambiance is perfectly matched by our staff. Dedicated personally to your event, our goal is to spoil you rotten! And that's exactly how you will feel after you've enjoyed the cuisine of Chef Philippe Boulout. Nominated for the James Beard Award as the Best Chef in the Northwest, Chef Boulout maintains his reputation as one of the culinary stars of the nineties. For a rehearsal dinner, wedding reception, or special event—relax and let The Heathman worry about the details.

A Heathman Management Group restaurant

THE HEATHMAN LODGE

7801 N.E. Greenwood Drive • Vancouver, Washington 98662
Contact: Catering Office (360) 254-3100 or (888) 475-3100
Business Hours: Mon–Sat 8am–5pm

Capacity: 5 to 300 people
Price Range: room rentals vary depending on food order; event room rates available
Catering: full-service, upscale catering
Types of receptions: elegant, sit-down or handsome buffet meals, hors d'oeuvres or simple cake and punch receptions, bridal luncheons and rehearsal dinners

Availability and Terms

The Lodge offers 4,500 square feet of private dining and reception space. The ballroom is divisible into three rooms, each with pre-function space. Two additional smaller banquet rooms are available as well. The Lodge also offers a 1,230-square-foot Presidential Suite and three large suites for more intimate receptions.

Description of Facility and Services

Seating: tables and chairs provided at no additional charge
Servers: included in cost of food or room rental
Bar facilities: host/no-host bars available; hotel supplies all liquor and bartender
Dance floor: available
Linens and napkins: available
China and glassware: included in cost of food, beverage or room rental
Cleanup: handled by the Lodge at no additional cost
Decorations: limited decorative items available at no additional charge; elaborate theme events can be arranged
Parking: ample free parking
ADA: meets all ADA standards; all banquet rooms are on ground level

Special Services

A night in one of the 121 guest rooms or 22 suites is a truly memorable experience. Old-world craftsmanship is evident in stretched leather lampshades and hand-crafted mirrors and frames. Hickory and pine furnishings lend comfort to the surroundings.

The Heathman Lodge is Vancouver, Washington's newest full-service upscale hotel. An unexpected urban retreat, the Lodge offers travelers and locals from the Portland/Vancouver area a blend of heart-felt service, business amenities and rustic, mountain lodge comfort. Inspired by authentic Pacific Northwest decor and cuisine, the Lodge provides each guest a calm refuge and a memorable experience.

HAND-HEWN HOSPITALITY

We invite you to take a virtual tour at www.heathmanlodge.com

Heritage House Farm & Gardens

Aurora, Oregon
Contact: Bill and Derolyn Johnson
(503) 678-5704 or (888) 479-3500
Shown by appointment

Capacity: 200–300 in a lovely garden setting
Price Range: varies depending on function and size of group; please call for information.
Catering: family prepared or bring your own professional caterer; prep area available; Heritage House can provide the rehearsal dinner or Sunday brunch following the event
Types of Events: lovely spring, summer and fall garden events including but not limited to weddings, receptions, family parties and events, business meetings and parties

Availability and Terms

Make reservations as soon as possible up to a year in advance. We can accommodate on shorter notice if the facility is not booked. Site is reserved with a one-third deposit. Liability insurance required. Only one event per day is scheduled.

Description of Facility and Services

Heritage House Farm and Gardens is a 61/2-acre hazelnut farm nestled halfway between Portland and Salem in the beautiful Willamette Valley. The house is a 1934 Colonial-style home decorated in country elegance and the grounds are lovely gardens and lawns surrounded by giant trees and nut orchards. The historic Aurora Colony is nearby for sightseeing and antique shopping, or take time to golf, view the beautiful Willamette River, or visit the Oregon Gardens.

Seating: tables and chairs for 250
Servers: caterer or renter provides licensed servers
Bar facilities: alcohol served by arrangement
Dance floor:dance area available
Linens and napkins: provided by caterer
China and glassware: provided by caterer
Decorations: table decorations arranged through caterer
Cleanup: provided by staff or caterer
Parking: ample parking is available
ADA: staff will accommodate

EXPERIENCE COUNTRY ELEGANCE FOR THE WHOLE WEEKEND

The bridal party can come and stay at the Heritage House for an extended event starting on Friday. Arrive in the morning or early afternoon and have plenty of time for making final arrangements. Have your rehearsal, dinner and an evening of relaxation together, including a professional massage for the bride and groom. On Saturday, spend a leisurely day preparing for the big event with family and friends. Leave the reception in a beautiful limo and spend your wedding night in a charming bridal suite at a local inn. Return to Heritage House the following morning for a delicious Champagne Brunch where you can open gifts and say farewell to family members and friends. A truly unique weekend event with no hurry or hassle. **One day events also available.**

 Please let this business know that you heard about them from the Bravo! Bridal Resource Guide.

Hilton Garden Inn®

Portland/Beaverton

15520 N.W. Gateway Court
Beaverton, Oregon 97006
Contact: Lisa Brown (503) 466-2604; Fax (503) 439-1818
Business Hours: 7:30am–6pm
Web site: www.hilton.com

Capacity: **Multnomah/Rose Garden:** up to 100; 1,236 sq.ft.; **Mt. Hood:** up to 30; 612 sq.ft.; **Two Boardrooms:** up to 12; 450 sq.ft.
Catering: full-service in-house catering
Price Range: $100 to $400
Types of Events: banquets, receptions, meetings, seminars, conferences

Availability and Terms

Reservations should be made as early as possible; credit card deposit required.

Description of Facility and Services

Seating: tables and chairs provided
Servers: provided
Bar facilities: full-service bar service available
Linens and napkins: provided
China and glassware: provided
Cleanup: provided by Hilton Garden Inn staff
Parking: ample free parking available
ADA: yes

BEAUTIFUL FOUR-STORY HIGH-RISE

A beautiful four-story high-rise with 150 guestrooms, The Hilton Garden Inn—Portland/Beaverton includes 14 two-room suites and four Jacuzzi suites, making it an ideal place to hold your wedding reception.

Conveniently located 12 miles west of downtown Portland and 20 miles west of the Portland International Airport.

Hilton
Portland

921 S.W. Sixth Avenue
Portland, Oregon 97204
Contact: Catering (503) 220-2552
Fax (503) 225-1480
Business Hours: Mon–Fri 8:30am–5:30pm
Web site: www.portland.hilton.com

Capacity: 12 to 1,200 people
Price Range: customized menus at varying prices
Catering: full-service catering
Types of Events: luncheons, hors d'oeuvres, served dinners and buffets

Availability and Terms

The Hilton Portland has many different reception rooms of varying sizes to accommodate any event from small rehearsal dinners to large wedding receptions. We feature our elegantly appointed new Pavilion Ballroom, ideal for 250 to 350 guests. Our new Broadway Room is suited for groups of fewer than 150 guests.

Description of Facility and Services

Seating: your choice of banquet rounds or informal cabarets
Servers: included in catering cost
Bar facilities: hosted or no-host bar; beer, wine, and champagne service; we provide all beverages, bartender, and servers
Dance floor: appropriately sized inlaid parquet dance floor
Linens and napkins: fine linens in coordinating colors; specialty linens also available
China and glassware: white china and stemmed glassware; ornate silver chafing dishes and urns
Cleanup: included in catering charges
Decorations: votive candles at no charge to complement your floral centerpieces
Lodging: complimentary deluxe room with champagne for the bride and groom; special group rate for your out-of-town guests; based on availability
Parking: parking available; costs vary
ADA: fully equipped to accommodate ADA requirements

We Accommodate All Your Needs

The Hilton Portland is a full-service hotel, conveniently located in the heart of downtown Portland. Our reputation for superior service is built on 75 years of combined banquet experience. We can accommodate your guest room needs, rehearsal dinner, and reception.

ON-SITE WEDDING SPECIALISTS

Our on-site Wedding Specialists will assist you in planning a perfect reception. Fresh, local cuisine and specialty menu items, custom-designed wedding packages, newly renovated guest rooms, and courteous, prompt service make The Hilton Portland your best choice!

Four Diamond

 Please let this business know that you heard about them from the Bravo! Bridal Resource Guide.

Holiday Inn

Portland Airport
Hotel and Trade Center

8439 N.E. Columbia Boulevard
Portland, Oregon 97220
(503) 256-5000; Fax (503) 256-5631
E-mail: HIPDXSALES@aol.com

Capacity: maximum of 1,200 guests
Price Range: customized to meet your needs
Catering: full-service catering on or off premise; wedding packages available
Types of Events: we offer a large number of rooms to accommodate your rehearsal dinner, ceremony or reception and will cater everything from a simple cocktail party to an elaborate, multicourse sit-down dinner

Availability and Terms

We offer a wide selection of rooms to fit your needs. Advance reservations are strongly encouraged. Deposits are required and are refundable with 60 days written notice.

Description of Facility and Services

Seating: all types of tables and chairs
Servers: staff included in catering cost
Bar facilities: full beverage service available; Holiday Inn Portland Airport to provide all beer, wine and liquor
Dance floor: cost varies per size of dance floor
Linens and napkins: variety of colors
China and glassware: white china and stemmed glassware
Decorations: silk plants, mirror tiles, votive candles, ficus trees and bud vases
Cleanup: included in price
Equipment: podium, risers and specialty props
Sleeping accommodations: 286 modern guest rooms with 17 suites; we offer special rates for your out-of-town guests
Parking: free parking for 900 cars
ADA: accessible

Special Services

Our professional sales and catering staff are ready to assist you with all your needs. Allow the Holiday Inn Portland Airport to take the stress out of your next event. The success of your event is our ultimate goal.

YOUR EVERY EXPECTATION WILL BE EXCEEDED!

The Holiday Inn Portland Airport is part of the John Q. Hammons Hotel Corp., one of the nation's largest. It has 286 modern guest rooms with the largest meeting facility 5 minutes from the airport. In addition to the 12 meeting and banquet rooms totaling 33,607 square feet of flexible meeting space, we have the ability to fulfill any client's needs or challenges. The staff at the Holiday Inn Portland Airport is well versed at accommodating your personal needs on the most special day of your life; you can rest assured that your every expectation for your wedding will be exceeded. We welcome the opportunity to give you 100% guest satisfaction.

25425 S.W. 95th Avenue • Wilsonville, Oregon 97070
Contact: Catering Department (503) 682-2211
Business Hours: Mon–Fri 8am–5:30pm; Sat 9am–noon

Holiday Inn SELECT

Capacity: up to 900 standing; 600 sit-down
Price Range: please ask our catering specialists for current menu prices; we are happy to customize a menu to fit your budget
Catering: full-service in-house catering
Types of Events: wedding ceremonies, receptions, rehearsal dinners, anniversary celebrations and family brunches

Availability and Terms

Five separate rooms are available to accommodate from nine to 900 guests. In addition, our Atrium with its various sized terraces can accommodate gatherings of up to 500 (perfect for ceremonies). Our catering specialists will be happy to assist with our current event policies.

Description of Facility and Services

Seating: tables and chairs for 600
Servers: staff included in catering costs; gratuity will be added to final bill
Bar facilities: full-service bar available
Dance floor: available at minimum charge
Linens and napkins: white linen tablecloths and napkins; special colors additional charge
China and glassware: white china and stemmed glassware
Decorations: silk flower arrangements, mirrors, oil candles, ficus trees
Cleanup: provided by the Holiday Inn Select
Parking: ample free parking available
ADA: banquet rooms and Atrium fully accessible; elevator to guest rooms; nine ADA compliant guestrooms

Special Services

The Holiday Inn Select Portland South offers 169 spacious comfortable guestrooms, including Executive Level accommodations. Other amenities include a full-service business center, indoor pool, whirlpool, fitness center, and on-site dining at the South City Diner and South City NightClub. We will provide a complimentary room for the bride and groom on their wedding night. Special guestroom rates available for out-of-town guests.

A "SELECT" BRAND OF EXCELLENCE

The **Holiday Inn Select Portland South** is the first "Select" brand of Holiday Inns in Oregon. Conveniently located off Interstate 5, only 15 minutes form downtown Portland, 26 miles from the airport, and 30 miles from Salem. Our professional catering staff "caters to your every need," from initial planning stages until the last guest leaves. "Let us take the stress off you!"

"STAY WITH SOMEONE YOU KNOW"

HOOD RIVER HOTEL & Pasquale's ristorante

102 Oak Avenue
Hood River, Oregon
97031

Reservations
(800) 386-1859

Sales
(541) 386-1900

E-mail: HRHotel@gorge.net; Web site: www.hoodriverhotel.com

Capacity: ballroom and mezzanine available; 5 to 250 guests
Price Range: price varies according to room, time of year, and menu selection
Catering: full-service in-house catering or off-premise
Types of Events: weddings, receptions, rehearsal dinners; informal hors d'oeuvres to formal sit-down dinners; off-site catering available

Availability and Terms

Hood River Hotel's ballroom can accommodate up to 250 people. Additional areas are available for groups of 20 or fewer. We suggest you book early to ensure availability. A deposit is required at time of booking to secure your date with the balance due the day of your event.

Description of Facility and Services

Seating: tables and chairs for up to 200 people
Servers and cleanup: included in catering cost
Bar facilities: full liquor service from Pasquale's Ristorante and Wine Cellar Bar; bartender included in price quote; extensive selection of wines and champagnes
Dance floor: accommodates up to 55 people
Linens and napkins: cloth linens available in a variety of colors
China and glassware: traditional pattern; assorted glassware
Decorations: floral supplies available upon request; early decorating by prior arrangement; some restrictions apply; in-house florist available
Parking: on-street and designated off-site parking
ADA: fully accessible

Special Services

- **Special Honeymoon Packages:** to suit budget and needs
- **Wedding Services:** on-site consultant and packages available to fit most budgets
- **Fireside Weddings:** have a romantic ceremony by a warm, crackling fire
- **Baby Grand piano and built-in stereo system**

EUROPEAN-STYLE CHARM

This charming European-style 1913 hotel offers 41 rooms and is listed on the National Register of Historic Places. Conveniently located in the heart of historic downtown Hood River and the Columbia River Gorge National Scenic Area, our banquet facility offers a unique location for your special event. Decorated in a wine cellar theme, the Hood River Hotel offers a full bar and the finest Italian and Northwest cuisine in the Columbia Gorge. Our warm European charm and friendly staff will ensure a wedding your guests will remember forever.

Hostess House, Inc.

10017 N.E. Sixth Avenue
Vancouver, Washington 98685
(360) 574-3284

Featured in *Modern Bride Magazine* as the place to have your wedding in the Pacific Northwest!

Open seven days a week; please call for an appointment

Capacity: chapel holds 200 guests; reception area holds up to 300 in good weather
Price Range: wedding and reception packages starting at $1,395 to $2,795; price depends on the day of the week, time of day and number of guests
Catering: full in-house catering and bakery
Types of Events: all types from cake and punch to sit-down dinners

Availability and Terms

A $500 deposit reserves your date and applies toward purchases. Reservations are taken as far as a year in advance; however, we can occasionally accommodate reservations on short notice.

Description of Facility and Services

Seating: as many chairs and tables as needed; plus patio
Servers: we provide all serving attendants and any additional personnel needed
Bar facilities: full-service bar and bartenders; we provide all alcoholic and nonalcoholic beverages and liquor liability
Dance floor: oak dance floor for 75 to 100 people; house DJ available for $100 for the first hour and $50 each additional hour
Linens and napkins: lace tablecloths and engraved napkins
Serviceware: fine china; long-stem crystal; silver serving pieces
Cleanup: Hostess House provides at no extra charge
Decorations: chapel and reception facility will be decorated throughout with floral arrangements in your colors. A 15 unit candelabra with flower arrangement, two sprays of flowers, and six pew arrangements decorate the chapel. A fresh flower arrangement will be at the guest book and fresh bud vases on every dining room table.
Parking: ample free parking provided; **ADA:** completely disabled accessible

INTRODUCING THE HOSTESS HOUSE...THE FIRST FULL-SERVICE WEDDING CENTER IN THE NORTHWEST

The candle-lit chapel seats 200 guests and looks out onto a beautiful garden with a waterfall. Now you can have the excitement and joy of a perfectly planned wedding with none of the work or worry. Our bridal consultants will assist you with every detail. The reception center is absolutely gorgeous! It has an indoor fountain, oak dance floor, and a fireplace. The covered decks open onto a lovely landscaped yard with a beautiful gazebo. The Hostess House—where the bride's wedding dreams come true! DIRECTIONS: We are located 10 minutes North of Portland. From I-5 North or South, take the 99th Street exit (#5) and go West two blocks. Turn right onto Sixth Avenue.

See page 232 under Bridal Accessories & Attire and page 329 under Ceremony Sites.

Hunter Creek Farm

14441 S.W. Wilsonville Road
Wilsonville, Oregon 97070
Contact: Angela or Marilyn
(503) 625-3424
Business Hours: 8am–8pm, 7 days a week

Capacity: 80 indoor
Price Range: $15 per person
Catering: in-house catering only
Types of Events: meetings, retreats, reunions, parties, weddings, and horse shows

Availability and Terms

A 50% deposit is required at time of reservation, with the balance due two weeks prior to the event.

Description of Facility and Services

Seating: 40 indoor
Servers: provided by caterer
Bar facilities: provided by caterer
Linens and napkins: white linen provided at no extra cost
China and glassware: provided by caterer
Cleanup: included in price
Parking: ample parking available
ADA: no handicap facilities to main house

Special Services

Five guestrooms with private bathrooms are available to the wedding party at a 10% discount.

PREMIERE EVENT LOCATION

Located on the Willamette River in Wilsonville, Hunter Creek Farm is a bed and breakfast and premiere event location on a 120-acre equestrian park. The home is 6,000 square feet and beautifully decorated in "Ralph Lauren" equestrian fabrics. Resembling an old English fox hunting lodge, the farm is complete with English gardens, a swimming pool, and pool house.

The Inn at Otter Crest

301 Otter Crest Loop • Otter Rock, Oregon 97369
Contact: Marilyn Ebe or Ginny Whiffen
(800) 326-5806; Fax (541) 765-2069
Web site: www.ottercrest.com

Capacity: **Winery, Conference Center and Restaurant:** five rooms serving from 10 to 300 people; **Cliff Top Suite:** up to 22 people; **Oceanside Patio:** from 10 to 300 people
Price Range: affordable; customized menus; packages to fit most budgets
Catering: full service in-house catering
Types of Events: indoor and outdoor oceanfront wedding ceremonies (even on the beach), all kinds of receptions and rehearsal dinners; free wine tasting with each event; light and tasty hor d'oeuvre selection; a variety of buffets available; formal and informal sit-down luncheons and dinners; special event celebrations, holiday parties, birthdays and anniversaries

Availability and Terms

We request a deposit equal to 30% of the function price with the balance due one week prior to the event. A full refund is made with 60 days notice.

Description of Facility and Services

Seating: round or rectangular tables, chairs, head tables and stages provided
Servers: well-trained, friendly and properly attired staff
Bar facilities: full beverage service available; host/no host; extensive wine list
Dance Floor: several sizes available
Linens and napkins: a variety of colors available at no extra charge
China and glassware: ivory china, flatware and clear glassware
Decorations: early access to facility for decorating or setup
Cleanup: included in price
Parking: complimentary adjacent parking
ADA: yes

Special Services

Just about everything is special about the Inn's 35 oceanfront acres. Over the years many memorable weddings have been performed on the front lawn, on the Inn's beach and in the oceanfront rooms. Here you'll find 30 rustic buildings tucked into the wooded hillside. There are covered walkways between the buildings and even a hillside cable car. The Inn's newly remodeled rooms and suites all have private patios and picture windows overlooking the ocean. Some have kitchens and fireplaces. Other amenities include a nature trail, private beach access, tide pools, tennis and basketball courts, outdoor swimming pool, spa, saunas, game and arcade room, fitness center, children's playground, a wonderful restaurant and our own winery. A short walk through the woods takes you to the famous Devil's Punch Bowl. Here a stairway leads to six miles of uninterrupted sand beach where agate hunting and surfing are daily activities.

Please let this business know that you heard about them from the Bravo! Bridal Resource Guide.

112 S.W. Second Avenue
Portland, Oregon 97204
Contact: Brad Yoast
(503) 227-4057; Fax (503) 227-5931

KELLS

PORTLAND'S IRISH RESTAURANT & PUB

E-mail: portland@kellsirish.com • Web site: http://www.kellsirish.com

---

Capacity: private banquet facilities located on second floor; capacities range from 15–150 and up to 300 reception-style
Price Range: varies according to room and services
Catering: full-service in-house and off-premise catering
Types of Events: We provide buffet and formal sit-down service for receptions, rehearsal dinners, business luncheons, cocktail and hors d' oeuvre parties, holiday and surprise parties, fund raisers and gala events.

Availability and Terms

The K Club is located on the second floor of the historic Kells building near the waterfront in downtown Portland. With the Irish ambiance, excellent service and outstanding food you've come to expect from Kells, the elegant K Club invites your guests to celebrate in the stately ballroom and mingle in the intimate Ulster and Cigar Rooms.

Description of Facility and Services

Seating: variety of seating customized to meet your needs from 15–150
Servers: included in service
Bar facilities: host/no host bar; largest single malt selection in the northwest, full range of micro beers, extensive wine list; fine cigars also available
Dance floor: we offer two separate locations for bands, a long list of our most popular local acts, electrical hook-ups available
Linens and napkins: included in service; inquire about our color selection
China and glassware: white china with glassware to complement
Cleanup: included with full-service catering
Decorations: discussion of your ideas and needs welcomed
Parking: parking for events may be made in advance, garages within close proximity
ADA: Kells first floor is ADA accessible; parties may be arranged for this space as well

PORTLAND'S FAVORITE IRISH RESTAURANT & PUB

Kells has become a Portland landmark since its opening in 1990. One of Portland's favorite nightspots, Kells offers a great menu of New World Irish cuisine mixing traditional favorites with fresh, northwest seafoods, produce, and all-natural ingredients. Kells also features live Irish music seven nights a week, a grand stone fireplace and comfortable cigar room. All this and the warm, friendly service and atmosphere of a genuine Irish Pub.

LAKESIDE GARDENS

16211 S.E. Foster Road
Portland, Oregon 97236
(3.4 miles east of I-205 on Foster Road)
(503) 760-6044; Fax (503) 760-9311
Business Hours: Mon–Fri 10am–2pm;
evenings and weekends by appointment
Web site: www.citysearch.com/pdx/lakesidegardens

Capacity: 225 people—sit-down wedding at gazebo; 180 people—sit-down wedding inside; 300 people—buffet reception; 120 people—sit-down buffet
Price Range: price is determined by the event and menu selection
Catering: full-service in-house catering only
Types of Events: elegant wedding receptions all year-round, birthdays, anniversaries, barbecues, corporate parties, business meetings, or seminars

Availability and Terms

Please make your reservations as early as possible; we recommend six months in advance. A $500 booking fee will hold the date and time frame scheduled for your event.

Description of Facility and Services

Seating: tables and chairs are provided; terrace and garden seating available
Servers: we provide all serving attendants
Bar facilities: beer, wine, and champagne; we provide beverages and bartenders
Dance floor: hardwood dance floor with electrical hookups for DJs and bands
Linens and napkins: linen tablecloths; linen and paper napkins available
Serviceware: fine china, glassware, and silver serving pieces available for your use
Cleanup: provided by Lakeside Gardens
Decorations: elegant building requires little decoration
Parking: plenty of convenient free parking
ADA: completely disabled accessible

THE IDEAL PLACE RIGHT IN YOUR OWN BACKYARD

Lakeside Gardens is a Private Event Facility situated on approximately seven acres. We schedule events year-round. Outside, Lakeside Gardens blends tall cedars, weeping willows, mute swans, and lakes surrounded by a garden paradise. During cooler weather Lakeside Gardens also offers a complete inside facility. Inside amenities consist of beautiful chandeliers, brass railing, an elegant oak and marble fireplace, a black ebony baby-grand piano, and mirrored wall that reflects an inspiring panoramic view of the lake and surrounding gardens. We are conveniently located only minutes from downtown Portland and the Portland International Airport. Lakeside Gardens offers superb catering. We are able to provide ice sculptures and other decorations to create the setting of your choice. A knowledgeable wedding consultant or program coordinator will work with you to plan and execute everything. Please call us for more details and personal assistance as you plan your next event.

LAKEWOOD CENTER FOR THE ARTS

368 S. State Street
Lake Oswego, Oregon 97034
(503) 635-6338
Business Hours: Mon–Fri 9am–5pm
Web site: http://www.lakewood-center.org

Capacity: 150 for sit-down dinner, 225 for cocktail party
Price Range: $450 for the room
Catering: provided by renter; kitchen available
Types of Events: banquets, receptions, reunions, office parties, business meetings.

Description of Facility

Lakewood Center is conveniently located on State Street (Highway 43) at the south end of Lake Oswego. The Community Meeting Room, on the lower level at the Center, has windows on two sides and is decorated with a forest green and cream color scheme. A full-catering kitchen is attached to the space. The room comes with tables, chairs and place settings for up to 150.

Availability and Terms

Reservations should be made as soon as possible, six months to a year in advance. A security deposit is required to reserve your date. This fee is nonrefundable if you cancel your date. Your room fee balance of $450 is due one week before your event. The security deposit will be refunded, 2–3 weeks after your event, if there is no damage and the room is clean.

Description of Reception Services

The Lakewood Center is the perfect facility for those who wish to coordinate the details for themselves or bring in their own consultant or catering company. The room is ideal for banquets, receptions, reunions, office parties and business meetings.

Seating: up to 150
China: place settings of plate, salad plate, coffee cup, water glass and silverware for up to 150 are included
Dance floor: room is carpeted; many groups dance on the carpet or rent a dance floor from outside sources
Decorations: please inquire; no tape, tacks, or nails please
Cleanup: done by the renter
Parking: paved lot behind facility
ADA: full handicap accessibility
Special note: the Center rents only the room, tables and chairs, and place settings for up to 150; items such as linens, silver, crystal, serving utensils, coffee urns, and dance floor need to be arranged with other vendors

MALLORY HOTEL

729 S.W. 15th Avenue • Portland, Oregon 97205
Contact: Catering Department (503) 223-6311
Business Hours: seven days a week

A RETURN TO ELEGANCE

When you wish to revive the era of gracious service and elegant surroundings, ***The Mallory Hotel*** is ready to accommodate you. Our banquet and reception facilities are spacious and beautifully appointed with *crystal chandeliers, mirrors and decorative gilding*. We have been creating memorable celebrations in Portland for more than 84 years.

Our ***Executive Chef, Ann E. Grassi***, leads a team of creative culinary professionals in designing menus specifically suited to your function. Whether you're planning a *sumptuous brunch buffet*, a *simple business luncheon*, a *cocktail reception* or an *elaborate five-course dinner*, we offer the best of *local ingredients* and *"au courant"* preparations to dazzle and delight. Our servers are professional, discreet and eager to assist your guests with any needs or desires. For groups from *eight to 125* our flexibility and dependable service results in satisfied clients who return time and again for special celebrations and events to remember. Please contact our Catering Department to schedule a tour of our facilities or receive details on available menus.

Capacity: 8–90 for sit-down meals; 125 for cocktail receptions and meetings
Price Range: varies according to menu selections
Catering: full-service, in-house catering only
Types of Events: weddings, receptions, rehearsal dinners, bridal showers, banquets, reunions, office parties, business meetings and seminars

Availability and Terms

Reservations are recommended six months to one year in advance. We accommodate groups on very short notice when space is available. A deposit is required at the time of booking with the balance due the day of your event. Deposit is refundable if cancellation is received at least 60 days prior to your event date.

Description of Facility and Services

Seating: sit-down service for up to 90 guests; standing service for up to 125 guests
Servers: professional serving staff included in catering cost
Bar facilities: full-service bar dispensed according to OLCC regulations; bartender provided at no additional charge for hosted or non-hosted bar
Linens: damask tablecloths and napkins provided; special orders accommodated
China and glassware: fine china and appropriate stemware included in cost
Cleanup: provided by The Mallory Hotel
Decorations: limitless possibilities
Parking: complimentary covered parking available at Mallory Park, across from the hotel on Yamhill.
ADA: full disabled accessibility

Special Services

With your reception, The Mallory Hotel will provide a complimentary Bridal Suite. With our 140 suites and large guest rooms, The Mallory Hotel can accommodate your out-of-town guests.

PORTLAND Marriott® DOWNTOWN

1401 S.W. Naito Parkway
Portland, Oregon 97201
Contact: Sales and Catering Department
(503) 226-7600 ext. 6563, (503) 499-6360; Fax (503) 226-1209
Business Hours: Mon–Fri 7am–6pm; Sat 9am–4pm

Capacity: up to 1,000 people
Price Range: price will be determined by event and specific menu
Catering: provided by the hotel exclusively
Types of Events: from intimate champagne receptions to elegant multicourse dinners, including rehearsal dinners and bridal showers; the addition of the beautiful Mount Hood Room offers a new view on Portland; overlooking the Willamette River and Mount Hood, the perfect room with the perfect view will enhance your special day

Availability and Terms

The Portland Marriott Hotel offers a wide selection of rooms to fit your specific wedding needs. Since most weddings occur on Saturdays, we suggest reserving your reception site as soon as possible.

Description of Facility and Services

Seating: tables, chairs, and head tables provided
Servers: included in price
Bar facilities: full beverage service available; Portland Marriott Downtown to provide all beer, wine, liquor, and bartenders
Dance floor: available at no charge
Linens and napkins: extensive linen selections at no charge
China and glassware: Portland Marriott Downtown uses only fine china, crystal, and silverplated flatware
Cleanup: included in price
Parking: limited valet parking available in hotel; plenty of public parking adjacent to hotel
ADA: yes

Special Services

The Portland Marriott Downtown provides **a complimentary deluxe upgraded king room the night of the wedding** for that special bride and groom.

WEDDING CELEBRATIONS

At Marriott, we bring something extra to the wedding party—a tradition of care, concern, and service that assures peace of mind for the bridal couple and a memorable reception for everyone. After playing host to hundreds of bridal couples and their families, Marriott has the art of reception planning down to a science. Let us assist you in planning the wedding celebration of your dreams.

THE MARSHALL HOUSE

1301 Officers' Row
Vancouver National Historic Reserve
Vancouver, Washington 98661
Contact: Frances Anderson (360) 693-3103
Business Hours: Mon–Fri 9am–5pm; Sat by appointment

Capacity: 25 to 225 inside; more if verandas or gardens are used
Price Range: $100 to $850
Catering: caterers from Marshall House's approved list only; caterers required for any food, beverage, or cake service
Types of Events: sit-down, buffet, hors d'oeuvres, cake and punch, or garden

Availability and Terms

You may rent as many rooms as you need (up to 4) to accommodate from 25 to 350 guests for as many hours as you need. Standard weekend rental periods are from 11am to 6pm, and from 6pm to 1am. Reservations should be made as soon as possible—six months to one year in advance for the busy summer months. A $100 deposit is required to hold your date.

Description of Facility and Services

Seating: antique tables and chairs
Servers: must be provided by caterer; one per every 50 guests/minimum of two
Bar facilities: champagne, white wine, and bottled or canned beer only (no hard liquor or kegs); must be served by an approved bartender; no self-serve alcohol
Dance floor: 20′x30′ hardwood dance floor; electrical hookup available
Linens and napkins: linen rental available
China and glassware: your caterer provides
Cleanup: we provide; extra charge for extra cleanup
Decorations: no tape, tacks, staples, or wire; you carry liability for damage; rooms not available for early decorating except within rental time
Parking: 60 spaces adjacent to building, additional parking one block away
ADA: yes

Special Services

The Marshall House encourages the unique and will be happy to help you create the perfect arrangements for your event. With four spacious rooms, the verandas, and the lawn, the possibilities are endless. Antique furnishings and candelabra are available at no extra charge. Linens, coffee urns, and punch bowls are available for rent. Call for a tour and an information packet. Our staff will assist you from planning through party.

IN THE ELEGANT VICTORIAN STYLE

Picturesque Officers Row on the Vancouver National Historic Reserve features 21 grand houses on 21 acres of lawn, trees, and gardens. The George C. Marshall House stands as a centerpiece on the Row in the historic Queen Anne style. With wide verandas, rich colors and textures, 11-foot ceilings, and a magnificent central staircase, the Marshall House is sure to provide a most elegant backdrop for your memorable day.

McMenamins EDGEFIELD

2126 S.W. Halsey • Troutdale, Oregon 97060; Contact: Sales Office (503) 492-2777
Business Hours: Mon–Fri 9am–5pm; Sat–Sun 10am–5pm, tours by appointment

---

Capacity: 200 people seated; 250 people reception style
Price Range: $100 to $4,000 food and beverage minimum required; based on size of room and day of week
Catering: in-house catering only; plated, buffet, and hors d'oeuvre; prices vary
Types of Events: wedding ceremonies and receptions, rehearsal dinners, bridal showers and parties, meetings, conferences

Availability and Terms

Edgefield has several beautiful and unique locations for wedding ceremonies and receptions, accommodating both small and large parties. Several large banquet rooms are available for receptions, seating between 100 and 200 people each. The movie theater makes an ideal room for ceremonies, or try a natural setting outdoors. Additional set-up fees for outdoor receptions and ceremonies. For the best availability, we suggest booking summer or holiday weekend events at least one year prior. Our dedicated wedding coordinators can assist you in booking and planning your event. Deposit equals 25% of estimated food and beverage total and is due 30 days after booking. An additional 25% is due 30 days before your event.

Description of Facility and Services

Seating: round and rectangular tables for assorted seating; cushioned banquet chairs
Servers: staff included in price; 17% gratuity added to bill
Bar facilities: full-service cocktail bar featuring Edgefield ales and wines
Dance floor: available in two banquet rooms
Linens and napkins: assorted tablecloth and napkin colors; no charge
China and glassware: china, glassware, and flatware; no charge
Cleanup: included in price
Decorations: client responsibility
Parking: free parking and lots of it!
ADA: 11 out of 12 banquet rooms are accessible

Special Services

Built-in stereo systems in most rooms; 103 bed and breakfast rooms; two on-site restaurants, three in summer.

EUROPEAN-STYLE VILLAGE

McMenamins Edgefield is the classic gathering place for weddings. The historical Main Lodge building is surrounded by specialty buildings with spectacular gardens and landscaping, making the 38-acre property a virtual paradise and providing beautiful backdrops for photographs. Included on-site is a winery, brewery, movie theater, gift shop, sports bar, artisans, special events and daily tours. Edgefield is 25 minutes from downtown Portland and only 15 minutes from the airport. Call the Group Sales Office for a complete banquet packet.

THE MELODY BALLROOM

615 S.E. Alder • Portland, Oregon 97214
Contact: Kathleen Kaad (503) 232-2759; Fax (503) 232-0702
E-mail: melody.ballroom@mci2000.com
Business Hours: Tue–Fri 10am–2pm or by appointment

Capacity: two rooms, up to 1,100 people; used separately, 300 and 800 people
Price Range: varies, please call
Catering: in-house catering and beverage services only
Types of Events: sit-down, buffet, theme, cocktails and hors d'oeuvres

Availability and Terms

The Melody Ballroom requires a room rental fee as a deposit to reserve your date. Reservations are accepted one year or more in advance. Catering cost must be paid one week prior to the event.

Description of Facility and Services

Seating: tables and chairs provided as needed
Servers: staff included in catering costs; gratuity on food and beverage
Bar facilities: full-service bar provided; host/no-host; liquor, beer, and wine
Dance floor: 30'x30'; 300 capacity; two large stages; can accommodate full touring bands
Linens and napkins: cloth and linen tablecloths and napkins; limited colors
China and glassware: china and glassware
Cleanup: included in catering cost
Decorations: no limitations; we can provide fresh flowers and limited decorating accessories
Parking: free street parking

Special Services

The Melody Ballroom rents on a per day basis, giving our clients the flexibility for decorating and music set up at your convenience. Our event coordinators will be happy to help you plan and execute your event to perfection…just ask.

EXTRAORDINARY FOOD AND FRIENDLY SERVICE WILL MAKE YOUR EVENT A SUCCESS!

The Melody Ballroom is a unique, historic facility, owned and operated by a professional chef. Our philosophy is to say "Yes!" and to make your event truly individual. We work with diverse menus and styles—even your favorite recipes! Our caring staff provides friendly service that will make your guests feel as if they were in your own home.

MILWAUKIE CENTER/ SARA HITE MEMORIAL ROSE GARDEN

5440 S.E. Kellogg Creek Drive • Milwaukie, Oregon 97222
Contact: Lin Dahl (503) 653-8100; Please call for an appointment

---

Milwaukie Center and the Sara Hite Memorial Rose Garden are located in beautiful North Clackamas Park. The new outdoor Rose Garden is available for weddings, receptions and photo opportunities. The Center is an air conditioned, nonsmoking facility; perfect for any size group up to 400 for a sit-down dinner. The Facility Use Coordinator will help to make your event a pleasant experience whether your event is out in the Rose Garden or inside the Milwaukie Center. We provide you with lots of choices.

ROSE GARDEN:

Capacity: to 150 people
Price Range: call for prices
Seating: chairs for 100; eight 6′ tables; 20′ x 20′ canopies available at an additional fee
Availability and Terms: call for schedule availability; a 50% deposit is required to hold your date

MILWAUKIE CENTER:

Capacity: North Wing: 200 standing, 125 seated; South Wing: 600 standing, 350 seated
Price Range: call for specific price information
Catering: use your own catering arrangements or use the Center's caterer with no additional cost for the use of the commercial kitchen
Alcohol: allowed with specific regulations; proof of liability insurance required; additional fee of $100
Availability and Terms: make your reservation as soon as your date is established; a 25% deposit is required to hold your date

Description of Facility and Services

Seating: chairs for 500; tables for 400; equipment request (number of tables and chairs) required at time of application
Servers: renter or caterer provides
Bar facilities: renter or caterer to provide bar, liquor, licensed server, and liability insurance
Dance floor: available; PA system also available
Linens and napkins: renter or caterer provides
China and glassware: Melamine china and silverware for 250; no glassware
Cleanup: renter responsible for removing all decorations and cleanup
Decorations: please discuss your decoration ideas with the Facility Use Coordinator
Candles: tapered and birthday candles are not allowed due to fire safety; limited votive candle use
ADA: yes

Special Services

The Milwaukie Center will have a Building Coordinator on duty during your event to assist with necessary details.

MONTGOMERY PARK

2701 N.W. Vaughn Street
Portland, Oregon 97210
Contact: Paula Person, event director (503) 228-7275
Office Hours: Mon–Fri 8:30am–5pm

Capacity: 15 to 1,200 people (up to 400 seated, 1,200 standing); 15,400 square feet
Price Range: $80 to $2,800
Catering: inside catering contracted to Food in Bloom; outside catering through one of four approved caterers: Jake's, The Best of Everything, Briggs & Crampton, or Eat Your Heart Out
Types of Events: weddings, receptions, buffets, meetings, trade shows, corporate events, business parties

Availability and Terms

Montgomery Park has two a large banquet facility, a beautiful atrium and two meeting rooms. Deposits or reservation fees may be required. Book up to one year in advance. Available hours are flexible.

Description of Facility and Services

Seating: tables and chairs provided (one setup included in room cost)
Servers: provided by caterer
Bar facilities: bar services and liquor provided by caterer
Dance floor: dance floor in the Atrium accommodates 500+ people with electrical hookup for bands or disc jockeys available
Linens, china and glassware: caterer provides
Decorations: ***no helium balloons*** or tape; table decorations must be obtained from caterer, florist, or other source
Cleanup: you must remove all materials you bring in; some or all of your deposit may be kept for damage or extra labor for cleanup
Equipment: podium, easel, table cloths, flip chart, whiteboard, overhead projector, phone service, and full audiovisual service available
Parking: 2,200 free spaces available on weekends and evenings

Special Services

An event coordinator, security or maintenance personnel will be available depending on the time of the event.

SOARING ATRIUM AND MODERN DECOR

Montgomery Park, a beautifully renovated historic building, features a 135-foot soaring atrium, a light airy atmosphere, and a contemporary black-and-white decor. It is an impressive site for your function. Montgomery Park is located in Northwest Portland at the bottom of the northwest hills, providing a beautiful setting for your special event.

MT. HOOD BED & BREAKFAST

8885 Cooper Spur Road • Parkdale, Oregon 97041
Contact: Jackie Rice (541) 352-6885
Office Hours: Mon–Fri 8am–7pm

Capacity: up to 200+ (indoors or outdoors)
Price Range: available upon request
Catering: local catering
Types of Events: receptions with country elegance, buffets, barbecues, weddings, wedding receptions

Availability and Terms

Four guest rooms and outdoor gardens are available for weddings and receptions. Deposit is 50% of total with balance due 30 days prior to event.

Description of Facility and Services

Seating: for up to 200+
Servers: service staff included with catering
Dance floor: available with electrical outlets; accommodates 200+
Linens: provided by caterer
China and glassware: provided by caterer
Decorations: early decorating possible; cleanup to be immediately after event
Cleanup: client and caterer responsible
Parking: off-street
ADA: limited accessibility

ENCHANTING COUNTRY SETTING WITH SPECTACULAR MOUNTAIN VIEWS

Mount Hood Bed & Breakfast has everything you need for your wedding or event. Situated on the north shoulder of Mount Hood just out of the Columbia Gorge, the facility offers spectacular views of Mount Hood, Adams and Rainier. Our 7,200-square-foot sports barn can be used to move to the indoors in case of inclement weather. Come see us on the sunny side of Mount Hood. A little more than one hour from Portland.

Visit our Web site at www.mthoodbnb.com

NEW SEOUL GARDEN YAKINIKU KOREAN B.B.Q. KOREAN RESTAURANT AND SALT & PEPPER CLUB

10860 S.W. Beaverton-Hillsdale Highway
Beaverton, Oregon 97005
Contact: Paul Rouse (503) 643-8818; Fax (503) 256-8800
Business Hours: 11am–2am

Capacity: up to 180

Price Range: from $10 to $30 per person depending upon menu and type of event; we have a price to fit any budget while maintaining the high quality expected; room rates also available

Catering: Asian/American cuisine catered in-house; dedicated to high standards, we deliver a menu ranging from convenient hors d'oeuvres to full banquet settings

Types of Events: from the most intimate business meetings and wedding receptions to full-blown car shows, we welcome the challenge to satisfy your needs and demands

Availability and Terms

The room should be reserved as far in advance as possible. A 50% deposit is required upon contract signing and all other terms will be explained at that time.

Description of Facility and Services

Seating: tables and chairs provided
Servers: provided; 18% gratuity requested
Bar facilities: full no-host bar available
Dance floor: large dance floor and stage are available with plenty of electrical outlets; music can be provided by our house DJ at a reasonable cost or you may hire your own DJ; large selection of international music available
Linens and napkins: white tablecloths with peach napkins; other colors available at cost
China and glassware: provided
Decorations: no limitations set; please allow plenty of time to set up prior to the event
Cleanup: provided
Audiovisual: audiovisual aids and podiums can be provided at cost
Parking: large parking lot located in rear of building
ADA: we are completely handicap accessible

EXCELLENCE IN SERVICE AND QUALITY

With a reputation for excellence in service and quality, a friendly staff, and a very competitive price range, you can rest assured that your experience at the New Seoul Garden and Salt & Pepper Lunge will be one of satisfaction and repeated comfort seven days a week. Everything goes better with a little Salt & Pepper.

 Please let this business know that you heard about them from the Bravo! Bridal Resource Guide.

NORTH STAR BALLROOM

635 N. Killingsworth Court
Portland, Oregon 97217
Contact: Harriet Fasenfest
(503) 240-6088; Fax (503) 240-8229
Business Hours: Mon–Fri 10am–2pm;
or call for an appointment
E-mail: northstar@teleport.com
Web site: www.northstarballroom.com

Capacity: from 20 to 375
Price Range: $75 to $1,500
Catering: on-site available, in-house with outside caterers welcome
Types of Events: sit-down dinners, buffet, cocktails and hors d'oeuvres, themes

Availability and Terms

Ballroom, salon/bar, dining room, reception area, private parlor and meeting room available. Rooms to be reserved up to two years in advance. A 50% deposit is required at the time of reservation, refundable under terms. A refundable cleaning/damage deposit is required.

Description of Facility and Services

Seating: tables and chairs provided for up to 300
Servers: caterer to provide
Bar facilities: bar available; caterer or bar service to provide liquor and liability
Dance floor: large maple floors up to 250; up to 220 volt
Linens and napkins: caterer to provide
China and glassware: caterer to provide
Cleanup: responsibility of caterer
Decorations: upon approval
Parking: free off-street parking available; valet parking can be arranged for an additional cost
ADA: handicap ramp to lower level; one handicap accessible bathroom

Special Services

The rooms are accessible for early decorating. Sound and lighting equipment available. Video services can be arranged at an additional cost.

URBAN SOPHISTICATION AND ECLECTIC MEDITERRANEAN STYLE

Not your typical romance and wedding? Then why choose a typical wedding hall? The North Star Ballroom is proud to offer a stunning new facility that is as unique as you are. Discover the hidden treasures of Portland's only "neighborhood villa," conveniently located just off I-5 less than ten minutes from downtown Portland. The North Star Ballroom has a variety of rooms that capture the spirit of its Italian Renaissance architecture. Very competitively priced with wedding packages available, the North Star Ballroom is a perfect choice for those contemporary celebrations of the heart.

O'CALLAHAN'S

RESTAURANT & CATERING

at
RAMADA INN
PORTLAND AIRPORT

6221 N.E. 82nd Avenue
Portland, Oregon 97220
Contact: Ann Conger
(503) 253-2400; Fax (503) 253-1635
Business Hours: Mon–Sat 8am–6pm

Capacity: Executive Ballroom: 300 sit-down, reception 350pp; Upstairs Ballroom: 200 sit-down, reception 250pp; rooms can be combined to accommodate up to 500 guests
Price Range: reception $11.95 to $21.95; banquets $9.95 to $21.95
Catering: full-service in-house and off-premise catering; references available
Types of Events: weddings, anniversaries, receptions

Availability and Terms

O'Callahan's offers two ballrooms, the Executive Ballroom (4,200 square feet) and the Upstairs Ballroom (2,800 square feet). Reservations should be made 6 to 12 months in advance. Reservations are made for five-hour segments. A 25% deposit is required to secure your date with the balance due 72 hours prior to your event. A 60-day cancellation notice is required for deposit refund.

Description of Facility and Services

Seating: chairs for up to 600 guests
Servers: appropriate service staff available
Bar facilities: full-service bar with bartender; portable bar available; liquor and liability provided by O'Callahan's
Dance floor: portable dance floor with 550 capacity; 110 and 220 outlets available
Linens and napkins: linen tablecloths and napkins available in a variety of colors
China and glassware: white china; variety of glassware
Decorations: early decorating (two hours prior) available; decorations to match our room colors available; please no scotch tape, thumb tacks or rice
Parking: ample free parking
ADA: bathrooms, elevators, and guest rooms

Special Services

A complimentary bridal suite is available for the bride and groom following their reception at O'Callahan's with a minimum purchase. We also offer group rates for your out-of-town guests.

THE POSSIBILITIES ARE ENDLESS!

O'Callahan's has been part of the Northwest scene for over 20 years. During that time we have catered numerous wedding receptions and rehearsal dinners—casual to very formal. We are also happy to cater your event off-premise. With our reputation for personalized and professional service…the possibilities are endless!

OAKS PARK
HISTORIC DANCE PAVILION

at Oaks Park

Portland, Oregon 97202
Contact: Volanne (503) 233-5777
Business Hours: Mon–Fri 8am–5pm

Capacity: dance pavilion with formal seating for 275; festival setup with dancing for 500; outdoor gazebo area for 1,000

Price Range: pavilion rental for a minimum of three hours at $100 per hour, five hours for $450, 10 hours for $700; outdoor gazebo area is $405 plus a $45 waste-removal fee

Catering: our in-house catering menus are individually designed to suit your own taste, personality, and style. Our goal is to give you exactly what you want. If you are using an outside caterer, we will charge you a fee of 20% of their final bill

Types of Events: full-line catering, buffet, hors d'oeuvres, and cake and punch

Availability and Terms

Our indoor facility is available for bookings on any day or evening. Our outdoor gazebo and grounds are extremely popular; please don't hesitate to call and inquire. A deposit of $250 is required on the day of booking.

Description of Facility and Services

Seating: we can formally seat 275 people

Servers: we can provide any equipment necessary and the personnel to guarantee your event will run smoothly and at a level of service you expect

Bar facilities: Oaks Park Association provides liquor at the liability of the renter; it is Oaks Park's policy to provide a staff bartender

Dance floor: 99′x54′ dance floor with a capacity for 400 people

Linens and napkins: all colors of linen and cloth napkins and tablecloths available for an additional cost

Decorations: we enjoy your personal style—and offer the bonus of fanciful historic carousel horses

Parking: ample free parking

ADA: yes

A LOVELY, ROMANTIC, AND HISTORIC SETTING

Join us in our historic riverside park on the Willamette River and let us create the perfect memory for you and your guests. Our beautiful lighted gazebo is framed by a forested setting and mystic city skyline backdrop. The gazebo offers a lovely, romantic setting for your wedding or reception. In case of chilly weather, our historic, multiwindowed dance pavilion is just steps away. Our facility is ideal for weddings, reunions, receptions, birthdays, and anniversaries. It is our policy to work with you and offer exemplary step-by-step service all during the celebration, allowing you to enjoy the day.

See page 330 under Ceremony Sites.

OLD LAURELHURST CHURCH

3212 S.E. Ankeny • Portland, Oregon 97214
Contact: Deborra Buckler
(503) 231-0462; Fax (503) 231-9429
Business Hours: by appointment only

OLD LAURELHURST CHURCH

Capacity: 200 seated; 350 partial seating/reception-style; 150–200 recommended during hot summer months
Price Range: $900
Catering: select from approved list or as per discussion with wedding coordinator (we try to remain flexible, but have strong recommendations due to previous experience with caterers)
Types of Events: receptions, management retreats, banquets, employee parties, meetings, seminars, and privately catered family gatherings, Christian celebrations

Availability and Terms

Please call for availability. A 50% down payment is required at time of booking. Booking and cleanup deposit is due two months before the event. Alcohol in moderation is allowed with licensed and insured servers/caterers; no beer or kegs.

Description of Facility and Services

Seating: 250 white wedding chairs; 18 round tables seat six to 10 guests each
Servers: arranged through caterer
Bar facilities: arranged through caterer
Dance floor: stage and floor area available
Linens: arranged through caterer
China and glassware: "Blue Willow" china available for rental through church; other types arranged through caterer or client
Decoration limitations: facility is well decorated; additional decorating allowed with the exception of tape, tacks, or nails
Cleanup: renter or caterer responsible for cleanup; we set up tables and chairs and can arrange cleanup for an extra charge
Parking: free parking on street and around Laurelhurst Park (one block away), and on Burnside (one block away)
ADA: limited due to the historic nature of the church; ramp from sanctuary to reception facility

Special Services

Side serving room is available. Reception facility conveniently located downstairs. Located in the historic Laurelhurst area, Old Laurelhurst Church is an outstanding example of the Spanish Colonial Revival-style of architecture.

OMSI
OREGON MUSEUM OF SCIENCE AND INDUSTRY

1945 S.E. Water Avenue
Portland, Oregon 97214
Contact: Event Sales Office
(503) 797-4671; Fax (503) 797-4566
Event Sales: by appointment

Capacity: 50 to 4,000
Price Range: call for cost estimates on rental fees and catering
Catering: exclusive, full-service in-house catering available; creative menus are based on budget requirements and/or type of food and beverages requested
Types of Events: social events; receptions set among the exhibits as well as sit-down breakfasts, luncheons and dinners; most areas offer a spectacular view of the downtown city skyline and the river

Availability and Terms
The riverfront science center has five exhibit halls: Turbine Hall, Changing Exhibit Hall, High Tech Hall, Life Science Hall and Earth Science Hall. For additional space and entertainment the Auditorium, Copeland Lumber Dining Room, Outdoor Courtyard, Murdock Planetarium and OMNIMAX® Theater are also available. A 50% nonrefundable deposit of estimated charges is due upon signing an agreement. The balance is due three days prior to your event.

Description of Facility and Services
Seating: tables and chairs in current inventory are available for use at no additional charge. Any equipment that OMSI does not have may be rented for you at an additional cost.
Bar facilities and servers: provided by Fine Host Corporation
Dance floor: may be rented from outside source
Linens and china: our Event Sales department strives to create events that are visually stunning. We provide a wide variety of specialty linens, china, tableware, and floral arrangements that will make your event at OMSI stand alone.
Parking: no charge
ADA: meets all ADA requirements

Special Services
Our experienced event planners will assist you with virtually all planning aspects of your event. Creative menu planning, outstanding service, specialty decor expertise and close attention to detail will provide you with a magnificent event—one your guests will not soon forget.

OMSI'S WORLD CLASS SCIENCE CENTER
OMSI's world class science center is available for private special events and meetings. The museum features interactive hands-on exhibits that will educate, entertain, and amaze your guests. Also featured: an OMNIMAX® Theater that shows educationally rich and thrilling motion pictures on its five-story domed screen; the Murdock Planetarium that features astronomy and laser light shows; and a 219′ submarine that is available for tours.

Visit our Web site:
www.omsi.edu/geninfo/eventsales

OREGON CITY GOLF CLUB

20124 S. Beavercreek Road • Oregon City, Oregon 97045
Contact: Event Coordinator
(503) 656-2846, (503) 656-0038
Business Hours: Mon–Sun 8am–6pm
E-mail: OCGCI@aol.com

Capacity: 125 seated; 160 standing; can accommodate additional guests depending on season
Price Range: $200 to $1,000
Catering: we work with an approved list of caterers
Types of Events: wedding receptions, bridal showers, private parties, baby showers, graduations, retirements, birthdays, tournaments, meetings, seminars

Availability and Terms

We suggest that you reserve as early as possible but we are sometimes able to accommodate parties on short notice. A deposit is required to secure your date.

Description of Facility and Services

Seating: round or adjustable tables with double padded white chairs for 125+ guests
Servers: appropriate staff will be provided
Bar facilities: host or no-host; beer, wine, champagne available; bartenders provided; compliance with all local and state liquor laws; liquor liability provided
Dance floor: available; CD player provided; electrical available
Linens: linens available; a variety of colors available from caterer for an additional cost
China and glassware: clear glass china available; variety of crystal glassware available
Cleanup: provided by Oregon City Golf Club
Decorations: no staples, nails, tacks or tape; artist's putty may be used
Parking: free parking
ADA: yes

Special Services

Our event coordinator will work with you in planning and executing all details, to make your event a total success.

SOCIAL EVENTS TO TOURNAMENTS

Oregon City Golf Club was built in 1922 and is the third oldest public golf course in the State of Oregon still in operation. With our newly remodeled clubhouse and banquet facility, we can handle all of your social events and tournament needs.

The Oregon Golf Club

25700 S.W. Pete's Mountain Road
West Linn, Oregon 97068
Contact: Catering Department (503) 650-6900
Business Hours: 8:30am–5pm
Web site: www.oregongolfclub.com

Capacity: up to 500 people sit-down dinner
Price Range: customized reception package
Catering: full-service, in-house catering
Types of Events: sit-down, buffet, cocktail and hors d'oeuvres, outdoor garden setting for receptions and ceremonies

Availability and Terms

Please make reservations as early as possible. Four rooms are available to meet your special needs. An advance deposit is required; payment is due seven days in advance.

Description of Facility and Services

Seating: tables and chairs provided for up to 500 guests
Servers: provided
Bar facilities: full-bar service provided
Dance floor: 18′ X 18′ floor; electrical available
Linens and napkins: provided; in all colors
China: fine white china provided
Decorations: we will be happy to discuss your specific needs
Cleanup: provided by The Oregon Golf Club
Parking: free parking
ADA: yes

Our private country club setting, the natural beauty and charm, the exceptional service and attention to detail will allow you to have a first-class event that you and your guests will thoroughly enjoy.

Nestled in the Willamette Valley against a backdrop of the majestic Cascade Mountain Range, The Oregon Golf Club boasts an exceptional reputation. Inspired by the Scottish traditions of golf's birthplace and enlivened by the beauty of the Pacific Northwest, our spectacular facility is an ideal location for your wedding and reception.

4001 S.W. Canyon Road
Portland, Oregon 97221
Contact: Gary Wilson or Lisa Schur
(503) 220-2789; Fax (503) 220-3689
E-mail: zoocatering@metro.dst.or.us
Business Hours: Mon–Fri 8:30am–5pm

OREGON ZOO

The Oregon Zoo has always been a dramatic, fun and surprisingly elegant place to host your special events. Our Cascadian-style banquet center is a wonderful choice for a romantic gathering in the heart of Portland's favorite playground. Like a private alpine lodge, our banquet center is grand yet intimate, accommodating up to 500 people for banquets or up to 800 reception guests. Warm colors, rich textures, and thick, plush carpets ensure the comfort of your family and guests. The Grand Staircase in the heart of the facility provides the perfect backdrop for keepsake photographs of the beautiful bride.

Join the couples who have discovered the zoo as Portland's ideal wedding and reception site. The Oregon Zoo is located on the MAX light-rail only five minutes from downtown. A portion of all event fees is used in endangered species research and protection.

Capacity: indoor up to 800; outdoor up to 6,000
Price Range: price varies according to menu selections
Catering: in-house catering
Types of Events: buffet or sit-down; weddings, corporate events, outdoor barbecues, indoor banquets, theme parties…anything is possible!

Availability and Terms

Our banquet room can accommodate up to 800 people. Our outdoor facility can accommodate groups up to 6,000. A deposit is required to confirm reservation. Book early, as our facilities are very popular.

Description of Facility and Services

Seating: tables and chairs included in cost
Servers: provided by the zoo
Bar facilities: host or no-host bar available
Dance floor: we can rent one for your event for an additional fee
Linens and napkins: assorted colors of tablecloths and napkins available at no additional charge
China and glassware: provided for indoor events; can be rented for outdoor events
Cleanup: included in catering costs
Decorations: no balloons allowed because of the animals
Parking: large lot adjacent to entrance
ADA: yes

THE OVERLOOK HOUSE

3839 N. Melrose Drive
Portland, Oregon 97227
(503) 823-3188, (503) 823-2525
Tours: Tuesdays 5pm–7pm

Capacity: winter (November-April) up to 75; spring, summer, and early fall months (May–October) up to 150
Price Range: call for current information
Catering: select your favorite caterer; we provide complete kitchen facilities
Types of Events: buffet, patio cocktails and hors d'oeuvres, cake and punch weddings and receptions

Availability and Terms

The home and grounds are included in a six-hour rental period, 11am to 5pm or 6pm to 12 midnight. Reservations may be made as soon as the date of your event is determined up to a year in advance. A deposit is required, with a portion refundable if we have a minimum of 30 days' notice. Rental fees are due 30 days in advance of the event. Tours are offered Tuesdays between 5–7pm.

Description of Facility and Services

Seating: tables and chairs provided
Servers: provided by your caterer or yourself
Bar facilities: you provide your own beverages and liquor liability; please, bottled or canned beer, wine, and champagne only—no hard liquor allowed
Linens and napkins: provided by your caterer or yourself
China and glassware: white china and glass punch cups and trays available
Cleanup: cleanup is your responsibility
Decorations: please inquire about restrictions or for details on early decorating
Parking: on-street parking available
ADA: facilities available

Special Services

Overlook House personnel are on site at all times to make sure everything is taken care of and running smoothly. The use of our serviceware, china, glassware, silverware, coffee pots, punch bowls, and ladles is included in the rental fee.

THE ROMANCE AND ELEGANCE OF A MANSION AND GARDENS

The Overlook House is a 1927 brick, English Tudor–style home located on more than an acre of beautifully landscaped grounds overlooking the Willamette River and the Portland West Hills. The grounds are graced by a rose garden and trellis, making it an ideal setting for an outside wedding and reception during the spring, summer, and early fall months. Inside, the beveled glass, original woodwork and fireplace make the living-room area a lovely site for an intimate wedding or gathering. The Overlook House is also an ideal setting for weekday business retreats.

NCP PANTHEON BANQUET HALL

5942 S.E. 92nd Avenue • Portland, Oregon 97266
Contact: Effy Stephanopoulos (503) 775-7431, Fax (503) 775-3068
Business Hours: Mon–Fri 10am–6pm; or by appointment

Capacity: up to 500
Price Range: various packages available; call for details
Catering: in-house catering
Types of Events: weddings, rehearsal dinners, bridal showers, birthdays, anniversaries, retirement, proms and holiday parties; corporate functions and business meetings

Availability and Terms

Our two banquet rooms are available any day of the week. Please make reservations as soon as possible, but we always try to accommodate receptions on shorter notice. Pantheon Banquet Hall accommodates up to 500 people and our smaller banquet room accommodates up to 80 people.

Description of Facility and Services

Seating: tables and chairs provided for up to 500
Servers: professional serving staff
Bar facilities: full-service bar; bartender
Dance floor: 18′x18′ up to 24′x60′; electrical outlets available
Linens and napkins: tablecloths and napkins in an assortment of colors
China and glassware: china and crystal glassware provided
Cleanup: provided by Pantheon Banquet Hall
Parking: ample parking available

WE MAKE WEDDINGS SPECIAL

Every wedding is special and exciting, says Effy, banquet coordinator, as we can focus on each bride attending to every detail to make this day the most perfect day of her life. Enjoy our finest cuisine prepared by our professional chefs. Also a private bridal room awaits you, along with a complimentary bottle of champagne or nonalcoholic champagne and limousine service to and from the Pantheon Banquet Hall, compliments of the owner, Sakis.

Fairytale Experience

"Anyone that employs your service can expect, after arriving in your MAGICAL COACH, to walk through your doors into a WONDERLAND of special treatment. The PRINCE AND PRINCESS are introduced with a spotlight entrance into the PANTHEON HALL, which is nothing less than CINDERELLA'S BALLROOM. I have many friends who still are discussing how this FAIRYTALE atmosphere was hidden in a structure centrally located in the middle of the Rose City."

~Mrs. Judy Stowell

 Please let this business know that you heard about them from the Bravo! Bridal Resource Guide.

PAZZO
RISTORANTE

HOTEL VINTAGE PLAZA

422 S.W. Broadway • Portland, Oregon 97205
Contact: Private Dining
(503) 412-6316
Business Hours: Mon–Fri 9am–5pm

Capacity: 140 people reception; 120 people seated
Price Range: varies with menu selection, call for details
Catering: full-service in-house and off-premise catering from Pazzo Ristorante
Types of Events: sit-down, buffet, hors d'oeuvres

Availability and Terms

The Hotel Vintage Plaza has banquet rooms available to accommodate functions of many sizes. These rooms are located on the second floor of the hotel and display the same European decor seen throughout the hotel lobby, restaurant, and guest rooms. Also available is the Pazzo Cellar which has the capacity for seating up to 72 guests, 80 for a reception The Pazzoria bakery can accommodate up to 25 people for an evening event.. We encourage you to reserve as soon as possible to secure your desired date. A deposit is required to confirm your space.

Description of Facility and Services

Seating: up to 120
Servers: serving attendants available; 18% gratuity
Bar facilities: full-service bar with liquor, beer, and wine provided
Linens and napkins: linen and cloth tablecloths and napkins available in ivory; specialty colors available upon request
China and glassware: ivory china; sheer-rim wine glasses and flute champagne glasses available
Cleanup: included in catering charges
Decorations: we have votive candles available for your use; we'll also assist you with any floral arrangements and decorations you may need
Parking: valet parking available; $5 per car for short-term parking; $15 per call for all day; parking garage located across the street for self-park
ADA: yes
Guest rooms: Hotel Vintage Plaza has 107 guest rooms and suites; each evening the hotel serves an Oregon Wine Reception in the lobby; call (503) 412-6312 for details

NORTHERN ITALIAN CUISINE IN SUMPTUOUS STYLE

From the warm and friendly greetings of the doorman to the pampering from our wait staff, our guests experience cozy European elegance and personalized service. Pazzo Ristorante offers exquisite food that embraces the warmth of Northern Italian Tuscan cuisine with artistic presentation and quality services. We will be happy to assist you in custom designing a menu to meet the needs of your function.

500 S.E. Butler Road
Gresham, Oregon 97080
Contact: Events Coordinator (503) 667-7500
Business Hours: Mon–Fri 8am–5pm
Web site: http://www.persimmongolf.com

PERSIMMON
COUNTRY CLUB
COMMUNITY

Capacity: 300 people
Price Range: varies
Catering: in-house by Persimmon Grille
Types of Events: weddings, receptions, rehearsal dinners

Availability and Terms

Persimmon features an elegant reception area for entertaining 300-person banquet facility. Reserve space up to one year in advance. A deposit is required to reserve space.

Description of Facility and Services

Seating: tables and chairs provided for up to 250
Servers: included in catering cost
Bar facilities: Persimmon has alcoholic beverages and bartenders available
Dance floor: accommodations available; electrical outlets available
China and glassware: white china; glass beverage ware available
Linens and napkins: white tablecloths and napkins; colors available at additional charge
Decorations: please inquire with events coordinator
Cleanup: courtesy of Persimmon
Parking: free on-site parking
ADA: disabled accessible

Special Services

Persimmon's precise attention to detail will assure your wedding day is flawless. Please inquire regarding accessibility for early decorating. Valet parking available at an extra charge.

THE PERFECT SETTING FOR WEDDINGS AND RECEPTIONS

Persimmon offers a wide variety of services in an elegant relaxed environment set among spectacular scenery overlooking magnificent views of Mount Hood.

PORTLAND ART MUSEUM

NORTH WING

1119 S.W. Park Avenue • Portland, Oregon 97205-2486
Contact: Food and Beverage Manager (503) 226-2811 ext 4291
Business Hours: Mon–Thurs 10am–4pm;
Call for an appointment

The Portland Art Museum's North Wing Building offers unique and magnificent rooms for any kind of gathering. Situated in the heart of Portland's Park Blocks, this architectural beauty features two large ballrooms, one banquet room, and several meeting rooms–each with a gracious and distinctive style! Arrangements can be made to view the current exhibition or tour galleries in conjunction with your event.

Capacity: 15 to 1,000 with very flexible configurations; or the entire building for up to 1,500
Price Range: varies according to room; please call for specific information
Catering: choose from our list of preferred caterers
Types of Events: every imaginable possibility, from wedding ceremonies, elegant receptions, full-dress balls, parties, and reunions to business meetings, seminars, fund raisers, training sessions and more; corporate sponsors enjoy additional benefits of using the Belluschi Building and the North Wing

Availability and Terms

Reserve your room up to one year in advance. A deposit confirms your reservation. Liability insurance and a nominal security fee are required.

Description of Facility and Services

Seating: tables and chairs available; choose from a variety of floor plans
Dance floor: hardwood dance floors and stages in all ballrooms
Linens, china, glassware, service and setup: all provided by caterer
Bar service: available through caterer
Decorations: elegant facilities need little decoration
Parking: available on street or in several nearby lots
ADA: accessible

**RESERVE THE PORTLAND ART MUSEUM
FOR A TRULY ARTFUL AFFAIR!**

PORTLAND CONFERENCE CENTER

300 N.E. Multnomah Street • Portland, Oregon 97232
Contact: Sales Coordinator (503) 239-9921
Business Hours: Mon–Fri 8am–5pm or by appointment
E-mail: info@portlandcc.com; Web site: www.portlandcc.com

Capacity: 20 to 400 sit-down, 700 for standing reception; 12 rooms ranging from 475 to 4,600 square feet

Price Range: various packages available; please call for specific information

Catering: full service in-house catering; off-site catering available; we will customize a personal menu for you or choose from one of our Chef's suggested menus

Types of Events: cocktail and hors d'oeuvres, buffets, sit-down luncheons or dinners, rehearsal dinners, ceremonies, receptions, anniversaries, special celebrations, holiday parties, proms and corporate functions

Availability and Terms

To ensure your special date in our newly remodeled Bridges Ballroom or in the coziness of one of our other rooms, we recommend making your reservation as early as possible; one year is suggested. We can accommodate events on short notice if space is available. You may reserve for afternoon or evening with a $500 deposit.

Description of Facility and Services

Seating: tables and chairs provided

Servers: provided in formal attire

Bar facilities: host/no-host bar(s); non-alcoholic beverages available; liability provided

Dance floor: built-in and portable dance floor; electrical hookups for band or DJ; large stage and PA system

Linens and napkins: linen tablecloths and cloth napkins provided in white or a variety of colors; skirting available in white, ivory, burgundy, royal blue or black

China and glassware: white china and glassware provided with catering

Decorations: need little decoration; table decorations and centerpieces provided; we handcraft our decorative bows in your wedding colors; fresh flowers and ice sculptures available

Parking: ample free parking; located on MAX line; **ADA:** main and lower level fully comply

Special Services

Our desire is to help you in planning for a successful and memorable event. We offer assistance during your planning including a two-week checklist before your special day to finalize all the details.

"YOUR EVENT IS AS IMPORTANT TO US AS IT IS TO YOU"

Portland Conference Center personnel are on site at all times to offer assistance and to service your entire event professionally. We welcome the opportunity to "Center" our attention on you and to individualize your event for a truly memorable affair.

Portland SPIRIT River Cruises

PORTLAND SPIRIT WILLAMETTE STAR CRYSTAL DOLPHIN

110 S.E. Caruthers • Portland, Oregon 97213
(503) 224-3900, (800) 224-3901
Web site: http://www.portlandspirit.com
E-mail: sales@portlandspirit.com

Offering spectacular views, outstanding service and first-class Northwest cuisine, prepared on board in each ship's galley. Our event planning services ensure that not one detail is overlooked, from a rehearsal dinner for 25 to an elegant sit down dinner reception for 340. A cruise on the **Portland Spirit**, **Willamette Star, or Crystal Dolphin** will guarantee the perfect place for your special day.

Availability, Price and Terms

The Portland Spirit vessels are available year round from downtown Portland. You may charter the entire **Portland Spirit** vessel or one-deck rentals are available. The **Portland Spirit** also offers public cruise schedules. The **Willamette Star** and **Crystal Dolphin** are available for private charter and offer limited public cruise schedules. Deposit and signed contract confirms cruise date. Prices depend on time of day, season of year and number of guests. NOTE: Capacity recommendations on each vessel depend on time of year, menu selected and type of wedding planned. Please call for specific recommendations.

Portland Spirit

130 foot, three level yacht, two outside decks
Available for full boat charter, one deck rental
Capacity: up to 540 guests
Seating: tables and chairs for 350, plus outside seating
Dance floor: large marble dance floor

Crystal Dolphin

130 foot, three level yacht, two outside decks
Available for private charter
Capacity: 90 guests
Seating: tables and chairs for 40, plus outside seating

Willamette Star

75 foot, two level yacht, two outside decks
Available for private charter
Capacity: up to 120 guests
Seating: tables and chairs for 80, plus outside seating
Dance floor: available

Description of Vessel Services and Facilities

Enclosed decks are temperature controlled
Linens: linen tablecloths and napkins provided
China: our house china and glassware provided
Servers: included with food and bar service
Bar facilities: full service bar, liquor, bartenders and liability insurance
Cleanup: provided
Parking: commercial and street parking available
ADA: limited with assistance

Pumpkin Ridge
GOLF CLUB

12930 Old Pumpkin Ridge Road
North Plains, Oregon 97133
Contact: Catering Director
(503) 647-4747; Fax (503) 647-2002
Business Hours: 8:30am–5pm
Web site: www.pumpkinridge.com

At Pumpkin Ridge Golf Club, every detail of your wedding reception will be made memorable through our unique artistry and style. Set on the edge of the beautiful Willamette Valley, yet convenient to downtown Portland, our gracious 18,000 sq. ft. clubhouse features dramatic architecture and an old Portland flavor. Ghost Creek Sunset Room, with open beam ceilings, skylights and a spacious patio provides an intimate setting with panoramic views of our championship courses. Our catering department offers professional event planning and culinary expertise. Our mission is to provide the utmost in customer service with a knowledgeable staff dedicated to fulfilling your every need.

Capacity: accommodates up to 200 guests; 250 with use of adjoining outdoor deck
Price Range: price varies according to menu selection
Catering: full-service, in-house catering provided
Types of Events: weddings, receptions, rehearsal dinners, bridal showers, formal sit-down, buffet, cocktail and hors d'oeuvres

Availability and Terms

Please inquire. A deposit is required; payment is due on or before the day of your event.

Descriptions of Facilities and Services

Seating: tables and chairs provided for up to 250 guests
Servers: service staff included in catering cost; 20% service charge is added to all food and beverage selections
Bar facilities: full-service bar provided
Dance floor: parquet dance floor available in a variety of sizes
Linens and napkins: provided; available in a variety of colors
China and glassware: provided
Decorations: a variety of centerpieces and room accents available
Cleanup: provided by Pumpkin Ridge Golf Club
Parking: convenient free parking
ADA: wheelchair access to all rooms

Special Services

At Pumpkin Ridge, each event is creatively designed, professionally serviced, and second to none. Escape to Ghost Creek Golf Course at Pumpkin Ridge and let us help you to create a celebration that's sure to be remembered for years to come!

The David Cole Queen Anne Victorian Mansion

1441 North McClellan
Portland, Oregon 97217
Phone 1-503-283-3224
Fax 1-503-283-5605

Capacity: 200 seated at outdoor gazebo (glassed in for winter months); 300 reception

Price Range: weekend, weekday and holiday rates available. Please call for specific price information; range from $300 to $1,750

Catering: select from closed list of six professional caterers for any food service (except cake); alcohol must be served by attendant; kitchen available for warming, but no on-site cooking

Types of Events: weddings, receptions, rehearsal dinners, buffets, cocktail parties, corporate meetings, fund-raisers, class reunions, picnics, birthdays, anniversaries, memorials, photo shots, movies, and many other events

Availability and Terms

The mansion is a 6,300-square-foot Victorian with a 42′ round enclosed gazebo. Reserve as early as possible. Reservations have a 90-minute and six-hour time limit per function. Available year-round, the mansion is conveniently located just minutes north of downtown Portland, just off I-5.

Description of Facility and Services

Seating: tables and chairs for up to 300 guests included in rental fee

Servers: provided by caterer

Dance floor: space for 200+ guests in the enclosed gazebo

Bar facilities: provided by Queen Anne

Cleanup: provided by the Queen Anne staff

Decorations: completely decorated in Victorian era antiques, silk floral garlands and arrangements throughout the home; meticulously landscaped gardens outdoors

Parking: plenty of free parking

Special Services

Lovely appointed dressing rooms for the bride and groom. Chauffeur-driven, 1951 Bentley, in Anniversary Silver, available by the hour.

A MAGICAL STORYBOOK PLACE

Every bride deserves perfection on her wedding day whether it is informal, formal, or a simple family ceremony. Easily accessible and very private, the Queen Anne Victorian Mansion is a beautiful location for creating your perfect day. Built in 1885 by David Cole as a wedding gift for his wife, the house is truly a work of art. The home is listed on the Historic Register. It features two-tone wood and spooled gingerbread throughout. It has three English coal-burning fireplaces and one of the largest private collections of Povy stained glass windows in the world. Come celebrate your special day with us!

Radisson®
HOTEL PORTLAND

1441 N.E. Second Avenue • Portland, Oregon 97232
Contact: Jennifer Bates, Director of Catering (503) 233-2401
Business Hours: Mon–Fri 8am–5pm
E-mail: Radis1@ix.netcom.com; Web site: www.radissonhotel.citysearch.com

---

Capacity: the Horizon Ballroom features over 2,600 sq.ft. of beautiful banquet space and includes a large foyer area that is perfect for your receiving line, buffet or guest bars

Price Range: many options available; please check with our catering department

Catering: the Radisson offers full-service in-house catering; we specialize in creative menu design to make your reception a beautiful experience

Types of Events: elegantly served luncheons and dinners, creative dinners and hors d'oeuvre buffets

Availability and Terms

Early reservations are strongly recommended. A deposit is due within 14 days of reserving banquet space. Remaining balance is due seven days prior to the reception. Guaranteed number of guests is required to be called in 72 hours prior to event.

Description of Facility and Services

The Radisson Hotel—Portland made its debut in August of 1999 following a 4.5 million dollar renovation. The banquet facilities received beautiful new carpeting, premium new banquet chairs and the addition of upscale chandeliers. The ballroom is located on the main level of the hotel and features private entrances.

Servers: professional service staff is included with reception package

Bar facilities: the Radisson can arrange for a hosted or no-host bar for your reception; our portable bars include full setup, mixed drinks, beer, wine, champagne and soft drinks

Dance floor: portable dance floors available

Linens and napkins: available in a variety of colors at no additional charge

China and glassware: white china, stemmed glassware

Decorations: early access for setup prior to your event; banquet staff will set up tables and chairs according to your specifications

Cleanup: included at no extra charge

Parking: ample, complimentary parking is available for your guests;

ADA: fully accessible

Bridal suite: with the selection of a full wedding package, the Radisson Hotel will extend a complimentary guestroom for the bride and groom on the evening of the reception; the guestroom includes a bottle of champagne/sparkling cider and a special truffle box for two

BACKED WITH EXPERIENCED RECEPTION AND MEETING COORDINATORS

The Radisson Hotel—Portland has a warm traditional atmosphere with a convenient location for you, your family and guests. We are near the Rose Quarter arena, Oregon Convention Center and shopping at Lloyd Center. The 10-story hotel has 238 guest rooms, each featuring a view of the city, the Willamette River, the West Hills or Mount Hood. We also offer a full-service restaurant and lounge. We look forward to making this a memorable day for you and your guests!

RED LION HOTEL®

VANCOUVER (At the Quay)

100 Columbia Street • Vancouver, WA 98660
360-694-8341 • Fax: 360-694-2023
www.redlion.com

Capacity: 14 meeting rooms to accommodate weddings and receptions from 10 to 600 guests; indoor and outdoor settings with riverview and patio seating available
Price Range: each event is individually priced with custom menu and services to meet your specific needs
Catering: full-service in-house catering exclusively
Types of Events: our events are as unique as our customers; offering a variety from light hors d'oeuvre receptions to elegant luncheon and dinner events

Availability and Terms

Please contact the sales and catering office to discuss space availability and terms.

Description of Facility and Services

Seating: tables and chairs provided by hotel
Servers: staff included in catering costs
Bar facilities: full beverage service; hotel provides all alcoholic beverages
Dance floor: complimentary; electrical outlets available; staging available for band or disc jockey
Linens and napkins: linen tablecloths and napkins in a variety of colors at no additional charge
China and glassware: white china; stemmed glassware
Decorations: lattice, silk plants, and votive candles; access for early decorating by prior arrangement
Cleanup: provided by hotel staff
Equipment: podiums, risers, and staging available at no charge
Parking: complimentary
ADA: all meeting rooms are accessible

Special Services

The Red Lion Hotel at the Quay offers 160 newly renovated guest rooms and 3 suites. Your guests will enjoy the many "extras," including coffee, coffee maker, iron and ironing board available in each room, no access charge for calling card calls and upgraded terrycloth towels. Special group rates are available for ten or more rooms per night.

EXPERIENCE THE DIFFERENCE

By selecting the Red Lion Hotel at the Quay, you will benefit from our unique and dramatic setting on the Columbia River, as well as our professional wedding consultants, who will assist you with all your planning needs. From menu planning to room decor and design, our experienced and friendly staff are trained to ensure a memorable and worry-free event. Our convenient location at the Washington/Oregon border situates us perfectly to accommodate friends and family from both states. Experience the difference of the Red Lion Hotel at the Quay and plan the most memorable day of your life!

THE REFECTORY

1618 N.E. 122nd Avenue
Portland, Oregon 97220
Contact: Catering Director (503) 255-8545
Business Hours: 10am–5pm

Capacity: up to 280
Price Range: hors d'oeuvres $12 per person; buffet $14 and up; sit-down dinner varies according to menu selection
Catering: full-service in-house catering available
Types of Events: receptions, banquets, rehearsal dinners and more

Availability and Terms

Reservations are recommended at least two months in advance. A $200 deposit is required, with a 30 day notice for a full refund in the event of a cancellation.

Description of Facility and Services

Seating: tables and chairs provided up to 280
Servers: provided
Bar facilities: full-service in-house bar
Dance floor: available
Linens: a variety of colors are available at no charge
China and glassware: available
Cleanup: provided at no charge
Parking: plenty of parking available
ADA: yes

CONVENIENT LOCATION

The Refectory will work with you to develop a special menu. We will also work with any size budget. We are conveniently located off I-84, just 10 minutes from downtown Portland. Our banquet room offers a private entrance and many other amenities.

1510 S.W. Harbor Way
Portland, Oregon 97201
Contact: Sales & Catering (503) 423-3112
E-mail: sales@RiverPlaceHotel.com
Web site: http://www.RiverPlaceHotel.com

RIVERPLACE HOTEL

Capacity: 10 to 400 guests; 400 reception; 200 sit-down meal
Price Range: varies according to room and services
Catering: meal prices starting at $15 per person for lunch and $24 to $50 for dinner; full-service in-house and off-premise catering
Types of Events: ceremonies and receptions; sit-down dinners and buffets; catered affairs outdoors in Tom McCall Waterfront Park or onsite courtyard

Availability and Terms

The hotel's ballroom as well as its waterfront Esplanade Restaurant and Grand Suite, Private Dining Room, and Courtyard are available for weddings and special events. Each provides a unique space whether for 10 or 400 guests. A nonrefundable deposit is required to confirm space.

Description of Facility and Services

Seating: variety of seating customized to meet your needs from 10 to 200
Servers: included as hotel service
Bar facilities: host/no-host bar; alcohol/nonalcoholic beverages available; liability provided
Dance floor: complimentary dance floor; electrical hookups available
Linens and napkins: white napkins and cloths; inquire about color selection
China and glassware: ivory china with wine-colored border and gold band; crystal glassware; only silver chafing dishes and flatware are used
Cleanup: included with full-service catering
Decorations: discussion of your ideas and needs welcomed
Parking: Master Account Parking may be arranged; garages within close proximity
ADA: fully accessible

Special Services

Silver candlesticks with white candles are provided by the hotel. Rooms are frequently available one-and-a-half hours prior to the function for early decorating—earlier if no prior functions are scheduled. Specialized menus are easily created to accommodate your tastes for whatever occasion you may be planning. We also have special guest room rates for your out-of-town guests and honeymoon packages.

A WATERFRONT LOCATION IN DOWNTOWN PORTLAND

The elegant RiverPlace Hotel overlooks the marina on the Willamette River, a perfect setting for a Northwest wedding.

SALEM INN

1775 Freeway Court, N.E. • Salem, Oregon 97303
Contact: Sales Office (503) 588-0515 or (888) 305-0515; Fax (503) 588-1426
Business Hours: Open 7 days a week

Capacity: *Capitol Room:* 621 sq. ft.; *meeting room:* 800 sq. ft. (accommodates up to 50 people)
Price Range: $125 per day; 10 or more rooms rented, meeting room is free
Catering: outside catering welcome
Types of Events: wedding receptions, reunions, seminars, meetings, corporate functions

Availability and Terms

No deposit required. Cancellation notice required 48 hours before function. Reservations should be made as early as possible.

Description of Facility and Terms

Seating: tables and chairs provided by Salem Inn
Servers: provided by caterer
Bar facilities: no bar facilities on site
Linens: fee for linens
China and glassware: dishes, flatware and glassware available
Cleanup: provided in rental fee
Parking: ample parking available
ADA: accessible

Special Services

Our friendly staff will strive to make your stay as comfortable and enjoyable as possible. We offer a complimentary continental breakfast each morning. Executive suites available.

CONVENIENT LOCATION

Located at the Market Street exit off I-5, the Salem Inn is close to the State Capitol, State Fairgrounds, Wallace Marine Park, Lancaster Mall and Volcanoes Stadium.
Directions: *I-5 south*, exit 256, turn right and hotel will be on your right. *I-5 north*, turn left, proceed one block and hotel will be on your right.

The Scottish Rite

Scottish Rite Center

709 S.W. 15th Avenue • Portland, Oregon 97205
Contact: Bill Stanger (503) 226-7827
Business Hours: Mon–Fri 8am-4:30pm or by appointment

Capacity: 50-400 sit-down or reception style
Price Range: call for price schedule
Catering: exclusively by Katering by Kurt, we are proud to offer full service catering by Kurt Struben, prior executive chef of the prestigious Essex House in New York

Availability and Terms

Advanced reservations are strongly recommended. A deposit is required at time of booking.

Description of Facility and Services

Seating: up to 400; table and chair setup included in room rental
Servers: provided by Katering by Kurt
Bar facilities: provided by Katering by Kurt; client may provide alcohol, but must have liability insurance
Dance floor: up to 250 guests; electrical available
Linens: available in most colors
China and glassware: white china and stemmed glassware
Decoration limitations: no rice or birdseed
Cleanup: provided
Parking: our own covered 155-space lot with attendant
ADA: accessible; elevator and ramp access

Special Services

At the Scottish Rite Center, we offer excellent catering exclusively by Katering by Kurt. We have a beautiful auditorium for ceremonies holding up to 580 guests. Gleaming hardwood floors expand our 4,500 square-foot ballroom. A dressing area is provided for the bride. The reception area includes a stage for the band or DJ of your choice.

BEAUTIFUL, WELL-PRESERVED BUILDING

The Historic Scottish Rite Center is a beautiful, well preserved building built in 1900. Located right next door to the Mallory Hotel makes it convenient for out of town guests.

traditional • charm • elegance

SETTLEMIER HOUSE

355 N. Settlemier Avenue
Woodburn, Oregon 97071
Contact: Sharon Walsh
(503) 982-1897
Business Hours: open by appointment

Capacity: inside the house: 60 to 85; outdoors: 300+
Price Range: starting at $400, facility rental varies; midweek discounts available
Catering: we recommend professional caterers or you may select your own
Types of Events: weddings, receptions, rehearsal dinners, buffets, cocktail parties, meetings, picnics, office parties, family reunions, fund-raisers, class reunions, birthdays, anniversaries, memorials, photo shoots, movies, and many other events

Availability and Terms

A 25% deposit is due at time of booking.

Description of Services and Facility

Seating: some tables and chairs provided
Servers: provided by caterer or client
Bar facilities: client provides bartender, beverages, and liquor liability; beer, wine, and champagne only—no hard liquor allowed
Dance floor: gazebo; capacity: 25+; electrical outlets available
Linens and napkins: provided by caterer or client
China and glassware: available in limited quantity
Cleanup: responsibility of client, unless other arrangements are made
Decorations: please inquire about restrictions and details on early decorating
Parking: free street parking

Special Services

The Settlemier personnel are on site at all times to answer questions and make sure that everything is taken care of and running smoothly.

A LOVELY ROMANTIC SETTING PLEASANTLY SITUATED IN THE HEART OF THE WILLAMETTE VALLEY

The Settlemier House is an 1892 Victorian home located on nearly an acre of beautifully landscaped grounds. The backyard is surrounded by a photinia hedge with a gazebo, offering a romantic and private setting for an outdoor wedding and reception during the spring, summer, and early fall months. It is our policy to provide friendly service—we want you and your guests to feel welcome and to have a truly memorable experience. The Settlemier House is located 30 minutes south of Portland and 20 minutes north of Salem, making it ideally accessible for all your guests.

Sheldon's Cafe
at the Grant House on Officers' Row

1101 Officers' Row
Vancouver, Washington 98661
Contact: Gary
(360) 699-1213
Business Hours:
Tues–Sat 11am–2pm, 5pm–8pm;
Sundays, weddings only

Capacity: 20 to 100+
Price Range: food starting at $12 per person; room charge $500
Catering: full-service catering available in-house or off premise
Types of Events: ceremonies and receptions, rehearsal dinners, family reunions, birthdays, anniversaries, meetings, etc.

Availability and Terms

House rental includes main dining room, sunroom, covered veranda, as well as the herb and flower garden patio. A $250 nonrefundable deposit is required to guarantee your reservation.

Description of Facility and Services

Seating: all indoor, veranda and patio seating provided
Servers: included in price; 15% gratuity on all food and beverages
Bar facilities: Cafe provides liquor, regional beers and wines
Dance floor: outdoor patio only; accommodates 40+ people
Linens: cloth and paper products available
China: fine china and glassware available
Decorations: the Grant House's historic elegance reduces the need for expensive decorations; we are glad to discuss your specific decorating needs
Cleanup: included at no extra cost
Parking: ample free parking; easy access to I-5
ADA: Yes

Special Services

We excel at helping you have a fun and memorable event. Save time and reduce stress by letting us host both the ceremony and reception.

Sheldon's Cafe is located in the historic and elegant Grant House on Officers' Row in Vancouver. Built in 1850 and listed on the National Register of Historic Places, the Grant House features wrap-around verandas, a main dining room with two fireplaces, a private dining room, and a sunroom that looks upon our herb and flower garden patio.

SHENANIGANS ON THE WILLAMETTE

4575 N. Channel • Portland, Oregon 97217
Contact: Michael Baker (503) 289-1597
Business Hours: Mon–Fri 8am–6pm;
Sat 9am–5pm; or by appointment
Web site: www.shenanigansrestaurant.com

Capacity: ballroom seats 400, 560 in entire facility; 800+ reception
Price Range: our complete menu packages start at $9.95 (lunch) and $14.95 (dinner)
Catering: full service, in-house Northwest specialty, custom tailored to your needs
Types of Events: buffet and sit-down breakfast, lunch or dinner, cocktail and hors d'oeuvres, offered for wedding ceremony and receptions, rehearsal dinners, birthday and retirement parties. Use our facility to impress family, friends and business associates for these and other events.

Availability and Terms

The entire facility includes four tastefully appointed rooms available for your use. Reservations should be made as soon as possible to ensure availability. A nonrefundable, nontransferable deposit is required within 30 days of confirming reservations.

Description of Facility and Services

Seating: all tables and chairs provided and set to your specifications
Servers: our professional staff is provided with a customary service charge
Bar facilities: full service, host/no-host bars include large oak bar for ballroom, variety of portable bars for smaller rooms
Dance floor: 1,200-square-foot oak dance floor located in ballroom with electrical hook ups
Linens and napkins: available in a variety of colors at no additional charge
China and glassware: white china and stemmed glassware at no additional charge
Cleanup: included in service
Decorations: Shenanigans' picturesque view requires little decoration. Table candles, mirror tiles, bud vases and punch fountain are provided at no charge. You are welcome to bring your own decorations.
Equipment: podiums, microphones, risers and easels provided by us at no charge
Parking and ADA: ample free parking; disabled access available

Special Services

Shenanigans' offers a wedding package consisting of hors d'oeuvres, as well as a variety of options and ideas. Our flexibility coupled with 50 years of combined experience is sure to make this special day a truly memorable and unique one.

SPECTACULAR RIVERSIDE SETTING

Shenanigans' is conveniently located on the scenic banks of the Willamette River, in the bungalow style Ports O' Call complex, only minutes from downtown Portland. Please come in and see for yourself the exquisite panoramic view and impressive hospitality that makes Shenanigans' the perfect place for the beginning of a life time of happiness. Exit 303 off I-5, follow the signs to Swan Island, left on N. Port Center, take immediate right and we're just to your left.

Sheraton Portland Airport HOTEL

8235 N.E. Airport Way
Portland, Oregon 97220-1398
Contact: Julie Bradford
(503) 249-7642
Business Hours: Mon–Fri 8am–9pm
E-mail: jbradford@sheratonpdx.com

Capacity: 25 to 450 seated; 750 standing
Price Range: $16 to $27 per person
Catering: full-service in-house and off-site catering
Types of Events: sit-down, buffet, cocktails and hors d'oeuvres, rehearsal dinners

Availability and Terms

The Sheraton features 16 reception rooms on the lobby level for entertaining. Facilities may be reserved 18 months in advance with a $500 deposit. Cancellations must be made at least six months in advance for a refund of your deposit.

Description of Facility and Services

Seating: tables and chairs for 700
Servers: included
Bar facilities: full-service bar with bartenders provided; Sheraton provides liquor, beer, wine, and champagne
Dance floor: included in price
Linens and napkins: large selection of colors at no additional cost
China and glassware: white china provided; all types of glassware provided
Cleanup: included in price
Decorations: Sheraton supplies centerpieces, silver punch fountain, white lace skirting on cake and beverage tables, large floral arrangement; special arrangements needed for early decorating
Parking: complimentary parking available
ADA: yes

Special Services

A special wedding night package is included with your wedding reception. Enjoy spending this evening in a deluxe guestroom, upgraded to a suite upon availability, enhanced with champagne and chocolates.

Newly Remodeled

Shilo Inn Suites Hotel

and Conference Center—
Portland Airport/I-205
11707 N.E. Airport Way
Portland, Oregon 97220-1075
Contact: Sales/Catering Office
(503) 252-7500, ext 270
Business Hours:
Mon–Fri 8am–5:30pm;
Sat by appointment

Capacity: 10,402 sq. ft. of flexible meeting space
Price Range: packages to fit most budgets
Catering: full-service at our deluxe hotel or your special location
Types of Events: ceremonies and receptions; rehearsal dinners and family brunches,too!

Availability and Terms

You are invited to visit our facility to discuss your needs.

Description of Facility and Services

Seating: banquets of up to 350 guests
Servers: professional, full-service staff for all events
Bar facilities: hosted or no-host bars and table service
Entertainment: musician and DJ referrals available
Dance floor: beautiful wood floor with minimal setup fee
Linens: included to complement your colors
China and glassware: included; styled to complement formal and informal themes
Cleanup: setup and cleanup by our staff
Decorations: chandeliers, mirrored walls, table and buffet decorations included
Accommodations: Four-diamond, full-service with 200 luxurious junior suites; in-room microwave, refrigerator, wet bar, coffee maker, iron and ironing board, three televisions, two vanities, data ports, voice mail and four phones with two lines; convenient in-room first-run movies, games and entertainment
Complimentary amenities: full breakfast, hosted social hour, *USA Today*, local phone calls, 24-hour coffee, fax service, popcorn and fruit
Complimentary services: 24-hour shuttle to the Portland Airport and MAX light-rail station, 24-hour pool, spa, steam room, sauna, fitness center and turn-down service; lounge with lunch and dinner entertainment and cigar bar. We will assist you in planning the reception or event of your dreams. We'll make you look good!
Parking: free parking available on-site
ADA: banquet rooms and guest suites

Reservations

Visit our Oregon coast resorts in Warrenton/Astoria, Seaside, Tillamook, Lincoln City or Newport. Or take a break in Bend. Phone (800) 222-2244 or visit our web site at www.shiloinns.com.

SILVER FALLS VINEYARDS

4972 Cascade Highway, S.E.
Sublimity, Oregon 97385
Contact: Duane Defrees
(503) 769-5056

Capacity: 150 inside, 300 inside and outside
Price Range: $350 to $850; limited to one event per day
Catering: your choice of caterer; excellent selection of caterers recommended upon request
Types of Events: weddings, receptions for any occasion, reunions, business meetings, company parties, proms, holiday parties

Availability and Terms

Reservations are recommended as early as possible for summer, fall, and holiday events. Deposit required.

Description of Facility and Services

Seating: tables and chairs provided for 80 guests; list of rental services available
Servers: provided by caterer or client
Bar facilities: bar facilities on premises; licensed caterer or client to provide bartender, liquor, and liability
Dance floor: inside dance floor; capacity: 75
Linens and napkins: ivory tablecloths and coordinating market umbrellas available
China and glassware: provided by caterer or client
Cleanup: responsibility of client or caterer; cleanup deposit required
Parking: ample free parking available
ADA: yes

Special Services

The facility includes a bridal party lounge with a mirrored wall, oriental rug and daybed. The vaulted and beamed reception area has a piano, built-in CD sound system, wood stove, French doors, faux marble floor and a stained glass entry. A galley kitchen is equipped with a range, refrigerator and microwave. Several charming bed & breakfasts are located within 10 miles of the site; a very nice motel is located just three miles away.

A GREAT PLACE FOR A GREAT TIME

Silver Falls Vineyards is an elegant, old-world rustic facility surrounded by a horse ranch, vineyard, and miles of rolling countryside. Conveniently located 12 miles east of Salem in a private setting, Silver Falls Vineyards is a unique, versatile place to hold your wedding and reception.

STOCKPOT RESTAURANT & CATERING COMPANY

8200 S.W. Scholls Ferry Road
Beaverton, Oregon 97005
Contact: Gary or Murray (503) 643-5451
Business Hours: 9am–2am DAILY

Capacity: indoors, three rooms; up to 350 guests
outdoors, two patios and the green; up to 600 guests
Price Range: will vary depending on food services required
Catering: in-house only
Types of Events: specialize in custom menus designed to complement your style of reception; a variety of buffets—traditional fare and many ethnic styles are available, as well as full-course sit-down dinners, hors d'oeuvre selections, or even a Southwest barbecue on the patio

Availability and Terms

The entire restaurant is available for private use on Saturday during the day. The patios overlooking the ninth green are available during the spring and summer months. Reservations are taken at your convenience with a $200 nonrefundable deposit at time of booking.

Description of Facility and Services

Seating: all tables and chairs provided
Servers: professional staff included in catering costs
Beverages: full beverage service offered; liquor liability included
Dance floor: available for you and your guests; ample electrical outlets for bands
Linens: provided with catering costs
China and glassware: a full selection of china and disposable available
Decorations: table decorations available; however, you may bring your own; rooms open for early decorating
Parking: free parking space for 600 cars; handicapped parking available

Special Services

Our desire is to give your reception those personal touches that reflect your style and personality. Menu planning, service, and other minute details are all part of the process. We don't forget whose wedding it really is.

PATIO OVERLOOKS THE GOLF COURSE

The Stockpot Restaurant is a unique catering facility with an elegant indoor reception room and spacious patios that overlook the ninth green. Enjoy your rehearsal dinner or wedding reception indoors, outdoors, or a combination of both. The Stockpot Restaurant at the Progress Downs Golf Course looks forward to making your event a great success.

The Sweetbrier Inn

7125 S.W. Nyberg Road (Exit 289 off I-5)
Tualatin, Oregon 97062
Contact: Sales & Catering Office
(503) 692-5800, (800) 551-9167; Fax (503) 404-1950
Web site: www.Sweetbrier.com
Office Hours: Mon–Fri 7:30am–5:30pm; Sat 9am–1pm

Capacity: 250 for dinner; 300 for reception
Price Range: creative, customized menus to fit your budget
Catering: full-service in-house catering
Types of Events: cocktails and hors d'oeuvres, buffets, sit-down luncheons or dinners, rehearsal dinners, wedding receptions, anniversary, special event celebrations, holiday parties

Availability and Terms

Four separate rooms are available; we can seat 250 for dinner or 300 for a reception. You can reserve for day or night.

Description of Facility and Services

Seating: tables and chairs
Servers: staff included in catering costs
Bar facilities: full-service bar available
Dance floor: 225 square feet of dance floor; PA systems and risers available
Linens: white linen tablecloths and colored napkins; white skirting
China and glassware: white china; assorted glassware
Decorations: creative catering staff to assist you
Parking: ample free parking
ADA: all facilities ADA accessible

Hotel Features

The Sweetbrier Inn offers 131 guest rooms including 32 luxury two-room suites. Honeymoon packages are also available.

PARKLIKE SETTING

The Sweetbrier Inn is conveniently located off I-5, and offers a bistro-style restaurant, a lounge featuring live jazz music, meeting and banquet facilities, and 131 guest rooms. The banquet rooms overlook a garden setting which provides the perfect atmosphere for a rehearsal dinner, reception or wedding. The spiral staircase in the lobby, or the garden area by the pool, offer excellent ambiance for those special photographs on your memorable day.

TALLINA'S GARDENS & CONSERVATORY

15791 S.E. Hwy. 224 • Clackamas, Oregon 97015
(503) 658-6148
Business Hours: Mon–Sat 8am–3pm
Web site: www.dollsupply.com
Closed to Weddings November 1 through April 30
Contact Our Facility For More Information

Capacity: Rose Garden, seating for 200; "The Park," seating for 300; Glass Conservatory, seating for 160

Price Range: $500 to $1,900

Catering: you provide caterer; kitchen is available for warming food, but no on-site cooking or barbecues please

Types of Events: weddings, receptions, anniversaries, birthdays

Availability and Terms

Conservatory includes a main room and dressing/rest rooms are available. The Gardens are open for viewing; please call for times available. The Conservatory is open for viewing Monday through Saturday; call for times available. It is best to call first for availability. A deposit of 50% of the total bill is required at the time of booking. Final payment is due three weeks prior to your event.

Times available to rent: Noon–5pm, 6pm–11pm, Noon–10pm or 11am–9pm. Additional time is $100 per hour or any part thereof.

Provided that cancellations are made six weeks in advance, we will gladly refund 75% of your deposit.

Description of Facility and Services

Seating: up to 300 chairs available (depending on area rented) and up to 20 round tables available (depending on area rented)

Servers: provided by caterer

Bar facilities: ONLY wine or champagne allowed; renter must provide liability insurance

Linens, china and glassware: provided by caterer

Cleanup: caterer or client to clean up; must be left as found to receive deposit refund

Decorations: please, no loose sequins, confetti, rice, birdseed, rose petals or potted plants, etc.

Parking: 150 paved parking and 200 grass parking

ADA: limited

Special Services

Complete gardens can be rented for pictures only for $50—provided not already rented.

BEAUTIFUL GARDEN SETTING

Tallina's extensive gardens are beautifully landscaped with over 1,200 rose bushes. The French rose garden, Oriental garden, cottage garden, English vegetable garden and five ponds are the perfect settings for a romantic wedding or any festive event. Our indoor Victorian Glass Conservatory gives you that outdoor feeling in colder months. We are now introducing "The Park," a wonderful natural grassy setting. Tallina's assures you of a setting that will forever enhance your most treasured memories.

 Please let this business know that you heard about them from the Bravo! Bridal Resource Guide.

TIFFANY CENTER

1410 S.W. Morrison
Portland, Oregon 97205
(503) 222-0703 or (503) 248-9305
Office Hours: Monday–Friday 9am-5pm.
Appointments recommended;
after hours and Saturday appointments available

Capacity: from 10 to 1,200 people; seven rooms and two elegant grand ballrooms ranging from 200 to 6,918 square feet

Price Range: call for price schedule

Catering: exclusively by Rafati's Elegance in Catering, prepared on-site in their commercially licensed kitchen; Rafati's full-service catering can assist you with your selection of the perfect menu for your wedding—from brunch to casual or formal reception services, all events are customized to reflect each bride's individual taste and style; personalized menu planning in all price ranges

Types of Events: wedding ceremonies, receptions, rehearsal dinners, private parties, dances, concerts, theater productions, exhibits, fund-raising events, corporate meetings and seminars

Availability and Terms

The Tiffany Center has three ballrooms with dance floors, stages and dressing rooms. Early reservations are suggested, but short notice reservations will be accommodated with space availability. A refundable deposit is required at the time of booking. Client must provide liability insurance.

Description of Facility and Services

Seating: table and chair setup included in room rental
Servers: provided by Rafati's Elegance in Catering
Bar facilities: provided by Rafati's Elegance in Catering; fully licensed
Dance floor: accommodates up to 700 people
Parking: convenient street and commercial lot parking; located on MAX line
ADA: all event rooms are fully ADA accessible

- Central air conditioning in second floor Ballroom; spot cooling available in fourth floor Ballroom

Special Services

The Tiffany Center's expert staff can provide you with complete event planning services. From candle and floral centerpieces, wedding cakes, decorated ice carvings, place cards and balloons to musicians and limo services and much more.

PORTLAND'S PREMIER WEDDING FACILITY

The Tiffany Center features traditional charm and elegance in a centrally located historic downtown building. Large ballrooms and cozy foyers together with gilded mirrors, gleaming hardwood floors and emerald green accents will provide you with an elegant setting for your wedding ceremony and/or reception. Our experienced, professional staff will provide you with everything you need to ensure that your once-in-a-lifetime event is a treasured memory.

See page 318 under Caterers & Ice Carvings.

Timberline

TIMBERLINE LODGE

Timberline, Oregon 97028
Catering Sales Office
(503) 622-0722; Fax (503) 272-3708
Business Hours:
Tues–Sat 10am–6pm
http://www.timberlinelodge.com

Capacity: up to 200 seated, four banquet rooms, outdoor patio
Price Range: packages begin at $32 per person
Catering: in-house only
Types of Events: ceremony, reception (buffet or sit-down), cocktails, lodging

Availability and Terms

The Raven's Nest, capacity of 175 theater-style, 75 for reception, is a loft-style room with cathedral ceilings and large picture windows, providing a perfect setting for a ceremony. Also available is the Main Lobby Patio, with majestic Mount Hood as a backdrop, for an outdoor ceremony. On the floor below the Raven's Nest, the Ullman Hall banquet room has a dance floor, picture windows and seating for up to 200 people. Silcox Hut is also available for up to 45 people. Packages are for a four-hour duration (from start of ceremony to end of reception) and include food and beverage services and a wedding cake. A deposit is required upon reservation. Contact the Catering Office for a complete wedding packet.

Description of Facility and Services

Seating: round tables and chairs are available for up to 200
Servers: Timberline has a full staff of professional servers and bartenders
Bar facilities: full-service bar available
Dance floor: 400-square-foot dance floor in Raven's Nest; 300-square-foot dance floor in Ullman Hall; electrical outlets available
Linens and napkins: cream or white tablecloths and napkins
China and glassware: fine china; appropriate glassware available
Decorations: two-hour setup time for decorating included; no confetti, glitter, rice or birdseed, please; inquire about special restrictions
Parking: Sno-Park permit required during winter months
ADA: disabled facilities available, with the limitations of a historic building

Special Services

Timberline, a National Historic Landmark, has 70 guest rooms available for your event. Your guests can enjoy the convenience of the ceremony and reception at one site plus the unique overnight experience this historic lodge provides.

TIMBERLINE—A CLASSIC FOR OVER 60 YEARS

For over 60 years, Timberline has been a favorite destination for millions of visitors from around the world. Located just 60 miles from Portland on the 6,000-foot level of Mount Hood, Timberline is the epitome of the classic alpine ski lodge. Unique lodging, gourmet dining and panoramic views of the Cascade Mountain Range welcome guests year-round.

Touch of Elegance

205 E. 16th Street • Vancouver, Washington 98663
Contact: Cindy Hammond (360) 694-3608
Business Hours: by appointment
Web site: www.touchofelegance.net

Capacity: 125
Price Range: $110 per hour
Catering: in-house or bring your own
Types of Events: wedding receptions, rehearsal dinners, birthdays, anniversaries, and business meetings

Availability and Terms

One large decorated room, setup and cleanup included in rental. A 50% deposit plus a $200 refundable damage deposit is due at booking. The balance is due one month before the event.

Description of Facility and Services

Seating: tables and chairs provided; 60" rounds and 8' conference
Servers: provided as needed
Bar facilities: provided by caterer or renter
Dance floor: available for an extra charge
Linens and napkins: available in limited colors
China and glassware: provided by caterer for an extra charge
Cleanup: provided
Parking: on-street parking available
ADA: yes

Special Services

Silver candle hurricanes, mirrored tiles, greenery, tulle and other assorted decorations available.

A SPECIAL EVENT DESERVES A SPECIAL SETTING

Tucked away on a quiet side street, walk through the doors of Touch of Elegance into the soft glow of brass chandeliers, a trace of trailing ivy, and your own personal touches that will make this your event. Tastefully decorated and arranged as required for your event, our staff will be happy to do all they can to make your day something special. Call Touch of Elegance for an appointment, and over a cup of tea and treats, we'll plan just the event you're thinking of.

Tuality Health Education Center

Facilities for your special events.

A member of the Tuality Healthcare family.

334 S.E. Eighth Avenue
Hillsboro, Oregon 97123
(503) 681-1700
Business Hours: Mon-Fri 9am-5pm

Capacity: rooms range in size from 270–3,100 square feet and can accommodate up to 400 people or 250 in banquet/seating format
Price Range: price varies according to event
Catering: choose from one of our preferred caterers
Types of Events: receptions, banquets, parties, meetings, seminars

Availability and Terms

A 50% rental deposit and signed license agreement reserves your space up to one year in advance. Day, evening and weekend space is available. Minimal kitchen fee per person.

Description of Facility and Services

Seating: tables and chairs provided and set up to your specification
Servers: provided by caterer
Bar facilities: provided by caterer
Dance floor: dance floor available up to 18' x 18'
Linens: provided by caterer
China and glassware: white Wedgwood china; variety of glassware available
Decorations: no rice, birdseed or confetti; enclosed dripless candles only
Cleanup: handled by caterer
Parking: ample free parking
ADA: fully accessible

Special Services

Choose from our preferred caterers who have access to our cold kitchen, china, silverware, glassware, and some table decorations. Early decorating my be arranged with the caterer. Equipment such as a CD player, rear or front screen projection of video, slides, computer screen or satellite broadcast may be rented. An audiovisual technician can be provided.

PERFECT FOR SMALL OR LARGE EVENTS

The Tuality Health Education Center features a beautiful sunlit foyer area that is perfect for cake and buffet service tables. The combination of skylights and foliage in our lobby is a perfect setting for your guests to mingle. Moveable walls allow for creating a space that is just the right size for your event.

 Please let this business know that you heard about them from the Bravo! Bridal Resource Guide.

THE WEDDING HOUSE

2715 S.E. 39th Avenue
Portland, Oregon 97202
Contact: Joan Ormsby (503) 236-7353
Business Hours: Mon–Fri 10am–4pm
evening appointment available

The Wedding House

Capacity: 100 seated for ceremony; up to 150 for reception
Catering: in-house catering available; outside catering services also welcome
Types of Events: weddings, receptions, anniversaries, parties, business meetings

Availability and Terms

Reservations are available at The Wedding House in six-hour segments; 10am to 4pm for morning bookings, and 5pm to 11pm for evening bookings. A nonrefundable deposit is required to secure your date and does apply to purchases. Balance is due two weeks prior to your event date.

Description of Facility and Services

Seating: tables and chairs provided as needed
Servers: included in catering cost
Bar facilities: host or no-host bar available upon request
Dance floors: available upon request; electrical outlets
Linens and napkins: white tablecloths and napkins; colors available upon request
China and glassware: available upon request
Cleanup: provided by The Wedding House
Decorations: please discuss decorating ideas with our staff; early access for decorating available by prior arrangement
Parking: free parking
ADA: yes

Special Services

If you prefer to have your wedding at your home and not at ours, we will be happy to assist in the planning and executing aspects.

- Catering
- Flowers
- Cakes
- Music
- Limousine
- Photography
- Wedding Dance Instruction
- Bridal and Formal Wear Boutique
- DJ Service
- Invitations
- Something special…just ask

COMPLETE WEDDING SERVICES

A beautiful historic home with a fireplace, ballroom, and large staircase with banister, The Wedding House will add romance to any elegant occasion. Kitchens and reception facilities are available for small and large groups. We offer complete wedding packages that can be catered to your individual needs.

THE WESTIN SALISHAN

LODGE & GOLF RESORT

Gleneden Beach, Oregon

7760 Highway 101 North • Gleneden Beach, Oregon 97388
Contact: Group Sales
(800) 890-9316; Fax (503) 764-3510
Web site: http://www.salishan.com

Capacity: 14,000 square feet of flexible meeting space for groups of 5 to 500
Price Range: price varies depending on event
Catering: full-service in-house catering
Types of Events: conferences, receptions, banquets, catered functions

Availability and Terms

Reservations are recommended six months to one year in advance.

Description of Facility and Services

Seating: tables and chairs provided for up to 600
Servers: one server per 25 guests
Bar facilities: full-service in-house bar
Dance floor: 400 sq. ft. dance floor available
Linens: a variety of colors are available at no charge
China and glassware: china and crystal available
Audiovisual: flipcharts, overhead projectors
Equipment: podiums, easels and risers available at no charge
Cleanup: provided at no charge
Parking: plenty of parking available
ADA: yes

Special Services

The Westin Salishan Lodge features 205 oversized guest rooms with fireplaces, private balconies, and ocean views; on-site massage, golf links, tennis courts, Westin Kids Club, putting course, and outward bound course.

EXPERIENCE YEAR-ROUND ATTRACTIONS OF THE OREGON COAST

The Westin Salishan Lodge and Golf Resort offers conference groups, individuals, couples and families a unique opportunity to experience the year round attractions and activities of the Oregon coast. Recreational activities include Oregon coast eco tours, hiking, beach combing, shopping at the local factory stores and marketplace, classic tours of the nationally renown wine cellar, wine tasting, horseback riding, tennis, golf, massages and storm watching. In addition to two unique on-site restaurants, Salishan is located within a seven mile radius of over 60 restaurants.

WILLAMETTE EVENTS CENTER AT THE LINN COUNTY FAIR AND EXPO

I-5 and Knox Butte Road • Albany, Oregon 97321
Contact: Jill Henderson
(541) 926-4314, (800) 858-2005; Fax (541) 926-8630
E-mail: fairexpo@co.linn.or.us
Office Hours: 8:30am–5pm; facility staffed 24 hours

Capacity: Willamette Events Center can accommodate up to 6,000 guests; conferences from 10 to 400 in 48,600 sq.ft.; three additional buildings totalling five acres under cover
Price Range: $40 to $1,600
Catering: in-house catering available; contracted and flexible
Types of Events: receptions, weddings, parties, showers, conventions, conferences, expositions, concerts and more

Availability and Terms

Currently booking into 2005. Please call for availability.

Description of Facility and Services

Seating: provided according to event; up to 3,000
Servers: provided; contracted
Bar facilities: contracted through caterer
Dance floor: available at market rate
Linens: available in a variety of colors
China and glassware: contracted
Decorations: some limitations apply; please inquire
Equipment: A/V carts, cords, podiums, sound; anything can be arranged
Parking: approximately 2,000 public parking spaces available
ADA: fully accessible

Special Services

Service is extreme here! On-site assistance with local contacts and arrangements. The Linn County Fair and Expo Center is a full-service conference center, exhibit hall, and fairgrounds facility with a professional "can do" staff.

In The Willamette Athletic Club

4949 S.W. Landing Drive • Portland, Oregon 97201

Contact: Catering (503) 225-1068

WILLAMETTE Cafe

Capacity: up to 250 for buffets; 100 for sit-down dinners
Price Range: $11 and up for food per person
Catering: in-house only
Types of Events: wedding receptions, rehearsal dinners, anniversaries, reunions, showers

Facilities

The Willamette Cafe in the Willamette Athletic Club offers three rooms accommodating up to 250 people, including a terrace with a view to the Willamette River.

Rates

A room charge of $250 takes care of everything except the dance floor. All tables are set with linen, fresh flowers and votives. All stemware, silverware and china are provided as well as all skirted tables. We'll provide a 12-foot skirted table for the wedding cake decorated with silver champagne bucket, silver candelabra, silver goblets and silver serving set. We'll also cut, plate and serve your wedding cake. All setup and cleanup are complimentary and there's plenty of free parking.

Minimum food charge is $11 per person. A $500 deposit is required to secure the facility. The deposit is refundable if notice of cancellation is given 90 days prior to event.

Description of Facility and Services

Servers: no additional charge including wedding cake cutting service
Gratuity: 17% service charge on food and beverage for buffets and 20% for plated dinners
Bar facilities: beer and wine—full-service bar available (minimum sales of $300)
Linens: linen skirting, tablecloths and napkins at no additional charge
China and glassware: bone china and crystal glassware provided at no additional charge
Dance floor: available at an additional charge
Cleanup: provided by Willamette Cafe at no additional charge
Entertainment: beautiful baby grand piano available; outside contractors welcome
Parking: ample free parking
ADA: yes

CUSTOMIZED SERVICE

The Willamette Cafe offers white tablecloth service and excellent food combined with years of experience catering wedding receptions and rehearsal dinners. All table arrangements, seating and menus can be customized to suit your specifications. Your every need will be attended to by our first class staff so that you, your family and friends can relax and enjoy the festivities of the day.

Willamette Gables

Riverside Estate
10323 Schuler Road
Aurora, Oregon 97002
Contact: Laurel and Scott Cookman
(503) 678-2195
E-mail: w.gables@juno.com
www.willamettegables.com

Wedding receptions and special events in an intimate country setting on the banks of the Willamette River

Willamette Gables is a five-acre country estate on the banks of the Willamette River, 30 minutes south of Portland and 30 minutes north of Salem. This beautiful southern plantation-style home provides the perfect backdrop for your wedding and reception.

The adjacent gardens overlook the meandering Willamette River, offering gorgeous views and solitude. Willamette Gables specializes in quality customer service and attention to detail.

Willamette Gables is shown by appointment only from 9am to 5pm. The property will not be shown if an event is in progress.

Capacity: 200 outdoors; 10 to 50 seated indoors; 100 reception-style indoors
Price Range: **weddings:** $2,000; **events:** based on size, space and time of day
Catering: choose your own caterer (we reserve the right to approve your selection) or choose from our list
Types of Events: weddings, receptions, picnics, garden parties, teas, anniversaries, private parties, meetings, seminars and retreats

Availability and Terms

Indoor facility is available year round; outdoor setting is available June through September. All reservations must be accompanied by a 50% deposit; the balance is due 45 days prior to your wedding.

Description of Facility and Services

Seating: indoor: tables and chairs provided for up to 50; **outdoor:** provided up to 200
Servers: provided by caterer
Bar facilities: caterer provides licensed bartender and liability insurance; beer , wine and champagne only
Linens and table service: provided by caterer; linens must be ground length
Setup and tear down: provided; caterers are expected to provide their own cleanup and trash removal
Decorations: many items are provided; little decoration needed; no rice, birdseed or confetti
Sound system: responsibility of client
Photographers: we suggest you choose a photographer who specializes in outdoor weddings and events
Parking: ample parking; parking attendants included in the fee

Special Services

- **Covered Area:** 40′ x 40′ canopy (upon request) for an additional charge
- **Wedding and Event coordination:** experienced assistance is available

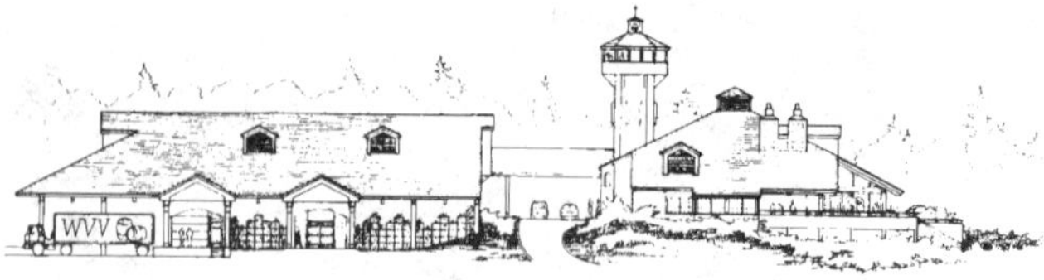

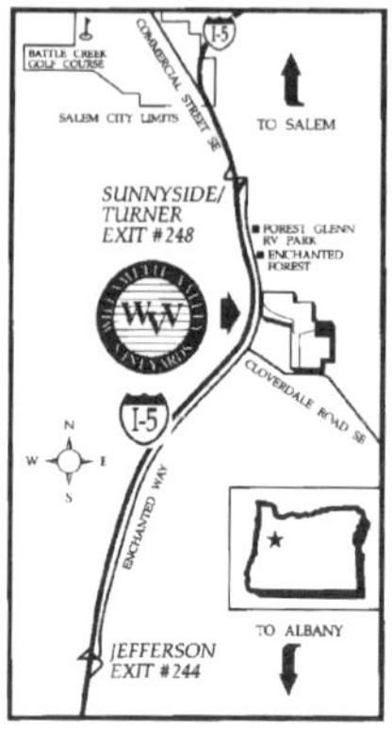

WILLAMETTE VALLEY VINEYARDS

8800 Enchanted Way S.E. • Turner, Oregon 97392
Contact: Hospitality Coordinator (503) 588-4024;
Fax (503) 588-8894; Toll free (800) 344-9463
Business Hours: 11am–6pm daily

Capacity: up to 600 inside and outside
Price Range: $150 to $1,800
Catering: exclusively by Willaby's Catering, prepared on-site; Willaby's full-service catering can assist you with your selections of the perfect menu for your wedding; all events are customized to reflect each bride's individual taste and style; Willaby's offers personalized menu planning in all price ranges
Types of Events: wedding ceremonies, wedding receptions, rehearsal dinners, bridal showers, bridal party luncheons and more

Availability and Terms

Reservations should be made as soon as possible. We require a 50% deposit at the time of rental.

Description of Facility and Services

Seating: tables and chairs are available
Licensed servers: Willamette Valley Vineyards arranges for wine servers for both indoor and outdoor events
Liquor liability: we are not licensed to serve any alcoholic beverages other than wine and beer on premise. Our award-winning wines are available for purchase in our tasting room.
Music and dance floor: amplified music is allowed, and dance floor areas are available both inside and outside the facility
Linens and glassware: available for rent
Cleanup: client or caterer to provide
Decorations: no nails, rice, or birdseed please
Parking: free parking available to Willamette Valley Vineyards patrons
ADA: access to restrooms, tasting room, and event rooms

Special Services

Specialty gift baskets and personalized neck labels attached to your choice of Willamette Valley Wines are available for purchase prior to your event. This personalized touch is a special remembrance for your guests and attendants. Complimentary tours by arrangement. Bridal registry is available in our tasting room.

PANORAMIC VIEW

Our newly built Visitor Center with panoramic view of the Willamette Valley and Coastal Range is the perfect location for any event.

WINDOWS
BANQUET & CATERING

SKY ROOM AND TERRACE

(City View Overlooking Portland)
Top Floor of the Holiday Inn Portland Downtown
1021 N.E. Grand Avenue • Portland, Oregon 97232
Contact: Sales and Catering Office (503) 820-4160; Fax (503) 235-0396
Office Hours: Mon–Fri 8am–5pm
Web site: holidayinnport.citysearch.com

Capacity: Ballroom: up to 250 people; Windows Sky Room: up to 150 people; Terrace: up to 100 people
Price Range: prices vary by size and length of stay; customized menus for your budget
Catering: full-service in-house
Types of Events: meetings, social events, seminars, receptions, sit-down, buffets, any custom event

Availability and Terms

Our Grand Ballroom holds up to 250 people and easily divides into four sections. For gatherings up to 200 people or more, choose our open patio/terrace, which overlooks the city of Portland. Adjacent to our terrace area, enjoy Windows Sky Room with views of the nightlife and city lights that show off the skyline view of Portland. Windows Sky Room is the perfect room for any special event. The cancellation policy varies according to the type of event.

Description of Facility and Services

Seating: tables and chairs provided and set up to your specifications
Bar facilities: full beverage service
Dance floor: dance floor and electrical hookups available at an additional charge
Linens: linens and cloth napkins available in a variety of colors, complimentary basis with catering
Cleanup: provided by hotel
Parking: complimentary parking

Special Services

Windows catering staff offers personalized attention to every detail of your reception including customized menu planning, private space for rehearsal dinners, and lovely honeymoon suites with a spectacular Portland city view for the bride and groom as well as special guest room rates for your out-of-town guests. You may also hold your wedding ceremony here.

ELEGANCE AND SPECTACULAR CITY VIEW

Windows is a full-service banquet facility. In addition to our 4,000-square-foot ballroom, Windows Sky Room with its panoramic view, is also available for private affairs. Our open-air terrace provides a beautiful setting for a wedding and/or a reception. Windows catering serves fine Northwest cuisine highlighting fresh foods of the Pacific Northwest. Whether an intimate gathering or a full reception, your event is special to us.

WINE COUNTRY FARM

6855 Breyman Orchards Road • Dayton, Oregon 97114
Contact: Joan Davenport (503) 864-3446, (800) 261-3446
Web site: www.winecountryfarm.com
Business Hours: 7am–10pm

Capacity: up to 300 outdoor, 80 indoor
Price Range: prices vary depending on size and type of event
Catering: no in-house catering available
Types of Events: weddings, receptions, fundraisers, class reunions, family reunions and many other events

Availability and Terms

A $500 deposit is required upon contract signing. A DJ is included in the package price; please inquire.

Description of Facility and Services

Seating: 300 chairs, 40 tables (8-top)
Servers: provided by caterer
Bar facilities: our own wine and beer; no hard liquor; we provide bartenders
Dance floor: 35′x35′ dance floor pavilion
Linens: cloth napkins available in limited colors; all linens included except napkins
China and glassware: wine glasses available
Decoration limitations: please inquire
Cleanup: provided at no charge
Parking: ample parking available
ADA: accessible

Special Services

Wine Country Farm also features a seven-bedroom bed and breakfast inn on the grounds. All overnight accommodations include the bountiful Country Farm Breakfast.

WELCOME TO WINE COUNTRY FARM

Wine Country Farm sits on a hill surrounded by our own vineyards with a spectacular view. Beautiful grounds with flowers, gazebo, and a 35′x35′ pavilion for dancing is available. We also raise Arabian horses, one of which can bring the bride in a buggy. We have a seven-room bed and breakfast to make your wedding truly relaxing. Changing rooms are provided for the wedding party. We have a spectacular setting in the heart of wine country, less than one hour from Portland and just a half-hour from Salem. Please call us for more information.

WITTENBERG INN

WITTENBERG INN

5188 Wittenberg Lane
Keizer, Oregon 97303
Contact: Richard Andres
(503) 390-4733, (800) 299-7221; Fax (503) 390-1108
Business Hours: Open 24 hours
Web site: www.wittenberginn.com

Capacity: seven banquet rooms; three will seat up to 160, four will seat up to 450
Price Range: varies with menu selection
Catering: in-house catering; award-winning chef
Types of Events: receptions, weddings, banquets, conventions, seminars, meetings

Availability and Terms

Rooms are reserved based on availability. A deposit is required at the time of confirmation with the balance due 30 days prior to the event. Deposits are refundable if cancellation is received at least 30 days prior to the function.

Description of Facility and Services

Seating: tables and chairs provided as needed
Servers: provided
Bar facilities: full-service bar
Dance floor: available for a charge
China and glassware: china and glassware provided
Linens and napkins: white linens provided; other colors available for an additional fee
Cleanup: provided by Wittenberg Inn
Parking: ample free parking available
ADA: ADA compliant

Special Services

- Gourmet continental breakfast
- 86 mini-suites with microwaves, refrigerators, and coffee makers
- Jacuzzi suites and romance packages available

We cater to weddings!

WORLD TRADE CENTER

Two World Trade Center Portland

25 S.W. Salmon Street • Portland, Oregon 97204

Reservations: (503) 464-8688 • Office Hours: Mon–Fri 8am–5pm

Capacity: inside: 400 reception, 300 seated; **outside:** 800 reception, 500 seated; **Flags riverfront space:** 125 reception, 80 seated

Price Range: please call for specific price information

Catering: we can host a rehearsal dinner or reception, or we can package your entire wedding, handling all the details for you!; full-service in-house catering available with creative and helpful event coordinators to assist you

Types of Events: sit-down, buffet, hors d'oeuvres

Availability and Terms

A variety of rooms are available to meet your specific needs. Choose between the glassed-in Mezzanine or our covered Plaza for your outdoor ceremony or reception. Our riverfront banquet space offers a fantastic view of the river and Tom McCall Waterfront Park. There is also a 220-seat auditorium for indoor ceremonies. Reservations are suggested at least six months in advance—particularly during spring and summer months. A 25% deposit of anticipated total expenses is required at the time of booking.

Description of Facility and Services

Seating: seating capacity based on room(s) selected and seating arrangement; table and chair setup included in rental price

Bar facilities: full beverage service provided

Dance floor: dance floor upon request at standard rental rate; electrical hookup for bands or disc jockey available

Decorations: creative theme events may be arranged

Parking: underground daytime and evening parking available in the building

ADA: all rooms are disabled accessible

INVITE YOUR GUESTS TO SEE THE WORLD

Imagine your special day at Portland's showcase—the World Trade Center! Located in the heart of the city between Southwest Salmon and Taylor streets, First Avenue and Naito Parkway, this award-winning facility has a commanding view of the beautiful Tom McCall waterfront and provides the finest in facilities. You'll enjoy our cooperative and helpful staff, prepared to do whatever it takes to make your special time a wonderful experience. Please call for a tour and complete information packet.

© red door studio • page 520

ILLUSION OF BEAUTY LAW

A law was passed in 1775 stating that a young woman couldn't wear makeup at her wedding. If she did, her marriage would not be considered legitimate, because the groom would have been "ensnared" by the illusion of beauty made by the makeup.

HELPFUL HINTS

- **Eat right and get enough sleep:** It gets very hectic prior to the wedding with all the planning and parties. Be sure to take care of yourself! You'll need every ounce of energy. Eat right and get enough sleep to look your very best on this special day.
- **Pamper yourself:** A couple of weeks before the wedding, take time to pamper yourself. Schedule a massage to relieve tension and stress. A facial is wonderful for your skin, but be sure to allow some time for your face to benefit from it. Avoid using unfamiliar products too close to the wedding in case your skin has an allergic reaction. Prepare your hands and nails with a manicure. A pedicure will do wonders for your feet and toes for the honeymoon.
- **Hair consultation:** When you have selected your headpiece, make an appointment for a consultation with your hairdresser. This allows time to experiment with different hairstyles that complement your face and work well with the headpiece. This way there are no "surprise" hairstyles the morning of your wedding. You and your hairdresser should agree on the style and look well in advance. Also make sure your hairstyle will look nice even when you take off the headpiece.
- **Makeup consultation:** A makeup consultation can help you apply makeup in a natural and flattering way to highlight your features. The photographer may ask for a heavier application for the photos. Ask the consultant how to obtain the best look without overdoing it.
- **Bridesmaid lunch and manicure:** A fun idea is to take your bridesmaids to lunch and then treat them to a manicure. This usually takes place a day or two before, or the morning of the wedding. For parties of three or more it is best to schedule an appointment at least three months in advance.
- **On-site beauty service:** Many salons and beauty consultants offer hairstyling and makeup for you and your bridesmaids at the ceremony site. Fees are based on services, number of people, and travel time.

For more assistance with staying organized during the wedding planning process, check out the Bravo! Wedding Organizer. Detailed question worksheets double as contracts. This step-by-step system will keep every detail of your wedding organized. To order, refer to the order form on page 24 in this Guide.

ATLANTIS SALON

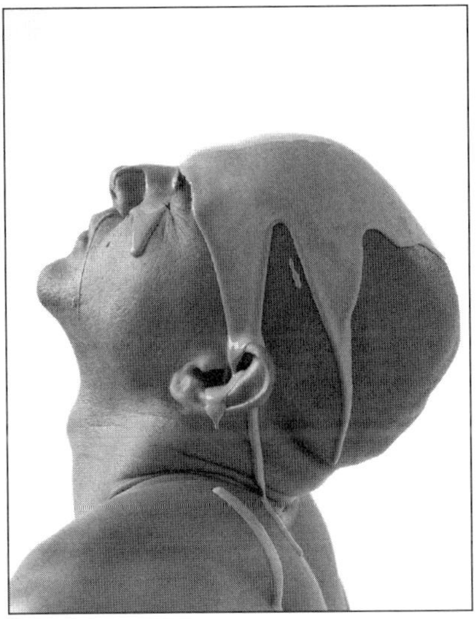

SPA

1126 S.W. Morrison
(503) 721-1576
Downtown Portland

Salon Options

* Hair Care & Design
* Spa Manicures
* Spa Pedicures
* Nail Extension
* Photostyling On-Site
* Enhancing Makeup
* Massage
* Occasion Styling
* Bathe Treatments
* Spa Services
* Bridal Packages
* Waxing

Spa Treatments

* **A DAY IN ATLANTIS:** Luxurious eight hour spa day includes lunch and photography
* **CREATE YOUR SPA PACKAGE:** Choose your own four services, includes luncheon
* **MASSAGE:** Deep tissue, Shiatzu, Swedish, reiki, pregnancy, hot stone–delight!
* **SEA SALT BODY SCRUB:** Exfoliating and detoxifying skin treatment–baby soft!
* **AUSTRIAN MUDD BODY WRAP:** Mineralizing and nourishing body wrap
* **CALMING BATH TREATMENT:** Infused chamomile and relaxing herbs soothe
* **REVIVING BATH TREATMENT:** Awaken the senses and mint revives the skin
* **SUMMER CITRUS MANICURE & PEDICURE:** Twist of citrus to any nailbed

Special Bridal Packages

Whatever stage you're in with your bridal planning, let the staff at ***Atlantis*** assist you. Our full-time bridal coordinator has 10 years experience with beauty planning for event groups large and small. With a large menu of services and personalized spa packages, ***Atlantis*** has the ability to accommodate *any* wedding group. Complimentary bridal consultations are always welcome.

Carpe Diem

By appointment only
(503) 244-2885, (503) 287-1272, (503) 515-5323

We are an ensemble of professional stylists/makeup artists, that come to you on location with experience. We are fully equipped to handle all of your needs down to the smallest detail.

Our Services include

- **A complimentary consultation** to discuss what your needs are, so that a proper package can be designed for you, and book any necessary appointments at that time.
- **A personal consultation** to discuss any haircare preparation (hair shaping, retexturizing, coloring, and conditioning treatment) necessary to be done prior to the wedding.
- **A trial run with the bride** to go over makeup selection and application as well as a practice style and headpiece placement.
- **A package designed** to suit your needs

On-site

- Bridal/formal up-do's
- Full makeup application
- Manicure/polish changes
- Assistance through the ceremony

Services in the Salon We Offer

- Haircutting
- Shampoo and styling
- Color and weaves
- Manicures and pedicures
- Artificial nail services
- Permanent waves and retexturizing
- Special occasion styling and up-do's
- Hairstyling lessons
- Color cosmetic application
- Eyelash tinting

Off-site Referrals for

- Facials/full body massage

30 day notice preferred.
Short notice inquiries and services are welcomed.
Deposit required.

VISA MasterCard and personal checks accepted.

Make-Up and Hair Design by

Tonya

13900 S.E. 180th
Boring, Oregon 97009
Contact: Tonya Powell (503) 658-4815

Let Tonya pamper you and the whole wedding party with her professional knowledge of makeup and hairstyling, for perfect portraits and a beautiful walk down the aisle. Tonya has over 15 years of makeup and hair design experience including film, print and runway, and has taught seminars in the United States and overseas.

Services Include

- **On-site** makeovers including beautiful hairstyling
- Consultation at no charge
- Assistant availability for large parties at low additional fee
- Haircut and color done prior to wedding if desired
- A calm nature and a great attitude to put you at ease

Perhaps you prefer a dramatic look for an evening affair or a more subtle touch for a morning ceremony—Tonya can tailor your makeover and hair design to fit your exact needs.
To set up a free consultation, please call at least two months in advance, however, Tonya does welcome last minute calls.

PARADISE

DAY SPA & SALON

2905 N.E. Broadway
Portland, Oregon 97232
(503) 287-7977
Web site: paradiseday.uswestdex.com

PARADISE BEFORE THE HONEYMOON

Seduce your senses, soothe your body, surrender your stress for the most important day of your life.

Our staff of professional licensed therapists and practitioners invite you and your chosen loved ones to our beautiful facility to be nurtured and beautified for your special day.

We Welcome You to Paradise

We are a unique spa and salon that caters to brides, grooms and your entire wedding party. Specializing in beauty consultation, wedding day hair and veil, makeup application, nails, etc. Our spa treatments complement your experience to soothe you with facials, massage and body treatments. When you visit our salon, you'll be in a vintage house with portraits of our satisfied bridal customers on the wall.

Bridal Packages

The Lotus Blossom is a package specifically designed for the bride. You'll receive a complimentary consultation, hairstyle, makeup application, and manicure—all done on the wedding day.

When Should You Schedule?

Brides should schedule their consultation one to two months prior to the wedding day. This will allow time for specific hairstyles (colors, cuts or perms) and to discuss your makeup and hair needs. On-site services on your wedding day are available with advance booking.

CALL FOR MORE INFORMATION ON OUR FULL RANGE OF SERVICES AND WEDDING BROCHURE. WE WILL BE HAPPY TO ASSIST YOU IN ANY WAY POSSIBLE.

As seen in the September 1999 issue of National Geographic Traveler Magazine as one of America's 24 best spas!

Professional Make-up Services

Kim Lane • Carrie Wilson
(503) 287-5205; Fax (503) 287-5299

We specialize in makeup only. At your location, we offer our seven years experience, including weddings, runway, print and film. We have had extensive training, in addition to working for MAC cosmetics for five years. We are knowledgeable in techniques for enhancing features on all skin tones and our expertise in color theory will enable us to choose the best colors for you and your wedding party. We work quickly and efficiently to eliminate any stress on your special day.

• On-site Services

- We use products specially formulated for film, video and photography
- Engagements, rehearsal dinners and other special events
- Entire wedding parties—including men and mothers, too
- Waterproof mascara and false eyelashes (if desired) at no extra charge
- Lessons available

In Advance

Prior to your wedding, we will meet for a consultation to discuss the details and choose your look. At this time we can schedule any additional appointments that will best suit the needs of you and your wedding party.

Notes

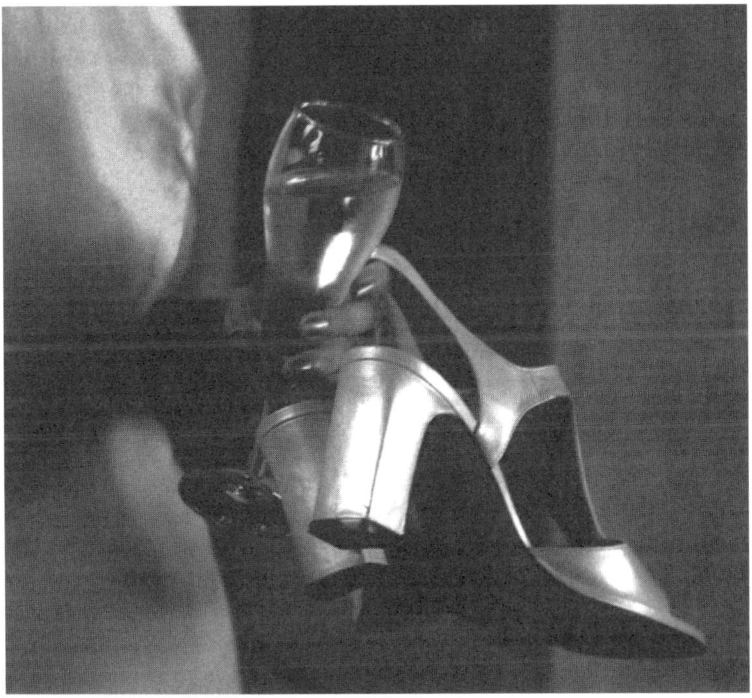

© Moments In Time Photography • page 507

Talismans

Talismans a bride may choose to wear or carry on her wedding day came about from a mix of tradition and superstition.

Something Old
to bring a sense of continuity

Something New
adds an optimistic note

Something Borrowed
the superstition that happiness rubs off

Something Blue
for purity, fidelity and love

A Penny In Your Shoe
to help ensure a life of fortune

HELPFUL HINTS

- **How to make candles burn slower and drip less:** If you plan to use candles at your event or wedding, put them into a freezer in a foil-wrapped box the night before. This prevents the candles from burning down too far while the photographer is taking formal portraits before the ceremony. An alternative is to bring an extra set of candles. You don't want it to look like the candles were already used before the wedding actually begins.
- **Guest-book pen:** Bring an extra pen for the guest book. Sometimes fancy plume pens run out of ink or don't write well. You want to make sure you have a complete list of who attended your wedding.
- **Money tree or money bag:** If you choose to have a "money tree" at your reception, it's a good idea to have envelopes on hand to put the money in. Guests can attach their gifts to the tree along with their names (no one likes to give an anonymous gift). If you choose the tradition of a "dollar dance," a money bag to carry on your arm will eliminate pin marks on your beautiful wedding gown.
- **The unity candle:** Unity candles used during the ceremony are not only symbolic, but can be enjoyed for many years to come to celebrate your anniversaries.
- **Wedding gown slips:** These slips can be very expensive to wear for just one day. Some shops have slips available for rent.
- **Shoes:** Comfort is number one—style is second. Find a pair of shoes that will be comfortable, and then customize them with lace, beading, and pearling. Clip-on accessories are also available to dress them up. If you buy a satin shoe, many stores offer free dyeing after the wedding so that you can wear them again.
- **Garters:** It is nice to buy two garters, one to throw and the other to keep as a fun memento.
- **Toasting goblets:** You'll find a variety of glass, crystal, pewter, or silver goblets and toasting glasses to choose from. You can have them engraved with your names or initials and your wedding date. Your florist will be able to provide decorations such as ribbons and fresh flowers to place around the stems of your glass or goblet. These are mementos you'll want to keep for years to come, or to pass on to the next generation.
- **Something old:** Ask your mother or grandmother for something she carried at her wedding: a lace hankie, Bible, or piece of sentimental jewelry you can wear or carry.
- **Bubble shower:** Provide containers of bubbles that can be blown as the bride and groom leave the ceremony. The bottles can be customized with the names and wedding date for guests to keep as a keepsake.

For more assistance with staying organized during the wedding planning process, check out the Bravo! Wedding Organizer. Detailed question worksheets double as contracts. This step-by-step system will keep every detail of your wedding organized. To order, refer to the order form on page 24 in this Guide.

NORDSTROM

Washington Square
9700 S.W. Washington Square Road
Tigard, Oregon 97223
(503) 620-0555

AT NORDSTROM, WE HAVE A BEAUTIFUL SELECTION OF FINISHING TOUCHES FOR YOUR SPECIAL DAY

From pearls to pumps, you'll find surprising selections for the beautiful bride. Plus, we have special occasion attire for the mother-of-the-bride or groom and the entire wedding party.

Hosiery

You'll find a variety of styles and colors to complement you and your attendants' bridal attire from Givenchy, Classiques Entier, and Donna Karan.

Fashion Jewelry

You'll enjoy an extensive selection of Austrian Crystal jewelry from Swarovski and Christian Dior, as well as freshwater pearl designs from Lily Rachel.

Fashion Accessories

Finishing touches for your bridal party are easy with our extensive accessory collection, including decorative hairpieces and satin gloves. We are also happy to place special orders for your individual needs.

Lingerie

Complete your trousseau with selections from our beautiful collection of bridal lingerie, including bustiers, garter belts with matching panties, peignoir sets and garters.

Handbags

Our handbag section features a unique selection of styles including satin, velvet, and beaded handbags from $28 and up.

Fine Jewelry

Whether you're shopping for an engagement ring or wedding set, you'll find a breathtaking array of contemporary and traditional rings. Custom jewelry designing is also available in selected stores.

The Wedding Cottage

Westside
4775 S.W. Watson Avenue
Beaverton, Oregon 97005
(503) 643-9730

Downtown
423 S.W. Fourth Avenue
Portland, Oregon 97204
(503) 827-4578

The most enormous selection of elegant accessories from economical to extravagant.

A trip to The Wedding Cottage is a must for anyone planning a wedding. The variety and beauty of the wedding accessories are like no other in the Pacific Northwest. There is so much to see, that brides return again and again.

The Wedding Cottage carries many lines including Beverly Clark, Marcela, Lillian Rose, Cathy's Concepts and the new Toccata line. Many items are custom-made or customized to fit a bride's individual or wedding theme.

An extensive amount of inventory is on hand. However, we take pride in our ability to special order items not in stock in the exact color or style needed.

Every bride receives a Bride's Card that allows her a $10 instant credit every time her cumulative purchases reach $100. Brides who do all their shopping at The Wedding Cottage find they have substantial savings.

- ♥ Bridal books and planners
- ♥ Guest and memory books
- ♥ Unity candles and holders
- ♥ Bridal jewelry
- ♥ Knives and servers
- ♥ Custom cake tops and charms
- ♥ Bubbles (8 varieties)
- ♥ Favors and candies
- ♥ Personalized napkins and ribbons
- ♥ Toasting goblets
- ♥ Cameras
- ♥ Invitations and announcements in over 60 books
- ♥ Bridesmaid and groomsmen gifts
- ♥ Plume and guest book pens
- ♥ Ring Bearer pillows
- ♥ Flower Girl baskets
- ♥ Garters, hankies, gloves
- ♥ Photo albums
- ♥ Custom veils, headpieces, and hats
- ♥ Purses and money bags
- ♥ Shower invitations and games
- ♥ Rehearsal invitations
- ♥ Specialty and Anniversary Gifts

Our main store is located in Beaverton, with a second smaller location in downtown Portland, inside the Ania Collection.

See page 401 under Invitations & Announcements.

Alameda Bridal Faire

5707 N.E. Fremont
Portland, Oregon 97213
(503) 282-4430
Business Hours:
Mon–Fri 10am–5:30pm; Sat 9am–4pm

© Photography by Fudge

YEAR-ROUND BRIDAL FAIRE

Wedding Flowers

Whether your wedding dreams include an enchanted garden, a cathedral or fireside at home, Alameda Floral can help make them come true. Free personal consultation to create the ambiance you want for your wedding day.

Photography

The photographer who captures the memories of a perfect day should be #1 on your list. Alameda Bridal Faire has only the best and we can help you here!

Travel Agency

We offer hundreds of packages of romantic travel for couples, from intimate hideaways to luxury cruises. Personal planning and service are top priority.

Wedding Gowns, Veils and Accessories

Our selection of the finest gowns and veils are available for viewing at all times. When it comes to accessories, we travel to New York to find the latest, fashionable and most reasonably priced toasting flutes, cake knives, guests books, pillows, and gifts for the wedding party.

Invitations

Receive the personal help and attention to detail that is so very necessary in ordering your printed stationery. The first that your guests will see of your style and taste.

Disc Jockey Service

Need a great DJ? Our goal is to provide a smooth flowing event where everyone has a good time! You will be amazed and excited to see how special your event can be.

Tuxedos

Excellent service combined with genuine joy for your event is the reason men of distinction rent their formal attire at the Alameda Bridal Faire.

Custom Cakes and Catering

Food your guests will be talking about for many years to come and dream wedding cakes delivered with pride and perfection.

To add to your shopping enjoyment,
we feature a full-service espresso bar and deli.

Magical Creations Boutique, Inc.

Serving Exclusively Size 14-7x

4240 N.E. Sandy Blvd.
Portland, Oregon 97213
(503) 288-5450
Business Hours Mon–Fri 10am–7pm,
Sat 10am–6pm Sun Noon–5pm
E-mail: MCBI1@aol.com

Location

Located in the heart of the historic Hollywood District, only 10 minutes east of downtown Portland and 15 minutes from Vancouver.

Premier Plus-Size Shop

As the premier plus size shop in the greater Portland area, we at Magical Creations Boutique have dressed many attendants, rubenesque mothers of the bride and groom, as well as brides who seek the one-of-a-kind or non-traditional look for their special wedding.

We serve exclusively size 14W–7X and provide a warm, supportive environment with comfortable, spacious fitting rooms, each equipped with a fan.

Styles and Price Range

In addition to formal wear, we carry lingerie, jewelry, accessories, active wear, natural fiber casual clothes and ethnic garments for all activities associated with the wedding. A wide variety of designs are featured, representing creations from small local designers to nationally known manufacturers, with prices ranging from $65–$325.

Catering to Your Individual Needs

Each of our customers are special to us. We are dedicated to providing individualized customer service to ensure a satisfying shopping experience. Allow us to assist you with your fashion needs and eliminate some of the special occasion stress!

We believe that Magical Creations Boutique creates an environment for plus size goddesses...where magic truly happens.

HELPFUL HINTS

- **Selecting your bridal gown:** Take the time to try on the various styles available at different shops. Most importantly, pick the dress you feel the best and most comfortable in. Many people will try to influence your preference one way or another. Just remember you're the one wearing it and your fiancé is the one you're wearing it for! **NOTE:** Allow at least six months to order your wedding gown.
- **Bridesmaid dresses:** There are several factors to keep in mind when selecting bridesmaid dresses. Colors and fabrics vary with the seasons. The style usually complements the bridal gown. The formality is based on whether it is a daytime or evening wedding. Choose a dress color and style that will be flattering on all the bridesmaids, and keep in mind that the main focus will be on the backs of the dresses during the ceremony.
- **Formal and evening attire:** Many bridal shops carry a nice selection of formal and evening gowns for special occasions and pageants. Bridal salons may carry one-of-a-kind gowns or a limited selection.
- **Guideline for lengths:** The bridesmaid dresses should never be longer than the bride's gown. The mother's dresses should never be longer than the bridesmaid dresses.
- **Headpieces and veils:** Pick a headpiece that enhances your face and hairstyle; it should complement, not overwhelm. If you attempt to press your own veil, be extremely careful. Press the veil between white tissue. Do not put an iron directly on the veiling. Ask about care when you buy the veil.
- **Accessories:** Most bridal shops carry a nice selection of bridal accessories, including garters, slips, gloves, jewelry, shoes, albums and guest books.
- **Looking good all day long:** You may want to consider the fabric for your dress more closely, depending on how long you will be in the dress. There is no way to avoid wrinkling a dress once it is put on; however certain fabrics wrinkle more easily. Here are a few ways to preserve your dress: Get dressed at the ceremony site, eliminate traveling in dress before ceremony, bring a stool to the ceremony site for sitting on, and make sure there is an aisle runner if you have a long train. Detachable trains and veils make it easier to travel about and dance at the reception. Just remember, this is a day to enjoy, don't worry if your dress is tattered and stained at the reception; with a cleaning and preservation service most stains and problems can be fixed.
- **Picking up your dress:** It might be smart to leave the dress at the bridal shop even if the dress is ready in far in advance of the wedding day. The bridal shop may be better equipped to store and keep the dress fresh and pressed.
- **IMPORTANT NOTE:** The following recommendations are for your protection: 1) be careful about where you buy your wedding dress. Ask your friends and family about where they went and what their experiences were; 2) make sure the delivery date of your dress is well in advance of your wedding; 3) get a copy of the order or receipt with a guarantee of delivery date to keep with your wedding records; 4) if a contract is used, **read it carefully** (even the fine print) before signing! If you have any questions or concerns about the company, check it out with organizations that keep track of the reputations of companies.

AniA Bridal Collection

419 S.W. Fourth Avenue
Portland, Oregon 97204
(503) 796-9170; Fax (503) 796-0008
Business Hours: Mon–Fri 11am–6pm
Sat 10am–6pm

AniA Bridal Collection is located in the heart of downtown Portland. We offer the largest selection of designer's gowns. Our sales team is totally committed to excellent customer service and has extensive knowledge on every bridal gown we carry. Some of the designers we carry are:

Anu Pam
Bolo Vasquez
Couture by Judd Wadell
Diamond Collection
Janell Berte
Jim Hjelm
Jasmine
Lezu Atelier
Manale
Maggie Sottero
Mia Callaway
Monique L'hullier
Mika Inatome
Pronovias
Ramona Keveza
Stephen Yearicks
Tomasina
Vera Wang
Watters & Watters
Youlin
And Many Others

Please call us for your personal appointment.

 Please let this business know that you heard about them from the Bravo! Bridal Resource Guide.

BELLE AND BOW TIE TUX

Bridal and Formal Wear

Northeast
4300 N.E. Hancock
(at 43rd & Sandy)
(503) 284-5969
Mon–Sat 9am–7pm

Eastside
Ross Center
11211 S.E. 82nd Ave.
(503) 652-7076
Mon–Sat 10am–7pm

Styles and Selections of Wedding Gowns

Over 60 gowns to select from in each store. We feature Alfred Angelo Dreammaker gowns.

Description of Wedding Gowns and Ordering

- **Colors:** white and eggshell
- **Fabrics:** satin, lace, taffeta and peau de soie
- **Styles:** chapel length, sweep train, street length, sheath, off the shoulder and more
- **Sizes:** 4 to 44 are carried in the store
- **Price range:** $350 to $1,500

It usually takes from three to six months to order your gown. A 50% down payment is needed upon ordering; deposits are nonrefundable.

Service

Alterations are done at our Northeast store. And for a $60 charge, you can bring your gown back for preserving and boxing.

Headpieces

Wreaths, face framers, hats and crowns are just some styles available at two of our three locations. **Price range:** $120 to $220.

Bridal Attendant Attire

Alfred Angelo bridesmaid dresses, sizes 4 to 44. **Price range:** $180 to $300. Alfred Angelo junior bridesmaid and flower girl dresses in sizes 3 to 12. **Price range:** $120 to $200.

Accessories

Bridal and bridesmaid gloves, jewelry and rental slips.

WEDDING GOWNS TO FORMAL WEAR

Two convenient locations in the Portland area, where we help with your bridal-attire needs from wedding gowns to formal wear. Come visit us today and see the number of ways Belle & Bow Tie can make your wedding day easier.

See page 263 under Tuxedos & Formal Wear.

THE BRIDAL ARTS BUILDING

10017 N.E. 6th Avenue
Vancouver, WA 98685
(360) 574-7758
Business Hours: Mon–Sat 10am–6pm;
open late Thursday night until 8pm;
Sun noon–5pm; closed most holidays

Styles and Selections of Wedding Gowns

Come visit and experience our truly elegant and complete Bridal Salon. We offer nationally advertised designer gowns at affordable prices. Select from over 300 gowns in stock. Bridal Arts also offers a beautiful line of rental wedding gowns and slips.

Ordering Your Gown

Allow three months after your gown has been ordered for delivery. A 50% deposit is required when you place your order, with monthly payments on balance available. Ask about our layaway plan. Rush orders are welcome.

Description of Wedding Gowns

- **Colors:** white, ivory, blush, pink and rum
- **Fabrics:** satin, taffeta, silk, lace, peau de soie and tulle
- **Styles:** cathedral, chapel length, sweep train, floor length, and street length
- **Sizes:** 3 to 44
- **Price range:** from under $300 to $2,000

Service

Because you are so special to us, we pay the sales tax for Washington buyers. We also include a garment bag to protect your gown, can store your gown until your wedding, and professionally steam your gown, so it's perfect for your wedding. We will match any other store's prices and services.

Headpieces

We offer a large selection of premade headpieces and veils, or can custom design one to your specifications. **Price range:** starting from $60.

Bridal Attendant and Mothers of the Bride Attire

We feature nationally advertised designer bridesmaid gowns in all the popular styles, fabrics, and colors. A 50% deposit is required for special orders. **Sizes:** 4 to 44. We cater to mothers for informal to formal attire for weddings. **Sizes:** 4 to 24. Also be sure to see our complete line of holiday and cruise attire.

Tuxedos

We carry the complete line of Black Tie Tuxedos. The finest quality at the best price...that's "Black Tie."

 Please let this business know that you heard about them from the Bravo! Bridal Resource Guide.

Exquisite Wedding Cakes

Our cakes are scrumptious. Always baked fresh—never frozen, and custom decorated to your specifications. $1.75 per serving for most flavors. Fresh-flower decor and fountain setups are available. We deliver and set up (fee depending on distance).

Bridal Arts Florist

Our florists truly specialize in gorgeous wedding arrangements at affordable prices. We will even meet with you at your church to design your flowers to your needs. Always a free toss bouquet with your order. We are "the" experts in this field. We have done hundreds of weddings—each one very unique and special.

Special Bonus

When you order both your cakc and flowers from us, we will waive the delivery and setup fee and include a fountain setup under the cake at no extra charge.

FULL-SERVICE WEDDING FACILITY

The Hostess House and Bridal Arts Building is the first full-service wedding facility in the Northwest. We have everything for your wedding, including a candle-lit chapel that seats 200 guests and an absolutely gorgeous reception center; wedding attire for the entire wedding party; dyed-to-match shoes; jewelry, gloves, and slips; invitations and imprinted napkins; party supplies and decorations; custom-designed cake tops and unity candles; gift shop and bridal registry; DJ services, musicians, and vocalists. Other services include catering, photography and video services, plus much more.

Directions: located 10 minutes north of Portland. From I-5 north or south, take the 99th Street exit (#5) and go west two blocks, turn right onto Sixth Avenue.

See page 154 under Banquet & Reception Sites.

BRIDAL, ETC.

2259 N.W. Ninth Street
Corvallis, Oregon 97330
(541) 754-7729
Business Hours:
Mon–Fri 10am-6pm; Sat 10am-5pm
After hours available by appointment

Let us help you find the gown of your dreams! The tradition of selecting your gown can sometimes be stressful. At Bridal, Etc. we like to make it an enjoyable experience. We have friendly consultants to help you with your selection. We even invite you to bring your camera and take pictures of the entire experience. Our five-way floor-to-ceiling mirror makes it easy for you to get the full effect of your selections.

Styles and Selection

Bridal Etc. has a selection of over 150 of the newest styles in sizes 6 through women's size 22. Our styles vary from the informal, the simple elegant to the traditional, in a price range of $200 to $1000. Our gowns are made from such fabrics as silk, Italian matte satin, shantung, tulle, organza, crepe and lace. We can special order your gown or you may purchase off the rack at a discount. In addition to our gowns, we carry over 75 veils in stock and also offer custom veil designs.

We provide a wonderful selection of bridesmaid dresses in a variety of styles, sizes and colors. Many of our bridesmaid dresses can be worn and enjoyed again and again. Our bridesmaid dresses range in price from $100 to $199. We also offer flower girl and mother of the bride dresses. In addition to our selection of dresses, we can offer the finishing touches including shoes dyed to match, jewelry, garters and invitations.

Making the Experience Fun

We make the selection of your wedding attire fun. We have trained consultants to meet each bride's needs. We are continuously receiving new stock and styles for the best selection. Layaway is available.

We are a member of the Better Business Bureau.

Bridal, Etc. has the selection that you want and the service you deserve! Come visit us soon.

Bridal Showcase

I-5 to Exit #9, next to Clark Co. Fairgrounds
Vancouver, Washington
Contact: Donna or Dorothy
(360) 573-2817 or (503) 289-6324
Business Hours: Tues–Fri 10am–6pm; Sat 9am–5pm

Styles and Selections of Wedding Gowns
Bridal Showcase carries gowns from 27 manufacturers. This special collection has been carefully selected for today's bride.

Ordering your Gown
It takes an average of four months to order your gown. A 50% deposit is required. Charges for cancellations of special orders are assessed.

Description of Wedding Gowns
All colors, fabrics, and styles. **Sizes:** 4 to 30, larger sizes upon request. **Price range:** $200 to $1,300.

Service
We have in-house alterations for your convenience. Charges for alterations will vary depending on what needs to be done. Complimentary steaming of gowns is included.

Bridal Attendant Attire
Dresses from sizes 4 to 24. **Price range:** $95 to $200.

Dresses for Mothers of the Bride and Groom
Moms can choose from a large selection of dresses in a variety of colors, styles, and fabrics in sizes 4 to 26. We also carry a large selection of petites. **Price range:** $70 to $350.

Accessories
- Headpieces
- Shoes
- Undergarments

Silk Beaded Gowns
We have a wide range of silk beaded gowns that are perfect for cruises, fund raisers, pageants, or any formal event.

FINEST MERCHANDISE AND CONSULTANTS
Our business truly serves the community from Salem to Seattle with the finest merchandise and consultants trained to meet each individual's personal needs. We're just 10 minutes from Portland, conveniently located next to the Clark County Fairgrounds. Take I-5 or 205, exit #9.

♥ *Member of Weddings of Distinction*

See page 253 under Dress Design, Alterations & Custom Veils.

Bride's World, USA & Ambrosia Catering

17943 S.W. Tualatin-Valley Highway
Aloha, Oregon
(503) 649-9583; Fax (503) 649-2399
Mon, Wed, Fri, Sat 11am–6pm;
Tues, Thurs 11am–8pm; Sun 11am–4pm
Web sites: www.BridesworldUSA.com; www.BridesworldUSA.net

Styles and Selections of Wedding Gowns

Bride's World USA offers hundreds of wedding gowns in stock for purchase. We feature gowns from many manufacturers, including beautiful gowns from tea-length informals to the traditional cathedral-length gown shimmering with thousands of beads and sequins. Special orders taken gladly.

Alterations Service

In-house alterations for your convenience. Charges for alteration will vary depending on work to be done.

Accessories

We have a complete line of bridal and bridesmaid shoes, bras, slips, gloves and jewelry. We also carry a wide range of ring bearer pillows, invitations, goblets, knives, and bridesmaid gifts. In addition, we carry the latest tuxedo fashions.

Description of Wedding Gowns and Ordering

- **Colors:** white, ivory, eggshell, pink, rum
- **Fabrics:** satin, taffeta, silk, shantung and more
- **Styles:** cathedral, chapel length, sweep trains and tea length; necklines include Queen Anne, V-neck, bateau, Sabrina and off the shoulder
- **Sizes:** 4 to 44
- **Price range:** $110 to $2,000

Special orders generally require two to four months to arrive. If your wedding is only a few weeks away, we're happy to call the manufacturer to see if they have the gown in stock, so we can get it in seven to ten days. A 50% nonrefundable deposit is required.

Ambrosia Creative Catering Cost and Services

Ambrosia Creative Catering offers a full line of catering services that are tailored to your needs. Choose from complete event packages (including crystal plates, linens and more) or let us design a package especially for you. Prices start as low as $9.95 per person for a full-service buffet, complete with wedding cake. Our staff provides complete setup and cleanup for your event. A deposit is required to secure your event date. A 15% gratuity will be added to the final bill. We provide a fully-licensed kitchen where your food is professionally handled and prepared.

Our Promise to You…

We promise to create an exquisitely designed occasion for you and your guests, with your budget in mind.. Ask to see our full-color portfolio and reference list.

We Do the Work…You Don't Worry

We take pride in helping you plan and design your special occasion.

ONE STOP CAN FULFILL ALL YOUR WEDDING NEEDS!

Charlotte's
WEDDINGS & MORE

8925 S.W. Beaverton-Hillsdale Hwy
Portland, Oregon 97225
(503) 297-9622; Fax (503) 297-9061
call for your personal appointment
Business Hours:
Mon–Fri 11am–8pm; Sat 10am–5pm

We are the "Dream Makers"

In our fairytale setting, a tradition carried on by Charlotte's Weddings, we help make your dream come true. We currently have over 500 gowns in stock that can be purchased off the rack or special ordered. Sizes: 4-48. Prices range from $150 to $2,500. Choose from famous designer gowns or from our "simply elegant" gowns at prices you can afford. You will find splendid attire for every member of your bridal party, from the maid of honor to the littlest flower girl, and styles that are appropriate for mothers and guests too. Not to forget the groom and his attendants, we will fit them in fabulous tuxedos in the most famous styles offered today.

Wedding specialties and services

- Professional bridal consultant who will give the personal attention you deserve; no waiting; private rooms with ceiling to floor mirrors in every room
- Elegant designer wedding gowns
- Large selection of informal dresses for garden weddings and other informal settings
- For the budget-oriented bride we have a budget room with prices under $500
- Discounts on bridesmaid dresses, invitations, tuxedos, and more with the purchase of a wedding gown
- Rentals of beautiful bridal gowns, which include a slip and minor alterations
- Wide selection of veils, hats, and headpieces (designer or custom)
- Wonderful selection of accessories—shoes, jewelry, hosiery, gloves, bras, garters, and bustiers
- Guest books, pens, cake tops, cake knifes and servers, and much more
- Professional seamstress who will work with you by appointment

INDIVIDUAL ATTENTION

At Charlotte's Weddings, everything is made so easy. You will have so much fun that you will not believe it until you experience it for yourself. Call and schedule an appointment, so that we can give you the professional assistance and attention you deserve.

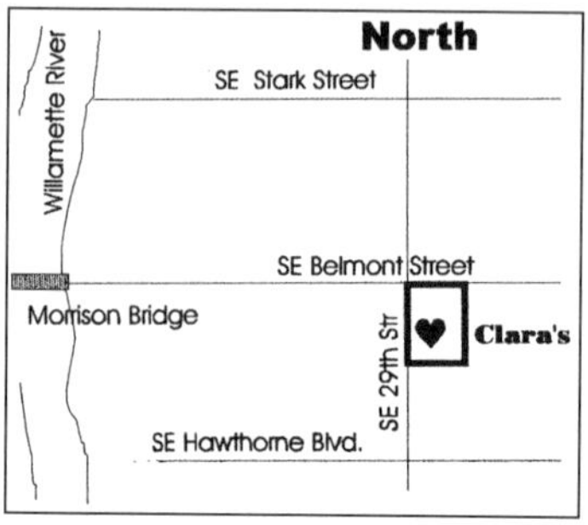

Clara's Wedding Establishment Ltd.

916 S.E. 29th • Portland, Oregon 97214
(at the corner of 29th and S.E. Belmont Street)
(503) 234-3484; Fax (503) 234-0404
Business hours: Mon–Fri 11am–8pm; Sat 10am–6pm
E-mail: claraswe@sprynet.com
Web site: portlandbridalshow.com/claras weddingest

EVERY BRIDE DESERVES A GUARDIAN ANGEL!

Clara's Wedding Establishment Ltd. is Portland's unique bridal shop. At Clara's, we take all of the stress out of planning your wedding.

Wedding Specialties and Services

- ♥ **Wedding gowns :** Clara's carries a wide range of the latest styles in veils and beautiful wedding gowns in sizes 4-48. We also custom-design and make gowns, veils, bridesmaid and flower-girl dresses. And when you purchase a bridal gown from Clara's, you receive a **free hour of limousine service** from Clara's Limousine Service.
- ♥ **On-site coordination:** Clara's offers on-site coordination to make your wedding day stress-free. We offer a five-hour package including rehearsal, ceremony and reception. And, you receive a **free hour of limousine service** from Clara's Limousine Service.
- ♥ **Free vendor coordination:** Clara's is truly the one place to come to plan your wedding. We offer wedding planning and vendor coordination at no cost to you. From start to finish, you can plan your entire wedding without leaving Clara's comfortable surroundings.
- ♥ **Accessories:** We have it all! Goblets, cake tops, guest books, pens, wedding-party gifts, ring pillows, and much more.
- ♥ **Limousine service:** White stretch limousines attended by well groomed, courteous, professional drivers. No minimum hours for weddings.
- ♥ **DJ Service:** Clara's own Ultimate Entertainment offers complete music for your ceremony and reception. Packages include music, lighting, bubble machine.

Visit our shop soon to learn more about our unique services. Brides are always encouraged to drop by Clara's at any time to relax with a cup of tea. Let us handle all of the details while you concentrate on making your dreams come true. We look forward to seeing you soon.

"LET CLARA'S BE YOUR GUARDIAN ANGEL!"

See page 453 under Disc Jockeys.
See page 542 under Transportation.

Divine Designs

437 N.W. 23rd
Portland, Oregon 97210
(503) 827-0667; Fax (503) 827-0668
Business Hours: Mon–Tues 10am–6pm;
Wed–Thurs 11am–8pm; Fri–Sat 10am–6pm;
October – May: Sundays 12:30–4pm;
Appointments required

Gown pictured by LAZARO

Divine Designs—the Showroom Collection with Style, Simplicity, and One-of-a-Kind Lines:

- Allin rae
- Amsale
- Bianchi
- Carmi
- Christo's
- Diamond
- Demetrios
- Galina
- Givenchy
- Janell Berte
- Jessica McClintock
- Jim Hjelm
- Jasmine
- Lezu Atelier
- Lazaro
- Monique L'Huillier
- Nancy Issler
- Nicole Miller
- Odessa
- Pricilla
- Reem
- Regalia
- Robert Legere
- Stephanie's
- Siri
- Vera Wang Gowns
- Watters & Watters
- And many more!

For more information call

Divine Designs (503) 827-0667

Custom Designs Offered.

Divine Designs will not be undersold.

Elegant Moments Bridal

Oregon City Shopping Center
1900 S.E. McLoughlin Boulevard
Oregon City, Oregon 97045
(Off I-205, Oregon City exit #9)
(503) 650-GOWN
Web site: www.elegantmoments.com

One of the Largest Bridal Salons in the Northwest

Premier Bridal Salon

Elegant Moments Bridal is true to its name. An atmosphere of elegance is only one part of the difference you can enjoy while selecting your wedding gown. With comfort in mind, the large fitting areas are perfect for a single bride or large groups. From our spacious dressing rooms and exquisite fitting areas, friends and family can relax in comfort and elegance. Selection, comfort, personal attention, and our commitment to service are only some of the reasons to visit us.

Newest Bridal Fashions

Our store is filled with the newest styles from many of today's top designers. We carry a wide selection of styles ranging from informal to formal, halter tops to long sleeves, and traditional to modern. We also provide a very complete assortment of bridesmaids, mother-of-the-bride, flowergirls and special occasion dresses.

Veils, Shoes, Jewelry, Gloves, Garters, and More

We have an extensive selection of veils, custom veils, bridal shoes, dyeable shoes, gloves and bridal accessories to put the finishing touches on your special day. Our knowledgeable bridal consultants will help you make your wedding day perfect. Our assortment of ring bearer pillows, garters, gloves, guest books and pens, unity candles, cake knife sets, toasting goblets, and attendant gifts make a visit well worth it.

Full-service Bridal

Come and experience the best full-service salon in the Northwest. Bridal consultants help you to find your fashion style and locate your ultimate wedding dress. We are here to serve our customers and we will always take the extra time you need to give you the service you deserve. Each gown is always hand-pressed and ready to walk down the aisle. Alterations are available by our on-site seamstress. Appointments are never needed.

WE LOVE WHAT WE DO FOR YOU... AND IT SHOWS

Come to Elegant Moments Bridal for the most important dress decision of your life and experience our commitment to giving you the personal attention that you deserve. Our bridal consultants are here to help you in all aspects of finding your perfect gown, wedding party attire, or just putting the finishing touches together for your special day. We truly love what we do for you and it shows.

Elsie's
VICTORIAN BRIDAL

739 S.W. Evans Street
Portland, Oregon 97219
Contact: Elsie E. Bartling
(503) 244-4098
Business Hours: Mon–Sat;
call for appointment

One-of-a-Kind Period Gowns
Elsie's Victorian Bridal designs one-of-a-kind period gowns from the early 1800s through the 1970s. "I specialize in natural-fiber fabrics and antique laces, hand crochet, and embroidery." Everything is custom made; nothing is manufactured. Select from over 60 dresses in stock or have a custom design made especially for you.

Ordering your Gown
Choose a dress available in the shop, or allow one month for the gown design you select to be made. A 50% deposit is required. Since each gown is custom designed, there are no refunds or exchanges.

Description of Wedding Gowns
- **Colors:** white, ivory, eggshell, pink, blue, lavender or rose
- **Fabrics:** silk, satin, lace, linen, cotton or net
- **Styles:** chapel length, sweep train, floor length or tea length
- **Sizes:** 6 to 20 (also custom orders)
- **Price range:** $295 to $1,995

Restoration of Antique and Vintage Gowns
In addition to custom designing wedding gowns, Elsie can restore antique or vintage gowns your mother or grandmother may have worn. All alterations to reconstruct and fit the gown to your specifications are done with expert handwork. Elsie's provides consultation on Old World customs and offers an ideal Victorian setting for wedding portraits.

Bridal Attendant Attire, Headpieces, Mothers' Gowns, and Parasols
Custom-order bridesmaid dresses in all sizes. **Price:** $250. Junior bridesmaid and flower-girl dresses by custom order. **Price:** $195. One-of-a-kind, custom-order dresses in all sizes. **Price:** $295 to $695. Victorian-style hats, antique headpieces, garlands, and headpieces of handmade silk roses to complement your dress are on hand or can be custom made. **Price range:** $225.

CREATING FAMILY HEIRLOOMS
For over 27 years, Elsie's Victorian Bridal has been designing for the bride who wants that nostalgic touch of "something old"—something unique and reminiscent of days gone by. Each one-of-a-kind gown is designed and made by Elsie with exquisite embellishments of handmade antique imported lace, hand embroidery, and French hand sewing, making it a timeless creation that will become a family heirloom to be treasured for years to come.

Fashion Expressions®

WEDDING AND FORMAL WORLD

130 S.W. Ellsworth
Albany, Oregon 97321
Contact: Joyce and Jim Nesmith
(541) 928-3617, (800) 336-3617
Mon–Sat 10am–5:30pm

© Gregory Dean Photography

Our Wedding Gowns

The impeccable good taste exudes quiet, discreet confidence and assures you a feeling of extravagant, timeless elegance. Whether you want a gown for a garden wedding or a traditional, formal gown for a church wedding, you can find over 125 different gowns from many major manufacturers. The gown of your dreams can be found at our store. We carry basque, A-lines and empire waistlines in satin, chiffon, crepe or organza fabrics. Gown styles are available in tank top, short sleeve and long sleeve with or without trains. Brides throughout the Northwest wear our gowns. Gowns are available in sizes 2 to 44, in white, ivory, rum pink and cafe.

Our Store

Located in historic downtown Albany, our bridal department is large, well lit and always has trained bridal consultants to help you select and try on gowns. Wedding planning ideas are shared with the bride and her mother to make it easier to develop their ideas into a workable plan. Weddings are a tradition at Fashion Expressions—celebrating 14 years of serving Oregon brides and grooms. We offer experience, uncompromising service and a strong loyalty to customers. A beautiful sign of the shape of things to come is evident in this season's fashions available at Fashion Expressions.

Headpieces

The crowning touch to your wedding look is your headpiece and veil. Many major veil designs are available. We also custom design veils for our brides.

Bridemaids, Flowergirl, Mothers

With over 60 bridesmaids dresses in store, plus hundreds more available in catalogs to select from, we can help you select the right dress to complement your wedding gown. It is the bridesmaids that add the background color for the bride. We will be carrying a new line of mothers dresses for spring and summer.

Tuxedos

The tuxedo selection at Fashion Expressions has over 70 tuxedos to choose from. Each groom can make a choice, from the collarless shirt to the classic black notch tuxedo, that will make his wedding outstanding. Groomsmen can wear a vest color to coordinate with the bridesmaids dress. Tuxedos are available in sizes 4 to 70.

Unique Business

For the rest of our lives we'll remember where we were and what we were doing as the 20th century passed into history. We want those memories to be good. A bride receives special attention at Fashion Expressions. The selection, personal attention, trained consultants and our desire to help you get the wedding of your dreams makes our store a very special place to shop.

For all your wedding and formal wear needs
A store with a good reputation and years of experience.

HERE WE GO AGAIN

9519 S.W. Barbur Blvd.
Portland, Oregon 97219
Contact: Chris Gauger (503) 244-0855
Business Hours: Mon–Sat 10am–6pm;
Thurs 10am–8pm; Sun noon–4pm
E-mail: hwga@europa.com
Web site: http://www.hwga.com

Congratulations on your upcoming wedding! This should be an exciting, fun time for you, planning your celebration. At Here We Go Again, we wish you much joy, happiness and the perfect wedding. We'd love to help!

Gorgeous Gowns!

Although our selection changes constantly, we get designer gowns such as Demetrios, House of Bianchi, Venus, Moonlight, Scaasi, Diamond Collection, Alfred Angelo, Jessica McClintock, Mori Lee and many others. Occasionally we have European designers as well. Our gowns come from a variety of sources. Most are consigned by women like you who, for whatever reason, don't wish to keep their gowns. Others come from bridal boutiques as overstock or floor samples. Still others come direct from manufacturers as overcuts or closeouts to supplement our stock and complete our size selection. We also feature a line of very reasonably priced, high-quality new gowns, which can be ordered in just your size.

Great Value

Don't think for a moment we accept just any gown for consignment! We carefully screen all gowns, accepting only current styles that are cleaned and in perfect condition. We know you don't have time to sort through a bunch of out-of-date dresses to find the few gems. We inspect each gown to ensure quality and often send them to be cleaned a second time if they don't meet our standards. We're as picky as you are!

Impeccable Service

Shopping for a gown should be a fun experience. You don't have to spend a fortune to be treated like someone special—we love helping you! Regardless of your budget or size, we want to help you find the perfect gown. At Here We Go Again, you'll find unexpected extras: expert in-house alterations, convenient 7-day-a-week hours, layaway and flexible payment options, and noncommission sales people who really care—not about making the sale but about helping you find what you want.

Wish List Service

Since our stock changes rapidly, we might not have your gown today. We understand you're busy and can't come in every week to check. Give us an idea of the styles you like and your budget, and we'll review incoming gowns for a match. If the right gown comes in, we'll call you! This simple service can save you time—and might get you the perfect gown.

Check us out on-line at http://www.hwga.com!

Jennifer's Creations

"Designing one-of-a-kind Bridal Gowns"

Located in Vancouver, Washington
Contact: Jennifer (360) 573-2933

"Design the Gown of Your Dreams"

Jennifer's Creations specializes in designing and creating the gown of your dreams! At your personal consultation, your ideas will be given "special attention" as you choose the details of your gown. Size is no problem as your gown will be custom fit to your individual body. A deposit of 50% is required to begin your gown, with the balance due upon completion.

Discount Bridal Service

As an authorized representative for "Discount Bridal Service Inc.®," Jennifer's Creations can help you to save hundreds of dollars on the gown of your dreams! Discount Bridal Service is the original "Personal Buying Service for Brides," enabling brides to save 20%-40% off the suggested retail prices of first quality wedding gowns, bridesmaids and more. Just provide the page number and issue date from a bridal magazine or the manufacturer's name. We will verify the style and give you our price. Gowns are paid in full at the time of order and will be shipped directly to you.

Alterations and Beadwork

Jennifer's has over 15 years experience in bridal gown design and alterations. She is also known for her "exquisite beadwork" and specializes in turning ordinary gowns into works of art!

Other Services

- Headpieces/veils: average cost $95-$125
- Invitations: 25% off retail prices
- Accessories: jewelry, gloves, bridal slips, guest books, pens and more!

Jennifer's Creations is committed to personal "one-on-one" attention.
Please call for your personal appointment!
Check us out online at http://members.aol.com/jcbridal/

Lelite Bridal Boutique
and
ANNA'S DESIGNER FABRICS

3970 S.W. Mercantile Drive, Suite 150
Lake Oswego, Oregon 97035
Contact: Anna Totonchy (503) 636-1474

Styles and Selections of Wedding Gowns
Lelite Bridal Boutique features elegant European gowns and accessories. Lelite is an exclusive Northwest importer from all over the world, as well as having dresses in stock and ready for order. Some of their exclusive gowns are:

- Harve from France
- Carolina Herrera
- Camela Sutera
- Alfred Angelo
- Dessy
- Melissa Sweet
- Currie Bonner

Dress Design and Alteration Services
If you cannot find the dress of your dreams, Anna and her staff of seamstresses will create any design the bride desires. For six years Anna's Designer Fabrics has offered only the finest in fabrics that are unique and different and from all over the world—France, Italy, England and India, as well as the United States.

Bridesmaid and Mother's Dresses
Our specialty is working with the bride on all the wedding attire, the gown, the bridesmaid's dresses and the Mother's dresses. Custom-design with brocades, satin, intricate hand beading and tulle. The fabric selection, alterations and measurements, and design all takes place in the shop.

Headpieces and Veils
The Boutique offers exquisite headpieces and veils; some of them feature real pearls, which the bride can have made into a necklace after the wedding. Extra fabric from dress alterations can create an incredible headpiece or headband to complement the wedding gown.

Lelite Will Take Care of All the Details
Anna will almost walk down the aisle with you, making sure your gown, bridesmaid dresses and mother's dresses are perfect. The secret to a beautiful gown is the fitting—even the most expensive dress will not look good without proper fittings and alterations. Anna and her staff will not allow a gown to leave the shop without all the proper steps that go along with making it look perfect.

When you
Dream of the perfect dress...

Rosewood Bridal

we can make it happen.

11545 S.W. Durham Road
Tigard, Oregon 97224
Contact: Gail Herschbach (503) 603-0363
Business Hours: Mon–Tues 11am–7pm; Wed–Fri 11am–5:30pm; Sat 10am–5pm
Web site: www.rosewoodbridal.citysearch.com

ROSEWOOD BRIDAL ESTABLISHED ELEGANCE

Magnificent Selection of Wedding Gowns

Whether you're looking for sophisticated silk, an elaborate organza or a simple design, Rosewood Bridal has many styles, fabrics and colors from which to choose. Rosewood Bridal features gowns from Mon Cheri, Eden, Mori Lee, Maggie Sottero, and many more of the top designers.

Special Services

We provide services including alterations for the bride and custom shoe dyeing. All fittings are done at Rosewood Bridal. Your gown can be stored at the shop until your wedding day, free of charge.

Bridal Attendant Attire

Rosewood offers a sophisticated line of bridesmaids' dresses from the most popular designers with a wide variety of styles, colors and sizes available through special order. You will also find a large selection of flower girl dresses in Cinderella styles of silk and satin. Not to leave out the groom, Rosewood Bridal carries an entire line of tuxedos for rent.

Accessories

Rosewood Bridal carries a variety of accessories that you'll need for the finishing touch, including shoes, gloves, headpieces and jewelry. And for last-minute items, look no further. You'll find everything from wedding books, pens, ring pillows, goblets and cake cutters.

Genuine Pampering and Nurturing

Rosewood Bridal never pressures a client or pushes for a sale. The Rosewood associates work as a team to meet each bride's needs. There's no sales commission, no competition to force a sale—just true care and concern shown through personal attention. "It's a tradition a bride shares with her mom and closest friends…we do everything we can to enhance that experience," says Gail Herschbach, owner.

When to Visit Us

Rosewood Bridal will help you find the perfect dress in time for your wedding. Although we recommend visiting the shop at least six months before your wedding. Rosewood Bridal can often rush an order or fit a bride at the last minute with a gown off the rack.

WEDDING Touch of Silk GALLERY

1515 Broadway • Vancouver, Washington 98663
(360) 695-6000; Fax (360) 695-2008
E-mail: touchofsilk@mindspring.com
Web site: www.touchofsilk.citysearch.com

A Wedding to Remember

There is no moment more anticipated than the one when you first appear in the doorway at the beginning of your ceremony. That one single instant of elegant perfection when the whole room sighs and your groom finds tears in his eyes. Let the caring staff at Touch of Silk help you to create this once in a lifetime experience.

Why Trust Touch of Silk?

Touch of Silk Wedding Gallery has been serving happy brides since 1979. There is no substitute for exceptional service and over 20 years experience in the bridal industry.

What You'll Find at Touch of Silk

- A large selection of dresses (over 300) in stock
- Everything to dress your bridesmaids, mothers, and flower girls
- Veils, gloves, shoes, jewelry, slips and more
- A full-service tuxedo shop
- On-site professional alterations
- Wedding Accessories: guest books, candles, pillows, toasting glasses and much more
- Invitations
- Wedding Rentals: candelabras, topiaries, floral baskets and more
- A full-service florist

Fabulous and Friendly

We're here to make your shopping experience a pleasant one. At Touch of Silk, our professional staff loves to assist brides with every wedding detail. We know what a stressful time this can be and are committed to providing whatever it takes to make you happy.

Helpful Hints

- The sooner you begin dress shopping, the better.
- Don't trust an internet company to provide you with a beautiful dress. Your worst nightmares can become reality, leaving you out of money and out of time.
- Listen to everyone's advice, smile appreciatively but make sure you are happy with the dress you choose.
- Have your dress altered professionally.
- Order your tuxedos at least two months prior to the wedding.
- Keep in mind that flowers add to the elegance of your wedding that is forever captured in your photographs.

Congratulations on your engagement from your friends at Touch of Silk

Tower BRIDAL

5331 S.W. Macadam Avenue
Portland, Oregon 97201
(503) 274-8940; Fax (503) 274-9843
Business Hours: Mon, Tue & Thu 10am–7pm; Wed 10am–8pm;
Fri 10am–9pm; Sat 10am–6pm; Sun noon–5pm

Congratulations on Your Coming Wedding

Your wedding day is one of the most unique and romantic days of your life. Planning your special day combines the talents of many people who wish to help make it the most memorable day for you to remember. Tower Bridal's friendly, well-trained consultants are dedicated to providing you and the members of your wedding party the best service available.

Wedding Gowns and Attendant Dresses

Our collection of gowns include romantic silk to traditional satin, crisp taffeta to floaty tulle. All are from designers you'll recognize from the pages of current Bridal Magazines: Priscilla of Boston, Galina, House of Bianchi, Jim Hjelm, Lila Broude, Alfred Sung and Alfred Angelo, to name a few. There are over 300 gowns to select from and they may be purchased from off the rack or you may special order to your specific size and color. Prices range from $150 to over $3,000.

Tower Bridal has a wide variety and selection of dresses that your attendants will enjoy wearing, available in all styles, fabrics and colors; from semi-formal to formal. Perfect complements to your gown and style. Flower girls and Mothers-of-the-Bride and Groom are not forgotten with a very special selection awaiting their choice.

Accessories

Veils, cathedral length or short and sassy; custom designed headpieces and tiaras from top designers; an excellent selection of shoes-all available in various fabrics and styles. We also offer lacy garters, lingerie, petticoats, ring bearer pillows, guest books and other select accessory items.

Special Service... with a smile

In-house alterations are available to give you that perfect fit with complimentary pressing to perfection, ready to go down the aisle. Charges for alterations will vary according to the work being done. Tuxedos, accessories and groomsmen gifts are available, the finest quality at the best price. Open 7 days a week with plenty of free parking.

We look forward to seeing you at Tower Bridal and we are committed to helping make your wedding day the happiest day in your life.

 Please let this business know that you heard about them from the Bravo! Bridal Resource Guide.

© Woodstock Photography • page 525

TRADITION

By the 14th century, the bride's garter became so highly valued that guests would rush the bride at the altar to gain the garter's possession.

•

Today, things have settled down considerably. Now the groom throws the bride's garter to the unmarried men at the reception.

HELPFUL HINTS

- **Dress design:** If you haven't found the dress of your dreams or if the dress you have in mind doesn't exist, take your ideas, pictures, and dreams to a dress designer. Designers offer a variety of options, taking a sleeve from one dress and a bodice from another to design a gown especially for you. Many expensive original designer dresses with designer prices can be copied, allowing you to stay within your budget.
- **Hemming:** Consult with a seamstress on hemming your dress. Many dresses can be lifted at the waistline to avoid taking lace off the entire hemline, and without distorting the lines and design of the dress. Also ask about ways to bustle up the train so it is comfortable and convenient for you to get around in at the reception.
- **Reserving alterations services:** As soon as you have selected your gown, be sure to make an appointment to reserve services for alterations. Many bridal-alterations specialists are booked months in advance. Your bridal shop can recommend a reliable seamstress or may have someone they work with. Brides should be prepared to pay for alterations and include this in their budget. They are never included in the price of the gown.
- **Making bridesmaid dresses:** You should buy the fabric all at once, even if each bridesmaid is paying for her own dress. Fabric comes in different dye lots and is difficult to match. Make sure that all the different fabrics you buy come from the same bolts to be sure everything matches. Remember to buy extra fabric, especially if you are working with delicate fabrics such as velvet or chiffon. This is not the time to come up short. Also, have the dresses made by the same seamstress to keep the dresses similar.

  NOTE: It's a good idea to make a demo dress in the style and fabric that you have selected, just to make sure you are getting what you want.
- **Length of bridesmaid dresses:** After you determine the length, hem all the dresses by measuring up from the floor. When marking the hemlines, be sure each bridesmaid is wearing the shoes she will be wearing for the wedding. This way, even though your bridesmaids are different heights, all the hemlines will align in the photographs.

For more assistance with staying organized during the wedding planning process, check out the Bravo! Wedding Organizer. Detailed question worksheets double as contracts. This step-by-step system will keep every detail of your wedding organized. To order, refer to the order form on page 24 in this Guide.

August Veils

Showroom located in:
AniA Bridal Collection
419 S.W. Fourth Avenue
Portland, Oregon 97204
(503) 788-5280; Fax (503) 788-5281
Web site: www.augustveils.com

Congratulations! In the near future you will be realizing one of life's most rewarding moments—your wedding. Rewarding? Yes! Stressful, most definitely! Here at August Veils we can appreciate the planning and endless attention to detail that contribute to a wedding. The kind of details that make your experience uniquely yours.

Experience and Attention to Detail

Our staff specializes in the kind of skills and experience to help you create the headpiece or veil that is just right for your occasion. Relax and let August Veils guide you through creative choices, playful suggestions, all guided by technical expertise that will help make your decisions a reality. Imagine creating an elegant headpiece embellished with Austrian crystals, pearls, and sequins. Working with your designer to incorporate lace from your gown, bringing together the past and present by adding memories from your mother's or grandmother's wedding dresses—the choices are only limited by your imagination.

Affordable Elegance

You'll be surprised at the affordability and luxury of your own custom design. All of our special attention and quality custom work does not take as much time as one might think. August Veils prides itself not only on its craftsmanship, but also in ensuring customers with prompt service. Quick turnarounds are no surprise to us!

Call today for more information on how you can begin your design experience, or visit our Web site for viewing and on-line ordering information.

"The veil is absolutely beautiful! It's so classy and I am glad that I found you guys!"

~ Adrienne Tourtelot

"You did a fantastic job and I am completely thrilled and pleased with it."

~ Heather Rainey

"You are so talented and I must thank you for being so wonderful to work with!"

~ Kathy Alvarez

fletcher artworks
ATELIER
and custom clothiers

1012 N.E. Birchwood Drive
Hillsboro, Oregon 97124
Business Hours: by appointment
Contact: Paula Smith-Danell
(503) 693-7725
Business Hours: by appointment

Services

We can help you create the dress of your dreams if you've been unable to find it or if you've found it but it is a costly haute couture original. If you have no idea what you want we can still help create a look for you that is unique.

We can create the perfect dress for you from just a drawing or one or more magazine cuttings; or you may want to peruse the vast fashion library for ideas, both contemporary or historical. If you are planning to wear your mother's or grandmother's dress but find you can't zip it up, we can alter or reconstruct the gown to fit you.

European Couture Experience

Paula has her bachelor's degree in Fashion Design from the American College for Applied Arts in London, England. She graduated summa cum laude and was awarded most outstanding graduate for her graduating class.

She has been in the fashion industry since 1984 and has been designing custom clothing and bridalwear since 1986. A portfolio is available for viewing by appointment, and references are available upon request.

Ordering your Dress

Please call for an appointment, and bring all your design ideas or plan to spend time looking through the many volumes of dress designs that Paula has spent years acquiring and cataloging. An estimate will be given at the time of the design selection, and a 50% deposit will be required when the dress is ordered. The balance will be due on receipt of the completed dress. Please plan on placing your order at least four months before your wedding date.

A series of measurements will be taken at our first meeting and will be turned into a flat pattern that will fit only you. It is helpful to bring the foundation garments that you are planning to wear as well as a shoe in the heel height that you are considering.

We will make a mock-up of your dress, so you can decide if this is the style you want. Any changes that you desire will happen at this point. Then it's on to the final fabric and final fitting, and you will have the dress of your dreams to wear on your special day.

Specializing in custom bridalwear
and women's tailored suits

Bridal Showcase

I-5 to Exit #9, next to Clark Co. Fairgrounds
Vancouver, Washington
(360) 573-2817 or (503) 289-6324
Business Hours: Tues–Sat; call for an appointment

Description of Service and Experience

Most manufactured gowns are made for women who are size 10 and 5’8” tall. Since most of us aren’t that size, it can be hard to find the perfect gown. Let Bridal Showcase fix it for you. From the simplest to the most difficult changes, our staff seamstress, Barbara Miller, can alter that dream gown to fit you perfectly. Custom-made gowns and complete makeovers of vintage gowns are also available. We begin with properly fitting bras to ensure a good fit, then design from a pattern, a sketch, or a picture of just an idea. We always make sure everything meets your specifications and tastes.

Our staff has years of experience in all areas of the bridal business. Our inventory of laces, appliqués, and trims makes selection easy. Come ask questions and look at our albums of previous projects and samples of our work. We gladly supply references.

Ordering and Cost

Most alterations take one week, but call for an appointment at least four to five weeks before your wedding. Custom-made and vintage-gown makeovers take 12 weeks, longer during the busy times of year. Each customer receives a firm bid in writing before any work is started.

♥ *Member of Weddings of Distinction*

Paper & Lace Studio

811 N.W. 20th Avenue, Suite 102-C • Portland, Oregon 97209
Contact: Constance Cooper (503) 417-8047
Business Hours: by appointment; days, evenings and weekends

Paper & Lace Studio was created by Constance for brides looking for tradition and value. *“Since I learned to sew at age ten, I have been using my faithful cast-iron machine.”*

Custom-Made Flower Girl Dresses

Save time shopping for that special little girl. Constance will design a beautiful dress just for her…made to fit and to coordinate with your wedding. Constance specializes in lace, ruffles and full petticoats. Your flower girl will be picture-perfect.

Vintage Bridal Gown Restyling

Constance will repair or completely remake your older gown. Family heirloom or an antique from a friend’s attic, she will carefully make it “new” again. Tip: Be sure to take “before” photos for keepsakes!

Fast and Fabulous Veils

No time to order your veil? Or have something in mind you can’t find in a shop? Constance will work with you to get the right look. Bring your headpiece—or help to design one.

Appointments and Ordering Are Easy

“Call for a consultation in my comfortable studio; sofa, coffee, private dressing alcove, and samples of my work! Ask about rush work…I’ll do my best to accommodate you.”

Starlight Gowns

Your Source for Custom Wedding Gowns

(503) 624-3737; Fax (503) 620-8728;
E-mail: ormike@aracnet.com
Business Hours: By Appointment Only

Close your eyes and dream of the perfect wedding gown---a gown that is breathtaking, allowing you to make your dream of that so special of occasions come true.

Services

We provide high quality, custom gowns at a surprisingly affordable price. Our gowns are handmade to your specifications. Each gown becomes a unique reflection of the woman who wears it. We can design a gown from a picture, or you can select gown types and fabric from our catalog. We will work with you to design an exceptional gown that is simply exquisite in appearance. Our combination of styling, quality materials, and detail in workmanship will make any off the rack dress pale in comparison. Rest assured you will have an affordable gown that captures your personality, a gown that fits you as only a custom dress can, and a gown that truly makes this extraordinary event magical.

Ordering and Cost

A down payment of 50% is required before the dress can be ordered. The balance will be due when we deliver your finished gown. We can recommend a number of experienced seamstresses for any needed alterations.

Notes

The Bride's Value

The bride's value was judged by

her beauty, ability to work, produce children,

and by the size of her dowry.

The more household goods, land,

and money the bride had in her dowry,

the higher esteem she was held in.

HELPFUL HINTS

- **Creating your own dress:** There are two reasons for creating your own dress: when you can't find exactly what you are looking for at a bridal shop (but know exactly what you want from pictures you may have seen), or if you want to save money by creating your wedding gown yourself or with the help of a seamstress. An additional way to save money is to purchase the lace, sequins, and beading at a fabric store or craft shop and sew it on yourself. If you don't feel comfortable with this, your mother or grandmother may enjoy taking the time to hand sew beading and sequins. An original gown becomes one of sentimental value to be treasured and passed on to future generations.
- **Finding a seamstress:** Your fabric store, friends, or family may be able to recommend a good seamstress or dress designer who specializes in bridal gowns or evening attire. Or look under the section in this book for alterations and dress design. It is a good idea to work with someone who has experience. Working with an inexperienced seamstress can be a costly experiment, with the prices of special-occasion fabrics and laces.
- **Mock dress:** Make the bodice pattern you've chosen in a less expensive fabric to be sure it is the style you want. Alterations in the pattern can be made at this time to check the fit to your figure. Ask your seamstress what the cost will be for this extra step.
- **Buy extra fabric:** Always purchase a couple of extra yards of fabric in addition to the recommended amount on the pattern. You may choose to change a feature or add accessories. To find the exact fabric dye lot can be difficult a couple of months later. When making bridesmaid dresses, purchase the fabric all at once, even if the bridesmaids are paying for their fabric individually.
- **Creative, time-saving ideas:** If you're making your wedding gown or special-occasion attire yourself, ask your fabric store for suggestions. The clerk can answer your questions, offer new ideas, and save you time. Some fabric stores may even offer classes and seminars on fabrics, helpful hints and special accessories you can create.
- **Bridal accessories:** Fabric stores may also carry headpieces, caps, frames, and veiling for you or your seamstress to create your own unique headpiece or veil. Inquire about all the additional accessories they may be able to provide.

For more assistance with staying organized during the wedding planning process, check out the Bravo! Wedding Organizer. Detailed question worksheets double as contracts. This step-by-step system will keep every detail of your wedding organized. To order, refer to the order form on page 24 in this Guide.

AMERICAN SHOWCASE
Fabric • Trim • Bridal

3604 S.W. Macadam Avenue
Portland, Oregon 97201
(503) 242-9373
Business Hours: Mon–Sat 10am–6pm

Whether you're a last-minute bride or planning months in advance, American Showcase offers unique bridal fabrics and supplies. Come visit our showroom and see why other fabric stores refer their customers to us.

Comments

"Ohhh…it's just like eating chocolate."
"There are other fabric stores, but I come here because of the personal service."
"You always know exactly what I need."
"You don't come in here just to buy fabric—you know you'll leave with a total look."
"You know more of what I need than I do."
"If they don't have what you need, they'll bend over backwards to find it."

"I've Heard So Much About American Showcase"

This we hear all the time. American Showcase Fabrics is known not only for its wedding and bridal supplies but also as the place for fabrics for Miss Oregon, Miss Teen Oregon, Miss Rodeo Oregon and other pageants.

From time to time you'll run into famous celebrities and designers from Disney, sports, TV, movies, stage, opera, skating and dance looking for that perfect thing.

We Provide

- The finest imported fabrics, trims, rhinestones, pearls, beads, tiaras, headpieces, veils, gloves, feathers and jewelry
- Custom sewing, specializing in brides' and bridesmaids' dresses and veils
- Alterations
- Women's resale
- Rental: bridal, pageant and evening dresses
- Famous, expert designers
- Specializing in bridal, performing arts, worldwide pageants and competitions of any kind
- Unique, hard-to-find and specialty fabrics
- 39 years in business

Wholesale/Retail

American Showcase offers a very generous discount of 30–40% off "Bridal Fabric Package" to all brides who purchase fabric from us for their entire bridal party. Special orders included!

PROMPT SHIPMENT ANYWHERE IN THE WORLD

Daisy Kingdom

134 N.W. Eighth Avenue
Portland, Oregon 97209
(503) 222-9033
Business Hours: Mon–Sat 10am–6pm; Sun 1–5pm

Fabrics and Patterns Available

- **Bridal-gown fabrics:** silks, satin, jacquard, brocade, taffeta, chiffon, organza, organdy, georgette, silk and cotton batiste, damask, velvet, dupioni, beaded and embroidered crêpes, and failles
- **Bridal gowns:** a selection of ready-made bridal dresses is available for try on and special orders; most dresses 30% off regular price
- **Patterns:** a full line of patterns available
- **Wedding party:** a large variety of fabrics for your bridesmaids, flower girls, and mothers of the bride and groom; from ornate to simply elegant, regardless of the season, you're sure to find the perfect fabrics **Price range:** $6 to $80 per yard. Special orders are encouraged.

Lace and Trims

- **Laces:** largest selection of beaded and plain Alençon and Venice laces in the Northwest **Price range:** $8 to $180 per yard.
- **Trims:** beaded or Venice frontal pieces, appliqués, pearls, sequins, ribbons, beaded fringe, and a large selection of trims

Headpieces and Veils

Unique finished headpieces and veils are available, or select from a full range of widths of illusion veiling. Many styles of wire and buckram frames are available to use with our extensive supply of flowers and pearl sprays.

Special Services and Bridal Accessories

Daisy Kingdom offers free demonstrations on bridal accessory design. For Daisy Kingdom customers, we have names of seamstresses specializing in weddings who are available to design or duplicate a gown or headpiece. Bridal gloves, garters, pillows, wedding books, slips, ribbon roses, and more are available.

AN EXCLUSIVE LOOK FOR YOUR WEDDING

At Daisy Kingdom, we've built our excellent reputation by carrying unique fabrics and accessories, providing superb service, and living by the philosophy of quality first! We enjoy working with brides to make sure they find the designs and fabrics to create the bridal gown and wedding party attire of their dreams.

Fabric Depot

700 S.E. 122nd • Portland, Oregon 97233
Contact: Bridal Department
(503) 252-9530
Visit our Web site: http://www.fabricdepot.com/

Fabrics and Patterns Available

- **Bridal-gown fabrics:** satin, brocade, shantung, taffeta, chiffon, organza, jacquard, georgette, Swiss batiste, damask, velvet, and linen.
- **Wedding party:** satin, taffeta, velvet, lamé, jacquard, silks, faille, crêpe, silk, and shantung.
- **Specialty silk:** dupioni, suiting, crêpe de chiné, beaded
- **Patterns:** full line of patterns available at 50% off every day

Lace, Trims and Accessories

Fabric Depot has almost every kind of lace in fabrics and trims. Many of our laces are available with beads and sequins, and in a large array of colors.

Laces: Galloon, Florence, Alençon, Venice, Chantilly, and embroidered organza

Trims: specialty trims include sequins, beaded dangle, satin piping, pearl edging, rhinestone strands, and button loops

Appliques and Motifs: huge variety of bodice motifs, collars, collar appliqués with and without beads and sequins

Buttons: large selection of fabulous special occasion buttons

Headpieces and Veils

We carry a large assortment of tiaras, hats, and headpieces. We also have a fabulous selection of tulle and netting in many colors and in 54", 72", and 108" widths. A variety of veiling including illusion, point de esprit, and Russian.

Special Services

The Palmer Pletsch International School of Serving Arts, located in our huge classroom, offers many specialized sewing classes to help with your bridal sewing projects, including classes in fit and couture sewing.

Discounts and Ordering

Fabric Depot offers a 40% discount off our already low retail prices when a "full bolt" (10–25 yards) is purchased. Special orders are available on most fabrics and notions.

OFFERING THE LARGEST SELECTION IN THE WEST

Fabric Depot has the largest in-stock quantities of fabrics, trims, and notions in the West. Our 40,000-square-foot retail store is an awesome display of every kind and type of fabric and notion available in the industry. Our fully stocked 30,000-square-foot attached warehouse allows us to provide large quantities of fabrics and notions.

Notes

© red door studio • page 520

THE BACHELOR PARTY

The traditional purpose of the bachelor party was to raise a special fund so that the groom could continue to go drinking with his buddies after the responsibility of the household budget had been taken over by the bride.

HELPFUL HINTS

- **Selecting formal wear:** There are a variety of formal wear styles available. The formal wear shop you decide to work with can offer suggestions for styles and colors that will appropriately fit the time of day. Even though etiquette books are very specific about what the groom and groomsmen should wear, in this day and age just about anything goes. Accessories to match the bridesmaid dresses are available for rent or purchase, or can be special ordered. Although the bride may help in deciding what the groom will wear, make sure that he is comfortable with the style selected.
- **Questions to ask:** Is the formal wear stocked locally? Are the locations convenient for the groomsmen? What is the price, and what does that include? Do you feel comfortable and confident that the formal wear store will deliver what you ordered?
- **Customized look for groom and groomsmen:** There are ways to bring out the personality of the groom and groomsmen and not sway too far from tradition. Paisley, plaid or polka dot cummerbunds and bow ties are a special flair that give a custom look. At the reception the groom can escape from the formal and put on sporty or Disney character accessories.
- **She keeps the gown, why shouldn't he keep his tux?:** A wonderful surprise for your groom is to purchase the tuxedo for his wedding present. This will make your groom feel as special as you do on the wedding day, with a tuxedo tailored to fit only him. There will be occasions to wear this tuxedo following the wedding day, many more occasions than a bride would have to wear her dress.
- **Buying a tuxedo:** Check into the purchase prices at your formal wear shop. If a tuxedo is worn four or more times per year for special occasions, it may be more cost-effective to own your own.
- **Final fitting and pickup date:** You must instruct each member of the wedding party to pick up his own tuxedo. Make sure they try on the entire outfit at the store. This will avoid the most common problem with formal wear—proper fit. If adjustments or replacements need to be made, they can usually be done right on the spot, or arrangements for substitutions can be made.
- **Out-of-town groomsmen and ushers:** If some of the groomsmen and ushers live out of town, the formal wear shop can supply you with measurement cards to mail back to them. Any clothing or alterations shop in the groomsman's home town should be able to do a complimentary fitting. It is imperative that these gentlemen take the time to try on their entire tuxedos when they pick them up!
- **Bring extra socks:** Have the groom buy a couple of extra pairs of socks to match the formal wear. Be sure these extra socks are on hand where the groomsmen plan to dress. It never fails that someone will show up with only white athletic socks. This may seem minor, but they stick out like a sore thumb in photographs.
- **Group rates and discounts:** Many formal wear shops offer special group rates, discounts or rebates for black-tie or black-tie-optional events. Ask about setting up a special rate for all the guests who will attend.

For more assistance with staying organized during the wedding planning process, check out the Bravo! Wedding Organizer. Detailed question worksheets double as contracts. This step-by-step system will keep every detail of your wedding organized. To order, refer to the order form on page 24 in this Guide.

BELLE AND BOW TIE TUX

Bridal and Formal Wear

Westside	***Northeast***	***Eastside***
8112 S.W. Beaverton-Hillsdale Highway	*4300 N.E. Hancock (at 43rd & Sandy)*	*Ross Center 11211 S.E. 82nd Ave.*
(503) 292-3557	*(503) 284-5969*	*(503) 652-7076*
Mon–Sat 8am–7pm	*Mon–Sat 9am–7pm*	*Mon–Sat 10am–7pm*

Formal Wear Styles

Twenty-seven different tuxedos to choose from, featuring Pierre Cardin, and Lord West. Some styles include tails; shawl collars; spencer waistcoats; double-breasted, notch, and peak lapels. Small boys' sizes available in most styles. Any style can be ordered for the larger sizes.

Price

- **Price range:** $75 to $95
- **Included** in price are coat, pant, shirt, shoes, jewelry (studs and cuff links), and all basic colors of bow ties and cummerbunds plus a few exotic ones
- **Optional items:** scarves, canes, gloves, and pocket squares reasonably priced
- **Alterations:** included in price and done in store

Ordering and Pickup

Reserving your tuxedos two months in advance is enough time. The groom and his party are registered upon ordering, and a file is kept to keep track of each person's measurement as he comes in. It is a must that each individual pick up his tuxedo and try it on. Usually, if there is a problem, a replacement can be made the same day.

Out-of-town Attendants

Belle & Bow can supply you with out-of-town sizing cards. These cards can be mailed to out-of-town attendants, who can get measured where they live and mail them back to the formal wear store where you registered.

Retail Accessories and Additional Services

The various retail items for sale are shirts, suspenders, vests, socks, pocket squares, top hats, scarves, gloves, jewelry, specialty bow ties, and cummerbunds.

Accessories in special colors can be ordered upon request. Belle & Bow Tie consultants can help you pick the suit appropriate for your wedding. We stock all tuxedos in our local Hollywood store, so last-minute orders are no problem.

ALL YOUR BRIDAL-ATTIRE NEEDS

We can help you with your bridal-attire needs from wedding gowns to formal wear for your entire wedding party. Come visit us today and see the number of ways we can make planning your wedding easier!

See page 231 under Bridal Accessories & Attire.

gingiss®
FORMALWEAR

Web site:
http://www.gingiss.com

You chose wisely.

Beaverton Town Square
(503) 643-7022

Clackamas Corner
(503) 653-7668

Vancouver Mall
(360) 256-6424

World's Largest Renter of Men's Formalwear

Formalwear Styles

Gingiss carries an assortment of name brands such as Lord West, Christian Dior, Perry Ellis and Oscar de la Renta. Our sizes range from 4 to 70. Because we have 275 stores nationwide, we have the ability to special order larger sizes and up-to-date styles to fit your wedding needs.

Price

Gingiss makes pricing easy. We run wedding specials each season. Gingiss offers a base price including coat, two styles of pants, standard tuxedo shirt in white or ivory, four choices of jewelry, solid color cummerbund and tie and suspenders. Then Gingiss gives you the option of upgrading using vests, hosiery, two styles of shoes, pocket squares, and button covers.

Gingiss Provides The Right Fit

Two people measuring the same person could come up with two different sizes. Why? Because measuring is an art not a science. At Gingiss, there is one nationwide measuring technique followed up with the final fitting one to two days before the wedding. If adjustments are needed to lengthen pants or shorten sleeves, it's not a problem. All Gingiss Formalwear consultants are trained to do alterations while you wait. *No appointments necessary.

Out-of-town Attendants and Guests

Out-of-town attendants are easy to handle with Gingiss Formalwear. Since we're the only nationwide formalwear specialist, we can ensure proper fitting for all your attendants, no matter where they live, through our Travel Tux Service.

Additional Services

Gingiss carries all merchandise in the stores. This allows us to provide try-ons, ability to do last-minute orders in as little as 20 minutes and fix an improper fit on the spot.

THE DIFFERENCE IN BLACK AND WHITE

With more than 275 stores and over 62 years of formalwear experience, the Gingiss name has been a hallmark of quality for more than half a century. When you register your wedding with Gingiss, you're assured of having the widest selection, the highest level of service and the most expert attention to detail and fit. We are "The Difference in Black and White."

Mr. Formal

24 Years of Wedding Excellence

27 locations—also serving Corvallis and Eugene area

GRAND AVE (503) 232-1542	**HOLLYWOOD** (503) 287-1725	**GRESHAM** (503) 667-6299
CLACKAMAS (503) 659-2337	**LAKE OSWEGO** (503) 636-8911	**PROGRESS** (503) 626-6483
HILLSBORO (503) 640-1838	**EAST SALEM** (503) 371-7970	**SOUTH SALEM** (503) 399-7989
MALL 205 (503) 254-1841	**BEAVERTON** (503) 643-2661	**VANCOUVER** (360) 253-9637
JANTZEN BEACH (503) 247-9301	**HAZEL DELL** (360) 574-7768	

MORE BRIDES TRUST MR. FORMAL'S WEDDING EXPERTS

Trust Mr. Formal's Formalwear Experience

- ✦ Trust our **24 year commitment to Wedding Excellence**
- ✦ Mr. Formal is the largest locally owned formalwear provider in the Northwest
- ✦ A Portland warehouse with an inventory of over 20,000 tuxedos
- ✦ Professionally trained Formalwear Consultants

Exceptional Quality and Selection

- ✦ Mr. Formal offers over 70 elegant tuxedo styles
- ✦ Tuxedos by top designers: Oscar De La Renta, Pierre Cardin, After Six
- ✦ The Northwest's largest designer vest collection including full back vests
- ✦ Tuxedo sizes from 4 to 70

Mr. Formal's Commitment to Value

- ✦ We have tuxedo styles that accommodate every budget
- ✦ Generous discounts are available on wedding invitations and bridal gown cleaning
- ✦ We offer a large selection of enhancement items to customize your look
- ✦ Our Price Promise: "We promise quality tuxedos at the best price available."

The Time Saving Convenience of Mr. Formal

- ✦ 27 convenient locations throughout the Pacific Northwest
- ✦ A web site to preview our extensive formalwear selection—www.mrformaltuxedos.com
- ✦ Out-of-town ordering is easy with our custom measurement cards
- ✦ Toll free number (800-284-4889) and in-store fax machines available
- ✦ A local warehouse that guarantees that last minute changes are never a problem

OUR PRICE PROMISE

Our policy is "buyer's assurance." We promise quality tuxedos at the best price. If you find a better price elsewhere, we will match that price on the same manufacturer and style.

View our latest formalwear collection at www.mrformaltuxedos.com and receive tuxedo discounts

Notes

GOWN PRESSING, CLEANING AND PRESERVATION

© Woodstock Photography • page 525

THE WEDDING TORCH

In ancient times the wedding torch

— a symbol of life and love —

was carried ahead of the bridal procession.

HELPFUL HINTS

- **Preparing your gown for the wedding day:** After alterations are performed on a new gown, have it cleaned, pressed, and padded with tissue so it is perfect and ready to go on your wedding day. Make an appointment for cleaning or pressing a new gown at least two weeks before the wedding.
- **Preserving your precious gown:** Your wedding dress is a sentimental and costly investment. Saving this investment means special handling, packaging, and dry cleaning by experts. You should not only clean the gown, but preserve and save its beauty as an heirloom for future generations. Many brides today have the pleasure of wearing their mother's or grandmother's dress on their wedding day because it was properly cleaned and preserved.
- **Dealing with stains:** When you bring your gown to your dry cleaner, it is important to point out any stains. Different stains require different treatments. Champagne stains in particular can be very difficult to discover, because they do not show up right away, but darken with age.
- **Choosing a wedding-gown specialist:** Today's wedding gowns feature beading, sequins, and pearls that require delicate care and special handling. Be sure to select a cleaner that specializes in gown cleaning and preservation.
- **Restoring heirloom dresses:** For brides choosing to wear an heirloom dress, don't be discouraged if it has become yellowed with age. In many cases a professional cleaner can restore the dress to 90% of its original color. Bring the dress in for an evaluation, and allow a month for this process to be done.
- **Avoiding common mistakes:** Avoid hanging your wedding gown over a prolonged time. This may cause the gown to stretch and sag. Fragile gowns should not be put in plastic bags, because moisture can form inside and promote mildew and fabric rot. Strong light, heat, or open air are other factors that will cause deterioration.

For more assistance with staying organized during the wedding planning process, check out the Bravo! Wedding Organizer. Detailed question worksheets double as contracts. This step-by-step system will keep every detail of your wedding organized. To order, refer to the order form on page 24 in this Guide.

Notes

© Real Mother Goose • page 279

Wedding Showers

The custom of giving wedding showers began in Holland, when friends or even entire communities gathered together to "stake" a young bride of modest means for all her household goods. The lack of dowry was considered to be an impediment to marriage.

HELPFUL HINTS

- **Unique shops for registry:** There are many wonderful stores where you can register. The china, glassware, flatware, and special accessories you select will be with you the rest of your lives. Look at the many registry stores in this book and remember, you can register at more than one.
- **Why you should register:** By registering, you let your family and friends know the gifts you would most like to have, and will ensure that what you receive will suit both your tastes and styles. Even if you and your fiancé can't imagine using fine china, stemware, and flatware in the near future, you'll appreciate them in years to come. It is very expensive to invest in formal china down the road. Family and guests enjoy giving gifts knowing they will be treasured and eventually passed on to future generations.
- **Mixing and matching:** Many shops allow you to mix and match your patterns to design your own dishware theme. Ask about ideas they may have. Most important, have fun selecting items that you and your fiancé will enjoy using.
- **When to register:** Soon after you become engaged is the best time to register. If your friends want to send engagement gifts, you can tell them where you are registered. Or for showers, your guests can select from a variety of items that you have on your "wish list."
- **Check with your registry:** It is a good idea to check your registry list periodically and keep it up to date with items you have received. Some gift givers will be making purchases in your behalf from other stores or will forget to let the store you are registered at know whom they are buying the gift for. It's nice for your guests to know what items you have or haven't received so they may plan their purchases accordingly.
- **Damaged items:** No business can be responsible for gifts that get broken after they leave their store. If gifts are damaged or broken, it usually happens in shipping. Packages that are carefully packed will reach you intact. However, if you find breakage upon unpacking, please call your delivery carrier (Postal Service or U.P.S.) for an inspection and claim. **NOTE:** Most shippers require that all packing, boxes, and wrappings be retained for inspection, so be sure to keep everything!
- **Thank-you notes:** It is important and proper etiquette to send thank-you notes immediately after receiving a gift. This way you let the gift giver know that the gift was received. Keep up with the many thank-you notes you will need to write, rather than waiting until after the honeymoon.

For more assistance with staying organized during the wedding planning process, check out the Bravo! Wedding Organizer. Detailed question worksheets double as contracts. This step-by-step system will keep every detail of your wedding organized. To order, refer to the order form on page 24 in this Guide.

carl greve

The Wonder of it All.

Second Floor Home & Gift Collections

731 S.W. Morrison at Park
Portland, Oregon 97205
(503) 223-7121; Fax (503) 223-9754
Toll Free (800) 284-2044
Business Hours: Mon–Fri 10am–6pm; Sat 10am–5pm
Web site: http://www.carlgreve.com

WHY IS CARL GREVE THE BRIDE'S FAVORITE STORE?

CHINA
- Bernardaud
- Calvin Klein
- Christian LaCroix
- Christofle
- Gien
- Hermes
- Lynn Chase
- Mottahedeh
- Pickard
- Raynaud
- Richard Ginori
- Rosenthal
- Royal Worcester
- Spode
- Vietri
- Villeroy & Boch
- Wedgwood

SILVER
- Christofle
- Gorham
- Jean Couzon
- Lunt
- Puiforcat
- Reed & Barton
- Retroneu
- Wallace

CRYSTAL
- Baccarat
- Hoya
- Kosta Boda
- Lalique
- Orrefors
- St. Louis
- Waterford
- William Yeoward

GIFTWARE
- Anichini Linens
- Annie Glass
- Mariposa
- Nambé

EXCLUSIVE TO PORTLAND: Bernardaud china, silver and crystal; Lynn Chase tableware; Hoya crystal; and William Yeoward crystal.

Services
- Table-Setting Seminars
- Exquisite Complimentary Giftwrap
- Interior and Home Design Services
- Designer Events and Trunk Shows
- Lavish Service
- A Knowledgeable Staff
- Exchanges Gladly
- Parking Validation

CARL GREVE
SECOND FLOOR HOME & GIFT COLLECTIONS
Bridal Registry • Distinctive Tablewares
Fine Bed, Bath and Table Linens • Distinctive Home Furnishings

COOK'S

CHINA, CRYSTAL & SILVER SHOP LLC

8538 S.W. Apple Way
(off Beaverton-Hillsdale Hwy. next to Jesuit High School)
Portland, Oregon 97225
(503) 292-4312 • Fax (503) 292-3908
Business Hours: Mon–Fri 10am–5:30pm; Sat 10am–5pm

Cook's features one of the largest selections of china dinnerware, crystal stemware, and flatware in the Portland area since 1984. Our knowledgeable staff will assist couples in selecting patterns that they will use during their lives together. Registering at Cook's will benefit you and your guests. Congratulations on your upcoming wedding and best wishes to you both.

Cook's Features

- Aromatique
- Arthur Court
- Belleek
- Dansk
- Denby
- Eureka
- Gorham
- Hagerty
- Henckels
- International
- Kirk Stieff
- Lenox
- Lunt
- Hutschenreuther
- Marquis
- Minton
- Nambé
- Noritake
- Oneida
- Pickard
- Portmeirion
- Reed & Barton
- Riedel
- Rosenthal
- Royal Albert
- Royal Crown Derby
- Royal Doulton
- Royal Worcester
- Spode
- Towle
- Villeroy & Boch
- Wallace
- Waterford
- Wedgwood
- Yamazaki
- and much more…

Cook's Services

- Specializes in everyday savings, quality, and service
- Features a modern, spacious showroom
- Employs knowledgeable bridal consultants to assist you with important selections
- Offers a convenient location with free parking
- (800) 574-1329 for your out-of-town guests
- Provides UPS delivery and gift wrap at a minimal charge
- Welcomes special orders at no extra charge

Bridal Registry/Completion Program

We offer a completion program which entitles all registered brides to an additional discount off already low prices on dinnerware, crystal and stainless/silverplate flatware patterns. This one-time purchase can include as many pieces as you need from our tabletop department and is good up to three months after your wedding. *An appointment is helpful to save you time.*

DISCOVER OUR VALUES!

Visit our Web site: http://www.cookschina.com

dish n dat

827 NW 23rd Avenue • Portland, Oregon 97210
phone: 503•279•8946; fax: 503•279•1509
Business Hours: Mon-Wed,Sat: 10am-6pm;
Thurs-Fri: 10am-7pm; Sun: noon-5pm

Bridal Registry for the Modern Bride

Featuring a unique selection of tabletop and accessories for your home, dish n dat offers gifts from all over the world. Crystal from Finland to stoneware from Japan, flatware from Germany to pottery from London. We go out of our way to find items you will not see elsewhere.

Our selection is very eclectic and ever-changing—you will always have new and exciting merchandise to choose from.

Offering personal, one-on-one service, we walk you through various options and assist you in organizing your ideas to create a table that fits your lifestyle. Also look to us for fun invitations, thank you notes, and decorations

A Sampling of the Lines dish n dat Carries

- iittala
- Boda Nova
- WMF
- Arzberg
- Swid Powell
- Calvin Klein
- Arabia
- Totem Design Group
- Ritzenhoff
- True West
- Cattarina Fadda
- Couzon
- Lunt Silversmiths
- Jonathan Adler
- Axis Paris
- Isamu Noguchi

HIP, URBAN TABLETOP AND HOME ACCESSORIES

Visit our Web site at
www.DishnDatInc.com

JCPENNEY

Clackamas
12300 S.E. 82nd Avenue
Portland, Oregon 97226
(503) 653-8830 ext. 231

Washington Square
9500 S.W. Washington Square Road
Portland, Oregon 97223
(503) 620-0750 ext. 234

Vancouver
8900 N.E. Van. Mall Drive
Vancouver, Washington 98662
(360) 254-3800 ext. 215

Salem
305 Liberty Street
Salem, Oregon 97301
(503) 585-4535 ext. 274

Eugene
300 Valley River Center
Eugene, Oregon 97401
(541) 342-6211 ext. 234

Also available at any of our 1,200 stores nationwide!
Call our national Gift Registry seven days a week: (800)-JCP-GIFT (527-4438)

How our Registry Works

JCPenney's complimentary gift registry offers you an opportunity to register at your convenience in your home or with one of our experienced consultants in our stores. In addition to what is available in our stores, we have gift registry catalogs and regular store catalogs to use when selecting your gifts. Our registries are immediately updated during the sale so as to eliminate gift duplication. JCPenney's toll-free number makes it effortless for family and friends to use our nationwide "SENDS Program" in the purchase and shipping of your gifts. Free gift boxes and wrap are also available for in-store purchases. Our consultants will assist you in the store with your selection of the items you and your intended have chosen for your future home. The process is quick and easy with the use of our scanners as you walk the store with the consultant. We also provide you with our "Registered At" cards to insert in your shower or bridal invitations. A complimentary wedding portfolio/planner is also given upon registration. Guest may also access your registry via the Internet at www.jcpenney.com.

The Best Way to Register

By registering with JCPenney, you can make your gift selections readily available to family and friends across the country. Just give us a call to make an appointment with one of our gift consultants. This ensures that you will never be rushed and the consultants can help you choose from a wide assortment of gift favorites found in our stores and catalogs. Although we recommend an appointment with a consultant, you may pick up a gift selection book from the gift registry and choose the "Do-It-Yourself" option if you are pressed for time. Whichever you choose, once you sign up, your gift list becomes easily accessible through JCPenney's nationwide gift registry network.

Returns and Exchanges

It's easy to return or exchange any gifts purchased through the gift registry at any of over 1,200 JCPenney stores. We have your gift registry on file for three months after your wedding, with a record of what items were purchased for you. Not only can we help you with your returns, but we can help you finish out items on your registry you wanted but did not receive. Handling returns or exchanges with your ease and satisfaction in mind is as important to us as selling you a gift that meets your needs. ***JCPenney Gift Cards Also Available!***

Items Available for Registry

- **Formal and casual china:** Mikasa, Noritake, Royal Doulton, Fitz & Floyd, Lenox, Pfaltzgraff, Villeroy & Boch, Nikko
- **Flatware and stemware:** Oneida, Reed & Barton, Towle, Wallace, Pfaltzgraff, Divinci, Royal Crystal Rock
- **Home accessories:** Martex, Croscill, Braun, Royal Velvet, Fieldcrest, Revere, Farberware, T-Fal, Crown Corning, Pyrex, Cuisinart, Kitchenaid, Oster, Braun, Black & Decker, Krups and many more

 Please let this business know that you heard about them from the Bravo! Bridal Resource Guide.

Kitchen Kaboodle

www.kitchenkaboodle.com

DOWNTOWN
SW 6th & Alder, second floor (503) 464-9545

BROADWAY
NE 16th & Broadway (503) 288-1500

CLACKAMAS TOWN CENTER
Across from Eddie Bauer (503) 652-2567

NORTHWEST
NW 23rd & Flanders (503) 241-4040

PROGRESS SQUARE
SW Hall Blvd. & Scholls Ferry Rd. (503) 643-5491

Order Toll Free: (800) 366-0161
e-mail: weddings@kitchenkaboodle.com

EVERY WEDDING IS SPECIAL. SHOULDN'T YOUR GIFTS BE, TOO?

Kitchen Kaboodle's Bridal Registry — like each of our convenient Portland area stores — is brimming with a dazzling array of the kinds of things that give your house its special character. The kinds of things that make your house a home.

We carry just about everything you'll need as you begin your lives together. From high-quality cookware to decorative accessories, gorgeous dinnerware to finely-crafted furniture, Kitchen Kaboodle carries a wide variety of:

- Dinnerware
- Barware
- Stemware
- Cookware
- Bakeware
- Kitchen Appliances
- Gadgets & Utensils
- Cutlery
- Cook Books
- Table & Kitchen Linens
- Candles & Candlesticks
- Decorative Accessories
- Lamps & Rugs
- Furniture
- Much, much more

UNIQUELY YOU

Looking for something out of the ordinary? Kitchen Kaboodle's the place. We're the exclusive Oregon retailer for many exciting items, and our buyers always work hard to uncover the kinds of unique items you won't find at the chain stores.

WE'VE DONE THE WORK SO YOU DON'T HAVE TO.

We know this is a busy time for you, so we burned the midnight oil to make sure our Bridal Registry is convenient and easy to use. Registry forms are available for you to complete at home or in the store. Each store updates your registry daily with items purchased at other locations, so your registry is always current. We'll even keep your registry list on file for one year following your wedding date.

WE'RE AT YOUR DISPOSAL

We're ready and willing to help. In addition to the Bridal Specialists available in each of our stores, our Bridal Consultant is available for free consultation. Call (503) 243-5043 ext. 208 in Portland or toll free (800) 366-0161 ext. 208. Our specialists will be happy to sit down, discuss your wants and needs, and recommend the products that will best meet those needs.

(503) 243-5043 ext. 208 or (800) 366-0161 ext. 208

MEIER & FRANK

BRIDAL REGISTRY
NATIONAL NETWORK
1-800-452-6323

Downtown *(503) 241-5158*	***Washington Square*** *(503) 620-3311, ext. 5158*
Lloyd Center *(503) 281-4797, ext. 5158*	***Clackamas Town Center*** *(503) 653-8811, ext. 5158*
Vancouver *(360) 256-4411, ext. 5158*	***Salem*** *(503) 363-2211, ext. 5158*

The Best Way to Register

After you've set a wedding date, make one with our Bridal Registry. Come in together, four to six months before your wedding. You can scan the gifts you most want and need with the help of our professional bridal consultants or on your own. Choose from our large selection of china, crystal, flatware, kitchen items, bed and bath linens and more. With so many options, you won't need to register anywhere else!

How Our Registry Works

Our complimentary computerized registry makes your gift preference list available at nearly 300 May Company Department stores nationwide. It's all part of our coast-to-coast network that's convenient for all your family and friends wherever they live. Your Meier & Frank registry will be available at any of these fine May Company Department stores:

- **Famous-Barr** in Missouri, Illinois and Indiana
- **Filene's** in Massachusetts, New York, Connecticut, Maine and New Hampshire
- **Foley's** in Texas, Oklahoma, Arizona, Colorado and New Mexico
- **Hecht's** in Washington D.C., Virginia, Maryland, North Carolina and Pennsylvania
- **Kaufmann's** in New York, Pennsylvania, Ohio and West Virginia
- **L.S. Ayers** in Indiana
- **Robinsons-May** in California, Arizona and Nevada

Our bridal consultants will answer all your questions and provide as much, or as little assistance as you would like. Purchases made for you are recorded instantly and removed from your list in order to avoid gift duplication. We will also provide announcement cards to inform you family and friends that you are registered at Meier & Frank.

Policies

- Damages/Duplicates: we will gladly exchange duplicates or damaged gifts.
- After-Wedding Completion Offer: as a special offer to our registered couples, we offer a completion-discount program to assist you in completing your registry.
- Tabletop Club Plan: use our plan to complete your china, crystal, and flatware patterns. When you purchase $100 or more, you'll have up to one year to pay without finance charge when a minimum monthly payment is made when due.

Services

Your bridal registry will remain in our computer for 13 months after the wedding. Update us if you receive gifts purchased elsewhere; friends and family enjoy the convenience of calling and getting an updated gift list as your anniversary approaches.

We can also help your out-of-town guests with their gift purchases with our convenient toll-free number. By calling (800) 452-6323.

See page 45 under Bridal Shows & Events.

The Real Mother Goose
Portland • Oregon

DOWNTOWN

901 S.W. Yamhill • Portland, Oregon 97205
(503) 223-9510

WASHINGTON SQUARE

9610 Washington Square • Portland, Oregon 97223
(503) 620-2243

Also located in the Oregon Market at the Portland Airport

We offer you the opportunity to let your wedding guests know about those unique items you've been dreaming of. At your convenience, come in and fill out a registry card with your chosen colors, themes or artists' work. We'll keep your information on file to guide your guests in their selection of a truly memorable wedding gift. Our knowledgeable and creative sales staff will help you choose items that you will love to receive and your guests will enjoy giving.

Everything you Need to Furnish your New Home with your Own Personal Style

- Fanciful and functional ceramics
- Art glass stemware
- Unique kitchen accessories
- Exotic wood humidors and jewelry boxes
- Creative lighting in wood, ceramic and glass
- One-of-a-kind garden accessories including fountains, lighting and chimes
- Handcrafted furniture

Services/Policies

- Layaway Available
- Gift Certificates
- Packing and Shipping
- Gift wrap available for a small fee

NO CASH REFUNDS, but exchanges gladly given within 10 days with a receipt or original gift box

See page 408 under Jewelry & Gifts.

ZELL BROS

Jewelers -:- Platinumsmiths

800 S.W. Morrison Street • Portland, Oregon 97205
(503) 227-8471 or (800) 444-8979; Fax (503) 223-8546
Business Hours: Mon–Fri 10am–5:30pm; Sat 10am–5pm

The Largest Selection of Fine China, Crystal, and Flatware in the Western U.S.

Mix Portland's early history with one of the city's most delightful traditions, and you have Zell Bros Jewelers. Since 1912, brides have been coming to Zell Bros to make their selections. Now we have more to offer than ever before! Choose from more than 450 patterns by over 100 manufacturers, for example:

- Royal Worcester & Spode
- Lalique
- Georg Jensen
- WMF
- Raynaud
- Saint Louis
- Nambé
- Wallace/Tuttle
- Allan Adler
- Denby
- Baccarat
- Thomas
- Buccellati
- Old Newbury Crafters
- Reed & Barton
- Swarovski
- Waterford Marquis
- Orrefors
- Kosta Boda
- Jean Couzon
- Hutschenreuther
- Ginori
- Laure Japy
- Philippe Deshoulieres
- Gien
- Lunt
- Crane Stationery
- Lladro
- Christofle
- Royal Crown Derby
- Waterford
- Rosenthal
- Versace
- Wedgwood
- Royal Doulton
- Herend
- Daum
- Royal Copenhagen
- Villeroy & Boch
- Haviland
- Coquet
- Oggetti
- Hermés
- PresenTense
- Puiforcat
- Limoge

Superior Personal Service

You can count on all the personal service you need and careful attention to detail. Here are just a few of the services we offer you:

- Bridal registry
- Complimentary gift wrap
- Full-service Stationery Department
- Exchanges gladly within 90 days
- Free jewelry inspection/cleaning
- Parking validation with purchase

WE HAVE EXACTLY WHAT YOU WANT.

See page 409 under Jewelry & Gifts.

© JaCiva's Bakery & Chocolatier • page 288

WEDDING CAKES

Wedding cakes can be traced back to ancient Rome.

A simple wheat cake or biscuit was

broken during the ceremony, with the

bride and groom taking the first bites.

The remainder was then crumbled over the bride's

head to ensure a bountiful life with lots of children.

HELPFUL HINTS

- **The wedding cake:** You'll find many flavors and styles of cakes to choose from. Visit several shops and compare quality, style, and prices. Also, sample different flavors of cakes to help in selecting the flavor you want. The baker is a specialist, so ask for advice and recommendations. Remember, each tier can be a different flavor. Make sure the portfolio and samples you are viewing are work done by the current baker on staff.
- **Order your wedding cake early:** Busy wedding months are June through September; you will need to order your cake four to five months in advance if you're getting married in the summer. At ordering time, you need only an approximate number of guests. Confirm the number two to three weeks before your wedding.
- **Figuring the amount:** The baker will be helpful in advising you on the amount of cake needed based on the number of guests. The price is usually based on a per-slice amount. Be sure to ask about tier sizes and serving portions—are they pieces or slivers of cake?
- **Cake knife, server and instructions:** Don't forget to bring a knife and server to cut the wedding cake or have the caterer supply them. Make sure your baker provides you with instructions for cutting and serving your wedding cake. Because of their size and elegance, wedding cakes can be tricky to serve. Appoint someone to be in charge of cutting and serving and supply that person with the instructions, or ask your caterer if their servers can be available for this task.
- **Fountain cakes:** If you've decided on a fountain cake, an 18-inch bottom is required; you may have to buy a larger cake than you need. Also keep in mind that a fountain cake must be close to a wall outlet.
- **Wedding cake tops & decorations:** Most bakeries and bridal accessory stores have a large selection of cake tops: hand-blown glass, figurines, or ornaments that are permanent keepsakes. Fresh-flower arrangements are very popular and can be coordinated with your baker and florist. If you have chosen colored decorations, bring some color swatches or samples when ordering.
- **Personalized mints** in your color theme are available for your wedding. This is a special touch you may want to consider for your cake table.
- **Edible place cards:** Place cards made from the finest chocolates or cookies are a personalized touch for a formal wedding dinner.
- **Serve the wedding cake:** If you have waiters at your event, it is recommended to serve the cake to each guest rather than just placing cake on a table. This way guests won't take an extra piece or expect seconds.
- **A smaller wedding cake:** To save dollars, order a smaller wedding cake and decorate it with beautiful fresh flowers, ribbons or sugared fruits. Then have sheet cakes to cut for guests. The wedding cake can stay in place until all the sheet cakes are gone.

For more assistance with staying organized during the wedding planning process, check out the Bravo! Wedding Organizer. Detailed question worksheets double as contracts. This step-by-step system will keep every detail of your wedding organized. To order, refer to the order form on page 24 in this Guide.

CHOCOLATERIE
Bernard C.™
Chocolates by Bernard Callebaut

4768 N.W. Bethany Blvd., Suite C-1
Portland, Oregon 97229
(503) 690-8982; Fax (503) 533-8178

440 Fifth Street, Suite A
Lake Oswego, Oregon 97034
(503) 675-7500; Fax (503) 675-0500
Web site: www.bernardc.citysearch.com
Toll free (877) 401-3950

A Sweet Thank-You

A wedding is a magical occasion and you want all of your guests to feel as special as you do. The elegant Bernard C. white, copper or gold mini-box of two-to-four chocolates is a distinct way to say, "thank-you." We will help you choose the perfect chocolates, such as heart-shaped with custom centers and can customize the boxes with the bride and groom's names (printing charges apply). We also have porcelain wedding boxes, perfect for one chocolate.

About the Chocolate

When Bernard Callebaut arrived in Canada from Belgium in 1982, his goal was to produce a line of chocolates with a quality never before experienced by North Americans. In 1998, he became the first North American to be awarded the "Grand Prix International Artisan Chocolatier" at the International Chocolate Festival in Roanne, France. In addition to the grand prize, he captured the award for the best chocolate to accompany fine wines. In 1999, he was awarded the "Prize of Excellence" at the same competition.

Callebaut, fourth-generation Belgian chocolatier, is renowned as an innovative creator of unique fillings for his chocolates. The centers the delicious chocolates are the freshest and highest quality available. The assortment consists of approximately 48 different centers with an additional 20 seasonal chocolates offered during the summer months and brandied cherries at Christmas. The chocolates do not contain any artificial additives in order to extend the in-store shelf life.

Where to Find Us

Ron and Barbara Cameron and Laura Adler invite you to try these irresistible chocolates at their Bernard C. Chocolaterie in the Bethany Village Centre. Take Sunset Highway (Hwy 26) to the Cornell-Bethany Boulevard (exit #65); turn right on Bethany Boulevard (north) for one-and-a-half miles to the Bethany Village Centre. We are *"under the clock tower."*

Our other location is conveniently located in downtown Lake Oswego—across from the Safeway parking lot on Fifth and "A" streets. We will be most happy to serve your wedding needs.

BEAVERTON BAKERY

12375 S.W. Broadway
Beaverton, Oregon 97005
Contact: Carrie Schubert
(503) 646-7136
Business Hours:
Mon–Fri 9:30am–6pm; Sat 8am–6pm

Types and Styles of Wedding Cakes

Beaverton Bakery has been famous for more than 30 years for beautifully decorated and delicious wedding cakes. We offer tiered wedding cakes in round or heart shapes. We also make European-style rolled fondant and marzipan cakes. Our fudge grooms cakes are a favorite. We offer wedding cakes sized to serve from 15 to 850!

Our large flavor selection includes such favorites as champagne cake, poppy seed, fudge, carrot, banana, German chocolate, French pastry and many more.

Cost

Our flat fee per cake includes several "extras:" free disposable pillar system, free cake-top ornament, and free delivery in the Portland Metro area Mondays through Saturdays. (There is a delivery fee for Sundays and holidays).

Ordering

Please order six to eight weeks in advance. A 20% deposit is required upon ordering. The balance is due two weeks before we deliver your cake.

Experience and Samples

Our wedding cake decorators and pastry chefs are among the finest in the area. They have the skill to create a truly memorable wedding cake for you. The schubert family has taken pride in their bakery products for over 30 years.

We invite you to visit our wedding cake showroom, where you can sample our cake flavors while you browse through our design portfolios. Our consultants will work with you to plan a special cake. No appointment needed; we welcome you Mondays through Saturdays.

Delivery and Instructions

We will deliver and set up your cake, provide instructions for cutting and even supply a cake knife and server (for an additional charge).

Additional Items and Decorations

We have our own in-house florist who can provide fresh flowers to decorate your cake. We also have a large selection of blown glass and other cake tops. We sell plain and decorated wedding mints, decorated sugar cubes, Jordan almonds, and mixed nuts. As well as our traditional decorated petit fours. Our bakery can provide cocktail breads, rolls, and Viennese pastries. We offer full-service catering, providing everything from hors d'oeuvres to full dinners.

 Please let this business know that you heard about them from the Bravo! Bridal Resource Guide.

THE CAKE AFFAIR BY JOYCE MOORE

(at the Chic-N-Deli)

11239 S.E. Division Street, Portland, Oregon 97266

Contact: Joyce Moore (503) 256-5131

Business Hours: Mon–Fri 11am–6pm; Sat 10am–5pm

Types and Styles of Wedding Cakes

At The Cake Affair, we offer many special designs and styles of cakes. Or, if you prefer, we can work with your ideas to create your own special look. One of our specialties is fountain cakes with satellite stairways or streamers. We pride ourselves on our tasty and attractive traditional cakes as well.

Flavors include sour cream white or chocolate, German chocolate, Lady Baltimore, poppy seed, carrot, and raspberry swirl. Filling flavors include lemon, cherry, pineapple, fudge, butter cream, mocha, raspberry, strawberry parfait, chocolate, champagne, and many more! A favorite is chocolate marble. The best way to choose the flavor for your cake is to come in and sample our delicious flavors—it may take a while, but it's worth it!

Cost

The Cake Affair has a wide variety of styles and sizes of cakes from which to choose. You can order the very affordable to the ultramodern cake or an elegant creation that will serve 500. Our charges are based on the size and complexity of the order. A flat fee per cake is payable in full one week prior to the wedding.

Experience

We have more than 28 years' experience in the Portland-Vancouver area and have been at this location for the past ten years.

Ordering, Delivery, and Instructions

Orders should be placed six to eight weeks before the wedding, but we can accommodate shorter-notice orders when necessary. We offer free delivery and setup within five miles of our location. An additional fee is charged for delivery beyond five miles. Complimentary cake-cutting instructions are provided with each order.

Additional Items and Decorations

We have an elegant selection of cake tops made of litec, as well as other affordable and beautiful styles and designs. Or if you prefer, we can build a cake top to match your wedding colors and specifications. Grooms cakes are another option available at The Cake Affair, offering you a tasty addition to the food served at your reception—a nice way to recognize the groom on this special occasion.

THE CROWNING TOUCH TO A PERFECT DAY

We want your cake to be the crowning touch to your perfect day. We encourage couples to come in and let us assist them in designing the wedding cake of their dreams! Our decorator takes personal interest in each order. Come in to view our photos and read thank yous from our many happy brides.

HANK'S PERFECTION BAKERY

661 S.E. Baseline
Hillsboro, Oregon 97123
Contact: Patty or Curtis (503) 648-4613
Business Hours: 6am–6pm

For your most special occasion, Perfection Bakery offers a wide selection of truly elegant, elaborate, and unique cake designs, and a knowledgeable staff to assist you in designing your perfect creation.

Our tradition of care and attention to detail has been passed along and refined for more than 65 years, using the finest ingredients available.

Our bakers and designers take pride in offering decadent cake flavors for your enjoyment. We offer the latest in shape designs from traditional rounds, to hearts, squares, rectangle and petal shapes.

We design the custom cake to your guest list needs, and the configuration to fill you heart's desire, including fountain stairs and unique stands.

Our personal one-on-one appointments allow you to sit and sample your cake flavors of choice and talk with a designer to determine your wedding needs.

We request orders 30 days in advance, but may accommodate shorter notice orders at our discretion. Full payment is required two weeks prior to delivery, with a full refund if canceled within five days of delivery the date.

Deliver and setup are free within the Hillsboro, Cornelius, and Forest Grove areas, with minimum mileage charges to Portland Metro Areas.

We encourage couples to come in and meet our knowledgeable and courteous staff and take advantage of our care and experience in planning your special day.

Perfection Bakery is a full-service bakery offering a full line of quality baked goods from pastries, cookies, breads, rolls and sheet cakes to fill your needs.

Call today for your appointment.

Helen Bernhard

"Baking your dreams come true since 1924"

1717 N.E. Broadway

Portland, Oregon 97232

(503) 287-1251

Business Hours: Mon–Sat 6am–6pm

Types and Styles of Wedding Cakes

Helen Bernhard Bakery is known throughout the metro area for beautiful and delicious cakes, pastries, and desserts. We use only the finest and freshest ingredients, including real butter. All our cakes are made from scratch and come in round or square shapes, stacked or separated by pillars. Flavors include Lady Baltimore, yellow butter, chocolate, banana, carrot, poppy seed, pink champagne, white chocolate, and apple spice. Filling flavors include lemon, raspberry, French cream, chocolate, pineapple, mocha, mint, apricot and strawberry. We have a variety of decorating options and offer an excellent selection of cake ornaments that will complement your color theme.

Cost, Ordering, and Delivery

A $10 nonrefundable deposit is requested when ordering your cake, with the balance due two weeks prior to the wedding. We recommend that you come in and select your wedding cake at least 30 days before the wedding. We always try to accommodate the bride's busy schedule, so we do accept orders on shorter notice. No appointment is necessary unless you need to talk directly to a decorator. Delivery throughout the Portland Metro area is offered at no extra charge.

Experience, Service, and Samples

Helen Bernhard Bakery has been providing the finest cakes and confections available in the Portland and Vancouver area for over 70 years through four generations of bakers. We recommend that you come in to sample the different flavors of cakes we offer and to review portfolios of our work. One of our friendly and professional staff members or decorators will be glad to sit down with you to help determine the type, size, and style of cake that will best fit your needs.

Additional Items and Decorations

As a full-service bakery, Helen Bernhard's can create a variety of baked goods for you, including petit fours, sheet cakes, chocolate Genache groom's cake, breads, Danish pastries, donuts, pies, cookies, and cheesecakes. We also have beautiful porcelain, glass, and traditional cake tops from which to choose that can add a crowning glory to your wedding cake.

SERVING OUR THIRD GENERATION OF HAPPY BRIDES

Helen Bernhard Bakery understands how important the wedding cake is to every bride and groom. A wedding cake is not only a long-standing tradition, but will also be the focal point of your reception. We have received great pleasure and satisfaction in creating cakes for many happy brides over the years and look forward to serving you. Let Helen Bernhard's make your wedding day a beautiful and delicious memory!

JaCiva's

BAKERY & CHOCOLATIER

4733 S.E. Hawthorne
Portland, Oregon 97215
(503) 234-8115
Mon–Sat 6:30am–6pm

United States Pastry Alliance gold medal winner
Winner of the Austin Family Business Award

Types and Styles of Wedding Cakes

If you're looking for a beautiful wedding cake, exquisite looking and luscious inside...A place where you can taste a variety of flavors and then select a different flavor for each tier...A place where you can get handmade mints to match your wedding colors...A place where you can get a special first-anniversary cake, just for the two of you, free...Then JaCiva's is your answer.

You can select a rich chocolate groom's cake or an assortment of Victorian tea pastries or chocolate truffles to make your rehearsal dinner or special-occasion event truly unique.

Cost, Ordering, and Delivery

Cost varies depending on the flavor, size, and style of cake. A $50 deposit is required, with the balance due two weeks before the wedding. Early ordering is suggested, especially for summer dates. JaCiva's delivers and sets up your cake free of charge in the local area. There is an additional fee for Sunday, private home and outside the metro area deliveries.

Chocolate and Other Gifts

JaCiva's offers a wonderful selection of wedding favors, groomsmen and bridesmaid gifts.

Wedding Accessories

Featuring the Beverley Clarke and Lilian Rose collection and others including; photo albums, ring pillows, pens, toasting glasses, cake and knife server, garters, etc.

"The cake must be a JaCiva's"
Bridal Connection July–August '96

CALL FOR A CONSULTATION WITH JACIVA'S "THE PERFECT PLACE TO FIND YOUR PERFECT WEDDING CAKE"

♥ *Member of Weddings of Distinction*

Renaissance Wedding Cakes

1160 S.W. McGinnis Court
Troutdale, Oregon 97060
Contact: Karen
(503) 492-4208; Fax (503) 492-2904
E-mail: rwedcakes@aol.com
By appointment only

Types and Styles of Wedding Cakes

If you're interested in personal attention to detail and pride in workmanship then come and see me. All my cakes are made from scratch, from the finest freshest ingredients. Cake flavors include my moist and luscious carrot and banana, white, butter, lemon, chocolate, German chocolate, poppyseed, spice, pink champagne and mocha. Some of our many fillings are lemon, raspberry, strawberry, fudge, cream cheese and cherry. There are a large variety of styles and shapes to choose from, and every tier can be a different flavor. You can have my light and creamy butter cream or my rolled fondant made from scratch.

Additional Items

Also available are groom's cakes, 1/2 sheets, 1/4 sheets, fountains, stairways, various cake stands and a large variety of ornaments that can be ordered for your convenience.

Cost

Cost is based on a per serving basis. A $50 nonrefundable deposit is required at time of order, with full payment due two weeks prior to the wedding. We like to have orders a month in advance, but we will always try to accommodate short notice.

Experience, Samples, Delivery and Instructions

I have 15 years experience in the Portland/Gresham area. Samples are available at consultations. Consultations are by appointment only. Delivery is available at no charge in the Gresham/Troutdale area. There will be a small charge for delivery elsewhere. Your cake will be boxed for delivery and cake cutting instructions are provided.

Personal Service Is Our Business

Renaissance is a family-owned business that believes very strongly in personal service. Give us a call—we will be glad to arrange a consultation.

YUM! YUM! YUM! YUM!

PIECE OF CAKE

PIECE OF CAKE

Established in 1979
Winner of Chocolate Safari 1991
7858 S.E. 13th • Portland, Oregon
Contact: Marilyn DeVault, food designer (503) 234-9445
Business Hours: New hours, please call

YUM! YUM! YUM! YUM!

AWARD WINNING! AWARD WINNING!

We provide elegant, classical wedding cakes and fun, unique designs that are custom tailored to your wedding dreams.

Gourmet Cakes from Piece of Cake

- **CHEESECAKE WEDDING CAKE:** decadent and beautiful. YUM! Choose from vanilla, chocolate marble, deep chocolate, amaretto, chocolate amaretto, praline and cream, grand marnier, lemon, German chocolate, Kahlua, and white chocolate.
- **AWARD-WINNING FANTASY CAKE:** voted favorite of the year. Each tier consists of cheesecake, choice of filling, and cake. What a surprise. YUM!
- **CARROT:** a wonderfully moist, spicy carrot cake made with pineapple. YUM!
- **IRISH OATMEAL:** a moist oatmeal spice cake with a real homemade texture. YUM!
- **DOUBLE CHOCOLATE FUDGE:** the chocolate lover's choice… made with coffee and buttermilk, this cake is almost black with chocolate. YUM!
- **POPPYSEED:** made with sour cream and filled with marionberries. YUM!
- **CREAM CHEESE POUND CAKE:** a dense pound cake, rich with cream cheese and butter. YUM!
- **APPLE RUM:** packed with apples, raisins, and walnuts, then frosted with cream cheese frosting. YUM!
- **BANANA PINEAPPLE:** moist banana cake complemented with a hint of rum. YUM!
- **ITALIAN CREAM:** coconut, pecans and a taste of Italy. YUM!

TASTE! YUM! Call (503) 234-9445 YUM! TASTE!

LOOKING FOR SOMETHING TO ADD TO YOUR PRE-WEDDING FESTIVITIES? ORDER ONE OF OUR BACHELORETTE OR BACHELOR PARTY CAKES.

CATERING ◆ CATERING ◆ CATERING ◆ CATERING ◆ CATERING

Vegan ◆ Vegan ◆ Vegan Wedding Cakes Yum!
Sugar Free ◆ Sugar Free ◆ Sugar Free Wedding Cakes Yum!

Marilyn and her staff are food designers, and the cakes are always a work of art.

© Joseph Photographer • page 501 • Capers Cafe & Catering Co. • page 303

Superstitions About Wedding Cakes

It's bad luck for the bride to

bake her own wedding cake.

•

The bride who samples her cake

before it's cut will forfeit her husband's love.

•

When the bride saves a piece of her wedding cake,

she ensures her husband's fidelity for life.

HELPFUL HINTS

- **Liquor laws and liability:** With today's strict liquor laws, it's always advisable to check into who assumes the liability for any alcoholic beverage service. Although the event facility and/or the caterer may carry liability insurance, the host or coordinator of the function may still be considered liable. Make sure all parties involved with the event are properly insured, and consult with an insurance agent to make sure you have appropriate coverage for yourself.
- **Banquet permits:** In Oregon and Washington, functions with private hosted bars featuring hard alcohol, beer, and wine are required to have a banquet permit. Many banquet sites are already registered with the states to serve alcoholic beverages, while others are not. If your banquet site requires you to purchase a liability waiver or banquet permit for the day, do it! It's for your protection. Remember that only Oregon Liquor Control Commission (OLCC) and Washington State Liquor Control Board (WSLCB) licensed food and beverage establishments can provide no-host bars. Call OLCC at (503) 872-5070 or WSLCB at (206) 464-6094 for more information. (Banquet permits can be obtained one week in advance of your function at any liquor store.)
- **Hotels and off-premise licenses:** Most hotels do not have off-premise liquor licenses, and their on-site licenses do not apply to events held on other properties. When planning an event at another site, make sure to obtain a one-time only license for any off-premise event.
- **Private hosted bars:** If you are serving hard liquor (alcohol other than beer or wine) at a hosted bar, you should consider having a state-licensed bartender. Licensed servers have a permit from the OLCC or WSLCB.

  If you have a no-host bar where money changes hands, the law requires that you have a server with a permit showing the completion of alcohol-server education.
- **Advantages of hiring professional beverage servers:** Beverage or catering service companies provide professionally trained staff who can handle complete bar services at your event. They take care of the purchasing, bar set-up and clean-up, serving, and liability. It may be worth the extra cost to ensure that the bar will be handled in a professional and legal manner. These people are trained to detect if someone should not be served more, or if someone is underage. This service also allows you to enjoy the event without worrying about your guests.
- **Beverages in bulk or case discount:** How do you get a good selection of beverages on a budget? Distributors, wine shops, and some stores offer variety and savings when you purchase in bulk. In some instances, unused beverages may be returned for a refund.
- **Area wineries:** Touring Oregon and Washington wineries can be a great place to find wines and champagnes. Spend a Saturday touring some of the wineries sampling the different varieties and select one that you and your fiancé will both enjoy.
- **Beverage-service equipment rentals:** Rental stores carry a variety of beverage-service equipment, including portable bars, kegs and taps, champagne fountains, and coffee makers.
- **Tired of punch and soda?** Try alternative beverages with a flair. Espresso bars feature a variety of drinks that you and your guests are sure to enjoy. They are also very "budget-friendly" in comparison to alcoholic beverages.

  Juice bars feature a wide selection of fresh-squeezed or specially mixed juices… everything from orange juice to exotic tropical concoctions.

HELPFUL HINTS

- **Determining the type of menu for your reception:** The time of day will help determine what you serve: for a morning wedding or event, you may want to serve a brunch menu; hors d'oeuvres are perfect for afternoon receptions; and a sit-down dinner or buffet is appropriate for evenings.
- **Favorite foods:** If you, your fiancé or families have favorite dishes or prefer certain types of foods, talk to your caterer about incorporating them into your menu. This extra attention to detail is always appreciated.
- **Menu selection and the weather:** Be certain that your menu selections will withstand your special day's anticipated weather. Avoid hot or heavy meals on muggy and humid days. High humidity may also wilt potato chips, cut cheeses, and similar foods. On hot days extra care should be taken to protect easily spoiled foods. Be especially careful with mayonnaise-based items, raw shellfish, and the like.
- **Catering guidelines:** To avoid running out of food at your reception, it is important to plan your menu carefully. Your caterer will be able to help you determine the best style of menu, with the correct amount of food based on your budget. Be sure to ask your caterer if they prepare any extra food for unexpected guests, and if there is an additional cost for this service. Always get a written estimate for the menu you have selected from the caterers you are considering. This estimate should include all food costs, rentals, labor, gratuities and taxes. Make sure the prices quoted will be valid at the time of your event!
- **Estimating how many people:** Determine your guest count as soon as possible, as all price quotes will be based on this number. Begin by requesting prospective guest lists from both your and the groom's parents. Then put together your own list. Once all the guest lists are combined, you can use the "rule-of-thumb" that 70–75% will attend to establish final guest count. We highly recommend that you include RSVP cards with your invitations whether you serve a formal sit-down dinner or a less formal buffet.
- **What the caterer supplies:** When it comes to supplying china, flatware, glasses, cups, saucers, and table linens, every catering company is different. Some will include the cost in their catering prices, while others will not. Ask each caterer you are considering how they handle this matter and make sure you fully understand all fees before signing a contract. What the caterer should supply is great service. They will coordinate all the details of your reception, including rentals, service staff, and referrals for other wedding-related businesses.
- **Serving the food:** After you have expressed your expectations for your reception, and have determined the flow of your party and time lines for the reception, your caterer will be able to suggest buffet table layouts and food start times. They may recommend that waiters serve hors d'oeuvres so that your guests can mingle, or offer you ideas about food stations which will create a more interactive reception for your guests. The important thing to remember is that you've planned well...Now it's time to leave the details of handling all the food service to the caterer so that you can enjoy your reception. The party is for you and your groom, and you should fully enjoy it without worrying about details that have already been delegated.

For more assistance with staying organized during the wedding planning process, check out the Bravo! Wedding Organizer. Detailed question worksheets double as contracts. This step-by-step system will keep every detail of your wedding organized. To order, refer to the order form on page 24 in this Guide.

PROFESSIONAL ICE CARVING

Sculptor: ***Christopher Huessy***
Contact: Dennise Huessy

Warehouse
(503) 557-0650

Office
(503) 654-0075

Traditional Sizes

• Full Size: 20″ by 40″ • Half Size: 20″ by 20″ • Individual Table Centerpieces
All sizes are available in clear or with color. Some specialty carvings include roses frozen in the ice. Carving detail generally lasts four to six hours.

Professional Background

Professional Ice Carving is a well-established full-time business. Our sculptor, Christopher Huessy, is a talented ice carver with over 25 years of experience. In addition to private affairs, we are currently servicing over 90 of the finest caterers, clubs, hotels, restaurants and professional organizations within the Portland Metropolitan area. Christopher is a leader in his industry, having custom designed and built his own ice block machine that produces 300-pound clear block ice, thus to ensure the quality of our product.

International Competition Medals and Honors

1999 – Gold medal – Lake Louise, Alberta, Canada
1998 – Competitor – The Nagano Winter Olympics Ice Carving Competition – Karuizawa, Japan
1997 – Sapporo Snow Festival – Sapporo, Japan
1996 – Gold medal – Anchorage, Alaska
1996 – Gold medal – Asahikaiwa, Japan
1994 – Gold medal – Fairbanks, Alaska

Christopher competes internationally to continue to offer "cutting edge" technology and to remain up-to-date on styles and trends.

Corporate Focus

Ice sculptures are a classic expression of prestige. Our ability to create an image in ice is as vast as your imagination. All sculptures are handcarved with artistic flair, and various images can be created for all kinds of events, from the "traditional" to "contemporary." We pride ourselves on our ability to reproduce business logos, complete with color. From practical shapes to extravagant masterpieces, you can rest assured you are in qualified hands.

Services

We take care of the details. What sets us apart is not just our ice carving but our consulting, delivery, safety, setup and expertise. Call for a personal appointment, and we'll be happy to assist you in creating an extraordinary event. We welcome your ideas and work with you to create the perfect affair!

Endorsements

Golf & Country Clubs
Columbia Edgewater Country Club
Multnomah Athletic Club
Oregon Golf Club
Portland Golf Club
Pumpkin Ridge Golf Club
The Reserve Vineyards & Golf Club

Hotels & Inns
Benson Hotel
DoubleTree Hotels
Hilton Hotel
Holiday Inns
RiverPlace Hotel
Timberline Lodge

Retail Chains
AT&T Wireless
Ben Bridge
Fred Meyer
Meier & Frank
Nordstrom
Safeway

INTEL • NIKE • OHSU • OMSI • OREGON CONVENTION CENTER • PSU • ROSE FESTIVAL ASSOC. • US BANK

We invite comparison

Rose's Tea Room

Full Service Event Catering
Business Office: 23501 N.E. 10th Avenue
Ridgefield, Washington 98642
(360) 887-3095
Fax (360) 887-3956
E-mail: rosestroom@aol.com
Web site: www.rosestearoom.com

Types of Menus and Specialties

Beautiful, elegant and unique, tea events are the ultimate expression of gracious hospitality. Modern tea is comfortable and enticing to the senses, encouraging good conversation and a lively exchange of ideas. Rose's Tea Room full-service catering offers a variety of tea events. Tea Brunches, Afternoon Tea Luncheons, Evening High Teas, Dessert Teas and Theme Teas can be tailored to suit any occasion and group size.

Rose's Tea Room teas are bountiful and satisfying meals. **Sample Menu:**

Cranberry Chicken Salad Puffs ◆ Classic Cucumber Tea Sandwiches Three Pepper Cream Cheese on Rye ◆ Almond Raspberry Frangipane Tarts Lemon Madelines ◆ Chocolate Dipped Hazelnut Crisps ◆ Cranberry Orange Poundcake ◆ Chocolate Dipped Strawberries ◆ Fresh Fruit ◆ Mad Hatter Scones Rose's Wild Blackberry Jam ◆ Blended Black Currant Tea

Rose's brings the charm of the tea room to you with china tea cups, exquisite layered table cloths, candles, and fresh flowers. Our Dessert Teas feature tea pastries fresh baked by Rose's Tea Room using only the finest ingredients available.

Cost

Prices range from $9.95 per person for dessert tea, depending upon size of group and menu requested. A 50% deposit is required to reserve your date, with the balance due 72 hours prior to the event. We ask for a guaranteed number of guests three days prior to the event.

Services

Rose's Tea Room caters business lunches, receptions, weddings, bridal showers, anniversary celebrations, and holiday parties such as our Colonial Christmas Tea. Tea, served buffet style, is a refreshing alternative to the cocktail party.

Rose's Tea Room excels in creating an atmosphere of gracious hospitality, where attention to detail and professional, kind service leave guests feeling pampered and happy.

In addition to catering, Rose's Tea Room offers Tea of the Month Club, Tea Time Gift Boxes, Rose's Wild Blackberry Jam, Huckleberry Preserves and our Tea Therapy Tin, available for delivery nationwide. (See our web site or call for more information.)

"This is the best food I have ever eaten."
— Esther Milligan, Woodland, Washington

"I have been to many teas, and this is the most food ever served to me. I loved it!"
— Becky Neuschwander, Burdoin Mansion, Battle Ground, Washington

AWARD-WINNING

A TASTE OF HOLLAND

JE MAINTIENDRAI

BAKERIES & CATERING

(Located inside West Linn Thriftway)
5639 Hood Street • West Linn, Oregon 97068
(503) 656-2981; Fax (503) 650-1230

A "Taste of Holland" Bakeries and Catering

- works with you in creating a one-of-a-kind masterpiece
- allows you to sample several different cakes and fillings
- provides highly skilled color matching from your samples
- creates the finest quality wedding cakes in the nation as judged by National Retail Bakers Association
- provide a free first anniversary cake
- provide expanded delivery outside of metro area for a nominal fee
- provide elegant catering for any occasion

Our award-winning bakery team will assist you in selecting from our large assortment of elegant Dutch pastries, gourmet cookies and breads to make your wedding day memorable.

Cost, Ordering and Delivery

We encourage you to come in to order your wedding cake. This allows you to view our portfolio and sample our quality. We request a 20% nonrefundable deposit with your order.

Ask about our

FREE

Anniversary Cake.

Accent on Events

918 S.W. Yamhill, Second Floor
Portland, Oregon 97205
Contact: Philip Sword or Barbara Abalan
(503) 227-4061
E-mail: accentevnt@qol.com

Full Service Catering and Special Event Production

- Wedding Receptions
- Theme Parties
- Holiday Parties
- Business Meetings
- Corporate Events
- Fundraisers
- Awards Banquets
- Reunions & Proms

Menus

Numerous menus available from which you may select or we will gladly custom design your menu based upon personal requests and budget.

Cost

Cost is dependent on menu and service selected (buffet or sit-down). Prices are per person and inclusive of staff, china, silverware, linens, etc. (except drop-off services). A 50% deposit required to confirm.

Alcohol

Fully licensed to serve all alcoholic beverages with complete liability insurance (hosted, no-host or combination).

Services

Experienced in all locations, from private homes to office buildings and outdoors. We provide only professional and skilled staff.

Accent on Events is the exclusive full-service caterer and event planner for the prestigious Adrianna Hill Grand Ballroom and provide services in the Portland Metro area. You are invited to call for information or schedule an appointment at Portland's most unique location to discuss your next event.

Affordable
Experienced
Innovative

Professional
Great Food
Easy

Special Fully-Inclusive Packages Available
with Rental of The Adrianna Hill Grand Ballroom

Great "Drop-Off" Food Services Available ♠ Receptions Ready-To-Go

See page 95 under Banquet & Receptions.

The Cuisine

Fabulous food is catered to your individualized tastes. All dishes are created by our personal chef and made with the finest ingredients.

Specialized Catering

Wedding Receptions, Rehearsal Dinners, Showers, Corporate Events, Holiday Parties, Business Meetings, Formal Banquets, Award Banquets, Elaborate Gift Baskets, Silver Platters, and Elegant Hors d' Oeuvres Mirrors.

Services

- Professional chefs, planners, and servers prepare for your special event.
- Elegant serving trays, baskets, and table decorations ranging from simple centerpieces to elegant displays are provided.
- Disposable dishware is included with no additional charge.
- Rental coordination of china, linens, silverware, etc., is arranged.
- Our "ALWAYS PERFECT" touch is added to every event.

Gifts

Impress your wedding party and friends with an ALWAYS PERFECT Gift Basket filled with fresh food, or an Elegant Hors d' Oeuvres Mirror. Local delivery is provided.

Cost and Terms

We offer free consultations and event planning. A 50% deposit is required to confirm the date of your event. Corporate accounts and all major credit cards are welcomed.

"Simple to Elegant Catering designed to meet your budget and needs"

Call for your Free Consultation
(503) 465-0400

Distinctive Catering

AN ELEGANT AFFAIR

P.O. Box 80013 • Portland, Oregon 97280
Contact: Melody
(503) 245-2802; Fax (503) 246-4309
E-mail: melodym@spiritone.com

Brides...You are cordially invited to An Elegant Affair...Your wedding!

Types of Menus and Specialties

Catering is our only business. An Elegant Affair catering will carefully plan, prepare, and present a tantalizing bill of fare created specifically to fit your wedding budget and needs. Whether it's a formal sit-down dinner, an intimate hors d'oeuvres reception, or a fabulous rehearsal dinner, we are committed to making your wedding an elegant one!

Services and Cost

- **Menu planning:** Our seasoned staff can prepare any type of cuisine in our fully licensed catering kitchen, and we are happy to design a menu that will suit your special occasion.
- **Estimating number of guests:** We can help you determine how many guests to expect to ensure accurate food quantities are ordered.
- **Cost:** Our prices are determined on a per-person basis and vary upon menu selection. A 25% deposit is required to reserve your event date. The balance is due before the event.
- **Beverage service:** Alcoholic and nonalcoholic beverages are available.
- **Linens and napkins:** Buffet table linen and skirting no charge; paper products no charge; white and colored linen tablecloths and napkins available.
- **Serviceware:** Silver serving trays available no charge; china, glassware, paper, plastic available.
- **Riverboat receptions and parties:** Available year-round on the Willamette.
- **Servers:** We supply experienced, professional servers and bartenders in formal black and white attire. Setup, serving, and complete cleanup of all food and beverages are always provided at no extra charge.

For your entertaining ease, let AN ELEGANT AFFAIR help make your special day a worry-free and memorable event.

(You'll find hosting a special occasion will never be easier or more enjoyable.)

Call today for a complimentary consultation!
(503) 245-2802

Applewood Catering

Chef Peter Leigh Gallin

HOOD RIVER, OREGON VANCOUVER, WASHINGTON

541.386.2144 360.260.0379

E-mail: applwood@pacifier.com

Specializing in Fresh Northwest and International Cuisine

Applewood Catering combines an international flavor with the colorful bounty of fresh Northwest ingredients to bring you healthy and unique menus tailored to fit any palate and budget. Chef Peter Leigh Gallin hand selects the freshest Northwest fruits, produce, meats and seafood to create a meal that will be an enchanting event. Combined with artistic presentation and refined professional service, your wedding will be an occasion you and your guests will never forget.

Full-Service Catering for Any Occasion—From Elegant to Casual

Applewood Catering is a full-service caterer able to work closely with you to ensure your wedding is the celebration you deserve. Whether you need catering for six or 600, we can arrange for every necessity; from all rentals and staffing, to cake, photographer and flowers, as well as the site.

Applewood Catering is experienced in large formal weddings, rehearsal dinners and elegant hors d'oeuvres as well as small intimate repasts and cooking classes. Let Chef Peter and Applewood's trained professional staff handle all the details to make your reception an event you and your guests will truly enjoy.

Chef Peter Leigh Gallin, Creative Catering since 1990

Chef Peter is a graduate of the renowned California Culinary Academy where he studied classical French cooking techniques. In addition, he has traveled and lived throughout the world where he has gained culinary influences from cuisines across the globe.

He is a devotee to better living through healthy eating and is a cooking instructor as well as a caterer. He has worked as Chef du Cuisine at numerous restaurants throughout the Rocky Mountains and now calls the Pacific Northwest home.

Serving Greater Portland, Vancouver and the Columbia River Gorge

Professionalism • Experience • Creativity

Applewood Catering
Call today for a consultation or brochure
(360) 260-0379 or (541) 386-2144
Applwood@pacifier.com

Barton Productions Catering

1822 N.E. 153rd Street • Vancouver, Washington 98686
(360) 574-7449; Fax (360) 573-9218 E-mail: ebarton@teleport.com

Hollywood and New York Style

Every Barton Productions Wedding Reception is carefully designed to fit the location, theme and style of your reception. For the **Elegant Cocktail Party**, start with Atwater's trained formal butlers in black tuxedos and white dinner jackets passing gleaming sterling trays of jewel-like hors d'oeuvres with a classy jazz trio and elegant black crystal and goldware. For the **Beautiful Victorian Banquet**, begin with the "back from the hunt" giant buffet with mountains of garlic roasted beef, whole turkeys and hams on several different levels of Italian marble combined with huge ferns, dozens of candles, and delicate gold ribbon woven through old fashioned ivory linens. The **Classic New York Dinner** butlered on elegant ecru and platinum china with sterling flatware, huge Pinot Noir wine glasses and giant rose centerpieces is another of the many special themes available for your "once in a lifetime" day! A wedding Luau, Caribbean, Northwest Rustic, Equestrian, Airplane, Beach, Mexican, Persian and French Country are just a few of the many other themes Barton Productions specializes in.

Glamorous Details Included at No Extra Charge

The "event of the year" that wows your guests is the goal of Barton Productions Catering for every wedding. All the extra details are included; buffet ferns, palms, candles, matching lame, cake table set-up, specially matched linens, butlers, bartenders, marble bar set-ups, and your special theme matched chinas, flatware, and crystal. A Professional Event Manager will coordinate all or any portion of your wedding reception details without extra charge.

Preferred Caterer in the Best Locations

Barton Productions Catering is a preferred caterer for various types of reception sites all over the Portland area, whether you are looking for a large Classical Roman ballroom like the **Portland Art Museum's Sunken Ballroom**, or the Victorian charm of **Arnegards' Winnington Ballroom** or the European elegance of **Hunter Creek Farm's Equestrian Estate** nestled on the Willamette River. The Marshall House, Pearson Air Museum, The Crown Ballroom, City University, The Burdoin Mansion, The Academy, The Jenkins Estate, The Grand Oregon Lodge, The World Forestry Center, A Night in Shining Amour, The Overlook House, Tallina's, and The Wedding House are just some of the many other locations in addition to your own private location or any of the area's many public sites.

Cuisine Your Family and Friends Will Like

With classics like the Giant Caesar Salad with Garlic Butter Parmesan Croutons, the three levels of marble Tropical Fruit Waterfall with Gran Marnier Chocolate Sauce, or the Sundried Tomato and Mushroom Rigatoni, combined with the Crab and Parmesan Stuffed Mushrooms, the Roasted Garlic and Pasta Skewers, and Roasted Pork and Pineapple Skewers with Cajun Barbecue Sauce, Barton Productions Catering will help you prepare a special menu that will please all your varied guests. **Call for a same day proposal faxed to you!**

Member of the Association of Catering & Event Professionals.

BLIMPIE

Contact: Tiffany Hugo

Westside
1923 S.W. Sixth Avenue
Portland, Oregon 97201
(503) 225-0538
Fax (503) 656-5513

Eastside
4124 82nd Avenue
Portland, Oregon 97266
(503) 771-3719
Fax (503) 656-5513

If you haven't had your occasion catered by us,
You haven't had the best by Blimpie!

Menu and Specialties

Blimpie offers a wide variety of sandwiches, salads, fresh baked cookies, and we can also provide ice cream or frozen yogurt cakes for any special occasion. Blimpie specializes in 3-foot and 6-foot Blasts made on homemade bread with your favorite fresh meats and delicious toppings. Blasts may be packaged with its own box and lining.

- 3-foot Blast feeds 15–20 people
- 6-foot Blast feeds 30–40 people

We also have "Blimpie Bites," a tray of our delicious three-inch subs to accommodate your party size with your choice choice of fresh meats and cheeses.

How about a "Blimpie Box"—a six-inch sub with your choice of chips, potato or macaroni salad and a fresh baked cookie, packaged with condiments and utensils in a convenient box. Order 10 "Blimpie Boxes," and the 11th is on us!

Cost and Services

Our cost is based per item. The balance is due upon delivery or pickup, with a 20% deposit due at the time of order. Our catering department would be happy to meet with you for a free consultation and sandwich, so you can experience for yourself how good Blimpie is.

Mention you saw us in the Bravo! Bridal Guide and receive a 10% discount!

CAPERS CAFE & CATERING CO™

12003 N.E. Ainsworth Circle, Suite A
Portland, Oregon 97220
Contact: Christian or Annette Joly
(503) 252-1718; Fax (503) 252-0178
Business Hours: Mon–Fri 7am–7pm
Web site: www.caperscafe.com

If You're Entertaining Very Important People… We Deliver

When you want to electrify a crowd, nothing causes quite the stir like food prepared by Capers Cafe and Catering Company. Bold, imaginative food… presented with both precision and panache. You've probably got some great ideas. So do we. And together we will plan an event that's destined to be remembered and implemented precisely as planned. All foods are prepared from fresh Northwest products with emphasis on taste and appearance.

Banquet and Reception Site

Capers is able to accommodate private rehearsal dinners and receptions up to 150.

Cost

Cost is based on the food selection and type of event. All costs are itemized and on a per-person basis. A 50% deposit is required upon confirmation of event. Cancellations may be made 10 days prior to the event.

Experience

With 25 years experience in the industry, Christian Joly has prepared international events for 2,000, as well as intimate dinners for two.

Services

Capers Cafe and Catering Company is a fully licensed and insured caterer, capable of providing any style of food and beverage that a customer may require. Seven days a week.

Food Preparation and Equipment

Capers Cafe and Catering Company prepares all foods with flair, putting heavy emphasis on taste and visual appearance.

Serving Attendants

To ensure a successful event, we provide all the necessary professionals to prepare, serve, and clean up. Gratuities are optional.

OUR FOODS AND SERVICES ARE 100% GUARANTEED

Capers Cafe and Catering Company is an extremely successful business because of its employees. Our staff believes in satisfying all the needs of our customers. We never take shortcuts and guarantee our foods and services 100%, or we return your money. ***We are at your service.***

CAROUSEL CATERING

223 S.E. 122nd Avenue • Portland, Oregon 97233
Contact: Catering Department (503) 261-9424; Fax (503) 261-2989
Web site: www.fountainsballroom.com
Business Hours: Tues, Wed, Thurs 9am–9pm or by appointment

"Stress-Free One Stop Wedding Planning"

Types of Menus and Specialty

Carousel Catering works with you to design a menu that suits your personality, style, and theme. We offer hors d'oeuvres, self-serve buffets, and sit-down meals. We cater anything from large sit-down dinners to a private party for two. All food is beautifully arranged and garnished with freshly carved centerpieces. We offer one stop planning—taking away your stress on the most important day of your life. We offer our own on-site facility located at The Fountains Ballroom. Ask about our photography, flowers, printing and decorating services.

Cost

Packages range from $6.95 to $40 per person. A nonrefundable deposit of $200 is required to reserve your date with the balance due 10 days prior to your event. A 20% gratuity will be added to the final food bill.

Services: On-site and off-site—We're located at The Fountains Ballroom

- **Wedding cakes:** each cake custom-made; choose from over 14 flavors and 12 fillings; each layer can be a different flavor at no additional charge.
- **Beverages:** assorted nonalcoholic beverages available; alcoholic beverages may be added to contract—we are fully licensed and insured; full bar, beer and wine service available
- **Dishes and glassware:** crystal dishes and cups; champagne, beer, and wine glasses available in glass or plastic
- **Linens:** coordinated linens, napkins, and table skirting; personalized paper napkins
- **Serviceware:** silver tea service; silver punch bowl, nut and mint trays, candelabras; silver champagne cooler and toasting glasses
- **Floral arrangements and ice carvings:** elegant floral arrangements for food and cake tables; specialize in freehand ice carvings, any size and design
- **Events:** we are wedding specialists; however, we also do corporate events from formal sit-down to box lunches.

See page 136 under Banquet & Reception Sites.
See page 485 under Photographers.

Restaurant and Catering
1331 S.W. Washington
Portland, Oregon 97205
Contact: Christine, Bob or Mercedes
(503) 223-0054

A Portland Favorite since 1979!

Cassidy's Restaurant is located in a historic building in the heart of downtown Portland. Our exceptional menu features regional cuisine of delicious seafood, premium-cut meats, fresh pastas, seasonal salads and more.

Full-service Catering

Cassidy's is experienced in catering all wedding-related events including rehearsal dinners, wedding brunches and full receptions.

Services

- **Food** From a sit-down dinner or extensive buffet to appetizers and desserts, we offer our fresh Northwest specialties. We'll help you plan a menu just right for your occasion.
- **Beverage** Cassidy's Restaurant is completely licensed and insured to serve alcohol and also offers a wide assortment of nonalcoholic beverages.
- **Cost** We are happy to work within your budget.
- **Staff** Cassidy's staff of experienced restaurant professionals also services our catered events.

Private Banquet Room and Full-service Restaurant

Cassidy's has a private dining room available for receptions and rehearsal dinners up to 50 people. During the afternoon, Cassidy's offers the entire restaurant facility to private parties for receptions up to 300 people.

RESERVE THE ENTIRE RESTAURANT FOR AFTERNOON RECEPTIONS!

See page 73 under Rehearsal Dinner Sites.

Catering At Its Best

Contact: Karla or Laura (503) 238-8889

Seriously Now...
Catering At Its Best takes quality seriously and continuously pushes it to higher levels. Offering unique blends of Northwest native flavors, uncompromised freshness and meticulous organization—our events and galas sparkle. Exacting standards, gracious professionalism, and a detailed understanding of artful, delicious presentation create wonderful celebrations!

They Say It's All in the Past—We Believe the Best is Yet to Come
Experience has groomed Catering At Its Best. Planning for the unforeseen, preparing for the "what ifs," and asking simple questions set the mark for professionalism. Members of our catering team are proficient, organized and thoughtful. The wait staff offers crisp, groomed service, artistic, bountiful presentation and thorough completion of all tasks. Behind the scenes, the Chefs create works of art with only top grade, fine quality ingredients. Quantities are carefully calculated—unpretentious abundance is the benchmark.

Atmosphere is for the Stars
Regardless of a location's character, the *atmosphere* can be formalized, refined or made to appear fun and festive. Catering At Its Best owns a full line of serviceware, provides color-coordinated linens and is a resource for creative props and decorations. Before each event, we meet at your site and finalize the arrangements to make floorplans flow freely, seating arrangements perfect, and the atmosphere glow. Creativity, ingenuity and experience help transform your ideas into realization, props into ambiance, banquet halls into gala ballrooms, and Mother Nature into paradise.

We Get Around!
Catering At Its Best has partied all over town! From your private home to a public park setting—we are adaptable to any environment. We are also approved to serve in major locations in and about Portland including The Central Library, The Jenkins Estate, The Sternwheeler Rose, The Portland Art Museum, The Laurelhurst Club, The Oregon History Center, Tallina's Garden and The Old Church. Catering At Its Best is the exclusive caterer for Kingstad Meeting Centers.

Welcoming One and All
Catering At Its Best is centrally located and is operating in an immaculate, fully licensed and insured commercial kitchen. We welcome our clients to visit our kitchen, discuss plans, and sample flavors and presentation.

Energized for the Future
Because brides and grooms rarely have a chance to eat at their own receptions, we prepare beautiful individual meals and a chilled bottle of champagne just in time to escape for the honeymoon!

Call Now!
As you plan your successful event, call Karla or Laura to learn more about Catering At Its Best's services.

Chef du Jour

Creative Custom Catering

Chef Nancy Crampton-Brophy

503 • 222-4553

1972 N.W. Flanders
Portland, Oregon 97209

NO THEME TOO EXOTIC; NO CUISINE TOO ESOTERIC

Types of Menus and Specialty
Our fare ranges from New Age/organic to classical decadence. We can design menus for casual or formal dining—from receptions and rehearsal dinners to bridal showers and anniversary dinners for two. We offer on- and off-premise catering. Ask about our honeymoon packages.

Think of Us for

LIFE CYCLE EVENTS	*CORPORATE FUNCTIONS*	*SOCIAL EVENTS*
Wedding Receptions	Company Picnics/BBQs	Teas/Brunches
Rehearsal Dinners	Holiday Parties	Cocktail Parties
Bar/Bat Mitzvahs	Grand Openings	Reunions
Birthdays/Anniversaries	Business Meetings	Retirements

Cakes
Wedding cakes from the simple to the elaborate; all types of flavors and fillings. Prices start at $1.50 per person. We also can create groom's cakes, first anniversary cakes and cakes for other special occasions. Call for an appointment to view photographs; samples available.

Cost
Reasonably priced. Free consultation and planning.

Experience
Chef du Jour Catering has been in business for eight years. We are the exclusive caterer for Congregation Beth Israel in Northwest Portland. We use the freshest available product and classical preparation techniques. Each menu is designed to meet the individual customer's desires and needs.

Service
Chef du Jour is a full-service caterer and can provide linens, glassware, centerpieces or anything else you need for your event. We have a professionally trained staff, attractive and healthy food and innovative food styling. We also offer decorating and florist services and pickup and delivery.

CATERING WITH A DIFFERENCE!

MasterCard VISA

Dale's Catering Service

Always in good taste!

2420 S.E. Belmont Street • Portland, Oregon 97214
(503) 234-9948; Fax (503) 236-9346

Specialized menus for each client since 1945

Experience

Dale's Catering has been serving Portland and the surrounding metropolitan communities since 1945. We pride ourselves on our commitment to our clients.

Types of Menus and Specialty

Dale's Catering will prepare food for any type of event from the most formal of weddings to large company dinners and sporting events. At Dale's Catering we believe that each wedding has its own unique personality and that the menu and service should reflect that personality. We can provide everything from formal wedding dinners served in courses to very simple hors d'oeuvres prepared, trayed, and delivered to your reception site.

Cost and Services

Because we are a full-service catering company, we can provide you with:

- **A menu designed especially for you.**
- **Equipment:** silver coffee and tea service, silver punch bowl, coffee urn, candelabras, cake knife and server, china, glassware, silverware, linens, linen napkins, paper and plastic supplies, tables, chairs, and much more are available.
- **Beverages:** Assorted alcoholic and non-alcoholic beverages are available. Dale's Catering Service is licensed by the OLCC to serve alcoholic beverages, and all of our bartenders have OLCC service permits.
- **Flowers:** We work with a local florist who can handle all of your floral needs.
- **Cakes:** We do not prepare cakes but will be happy to recommend three custom bakeries, and we can facilitate the ordering and delivery of your cake if you wish.

The cost of catering for your wedding will be determined by the menu, the number of guests, and the service requested. When we supply alcoholic beverages, you will be billed for the amount used.

An advance deposit of $500 is required one month prior to your wedding. You will be billed for the balance the first business day after the event, and the full balance is due upon receipt of the invoice. If you must cancel, your full deposit will be refunded if we are given 72 hours notice.

Comments From Our Clients

"Thank you for a job beautifully done." *S.B.—Portland*

"The food was wonderful. It was a perfect day and a perfect wedding." *K.V.—Vancouver*

"Thank you for the wonderful service. The food display was fresh, crisp and colorful." *C.P.—Portland*

Visit us at our Web site:
www.citysearch.com/pdx/dales

DeAngelo's Catering and Events

14297 S.W. Pacific Highway • Tigard, Oregon 97224
Contact: Steve DeAngelo (503) 620-9020
Available for catering seven days a week
Call for store hours

Types of Menus and Specialtics

DeAngelo's offers all types of menus from self-serve buffets to full-service formal sit-down affairs. We are well-known for our Pasta Bars. On-site cooking is always a hit with attendees. All foods are prepared from scratch. Low-fat and vegetarian menus are happily accommodated. A wide range of ethnic menus are available, such as Asian, Italian, Mexican, African, and Caribbean. Give DeAngelo's Catering a call when planning your wedding reception.

Cost and Experience

Price is based on a per-person basis for full-service events; however, many other options are available. DeAngelo's Catering prides itself on quality food at an affordable price. Delivery available. Food tasting and references provided upon request. Free consultation.

Services

DeAngelo's is licensed and insured to serve alcoholic beverages. Complete event coordination and site-analysis service available. To complete your event, all full-service buffets are decorated at no charge.

Presentation and Service Staff

All foods are exquisitely presented using copper chafing dishes along with granite and marble tiles and slabs. Service staff is available for all types of events. Attire is always appropriate.

Approved Caterer for the Following Locations

- Arnegards
- Portland Art Museum
- Canterbury Falls
- Central Library
- The Crown Ballroom
- Elk Cove Winery
- Jenkins Estate (main house and stable)
- Marshall House
- Queen Anne Victorian Mansion
- World Forestry Center

Other Sites which we are Familiar with

- Lakewood Center of the Arts
- The Laurelhurst Club
- Leach Botanical Gardens
- Metger Park Hall
- Oaks Park
- Scouters Mountain Lodge
- Senior Centers: Oregon City, Sherwood, Tigard, Wilsonville
- Sokol Blosser Winery
- North Star Ballroom

A founding member of the Association of Caterers and Event Professionals

FLEXIBILITY TO MEET YOUR NEEDS

DeAngelo's is always willing to work with clients to find a menu that fits within their budget and menu guidelines. We offer flexibility to adapt to special needs and requests. With our wide range of menus and services, we can accommodate your requests.

Decorations provided FREE with all full-service buffets!
Visit our Web site: www.cateringbydeangelos.com

Delilah's Catering

833 N.W. 16th Avenue
Portland, Oregon 97209
Contact: Linette True (503) 243-3324
E-mail: delilah@teleport.com
Web site: http://www.teleport.com/~delilah

Classic or Trendy

Your reception reflects your style, just as your bridal gown, flowers and music do. The food we prepare and the table we set show your guests the care you've taken to celebrate your wedding day.

Cuisine

- **Northwest:** Freshly prepared local seafood, meats, fruits and vegetables, changing with the season
- **International:** Authentic ethnic dishes including European, Mediterranean, South American and Asian.
- **Regional American:** Southwestern, Cajun, Heartland, Eastern Seaboard and Southern

Menus

Buffet or formal table service? Brunch, lunch, mid-afternoon or dinner? Winter, spring, summer or autumn? Indoor or outdoor? Cuisine? With this many factors involved in an event, our menus are custom designed to suit the event. Delilah's encourages you to mix and match cuisines to include your favorite dishes. Tasty vegetarian options are available.

Services

- **Staff:** professional waiters, licensed bartenders, chefs for on-site cooking or carving, on-site coordinators
- **Table settings:** china, linen, silver and crystal are available
- **Decoration:** ice carving, floral design, formal or rustic displays
- **Outdoor:** canopies, tents, dance floors, arches, tables, umbrellas and chairs in many styles

Exquisite Presentation

Our luscious food merits a beautiful presentation. We artfully arrange and garnish our dishes to be a focal point for your reception.

DELILAH'S GIFT TO YOU

We know how exciting your wedding day will be, so we prepare a basket as a gift from Delilah's filled with goodies from your reception, for the two of you to enjoy when you're alone.

EAT YOUR HEART OUT CATERING

Monica Grinnell, Proprietor since 1975
1230 S.E. Seventh
Portland, Oregon 97214
Kitchen/Voice Mail: (503) 232-4408
Fax (503) 226-0405
E-mail: eyho@europa.com

Types of Menus and Specialties

Who better to cater your wedding reception than the co-author of ***Newlywed Style: The Cookbook***, first in a series of life-style books for newly married couples. **Eat Your Heart Out Catering** was created in 1975 by two brides, who produced three brides-to-be along the way. Maybe you want to be involved in the menu, or just sit back and be dazzled by choices ranging from **baron of beef with Oregon Pinot Noir sauce and baby baked potato bar to caviar eclairs with lemon cream**. Recommended by **major facilities** including Montgomery Park, World Forestry Center, Jenkins Estate, The Marshall House, Portland Art Museum and Central Library among others—we specialize in all cuisines: ethnic, traditional, or more adventuresome with Northwest fresh products. At the heart of it, Monica Grinnell, the owner, was trained as an interior designer, so **food design and presentation** are as important as the **delicious flavors** we create. Most of all, we specialize in you because we know that **you** want to remember your wedding reception as a wonderful experience, from planning the look and the menu, to the moment you leave your reception with a beautiful food basket tucked under your arm.

Experience

Eat Your Heart Out Catering has had the pleasure to be hired by some of the finest corporations and private clients in the Northwest. Our experience includes 20 years of planning catering events; designing and packaging a line of herbed vinegars; cooking with such noted chefs as Julia Child, Marcella Hazan, Craig Claiborne, and Pierre Franey; teaching cooking classes; and appearing on local television demonstrating and teaching cooking techniques. We would be glad to furnish you a client list or recommendations, and we are happy to show you our beautiful **portfolio**.

Food Presentation, Equipment and Staff

Eat Your Heart Out Catering is a full-service caterer. We provide **dishes**, **linens**, disposable products if you need them, all **serving pieces** both traditional and unusual, **flowers**, **ice sculptures**, even props for **special themes**. Our staff includes **bartenders**, **servers**, even a substitute **"Auntie"** to cut the cake, so yours can enjoy the reception. Most importantly we give you the **confidence** to make your dreams become a reality.

WHAT MAKES US SPECIAL

You make us special. You're going to be whirlwinded, waited on, waited for, honeymooned, brided, groomed–kaazaam, you're married! And **Eat Your Heart Out** will be a part of it. Watch for our new book, *We're Married Let's Eat, simple cooking and entertaining for your first year together.*

FABULOUS FOOD BY NANCY TAYLOR

936 S.E. Ankeny Street, Suite A
Portland, Oregon 97214
Contact: Nancy Taylor
Kitchen/Voice Mail (503) 515-2824
Fax (503) 226-6364

Types of Menus and Specialty

Fabulous Food has been in the catering business since 1982, with a fine reputation for producing stress-free entertaining. Nancy's formal training includes classes in France at LaVeran and Le Cordon Bleu and in California from great chefs such as Julia Child, Julee Rosso, and Sheila Lukins of The Silver Palate. Fabulous Food believes in using the best quality ingredients and serving them with style. Whether the occasion calls for a backyard barbecue or formal French dinner service, we'll work with you to create the menu and details that will make your wedding or special event a fabulous affair!

Services

Nancy is happy to sit down with you and help plan details, from recommending an appropriate location to choosing and arranging for the rental of table linens in your color scheme. She prides herself on being flexible when working with her clients so the end result is a great event! After helping two daughters through their weddings, Nancy knows what wedding plans involve and enjoys every aspect.

Cost

The cost is based on a per-guest count and will vary according to your menu selections. A deposit of 50% is required two weeks in advance, with the balance due the day of the event.

Food Preparation and Equipment

We will provide all the service equipment you need from a wide collection of styles, including black lacquer, antique silver, brass, copper, baskets, and more!

Serving Attendants

We will provide all service staff needed, and also will take care of setup and cleanup of food and beverage services. We are fully licensed by the Oregon Liquor Control Commission and provide professionally trained staff.

THE FOOD IS TRULY FABULOUS

Fabulous Food has planned successful parties and receptions ranging from small affairs in private homes to large corporate festivities for U.S. Bank, *Life Magazine*, Air Touch Cellular, Nordstom, and Zell Bros Jewelers. All of Nancy's clients speak highly of her professional attitude, friendly smile and dependability, but most of all they say, "The food is truly fabulous."

♥ *Member of Weddings of Distinction*

Four Seasons Catering

Contact: Kevin Danley
(503) 674-2812

Receptions Without Limitations

Four Seasons Catering specializes in unique wedding receptions that include formal sit-down dinners, casual summer brunches, bountiful hors d'oeuvre buffets, and beautiful dessert buffets. Whether a garden party wedding for 30, or a formal reception for 300 in an historic wedding hall, Four Seasons Catering will create an atmosphere that every guest will remember. Imagine a summer reception at a local vineyard with a menu including flavorful hors d'oeuvres such as Jamaican chicken skewers, goat cheese tarts with grilled vegetables, and smoked salmon crostini.

Creating an Event with Individual Style

Each wedding menu is customized to meet the bride and groom's individual needs. Our staff will meet with each couple to ensure that every detail will be attended to. Following an initial consultation, an itemized estimate will be prepared. Four Seasons Catering can also provide a full line of dinnerware and glassware, linens, floral arrangements, tables, chairs, outdoor lighting, and canopies. All servers are professionally attired, and primed to provide each guest with a memorable event. Four Seasons Catering servers are responsible for setup as well as cleanup.

Attention to Detail Makes Each Event Special

At Four Seasons Catering, each wedding reception is carefully executed to achieve an unforgettable event. Small details create a reception with individual flair, from custom-made napkins to match the bride's color theme, to gift boxes of handmade chocolate amaretto truffles for each guest to take home.

"I'd always enjoyed the idea of entertaining, but working out the technical difficulties was a problem. When I discovered Kevin Danley with Four Seasons Catering, all my problems were solved. I have used Four Seasons Catering for small, intimate dinner parties to large, full-scale corporate affairs, never once being disappointed."

—Curtis Barber, Evolution Hair Design

"Four Seasons Catering catered our daughter's wedding reception. Kevin Danley met with us to hear exactly what the bride really wanted for her reception. He listened to her ideas and incorporated a plan that made our event very elegant. The day of the wedding we had nothing to worry about as Kevin took care of everything."

—Phil and Marsha Cavin

IZZY'S CATERING

Eastport Plaza	*Gateway Mall*	*Gresham*
3846 S.E. 82nd Avenue	*1307 N.E. 102nd Avenue*	*225 N.E. Burnside*
Portland, Oregon 97260	*Portland, Oregon 97220*	*Gresham, Oregon 97030*
Contact:	*Contact:*	*Contact:*
Debbi Schall or Robert Lampson	*Carol Pratt*	*Chris Wiser*
(503) 771-9919	*(503) 255-6364*	*(503) 667-7972*

Types of Menus

Buffet: We specialize in offering a high-quality buffet with an outstanding presentation at a very affordable price. We can feature Izzy's traditional buffet which includes a variety of pan and thin crust pizza, chicken, baked beans, mashed potatoes, wild rice stuffing, cinnamon rolls, salads, desserts and more. We can also customize a menu featuring a wide variety of entrees that are not typically on our restaurant menu. Please call for more details. We are very flexible, conscientious and affordable.

Appetizers: We also can serve you a wide variety of appetizer platters for your special event.

Restaurant Facilities

We have a variety of banquet rooms in our three eastside locations that can comfortably accommodate groups from 20 to 75 for rehearsal dinners, bridal luncheons, or small receptions. Larger portions of the restaurant can be reserved during selected off-hour times.

Catering Services

We have an experienced event coordinator on our staff to help assist you with any of your wedding planning needs.

Cost

On-site

- $6.49 lunch, $8.29 dinner for our traditional Izzy's buffet *
- Prices will vary for customized menus depending on menu items selected.

Off-site

- Pricing on catered buffet packages will vary depending on party size, menu selection and amenities, but packages typically range from $7–$10 per person.

* *Price valid as of January 1, 2000*

JAKE'S CATERING AT THE GOVERNOR HOTEL

611 S.W. 10th Avenue
Portland, Oregon 97205
(503) 241-2104; Fax (503) 220-1849
Web site: http://www.mccormickandschmicks.com

Type of Menus and Specialty

Jake's Catering at The Governor Hotel is a division of McCormick & Schmick Management Group and "Jake's Famous Crawfish." Jake's is one of the most respected dining institutions in the Portland area, and Jake's Catering at The Governor Hotel upholds this prestigious reputation.

Known for offering extensive Pacific Northwest menu selections, including fresh seafood and fish, pasta and poultry dishes and prime cut steaks, Jake's Catering at The Governor Hotel has the flexibility and talent to cater to your needs.

From stand-up cocktail/appetizer receptions to fabulous buffet presentations, to complete sit-down dinners for groups and gatherings of all sizes, Jake's Catering at The Governor Hotel is always poised and ready to serve.

Enjoy delicious hors d'oeuvres and entrees, delectable desserts and specialty theme menus (upon request), all prepared by our talented chefs and served by our friendly and professional staff.

Customers are encouraged to review our catering menus and to tour the elegant banquet facilities at The Governor Hotel to fully appreciate the total scope of menu options, facilities, and full-service capabilities.

Cost

We base our cost on a per-person count and the type of menu developed. We require a 50% deposit to confirm your event and payment in full 72 hours prior to event for estimated charges. We ask for a guaranteed number of guests three business days prior to the event.

Services

Jake's Catering at The Governor Hotel is the exclusive caterer at The Governor Hotel, which features nine exquisite banquet rooms with an Italian Renaissance decor and the capability to host groups from as small as 10 people up to 450 (seated) and 600 (stand-up reception).

Jake's Catering at The Governor Hotel provides off-premise catering services.

A REPUTATION FOR QUALITY AND A RESPECT FOR TRADITION

This is the motto for Jake's Catering at The Governor Hotel and McCormick & Schmick Management Group. You are guaranteed the finest quality of food and presentation, a friendly and professional staff, and a personalized customer service. Trust your important event to one of Portland's long-time favorites to ensure a truly memorable and successful experience.

See page 140 under Banquet & Reception Sites.

LONDON CATERING

3220 S.E. Milwaukie
Portland, Oregon 97202
Contact: Charles Barker
(503) 234-1978
Fax (503) 239-7168
Business Hours: 8:30am–5pm

Types of Menus and Specialty

AFFORDABLE! London Catering offers a wide variety of unique and delicious menus designed to meet your personal tastes and budget. Award-winning chef Charles Barker prides himself on preparing only the finest products for your events. All menu items are prepared fresh, including our wonderful homemade breads and desserts. You may choose from one of our established menus or we would be delighted to create the perfect menu for your special affair.

Services

SERVICE! The catering managers of London Catering will assist you every step of the way from initial consultation through to the completion of the event. Our services include:

- Menu planning
- Fully licensed to serve alcoholic beverages
- Gracious and professional service staff
- Rental coordination (including china, silverware, glassware and linens)
- Props and decorations: from simple centerpieces to elaborate theme environments

Location

ACCOMMODATING! London Catering offers a new private conference and adjoining dining room to be used for both personal and professional receptions or conference meetings. Special features include:

- An exquisite central courtyard and fountain surrounded by lush foliage
- Space accommodations: Conference room capacity for sit-down meals is 30 guests and for standing receptions, 50 guests. During summer months, the courtyard can seat or stand 20 additional guests

Reservations for the location can be booked by calling London Catering at (503) 234-1978.

Cost

CALL! You will be delighted at how affordable your event will be when catered by London Catering. The cost of your event will depend upon many factors, including the menu selected, type of service, rentals and decorations. Our catering managers will work diligently to ensure your event is produced within the guidelines of your expectations and budget. Events are priced on a per-person basis including all menu items and services. A deposit of $250 will hold the date for your event.

Food Preparation and Equipment

DELICIOUS! London Catering is known for its famous homemade cuisine often offered among beautiful floral presentations, combining to create an artistic display of your chosen menu items. We can provide all required equipment from a full silver service to French country baskets to unique and colorful linens.

Serving Attendants

COURTEOUS! The staff at London Catering takes great pride in satisfying your guests. We will provide all labor required for your reception, including event setup, service, bartending and cleanup crews.

1513 S.E. Third Avenue
Portland, Oregon 97214
Contact: Hollis Harris
(503) 232-8172; Fax: (503) 232-8173
Business Hours: Mon–Fri 10am–4pm;
evenings and weekends by appointment

The Wedding of Your Dreams

From simple coffee and cake presented beautifully, to complete sit-down dinners for your entire guest list, we pride ourselves on our ability to make your wedding day everything you want it to be…all within the budget you've set.

Our wedding consultant will work with you to coordinate your menu, your color scheme, and we also have an incredible floral designer to complete your perfect arrangements. We can provide a complete selection of paper or china service, table linens to coordinate with your wedding colors, and silver coffee and tea service.

Specialty Services Offered

Once upon a time, train travel was not only the fastest, most efficient way to cross the continent...it was also the most elegant. And central to the experience was the dining car.

Fine linen, silver coffee service, and immaculate porters in crisp white uniforms created a standard of service never before…or since…seen in the industry.

Trained in everything from the art of knowing the precise moment to approach a table to the finer points of when to bring the next course, Porter's played an integral part of the entire experience.

It is that more gracious era that serves as an inspiration for Porter's Catering. From the unmatched cuisine to the elegant service and gracious presentation, Porter's will please your palate, your eye, and your sensibilities with impeccable attention to every detail.

Cost and Terms

We will work within your set budget. Prices start at $10 per person and go up to $30 per person. At the time of booking, a 25% deposit is required to secure your date with the balance due the day of the event. The deposit is refundable with a 60 day cancellation notice.

WE MAKE WEDDING DREAMS COME TRUE

No matter what size your wedding, from formal to down-home Texas style barbecue, Porter's turns your wedding dreams into realities.

RAFATI'S

Elegance in Catering

TIFFANY CENTER
1410 S.W. Morrison, Suite 600 • Portland, Oregon 97205-1930
(503) 248-9305; Fax (503) 243-7147
E-mail: rafatis@vr-net.com; Web site: rafatis.citysearch.com

Types of Menus and Specialty

Rafati's full-service catering staff can assist you with the selection of the perfect menu for your function. From brunches, picnics in the park, formal dinner service, elegant afternoon tea in sterling silver to the most formal or casual of wedding receptions—we've done it all. Our portfolios are filled with pictures of our work—Northwest and other American Regional cuisines to Continental and Ethnic, mirror displays of whole decorated salmon, seasonal fruits and grilled vegetables, theme buffet presentations, formal dinner services and elegant hors d'oeuvres passed on silver trays.

Cost

The cost is determined by the menu selection, level of desired service and number of guests.

Experience

Operating under the Rafati's name since 1983, our actual catering and food service experience spans more than 25 years. Experience has made flexibility our hallmark.

Food Preparation and Equipment

Rafati's specializes in delicious, freshly prepared foods set in an elegant, lavish and stylish display. From silver, copper, crystal and mirrors to baskets, china, fresh flowers and theme props—we provide all service equipment needs.

Special Services

Service attendants: trained, professionally uniformed service staff to set up, serve and clean up; OLCC licensed, professionally uniformed and equipped bartenders

Beverages: we offer full liquor, extensive wine and champagne selections, bottled and keg beer (domestic, micro and imported) and a full selection of chilled non-alcoholic beverages; OLCC licensed with liquor liability insurance

Dishes and glassware: china, glassware standard, disposables on request

Napkins and linens: linen cloths, napkins and table skirting in range of colors; paper products in selection of colors

Other: fresh flowers; table, hall and theme decorations; ice carvings—full event services.

WHEN GOOD TASTE AND EXPERIENCE COUNT ...COUNT ON RAFATI'S

Rafati's is the exclusive caterer for the Tiffany Center—a centrally located, historic building featuring event floors of traditional charm and elegance with gilded mirrors, polished woods and emerald accents. From our fully licensed commercial kitchen we also provide elegant catering services to many other facilities and venues in the Portland Metro area. Our attention to detail, safe food-handling practices, award-winning chefs, trained professional servers, bartenders and experienced event planners are all dedicated to ensuring your freedom! Freedom to enjoy one of the most momentous days of your life.

Salvador Molly's
World Party Catering

Contact: Rick Sadle or Bob Love
(503) 297-9635
E-mail: catering@salvadormolly.com

Unique Catering for Unique People

Weddings • Rehearsals • Special Events

Take a Culinary Journey…

- Off to Boston Bay Jamaica for an authentic wood smoked jerk-seasoned dinner.
- Sail the South Pacific for a seaside Polynesian feast.
- Travel the Mediterranean countryside, Chianti in hand and dine on saltimbocca with fresh olive bread.
- Venture the backroads of the Americas and enjoy Northwest cedar plank salmon, authentic handmade tamales, or some good ole' slow-smoked Texas BBQ.

Services

Our catering department will help you with all the details to make your wedding day memorable and uniquely yours. We will assist with site selection, theme decor, entertainment, menu planning, prop and table rental. Professional wedding planners are available to assist with every important detail.

Cost

Price is based on a per person guest count, food selection and service requirements.

West Hills Catering Company

503.228.6822

Visit our Web site:
www.whcc.citysearch.com

Colleen Ann Schultz
Event Coordinator

Kevin D. Davin
Executive Chef

Portland's Premier Catering Service

Make your wedding reception the talk of the town! With over 40 years combined experience, Executive Chef Kevin Davin and Event Coordinator Colleen Schultz have teamed up to bring catering excellence to Portland. West Hills Catering Company features praise-winning cuisine and first-rate service.

Chef Davin—a consummate professional with a classic European culinary education will create an exclusive menu, tailored to your tastes.

Colleen will tend to all your wedding reception details. From helping you find the perfect location to decorations, custom linens, and silver, her experience will set your mind at ease.

Concerned About What To Serve?

There is no need to settle for a standard package offered by many clubs, caterers, or hotels. West Hills Catering Company offers an extensive variety of menu choices. Or we'll create a customized menu just for you.

We Are Experts At Taking The Show on the Road

Let us transform any site from ordinary to extraordinary! We use only state-of-the-art food preparation, handling, and transportation equipment. This ensures the safest and highest product quality.

Call for Menus and Compare Our Value

Our per person menu pricing is inclusive of service personnel, china, flatware, glassware, beautiful silver serving pieces and candelabras, linens, setup and cleanup.

You do not need to worry about any hidden charges—there are none! Elegant, full-service wedding buffets start as low as $10 per person.

Complete Wedding Reception Planning

Beyond fine cuisine and outstanding service, West Hills Catering Company also offers complete wedding staging, full liquor license, ice carvings, floral arrangements, entertainment, tents, canopies, and more!

Thank you for considering West Hills Catering Company. We truly believe you will feel very comfortable with us and we look forward to being of service to you. Please phone Colleen Schultz. She'll be happy to discuss your plans or answer any questions you may have.

Put West Hills Catering Company to work for you.
We do the work, and you take the bow.

YOURS TRULY CATERERS

1628 S.W. Jefferson Street
Portland, Oregon 97222
Contact: Barbara
(503) 226-6266, (877) 753-4214; Fax (503) 226-7616
Web site: yourstrulycaterers.citysearch.com

A PORTLAND TRADITION WITH A STANDARD OF EXCELLENCE

Menus

At Yours Truly, we specialize in preparing menus to suit each client's needs, always keeping in mind an elegant appearance as well as superb taste…from simple fare to dishes that please the most discriminating palate.

Services and Staff

Yours Truly has been successfully catering Portland's most exciting events for over 57 years. For everything from breakfast meetings to formal dinners—from business luncheons to corporate picnics, open houses to Christmas parties, Oregonians have relied on Yours Truly. Owner Barbara LaValla (former hostess on Channel 6's *KOIN Kitchen*) utilizes her outstanding culinary and catering skills to help prospective clients plan the "perfect" event.

Yours Truly prides itself in providing the most fully trained, efficient, and professional staff. We are licensed and insured to serve wine and beer as well as a full bar!

Equipment…Included Free of Charge

- Linens for food, cake and bar tables
- China (paper products for picnics)
- Glassware
- Silverware
- Punch Bowl (if desired)

Silver Wedding Pieces

Candelabra
Champagne Bucket
Cake Knife and Server
Nut and Mint Dishes
Toasting Goblets
Coffee Service

Receive a free "Bride's Basket" for you and the groom!

Call Yours Truly today!
(503) 266-6266

When your special event arrives you'll be able to relax and…
Feel like a guest at your own party!

Notes

© Holland Studios • page 495

Wedding Ring Finger

In the 19th century it was believed that a main artery ran from the fourth finger of the left hand directly to the heart, making that finger the perfect appendage on which to wear the wedding ring.

HELPFUL HINTS

- **Remember the marriage license:** Don't forget to bring the marriage-license packet to the wedding! Assign this task to a trusted friend or family member. A ceremony is not legal and complete without this—some ministers will even make you go home to get it while everyone waits.
- **A handkerchief is a must:** Include a handkerchief in your wedding attire, or have your maid-of-honor carry one for unexpected tears.
- **Make your ceremony special:** The minister or priest can help to make your wedding ceremony meaningful for both of you. Ask how you can personalize the ceremony—writing your own vows, selecting special songs, etc.
- **Ring-bearer pillow:** Practice tying the rings to the pillow so that they will stay on during the walk down the aisle, but will slip off easily during the ceremony.
- **Plan how to start the music:** Prelude music is a nice touch as the guests are being escorted into the church. To start the processional music, have someone signal the musicians at the appropriate time. Setting a specific time doesn't always work because guests are still coming in, or delays get in the way of starting the ceremony on time. One way to handle this is to have your clergyman signal the musicians to start the processional music after a nod from the father of the bride. Also provide your priest, judge, or pastor and the musicians with a cue sheet. The person officiating can unknowingly cut your well-planned music.
- **Approve your music selections with clergy:** Make sure your clergyman is aware of your music selections. Ask whether there are any restrictions on music. Some ministers or priests insist on approving all the music prior to the ceremony. Your favorite love song may seem offensive to the clergyman; neither you nor your musicians will enjoy any last-minute confrontations.
- **Check all the rules:** Make sure you know all the rules and restrictions about the church, chapel, or synagogue. Some have strict rules about photographs or videotaping, candles, and music. Sit down with the clergyman and discuss your ceremony from start to finish, so that any details can be worked out early.
- **Obtaining a marriage license in Oregon:** You must be at least 17 years of age or have written consent from a parent. No exams or blood tests are required. If divorced or widowed, please consult the Marriage License office by calling (503) 248-3523. Cost is $60 with a three-day waiting period. License is valid for 60 days.

For more assistance with staying organized during the wedding planning process, check out the Bravo! Wedding Organizer. Detailed question worksheets double as contracts. This step-by-step system will keep every detail of your wedding organized. To order, refer to the order form on page 24 in this Guide.

CRYSTAL SPRINGS RHODODENDRON GARDEN

S.E. 28th North of Woodstock
Mailing Address: 7215 S.E. Hawthorne
Portland, Oregon 97215
Contact: Rita Knapp, Event Coordinator
(503) 256-2483
Web site: www.bravowedding.com/pdx00/crystal springs
Business Hours: please call for appointment

Capacity: 125 indoor, 300 outdoor
Price Range: varies according to size and time use (must include setup, takedown, rehearsal time, ceremony/reception, and photography session)
Catering: no kitchen; catering by family or caterer; separate entrance for deliveries
Types of Events: weddings, receptions, reunions, Bar/Bat Mitzvahs, seminars, memorials; mainly on lawn; rustic building available in rainy weather

Availability and Terms

Outdoor events may be scheduled mid-April through mid-September. In the event of inclement weather, building may be used. Reservations are accepted up to one year in advance. Fee is 50% of agreed terms, balance due 30 days prior to event date. For cancellation, a sliding scale for 90, 60, and 30 days ahead.

Description of Facility and Services

Seating: tables and chairs for 75 available to rent on-site; larger groups must get tables and chairs from rental company
Servers: provided by caterer
Bar facilities: alcohol by permit only, with licensed bartender
Dance floor: rustic floor for indoor facility; floor may be rented for outdoors; 70 decibel sound restriction
Linens, china, and glassware: provided by caterer
Cleanup: site to be clear of refuse–dumpster on site; refundable deposit
Decorations: no tiny metallic pieces, please; only birdseed for confetti
Parking: two parking lots
ADA: new ADA entrance path, limited vehicle access via service road

Special Services

Building may be used for dressing if not used for reception or serve as your "base of operations."

WORLD-CLASS BOTANICAL GARDEN

This world-class botanical garden bounded by a sparkling lake filled by 13 natural springs invites a wide variety of both water and land birds. Lush greenery of mature trees and shrubs combine with winding pathways to provide unsurpassed beauty throughout spring bloom season and summer, followed by outstanding fall colors. Three "created" waterfalls enhance the garden's natural beauty. An atmosphere of peace, seclusion, and solitude pervades the garden.

OLD LAURELHURST CHURCH

3212 S.E. Ankeny
Portland, Oregon 97214
Contact: Deborra Buckler
(503) 231-0462; Fax (503) 231-9429

Old Laurelhurst Church is located at the corner of 32nd and Ankeny, in southeast Portland, just one block south of Burnside, half a block from the Music Millennium store, centrally and conveniently located. The church rose garden and beautiful Laurelhurst Park, just one block from the church, are favorite sites for wedding photography. Parking is available one block east around the park, and one block north on Burnside Avenue. Attractive wheelchair access is available through the rose garden.

Built in 1923, Old Laurelhurst Church is an outstanding example of the Spanish Colonial Revival-style of architecture. With an arcaded entrance, culvilinear gables and domed corner bell towers with round-arched openings, the church features wrought-iron calconet and 11 magnificent cathedral-quality stained glass windows. The live acoustics and warm ambiance provide an intimate feeling complementing the long and stately aisle in the sanctuary, which features the ornate original wooden beams and trim.

A nondenominational Christian church, Old Laurelhurst Church seeks to be of service to the community. The church is available for weddings, receptions, concerts, seminars, and community events. The sanctuary acoustics have been acclaimed by musicians and speakers. The church allows couples to bring in the Christian minister of their choice to officiate, or will provide referrals. Brides may have their musicians perform in front or in the balcony.

Prices range from $450 to $750 for a three to five hour time slot including up to one and a half hours of rehearsal time, large dressing rooms for the bride and groom, snack room, gold-leafed unity candle table, grand piano, Allen computer organ, a quality sound system with CD player holding up to five discs, cassette player, gold-leafed table in flyer, guest book stand and podium. A 50% deposit is required at the time of booking. Selected items including candelabras, candle accessories and pillars are available for an additional charge.

Couples may book the the on-site reception facilities separately or have their reception at another facility. The reception hall accommodates up to 250 guests and includes a stage and dance area, separate serving room, and a commercial grade kitchen for approved caterers from our list.

Appointments by phone are required to view and tour the facility. Please contact Debbie Buckler.

A more detailed description of the reception facility is on page 172 of this Bravo! guide.

The Burdoin Mansion

For Weddings &
Special Occasion Celebrations

18609 N.E. Cramer Road
Battle Ground, Washington 98604
Contact: Rob or Becky Neuschwander
(360) 666-4828
Business Hours: Tues–Sat 10am–5pm;
closed Sunday and Monday

All the Elegance and Grace of the Victorian Era

The Burdoin Mansion is a unique turn of the century Victorian colonial mansion, situated in a storybook setting of forest and country homes. The mansion can accommodate up to 100 guests indoors, 200 outdoors.

Pastor Rob Neuschwander has been a licensed minister and sought after vocalist in the Portland/Clark County metropolitan area for over 10 years. He has officiated or participated in over 200 ceremonies and is currently pastoring in Vancouver. Please call for additional information or to receive a brochure.

CANBY PIONEER CHAPEL

N.W. Third and Elm
Canby, Oregon 97013
Contact: Darlene Key (503) 263-6126
Viewing hours by appointment

This is the chapel for the couple who wish to have their marriage memories cherished in the romance of a Victorian country church. Built in 1884, this turn-of-the-century, traditional, steepled church features ornate interior walls of pressed tin in white, with a vaulted ceiling and leaded stained-glass windows. Both the side lawn and front stairway are perfect locations for additional wedding portraits.

The chapel will seat up to 120 guests. The basic fee includes rehearsal time plus four hours on your wedding day. You may select your own minister and musicians, or we will be happy to provide you with a list of referrals.

When it comes to something as special as your wedding, the church or chapel you select will set the tone for the day. We'll work closely with you to make sure everything is just as you've always dreamed it would be.

The Carus House

Historic Wedding Chapel

23200 S. Highway 213
Oregon City, Oregon 97045
(503) 631-7078; E-mail: carushs@aol.com
Business Hours: Please call for an appointment

Historic Elegance • The Carus House Wedding Chapel is a beautifully restored Queen Anne Vernacular-style chapel originally constructed circa 1880. A registered historic landmark, it is located just outside of historic Oregon City. **Intimate and Romantic** • Our main chapel seats 145 guests and includes hardwood floors and a romantically adorned arbor. A small indoor reception area contains four tables with linens, seating six guests each, and two bar tables. Our main chapel area is also available for setup as a reception area to accommodate your needs. A full kitchen is available for your catering needs. Our beautifully landscaped garden area includes a large pavilion tent, seating 100^+ guests and is available for your wedding or reception. Our package price includes chairs, an oak podium, altar baskets, candelabras, and a brides' dressing room with a private balcony. Covered walkway and disabled access are provided as well as ample parking. A sound system is available or there is ample space for your own soloist or DJ. Easy access from I-205, take the Park Place exit (#10), continue south on highway 213 for approximately 7-1/2 miles, we are located on the left side of the highway just past Carus Road. Call for more information, we would be glad to schedule a tour of our facility.

CHRISTIAN LIFE CHURCH

Conveniently located five blocks off I-205,
Exit #12 (Clackamas/Estacada exit)
9215 S.E. Church Street
Clackamas, Oregon 97015
(503) 655-1224
Please call for an appointment to view

This delightfully quaint historic church provides the perfect atmosphere for a romantic wedding. Several brides have called Christian Life Church their "Little House on the Prairie" church. It is what many people think of when wanting a wedding in a historical church setting.

Built over 100 years ago, Christian Life Church is a registered historic landmark. It has recently been restored to its original character and charm. One Christian Life Church tradition is for the bride and groom to pause on the way out to ring the historic bell in celebration. The church seats up to 120 people and is available for those desiring a traditional or contemporary wedding. You may select your own Christian minister, or we will happily provide referrals.

We understand that your wedding day can be busy, but it need not be rushed. The modest fee includes four hours, giving ample time for the rehearsal, decorations, dressing, ceremony and keepsake portraits. Be a part of the legacy of happy memories in the oldest church in urban Clackamas County at Christian Life Church.

FIRST CONGREGATIONAL CHURCH

United Church of Christ

Rev. Patricia S. Ross
Rev. John Paul Davis III

1126 S.W. Park Avenue
Portland, Oregon 97205
(503) 228-7219
Business Hours: Mon–Fri by appointment

For more than a century, brides have selected First Congregational Church, United Church of Christ, as the perfect site for their wedding ceremony. A beautiful sanctuary, filled with handcarved woodwork and magnificent stained-glass windows, provides a special setting for a wedding of any size. A First Congregational Church minister will officiate at your ceremony, and our organist and wedding coordinator will assist you with your ceremony plans.

Located in the South Park Blocks in downtown Portland on the corner of S.W. Park and Madison, First Congregational Church is a Portland Historic Landmark and is listed on the National Register of Historic Places. The church is known for its Venetian Gothic architecture and the red-roofed bell tower that can be seen from many parts of the city. And yes, the church bell, obtained in 1871, will ring before and after your ceremony. For additional information, please call 228-7219, Monday through Friday.

Hostess House, Inc.

10017 N.E. Sixth Avenue
Vancouver, Washington 98685
(360) 574-3284

Featured in *Modern Bride Magazine* as the place to have your wedding in the Pacific Northwest!

Open seven days a week; please call for an appointment

The Hostess House is the only facility in the Pacific Northwest that was designed and built especially for weddings. The candlelit chapel seats 200 guests and looks out onto a beautiful garden setting with a waterfall.

Although we primarily provide wedding and reception accommodations, ceremony packages are available. We offer four packages ranging in price from $150 to $500. Our packages includes our nondenominational House Minister, or your own minister is most welcome! DIRECTIONS: We are located 10 minutes North of Portland. From I-5 North or South, take the 99th Street exit (#5) and go West two blocks. Turn right onto Sixth Avenue.

See page 232–233 under Bridal Accessories & Attire
See page page 154 under Banquet & Reception Sites

MCLEAN HOUSE AND PARK

5350 River Street
West Linn, Oregon 97068
(503) 655-4268

The McLean House is a lovely 1920s home that borders the beautiful Willamette River in West Linn. The interior includes hand-crafted woodwork, charming fixtures, fireplace, spacious rooms, a sun-drenched conservatory, and a complete kitchen. The **2.4-acre park** surrounding the McLean House is a cornucopia of majestic evergreens, mighty deciduous trees, well-groomed gardens, large grassy expanses, winding trails, and secluded spots.

Through every season of the year, the McLean House and Park is the site of wedding and anniversary celebrations, family gatherings, class reunions, company meetings, seminars, formal and informal dinners, fund raisers, and religious services. **Guest capacity is 100.**

The McLean House and Park is owned by the City of West Linn and managed by the Friends of McLean House, a nonprofit organization dedicated to preserving the McLean House and grounds as well as making it a useful part of the surrounding communities.

For a special tour of the house, please call for an appointment Monday through Friday.

"THE GROVE" AT OAKS AMUSEMENT PARK

Portland, Oregon 97202
Contact: Volanne Stephens
(503) 233-5777
Business Hours: Mon–Fri 8am–5pm

"The Grove" located within historic Oaks Amusement Park, offers a unique, beautiful, quiet, wooded ceremony and reception site. The lovely, lacy outdoor gazebo provides the perfect setting in which to create special memories of your important occasion. "The Grove" is ideal for weddings, family receptions, anniversary celebrations and more. It is our policy to work closely with you, offering exemplary step-by-step service, allowing you to relax and enjoy the day.

Menus, all created by our in-house catering staff, are individually designed to meet your expectations, style, and tastes.

No surprises, just fun and best wishes!

See page 171 under Banquet & Reception Sites.

OAKS PIONEER CHURCH

455 S.E. Spokane
Portland, Oregon 97202
Contact: (503) 233-1497; Fax (503) 236-8402
Call for an appointment to view
our newly refurbished chapel.
Web site: www.oakspioneerchurch.com

Oaks Pioneer Church is located on the southern edge of Sellwood Park. The non-denominational church is managed by the Sellwood-Moreland Neighborhood Association. With seating for 75 guests plus the wedding party, it has been Portland's most popular intimate wedding chapel for many years. Prices start at $150.

Designated a national historic landmark, the church was built in 1851. The interior is finished in diagonal strips of natural wood. Two original pews are still in use and a carefully restored antique pump organ is available for the "Wedding March"–or more contemporary selections–as the bride comes down the aisle. An intricate stained glass window located above the altar is everyone's favorite photo backdrop! Newly installed air conditioning keeps the chapel comfortable in hot weather. An added wing houses modern dressing rooms for the bridal party.

Overlooking the Willamette River, the location of Oaks Pioneer Church provides an attractive natural setting as well as numerous excellent sites for outdoor photographs. The nearby S.M.I.L.E. Station, also a project of the neighborhood association, (234-3570) is available for receptions. Both the church and station are disabled accessible.

THE OLD CHURCH

THE OLD CHURCH SOCIETY, INC.

1422 S.W. 11th Avenue • Portland, Oregon 97201
Contact: Trish Augustin
(503) 222-2031; Fax (503) 222-2981
Web site: www.oldchurch.org
Office Hours: Mon–Fri 11am–3pm; Sat by appointment

The Old Church, located at S.W. 11th and Clay streets, has been a Portland landmark since its completion in 1883. On the National Register of Historic Places since 1972, it no longer serves Portland as a dedicated church but as an independent historical society. As a non-religiously affiliated church building, it allows each couple the opportunity to bring in the officiator of their choice. The Old Church stands as a striking example of Carpenter Gothic architecture with its Corinthian columns supporting a cathedral ceiling. The original ornate stained-glass windows filter the afternoon light into the chapel. Hand-carved pews surround the center aisle and slope to the altar area, giving an intimacy to the chapel that belies its 300-person capacity. A historic Hook & Hastings tracker pipe organ adds a warm ambiance to your wedding. Kinsman Hall, adjacent to the chapel, holds 200 for a standing buffet. Experienced wedding coordinators will assist you during your rehearsal and ceremony. Call The Old Church to schedule an appointment to discuss your wedding plans.

TIGARD UNITED METHODIST CHURCH

9845 S.W. Walnut Place
Tigard, Oregon 97223
(503) 639-3181; Fax (503) 639-5141
Contact: Pastor Wesley Taylor or Pam Dragon

Our fully remodeled and expanded sanctuary, equipped with a state-or-the-art sound system, seats up to 500 people. Warm, cheery colors, flexible seating, a grand piano and organ highlight the Tigard United Methodist Church. A large bridal dressing room is available. In addition, a chapel is available for small weddings.

Our three reception areas, including the main hall, can handle upwards of 400 guests, depending upon your needs (full dinner buffet planned, dance floor).

Please call the church office for more information or to request a wedding information book (503) 639-3181. Our church staff and wedding coordinator are ready to help with your plans.

WEST HILLS UNITARIAN UNIVERSALIST FELLOWSHIP

Wedding Celebrations in the forest at
8470 S.W. Oleson Road
Portland, Oregon 97223
Contact: Sherry Roark
(503) 293-3161
whuufrental@altavista.net

Our sanctuary, nestled among tall fir trees, seats 175 guests. Three walls of windows allow the natural landscaping and woods to encircle your special ceremony, creating a peaceful ambiance. A grand piano, moveable wooden pews, and hardwood floors add to the charm of the sanctuary. West Hills has ample parking as well as disabled access. Ceremonial facilitators are available to assist you upon your request.

We offer a wedding package for $375 which includes rehearsal time and six hours on the day of your wedding. The sanctuary only, with rehearsal time and no reception, is available for $225. Reception facilities are available in Forest Hall. Adjacent to the sanctuary, the hall has a piano and overlooks the woods and courtyard. We have a fully equipped kitchen and an additional room, allowing plenty of space for your catering needs. West Hills is also available for parties, retreats, memorial services and personal events.

Woodland Chapel

"A Tradition"

582 High Street S.E.
Salem, Oregon 97301
Contact: Office coordinator (503) 362-4139
Business Hours: Tues–Fri 10am–3pm

Woodland Chapel features a tree-shaded private park and intimate creekside setting. Our wedding chapel facility includes a lovely sanctuary featuring an unusual stained glass window and an arboretum. Our chapel and grounds are the perfect place for your wedding day photographs. The Chapel seats 125 guests in air-conditioned comfort.

The Rev. Manon Hamile will custom tailor your wedding to suit you. Our wedding staff consists of a wedding coordinator and sound technician available to respond to all your wedding questions and desires. For your convenience, a reception hall with a fully equipped kitchen is located downstairs. Larger reception facilities are located nearby. Conveniently located in downtown Salem with plenty of free parking available.

Woodland Chapel is a non-denominational church that promotes successful living based on the truth that each person is an expression of God. It provides a center for learning and practicing the recognition of self-worth in an atmosphere of love and fellowship. It teaches that there is a power of Good in the Universe, available to all.

Notes

Notes

MARRIAGE

My most brilliant achievement was my ability to be able to persuade my wife to marry me.

— Winston Churchill

MINISTERS

A Bonding of Love

REV. ROBERT BONDS

(503) 781-9482

© Adams & Faith Photography

Your moment in time. Your personal sacred ceremony in your own special way. Traditional or creative in a setting of your choice or we will be happy to assist. We also offer a family blending ceremony for those who have children from a previous marriage. Short notice is accepted. I provide an informal get-acquainted session to go over details. I am a nondenominational minister licensed to perform ceremonies in Oregon and Washington.

REV. SHARON K. BIEHL

(503) 653-2013

Creative, personalized wedding ceremonies. It's your day, so it should be your way! I specialize in traditional, nontraditional, religious, or nonreligious ceremonies tailored to fit your wishes and beliefs. As a nondenominational minister, I can be flexible to the situation, and I'll be glad to perform the ceremony at a site of your choice. There is no charge for an initial meeting to discuss your plans for the ceremony. At that time we'll be able to determine exactly what you want and discuss the costs. Call for an appointment anytime between 8am and 10pm. **Licensed to perform weddings in Oregon and Washington.**

REV. DIANA EVANS-BAXTER

(503) 626-3552

Your wedding ceremony is a rite of the heart where you as a couple come before your family and friends to celebrate this very special time in your life. Let me assist you in creating a traditional or non-traditional ceremony that will make your wedding day a beautiful and memorable occasion.

Call me for a complimentary "get acquainted" session. Fees vary, beginning at $100. Optional pre-marital counseling is available. Please call between 8 a.m. and 10 p.m.

Please let these ministers know that you heard about them from the Bravo Bridal Resource Guide.

Heartfelt Expressions

REV. LYNNE YON-STARK

4610 Fuhrer Street NE • Salem, Oregon 97305
(503) 390-9056 or (800) 779-7167

I believe this is your day, your once in a lifetime dream, an opportunity to share an intimate expression of your union. My goal is to help your unique vision of this special day become reality. Some weddings are elaborate and very formal, some simple and private. Each couple's needs are unique, which is why my motto is Your Wedding-Your Way. Together we can compose your vows and create your very personal wedding ceremony. I also offer prepared vows to couples who prefer to have theirs created for them. You choose your own special setting, backyard–beach–forest–park hot air balloon–church. Prices, gladly discussed, vary according to services provided. Please call and let's work together to create your wedding-your way.

REV. GARY CONKEY
REV. CATHERINE CONKEY

Heart-Centered Ceremonies

(503) 234-6851

Lovingly personalized wedding ceremonies. We specialize in creating a wedding ceremony that is unique to you and to your relationship, one that will become a moving and memorable experience for you and for your guests. Our goal is to have your guests tell us the ceremony sounds as though we wrote it just for you.

As nondenominational ministers, we are both open to performing a variety of ceremony styles and we have creative ideas to make your day extra special. We are licensed to perform weddings in Oregon and Washington at the location of your choice. Our fee is $100 and includes a planning session and officiating your wedding. Rehearsal time additional.

REV. GLORIA DAILY

(360) 574-2046

Licensed to perform weddings in either Oregon or Washington. I offer a traditional ceremony. I am a nondenominational minister, therefore able to be flexible and work with the bride and groom to personalize their ceremony. I am flexible to their ceremony site, whether it be at a church, home, park, or garden. Attire is always appropriate to the occasion. A meeting prior to the wedding is suggested but not required. There is no charge for the initial consultation. Fees begin at $75. Call for an appointment.

REV. DR. ASHLEY L. MCCORMACK

Interfaith Spiritual Center, Founding Member
Ordained Nondenominational Minister
(503) 977-6507
E-mail: gather@hevanet.com; Web site: www.hevanet.com/gather

Ashley's ministry is focused on the ancient spiritual practice of relationship. She facilitates workshops and writes about relationship as a spiritual art form, where she uniquely combines eastern and western philosophy and practices.

Ashley has been referred to as a calm presence, who is both insightful and organized.

Ashley is available to perform marriage and vow renewal ceremonies and ceremonies of union. Ceremonies may be traditional, eclectic, or interfaith and are created to reflect each couple's lifestyle. Premarriage counseling is also available. Call for an appointment between 7a.m. and 9p.m.

THE REVEREND
MR. ROBERT C.A. MOORE

Unitarian Universalist Minister

529 N.W. 18th
Portland, Oregon 97209
(503) 223-0487
E-mail: RCAMore@aol.com

I've been marrying people since 1965 when I was in seminary. As you would expect from a Unitarian, I have no credal requirements for you. Instead, the three of us will talk about what marriage means to you and organize an artful, tasteful and significant celebration of that meaning that all of us like. I avoid rehearsals and am particularly responsive to couples who have special places in mind for the wedding. My fee is $125 plus out-of-area travel and any other expenses.

"PASTOR BOB" HUTCHINSON

(503) 537-9726
Fax (503) 537-9726

Pastor Bob and his wife, Lois, share in planning your wedding ceremony. Pastor Bob is the creator of "The Family Blending Ceremony." Couples being married who have children from a previous marriage take vows focusing on loving and caring for one another's children. Inside weddings include the lighting of "The Unity Candle," while outdoor weddings include "The Communal Drink," a ceremony created by Pastor Bob. For a beautiful wedding ceremony by a minister with a wonderful sense of humor, call Pastor Bob.

JOHN L. RIGGS, JR.

(503) 656-3893 message phone; (503) 557-8557
Located in Oregon City-Portland area

Nondenominational minister with a sense of humor and the ability to ease your worries. Licensed to perform in Oregon and Washington. Available for weddings during weekdays too. Formality of the ceremony can be varied according to your wishes and beliefs. Meeting with the bride and groom is recommended to discuss standard or personalized marriage vows. References from happy brides and grooms provided on request. Prices vary according to services provided and are discussed gladly. Ceremonies performed in the past include those for ordinary hard-working couples, professionals and celebrities. All receive the same treatment for a realistic fee.

PASTOR REBECCA SANDERS

(503) 698-1199

Rebecca is a minister, licensed to officiate weddings in both Oregon and Washington. She will work with you to create the personalized wedding ceremony that you want, and one you are happy with. Her fee is reasonable and includes all of the following:

- ♦ License information
- ♦ Phone availability/support
- ♦ At least one planning session
- ♦ Vow preparation/options
- ♦ Attending your rehearsal
- ♦ Copy of ceremony prior to wedding, if requested
- ♦ Personalized copy of your vows
- ♦ References provided upon request

Please call to request an information guide detailing more of her services, or to schedule an appointment.

REV. ROBERT H. THOMAS

UNITED METHODIST CHURCH

12820 N.W. 33rd Avenue • Vancouver, Washington 98685
(360) 573-7725

Licensed to perform weddings in Oregon and Washington, I will be happy to perform your wedding at the location of your choice. At our initial meeting, we will discuss whether you want a traditional Christian service or if you would prefer to create your own. Each wedding is personalized to suit the couple. Premarriage counseling is available but not required. My fee for planning, rehearsal and officiating at your wedding ceremony is $125.

REV. KATE VERIGIN

(503) 768-9320 • E-mail: katev@europa.com

Kate McKern Verigin, a licensed nondenominational minister, creates ceremonies that celebrate all aspects of life—marriage, family blessings, baptisms, retirement, landmark birthdays and anniversaries, and memorial services. Weddings are her specialty.

"A wedding ceremony is the ultimate ritual, a true rite of passage ceremony. My wedding ceremony is an intricately designed tapestry, interwoven with a variety of spiritual philosophies and cultural traditions. It creates a soulful expression of love and celebration for ***everyone*** *in attendance."*

~Rev. Kate Verigin

A fee of $150 is charged for the wedding ceremony, plus one premarital planning session. Your personal needs and desires will be incorporated into her highly praised marriage ceremony. Kate also is an EMMY Award-winning television writer/producer, publicist, author, inspirational speaker, spiritual counselor and mentor, wife, step-mom and cat lover.

MARKY KELLY AND ALAN WINTER

Licensed Ordained Non-Denominational Ministers

(503) 287-8737

We are a couple who enjoy the experience of blessing others as they set out on a shared journey. Alan has been weaving the meaningful traditions of his clients into universal ceremonies for over 20 years, while Marky has a spiritual "un-focus," encompassing many non-traditional forms of belief and practice. And in our combined process, there is room for both solemnity and joy. We perform all manner of ceremonies; our interest is in the dynamic declaration of loving people's commitments to one another. You are welcome to meet with either or both of us, to design a ceremony which provides a sacred container for others to witness and celebrate your union. The initial consultation is free, and there is no additional charge for employing both of us to perform your ceremony. In our shared path of simple living, we often make use of "two-fer-one" specials. What a delight to pass it on!

Notes

© Mr. Dovely • page 343

FACT

The bride and groom must make a public pronouncement that they want to marry this particular partner. By saying the words, "I, Mary, take thee, John" and vice versa, the wedding ceremony becomes legal.

Butterfly Magic

Release Elegant Live Butterflies
At Your Wedding!

For information or a brochure call (503) 774-9288

Add Fairytale Magic to Your Wedding!

A butterfly release is designed to make your special occasion enchanting and unforgettable. On that special day, we will deliver the butterflies to your event where you will distribute one box containing a butterfly to each guest. The guests will then release the butterflies at a specially designated moment and read time-honored "fortune cookie-type" passages about love, friendship, life or nature. A butterfly release occasion is great fun for all since it lets your guests participate in your wedding.

About the Butterflies

The butterflies are indoor-bred by the Northwest's most experienced butterfly company. The butterflies are well treated and are fed the day of the event, and there is no need to raise the butterflies yourself.

Samples of Messages Inside the Butterfly Boxes

- ♥ To find joy in another's joy: that is the secret of happiness.
- ♥ Real love begins when we expect nothing in return.
- ♥ A successful marriage requires falling in love many times with the same person.
- ♥ Of all the music that reaches farthest into heaven, is the beating of a loving heart.

Butterfly/Dove Combination Package

Now you can experience both butterflies and doves together at a very special price!

Reservations

To best ensure your reservation, it is recommended you order 6–8 weeks before your wedding. A 50% deposit is required at the time of the order and the balance is due 15 days before the event.

Availability

Butterflies: May–September
Doves: all year

See Dove Magic, page 344.

DOVES AND BUTTERFLIES FOR RENT

MR. DOVELY

(503) 643-9730

Doves for Display and/or Release

With 14 years of experience Mr. Dovely is best known for his promptness, professional appearance—always arriving in a tuxedo and white gloves—and the attractiveness of his birds. The birds are clean, healthy and well-trained. Your guests will not soon forget the show of doves circling several times overhead before heading back to their home.

The release of doves at special events is an age-old tradition. The dove is a symbol of our love, our joy, and our hope. The release of doves (from gift wrapped boxes or cages) during a wedding or the display of doves in gilded cages at the church or reception makes a wonderful addition to any wedding.

A gentle butterfly release for a peaceful, quiet garden setting.

Availability and Cost

The doves fly from February to September, and cages of doves are available year 'round. Doves can fly up to 100 miles. Please call for a price quote.

Reservations

Please make your reservations early. The doves book quickly, particularly during the summer months. Gilded dove cages, and pictures of gift wrapped doves and doves in flight, are available at The Wedding Cottage at 4775 S.W. Watson Avenue, Beaverton, Oregon. Please call or stop by for more information.

Dove Magic

Express Your Love
By Releasing Snow-white Birds

For information or a brochure call (503) 774-9288

"The Dove"— a strong but swift flyer;
yet, a gentle and devoted lover.
A perfect symbol for everlasting love.

Doves for Display

Doves in gorgeous gilded cages can be placed by the entrance-way of your church or reception site to delight your incoming guests. Doves by the guest book or gift tables at your reception site will also set your guests a flutter.

Doves for Flight

What could be more memorable than the breathtaking sight of snow white love birds circling the horizon and flying off into the heavens in celebration of your new beginning? Your guests will be awed by their grace and amazed at the unique way you have concluded your ceremony. Our white birds at Dove Magic are the healthiest and most spirited available.

Written Dove Introductions

Choose from many poetic ceremony introductions.

Butterfly/Dove Combination Package

Now you can experience both butterflies and doves together at a very special price!

Availability

The doves book on a first come, first serve basis throughout the year.

See Butterfly Magic, page 342.

DOVE TALES

"CREATING MEMORIES FOR YOU"©

Contact: Alyce Dingler (503) 663-4229 or Rich Steele (503) 663-0123

Doves

Enhance your special day with the traditional and eternal symbol of LOVE…DOVES.

During your wedding or reception, we can:

- Release white doves to fly
- Beautifully display live doves
- Send a special message to someone on the wings of a dove

Availability

Doves are available any time during the year for display. Doves released for flight are available early spring through late fall (winter possible depending on severity of weather). All doves are trained to return home after being released.

Reservations

Are required at least two weeks in advance. However, we recommend you reserve early to ensure availability.

Cost

Price varies according to the number of birds, time of day, location, distance and special arrangements required. Please call (503) 663-4229 or (503) 663-0123 for a price quote based on your requirements. A 50% deposit is required at the time of booking.

People Say

"Your beautiful white doves made our wedding memorable and unique. Our guests stood in awe as the birds took flight in honor of our special day. Thank you." said Kim Pascual (bride)

"Your doves soaring above the thousands of women set the stage for the 1998 Race for the Cure," said Stephanie Koenig, Race for the Cure Marketing Chairperson. *"Our hearts and spirits flew on the wings of your birds as they lofted toward the sky. We look forward to working with Dove Tales again in 1999."*

In our tradition of
"Creating Memories For You"©

Notes

© red door studio • page 520

Flower Petals

Flower petals strewn down the aisle were used to put a protective layer between the floor and the bride's feet, guarding her from the evil ground monster.

HELPFUL HINTS

- **Kinds of party supplies:** For the biggest party of your life, be sure to stop by a party supply shop. You will discover fun ways to decorate, from crepe paper to balloons in every color imaginable. A party-supply store can help you with special themes and ideas for decorating tables, walls, ceilings, and floors!
- **Wedding accessories and decorations:** If you're looking for wedding bells, streamers, banners, or car decorations, you'll be sure to find them at a party specialist shop. Matching tablecloths, napkins, paper plates, and cups will coordinate your reception. Some shops can provide imprinted napkins, matches, ribbons, and balloons.
- **Case or bulk discounts:** Be sure to inquire about discounts when buying large quantities of items. You may want to consider renting a tank of helium so you can coordinate your own balloon decorations for the reception and save money.
- **Bridal accessories:** Some party shops have bridal accessories including cake knives and servers, unity candles, toasting goblets, ring-bearer pillows, and gift ideas for bridesmaids and groomsmen.
- **Special-occasion decorations:** Party shops carry a large selection of party decorations and accessories for weddings, birthdays, anniversaries, etc.… Theme-coordinated decorations are very popular—matching plates, napkins, cups, invitations, and other accessories such as guest books and photo albums. Gift supplies include coordinated wrapping paper, ribbon, gift bags, tissue, cards, and more.
- **Balloon ideas:** Balloons are an inexpensive means of decorating while providing a dramatic visual effect. They can also be used to hide flaws in walls or ceilings. Balloons can be sculpted to create special effects—in heart shapes or any shape you desire. Arches made with helium balloons create a special effect over entrances, dance floors, and buffet tables. A fun idea is to have a balloon release with special notes inside. **NOTE:** Some reception facilities do not allow balloons. Check to be sure they are allowed before you place your balloon order.
- **Colors of balloons:** Your special wedding colors can be created by placing a balloon of one color inside another of a different color.
- **Imprinted balloons:** Balloons can be imprinted with your names and wedding date, or anything else you choose. One couple released balloons with their name, wedding date, and telephone number on them, and received calls from all over, wishing them well.

For more assistance with staying organized during the wedding planning process, check out the Bravo! Wedding Organizer. Detailed question worksheets double as contracts. This step-by-step system will keep every detail of your wedding organized. To order, refer to the order form on page 24 in this Guide.

A TO Z PARTY RENTAL

995 Commercial Street, S.E.
Salem, Oregon 97302
Business Hours: Mon–Sat 7:30am–5:30pm; Sun noon–4pm
(503) 585-7782; Fax (503) 362-8647

A to Z Party Rental is a full-service, special event supplier. Our large inventory of equipment and supplies will ensure a successful event.

Knowledgeable Staff

Our staff will work with you to sort out the details for your event. Years of experience are at your disposal with proven success. You can count on receiving your rentals and purchases as ordered and ready for use with no worries or hassles. Our job is to make you a guest of your own party or event.

Ordering and Delivery

Our delivery rates are determined per zone and amount of time and man-power required.

Equipment and Accessories

- Tables and chairs
- Canopies
- Candelabras and pew abras
- Fencing and panels
- Audiovisuals
- Food preparation equipment
- Barbecues and crab pots
- Silk arrangements
- China and glassware
- Cutlery
- Arches
- Party lighting
- Chafers, trays, salad bars
- Stanchions, traffic cones
- Balloon bouquets
- *Please call for complete list*

Merchandise

- Items available in 23 colors:
  Plates, cups, napkins, cutlery, tablecovers, and tablerolls
- Balloons, balloon bouquets, candles, and arches also available

**We Can Special Order Merchandise For You—
Ask For Details!**

DELIVERY SERVICE AVAILABLE

1400 N.W. 15th Avenue
Portland, Oregon 97209
(503) 294-0412; Fax (503) 294-0616
Business Hours: Mon–Sat 8:30m–6pm
Appointments available any hour

Services

West Coast Event Productions is the Northwest's premier idea center for all events and special occasions. We specialize in the custom planning and design of event staging, lighting, sound, special effects, tabletop décor, and event and theme production. We are able to tailor your wedding to mirror your vision. We are here to help you make all your important event planning decisions. Please feel free to visit our newly designed showroom. Browse for ideas with our Photo Inventory Books. We have many of our specialty props, catering items and equipment displayed to aid in your event planning.

Rental Items Available

Table art: West Coast Event Productions features the Northwest's most outstanding selection of specialty linens and tabletop décor. Choose from designer florals, theme print linens, damasks, hand-painted tabletops and unique floral arrangements, along with a complete palette of solid colors with coordinating napkins and runners. Ask about our specialty chair covers and gold ballroom chairs. Choose from fourteen different china patterns.

Custom themes: West Coast designers work in tandem with your project manager to create the perfect environment or individual features, which solve design problems or enhance the mood of your event. Between our Portland, Bend and Las Vegas locations, our collection of sets and props is one of the largest available outside of Hollywood. And what we do not have already, we can build to your specifications. The West Coast reputation is one of total commitment to quality work, creativity and thorough professionalism in everything we do.

Wedding accessories: select from several styles of candelabras, brass and silver table candelabras, brass and contemporary full standing candelabras; wedding aisle and carpet runners; custom chuppahs; gazebos and arches; wood, ceramic, marble finish and Grecian columns; table accessories include urns, vases, hurricanes, votives, cherubs and table lamps.

Table Top: West Coast's unique approach to table top design affords you an unusual selection of ideas. Indoors or out, big or small, with fountains and waterfalls, non-floral theme centerpieces, topiaries, statuary, sculptures, garlands, opulent bouquets and leafy accents, our designers will create a magical focal point for your tables and buffets.

Millennium: Like never before, West Coast offers spectacular ideas for the upcoming New Years celebrations in several categories: Elegant, Futuristic, Theme, and Contemporary. Our collection of special effects equipment will add that needed "wow" at the stroke of midnight. Plan early for the best selection!

West Coast Event Productions

We are dedicated in providing you with a service that is unmatched anywhere else. By providing a number of services in one location we are able to handle the all your special needs and requests. It is our personal attention to detail, client devotion and experience in the event rental and production field that has propelled West Coast Event Productions into one of the most celebrated "entertainment" companies in the Northwest.

FLORISTS AND BALLOON DECOR

© red door studio • page 520

The Bride's Bouquet

The first flowers carried by brides were a combination of fragrant herbs whose strong aromas were purported to keep evil spirits at bay. As time passed, flowers were added and came to represent the bride's virginity, femininity, and fragility.

HELPFUL HINTS

- **Selecting a florist:** Most florists have a portfolio of their work. Choose a florist who will spend time with you. If the florist has not been to the site before, you may want them to do so to view the decor they will be working with. This ensures that they design your arrangements to match the surroundings and can be very helpful when you are discussing your ideas and needs with them. Ask for references to see what customers say about what was promised and what was actually delivered. Your florist can also inform you about what flowers will be in season and styles that will appropriately fit your theme and budget.
- **Develop a plan:** Think about your floral design and decorations and write it down. Determine what you will need for the various people involved, arrangements for the church, and decorations for the reception. Consider your budget. Ask several florists for formal bids based on your outline. Then determine which florist and budget you feel most comfortable with.
- **Meeting with the florist:** You should meet with your florist as soon as possible. A florist can only commit to a limited number of weddings or events, especially during the busy summer months. Be sure to bring color swatches of the exact colors you've selected.
- **Being prepared for your florist:** When meeting with your florist it is good to bring ideas to your first meeting. Although the florist may have photos of arrangements and bouquets or books, it is important to give a sense of what you are looking for. Take advantage of the florist's expertise. Be sure to tell the florist or designer if there are flower types that you absolutely do not like (i.e. carnations, baby's breath); also let them know what you love!
- **Flower shades and colors:** Colors and shades can be challenging when selecting flowers. If you select burgundy roses—beware, your burgundy may be the grower's "deep red". Always use a fabric swatch or ribbon sample to show your florist the exact color you are thinking of. The florist will help to tie the entire theme and mood of your wedding with the floral decorations and bouquets.
- **Throw-away bouquet:** Consider having a throw-away bouquet. When it comes time to throw the bouquet, many brides wish they had an alternative so that their own bridal bouquet could be preserved.
- **Mothers' corsages:** It is recommended that mothers and grandmothers wear wrist or purse corsages. This eliminates pin marks in a beautiful silk or chiffon dress. A shoulder corsage has a tendency to pull down on lightweight fabric, giving a beautiful dress an awkward look in photographs. Be sure to ask your florist to bring extra pins for corsages and boutonnieres.
- **Delivery and setup of flowers:** It is very important that your flowers be delivered at the right time. They shouldn't arrive earlier than necessary, since some facilities are not air conditioned and certain flowers deteriorate rapidly. If your flowers must be in place at a certain time, tell your florist what time they'll be needed. Always put the location and date on your contract, as well as the desired time of delivery so to prevent questions or last-minute problems. Check to see if the bid includes setup and delivery. If it doesn't, allow extra in your budget.

For more assistance with staying organized during the wedding planning process, check out the Bravo! Wedding Organizer. Detailed question worksheets double as contracts. This step-by-step system will keep every detail of your wedding organized. To order, refer to the order form on page 24 in this Guide.

BALLOON MANIA

1417 N.W. 138th Circle
Vancouver, Washington 98685
Contact: Rita Stromme
(360) 573-5465
Business Hours: day or evening appointments available

Design Ideas

Balloons are the perfect decorating alternative for any occasion or event. Arches, swags, columns and sculptures can highlight the focal points of your reception and give the room an air of festivity and elegance. Balloon centerpieces can be created for the dining, buffet and head tables with a special theme if desired.

Imagine how balloons can enhance your wedding photographs! They are available in an artist's palette of colors. Call for a free consultation and we can show you color samples. It is helpful to bring fabric and color swatches. You can browse through our extensive portfolio filled with design ideas and samples of Balloon Mania's work. We can then discuss ideas that will make your wedding just what you have envisioned. It is ideal to meet at the event site to determine the appropriate decor.

Cost and Terms

Appointments for a consultation should be made two to three months in advance if possible. Upon confirmation, a 50% deposit is required with the balance due two weeks prior to the event.

Experience

Enthusiasm and experience enable Balloon Mania to provide the personalized service you desire to make your wedding beautiful. Rita Stromme is a member of the Vancouver "Wedding Link", and the first Certified Balloon Artist in Southwest Washington.

Here are Some Quotes from our Satisfied Customers

"Thank you very much for all your help and creative ideas. It's been a pleasure working with you."

"I wanted to tell you how beautiful the balloons were for Kelly's wedding. She was thrilled. Thank you for your special touch to our celebration."

"I can't tell you how much it added to have such beautiful accents with your balloons—they really were perfect."

BALLOONS ADD FESTIVITY AND ELEGANCE

The Final Touch

Floral Design & Balloon Decor

Contact: Wynn and Lindy Bell (503) 579-9499, Shop (503) 579-5999
Web site: www.balloonsandflowers.com

Specializing in elegant and affordable wedding decor since 1987

Individual Item Pricing or Package Pricing

Balloon Packages: $295 • $495 • $995
Floral Packages: $350 • $600 • $950
(Check our Web site for package details)

Wynn and Lindy Bell, Certified Balloon Artists

International Balloon Arts Convention
1997 Large Sculpture–First Place
1998 Large Sculpture–First Place

Wynn and Lindy's decor designs have been featured in:

Special Event Magazine
The CBS Morning Show
Modern Bride Magazine
Signature Bride Magazine
Weddings With Style Magazine

Visit our Web site to view our full collection of exciting and creative decor ideas and designs: www.balloonsandflowers.com

FREE Consultation when you mention this ad

BRIDAL BLOSSOMS

A Wedding Florist Who Also Specializes in Flower Preservation

Contact: Shirley Keller
(503) 297-3042; Fax (503) 297-0459
Business Hours: Mon–Sat by appointment
E-mail: shirley@bridalblossoms.com
Web site: www.bridalblossoms.com

Throw Your Bouquet Our Way and Keep The Romance Forever!

There is one wedding memento you may not have realized you could save. It is your bouquet. Now, at Bridal Blossoms, you can capture the beauty and color of just-picked flowers for years to come. Preserve those floral memories beautifully arranged under glass with other keepsakes that you choose: a bit of lace, your grandmother's cameo, the groom's bow tie and boutonniere. Plan to include something with your names and the wedding date, which allows your special memories to live on as a romantic reminder of your wedding day. Bridal Blossoms offers a variety of designs in domes and hexagons to set on a table. They range from 4″x7″ to 12″x23″ and you have a choice of oak, fruitwood, or brass base. Or, you could choose the popular oval frame with convex glass and many choices of finishes, designs, colors, and sizes to enhance any floral arrangement and complement a wide variety of personal tastes. Custom-made rectangular frames are available in the size of your choice. Corner curio cabinets are also available. Each arrangement is one of a kind, personalized for you. Your flowers will be displayed in their three-dimensional beauty and entirety. Many brides choose to use the bridesmaids' dress fabric or fabric from their own gowns for the background.

Pre-planning

You will have to view a preserved bouquet to appreciate the beauty of this treasured keepsake. Call for an appointment before your wedding, so we can estimate the cost and give you instructions on the care of your bouquet. Protect them as you would a fresh vegetable. The fresher the flowers, the better the end results (NEVER FREEZE FLOWERS). For local weddings, designate someone to bring the flowers to Bridal Blossoms after the wedding (usually we receive the flowers from a Saturday wedding on the following Monday or Tuesday). Shirley Keller, designer at Bridal Blossoms, has been preserving bouquets since the early 1980s. Her specialty is wedding flowers, so the addition of preservation was a natural to follow. This is our 25th year in business here in Portland. Shirley started her four-year floral apprenticeship in 1959.

Bridal bouquet preservation is a great gift idea. Gift certificates are available.

COMPLETE WEDDING FLORIST

Bridal Blossoms designs fresh or silk flowers for the complete wedding, tailoring each package to each bride's needs and budget. Be sure to bring fabric swatches along with your ideas for the wedding you envision. No ideas? Then let us help you. We have a portfolio of photographs and plenty of floral books pertaining to weddings to help you choose which flowers and designs will best enhance your personality and taste. This is your wedding, and our goal is to work with you to personalize your flowers. Bridal Blossoms recommends reserving your date as soon as possible as we do limit the number of weddings per weekend. The initial consultation is free. Let us help your wedding "Blossom."

IMAGE

Custom Floral Design

Fresh & Freeze-dried Flowers
Bouquet Preservation
8010 Aumsville Highway S.E.
Salem, Oregon 97301
Contact: Michelle Fowler
(503) 749-9173
Fax (503) 749-3155
E-mail: ImageCF@gte.net
By appointment, days or evenings

photo by Mark Rempel

At IMAGE, we offer beautiful fresh or freeze-dried wedding flowers, as well as bouquet preservation services. Or, you may opt for the best of both worlds: let us create stunning fresh floral bouquets and arrangements for your wedding, then preserve your bridal bouquet or other special flowers for a lifetime of beauty. As floral artists, we treat each arrangement as an individual work of art that reflects your personal style.

Fresh Flowers

Whether the look you're after is light, bright and casual, or you lean more towards understated elegance, we work with you to fulfill your image of the perfect wedding. Your floral consultant is the same person who designs your wedding flowers, and sees that they arrive at the ceremony in perfect condition.

Freeze-dried Flowers

You may choose to carry preserved flowers on your wedding day. For our freeze-dried designs, real flowers are picked at the height of beauty—then frozen and preserved—to be transformed into lovely bouquets, exquisite floral headpieces, cake toppers, corsages and more.

Keepsake Preservation

We utilize the latest technology to preserve your wedding flowers in a stunning display of color and texture. Nearly any of your wedding flower arrangements can be preserved. We offer a beautiful selection of domed frames and shadow boxes to personalize and protect your flowers. You may choose to add bouquet preservation to your bridal shower or wedding gift list; we offer gift certificates for preservation in any dollar amount.

Terms

A deposit of $50 holds your wedding date, and is applied to your balance. A deposit of one-half the wedding is due a minimum of two months prior to the wedding date, with the balance due two weeks prior to your wedding at your final consultation.

Call today to receive our full-color brochure and to schedule your consultation.

Country Hill Gardens

Specializing in Freeze-Dried Rose Petals

33300 S.E. Peaceful Lane
Estacada, Oregon 97023
(503) 630-5775
Business Hours: Mon–Fri 9am–6pm; Sat 10am–4pm
We will ship direct to you.

Just picture this—being showered in rose petals by your family and friends—what a photo shot! Add these elegant details to your special day. Our rose petals are freeze-dried and have may uses. We will custom mix the petals to coordinate with your color scheme.

Design Ideas

Rose petals are stunning when used on the aisle way, and will make a lovely statement filled in paper cones as favors. They are a must for the flower girls. These petals are beautiful on your table tops at the rehearsal dinner and wedding reception. They can also be used around the wedding cake. And what a great idea to have for the honeymoon suite, to scatter about, truly romantic!

An Elegant Detail

These rose petals do not turn brown or disintegrate. They may be ordered in advance for ease of mind and stored. The rose petals vacuum up and also are biodegradable. Truly and elegant detail for your special day.

Services

We will mail direct, or can meet with you in person to get swatches of your colors. Many times we will use other flower petals mixed in with our rose petals to get the right blues and yellows, and they are beautiful!

Sweet Memories

Based on availability, we can freeze-dry your bouquets and if you'd like, we would be happy to work up a custom wreath or swag for your home. It is truly a useful decorating item with sweet memories.

A Floral Motif LLP

Serving Portland Metro and surrounding area
Contact: Tammy Yamamoto or Heather Holien
Please call for a private consultation
(503) 772-3324

photo by Brides' Choice

Your Wedding Flowers

Set the stage for your dream wedding. Beautiful and memorable, your flowers will make the difference. Your flowers should reflect the style of your wedding which will be captured in your wedding photos forever. It is important to us that your wedding is everything you've ever dreamed.

Personalized Services

- Consultation scheduled in the privacy of your home—uninterrupted and focused on achieving the look you want
- Select from our up-to-date wedding design books with hundreds of styles, or we'll bring your ideas to life. As professionals, we offer help if undecided on color or style.
- Pew bow design—any color desired
- Delivery and setup of items ordered

Wedding Flower Packages

Intimate Garden $365
Traditional Bride.......................... $705
Grand Elegance.......................... $1,200
Or customize to your own floral needs

Terms

Upon confirmation, we only require a 25% deposit with balance due two weeks prior to the occasion.

Always Happy Brides

"Thanks again for your beautiful work at our wedding. You were so attentive and thoughtful all the way through, and the end product was spectacular. Everyone is still raving about the flowers." ~ D&F 1998

"Thank you again for the beautiful flowers! They were wonderful and many people commented on them. The bouquets were perfect. If you ever need a reference, please feel free to call me!" ~ J&C 1998

Balenda's Flowers

1924 S.E. Tanager Circle • Hillsboro, Oregon 97123
Contact: Balenda Weisskirchen
503.693.6086

Business Hours: Please call for an appointment
(days or evenings available)

A Wedding to Remember

With over 16 years of wedding floral design experience, Balenda's Flowers will provide the personal touch you so richly deserve. Our experienced staff will accommodate all of your needs so the wedding progresses flawlessly.

Whether you choose silk or fresh flowers, we will assist and advise you in your selection so your wedding turns out just the way you have always dreamed.

No matter what your budget, Balenda's Flowers can provide you with wedding memories that will last a lifetime.

Some of the services that we provide include:

Wedding Flowers

- Victorian, Contemporary or European
- Silk or fresh
- Your personal ideas or choose from many design books

Services Offered

- Set-up and delivery by an experienced designer
- Transporting flowers from wedding to reception site
- Pinning of corsages and boutonnieres at no extra charge

Cost and Terms

Costs vary with types of flowers and size of bouquets. A 20% non-refundable deposit is required with the balance due 3 weeks prior to the wedding.

Free Floral Gift with booking if you mention this ad.

4201 N.E. Fremont • Portland, Oregon 97213
Contact: Pattie Scarpelli, Amy Walling, or Doug Lotz
(503) 281-5501
Business Hours: Mon–Fri 8am–5:30 pm; Sat 8am–3pm

Wedding Flowers

At Beaumont Florist we can do any wedding size from one simple bouquet to an extravagant affair.

Services Offered

- **Rehearsal dinner flowers:** centerpieces
- **Wedding-party flowers:** bridal and bridesmaid bouquets, flower-girl basket, headpieces, toss bouquet, boutonnieres, corsages
- **Ceremony flowers:** altar bouquets, pew decorations, garlands, and candelabra arrangements
- **Reception flowers:** buffet, serving and cake-table arrangements, guest book flowers, fresh flower decorations for the cake

Cost and Terms

We require a 25% deposit to book your wedding date with the balance due two weeks before the wedding. Delivery and setup are complimentary in the Portland metro area. Please call to make an appointment for consultation, so we can give you our undivided attention.

WE MAKE WEDDING DREAMS COME TRUE

Our design staff has a combined total of 55 years experience. We take great pride in meeting our customer's complete satisfaction. Feel free to bring in your fabric swatches, pictures, and dreams, and we will design a wedding to match your color scheme and budget.

Becky's Country Garden

13700 S. Mueller Road
Oregon City, Oregon 97045
632-7303

A Floral Package for Your Wedding Beginning at $249

Green fields hug the land like a familiar quilt, an orchard appears with tree after tree in perfect symmetry, towering pines line the horizon. Your worries fall away as you drive along the hinterland road toward Becky's Country Garden. This peaceful setting is the perfect place for you to choose the flowers for your wedding day.

Just 10 minutes from I-205 south of Oregon City and you have arrived for your appointment. Owned by mother and daughter team Kathy Cook and Becky McEahern, the business is located on an acre of lovingly-tended land where dahlias, gladiolas, sweet peas, snapdragons, lilies, roses, herbs and greenery grow—all to be used in the floral designs. A white lattice gazebo, swing, arbor and archway grace the pastoral setting, adorned by a brook tumbling into a pond.

The shop is filled with cut flowers and floral designs—the perfect place to choose the flowers for your wedding. Becky's Country Garden's floral packages begin at just $249 and includes bouquets for the bride and maid of honor, two mothers' corsages, four boutonnieres, and two large altar arrangements. *"Brides are amazed at our prices,"* says Becky. *"Most say they've been quoted $200 for the bridal bouquet alone."*

If you need more bouquets, corsages and boutonnieres, Becky and Kathy will adjust the package to meet your needs. The duo easily design flowers for large, elaborate weddings, or for smaller, intimate celebrations. No matter the size of the wedding, they put their hearts into creating exactly what each bride wants.

Once you leave the shop at Becky's Country Garden, you'll put all the worries about flowers for your wedding day behind you. You'll know you will have the flowers of your dreams, at a price you can afford. Call Becky at (503) 632-7303 to schedule your free consultation.

Terms

Becky and Kathy recommend that you bring pictures, swatches or any ideas that you may have to the complimentary consultation so that they can best meet your needs. The terms are a $50 nonrefundable deposit to reserve your wedding day (which is applied to your order) and the balance is due two weeks before the wedding.

Rental Items and Decorations

We have the following items available for rent: aisle carpet, candelabra (in brass or white), wedding arch, Roman pillars (two sizes), tall white wicker baskets, brass baskets and free standing style altar holders. All $25 each pair, one arch or one aisle carpet.

Visit our Web site:
www.bctonline.com/users/flowers.

Blooming Bouquets

A Unique and Romantic Florist

Westside
Kelly Cruickshank
(503) 626-4333

Eastside
Linda Negus
(503) 254-3281

E-mail: BLOOMINGBOUQUETS@juno.com

Elegant Wedding and Special Occasion Florist!

❀ Complete Wedding Party ❀ Ceremony ❀ Reception ❀ Cake ❀
❀ Event and Rehearsal Dinner Flowers ❀

- **Bridal Party Flowers:** bridal bouquets that are unique and one of a kind. Bridesmaids, flower girl bouquets, hair flowers, corsages and boutonniere
- **Ceremony Flowers:** altar bouquets, pew decorations, candelabras, gazebos, unity candles, garlands, arbor arches, topiaries, chuppas and pagalla decorations
- **Reception Flowers:** fresh floral cake decorations, cake table, buffet, serving and guest table bouquets

Costs and Terms

We are very conscientious about working with a budget and are able to give you more flowers at a more comfortable price. Every stem we purchase is used for your wedding only, giving you full and gorgeous bouquets. We never skimp. A nonrefundable deposit of $50 holds the date of your wedding.

Consultations

We have an extensive portfolio for you to look at during a free consultation. We have many creative, fresh and original ideas to make your wedding and reception one of a kind.

WEDDINGS ARE OUR AREA OF EXPERTISE

Blooming Bouquets has more than 15 years of design experience with a unique and romantic style. We can create any design you want, from romantic to contemporary wildflowers to orchids. We offer very personal attention in a comfortable atmosphere with attention to every detail. We take extra time to listen to your needs and fit your flowers to your style. We have done flowers for Portland's Rose Festival and have appeared on *AM Northwest!*

Please call for a free consultation.

"for Wedding Bouquets that are as beautiful and timeless as the love that you have for each other."

Mention this ad and receive a free toss bouquet with order!

Bouquets & Balloons

1256 N.W. 175th Place • Beaverton, Oregon 97006
Contact: Cheryl Skoric, CBA (503) 629-5827; Fax (503) 645-9404
Oregon's first Certified Balloon Artist
Business Hours: to suit your schedule,
day or evening by appointment

Let Bouquets & Balloons Make Your Dreams Come True!

Being a freelance designer, Cheryl is able to focus her attention on you. Her creativity and experience enable her to help you plan custom floral and/or balloon designs that will beautifully reflect the theme and feel of the wedding or special event on any budget. Cheryl has 12 years experience as a florist and eight years experience in balloon design. She is a staff member of the International Balloon Arts Convention, and she continues to educate herself by attending conventions nationwide. Come in for a FREE consultation and review samples and portfolios of her work.

The personal consultation, visiting the church and reception sites, and pinning on the corsages and boutonnieres are all complimentary. Cheryl is there to make sure all the finishing touches are perfect.

Cost and Terms

Flowers: Costs vary with types of flowers and size of arrangement.
Balloons: Costs vary due to size and type of balloon used
Arches: spiral, pearl, fishbone
Sculptures: bride, groom, swans, rings, hearts, wreaths and anything else you can dream up
Canopies: full balloon canopy, heart of tulle canopy, Cinderella canopy
Special effects: exploding balloons, exploding walls, confetti cannons and more!

Upon confirmation, a 25% deposit is required, with the balance due two weeks prior to your event.

Quotes From Our Satisfied Customers

Seen in March/April '98 *Bridal Connection* page 33: *"Cheryl did a fantastic job. I have really high expectations-and I've never seen flowers as beautiful."* — Jennifer (Kosta) Walsdorf

"Wow! I guess the delivery made a huge impression. I know we settled on $60, but due to the overwhelming reaction, I think it's worth a few more dollars. Thank you for such a terrific job on such short notice." — Scott Gee, ABC

Burkhardt's

European Flower Shoppe Ltd.

2155 NW 185th Avenue
Hillsboro, Oregon 97124
645-6492

To have and to hold from this day forward…

Flowers reflect the bride and groom's shared vision of their wedding day. Vow to celebrate this most important of life's landmarks in a setting designed to fulfill your desires.

During the exciting months ahead, let Burkhardt's be your guide in planning the perfect wedding. We ask that our brides call to schedule a consultation appointment. During your consultation, we will listen to your ideas and learn what style you want us to assist in creating. Enter Burkhardt's with your dream wedding in mind, let our floral consultants guide you in selecting accents that emphasize your priorities. We let no detail go unattended in coordinating each element of your event. Whether you have chosen a theme suggesting casually intimate or elegantly traditional, from an outdoor garden to a lavish gala event, you and your guests will long remember the warmth and ease of your special day. You'll be surrounded by the beauty of your flowers from Burkhardt's European Flower Shoppe.

Burkhardt's has been located in the Portland area since 1982. We have seen many mothers and grandmothers return with their daughters to plan upcoming wedding celebrations.

Burkhardt's offers full florist services with delivery and a designer on site. Applied to your balance, a 25% nonrefundable deposit will hold your delivery time and date with the remaining balance due two weeks prior to the event.

With your bridal reservation, receive your hand-tied toss bouquet complimentary with the mention of Bravo!

BURLINGAME Flower Shop

246-1311

FLOWERS TO SUIT THE OCCASION

8605 S.W. Terwilliger Blvd.
Portland, Oregon 97219
Contact: Violet or Jan Patella (503) 246-1311
Business Hours: Mon–Fri 8am–6:15pm; Sat 8am–5:30pm

Wedding Flowers

Our wedding flowers are created to fit the individual and her unique personality. Selected staff will work personally with each bride, designing everything to fit her and her needs. For over 40 years, we've worked with all kinds of budgets from small to large, and we'll be happy to show you how to get the most from your wedding or event flower budget. Come in for a consultation and to review samples and portfolios of our work.

Services Offered

- **Rehearsal-party flowers:** table arrangements, garden baskets, and more
- **Wedding-party flowers:** bridal and bridesmaid bouquets and headpieces, flower-girl bouquets and baskets, men's boutonnieres, corsages
- **Ceremony flowers:** altar bouquets, candelabra arrangements, pew bows, etc.
- **Reception flowers:** buffet, serving, and cake-table arrangements; guest-table arrangements; fresh cake flowers

We recommend you provide us with color and fabric swatches so that the floral arrangements we design for you will complement, blend, and accent your wedding and reception settings as well as you and your attendants' attire.

Cost and Terms

Burlingame Flower Shop requires a 25% deposit when placing the wedding order, with the balance due one week prior to the wedding date. We ask our brides to schedule an appointment for a comprehensive consultation to discuss her floral needs. We feel you deserve our full attention without interruptions. Our services should be reserved as soon as possible.

Specialties, Rental Items and Decorations

Burlingame Flower Shop carries a large selection of unique flowers for you to choose from for your event. Trained, experienced personnel are available to work with you personally to provide you with the European to traditional styles you prefer. We pay special attention to flowers, plants, and natural materials to enhance your worship settings. For the finishing touches at your ceremony and reception sites, Burlingame Flower Shop has candelabra and other wedding props available for rent. We work with each bride to make sure she has just what she'll need.

WE DESIGN FLOWERS TO FIT YOU AND YOUR NEEDS

Burlingame Flower Shop has been serving the needs of bridal couples in the Portland metropolitan area for over 44 years. Because each customer is unique and special to us, we work hard to ensure they always get the kind of service and craftsmanship they deserve. Your flowers for this very special day should reflect your style and personality. We'll take the time and care to make sure they do!

CRYSTAL LILIES

Exquisite Floral Artistry

at Embassy Suites Hotel Downtown
337 S.W. Pine Street
Portland, Oregon 97204
(503) 221-7701

Studio
134 S.E. Taylor Street
Portland, Oregon 97214
(503) 239-4553; Fax (503) 242-2563
Web site: www.crystallilies.com

© Holland Studios

Exclusively Weddings

Personal Consultations

As a Floral Specialist dedicated exclusively to the art of creating floral enchantment for weddings, my highest priority is for my artistry to reflect your unique style and taste.

We offer ideas suited to your own distinctive personality, and we will help you visualize the floral magic that will transform your chosen date into one that is truly yours alone. More than any other single element of your wedding, your flowers can elevate the ambiance from the everyday to the extraordinary.

Premiere Service

With more than 15 years experience in floral artistry for weddings, Crystal Lilies has earned a reputation for outstanding personal attention to each couple's special needs, including on-site floral analysis of your chosen location(s). Every detail of our floral artistry will be customized to coordinate perfectly to the mood, season and setting of your wedding.

Extraordinary Artistry

Staying in the fore of emerging floral trends and innovations, we take special pride in the accolades we continually receive for the stunning originality of our work. Along with breathtaking beauty, our talent for creating original masterpieces in floral design is the hallmark of our signature style.

We are skilled in a wide range of motifs, from European to contemporary, from understated elegance to baroque opulence, including hand-tied bouquets, altar arrangements flowing from Grecian style urns, ornate cake decorations, English countryside garlands and indoor and outdoor arches, gazebos and topiaries. The possibilities are as unlimited as your imagination.

Terms

A 20% deposit is requested to reserve our time for your special day, with the balance due three weeks in advance of the wedding date.

For a personal consultation, contact Kimberley for an appointment.

www.crystallilies.com

EDEN FLORIST & WEDDINGS

1037 N.W. 23rd Avenue
Portland, Oregon 97210
(503) 221-1847
Fax (503) 223-8931

CLACKAMAS FLORIST & WEDDING

10117 S.E. Sunnyside Road Suite L-1
Clackamas, Oregon 97015
(503) 652-9991
Fax (503) 652-9998

Our wedding packages are as unique as the couples who walk through our doors. We strive to meet the needs of all our clients. With over 30 years experience we are able to guarantee that from beginning to end, from the rehearsal to the reception, you will have the wedding flowers of your dreams.

Consultation

Please call to set up an appointment to meet with our floral design staff and plan out your special day.

Wedding Party Flowers

From the bride and groom, to the bridesmaids and flower girls—we can provide all the flowers for the wedding party. We also provide headpieces, boutonnieres, corsages, and many other accessories needed to walk down the aisle.

Ceremony Flowers

Whether you are having an indoor wedding with altar flowers and pew bows, or an outdoor garden wedding with an arch, we can make it the experience of a lifetime.

For Your Reception

We love to do table centerpieces, balloon decorations, flowers for the bride and groom's table, and let's not forget the decorations for the cake and buffet table.

Cost and Terms

To have the wedding flowers of your dreams, we invite you to come in for a consultation and meet with our design staff. We require is a 20% deposit to reserve the time and date of your special day. Your deposit will be applied to the balance of your wedding flowers.

Rental options are available to those couples choosing to have silk flowers, wedding arches, a fabulous spiraling candelabra holding 24 candles on each stand. Come in to see our fabulous selection.

We look forward to meeting with you and planning out your special day!

© Stewart Harvey

FABULOUS WEDDING FLOWERS LTD.

6010 S.W. Corbett • Portland, Oregon 97201
Contact: Cydne Pidgeon, AIFD (503) 246-6522; Fax (503) 768-9163
By appointment; days or evenings

Your Flowers

If you feel you are too individual to be put into a package, we need to talk. As a member of the prestigious American Institute of Floral Design, I believe every bride deserves an original creation, and over a cup of tea in our elegant new studio, you can pore over our extensive portfolios of photos and references while we plan all the special details that will make your wedding unique. As Portland's premiere wedding florist, our creativity and exceptional flair for color and proportion will surround you with outstandingly photogenic arrangements that will complement your gown, the season, and the wedding and reception sites. From custom veils with fresh flowers to gazebos that drip with fresh wisteria, accomplishing your dreams is our mission. Even Valentine's and Mother's Day weddings are always available if you book early.

Services and Specialties

We have Portland's largest collection of exclusive props and rentals, from coordinating suites of ornate or classic pillars, urns, and cherubs in old garden cement, antique ivory, verdigris and gold-leaf finishes, custom-designed aisle and altar candelabra, lighted topiaries, garden arbors, fountains and French-wired aisle ribbons. Unforgettable cakes, adorned with fresh flowers, are presented on special tables draped in antique French lace, silk, moiré, brocades, even galax leaves for a garden setting, or under our wrought-iron cake arbor.

Our two extensive cutting gardens are overflowing with fragrant antique and English roses, lavender, rare and beautiful perennials, and foliage grown especially for your wedding. If your budget is limited, ask about our Elegant Simplicity plan—you can still have a lush and imaginative presentation of top-quality fresh flowers!

Terms

A 25% deposit is required with the balance due two weeks before the wedding. We recommend securing our services as soon as possible as we will not overbook a weekend. Delivery and setup charges vary with the complexity of the setup and distance travelled and always include a designer—your guarantee of perfection!

THE WEDDING OF YOUR DREAMS

Your wedding is the culmination of all your hopes and dreams and probably the biggest party you will ever throw. We would love to enhance the passion and perfection of your day by surrounding you in the magic of Fabulous Wedding Flowers.

Member, Gala Events Group, Inc.

Flowers & Stuff

Milwaukie, Oregon
Contact: Craig or Stacey McCollam
(503) 786-7231
Business Hours: Please call for an appointment

© Photography By Craig

About Us

As Husband and Wife, we work together to create a wedding day to remember. Filled with the soft, fresh beauty of flowers, we capture those treasured moments forever with photographs that reflect your personality. We bring an artistic elegance to your custom flowers and photography. We love working together and truly enjoy helping you create a spectacular day.

What We Do

In a relaxed and quiet atmosphere, both Craig and Stacey will meet with you at a time convenient for you. Weekend and evening consultations are available for your busy schedules.

Stacey will spend time getting to know what you envision for your wedding flowers. From that vision, she will help you choose the flowers that fulfill your dreams and create a wedding day filled with the romance of flowers. Everything from a tulle draped aisle, to your custom bridal bouquet, to a handmade head piece for the littlest of flower girls, is created with artistic and loving attention to the smallest of details.

Craig will also take the time to help you choose a photography package that is right for you. Your wedding portraits will reflect the love and warmth of your special day. Whether you are planning a formal affair or a casual garden wedding, Craig's relaxed, casual style will capture your personality in portraits that you and your family will cherish for a lifetime.

About You

It is a wonderful time for you...filled with the excitement and anticipation of your wedding day. Let us help you create a day to cherish forever. Consultations are complimentary. To make an appointment to meet with us and view our portfolio of work, give us a call at (503) 786-7231.

As Husband and Wife we love working together and look forward to being a part of your Wedding Day!

Flowers by

Jacobsen's

"The Northwest's Family-owned Wedding Specialist for Over 25 Years"

435 N.W. Sixth Avenue
Portland, Oregon 97209
(503) 464-1234, (800) 343-1235
Fax (503) 464-1218
E-mail: info@jacobsens.com
Web site: www.jacobsens.com

◆ Flowers ◆ Photography ◆ Videography ◆
◆ Music ◆ Event Rentals ◆ Open 7 Days a Week ◆

Wedding Flowers

Exquisite bridal bouquets, attendant and flower-girl designs, candelabra designs, pew decorations, boutonnieres, corsages, and specialty pieces. We are well known for our international flowers and designers, including European, Oriental, Hawaiian, and contemporary.

Reception Flowers

Centerpieces, garlands, arches, topiaries, buffet and table designs.

Rental Services

We offer a complete line of wedding and reception accessories such as Roman pillars, candelabra, and arches.

Costs

We will tailor our services to fit your needs. Call and make an appointment with one of our consultants. We provide exceptional references.

Some Extra Services We Provide

- Open 7 days a week with real people on weekends
- Fabulous gourmet baskets
- We have a liquor license
- Daily Portland and Vancouver metro area delivery

Flowers by Van Go

designs by

PATRICE NEWHOUSE

617 N.W. 94th Street
Vancouver, Washington 98665
(360) 576-3835, (800) 280-4783
Web site: http://www.weloveweddings.com/vango

Your Wedding Flowers

As a wedding specialist, Flowers by Van Go offers a unique talent for interpreting the needs and desires of the bride and turning it into the wedding of her dreams. My extensive experience with weddings enables me to assist you in designing your wedding so that no detail is overlooked. My goal is to design each arrangement to enhance and complete the look of your wedding.

You will be working with someone who is passionate about what she does, and my enthusiasm and dedication will give you the confidence that everything possible will be done to make your day perfect.

Personalized Services

- Free consultation—uninterrupted and focused only on you and your wedding party.
- On-site consultation after booking (wedding and reception site).
- Extensive resources of wedding props, tents, tables, chairs and an array of plants and waterfalls.

Free Toss Bouquet

A toss bouquet designed as a topiary of your wedding flowers. This piece alone is a work of art and it is my gift to you as a thank you.

I stand by my work and use only the finest of quality of flowers, ribbons and all other products used for your wedding. My goal is to give you the best value for your money.

Cost and Terms

A 25% deposit is required at the time of booking with the balance due three weeks before the wedding.

Visit our Web site:
www.weloveweddings.com/vango

PORTLAND'S LEADING FLORIST FOR OVER 90 YEARS

flowers
TOMMY LUKE

1225 N.W. EVERETT, PORTLAND, OREGON 97209
phone 503.228.3140 *toll free* 800.775.3140 *fax* 503.778.5544
monday-friday: 7:00AM - 7:00PM *saturday*: 7:00AM - 4:00PM

Wedding Bells Are Ringing

Naturally, you want your wedding to be the most memorable day of your life. At Flowers Tommy Luke, we'll do everything we can to make your day shine. We begin by listening to your needs and desires for the big day. Then we develop an individual package to fit your budget and your dreams. We offer a 100% guarantee. To see a portfolio of our floral work, stop by our Northwest Everett location in the Pearl District.

The Price Tag

Our costs vary as each wedding is unique. A 25% deposit is required at the time of booking, with the balance due 10 days prior to event. We can deliver and set everything up for you.

For Rent

The following items are available for rental: aisle carpet, candelabra (in brass, wrought iron or silver) wedding arches, chuppa, kneeling benches, centerpiece containers, and silver bowls. Silk flowers and additional wedding decorations are also available.

A Portland centerpiece for over 90 years

We've been bringing flowers to Portland since 1907. You'll find our arrangements to be full, creative, unique and beautiful. If there's one thing we're enthusiastic about, it's flowers. To place an order give us a call or visit our new location in the Pearl District.

 Please let this business know that you heard about them from the Bravo! Bridal Resource Guide.

EUROPEAN FLORAL DESIGN

FRANÇOISE WEEKS

503.236.5829

What is European Floral Design?

In recent years European Floral Design has received a warm reception in the Pacific Northwest. The style is characterized by simple and harmonious floral compositions using a wide variety of flowers and foliage. The look is natural, yet vivid and exciting.

Françoise Weeks Florist

Françoise Weeks was born and raised in Belgium, where flowers are a part of everyday life. Her passion and enthusiasm for flowers were nurtured from an early age - Françoise has over 20 years of training and experience as a European floral designer. Since she opened her business here in Portland four years ago, her elegant and pleasing designs have attracted attention from wedding consultants, caterers, and photographers. And brides appreciate her personalized and artistic attention to detail.

Inspired by Flowers

I visited Françoise in her studio early one morning in April. She was in the middle of preparing for a wedding and the delicate fragrance of sweet peas and lily of the valley, combined with the intoxicating scent of lilacs and oriental lilies filled the room. Vases with soft colored spring blooms brightened the workbench, while vases of tall stems of cherry blossoms and stunning delphiniums lined the floor. As she lead me around tables brimming with hand-tied bouquets, altar arrangements, garlands and centerpieces she explained, "Every wedding is unique. And working with a bride to choose the right arrangements for her wedding is really exciting!"

As I left, we stepped out into a colorful spring garden, which seemed like an extension of her studio. A worn brick path meandered through the flower beds. "The garden is a constant source of inspiration," said Françoise. "I love the process of arranging interesting shapes, different textures and complementary colors to satisfy every bride's dream."

~ Shannon Spence

Terms

Consultations are by appointment only. A 20% deposit is requested to reserve your wedding day, with the balance due two weeks prior to the wedding date.

Geranium Lake Flowers

Gorgeous Flowers

U.S. Bancorp Tower • 555 S.W. Oak • Portland, Oregon 97204
(503) 228-1920 • (800) 228-1920 • Fax 240-6362

CREATIVE, FRESH, ELEGANT AND UNIQUE AS THE BRIDE AND GROOM

Geranium Lake Flowers is not your ordinary flower shop. We take pride in designing flower arrangements that reflect each couple's unique style and taste. We are knowledgeable, creative and professional with a wide range of experience.

Choosing from our own gardens and a full range of urns, arches and other interesting props, we create arrangements for any size wedding and budget.

We guarantee that your flowers will be fresh, fabulous and designed with care or we will replace them.

GERANIUM LAKE FLOWERS
Gorgeous Flowers

Conveniently located in the US Bancorp Tower

Lake Grove Flowers

(Flowers to touch the heart)
15630 S.W. Boones Ferry Road
Lake Oswego, Oregon 97035
Contact: Kumiko Jones
(503) 635-2094, (800) 635-2040
Fax (503) 635-0090
Business Hours: Mon–Fri 8am–6pm;
Sat 8am–4pm; closed Sunday

With You in Mind

Your wedding day is very special for all of us at Lake Grove FLowers. We understand this day that you have dreamed about always. The friendly and talented staff loves the romance of two people in love and feels honored to create something wonderful for each couple.

As one of Lake Oswego's most prominent design stores, our staff is proficient in creating your vision, from contemporary elegance to the most romantic and traditional styles. We welcome any size event, from the intimate home ceremony to the grand ballrooms. For ease and continuity, we always welcome and enjoy working with you on rehearsal dinners, showers and any social event surrounding your wedding.

Lake Grove Flowers invites you to come in for a complimentary personal consultation. Please call us to set up a time to discuss your ideas with a designer and to browse through our many photographs and catalogs.

Terms

Lake Grove Flowers' complimentary consultation recommends that you bring swatches and any magazine clippings that have caught your eye. Our terms are 25% down when the wedding is booked, and the balance due two weeks before the wedding. We recommend securing our service as soon as possible, as we cannot overbook a weekend.

Marsa's Flowers & Gifts

4930 Baseline Road
Parkdale, Oregon 97041
Contact: Marsa Routson (541) 352-6722
Fax (541) 352-6552
Business Hours 10am–6pm

Gifts • Flower Arrangements

Fresh • Silk • Dried • Weddings • Funerals • Special Occasions • Parties
Garden Supplies • Quilts • Specialty Pottery • Works by Local Artists

Every Wedding is Unique

Every wedding is unique to that particular couple, and is an expression of their own style and desires. With eight years of experience in wedding design, my job is to tailor the wedding that each couple personally wants. From designs to budgets, I work to make this a special day.

Services Offered

From country garden weddings to large formal church weddings, we have experience and a large library of design books and manuals for the bride to choose her style. Boutonnieres to Candelabras, to the bride's bouquet and reception tables, we are a full service florist

Cost and Terms

Wedding consultations are by appointment and a 25% deposit is required to reserve your wedding date. The remaining fee is due two weeks before the wedding. Reserve early-only one wedding per weekend is scheduled.

Specialties and Services

Free delivery and pinning on of corsages and boutonnieres is included, if requested. I will meet with the bride up to three times, to make sure that all is as she wants and everything is fine-tuned.

Rental Items

Candelabras, large and small wicker baskets, and Roman pillars are available to rent.

Surrounded by the Beauty of Nature

Located in the upper Hood River Valley and at the end of the Mount Hood Railroad, Marsa's Flowers & Gifts is surrounded by the beauty of nature that gives us our inspiration. Flowers are nature's masterpieces and what better way to express your love for each other and hopes and dreams for the future. Let us make your wedding one to remember in the years to come.

Sharon's Nostalgia

Contact: Sharon Cochran
(503) 641-6396

11400 S.W. Bel Aire Lane
Beaverton, Oregon 97008

Wedding Flowers

You are special and your day should be as unique as you want it to be. With over nine years as a licensed designer specializing in color, contrast, imagination, creativity and how these relate to the total feel you would like. This can be created from your own ideas or from the pages and pages of designs and settings we have personally done and have available for you to view. YOUR dress, YOUR colors, YOUR ideas…not someone else's.

Specialties and Services…You

English settings, romantic designs. We have arbors, arches, urns, french and wired specialty ribbons, isle designs from simple to draped elegance, altar settings and pillars. (If we don't have it, we know where to get it.) We are happy to move your flowers from the church to the reception.

We will be glad to work with you and your family to incorporate your bridal shower, bridesmaids luncheon, rehearsal dinner or whatever events surround your special day. We can do this in one theme, or vary it as you desire.

Consultation

Initial consultation is at no cost. Once your wedding is booked, and our small fee is taken, further consultations are scheduled as often as necessary.

Cost and Terms

Cost is determined by type of flowers, as well as size and number of arrangements. As stated above, each bride is individually cared for. A booking and delivery fee is taken, with final payment due two weeks before the wedding.

I LOVE WHAT I DO AND I CARE ABOUT YOU

We cater to the smallest, simplest of weddings, or can present the biggest party you want to give. We are a family-owned and -operated small business. Our goal is to help you be elated on this day that is so special.

(503) 641-6396

WISHING WELL FLORAL & GARDEN ART

21530 Willamette Drive
West Linn, Oregon 97068
Contact: Janine Voll (503) 557-3823
Fax (503) 557-0243
Business Hours:
Mon–Fri 9am–6pm; Sat 10am–5pm

IT'S YOUR SPECIAL DAY, LET US HELP YOU MAKE IT SHINE!

At Wishing Well, our goal is to help the bride feel comfortable, welcome and understood. **We listen!** Helping a bride to shine and express her own personal style is what we do best. You are a unique individual. Your wedding flowers should reflect that!

We Offer Many Styles to Make Your Vision a Reality

The **WILDFLOWER** look: earthy, fresh from the garden, understated and light hearted; the **EXOTIC** look: tropical, clean lines, Asian-inspired and adventurous; the **ENGLISH GARDEN** look: opulent, full blooms, old fashioned, perennial and romantic; the **AMERICAN TRADITIONAL** look: colonial influences, seasonal touches, tried and true.

Come in for a **FREE BRIDAL CONSULTATION**. Call and make an appointment for a 30 minute, personal, one-on-one meeting. Feel free to bring in pictures, magazines, swatches, and any other ideas you may have. A deposit of 25% will reserve your wedding day. Once the wedding has been booked, we offer on-site consultations. This allows us to work with you on specific ideas to suit the locations perfectly.

We have a variety of **UNIQUE ITEMS** available to rent; ivy arch, wrought iron stands, centerpieces, urns, pedestals and more. And if we don't have it, we can get it.

Remember, it's your special day. We care about you and your wedding dreams. We have lots of enthusiasm, creative ideas and the expertise to make it happen!

Mention this ad and receive a free toss bouquet.

Come visit us on our Web site at**: www.wishingwellfloral.com**

HONEYMOON, TRAVEL AND ACCOMMODATIONS

TRAVEL AGENCIES • BED & BREAKFASTS • HOTELS • RESORTS

© Holland Studios • page 495

FLINGING THE STOCKING

A custom passed down by the British started when guests would invade the bridal chamber and vie for the bride's and groom's stockings. They then took turns flinging the stockings at the newlyweds, with the belief that whoever landed the stocking on the bride or groom's nose would be the next person to marry.

Unforgettable HONEYMOONS

Romantic Travel for Couples

5707 N.E. Fremont Street • Portland, Oregon 97213
Contact: Reneé Duane
(503) 249-8444, Toll-free (888) 343-6413

Hundreds of Romantic Honeymoon Packages…to fit every budget!

Local to worldwide. We offer the widest range of honeymoon travel packages available. Our clients have honeymooned in quaint Northwest inns to exclusive private island hideaways in the South Pacific.

Our Service…a step beyond the ordinary

Informative Consultations—Honeymoon Consultant Renee Duane works closely with each couple, personally meeting and consulting with them several times before plans are finalized. She offers a lifetime of travel experience and first-hand knowledge of many of the destinations that couples most often choose for their honeymoon. Renee provides each couple with tips and suggestions on what to see, where to dine and what to pack.

Free Honeymoon—bridal registry

Your dream honeymoon becomes reality with our fabulous new registry program. We provide elegantly designed cards to be distributed to your wedding guests. Well-wishers can contribute to your honeymoon by ordering travel gift certificates.

Couples Only—All-inclusive Resorts…everything is included!

Honeymoon couples love the all-inclusive resorts that allow them to completely relax in a beautiful resort that includes all meals, drinks, activities and even tips! Just listen to their comments: Couples resort–Jamaica ***"An amazing resort…had the time of our lives."*** Gary and Christy; Sandals—Dunns River ***"An awesome place…we had a blast!"*** Tim and Brandi

HONEYMOON CRUISES AND CRUISE SHIP WEDDINGS

As members of the **Cruise Lines International Association** we represent every cruise line in the world. By working closely with major cruise lines, we are able to provide and offer special discounts, free upgrades, on-board credits and gifts to honeymoon couples. We also can arrange cruise ship weddings.

Worldwide wedding arrangements. We assist in arranging intimate or extravagant weddings just about anywhere in the world. We can also arrange for group travel discounts for all of your guests and loved ones.

Call for a free "Ideal Destination Planner"

Unforgettable Honeymoons

Romantic Travel for Couples

5707 N.E. Fremont Street
Portland, Oregon 97213
Contact: Reneé Duane
(503) 249-8444, Toll-free (888) 343-6413

© Namale Resort 1998

WORLDWIDE WEDDING ARRANGEMENTS

Intimate to Extravagant • Honeymoon/Wedding Packages • Group Travel Discounts

Romantic Hawaii...waterfalls, tropical gardens and beach weddings

Wed at sunset on one of Maui's pristine beaches...or choose a private lush garden in Kauai. Basic packages start at $375 per couple and include minister, photographer and 18 photos. A la carte add-ons include musicians, conch shell blowers, private candlelight dinners on the beach, flowers and much more. Beautiful waterfall locations also available. Hundreds of romantic honeymoon packages and condo/car packages available at wholesale rates.

Exotic South Pacific...authentic island-style weddings

Imagine being whisked away on a glass bottom boat to a deserted motu (tiny private island) to enjoy an unforgettable, traditional island-style wedding! Afterwards...relax in your own beachfront villa with private pool overlooking pure paradise. We offer a variety of affordable wedding packages in the Cook Islands and Fiji. Packages begin at $595 per couple. Accommodations: private island hideaways, luxury resorts, rustic bungalows (cheap!), intimate cruises and yacht charters.

The beautiful Caribbean Islands...St. Thomas to St. Lucia

There's nothing like the crystal clear warm waters of the Caribbean. The choices for wedding locations are limitless...white sand beaches of the Virgin Islands, cliffside romantic gazebos in Jamaica. Luxury yachts in the British Virgin Islands! Basic packages start at $395 per couple.

Complimentary weddings...with your honeymoon

We represent many luxury resorts and hotels that include a beautiful wedding ceremony, flowers, cake, and much more at no additional charge. Choose from Grand Lido, Sandals Resort and "Couples" in Jamaica.

Cruise ship weddings...luxury ships to private yacht weddings

Combine your wedding with a romantic Caribbean cruise! You can have your ceremony on the ship while in port at Miami or Fort Lauderdale... As members of the Cruise Lines International Association we represent every cruise line in the world and closely work with local representatives to give our clients the special rates and treatment they deserve!

ASK US ABOUT WEDDINGS IN CABO SAN LUCAS, MEXICO, AFRICA, BALI AND MUCH MORE!

McMenamins
EDGEFIELD

2126 S.W. Halsey
Troutdale, Oregon 97060
Contact: Sales Office (503) 492-2777
Business Hours: Mon–Fri 9am 5pm; Sat–Sun 10am 5pm; tours by appointment
E-mail: edge@mcmenamins.com; Web site: www.mcmenamins.com

McMenamins Edgefield is an unforgettable Northwest experience offering the best in food, beverage and relaxation. Originally built in 1911 as the Multnomah County Poor Farm, it is now on the National Register of Historic Places. The historical Main Lodge building is surrounded by specialty buildings and spectacular gardens and landscaping.

Accommodations

Edgefield offers over 100 bed and breakfast rooms furnished with cozy and inviting decor from the turn of the century. Televisions and telephones are absent from rooms, encouraging a tranquil retreat atmosphere. Romance Package available: bottle of Edgefield Sparkling Riesling and two champagne flutes; massage oil, candles and chocolates.

Amenities

- Room rates include a full breakfast in the Black Rabbit Restaurant
- Licensed massage therapist on site; aromatherapy baths
- 18-hole, 3-par golf course surrounding the property
- Winery with tasting room
- Brewery
- The Power Station Pub & Theater (classic English pub)
- Spectacular grounds and gardens on 38 acres
- Artwork painted by 15 different artists
- Amphitheater
- Distillery

Location

Edgefield is located 20 minutes from downtown Portland, five minutes from the Columbia River Gorge National Scenic Area and 15 minutes from Portland International Airport.

See page 163 under Banquet & Reception Sites.

Brightwood Guest House

BED & BREAKFAST

Mount Hood, Oregon 97011

Your Host: Jan Estep

(503) 622-5783, (888) 503-5783

"THE PERFECT PLACE TO SPEND THE FIRST NIGHTS OF THE REST OF YOUR LIFE TOGETHER"

"Peaceful, Private, Romantic..."

Situated on a two-acre portion of the historic Barlow Trail, surrounded by a clear mountain stream and tall firs, The Brightwood Guesthouse works magic to soothe the wedding weary. A Japanese garden harmonizes pleasantly with the cedar paneled oriental-furnished interior. Carpeted and comfortable living room, well-stocked kitchen, large bath, and sleeping loft with full-sized featherbed (audio provided by the waterfall outside) are yours to enjoy. Complimentary gourmet breakfast can be served on the private deck beside the koi pond or inside while watching wedding videos. Bikes and helmets are supplied as are washer/dryer, watercolors, bird and fish food, your daily *Oregonian*, and much more.

Special Services and Honeymoon Packages

Mount Hood offers secluded hikes, golf, tennis, skiing, and great restaurants. Limo service is available to airport; van shuttle to skiing. Honeymoon lodging packages begin at $106. Keepsake Basket begins at $40. Please call for details.

Pacific Rest
Bed & Breakfast

1611 N.E. 11th • Lincoln City, Oregon 97367

Contact: Ray and Judy Waetjen (541) 994-Beds (2337)

E-mail: jwaetjen@wcn.net; Web site: http://pacificrestbb.hypermart.net

Take a Journey Back to Simpler Times...

At Pacific Rest Bed & Breakfast, located four short blocks from the beautiful Oregon Coast, you'll find respite for the spirit as well as for the body. Two unique suites, both with private baths and sun decks, make Pacific Rest ideal for a romantic getaway or honeymoon. Built especially for a bed and breakfast, Pacific Rest is a newer home with a "coming home" feeling.

Restaurants, antique shops, and outlet malls are within walking distance. Seven miles of wonderful beach and beautiful Devil's Lake are just a short stroll away.

Special Services and Honeymoon Packages

Suites begin at $90, including a full, gourmet breakfast by candlelight. Honeymoon packages are available—please call for details.

Pacific Rest Cottage, located across the street, sleeps up to eight and features a Jacuzzi, wood stove, and all the amenities of home (fully equipped kitchen). Gift certificates available.

Come and be pampered ~ Escape to Pacific Rest

Hood River Hotel & Pasquale's ristorante

102 Oak Avenue
Hood River, Oregon
97031

Reservations
(800) 386-1859

Sales
(541) 386-1900

E-mail: HRHotel@gorge.net; Web site: www.hoodriverhotel.com

Description of Hotel

This charming European-style 1913 hotel is listed on the National Register of Historic Places. After complete restoration in 1989, the hotel has retained its turn-of-the-century character, yet offers the conveniences of a modern inn. One might choose from a lace canopy or brass bed, a view of the Columbia River, or one of our larger suites. Amenities include our wine cellar and meeting and event space for up to 200+ guests. You will want to make time to visit our fitness, Jacuzzi, and sauna facility. Pasquale's Ristorante offers breakfast, lunch, and dinner. We specialize in fine Italian and Pacific Northwest cuisine with menu items from pastas to wild game. After dinner, enjoy a cappuccino or cocktail by the fireplace. Pasquale's is the perfect place to relax after a day's adventure. The Hood River Hotel provides you and your guests a unique establishment, staffed to cater with a personal touch and offering wonderful food to remember us by.

Location

Conveniently located in historic downtown Hood River in the heart of the Columbia River Gorge National Scenic Area, the Hotel offers easy access to movie theaters, restaurants, and shopping. For those looking for outdoor adventure, the area offers windsurfing, white water rafting, skiing, swimming, golfing, and more.

Honeymoon Packages and Pricing

Enjoy a romantic evening in a lace canopy bed or suites. Custom-designed honeymoon packages to suit your budget and needs. Packages can include a chilled bottle of champagne or breakfast in your room, floral bouquet, movie for two, late checkout and a romance basket of massage oils, bath bubbles, customized glasses, and more.

Other Amenities

- 32 guest rooms
- Jacuzzi, sauna, and exercise facility
- Full-service restaurant and bar
- Banquet room accommodating up to 200+ people
- 9 suites with kitchen
- Wine cellar
- Air conditioning

Special Services

For your convenience, the Hood River Hotel offers free transportation to the Hood River Airport.

See page 77 under Rehearsal Dinner Sites.
See page 153 under Banquet & Reception Sites.

The Benson
HOTEL · PORTLAND

309 S.W. Broadway
Portland, Oregon 97205
(503) 228-2000; Fax (503) 226-4603
Office Hours: Mon–Fri 8am–6pm
Available all other times by appointment
Web site: www.bensonhotel.com

© Dick Busher

Description of Hotel
The Benson Hotel has long set the standard for elegance and service in Portland. This classic building in the style of the French Second Empire has undergone restoration, is registered as a national historic site, and is a Portland landmark. The look of the lobby features the elegance of marble in handsome accord with smooth circassian walnut highlighted by the glimmer of crystal accents.

Location
The Benson Hotel is located in the heart of Portland's retail, financial, and arts district on the corner of Broadway and Stark.

Special Honeymoon Package
Our "Champagne Kisses" package includes a night stay in a Penthouse Suite overlooking the city of Portland.

Amenities and Services for Family and Friends
The Benson is unparalleled in service and atmosphere. Our luxuriously appointed deluxe accommodations are in classic style in anticipation of your total comfort. We are here to cater to every your wish, be it for the bride and groom, out-of-town guests, or clients. You need only call us for a wide array of special services, including in-house exercise room, 24-hour room service, and clef d'or concierge. The Benson Hotel staff will delight in assuring that your stay is a memorable one.

Of course, no stay would be complete without a visit to our famed London Grill. In addition, the handsome Lobby Court features the soothing sounds of local jazz talent. We are fully equipped for large gatherings, with classic facilities for up to 400 people. Our experienced catering and banquet staff are prepared to help you with everything from planning to presentation, serving in style to your exact specifications.

PORTLAND'S GRAND TRADITION
The Benson Hotel summons together the grandeur of times past with a freshly appointed ambiance that is in perfect harmony with contemporary lifestyles. Call us for details, we'll be happy to make all the arrangements for a most memorable stay.

See page 104 under Banquet & Reception Sites.

COURTYARD
Marriott®

TIGARD COURTYARD BY MARRIOTT

15686 S.W. Sequoia Parkway
Tigard, Oregon 97224
(503) 684-7900
Fax (503) 620-3142

HILLSBORO COURTYARD BY MARRIOTT

3050 N.W. Stucki Place
Hillsboro, Oregon 97124
(503) 690-1800
Fax (503) 690-0236

Courtyard by Marriott offers the finest service and accommodations for both business and leisure travelers at affordable rates. Exceeding our guests' expectations and fulfilling their needs is the standard for our success.

Locations

Tigard: *Courtyard by Marriott—Tigard* is conveniently located right off I-5, exit 291, on the corner of Upper Boones Ferry and Sequoia Parkway. The hotel is a short distance from shopping at Washington Square Mall and local restaurants.

Hillsboro: *Courtyard by Marriott—Hillsboro* is conveniently located off Highway 26, exit 64, nine miles west of downtown Portland. A 13-screen movie theater is across the street and just a block away from Tanasbourne Shopping Center and restaurants.

Amenities

- voice mail
- phones with dataport
- indoor pool and whirlpool
- coffee makers in every room
- daily housekeeping
- remote control cable television
- weekday valet and coin-operated laundry service
- full-service restaurant and lounge
- complimentary corporate shuttle (2-mile radius)
- exercise facility
- full-size irons and ironing boards in every room
- meeting rooms with in-house catering
- in-room hairdryers
- ergonomic desk chairs

(Ask us about group discounts for 10 or more rooms)

For reservations
call (800) 321-2211

S.W. Tenth at Alder
Portland, Oregon 97205
(503) 224-3400 or (800) 554-3456; Fax (503) 224-9426
E-mail: governor@transport.com; Web site: http://www.govhotel.com

THE GOVERNOR HOTEL

Romantic, Boutique Hotel In The Heart Of It All

Discreet luxury awaits the newly married and their families in the elegant, turn-of-the-century Governor Hotel. Featuring 100 rooms, including 28 suites, this centrally located hotel offers lodging options that may include jet spa baths, terraces with city-scape views, or fireplaces. Combining services such as 24-hour room service, concierge services, twice-daily maid service with evening turndown, laundry and dry cleaning services, shoe shine, morning newspaper, and coffee in the lobby, The Governor offers a place of charm and style in which to prepare for and unwind from the event of a lifetime.

Special Packages and Pricing

The Governor Hotel's Romance Package is available for honeymoon or anniversary guests. Package prices vary depending on room selection and number of nights. Call (503) 224-3400 for pricing and details.

The Hotel also offers group rates for wedding parties. Families and friends will enjoy the downtown location close to shopping, city attractions, dining, the arts, and entertainment. Group rates vary. Call (503) 241-2106 for details.

Banquets and Catering

The Governor's West Wing is the former historic Elk's Lodge building. Here guests may create banquets and catering events that complement the love and magic of the wedding day. Superbly hand-crafted rooms serve from 6 to 600 for elegant seated meals or energizing standing receptions. Jake's Catering at The Governor will assist in all phases of planning and preparation, and will also accommodate off-site catering plans. Call (503) 241-2125 for information and details.

Hotel Ambiance and Services

Built in 1909, and fully restored to its original grandeur, The Governor Hotel is listed on the National Register of Historic Places. The striking exterior of terra cotta and white brick is an architectural beauty. A wood-burning fireplace, hand-painted sepia-colored murals, and traditional furnishings create a warm Northwest impression in the lobby. The restaurant and bar, Jake's Grill, is located off the main lobby. Offering traditional American cuisine, the restaurant has been named "one of the city's best" by *Condé Nast Traveler* magazine.

Historically tailored guest rooms and suites create a residential feel where guests may graze from private bars and relax with movies or cable TV. For a small fee, fitness-minded guests may enjoy privileges at the hotel's on-site, full-service, adult-only athletic club.

Notes

INVITATIONS, ADDRESSING AND CALLIGRAPHY

© Mount Burns Photography • page 509

BECOMING ENGAGED

The act of engagement has been symbolized in many different ways. During the Middle Ages, an engagement was assumed if a woman drank wine or another alcoholic beverage with a member of the opposite sex. In American colonial times, a couple who shared food in a kitchen were thought to be engaged.

HELPFUL HINTS

- **Where do you draw the line with the guest list:** The bride's family, groom's family and bride and groom generally each develop a "wish list". Then the list is narrowed down closer to the attendance you have budgeted for. Usually the attendance will be between 60-75% based on if family and friends live in town or not. A good rule of thumb to narrow down the list—if you haven't made contact with the person in the last year, leave them off.
- **Single Friends and Guests:** If friends are single, you are not obliged to invite their guest or escort. If you do decide to invite their guest, find out the name and address and send them an invitation separately. It is recommended to not write "and Guest" on an invitation. If a couple is living together, then you can send one invitation with both their names listed alphabetically.
- **Don't forget to send invitations to:** Remember, even though special people are playing a role in your wedding you do need to send invitations to them: parents, grandparents, clergy, attendants and immediate family. A good idea is to even send an invitation to yourself to track the date guests will receive the invitation.
- **Number of invitations needed:** When figuring the number of invitations to order, combine the lists from the bride's parents, the groom's parents, the bride, and the groom. The mother of the bride or the bride should discuss with the groom's mother the number of invitations available to the groom's family. When the lists are compiled, any additions, deletions, and corrections can be made by everyone.
- **Invitation styles:** Thousands of invitation styles are available: traditional, contemporary, custom designs, some with double envelopes or a folding invitation sealed with a sticker. When it comes time to select your invitations, pick the one that best suits your tastes, personal style, and budget. This is the first presentation of your wedding to both your family and guests.
- **Ordering your invitations:** Ideally, you should order your invitations three to four months before the wedding to allow enough time for delivery. Some shops offer quick-print service in one day to one week. Invitations should be sent three to four weeks before the wedding. Ask if you can get the envelopes in advance for addressing. It's fun and time-saving to have an addressing and stuffing party.
- **Wording the invitation:** When you order, be sure to work with a shop that specializes in invitations. These experts can help you fill out the complicated order forms, and will help you with correct wording for the invitation.
- **Correct spelling of names:** Etiquette books cover proper addressing of both inner and outer envelopes. Before addressing your envelopes, make sure you double check on your master list for the CORRECT spelling of names.
- **Engagement announcements:** They are always a good idea to send, especially for out-of-town guests.
- **Calligraphy and addressing:** Invitations can be hand calligraphed or by machine. This adds a very personal touch to your invitations.
- **Custom hand-crafted and graphic designed invitations:** Invitations can tie in with the decor. Unique ideas include your own wedding wine and/or beer labels.

For more assistance with staying organized during the wedding planning process, check out the Bravo! Wedding Organizer. Detailed question worksheets double as contracts. This step-by-step system will keep every detail of your wedding organized. To order, refer to the order form on page 24 in this Guide.

Calligraphy by Jennifer

503-658-4211

Calligraphy Styles

Choose from a variety of styles for your special day including italic, uncial, foundational, and black letter. My calligraphy is always handcrafted and never computer generated.

Custom Services

My services include:

- Invitation and announcement addressing for all occasions
- Original invitation design
- Thank you notes
- Place cards, menu cards, wedding programs
- Wedding album fill-ins
- Poems, songs and quotations
- Certificates and awards
- Your choice of paper and ink color

I can coordinate the design and lettering of your complete wedding set, beginning with the invitations and ending with the thank you notes. Coordination of printing services is available, if necessary. Calligraphy adds sophistication, grace, and elegance to your special occasion.

Cost and Ordering

I offer unique, customized wedding invitations to fit your style and budget. Generally, you should place your order four to five months in advance, although rush jobs can be accommodated. I require a 50% deposit with the balance due upon delivery.

For one-on-one service and extra attention to details, please give me a call today to set up an appointment and to view samples! Add a touch of elegance to your special occasion… Calligraphy by Jennifer.

Mention the *Bravo! Bridal Resource Guide*
and receive a $10 gift certificate toward your purchase!

Visit my Web Site at http://pages.prodigy.net/jenscribe/jenscribe
E-mail: jenscribe@prodigy.net

"Serving Northwest brides since 1946"

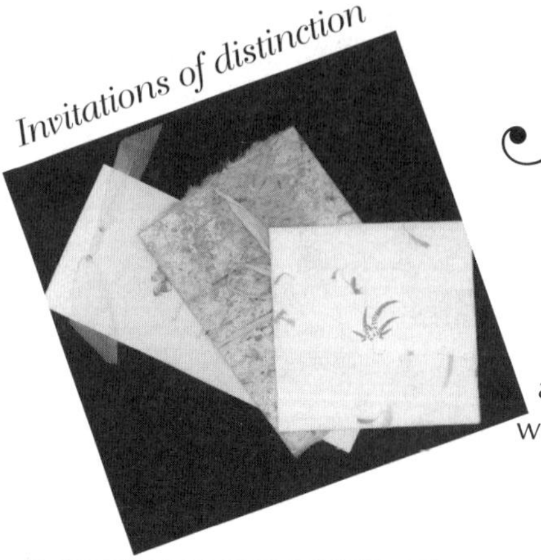

Anders
Printing Company

(503) 232-5842
Fax (503) 238-5940
3402 S.E. Division Street
Portland, Oregon 97202

andersprinting@worldnet.att.net
www.weloveweddings.com/anders
Monday–Saturday
Evenings by appointment

Specializing in…

- Custom designed invitations
- Engraved invitations
- Traditional invitations
- Personalized service
- Quick turnaround

Selections and Styles of Invitations

We carry over 50 major catalogs. Papers include 100% cotton fiber papers, recycled papers, parchments, vellum as well as handmade and more. Our specialty is custom invitations at affordable prices.

Special Services

Our trained consultants are here to help you through every detail of your invitations, from the beginning of the selection, etiquette of wording and ways of saving you money!

Cost and Ordering

Invitations start at $50 per 100. This price includes printed invitations, double envelopes, and tissue. It is recommended to order your invitations at least three months prior to your wedding day. Depending on the quantity and specifications of your orders, Anders can have them to you in as little as three days to two weeks. A 50% deposit is requested when placing the order, with the balance due upon delivery.

Other Services

Anders also offers a variety of thank you notes, wedding programs, imprinted napkins, ribbons, and matchbooks. Consider personalized stationary for attendant gifts as well.

Mention the Bravo! Resource Guide and receive 25% off your printed catalog wedding invitations.

Hallmark GOLD CROWN

ANDREW'S

Fisher's Landing Market Place
2100 S.E. 164th Avenue
Vancouver, Washington 98683
(360) 892-7773

11505 N.E. Fourth Plain Road
Vancouver, Washington 98662
(360) 254-5885

Selection and Styles of Invitations

Your wedding is a personal expression of your personality, style and dreams. Whether you select a traditional or contemporary style ... one with your photograph ... or something in between, we have a multitude of invitation choices in a variety of price ranges from several companies including Carlson Craft, Regency, Stylart and Hallmark's Wedding Collection featuring Precious Moments and exclusive Crown Collection designs. These albums also offer a wide selection of invitations suitable for special events and parties.

Wedding Accessories

Andrew's Hallmark can help you select your accessories—cake servers, toasting glasses, albums, frames, guest books, garters, ring bearer pillows, gifts for attendants, thank yous, napkins, cake tops, programs, plume pens, unity candles, map cards, scrolls, envelope seals, decorations and even a variety of items that can be personalized.

Personal Service

"Discover the Difference" is the motto for the Andrew's Hallmark stores. Our fully trained staff of Wedding Consultants guarantees excellent service and a personal touch second to none. We'll assist you as you choose your invitations and help you select your wording. Before you leave, we'll make sure we've helped you meet all your needs. We carefully double check all orders before they leave the store. When your order arrives, it is checked again and counted to make sure everything is perfect.

Additional Services

IN A HURRY? That's not a problem. With our in-store computer, we can create professional invitations for all occasions while you wait. RUSH service also is available for orders from our albums. We offer local imprinting on album covers and napkins purchased at our stores. With your Hallmark Gold Crown Card, your purchase earns you points toward FREE Hallmark merchandise.

Complete Wedding Printing, Inc.

Portland
2236 N.E. 82nd Avenue
(503) 252-6222

Beaverton
117th and S.W. Canyon Road, Suite E
(503) 646-0821

Open Mon–Fri and Sun;
evenings by appointment

For **Stress Free** ordering and **Quick** turnaround come to **Complete Wedding Printing.**

Personal Service A Part Of Our Tradition!

All Major Books • Custom Designs • Your Design

The Personal Touch

Complete Wedding Printing is a locally-owned, specialty print shop. We are proud to offer an in-house printing facility along with one of the largest selections of wedding invitations from associated suppliers. The hallmark of our business is the "personal touch." If a bride wants a unique invitation with her artwork or calligraphy, we are glad to create the invitation she wants.

Competitive Prices

Shop and compare Complete Wedding Printing's personally printed invitations, prices and services, or choose from all the major books. We will work within your budget!

Personalized Printing

It's your wedding and we encourage you to do it your way, by creating the perfect wedding invitation. Our professional consultants are able to work with you to create your own special invitation. Using your design, ideas, artwork or photo our skilled printers can produce that unique image that is you. Whether printed personally or printed from a supplier, invitations with a rich appearance, raised lettering and a wide selection of designs are available. We also feature the popular layered look, using handmade paper.

Accessories

Many different accessories are available to personalize your wedding. These range from custom printed wedding programs, matches, napkins, ribbons, thank-you's, photo tissues to toasting glasses or unity candles. We are glad to provide that special accessory you need.

When placing your order, please mention that you saw this listing to receive 20% off on your invitations, and 50 FREE Thank-you's.

ETCETERA
GIFTS & PAPERS

1724 N.E. Broadway • Portland, Oregon 97232 • (503) 249-6864
Business Hours: Mon–Sat 10am–6pm; Sun Noon–5pm

Selection and Styles

Crane, William Arthur, Regency, Chase, Oblation and many more…We have over 30 books of invitations and announcements to choose from with styles that range from casual to elegant. We can also help you with custom printed invitations for bridal showers, engagement parties and rehearsal dinners. We offer a nice selection of boxed shower and party invitations in our stationery department.

Additional Services

Our friendly and experienced consultants can help you choose just the right invitation for your budget, and can assist with the wording to make it special. We also have a great selection of guest books, unity candles, goblets, photo albums, cake knife sets and unique attendant gifts.

Cost

Etcetera offers an excellent selection in all price categories. **We offer 10% off all custom wedding invitation orders.**

Ordering

We can have your invitations within a week to 10 days, and also offer overnight delivery if needed. We do ask for a 50% deposit when finalizing the order. We can work within your time frame, but it is always good to allow yourself extra time—eight to ten weeks, if possible.

A Delightful Place Offering Attention to Detail

Choose your special invitation in the comfort of our bridal section. Take as much time as you need to make your choice—we can even make evening appointments if necessary. Our shop offers you attention to detail and everything you need, from thank you notes to place cards and accessories. You will find our shop a delightful place to browse around—and you may even wish to register for some of our unique wedding gifts.

OBLATION
papers & press

516 N.W. 12th Avenue • Portland, Oregon 97209
Between Glisan and Hoyt, in the heart of the Pearl District
Tel. 503.223.1093 • Fax 503.295.7144
Web site: www.oblationpapers.com

Invitations Extraordinaire!

A New Place for Paper Lovers in the Pearl District

• Custom Wedding Invitation Gallery
• Hand-Papermaking Studios
• Letterpress Printing

We Love New Ideas!

Our experienced staff is poised to help you propel your great ideas into an artful expression of the couple you're about to become.

We offer a select handful of books filled with the most beautiful invitations imaginable:

Oblation Papers & Press • Clover Creek • Crane's • Take Notice

William Arthur • Twinrocker • Anna Griffin

Wax seals, Italian photo albums, fountain pens from Paris, hand-bound guest books, and hand-dyed silk ribbons can add a richness to your personal story.

Visit our Studios

Come visit our studios, where exquisite papers are made each day. Choose the fresh flower petal inclusions we place into your invitations, or compare the textures of olive green mango paper with creamy white Italian Amalfi and sheer gold-flecked unryu from Japan.

Letterpress

This fine method of printing is more sought after than ever, with its debossed, dimensional quality that offers an integrity not found in the world of quick print. Come view our century-old cast iron presses in action, and begin to make your own impressions.

Paper & Lace Studio

811 N.W. 20th Avenue, Suite 102-C • Portland, Oregon 97209
Contact: Constance Cooper 503.417.8047
Business Hours: by appointment; days, evenings and weekends

Paper & Lace Studio

Constance created Paper & Lace Studio after working as a bridal consultant in some of the busiest shops in Portland. She recognized that brides need an invitation studio where they can set their own hours, shop in quiet relaxation, and receive the professional attention this detailed process deserves.

Paper & Lace Studio is located in the charming carriage house of a historic Northwest mansion, convenient to downtown and freeways.

Specializing in Tradition

If you prefer classic styles, Constance will show you the always-elegant genuine "engraved invitation." A technique dating back to the 17th century, here is the ultimate in beauty with a sense of history. Your wedding invitation is engraved on a custom-made metal plate, then special ink is applied into the engraved plate, and finally each invitation is carefully pressure-printed on high-quality 100% cotton "watermark" paper. This process results in unique raised lettering with timeless formality, just right if you'd like to send your guests the same kind of invitation used for centuries. In fact, because engraving is the style of invitation used for royal weddings, any bride wishing to use a family coat-of-arms may request to have it embossed on her wedding invitation; Paper & Lace Studio will be glad to order it.

A Variety of Styles

For couples who like a dramatic or romantic theme, Paper & Lace Studio carries a wonderful selection to express your personal style. For example, Constance will help you with a modern invitation on bright white paper with bold red lettering and envelopes lined in shiny silver…or a dreamy Victorian confection on rose-patterned candlelight paper with sage-green ink and envelope liners to match. Paper & Lace Studio also offers an entire album filled with meaningful choices for African-American weddings.

Etiquette and More

Constance is glad to help with etiquette questions, and special situations such as ensuring the correct wording for invitations to a Jewish or military wedding or a Nuptial Mass. *"I am sensitive to a couple's wish to keep important traditions in their family, whether that is related to their faith life, ethnic heritage, or other history."*

Paper & Lace Studio helps brides with wedding programs, favors, napkins and carries a boutique selection of exclusive handmade ring-bearer pillows, garters and veils you won't see anywhere else.

Call for an Appointment

Call Constance to schedule an appointment to fit your schedule. Some brides shop for invitations alone, while others order with the groom or with their mother. *"I designed my studio for comfort, and I have plenty of coffee cups for you. I want you to have a fun and memorable experience as you plan how to invite your guests to your wedding, and I will be sure your order is absolutely accurate."*

PaperPlus®

TIGARD
11105 S.W. Greenburg Rd.
(503) 684-1892

PORTLAND
835 E. Burnside
(503) 238-3607

EUGENE
1090 Bailey Hill Rd.
(503) 345-3223

Business Hours: Mon–Fri 7:30am–5:30pm; Saturdays 9am–2pm

Why Ready-to-Print Invitations and Announcements?

- **You Get Selection!**
  Paper Plus has over 200 designs and formats in stock and ready to print. Choose from formal, romantic, elegant, or plain and simple styles.
- **You Get Uniqueness!**
  When you pick the design and the printer, you have the ability to customize your invitation.
- **You Save Time!**
  By dealing with a local printer you can have your invitations in as little as a day or two.
- **You Save Money!**
  You only pay for the stock, the printing, and production cost. No sales agent mark-up and no shipping!

SHARING A SECRET…

Paper Plus is well-known for their printing and office supplies but their great selection and low prices on wedding supplies may be one of Oregon's best kept secrets.

Snead's PARTY TIME Rentals & Decorations
"ONE STOP PARTY SHOP"

141st & Tualatin Valley Highway
Beaverton, Oregon 97005
(503) 641-6778
Mon–Sat 7:30am–6pm; Sun 8am–4:30pm

Selections and Styles of Invitations

Sit down and relax in the quiet of our wedding room and browse through 19 albums from traditional to contemporary designs. Our suppliers offer beautiful craftsmanship featuring embossing, engraving, and thermography on bristol, vellum, mirrorkote, parchment, linen, foil, and laid finish with many using recycled paper. You will have many choices in lettering style and ink color. If you prefer, you may design and compose your own to make your wedding more personal.

Special Services

Our experienced wedding consultants check to make sure every detail is correct and that you are communicating with your family and guests in the mood you want for your wedding—all the while remaining within your budget. We can also assist by suggesting compatible wedding accessories and gifts for attendants along with an extensive selection of church and reception rental items and decorations.

Ordering and Cost

Allow ample time to receive and address your invitations. You need to mail them four to six weeks prior to the wedding. Although we can provide emergency three-day service, the average time is two weeks. Prices range from economical to upper moderate. We require a 50% deposit with the balance due on delivery.

Other Services

- **Imprinting is our specialty!!** We provide in-house quality imprinting of your napkins, ribbon, etc. Assorted type styles and colors, wedding symbols and emblems. Our selection of bulk-pack napkins is extensive.
- **Memories book:** an album of anniversaries from 10 to 60 featuring invitations, thank yous, beverage napkins, place cards, and ribbons.
- **Occasion book:** an album for holidays, religious celebrations, new baby, schools, sports, recitals, birthdays, retirements, galas, bon voyage, open house, picnics, and fund raisers, featuring regular and photo invitations, napkins, guest towels, coasters, matches, place cards, and ribbons.
- **Professional images:** an album for business stationery, office and specialty products, featuring business cards, letterhead, envelopes, statements and other forms, computer laser paper, announcements, folders, labels, signs, and specialty advertising.

CUSTOMER SERVICE AND SATISFACTION

Established in 1964, we pride ourselves on customer service and satisfaction. Please give us the opportunity to serve you!

See page 536 under Rental Items & Equipment.

TOWNE PAPERS

Social Stationery, Invitations & Gifts

9 N.W. 23rd Place
Portland, Oregon 97210
(503) 224-6156; Fax (503) 224-3616
Business Hours: Mon–Fri 9am–6pm; Sat 10am–5pm; Sun Noon 4pm
E-mail: townepaper@aol.com

Selection and Styles

Traditional or contemporary, Towne Papers has a huge selection of invitations for every style in a wide range of pricing. We specialize in finding the perfect invitation for your wedding. We have access to hundreds of vendors around the world. Paper lines include: Cranes, William Arthur, Regency, Lallie and Elite.

Special Services

We offer in-house printing with same day service available. Towne Papers also has Business Stationery, Holiday Cards, Corporate Gifts and Gift Wrapping Services available. Printed napkins, matches, and ribbon add a special flair to your event. If we do not have it, we'll find it!

Personalized Service

Just let us know what your needs are and one of our experienced sales consultants will take care of it for you. We specialize in the unique. We can help you over the phone, by appointment, or just drop in!

Towne Papers has been in business for over 18 years and is owned and operated by a meeting planner of 10 years who understands the need for flexibility, creativity and interesting time constraints when it comes to planning your event. Conveniently located in Uptown Shopping Center and open seven days a week to serve you!

The Wedding Cottage

Westside
4775 S.W. Watson Avenue
Beaverton, Oregon 97005
(503) 643-9730

Downtown
423 S.W. Fourth Avenue
Portland, Oregon 97204
(503) 827-4578

The most enormous selection of elegant accessories from economical to extravagant.

The Wedding Cottage is known for having the most beautiful invitations as well as the largest selection in the Portland area. With over 14 years of experience, The Wedding Cottage is able to help brides with those tough etiquette questions, and wording for traditional and contemporary invitations, announcements and receptions.

Selections and Styles

The selection of paper is enormous, with over 60 books containing hundreds of invitations from which to choose. Handmade papers, vellum overlays, tea length, and of course 100% cotton papers are just some of the choices. All can be printed in a variety of fonts and ink colors. We stock beautiful ribbons that can be used on invitations, too.

Personalized napkins and ribbons are printed in-house with a large selection of colors available. Rehearsal dinner and shower invitations along with thank you notes, place cards, and table cards are all in stock. We also offer blank invitation and ceremony program stock.

Ordering

Our knowledgeable staff provides excellent customer service and individual help in writing your invitations. Printed orders are generally back within two to three weeks, depending on the invitation. However, some can be received within two to three days, if needed. Of course allowing plenty of time is always best—three to four months prior to the wedding is recommended. Invitations are mailed out four to eight weeks before the wedding, depending on the situation.

Our main store is located in Beaverton, with a second location in downtown Portland, inside of the Ania Collection

Mention the Bravo! Resource Guide and receive a free packet of thank you notes.

See page 226 under Bridal Accessories & Attire.

Notes

© Moments In Time Photography • page 507

ORIGINS OF THE ENGAGEMENT RING

The giving of an engagement ring was considered to show commitment on the groom's part to purchase the bride. The use of rings within the wedding ceremony can be traced back to the ancient Egyptians and Romans.

YOUR GUIDE TO GEMSTONE VALUE AND QUALITY

For most couples, the bride's engagement ring is the first major piece of jewelry that they have ever purchased. When you're making a purchase of this size and for something that the bride will wear for the rest of her life, it's nice to know what the jeweler is describing and what exactly you're getting.

The stone you select as the centerpiece of your engagement ring is judged by four distinct factors that combine in a number of ways to arrive at its value. These factors are commonly referred to as the Four Cs.

CARAT WEIGHT: The weight of all precious stones is expressed in carats. Originally, the word carat was derived from a natural unit of weight, the seeds of the carob tree. Traditionally, gemstones were weighed against these seeds, but in more recent times, a standardized system has been developed by which one carat equals 0.2 grams, or one-fifth of a gram. The carat is then divided into 100 "points," so that a gemstone of 25 points equals a quarter carat, or a gemstone of 50 points equals a half carat, etc.

CLARITY: Virtually every diamond (the most common stone selected for an engagement ring) has some minute traces of noncrystalized carbon, the element from which they were formed. In most cases, these traces of carbon are not visible to the human eye but become apparent under magnification and are referred to as "inclusions." These inclusions are actually nature's fingerprint and are what make every diamond different from another. Therefore, the freer the diamond or other gemstone is of inclusions, the rarer the stone will be, causing a higher value to be placed on the stone.

There are three major international grading systems for classifying diamonds—GIA, CIBJO, and HRD. A stone is termed flawless by the GIA if it is without inclusions internally or externally. The other systems use the term "loupe clean," or internally flawless.

COLOR: When it comes to diamonds, most of us don't think in terms of colors available, but diamonds do cover the spectrum of colors. While the majority range in color from a barely perceptible yellow or brownish tint, the really rare stones are described as "colorless." Even rarer diamonds, which are sometimes referred to as "fancies," can be found in shades of green, red, blue, or amber.

CUT: Of all the ways diamonds are rated, this is the one that man directly has an impact on. How each diamond is cut will directly affect its fire and sparkle, since it is the cutter's skill that ultimately releases the beauty of each stone. It is the talent, artistry, and years of experience of this person that enable the stone to make the best use of the light by allowing it to reflect from one facet to another and then disperse through the top of the stone. The better the cut, the more brilliance and sparkle you will see in the stone you select.

For more assistance with staying organized during the wedding planning process, check out the Bravo! Wedding Organizer. Detailed question worksheets double as contracts. This step-by-step system will keep every detail of your wedding organized. To order, refer to the order form on page 24 in this Guide.

DESIGNER JEWELRY
SHOWCASE

One S.W. Columbia Street, Suite 0002
Portland, Oregon 97258
(503) 241-9389; Fax (503) 222-1310

Fine jewelry is fine because it is built to last for generations. That is what you will discover at Designer Jewelry Showcase. We showcase nationally recognized designers whose quality is as important as ours. You will *find new designer* platinum and 18k wedding rings as well as many different styles of men's custom platinum wedding bands. If by chance you do not see the wedding ring of your dreams, we will custom design and manufacture your ring according to *your* specifications. *Come in* and *experience the difference.*

Designer Jewelry specializes in ideal cut diamonds A.G.S.–G.I.A. certified. Our emphasis is on finer quality, color, clarity and cut. We help our clients to become informed buyers. We show diamonds unmounted and in the proper lighting so that their 4 Cs can be determined accurately.

Cut

Designer Jewelry feels that the cut is the most important and overlooked factor in determining a diamond's value and beauty. As Master Diamond Cutters, we are especially qualified to educate you in the finer details of cut.

The Ideal Cut: When a round brilliant diamond has been cut to "ideal" proportions by a master cutter, it is a splendor to behold.

The Ideal Cut Diamond describes a round brilliant diamond that has been cut to exact and mathematically proven proportions. Its symmetry, with 58 exactly placed facets, produces the ultimate in lustre and beauty. When a diamond is cut to the ideal proportions, all of the light entering from any direction is totally reflected through the top and is dispersed into a display of sparkling flashes and rainbow colors.

Cost

As a direct importer, Designer Jewelry is especially qualified to select the finest cut diamonds at the most competitive price. Cost is relative to quality, size and cut. Diamond prices will start to compound with increases in size. Our international experience gives us the ability to draw upon worldwide resources in locating rare and important diamonds. As a result, we have enjoyed a high rate of repeat and referral business.

Fred Meyer JEWELERS

"For All Those Special Times"

Now in most major malls!

Call for a location near you.

(800) 858-9202

For Your Wedding

Fred Meyer Jewelers goes to more weddings in the Northwest because you choose from one of the largest wedding ring collections, you will discover an impressive selection of classic and contemporary engagement rings, wedding sets and solitaires. A collection of unmounted diamonds in all shapes and sizes with an unrivaled selection of 14kt. and 18kt. gold settings. Fred Meyer Jewelers also offers the reassurance and protection of an independent appraisal on unmounted diamonds 1/4 carat or larger.

Custom Design and Jewelry Restoration

Fred Meyer Jewelers have custom design specialists on staff. Our in-store goldsmiths specialize in restoring keepsake jewelry or transforming an old treasure into a new beautiful creation.

Gifts for Wedding Attendants

- **Groomsmen:** men's accessory jewelry
- **Bridesmaids:** ladies fashion accessories, earrings, pendants and bracelets

Other Jewelry

Helpful gift hints for the bride or groom: diamond earrings, bracelets and neckwear for her; men's accessory jewelry, 14kt gold chains and bracelets, or quality watches from Seiko, Citizen, and Pulsar for him. Don't forget Mom, Dad, friends, and relatives who especially helped to make your wedding day perfect. Thank them with specially selected gifts.

Service: Financing and Guarantee

Fred Meyer Jewelers 30-day money back guarantee ensures your complete satisfaction with every purchase, and your diamond is protected against loss for as long as you own it (see our store for complete details). Our "Diamond Standard" includes free inspection, free cleaning, trade-in value, and guarantee against diamond loss. You can pay for your jewelry the easy way with our convenient revolving charge card.

Quality and Affordability

We're committed to quality and affordability. The selection of a wedding set is the ultimate expression of your hopes, dreams and promises. Fred Meyer Jewelers makes your selection easy with the Northwest's largest collection of exquisitely designed wedding rings in classic or contemporary designs. Or have our master goldsmith design a unique ring especially for you. We believe no sale is ever final until you, our customer, is completely happy. So come to Fred Meyer Jewelers and celebrate all those special times!

 Please let this business know that you heard about them from the Bravo! Bridal Resource Guide.

JLA NORTHWEST JEWELERS

8235 S.E. 13th Avenue • Portland, Oregon 97202

Located in the Old Sellwood Square

(503) 231-0090; Fax (503)231-0095

E-mail: jla@spiritone.com; Web site: www.jlanw.com

Business Hours: 11am–5pm Tues–Sat;

other hours reserved for private appointments

Specialty

JLA Northwest Jewelers specializes in **platinum** wedding bands and engagement rings, from antique-estate diamond jewelry to modern, custom-designed platinum wedding sets ranging in price from $250 and up.

Types of Jewelry Sold

Engagement rings, wedding bands, precious and semi-precious stone jewelry, earrings, bracelets, pendants and necklaces, custom designed and handmade fine jewelry, pearls, cufflinks and studs.

Shapes and Kinds of Stones Available

We specialize in diamonds in all shapes, sizes and qualities at wholesale prices. Our diamonds are GIA (Gemological Institute of America) or EGL (European Gem Lab) certified. We also carry an inventory of Sapphires, Rubies, Emeralds and other precious and semi-precious stones.

Custom Design

Designer Judith Arnell has been in the wholesale jewelry business for 26 years as a designer and manufacturer of fine jewelry. She will personally work with you to design the perfect, one one-of-a-kind piece of jewelry to enhance your image…at a reasonable price! Please stop by our studio to view our work and discuss your jewelry needs in a comfortable atmosphere.

Our Mission

Our mission is to make sure our customers get the best product at the lowest possible price. Making you a satisfied customer is always our priority…and we are confident that we cannot be undersold.

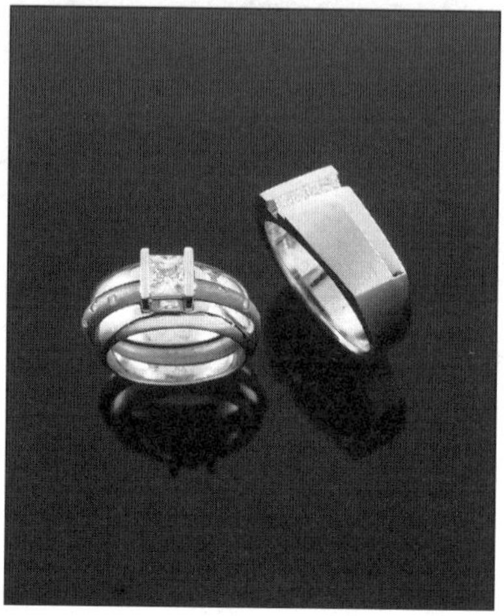

DOWNTOWN

901 S.W. Yamhill • Portland, Oregon 97205
(503) 223-9510

WASHINGTON SQUARE

9610 Washington Square • Portland, Oregon 97223
(503) 620-2243

Also located in the Oregon Market at the Portland Airport

Specialty Wedding Sets

We represent more than 25 jewelry designers with custom design service available at our downtown location. Engagement rings and wedding sets can be created in 14K or 18K yellow, rose or white gold and platinum. Large selection of original designs available and a friendly, knowledgeable staff to assist you. Loose diamonds and gemstones can be matched with designs in stock, or our on-staff designer can design something especially for you. Wedding rings from $250, plain bands from $65.

Gift Ideas for Bride, Groom and Attendants

Extensive collection of original and handcrafted fine jewelry, ceramics, art glass and exotic wood accessories that the wedding party will love to receive.

Services/Policies

- Layaway Available
- Gift Registry and Gift Certificates
- Packing and Shipping
- Gift wrap available for small fee

See page 279 under Bridal Registry & Gifts.

SINCE 1912

ZELL BROS

Jewelers - Platinumsmiths

800 S.W. Morrison Street • Portland, Oregon 97205
(503) 227-8471 or (800) 444-8979; Fax (503) 223-8546
Business Hours: Mon–Fri 10am–5:30pm; Sat 10am–5pm

WE'VE HELPED PORTLAND KEEP 88 YEARS OF WEDDING PROMISES

Zell Bros, the Largest Full-service Jewelry and Tabletop Store in the West

Zell Bros is a wedding tradition. When we opened in 1912 in a small storefront near Union Station, Zell Bros made a promise: to consistently offer the most beautiful jewelry and the highest quality diamonds available. Choose from our large selection and let one of our expert on-staff designers create unique rings just for you. We've helped generation after generation of Portland brides and grooms keep their promises of finding "just the right" rings.

Shapes and Kinds of Stones Available

You name it, we have it. From the most brilliant diamonds, to lustrous pearls, rubies, and sapphires. All birthstones are available, too.

Custom Design and Jewelry Restoration

Our extensive, in-store manufacturing department is staffed with expert jewelers, designers, diamond setters, platinumsmiths, and watchmakers. We will create anything you can imagine, or restore, remodel and repair your treasured heirloom pieces.

Gift Ideas for Bride, Groom, and Attendants

Let our staff of expert gift consultants guide you throughout three floors in your quest for excellence.

Service is our Most Important Product

Here are a few things we offer:

- Our famous gift wrap
- Free diamond inspection
- Free jewelry cleaning
- Credit options
- Bridal gift registry
- Full-service Stationery Department
- Exchanges gladly within 90 days
- Parking validation with purchase

LET US HELP YOU KEEP YOUR PROMISE

See page 280 under Bridal Registry & Gifts.

Notes

© Strong Photography • page 523

ENSURE GOOD LUCK

During the Elizabethan era, to ensure good luck,

the bride and groom were encouraged to

kiss over a stack of small sweet buns that

formed a centerpiece on a table.

It was the French who, in the 17th century,

started to frost the stack of cakes with a

white sugar frosting so that they would stay upright.

Thus was born the tiered wedding cake

that brides use today.

Northwest Artist Management

Musicians, Concerts & Fine Events

6210 S.E. 41st Avenue
Portland, Oregon 97202
Contact: Nancy Anne Tice • Phone/Fax (503) 774-2511
Business Hours: Mon–Fri 9am–6pm
E-mail: nwartmtg@teleport.com; Web site: www.nwmusicpro.com

Entertainment Consultant Services

Since 1989 Northwest Artist Management has been proud to offer the finest in classical, jazz, and international music for weddings and all fine occasions. From Arias to Zydeco, soloists to elegant dance bands and hot jazz ensembles, we can accommodate just about any entertainment need or musical preference, including assistance with technical details.

Specialty

We represent only the finest Northwest artists whom you can select with complete confidence, knowing they are as dedicated to creating special memories as you are! We offer string quartets, brass ensembles, classical soloists, and vocalists of all kinds, a wide variety of dance bands, jazz ensembles, and international music such as Italian, Irish, Mediterranean, Middle Eastern, Flamenco, Mariachi, Reggae, the Blues, Latin Salsa, Caribbean, and Cajun/Zydeco to suit most budgets.

Budget and Terms

Northwest Artist Management can accommodate any budget, ranging from $150 soloists to a large big band or orchestra. Reception bands and ensembles average between $350 and $1,500, depending on size, type, and reputation of the group.

How Much Can We Save?

Our commission is built into the artist's fee. We consult with you to determine just exactly what your preferences are, and can usually offer several choices from which to choose. We provide complete promotional materials, photos, demo tapes, references, and frequently, live performance observation possibilities so you can be assured of making an informed and confident decision.

How Far In Advance Should We Meet?

We have provided musicians as late as the day of the wedding, but usually prefer to consult with you six to nine months in advance. To engage certain groups, a one-year-in-advance reservation is advisable so you won't be disappointed, especially if your wedding is on a Saturday in August.

Experience

All of the artists on our roster are gifted, polished professionals with years of experience in helping couples "custom-design" every detail of their wedding music. We are knowledgeable about all music from the grand Baroque period to the hottest Top 40. We are available to consult with you personally to help you select the perfect repertoire that will create and enhance the romance and magic of your special day, and accommodate the needs of your guests. We offer only the best, because you deserve nothing less!

Member of:

Weddings of Distinction, Jazz Society of Oregon,
Portland Oregon Visitors Association, Washington County Visitors Association

THE FIRST DANCE

The traditional bride and groom's first dance represents the start of their new life together. After the first dance together, the bride dances with her father and the groom with his mother.

HELPFUL HINTS

- **Deciding on a band:** Every band should have a music list available for you to review. This will be helpful in deciding on a band. You may want to ask if the band is currently playing somewhere, then you can listen to their music style live and see their stage presence before you make a final decision.
- **Reserving a band:** Reserve a band or orchestra for your reception immediately. There are only a limited amount of Saturdays available, especially in peak wedding seasons. Popular bands and orchestras are often reserved up to a year in advance.
- **Setup requirements:** The formality, facility, and size of your event will determine the type of music that is appropriate. Inquire about whether the site can accommodate dancing and has the area necessary for the musicians to set up and perform. Be very specific about getting the space and electrical requirements from the band so that you can accurately relay the information to your contact person at the facility.
- **Cut-off hours:** When you make all the final arrangements with your facility, be sure to ask if they have any specified time cut-offs for music. Some facilities require that music be stopped as early as 10pm for the comfort of neighboring homes, businesses, or other guests.
- **Background music and dancing music:** Remember when reserving your music that the first hour of your reception or event is a time for introductions and mingling with guests. If your band begins playing immediately, you'll want to make sure that the music is background-type music that doesn't overwhelm and interfere with mingling. The band can be instructed at a certain time or by signal to pick up the pace of the music for dancing.
- **Keeping the flow going at the reception:** It is a good idea to have a liaison between the bride and groom and the band. This person can instruct the band when it's time to play the "first dance" song. Many times the band leader will act as master of ceremonies, announce the cake cutting, throwing of the bouquet, and the garter toss. The best man may be the person to do this since he will be close at hand to coordinate the order of events with the bride, groom, and parents. This will help the day to flow smoothly for the bride and groom.
- **Band breaks:** How many breaks will the band be taking and for how long? Will there be music provided during this downtime? Will the musicians require food and/or beverages? This could effect your total count to the caterer.
- **What kind of band is appropriate:** for a wedding with 50-75 guests, a three-piece band is appropriate; for 75-200, a four- to six-piece band works well.
- **Saving on music:** The best way to cut music costs is to have your wedding in off-season: January through March, Sundays, early in the day. Musicians will be more willing to negotiate prices if it doesn't conflict with another high paying booking.
- **NOTE:** Make sure your contract is sound, and that your event won't be bumped for a larger engagement. A deposit is usually required.

For more assistance with staying organized during the wedding planning process, check out the Bravo! Wedding Organizer. Detailed question worksheets double as contracts. This step-by-step system will keep every detail of your wedding organized. To order, refer to the order form on page 24 in this Guide.

Sinatra Swing, Inc.

From supper-club swing to dance floor romance.

"...STYLE AND PANACHE..."
—Jenni Minner, Performing Arts Coordinator, Portland Saturday Market

"...EXCELLENT..."
—Al Kendall, Entertainment Chairman, BPOE

"...COURTEOUS AND RELIABLE...COVERS SINATRA BEAUTIFULLY..."
—Eric B. Allen, Restaurant Manager, Willamette Athletic Club

"...TOP OF THE LINE..."
—Carmen Eastman, President/CEO, Eastman Entertainment

Make Your Wedding Swing!

Entertainer Johnny Martin brings 20 years of experience to the stage. He's made quite a splash at the Multnomah Athletic Club, Columbia Edgewater Country Club, Waverley Country Club, Queen of the West Cruise Line, and various Oregon casinos—to name a few.

Widely recognized as an emerging vocal talent in Portland.

Something Old, Something Borrowed, Something Blue-eyed

Sinatra swing as performed by Johnny and backed up by the finest musicians in town.

Not a variety act. Highly specialized swing music made popular by great artists such as Nelson Riddle, Billy May, Cole Porter, and Sammy Cahn. Brings all generations to the dance floor.

A Day Like This Should Be Special

Make your reservations now. Advanced booking recommended. Whenever there's a need for highly specialized music and entertainment.

SUMMER WIND • LET'S FALL IN LOVE
HELLO YOUNG LOVERS • SOUTH OF THE BORDER
COME FLY WITH ME • OLD BLACK MAGIC
NIGHT AND DAY • UNDER MY SKIN
WITCHCRAFT • LADY IS A TRAMP

Call for a free demo tape or live performance video.
E-mail: micstand5@aol.com

BYLL DAVIS & FRIENDS

(503) 644-3493

Type of Music

Byll Davis & Friends offers complete flexibility in all styles and eras of music, including ethnic, Big Band, good time rock 'n' roll and Top 40.

Instrumentation

Byll Davis can accommodate your needs with one to eight musicians. Dress is usually formal, but we'll dress to suit the occasion. Call for more details.

Experience

Byll Davis has a master's degree in music, has participated in several successful road tours and has led and performed in bands that specialize in Big Band, rock 'n' roll, Top 40 and variety and society musical styles. The Byll Davis & Friends ensemble has performed in literally thousands of engagements locally for a wide variety of events and audiences.

Musical Style and Audience Rapport

The following comments represent the kind of feedback Byll Davis & Friends receives:

"Byll, you were fabulous as always and a delight to work with."

"It was the perfect band for the evening…many, many compliments from our guests."

"Your selections for our event were based on your ability to adjust and come through with what people like."

"Your music was so good it made it difficult to keep the outsiders from crashing in."

Free Consultation

If hiring a band is new to you, or if you want to find out more about Byll Davis & Friends, make an appointment to meet with Byll. The service is free, the information invaluable.

Cost and Terms

Prices, space and electrical requirements will vary depending on the size of the band and location of engagement. Please call for additional information.

RELIABLE
APPROPRIATE
PRICED RIGHT
FUN ! ! ! !

(503) 644-3493

Cúl an Tí

67 N.E. Meikle Place
Portland, Oregon 97213
Contact: Cary Novotny (503) 236-9781
E-mail: culanti@aol.com
Web site: http://members.aol.com/culanti/

ROUSING IRISH AND CONTEMPORARY FOLK MUSIC

Three strong instrumentalists make up this compelling ensemble, which combines the best elements of traditional Irish dance music with exciting, modern Celtic stylings. Bass and acoustic guitars blend with vocals, accordion and red-hot fiddle in fresh arrangements of traditional Irish music, perfect for dancing and celebration. Cúl an Tí—"cool ahn tee"—performs a broad range of music, including slow ballads and waltzes, lightning fast jigs, reels, polkas, bluegrass, American folk music, and a modest selection of classic rock. The band plays throughout the Pacific Northwest; appearances include the 1998 Portland Celtic Festival, the Portland Celtic Minifest, The Bite festival of Portland as well as countless dates in venues such as Kells and Biddy McGraw's in Portland, and Conor Byrne's Pub and Kells in Seattle.

Reception Options

Cúl an Tí is well connected in Portland's folk-music community, allowing them to invite additional top-notch musicians into the line-up if requested. Instrumentalists, singers, even Irish dancers and callers (to teach dance steps to your guests) are available to help create an even more spectacular performance. Scaled-down versions of the band (solo or duo format) are also available, for those on a thrifty budget.

Ceremony Options

Cúl an Tí can provide the soft and subtle melodies to help make your ceremony a moving and memorable event. They offer a wide variety of beautiful musical combinations, including classical and fingerstyle guitar, violin, male and/or female vocals, bass and Irish tin-whistle. Special requests for the processional/recessional are encouraged.

Special Services, Costs and Terms

Cúl an Tí's P.A. system is available for toasts and announcements; recorded music can be provided during breaks. Fees are determined on an individual basis, according to length of performance, location, and amplification requirements. All necessary details are included in contract. Demo tape and references are available upon request.

LIVELY, UPLIFTING MUSIC IN THE SPIRIT OF CELEBRATION

Give Cúl an Tí a call—they will help you find the right combination of ceremony and reception music to help make your wedding day a joyous and successful event.

DAVID COOLEY & THE HARD SWING BAND

P.O. Box 2086
Vancouver, Washington 98668
PORTLAND (503) 227-1866
VANCOUVER (360) 693-1707
Fax (360) 693-4057

Type of Music

Referred to as "the Frank Sinatra of Portland," (Phil Smith, Oregonian) David Cooley's brand of Swing and Big Band vocals are the Northwest's finest. His recent release, "Fly Me To The Moon," on CD and cassette, is an impressive collection of popular Swing standards. In addition to Swing music, the band's repertoire also includes Rock 'n' Roll, Rhythm and Blues. The group provides background music, dance music and ceremony music. Special requests are welcome. Please call for more information.

Experience

David's 15 years as a singer and band leader guarantees you the perfect sound, style and pace for your reception. He understands what an important effect the band has on a successful reception. His performance credits include venues in Europe, Asia, Hawaii, Canada and the United States.

Instruments

The group may be booked in several different ways: from a trio, quartet, five or six-piece, all the way to the renowned 11-piece band featuring the Hard Swing Horn section. These variations allow great flexibility in choosing the appropriate sound, style and price range for your reception music.

Special Services

David Cooley is an excellent MC. He will help coordinate announcements, first dance, bouquet toss and other special activities. David will be at your service to help in every way possible.

Cost and Terms

Pricing is flexible according to the size of the band, venue and location. Please call for an estimate and more information.

Commitment

David Cooley's commitment to excellence in musical services extends beyond the reception itself. Advance planning and last-minute changes are accommodated with every means possible—no detail is too small.

Credits

OREGON SYMPHONY • OMSI • PORTLAND CENTER FOR PERFORMING ARTS MULTNOMAH ATHLETIC CLUB • MUSEUM AFTER HOURS • UNIVERSITY CLUB SALISHAN LODGE • PORTLAND HILTON • SEATTLE SHERATON • FOUR SEASONS OLYMPIC, SEATTLE • WASHINGTON ATHLETIC CLUB • GOVERNOR HOTEL • THE RACQUET CLUB • BENSON HOTEL • PORTLAND MARRIOTT • WAVERLEY COUNTRY CLUB • PORTLAND GOLF CLUB • SKAMANIA LODGE

If you're looking for a very special accent at your wedding, call now.
***David Cooley & The Hard Swing Band** offers a classic musical atmosphere with all the style, charm and spirit to make your celebration unforgettable.*

RAMSEY EMBICK BAND

Contact: Nancy Anne Tice
Phone/Fax (503) 774-2511
E-mail: nwartmtg@teleport.com
Web site: nwmusicpro.com

Types of Music and Demo

Ramsey Embick is an exceptionally talented musician who plays all styles of music from the 40s to the 90s. His repertoire includes Latin, Jazz, Big Band, Jump Blues, Hip Hop, R&B, Rock n' Roll, Oldies and lots of sizzling contemporary hits. From sensitive, romantic ballads, to high energy dance numbers, his music is sure to keep the party flowing smoothly and the dance floor full.

Instruments

Ramsey Embick can provide a versatile ensemble to fit most situations from a trio of keyboards, bass and singing drummer, to quartet or quintet with either female vocalist and/or saxophone. Larger groups with percussion and other instruments are available as the budget allows. Ramsey Embick is an elegant soloist, and can also provide duo or trio jazz for background or cocktail.

Experience

Ramsey Embick toured 25 countries around the world for four years as Music Director for the Pointer Sisters. He has also worked with other musical giants such as Jennifer Holliday, Gladys Knight, Michael Jackson and the Commodores. His many years of playing the world's major concert venues have given him the polish and sophistication to handle any musical situation from solo to playing with 18 piece Big Bands, with confidence and style. Since moving to Portland in 1994, he has played in all the best venues for numerous corporate, private and bridal clients, as well as playing at the hottest jazz clubs and local festivals. Besides heading up his own band, he works frequently with the Bobby Torres Ensemble, and the Carlton Jackson/Dave Mills Big Band. Other local engagements include Linda Hornbuckle, Mel Brown, the Linn Sisters and arranging for Gino Vanelli. His 1996 CD, "Getting Your Feet Wet," by his own jazz trio, in a smooth, contemporary Latin groove was released to rave reviews.

Special Services

Ramsey is happy to play your requests. He designs his set list to suit the needs of your special day and serve as MC. You are welcome to use the PA for toasts and announcements.

Cost and Terms

Competitive rates vary depending on group size, date and time of year, playing time and location. Call for quote and free promo and demo materials.

The Critics are Unanimous:

"Outstanding, absolutely wonderful, spectacular presentation, beautiful and technically dazzling keyboard work. Incredible!!" Let the Ramsey Embick Band put the superlatives into your next musical celebration!

JANICE SCROGGINS/GARY HARRIS QUARTET

Contact: Nancy Anne Tice
Phone/Fax (503) 774-2511
E-mail: nwartmtg@teleport.com; Web site: www.nwmusicpro.com

Types of Music and Demo

Celebrated jazz, blues and gospel pianist, **Janice Scroggins** has teamed up with **Gary Harris** on sax and flute to form a lively and sophisticated instrumental quartet that plays jazz, blues, rhythm and blues and funk favorites for listening and dancing. If groovin' to the hits of Duke Ellington, Cole Porter, Marvin Gaye, Otis Redding, The Temptations, Glenn Miller, Kenny G., Stevie Wonder or Gershwin is your idea of a great time, please call for a free demo, promotional kit and references.

Instruments

The instrumental quartet consists of keyboards/synthesizer, bass, drums, saxophones and flute. A vocalist may be added as the budget allows.

Experience

Janice Scroggins and **Gary Harris** have dazzled audiences at concerts and festivals in Russia, Europe, Japan, Mexico, Hawaii, Africa and all over the United States and Canada. Janice has opened for Bill Cosby, BB King, Ray Charles and Taj Mahal. Gary has played with The Temptations, Four Tops, Lou Rawls, Manhattan Transfer, and George Benson. Janice's *Scott Joplin* album was nominated for a Grammy Award in 1988, and she has been the recipient of the Cascade Blues Society, Muddy Waters Award three times. Locally, Janice has played with Linda Hornbuckle, Lloyd Jones, Curtis Salgado and Norman Sylvester; Gary plays with Leroy Vinnegar's Quartet, and several big bands, and they both play and tour with Obo Addy. Gary has recorded the California Raisins theme for Will Vinton Studios on Atlantic Records. Both have played for countless weddings and private parties. Their quartet blends and combines all of their respective experience into a tight and polished ensemble that is sure to get you up and dancing!

Cost, Terms and Special Services

Competitive prices based on date, time, length of engagement and size of group. All details outlined in contract. Call for quote. They welcome your requests including ethnic favorites. They are happy to serve as MC if you wish. Tuxedo is standard attire for weddings, unless otherwise specified.

ELEGANT, SMOOTH AND SOPHISTICATED. STYLISH, HIP AND GREAT FUN

This band knows exactly what to do to ensure the music will be the best it can be!

JAY HARRIS & SAM BAM BOO

ISLAND STEEL DRUM DANCE BAND

Formerly Jay Harris & Rockita

Contact: Nancy Anne Tice
Phone/Fax (503) 774-2511
E-mail: nwartmgt@teleport.com
Web site: www.nwmusicpro.com

Type of Music and Demo

Sam Bam Boo plays a unique blend of calypso, reggae, and island-style renditions of many types of popular music (blues, jazz, rock, even classical!), which they call "Rockalypso"! Much more than just a "steel drum band"—imagine your favorite Beatles, Elton John, Santana, Billy Joel, James Taylor, Sting or Van Morrison tunes played with that distinctive Caribbean flavor that makes you think of bright colors, steamy tropical nights, palm trees and exciting times on the dance floor. They also play all of your favorite island hits from "Jamaica Farewell" to "Day-O." Bob Marley, The Beach Boys, and Jimmy Buffett are well represented. Think of a festive "Island Carnival" and you have Sam Bam Boo. They also have a Limbo Stick and will teach you how to "Do the Limbo", an activity guaranteed to enliven any event! Call for free promotional package, demo, references, and song list.

Instruments

Sam Bam Boo is a trio that blends the bright, captivating tones of the steel drum with percussion, and bass and guitar. They frequently add a sax player when the budget permits. They are a surprisingly versatile ensemble with a full, rich sound. All the players also sing and wear tropical attire to complete the island look.

Experience and Special Services

Sam Bam Boo band members have played for hundreds of private parties, weddings, and corporate events in their many years on the band stand. They have played in every conceivable setting from boats, barns, and beaches, to parks, festivals, gardens, museums, wineries, mountain resorts, and all manner of commercial establishment…always with rave reviews and consistent invitations to return. They are pleased to serve as master of ceremonies and to play as many of your requests as possible. You are welcome to use their PA system for announcements. All ensemble members are talented, professional musicians, who are easy and fun to work with. You can trust your special day to Sam Bam Boo.

Cost

Sam Bam Boo is a highly affordable ensemble. Rates based on location, ensemble size, playing time, and season of year. Call for price quotation. We always use contracts.

KIM RALPHS & COMPANY

(503) 282-3421

Sinatra, Swing & More!

Imagine the lush soundtrack to *Sleepless in Seattle!* Classic and timeless. Band leader, **Kim Ralphs**, has assembled a fine group of professional musicians that specialize in the elegant and sophisticated music of the 1930s and '40s. They play quiet and tasty jazz instrumentals and the romantic love songs of Tony Bennett, Frank Sinatra, and Glenn Miller. For your dancing pleasure, they offer Big Band Swing and smooth Latin and Bossa Nova favorites.

In a more contemporary vein, they know all of Kenny G's most memorable hits. When you really want to take the temperature up, they can pump out some '50s and '60s rock. Kim Ralphs & Company are polished and versatile professionals who offer a wide variety of musical styles. They are always happy to accommodate your special requests to ensure your event is a success.

Kim plays **piano**, key-bass and various electric keyboard sounds such as **vibes** and **marimbas**. **Sax and flute, drums and vocals** complete the sound. The size of the group can expand to fit your budget. Both male and female vocalists are available, or the band can play only instrumentals, if you prefer.

Since 1985, Kim and his group have performed at the finest hotels and country clubs, and have been recommended by the best event planners and booking agencies. They are always happy to make announcements for you and help coordinate your party. Standard attire is black tuxedos. Let Kim Ralphs & Company create a warm and sparkling atmosphere for your next special event!

LISTEN TO WHAT THE PROFESSIONALS SAY:

"Kim is a fine pianist...and I always enjoy seeing him here."
Dennis Yamnitsky, F&B Manager, **Oswego Lake Country Club**

"Kim plays here often, and always does a great job...highly recommended."
Susan O'Neil, **Waverley Country Club**

"All the music that I have listened to over the years and all the conventions that I have gone to, I can truly say that this band was the best!"
Colleen Greenen, Convention Sales Manager, **Portland Oregon Visitors Association**

"Impeccably professional and experienced... a pleasure to work with."
Nancy Tice, **Northwest Artist Management**

THE MILLIONAIRE$

c/o Berkshire Snow Productions
P.O. Box 14159
Portland, Oregon 97293-0159
(503) 235-3071, (503) 284-1186
E-mail: berksnow@teleport.com

Good Time R&R, R&B, Blues,
Oldies and more, 40's thru 90's

Types of Music and Demo

The Millionaires bring a wealth of musical experience to your wedding reception or special event. With a repertoire that covers the history of rock 'n' roll, The Millionaires let the music speak for itself and the fun begin. From the days of Big Joe Turner and Howlin' Wolf, when the blues began to rock, through the hits of Elvis Presley, Roy Orbison and Chuck Berry and on to the British Invasion with the Rolling Stones and Beatles.

The Millionaires play the best of rock 'n' roll, rhythm and blues, blues, country and more—familiar songs from the '40s to the '90s. Our demo is available upon request.

Instrumentation and Personnel

We feature three male lead vocalists, accompanied by the classic four-piece format of electric guitar, Fender bass, electric piano/synthesizer/Hammond organ and drums.

Experience

Michael Kearsey, Don Heistuman and Jim Stein are backed by drummer Fred Ingram. These musicians have been members of some of the best loved groups in Oregon including Nu Shooz, Upepo, Diamond Hill, Razorbacks, the Larry Mahan Band, Saint Champagne, the Blue Devils and the Brothers of the Baladi. The Millionaires have played weddings, corporate events and club dates since 1992.

Musical Style and Audience Rapport

The Millionaires love to entertain and deliver songs that you love to hear. We will work with you to customize our sets to please the wide-range of ages that may be at your event and include styles from decades of great popular music. We are always happy to provide specialty songs that are most important to our clients. The bottom line for The Millionaires is to create the best musical memories for your needs.

Cost and Terms

Our prices will vary based on location, season, availability, length of engagement and special services you may need. We are flexible because we are The Millionaires!!

Opus 5

The Dance Band!

6210 S.E. 41st Avenue
Portland, Oregon 97202
Contact: Nancy Anne Tice at
Northwest Artist Management
Phone/Fax (503) 774-2511
E-mail: nwartmtg@teleport.com
Web site: www.nwmusicpro.com

Type of Music and Demo

OPUS 5 members combine many years of national and international touring and performing experience into a versatile, polished, and sophisticated dance band perfect for weddings, receptions, dinner and dancing, corporate entertaining, and elegant celebrations of all kinds. They are equally at home with Jazz, Pop, R&B, Country, Rock 'n' Roll, and the romantic, sentimental favorites of the past. Call for demo tape, photos, group résumé, play list, and references.

Instruments

OPUS 5 is a five-piece group with an extremely talented female lead vocalist. Instruments include keyboard/synthesizer, bass, drum, and guitar. Band members provide terrific lead vocals and smooth harmonies. They dress in formal attire unless you request otherwise to suit the occasion.

Experience, Music Style, and Audience Rapport

The members of OPUS 5 have played for hundreds of weddings over the years and know just what to do to keep your guests happy. They have played in places such as Oregon Symphony Gala, Atwater's, Oswego Lake Country Club, Columbia Gorge Hotel, The Governor Hotel and Benson Hotel, and at many local wineries and festivals. OPUS 5 is as dedicated to making special memories as you are. Accordingly, their play list is designed to perfectly suit the ambience of your special event, making sure the volume is just right and you and your guests have the time of your lives!

Special Services, Cost, and Terms

OPUS 5 encourages your special requests, including ethnic favorites. You are welcome to use their PA system for announcements and toasts. They will also serve as Master of Ceremonies for all dance traditions, bouquet and garter toss, etc. Taped music is provided for breaks. OPUS 5's prices are highly competitive and quoted individually, based on playing time, location, and season of the year. Details such as deposits, overtime, and cancellation charges are explained in their contract. Call for quotation.

Setting Requirements

Whether indoor or out, the band needs two 110-volt electrical outlets. Any outdoor engagements must have an awning or tent to cover the band. OPUS 5 prefers to set up several hours before the event if possible.

EXPERIENCE AND FLEXIBILITY

A thoroughly professional attitude helps ensure OPUS 5's success and popularity with its clients. The energy, elegance, and sparkle they bring to the bandstand are sure to enhance the mood and festive atmosphere of your next special event.

Patrick Lamb Productions

544 N.E. Thompson, Suite A
Portland, Oregon 97212
Contact: Amy Maxwell
(503) 335-0790; Fax (503) 335-9074
Sax Line (503) 650-7138
E-mail: lamb@teleport.com

VISA MasterCard

Types of Music and Demo

Imagine the sound of sweet saxophone permeating the atmosphere of your wedding. Patrick is versatile and plays music appropriate for the occasion including jazz, blues, motown, 70s retro, disco and original music of his own. His recent invitation to play at the White House and appearances at major festivals around the U.S. have given his career momentum. His new release, *For the Love* CD, is commercially available, and recently made "Top 10 in the Northwest" for Northwest bands. Patrick has a funky, versatile group which can tune itself for the needs of almost *any occasion*. From the traditional, relaxed background jazz which is needed for a dinner party, to the 70s party down retro and motown, Patrick's band is a consistent crowd-pleaser. Please call for a promotional package, demo tape and/or more information.

Instrumentation and Personnel

High quality professional musicians including saxophone, vocals, bass, drums, guitar, percussion, piano/organ as appropriate for the size and intimacy of the occasion.

Experience

You might be familiar with Patrick's music from his many appearances which include: The Mount Hood Festival of Jazz, The Bite, The Newport Jazz Festival, Hillsboro Concert in the Park, Lake Oswego Concert Series, Nordstrom, or the private parties he has played including one for FOX 49. Or you might have heard his new "Top 10 in the Northwest" release on KKJZ and KINK. Patrick has also toured and recorded with recording artists Tom Grant and Grammy recipient Diane Schuur, opening at festivals for people like Kenny G., Wynton Marseilles, Branford Marseilles, B.B. King, and many others. Patrick has experience in all aspects of the music business form touring, recording, and playing for all kinds of different occasions.

Cost and Terms

Prices are competitive and computed on an individual basis depending on month, day, time, and length of engagement. Our PA and lighting systems arc always available for your use. Call for quotations.

Testimonials

"Patrick Lamb's music adds so much to any event or to any venue. He is someone you want to follow and listen to wherever he plays. Any event or venue would greatly benefit from his appearance because of his reputation, his crowd appeal, and the draw that he brings in. Patrick Lamb is simply the greatest!"

—Teri Joly, CFI, Portland, OR

"I want to thank you for your beautiful holiday performance at the White House. Your appearance helped to make our 1996 Christmas holiday program truly memorable."

—Ann Stock, social secretary, White House, Washington, D.C.

STAGE III

Contact: Nancy Tice
Phone/Fax (503) 774-2511
E-mail: nwartmgt@teleport.com
Web site: www.nwmusicpro.com

Type of Music and Demo

Stage III is an incredibly versatile trio of experienced, talented musicians that play all styles of music from the marvelous Big Band Swing Era of the '40s and '50s, to the exciting contemporary hits of the '90s. This includes '50s and '60s nostalgia favorites, classic rock, country, Latin and jazz standards, rock 'n roll, blues, and plenty of romantic ballads, perfect for listening and dancing the night away. They provide rich vocal harmonies and a solid sense of fun sure to keep the dance floor full. STAGE III welcomes your requests. Call for a free promotional package, song list and demo tape.

Instruments

STAGE III is a trio of two men and a female who provide superb lead and harmony vocals, as well as playing live on stage, keyboards, soprano, alto and tenor saxophones, trumpet, flute, conga with full percussion accompaniment, lead and acoustic guitar, along with all digital sound and lighting. It is hard to believe that such a full and complete sound comes from only three musicians!

Experience

Band leader, Ron Barnes, has performed nationally and locally for over 20 years. From the Grand Ole Opry to Disneyland, Ron has worked with entertainers such as Three Dog Night, Hank Williams Jr., the Osmond Brothers, the Kingsmen (Louie Louie), and Del Shannon (Runaway). He has performed for countless fairs, festivals, weddings and special events. Mike Reif, guitarist, has also performed for over 20 years in casual, Big Band and blues bands, and Jann-Marie has toured and worked with the gospel rock group, New Life, as well as with casual bands specializing in Classic Rock and R&B styles. She has also appeared with national artists such as Pat Boone and Andrea Crouch. You can feel confident trusting the music on your special day to STAGE III. They will work closely with you to play the kind of music that will make your event truly unique, special, and memorable in every way. STAGE III knows how to "read the crowd" and adjust the tunes and volume to suit the needs of you and your guests.

Special Services

STAGE III will provide taped music for breaks and serve as Master of Ceremonies if you wish. You are welcome to use their microphones for toasts and announcements. Tuxedo or less formal attire as requested.

Costs, Terms and Setting Requirements

STAGE III provides a full band sound without the full band price. Price is highly competitive depending on date, time and location of the event. All terms specified in contract. Please call for quotation. STAGE III prefers to set up at least three hours before the event. Two 20 amp power outlets and a stage area of 20' x 10' preferred.

STAGE III provides the sizzle, energy, romance and sophistication that assures your next special event will be a smashing success!

SWINGLINE CUBS

0755 S.W. Miles Street
Portland, Oregon 97219
Contact: Teddy Deane (503) 246-4739
E-mail: swingcub@teleport.com
Web site: swinglinecubs.com

Types of Music

We play all types of swing (especially jump swing), '60s Motown, '70s hits, rhythm & blues, awesome renditions of standards and ballads, and all varieties of rock 'n' roll as well as contemporary pop and jazz. We also have CDs commercially available.

Instrumentation and Personnel

Exceptional lead female and male vocals with vocal backups accompanied by sax/clarinet/flute, piano/organ/synthesizer, trumpet, guitar, bass, drums and percussion.

Experience

In the last 15 years, we have played for well over 1,000 events of all kinds. Our client list includes: Portland Trail Blazers, Peter Jacobsen Productions, Oregon Symphony, Hewlett Packard, NIKE, Intel, Jantzen, Boys and Girls Aid Society, American Cancer Society, Doernbecher Children's Hospital, Komen Foundation, University of Oregon, Oregon Health Sciences University, University of Portland, Mayor Vera Katz, Portland Oregon Visitors Association, Reed College, The Bite, Rose Festival, Fort Vancouver Fourth of July, USA network movie, "The Haunting of Sarah Hardy"... and hundreds more.

Musical Style and Audience Rapport

The primary goal of the Cubs is to make your reception or event as enjoyable and memorable as possible. We are especially responsive to volume considerations. We will provide you with soft music for conversation and enthusiastic, energetic music for dancing.

Special Services

Ethnic music and special requests are gladly accepted. We can MC any activity from bouquet toss to door prizes. Our PA and lighting systems are always available for your use.

Cost and Terms

Prices are competitive and computed on an individual basis depending on month, day, place, time, and length of engagement. Call for quotations.

LOVE OF FESTIVITY

The "Cubs" are composed of personnel with a flair for elegance and a love of spontaneity and festivity. We cherish playing standards from the heart, but we absolutely love playing music that gets people moving, dancing, and celebrating.

WE'RE REALLY SERIOUS ABOUT THIS WHOLE BUSINESS OF HAVING A GOOD TIME!

TRUE FRIENDS, FEATURING MARILYN KELLER

Contact: Nancy Anne Tice
Phone/Fax (503) 774-2511
E-mail: nwartmtg@teleport.com

Types of Music and Demo

Vocalist, **Marilyn Keller** brings sparkle, grace, excitement, and a wealth of experience to the bandstand. Known for her "riveting stage presence, and killer renditions of gospel/blues," her repertoire also includes jazz, big band hits, rhythm and blues, Motown, rock 'n' roll, funk and contemporary pop favorites. Her ballads are haunting, soulful and tender, but she "gets down" with the best of them in all kinds of high energy tunes that are so much fun to dance to. Call for free promotional package, demo, song list and references.

Instruments

True Friends is a five-piece band consisting of keyboard/synthesizer, bass, drums, guitar and Marilyn on lead vocals. Band members add great harmonies. For smaller events, they can perform as a quartet, or add horns as the budget allows. Her exquisite vocals are frequently requested for wedding ceremonies.

Experience, Style and Audience Rapport

Marilyn Keller has performed for countless weddings, corporate parties, music festivals, at wineries and with many of Portland's finest musicians, including, Tall Jazz, Ron Steen, Tom Grant, The Swingline Cubs, Don Latarski, and Michael Allen Harrison. She and her band have played for a weekly jazz church service at Augustana Lutheran Church for six years. She has opened for the legendary Ray Charles, sung the National Anthem at a Portland Trail Blazer game, and has been guest soloist with the Eugene Symphony Orchestra. Her warm, confident and easy-going style enables her clients to relax and have a wonderful time whenever she and her band perform.

Special Services

Marilyn Keller welcomes your special requests, invites you to use the microphone for toasts and announcements, and is happy to serve as MC for all of the special wedding traditions, including first dance and bouquet toss.

Cost and Terms

Price is highly competitive, and based on date, time, location and length of engagement. All terms are outlined in contract. Tuxedo is standard attire for weddings, unless you specify otherwise. Call for quote.

ADD SOME MAGIC...

Marilyn Keller is at ease in any setting from intimate piano bar to large concert hall or festival stage. Let her add some magic to your next special event.

© red door studio • page 520

ANCIENT GREEK TRADITION

Instead of figuring their ages from their birthdates, ancient Greek women determined their ages from their dates of marriage.

HELPFUL HINTS

- **Deciding on a disc jockey:** Be sure to meet with disc jockeys in person. Make sure the person you meet is the one you are hiring for your event. Ask to see the equipment and portfolios or presentations of their shows so you know what to expect. If they do more than one show per day, check to make sure they have the appropriate equipment setups for two or more shows. The disc jockey should be able to provide you with a list of music available so that you can preselect favorites you would like played. Be sure there is a good mix of music so that people of all ages can enjoy and participate.
- **Written contract:** It is advisable to get a written contract stating exactly what you have agreed upon: date, number of hours, types of equipment, who will be doing the show, the total cost, what is included, and so on.
- **Master of ceremonies:** Be sure to ask whether your disc jockey can act as master of ceremonies at your reception. This will help the flow of events like cake cutting, throwing of the bouquet, garter toss, and announcing the first dance. One disc jockey recommends that the toast to the bride and groom should immediately be followed by the "first dance." This breaks the ice and gets the party going, especially when the rest of the wedding party is invited to the dance floor during or after the first dance.
- **Volume of music:** Discuss with your disc jockey the volume you wish and the selection of music. Keep the volume of music low for the first hour of your reception, allowing guests to mingle and ensuring that the level is comfortable for older guests. Then when the dancing begins, the volume can be raised.
- **Setup requirements:** Inquire about whether the site can accommodate dancing. Find out whether your disc jockey needs early access to the room and what the space and electrical requirements are. Make sure your facility contact knows about these needs and that they can be met.
- **Cut-off hours:** When you make all the final arrangements with your facility, be sure to ask if they have any specified time cut-offs for music. Some facilities require that music be stopped as early as 10pm for the comfort of neighboring homes, businesses, or other guests.
- **Special effects and requests:** Most disc jockeys are glad to play special songs if they are requested. Also inquire about any special effects they can supply, such as lighting, strobes, mirror balls, and fog.

For more assistance with staying organized during the wedding planning process, check out the Bravo! Wedding Organizer. Detailed question worksheets double as contracts. This step-by-step system will keep every detail of your wedding organized. To order, refer to the order form on page 24 in this Guide.

A.A. TWO'S COMPANY DJ SERVICE

P.O. Box 68211 • Portland, Oregon 97268
Contact: Chris Tjaden
(503) 786-9090
E-mail: djtwosco@ptld.uswest.net

Type of Music

We supply your event with a wide range of music. You may choose from the '50s, '60s, '70s and '80s. big band, ballroom, jazz, country and Top 40. Our collection contains over 18,000 title songs, all on compact discs and mini discs. We play to you and your guests.

Demo and Equipment

Our equipment is state-of-the-art with a clean professional look. We will give you a full, high-quality sound at a level you want. Our lighting adds a special effect to your event. Upon request, we will mail you a promotional package, including photo, that will answer all of your questions.

Experience and Attire

With over 25 years experience in the entertainment industry, A.A. Two's Company knows what it takes to make your event a success. We always dress in appropriate attire for your occasion.

Cost and Terms

We prefer to speak with each client and ask a few questions about their plans for the event. We then describe our service and quote a price. A deposit is required with the signing of the agreement. As always with any special event, it is best to book as early as possible.

Special Services

We help coordinate all the events during your wedding reception. We will make any special announcements during the event. Our cordless microphone is always available to you and your guests. Special requests are always welcome before and during the event. For the adventurous group, we are happy to get out on the dance floor and teach your guests the "Macarena", "Electric Slide" or even the "Octoberfest Chicken Dance."

QUALITY SERVICE IS OUR GOAL

A.A. Two's Company is a unique husband-and-wife team who pride themselves on providing quality service. We feel every event deserves our focused attention, so we only book one event per day. Our goal is to make your event a total musical success.

A DANCING PENGUIN MUSIC

LIVE MUSIC & DJ

(503) 282-3421

A Dancing Penguin Music owner, Kim Ralphs, is a professional pianist and DJ with over 15 years of experience entertaining Northwest audiences. His company is very well known and respected in Portland. This outstanding reputation was built with great customer service and attention to detail. He listens to you!

Playing the right song at the right time keeps the dance floor full and your guests happy. Swing, rock, disco, 80s, country, jazz…It's up to you!

You'll have total control of music style and volume.

You'll hear your favorites and special requests.

Master of ceremonies and help coordinating your event are included.

Black tuxedo is standard attire.

LISTEN TO WHAT THE PROFESSIONALS SAY:

"Kim plays here often, and always does a great job…highly recommended."
Susan O'Neil, **Waverley Country Club**

"Kim is a fine pianist…and I always enjoy seeing him here."
Dennis Yamnitsky, F&B Manager, **Oswego Lake Country Club**

"Whenever I need a DJ, A Dancing Penguin Music is the first company I call."
Nancy Tice, **Northwest Artist Management**

"I've recommended Dancing Penguin Music for years. Real professionals."
Diane Parke, event planner, **Occasions Etc. Inc.**

"Kim's piano and DJ combination really adds a touch of class to your event."
Charlotte Seybold, event planner, **Special Occasion Consulting**

Live piano with a DJ will make your event special!

A+ Mobile Music

Formerly SoundChoice Mobile Music
Kimberly Fogg
Professional DJ/MC, Line Dance Instructor, Vocalist
Office (503) 408-5728; E-mail: AplusMobileMusic@aol.com

SoundChoice Mobile Music has changed its name to A+ Mobile Music. *Why? To give my clients the best sounding equipment and the most options a DJ can offer. Many extras are offered to make your event a big hit and stress free! With over 15 years as a performer, I am very capable of performing the Master of Ceremony duties so all you have to do is enjoy yourself! I'm proud to be able to offer so much to my clients at such a reasonable price!*

♪ **1,200+ CD** Albums ranging from the roaring '50s & '60s swing, to today's chart toppers of country, rock 'n' roll, dance, alternative, blues and R&B. A current song list is available for requests. **This is *your* event; I play it anyway you like!**

♪ I use only **professional rack mounted equipment** in a slick stand-alone unit. To achieve the best sound quality, I use a large Yorkville 4-speaker system. A **Shock Resistant** dual CD player is used to withstand any amount of shaking your guests can create on the dance floor. Back-up equipment is handy at all parties for any emergencies that may arise.

♪ ***Special Options:*** Demo tape of wedding songs, lighting, fog machines, bubble machine and a quality cordless mic is offered at **no extra cost to you!** Karaoke services available for a small additional fee.

♪ **Six years of experience giving line dance lessons** and I can teach any "two left feet" anything from the Boot Scootin' Boogie to the Macarena.

♪ **Ceremony music services available.** I can help organize and provide a microphone for the Minister if needed. If you are looking for a **vocalist,** I would be happy to provide you with a demo tape of my songs. **I guarantee the first dance at weddings.**

♪ A+ Mobile Music would be happy to meet with you for a **free no obligation consultation.** I feel it's important to meet any DJ before you book a date. To ensure you get top-notch quality, all meetings and performances are done by myself and I book only one event a day.

♪ Packages begin at $380 for four hours and $30 each additional hour. It is straightforward, with no hidden costs. All booked dates are contracted. (Set up and tear down are not part of the four hours.) References available upon request. **A discount is offered for Sunday bookings.**

References Speak for Themselves

"My daughter's graduation party had over a hundred graduating seniors in attendance. Kim handled the requests with compassionate efficiency. She partied with the guests and made them feel a part of the event. Many of them stopped at the end of the night to comment just how at home Kim made them feel. It is my most heartfelt feeling that Kim made the party into a lifetime memory."

—Dr. Michael Booth, DVM

A.D.S. PROFESSIONAL

DJ Music Service

15010 S.E. McLoughlin Boulevard
Milwaukie, Oregon 97267
Contact: David B. Patterson
(503) 659-7808

Type of Music

Our disc jockeys are specialists in music from light jazz, big band, '50s, '60s, '70s, '80s, '90s, country, and the latest current hits. Special arrangements can be made for a variety of different ethnic music. As our customer, you will have total control over the style of music and the volume at which it is played.

Demo and Equipment

A.D.S., Inc. uses only professional sound equipment to ensure reliability and the highest sound quality. Our systems are built into custom cabinets and can accommodate most situations indoor and outdoor. Our music sources include CDs, tapes, and records.

Experience

A.D.S., Inc. has been a full-time disc jockey service for over 20 years. We have been a member of the Disc Jockey Association of America and are currently instrumental in forming the Northwest Professional D.J. Association. We are dedicated to providing our customers with the most outstanding and professional service available. Each year we are honored with the privilege of supplying music for over 350 wedding receptions, company functions, and special occasions. Our clients include KISN Radio, Multnomah Athletic Club, Toyota Motor Company, Intel, Nike, Yoshida Group, and Boly Welch Agency. A.D.S. has also been on the entertainment board of directors for the March of Dimes Walk-a-thon from 1990-1997.

Cost and Terms

Prices vary according to month, day, time, and location of your event. A deposit is required to hold date, with the balance due the day of your function.

Special Services

Our special service includes custom lighting packages. A.D.S. can arrange other forms of entertainment to enhance your function such as magicians, impersonators, comedians, and dance instructors. Please call to make an appointment for a free consultation to discuss our special services.

EXPERIENCE AND DEDICATION TO EXCELLENCE

Our goal is to make your event a total musical success. Our strategy is to be the navigator for your party, leading your guests through a smooth blend of music, lights, and communication of all the special events at your function.

All About Music DJ Company

P.O. Box 20625
Portland, Oregon 97294
(503) 408-7857
E-mail: aamdjcompany@earthlink.net

Type of Music

All About Music DJ Company has a wide variety of music that enables us to play whatever you and your guests request. Our music collection includes everything from Jazz to Country to New Age to Top 40. **We have it all!** We will discuss your event with you in detail so that when your big day arrives, the music will be perfect!

Equipment

Our state-of-the-art digital sound equipment ensures a crisp, clear sound for you and your guests to enjoy. The system is compact and will fit in an 8-foot by 4-foot space easily with a standard electrical outlet. Our system components are manufactured by industry leaders, including: Gemini, Sony, QSC, and American DJ. Lighting and special effects are available for your event upon request.

Experience

We love our job and it shows! Our goal is for you and your guests to have a great time. So sit back, relax, and let us entertain you. We have been disc jockeying for over five years, and know how to get everybody dancing! We are professionals, dressing in appropriate attire for every event.

Cost and Terms

We vary our services to fit your needs, with packages starting at $395 for a 3-hour production. A 50% deposit is due at contract signing in order to hold your date, with the balance due the day of your event.

Special Services

Our staff of professionals will help to coordinate activities during your event and keep them running smoothly. Our DJs act as masters of ceremony, making announcements to notify your guests of special activities throughout your event. Our microphone is always available to you or your guests. We encourage requests throughout the event, and are happy to provide instruction for audience participation dances.

For more information call us or visit our web site. We can send you an information packet, including a list of our most popular songs, or schedule an appointment with you to discuss your plans in detail.

Visit our web site at http://home.earthlink.net/~aamdjcompany.

We look forward to hearing from you soon.

ALL-WRIGHT MUSIC CO.

P.O. Box 3282
Portland, Oregon 97208
Contact: Eric Wright
(503) 452-0040
Web site:
http://www.bravowedding.com/pdx00/allwrightmusic

All Wright Music!

We love music! AWM DJs mix music from every era—Big Band to '90s top dance hits. Our collection also includes ballroom, disco, club hits, Latin and Top 40. We send out a detailed questionnaire to find YOUR wants and needs because every reception is unique. We also encourage all guests to make requests.

Sound and Lighting

Our sound and lighting systems are custom-built in Portland. The systems are compact and detail-finished for professional appearance. Lighting systems are designed for each reception and are always included in the wedding package!

Experience

All Wright Music Disc Jockeys have performed at over 3,500 events. Weddings are our favorite because they are true celebrations! We have also performed at private celebrations for celebrities, including Kevin Costner and Sylvester Stallone. AWM has been flown all over the USA to create magical, festive receptions. Our résumé speaks for itself!

Cost and Terms

We speak with each client to find out the specific wishes and needs for their event. Please call me for a free personal consultation—brochures and information will always be mailed upon request.

Our Guests Have Spoken

"It has been over two years, and people still remember our reception as the best they've ever attended!"
—Mrs. R. Roake

"For the fifth year, you've made our annual event a true success! You are our 'Mr. Music!"
—Julie Papen/Special Events, NIKE

"Thanks for the GREAT job! My daughter's night was truly memorable. Best wishes for success!"
—Former Governor Neil Goldschmidt

"Thank you for a fabulous evening! Our night was pure magic! Your music was outstanding!"
—Audrey Stewart, *Bridal Magazine*

It is your day!
Let us help you turn your reception into
a party of elegance, excitement, and lots of fun!

AM Productions

Disk Jockey Service

Since 1988

Northwest Professional DJ Association

Contact: Leland Moyers

Portland: (503) 233-9077

Type of Music

AM Productions will make available for you and your guests their exclusive *Song Title Catalog.* The catalog contains thousands of danceable requests from the roaring '40s to Top 40s, Country and Western to the Bunny Hop. We can also perform ceremonies and provide live musicians for your event.

Demo and Equipment

Our brochure will answer all your questions. We use only state-of-the-art rack-mounted components from the leaders in sound equipment: Sony, EV, Ross, Peavey, Crest, Gemini and QSC.

Experience

We love doing what we do! Whether the situation calls for informal attire, a tuxedo, or anything in between, we will be appropriate. The key to disc jockeying is the ability to respond to all age groups and to have the backup resources to do it well. We have this and more.

Cost and Terms

Disc jockey package prices begin at $295. A $100 deposit is required to hold your date. Our event schedule fills quickly, so please call as soon as you know your date.

Special Services

Our disc jockeys are happy to make any special announcements and encourage song requests from you and your guests. Karaoke and lighting also available.

Setting and Requirements

One 110-volt power outlet and 4′x6′ of space are all we require.

CUSTOM-TAILORED MUSIC FOR EACH EVENT

AM Productions specializes in ***"Custom tailoring music for each event."*** We pride ourselves on playing the music that you request as well as having extensive use of compact discs. From the day you inquire to the day of your wedding, we will be available to help make your event as special and memorable as we possibly can. Call us today!

AM Productions is a participant of the Better Business Bureau Mediation/Arbitration Program and a member of the Northwest Professional DJ Association.

Visit our Web site:
www.ampcenter.com

Anthony Wedin Productions, Inc.

DJ Entertainment • Slide Show Presentations • Audio/Visual Support

1665 Edgewater Court
West Linn, Oregon 97068
Contact: Anthony Wedin (503) 557-8554
Visit our Web sites:
awp.citysearch.com
www.bravowedding.com/pdx00/anthony wedin

Member of the Northwest Professional DJ Association

WHY HIRE A DISC JOCKEY WHEN YOU CAN HIRE AN ENTERTAINER?

Type of Music

Anthony Wedin Productions provides a wide variety of music from the '40s to the '90s. All music is on compact disc to provide clear quality sound with a quick request time for you and your guests. A song list is also provided so you can pick out your favorite dance music months before your wedding.

Demo and Equipment

Just as you have high standards for your wedding day, Anthony Wedin Productions has high standards for its sound equipment. Professional sound equipment is always used to ensure a day of stress-free fun and enjoyment. Each sound system comes with a wireless microphone and optional dance lighting at no charge.

Experience

Anthony Wedin and his staff are trained to be an interactive part of your special event. We have the music and the music knowledge to make your wedding day exciting and one to remember. We have been creating fun and successful receptions for brides and grooms since 1988. Dress is always tuxedo, unless you request casual attire. Anthony Wedin and his staff are also members of the Northwest Professional Disc Jockey Association, Gala Events Group, and the Association for Catering and Event Professionals.

Cost and Terms

Prices start at $325 and vary depending on date and time of the function. Disc jockey and slide show presentation packages also available.

Slide Show Presentations

Anthony Wedin Productions can also compose a slide show presentation for your reception that will be the envy of all and create a lasting and unforgettable memory. The presentation is shown live at your reception, and you are given a video to cherish through the years. Packages available. Call for details.

Setting and Requirements

Music for both the ceremony and reception can be provided either indoors or outdoors. All that is needed is a banquet table and a standard outlet.

WHY ANTHONY WEDIN PRODUCTIONS?

Anthony Wedin and his staff's professionalism and attention to detail will make your wedding day worry-free. Acting as master of ceremonies and coordination of the day's activities are all part of the services provided. The enthusiasm is contagious and your guests will remember your wonderful day as one of fun, laughter and lively entertainment.

 Please let this business know that you heard about them from the Bravo! Bridal Resource Guide.

Celebrate with...

Big Mo Productions™

Custom DJ Services

(503) 492-2851; (888) 449-5099 toll free
E-mail: DJExtra@aol.com
http://www.weloveweddings.com/bigmo

Type of Music

Vast collection of danceable romantic and fun music for all ages from the 20s to the NEXT MILLENIUM'S current hits. Our music library has over 21,000 titles. Music styles include, but are not limited to: Contemporary and Traditional Wedding Ceremony, Country, Cajun, Big Band/Swing, Reggae, 50-60s, 70s, 80s, 90s, Classical, House, Rock, Disco, R&B, Motown, New Age, Jazz, Top 40, Holiday, Cultural and Ethnic Specialties.

Equipment

Only state-of-the-art Professional Equipment, Concert Quality Speakers, and Digital Compact Disc Technology ensuring CLEAR AND SUPERIOR music for any size hall or facility.

Experience and Attire

Tuxedo, Western, Casual or Theme attire as you desire. Big Mo Productions is solely owned and operated by Mel "Big Mo" O'Brien. Allow Big Mo to send recent references to answer all your questions about experience, professionalism and meeting his client's needs and desires.

Here is a sampling of what our clients have written about our services:
•"I can't thank you enough. Everything was PERFECT." • "You (Big Mo) fulfilled your contract above and beyond." • "Everyone had a GREAT time!" • "I am recommending you to family, friends and EVERYONE!" • "The evening was wonderful! Thank you." • "The most memorable parts of our reception occurred on the dance floor." • "Thank you for getting everyone involved, including the children."

Cost and Terms

Very competitive rates. Only $75 books your date. Booking deposits are conditionally refundable. No "hidden charges." No "up selling." No charge for travel, setup or breakdown time. We do not charge a full-hour rate for partial hours of service.

Special Services

FREE personalized 10″ x 12″ framed Custom Labeled Golden Record on Velvet of your First Dance as husband and wife. FREE give-aways for "the little ones" at your reception. Five-plus hour receptions: FREE Effects Lighting for evening and indoor receptions. New high-tech "non-smoke"—no heat or odor—hazer/fogger available. Big Mo Productions recognizes that YOU are "the STARS" of your reception, NOT the DJ.

"Quality, Value, Service…and Fun"

COMPLETE MUSIC®

DISC JOCKEY SERVICE

Need a Great DJ?®
Call the Professionals.

Contact: David Gard

Portland (503) 639-8628 • Salem (503) 378-7975

http://www.cmusic.com

Northwest Professional DJ Association

Ceremonies & Receptions

Type of Music

Complete Music takes great pride in being the finest and largest entertainment service in the nation. We are here to please our customers so they can be certain that their event will be cherished by everyone who attends. We bring to every event selections of the most popular music from the Big Band Era through today's Top 40 hits. Every song listed in your music catalog will be brought to your event, including the most recent hits. Call for a FREE catalog and video showing all your entertainment options.

Equipment

Our service includes Complete Music's professional sound system, our entire music library, a wireless microphone and our computerized lighting effects. Your DJ will act as the Master of Ceremonies for all your important events and will perform many audience participation dances at your request.

Experience

Complete Music was established in 1973 and has become the nation's largest due to the personal care taken in tailoring each reception to each bride and groom's wishes. We customize our service to fit your expectations and guarantee the results to your satisfaction.

Cost and Terms

Complete Music's fees are based on a five-hour program, which includes dinner music, background music and dance music along with a FREE computerized light package, which add to the smooth flow of your reception. Complete Music can also provide the music and/or equipment for your ceremony. Call us for our cost and deposit requirements.

Setup

Your DJ will arrive at least one hour prior to your event for setup. This allows the DJ time to prepare for your special event. All that we require is a standard six-foot banquet table and one electrical outlet.

Complete Music's Goals

Our first goal is to ensure that everything runs smoothly and according to your plans. Our second goal is to make certain that all your guests have a good time. Call Complete Music and allow us to find out what your needs are, so that we can combine your ideas with our experience to provide you with a unique reception.

Decades Mobile Music

6312 N. Willamette Lane
Portland, Oregon 97203
Contact: Brian Darby or Loretta Korsun
(503) 283-4886; Fax (503) 283-4857

Type of Music

The act of celebration has been associated with dancing since the dawn of time. When you invite Decades Mobile Music to your event, you and your guests can relax and celebrate as we play favorites for everyone— from the youngsters to the young-at-heart! We stock popular dance music and Top 40 for every decade: from the '40s, '50s, '60s, '70s, '80s, and '90s.

We will also act as Master of Ceremonies, if you request, so that every part of your special event flows smoothly.

Song List and Equipment

We provide a song list to help you select your favorite music. Our equipment is the latest professional gear, and all recordings are on compact disk. This assures the clarity that makes music enjoyable at any volume level you and your guests prefer.

Experience and Attire

Others talk… WE LISTEN! Our Event Coordinator is at each engagement to ensure smooth flow and good communication between the host, guests and DJ. We tailor our services to meet your specific needs; your agenda is ours. Our skilled people and people skills make the difference. In addition to drawing on a great depth of knowledge for appropriate music selections, our DJs will play requests (can't remember the name?… hum a few bars!) and dedications. Our Event Coordinator will make announcements, pick up requests, respond to schedule changes, and keep the celebration going! Attire is normally a jacket and tie. We are happy to wear whatever is appropriate for your event.

Cost and Terms

A three-hour show starts at $350. A $100 deposit is required. Additional hours are $75. Lighting and props can be added to make your event more memorable. Special music requests, made in advance, are always free. You are given a written agreement to assure our services will match your expectations.

Setting and Requirements

We arrive at least an hour before the show to setup and test. This allows us ample time to adjust for local conditions. We require two standard 120v outlets, more if lighting is used. A space of 10′ x 8′ is necessary, indoors or out.

A Party in Every Package

DeeJay Entertainment

Specializing in Weddings

503/295-2212 ▪ Toll Free 1-800/963-6968

Visit our Website:
www.deejayentertainment.com

Featuring Portland Radio DJs:

K103 fm Z100

Type of Music

DeeJay Entertainment can play a variety of hit music at your wedding reception, including top 40, country, 70s/80s retro, classic rock and oldies. Every crowd is different and DeeJay Entertainment reacts with the appropriate selections.

Experience

Featuring Portland Radio DJs, DeeJay Entertainment is fortunate to represent some of the most experienced and professional disc jockeys available in the Portland-metro area.

Demo

Call today and we will mail or fax you a brochure that includes references and a sample song list. Prior to scheduling your event with DeeJay Entertainment, we will discuss the range of music you like, and the presentation style. This will help us create the mood you desire for your reception. We set up our own state-of-the-art sound equipment and make announcements to keep your guests informed. We eliminate all hassles so you can focus on your special day! DeeJay Entertainment can also provide music at your wedding ceremony.

Costs and Terms

Saturday events scheduled between May 1–September 30, and December 1–31 are $450 (4 hours or less). All other dates are $400 (4 hours or less). Each additional hour is $75.

Thirty percent deposit is required to hold your date with the balance due prior to the start of the reception. VISA, MasterCard, and American Express gladly accepted.

PROFESSIONAL...

EXPERIENCED...

RECOMMENDED...

Eighty percent of the events scheduled with DeeJay Entertainment are referrals, so we encourage you to check on availability as soon as you have set a date. We hope to have the opportunity to serve you and invite you to call anytime with questions or to schedule an appointment with one of our representatives.

Find out why so many of our past clients refer other people to DeeJay Entertainment!

ENCORE STUDIOS

Portland, Oregon
(503) 255-8047
E-mail: encore@webcombo.net
Web site: www.bravowedding.com/pdx00/encore-dj

We'll coordinate your reception for you! Music sets the mood for any occasion and is particularly important during your ceremony or wedding reception. Whether you need disc jockeys or musicians, let us assist you in providing the music you want for your wedding ceremony and/or reception.

Type of Music

For your listening pleasure and convenience, we provide music of all styles and have a huge library of music from the 20s to the 90s in all eras: Top 40, Country/Western, Jazz, Classical, Rock 'n' Roll, Motown, Rhythm & Blues, Swing, Ballroom, Big Band, Rap, Reggae, Disco and Ethnic. Your favorites are always welcome!

Equipment and Demo

We have state-of-the-art mobile equipment which sets up quickly in a 6′ x 6′ area with a standard 110-volt outlet. You are welcome to a private or live viewing.

Experience and Attire

With over 20 years of experience, you are assured of knowledgeable service with our professional and fun disc jockeys. We are not only disc jockeys but masters of ceremony as well, ensuring your wedding runs smoothly and successfully. We play the music you want to hear, and our packages are designed for every budget and musical preference. Casual or theme attire, tuxedos or suits and ties are available.

Cost and Terms

Wedding packages are $595 for four full hours of playing, with no hidden or extra costs. Ceremony music only is only $100.

Special Services

Special lighting, strobes, spots, mirror balls, ropes, and fog available for special effects.

Should you prefer live music for your entertainment needs, please ask one of our consultants for assistance.

PORTLAND RADIO PERSONALITY KEN O'BRIEN

KEN O'BRIEN PRODUCTIONS

P.O. Box 69541
Portland, Oregon 97201
(503) 846-0684, cell (503) 380-7219

As a radio personality for years I've worked with and entertained thousands of people. Anyone can play a CD player and pretend to be a DJ. **Ken O'Brien Productions** has earned the respect and admiration of hundreds of brides, grooms and their families for years. If you take a highly experienced radio personality, nightclub DJ, a master of ceremonies, and mix in a lot of personality and energy, you get an **Entertainer**.

We will coordinate and choreograph your wedding ceremony (no matter what your religion). We personalize this special moment to fit your family. Your reception is meant to be the party of the year. **Ken O'Brien Productions** will make it just that.

Ken O'Brien Productions is very well known for their hands on, get involved personalities. But remember, you are the show and everyone will know it.

Type of Music

Ken O'Brien Productions provides music from the hit parade era of the '40s, to the sock-hop-doo-wop jitterbuggin' of the '50s, to the Motown and British invasion of the '60s, to the classic rock-disco and funk era of the '70s, and up through the '80s rock and top 40 and country hits of today.

Experience

Ken O'Brien Productions has 16 years of master of ceremony and DJ experience. His DJs and MCs are the most energetic, mature **Entertainers** in the business.

Special Care

Ken O'Brien Productions takes all the stress and confusion away from you and your family on this special day as your master of ceremony and DJ with attention to detail.

Appointments

Ken O'Brien always meets with clients at their place of choice. It is important to get to know your DJ/MC before booking your date. Call to setup your appointment with **Ken O'Brien Productions**.

MOBILE MUSIC ENTERTAINMENT SERVICES

Since 1978

Professional DJ Services...

Contact: David Efaw
(503) 692-4498; Fax (503) 612-9433

Now serving the Salem Area
Contact: Jayson Yates (888) 951-4500

Type of Music
Mobile Music has over 300 hours of music we bring to each event. Music selection ranges from big band, '50s, '60s, '70s, '80s, country, Top 40, rock, and jazz. We always play the music you want, and of course we play requests.

Equipment
The sound systems Mobile Music uses are custom built for mobile use. You won't find any home gear in our systems. The systems are compact and can be set up in 20 minutes. We do have larger setups for functions up to 5,000 people.

Experience
Mobile Music has been in business since 1978. We provide music and entertainment at over 1,000 events each year. We base our business on providing friendly, professional service to our clients. What you want comes first with us.

Cost and Terms
The basic package starts at $325 for three hours and $75 for each additional hour. Mobile Music also has light shows and other special effects available for rent. A 20% deposit and a signed contract hold your date for you.

Corporate Events
For corporate events, Mobile Music has a wide variety of activities, including **karaoke, contests and games**—all hosted by a professional master of ceremonies. Please call for more information and rates on packages.

Special Services
Mobile Music uses only professional mobile disc jockeys and club DJs from around the Portland area. Whether you want a life-of-the-party DJ or just music, we have the disc jockey for your event. Band packages also available.

Setting and Requirements
The standard setup requires a 10′ x 4′ space. Larger systems and lights require additional space. A 110-volt AC outlet is needed for power.

MUSIC THE WAY YOU WANT IT
We at Mobile Music pride ourselves on providing quality music the way you want it played. We use only professional disc jockeys with experience, who will help make your event everything you want it to be. If you have any questions or special requirements, feel free to call.

David Efaw

FOR THE PARTY YOU WISH WOULD NEVER END!

Music Express

Music Express
Mobile Disc Jockey Service

The Willamette Valley's Premiere Mobile DJ Service

Contact: Eric or Sheila Mousel, husband and wife DJ team
(503) 362-7216, (800) 222-7216
Web site: www.musicexpressdjs.com
E-mail: fun@musicexpressdjs.com
Portland • Salem • Eugene

As the Willamette Valley's premiere mobile disc jockey service, Music Express is dedicated to making your wedding reception the one that everyone wishes would never end! Your DJ plays an important role in setting the mood for your reception. Whether you are looking for something light and classy or you want a party that everyone will remember, Music Express has what you're looking for.

Experience and Attire

Music Express will provide you with two of the area's best disc jockeys for your reception. A pair of experienced professionals at your reception allows a greater level of guest interaction and results in a much smoother event. Music Express DJs are trained wedding specialists, familiar with all types of music and fully capable of acting as your Master of Ceremonies. Our DJs really know how to get a party going. The attire will be formal unless otherwise requested.

Types of Music

We have the music to satisfy almost any request, from the 30s to the 90s. We bring thousands of hits—from pop and country to big band swing and good old classic rock n' roll—to every reception and all on CD. We prefer to arrange a meeting to get to know you a little bit and will determine our playlist based on your requests. The music played will be customized for your tastes and desires and will be set at the volume you choose. You set the mood.

Equipment

We use only professional mobile DJ equipment that looks and sounds great! The equipment is customized to fit the needs of the event and is presented tastefully. Our setup will not detract from the decor of your reception. Minimum setup requires one 6′ or 8′ banquet table and a standard 110-volt outlet.

Cost and Terms

Our prices are competitive. Reception packages range from the very basic to the very best and are based on your needs and desires. Ceremony/reception packages are available. A minimum $100 deposit is required with signing of a reservation agreement. Credit cards and personal checks are accepted.

Call Music Express for
the party you wish would never end!

NOTE WORTHY MUSIC

2233 N.E. Mason
Portland, Oregon 97211
Contact: John Mears (503) 284-3961

Types of Music

At Note Worthy Music we offer the music you want—and at a price that is affordable. We draw from any era of music that you desire! Whether you want Big Band, jazz, country, classic rock or Top 40, we will meet your needs. Because this is your event we will do everything to make it special. Our disc jockeys will meet with you to discuss any special needs.

Equipment

Note Worthy Music uses top of the line equipment to provide you with crystal clear music from our vast CD collection. Music volume is constantly monitored for your listening pleasure.

Services

Our disc jockeys will serve as your master of ceremonies if you desire and will dress according to your theme. With 15 years in the music industry, we will help make your special day a truly wonderful experience.

To enhance your special day we usually have soft background music provided as your guests enter your reception. As the party progresses we will announce special moments such as cutting of the cake, throwing of the bridal bouquet, shooting of the garter and the couple's first dance. As the reception continues the music is constantly monitored for both volume and style that you desire. From soft jazz to rock 'n' roll, it's all for you!

Our disc jockey services are provided for either indoors or outdoors. All that is needed is a standard wall plug and one banquet table.

Satisfied Customers are Saying

"Thank you for making our 50th wedding anniversary party such a wonderful occasion. Everyone enjoyed your musical selections which made for great dancing as well."

~Jo and Slats Austin, Forestry Center

"Thank you for the great music at Bob's birthday, and for the music you have provided for our Optimist dances. Everyone always enjoys your wide selection of music."

~Adele Hemstreet, President, The Optimist Club of Lloyd Center

"Our wedding would not have been the same without your services—Thanks again!"

~Robert Heinrich

"John, not only were you easy to work with but very accommodating to all our special needs for our wedding reception."

~Shelly Vanness

BRAVO! SPECIAL **$75 off**

Three hours for $275
$30 each additional hour

Omega Audio

Mobile Disc Jockey Services
1332 S.E. Carlton
Portland, Oregon 97202
Contact: Earl Forster, Owner
(503) 235-2743
E-mail: OmegaAudio@aol.com

"Thank you for all your help and professionalism in planning our wedding. We had a wonderful evening and everything was so beautiful and perfect. We will definitely recommend Omega Audio to all of our family and friends." —Denise and Todd Saperstein

Experience

Omega Audio has been providing reasonably priced, top quality mobile music and lighting services for over 18 years. Our disc jockeys are professional in both attitude and appearance. We are ready to work with you to ensure that your event is everything you want it to be.

Type of Music

Omega Audio brings a tremendous selection of the most loved songs in America to your event. From hits of the '20s right up to today's chart-busters, we play the music you want to hear. Requests from your guests are always welcome, and our disc jockeys are happy to act as master of ceremonies.

Equipment

Our disc jockeys use systems with professional grade equipment to provide a state-of-the-art experience. We have sound systems to suit whatever size room your event requires. Thinking about an outdoor event? Omega Audio can accommodate!

Special Services

We can bring any room to life with lighting and special effects such as intelligent lighting, mirror balls, strobes, fog and much more. For added excitement, we have **Karaoke, Dance Lessons, and Casino Gaming,** as well as outdoor inflatable games for kids.

Cost and Terms

Packages start at $395 for four hours of uninterrupted music; no charge for set-up time. The rate for each additional hour is $75. A minimum deposit of $100 is required upon signing the contract. Be sure to reserve your date as far in advance as possible—it's never too soon to hire the best.

Everything you choose for your wedding day is a reflection of your dreams. We at Omega Audio would like to make those dreams come true!

On The Go! Productions

6611 N.E. Wygant Street
Portland, Oregon 97218
Contact: Rudie Kerchal
(503) 281-9628 or (503) 281-5506
Web site: onthegoproductions.com

Type of Music

On The Go! Productions' library covers music from the '40s Big Band era to the '50s, '60s, '70s, '80s, and '90s, dance music, and the best country and current top 40 hits.

Equipment

We use commercial veritable pitch CD players, live music mixing consoles, Technique's turntables, Pro Audio speakers and amplifiers, full service lighting, and dance floors.

Experience

On The Go! Productions was established in 1976. We have performed at over 5,000 receptions and corporate events in the last 24 years. References and personal DJ information is available.

Cost and Terms

Our standard package starts at $275 for three hours of continuous music. Additional hours are $50. You may add karaoke to any package for an additional $100. A variety of packages are available—please call for additional information and a free brochure.

Special Services

Our disc jockeys are employees of On The Go! Productions. They are trained to be high-energy master of ceremonies. We meet every bride and groom in order to tailor our services to their personal requirements.

We furnish everything needed to perform for your event. All tables are draped and skirted to give a classy appearance at your event. We take pride in what we do and that is reflected in how we dress, our equipment, and our attitudes.

WHEN IT SOUNDS AND LOOKS THE BEST…
IT'S *ON THE GO!*

On The Go! Productions is owned and operated by Rudie Kerchal, a second generation musician with over 24 years of experience in the wedding industry. Your wedding day is the most important celebration you will ever experience. Should you honor us by choosing On The Go! Productions to provide your reception entertainment, we pledge to pull out all the stops to make it a celebration you will long remember! You deserve it. Call today at (503) 281-9628 or (503) 281-5506 to tell us more about your wedding plans.

SAILING ON PRODUCTIONS

Professional Shows for All Occasions • Extensive Musical Selections

1003 S.E. 105th Avenue • Vancouver, Washington 98664

Contact: Rocky Rhodes

(877) 340-1668, cell (360) 608-0677, Phone/Fax(360) 254-2111

E-mail: rockyrds@teleport.com; Web site: teleport.com/~rockyrds

---

Type of Music

With over 2,000 CDs and 16,000-plus karaoke songs, Rocky & Associates can provide music not only from the '40s to current popular hits, but Ethnic music as well (e.g. Hispanic, Hawaiian, Italian, Japanese, Greek, Jewish, etc.).

Demo and Equipment

With a state-of-the-art system, which includes special effects sound and lighting, Rocky can cater your look and sound to be intimate or Vegas-style. Designed to fit in all settings with a look of class, professionalism is the word.

Experience

A Pacific Northwest tradition since 1983, Rocky brings years of experience to every event. Having performed nationally since the 1960s, Rocky has a resume and portfolio to prove why brides have changed the date of their wedding to fit his schedule. All attire is appropriate for the occasion.

Cost and Terms

A basic four hour show is $350 with a $50 an hour overtime charge. But if the overtime is booked in advance, the cost is only $25 an hour. A 50% nonrefundable deposit is required in advance. Except for extreme distances, there is no charge for travel and setup, and all special effects and karaoke are included.

Special Services

There is no limit to Rocky's services, and mothers love to see him take over. As a wedding coordinator, he is one of the best. Using remote mics, Rocky helps keep the event running smooth and eventful.

Setting and Requirements

There is no setting too demanding for this show. The only needs are one electrical outlet and a space of at least 6"x8." Anything more is a luxury but not a need.

Versatility

The uniqueness to Rocky's show is his versatility and one-on-one service to each client. No two parties are exactly the same, and Rocky's ability to adapt to each client's need has made him marketable worldwide. No request is too difficult, and if we don't have it, you can bring it to be played. Only the client's satisfaction is the main concern of Sailing On Productions.

Signature SOUND

Mobile DJ Service

"The Wedding Reception Specialists"

P.O. Box 65616
Vancouver, Washington 98665
(800) 903-3830; Fax (800) 328-3930
E-mail: info@ssdj.com
Check out our Web site at: www.ssdj.com

Type of Music

Our high-quality digital music library contains a huge selection of music, enjoyable to all ages. Special requests are always welcome. This will ensure that you and your guests have a fantastic wedding-day experience.

Demo and Equipment

We invite you to call our office for a complimentary consultation. At this time, you can meet your prospective disc jockey, go over our extensive music lists, and arrange any extra details for your special day. You can rest assured that our sound and lighting systems use only the finest professional gear. And our setup appears tasteful, without unsightly cords everywhere.

Experience

Signature Sound disc jockeys have performed from coast to coast, and have an extensive background entertaining all types of people. Our references include the Portland Trail Blazers, Intel and more. From traditional to modern, extravagant to simple, we can make your wedding reception uniquely yours.

Cost and Terms

Our wedding packages range in price from $299 to $999. We offer many options, including exciting lighting packages, bubble machines, extra hours of dance music, and ceremony music and sound systems. A 10% deposit and a signed contract are the only requirements to reserve your date.

Setting and Requirements

We can perform at any location, anytime. From the Benson Hotel to your backyard, we've "been there…done that." A typical wedding reception requires a normal 110-volt outlet, and a table at least six feet in length, with tablecloth and skirting to match the other tables. If we need to provide our own table, just let us know!

Why Choose Signature Sound?

It's your wedding day, and you're the center of attention, not us! All DJ advertisements may look alike, but all DJs don't necessarily perform the same. Our full-time office staff, experienced and talented disc jockeys, large music library, and premier sound and lighting equipment make the difference between an extraordinary day and "just another wedding."

SUNRISE ENTERTAINMENT SERVICES

Mobile DJs & Lighting

2905 18th Avenue • Forest Grove, Oregon 97116
(503) 357-6699, (877) 710-1600
Fax (503) 357-2899, (877) 710-1800
E-mail: joeybdj@sunrisedjs.com
Web site: www.sunrisedjs.com

A.D.J.A.

Nicole and Joe Burruss, owners and proud members of the American Disc Jockey Association. We are also fully insured for your protection!

Type of Music

Wow! Where do we begin? We have every kind of music imaginable! We offer traditional and contemporary ceremony music. We offer ballroom, classical, big band, and swing music—both original and modern. We also offer one of the most complete varieties of music from the '50s, '60s, '70s, '80s and '90s!

We provide a detailed, easy to use directory of all our music for your guests to make requests from. We understand that your guests may range in age from 5 to 105 years old! That's why we believe it is just as important to have a *quality* selection as it is to have a *large* selection.

Equipment

We use nothing but the best! All of our systems are digital, and use only CDs. If you prefer a discrete, high quality system with elevated speakers on stands, we've got them. If you prefer a larger set of speakers with earth shaking bass, we've got them. If you need a sound system big enough to fill a stadium with thousands of people, we've got you covered. We will customize the sound to fit your event.

Our systems are never under-powered or distorted. On the other hand, you won't have to worry about the music being too loud during the times when it shouldn't be! We have wireless microphones available upon request. We use a device called the "Feedback Destroyer Pro," which virtually eliminates all forms of irritating feedback caused by microphones (great if you need us to provide the sound for your singer).

We offer a wonderful selection of special effect lighting including romantic multi-colored mirror balls, high tech effect lighting, intelligent lighting, truss systems spanning 15-foot lasers, fog machines, hazers, and bubble machines. You can choose a standard light package or we will work with you one-on-one to customize a light show to your exact specifications.

Experience

We have over 15 years experience in the entertainment business! Although not all of our DJs are as fortunate to share the extensive experience that we have, we can assure you that we have the best DJs in the trade! The first thing that we look for when we hire our DJs are good people skills. Secondly, we look for DJs with a great love and knowledge of music. Once we've selected our DJs, we put them through an extensive training program to make sure that they arrive properly trained and dressed for your event. Still not enough? Ask us for a list of our references and find out what our previous clients have to say about us!

Submit Everything Online!

You can select and submit your choice of chart topping musical hits, organize the online reception planner to choose your exact order of events, print online contract copies, and much, much more!

Do Not Hire A DJ
Until You've Been To: www.sunrisedjs.com!

Clara's Own
ULTIMATE ENTERTAINMENT
Portland's Premier
Full Service DJ Company
916 S.E. 29th Avenue
Portland, Oregon 97214
(503) 234-3055, (888) 332-6246
E-mail: Claraswe@Sprynet.com

ULTIMATE
ENTERTAINMENT
Mobile Disc Jockey Service

Find Us On The Web: portlandbridalshow.com/claraswedding

Type of Music

We feel strongly about giving you the right music. Songs that are proven to get your guests up and dancing. That's why we provide you with a catalog of the biggest party songs of all time. Choose from any era… Big Band, Country, '50s & '60s, '70s & '80s, R&B, Top 40, Classic Rock and more! All music is on compact disc to provide clear digital sound. Special requests are always welcome.

Equipment

What's great music without great sound? At Ultimate Entertainment, we use sound systems that contain the finest audio components available. Sound checks are made before guests arrive to ensure excellent sound at every location, both indoors and out. We have a wireless microphone at every event for your convenience. For nighttime functions, a dazzling array of lighting is an option you may choose to enhance your celebration. From the smallest backyard to the largest banquet hall, Ultimate Entertainment has the equipment to handle any situation effectively and efficiently.

Experience

Music and entertainment is the most important factor to the success of any event. When you choose Ultimate Entertainment, you get more than a DJ, you get our experience, quality, and professionalism. We are actively involved before, during, and after your event. This is why we stand by our reputation as "Portland's Premier Full Service DJ Company."

Cost and Terms

Ultimate Entertainment offers two different packages to choose from:

- **Package A includes**: four hours of entertainment, Disc Jockey in formal attire, all of your announcements, and a bubble machine. Our price to you… $375.
- **Package B includes:** All of the above, plus a dazzling light show, and a FREE hour of limousine service compliments of Clara's Limousine Service. Our price to you… $499.

Only a $50 deposit holds your date. Additional entertainment hours are available for only $80 per hour. We also provide music for ceremonies starting at $100. Please call for your free hour consultation with video presentation.

Special Services

Our disc jockeys are trained event coordinators and will handle your special activities during your reception. Whether you are looking for an "interactive DJ" or a "low key DJ," our DJs can help you with your event. Ultimate Entertainment also has: karaoke, special effect lighting, fog machines, snow machines, and party kits (novelty items...leis, sunglasses, inflatable guitars, saxophones, and beach balls).

See page 238 under Bridal Attire.

Notes

MUSICIANS AND VOCALISTS

© Eleanor Glorioso Photographer • page 493

Sweet Dreams

Legend has it that unmarried guests who sleep with a piece of the grooms cake under their pillows will dream of their future spouses.

HELPFUL HINTS

- **Live music sets the stage:** Live music adds to the ceremony and can be as soft or dramatic as you choose. There are a variety of musicians to select from: individual pianists, harpists, trumpeters, mandolin trios, string quartets, and brass quartets—just about any combination you would like. Most musicians are very affordable and will accommodate your requests.
- **Be creative with your selection of musicians and songs:** You'll enjoy selecting music with special meaning for you and your groom. If you can't decide, talk with some of the musicians, listen to their demo tapes, and view their song lists. Musicians are usually very helpful and will gladly offer ideas and suggestions to make your wedding special and meaningful.
- **Approve your music selections with clergy:** Make sure your clergyman is aware of your music selections. Ask whether there are any restrictions on music. Some ministers insist on approving all the music prior to the ceremony. Your favorite love song may seem offensive to the clergyman; neither you nor your musicians will enjoy any last-minute confrontations.
- **Be sure to find out about the musicians' requirements:** They may need to set up and warm up before the event begins. Make sure the ceremony or event site is open at least one to two hours earlier. A music rehearsal may conflict with your photographs, but the solution is to plan ahead and inform the musicians and the photographer of each other's needs.
- **Amplification equipment:** Help the musicians coordinate any necessary amplification equipment. Find out ahead of time if the church or hall has a PA system. If so, ask whether the church will permit you to use the system for your wedding. Find out whether it is compatible with the musicians' equipment (many churches have older systems with incompatible microphones).
- **Plan how to start the music:** Prelude music is a nice touch as the guests are being escorted into the church. To start the processional music, have someone signal the musicians at the appropriate time. Setting a specific time doesn't always work because guests are still coming in, or delays get in the way of starting the ceremony on time. One way to handle this is to have your clergyman signal the musicians to start the processional music after a nod from the father of the bride. Also provide your priest, judge, or pastor and the musicians with a cue sheet. The person officiating can unknowingly cut your well-planned music.
- **Saving on music:** The best way to cut music costs is to have your wedding in off-season: January through March, Sundays, early in the day. Musicians will be more willing to negotiate prices if it doesn't conflict with another high paying booking.
- **Hire for both ceremony and reception:** Most musicians can perform both at the ceremony and reception. For instance a string quartet can be hired for the one-hour ceremony for $325 and then each additional hour at the reception would be $75 per hour. This would be nice for greeting guests, mingling and dinner music. Ask your musician if he can do both; some individual musicians have pieces that they can add on to make a trio.

For more assistance with staying organized during the wedding planning process, check out the Bravo! Wedding Organizer. Detailed question worksheets double as contracts. This step-by-step system will keep every detail of your wedding organized. To order, refer to the order form on page 24 in this Guide.

Michael Allen Harrison

P.O. Box 30448
Portland, Oregon 97294
(503) 255-0747
Web site: www.mahrecords.com

Types of Music

Composer/pianist Michael Allen Harrison is an international recording artist who resides in his hometown of Portland, Oregon. Over the last 15 years Michael has released 20 albums of his signature adult contemporary style of new age, classical, pop and jazz. He has also released five Christmas albums and an album dedicated to Gershwin and other artists of that era. His music is heard around the world and locally on KINK FM 102, KKJZ, KMHD, K103, and regularly as the leader of the Good Day Oregon Band on KPTV Channel 12 Good Day Oregon Show. Michael has written and performed his music with orchestras, ballet companies, motion pictures, short films, commercials, and is the featured guest artist for the Celebrity Forum lecture series where he has opened for Walter Cronkite, Jerry Lewis, Collin Powell, Margaret Thatcher, Jerry Spence, Cokie Roberts and James Whitmore.

Experience and Demo

Michael has been performing professionally for 15 years. One of the Northwest's favorite pianists, he regularly plays a rigorous schedule of show and concert dates in the U.S. and abroad. Still he makes time to play weddings, corporate parties, and special events as well as two quite unique and personal services, Fireside Concerts and Dinner with Michael. Fees vary depending on whether he plays piano solo or is joined by part or all of his band. Michael loves to play his original music as well as the favorites and wishes of his clients. He will also write and sing new original music created specifically for a bride and groom or to celebrate a special occasion upon request. We have created several personalized gift packages for wedding parties, corporations and small companies—especially nice for the holidays. Please call for quantity and pricing. Information, demos, photos, and promotional material can be requested over the phone at (503) 255-0747 or though our web site at www.mahrecords.com.

Harpist Ellen Lindquist

© Adams & Faith Photography

(503) 626-4277
Web site:
www.bravowedding.com/pdx00/ellenlindquist

DISCOVER THE AMBIANCE AND ELEGANCE OF HARP MUSIC AT YOUR WEDDING AND RECEPTION

Types of Music

Harp music adds elegance and magic to any wedding and reception. Ellen's repertoire spans many decades to include Classical, Love Songs, Movie Themes, Show Tunes, Oldies and New Age. Her repertoire ensures each wedding and reception is personal and unique.

Harp Music is Perfect for

- Ceremonies
- Receptions
- Rehearsal Dinners
- Engagement Parties
- Bridal Showers
- Bridal Luncheons

Experience

With over 19 years of professional experience, Ellen knows what her clients want and expect. She has played at hundreds of weddings and receptions. She has played at most of the bridal sites in Portland/Vancouver and can make suggestions to the bride/groom to enhance their wedding day. She has played with the Columbia Symphony, Portland Chamber Orchestra, Eugene Symphony, Oregon Festival of American Music, Ernest Bloch Music Fest and Peter Britt. Her experience includes working on cruise ships, hotels in Japan and she has played with celebrities from Kenny Rogers to the Moody Blues. She was trained at the Music Academy of the West, Julliard School of Music in New York and California State University Northridge.

LET HARP MUSIC CREATE THAT EVERLASTING MEMORY

Call for a free brochure, references and prices. Harp/flute also available.

Musical Elegance

Elaine Seeley

·HARPIST·

(503) 636-0349
Web site: www.bravowedding.com/pdx00/elaineseeley

Types of Music

No musical instrument compares to the harp when it comes to bringing style and beauty to complement your special occasion. Elaine Seeley has played for many types of events and locations including:

- Weddings and Receptions
- Open Houses
- Corporate Events
- Restaurants and Hotels
- Banquets
- Private Parties

Ms. Seeley's varied and extensive solo repertoire includes classical music, rhythmical arrangements, and popular show tunes. Also available are duo combinations—harp and flute, harp and violin, and harp and voice.

Experience

Ms. Seeley is a harp instructor at Lewis & Clark College and former music specialist at Oregon Episcopal School. Her professional background is impressive. Her affiliations include the following orchestras:

- Portland Opera
- Oregon Symphony
- Vancouver Symphony
- The Musical Theater Company
- Ballet West
- Chamber Music Northwest
- Sunriver Music Festival

Education

Ms. Seeley acquired her B.A. degree in music education at the University of Southern California. She has an M.F.A. in harp performance from California Institute of the Arts.

Cost

For a personal quotation and consultation regarding music for your event, please call Elaine Seeley at (503) 636-0349.

**AN ELEGANT ACCOMPANIMENT
TO YOUR EVENT**

AARON MEYER - VIOLINIST

THE TIMELESS
ELEGANCE OF
BEAUTIFUL
VIOLIN FOR
YOUR WEDDING

SOLO OR ACCOMPANIED, CALL TO RESERVE YOUR DATE - 503.221.4266

Type of Music

Aaron Meyer's music ranges from traditional, classical music and jazz standards, to his own unique blend of original, pop, and world music. He can perform solo, in a duo, or with his band featuring accomplished singers and guitarists Tim Ellis and Jeroan Van Aichen. Aaron's versatility is evident in that he has appeared with many Portland bands including Pink Martini and with Michael Allen Harrison. Aaron regularly performs on KPTV Channel 12 Good Day Oregon Show, concerts and events throughout Oregon, and as a featured guest artist for the Celebrity Forum lecture series where he has opened for Walter Cronkite, Jerry Lewis and Collin Powell.

Experience

As a soloist with the Philadelphia Orchestra at the age of 11, former member of the band Pink Martini, guest artist on Cunard Cruise Line, and current member of the Michael Allen Harrison band, Aaron has gained the experience to entertain and provide appropriate music for wedding ceremonies, receptions, corporate functions, and concerts. Most recently, Aaron performed songs from his latest CD "Seasons of Peace" in New York City at the United Nations building and at the World Peace Conference in The Hague, Netherlands. Aaron has been playing at weddings for many years and enjoys contributing to the elegance with his music on this very special day. Call for cost, photos, demos, or press packets.

Check out where Aaron is playing next at:
www.violin.citysearch.com

For that perfect wedding...

The Stradivari String Quartet

Winchester Enterprises
(503) 232-3684
Fax (503) 236-2920
Hugh Ewart, Assoc.
Concertmaster Emertus
Oregon Symphony

Types of Music

For that perfect wedding or event...perfect music by The Stradivari String Quartet for ceremonies and receptions in your church, synagogue, private club, residence, or garden. The style is elegant, distinctive, and affordable. Information packet including music list available upon request.

Experience

Distinguished wedding music since 1961. Our clientele has included prominent Northwest social and business leaders. In 1980 Stradivari String Quartet appeared in the Paramount motion picture "First Love" filmed on location in Portland.

Cost

Call for current prices and availability.

CHARMING AMBIANCE

"The Stradivari String Quartet added a charming ambiance to the event."
Barbara Jordan
The Oregonian

Call for your FREE demo cassette.

TOM MCCORMACK/DREAMSPEAKER

P.O. Box 3138 • Wilsonville, Oregon 97070
Contact: Tom McCormack (503) 402-1823
E-mail: legendteller@hotmail.com

The Storyfellow accentuates ethnic stories from indigineos cultures. He brings the grail cup to life creating an alchemical wedding and divine marriage of your spirits. Regardless of your theme or specific needs, this dreamteller will customize stories, poetry and flute music to make your sacred rites memorable. McCormack is an award-winning master storyteller who animates dialoguing characters through selected tales. He has received international honors for his Native American legends performances.

Music

Tom plays all of the indigineos flutes of world cultures. He'll make your wedding literally a "dream come true," playing the Didjureedu from Australia. Or you may wish for him to sing a Native-American wedding song interspersed with clapper-stick, drum and rattle.

Experience

This legendteller professionally tours international venues, performing to the Maori's in New Zealand. Since 1988, he has presented performance art with an uncompromising standard of excellence. He was honored by Indian leaders at the 1995 Dreamspeakers Indigineos Festival in Canada. Then he was a workshop presenter at the Tribal Chiefs Spirituality Conference. In 1996 he won a Parent's Choice Gold Award for his audio recording, "Tales For Western Tribes." Local and national references available upon request. His versatility has enabled him to present to small groups on up to 6,000.

Cost

This myth-teller will create legends, poetry and flute music to the specific desires of the couple for their wedding day…carefully timing the segments to the proceedings. After consultation, a rate quote will be given. Fees depend on the duration, location and requirements of the event. A contract is provided explaining the services and details.

A DANCING PENGUIN MUSIC

FLUTE/SAX & PIANO

(503) 282-3421

Ceremonies

Imagine 20 to 30 minutes of relaxing flute and/or sax, accompanied by piano, to create the perfect atmosphere for your bridal entrance. Classical, jazz, or popular music, your choice. A portable electric piano and sound system are available and can be set up inside or out. We can even provide a cordless lapel microphone for your minister.

Receptions

Beautiful, volume-appropriate dinner music can be followed by more lively upbeat material if you choose. Requests are gladly taken. Drums and vocals can be added for dancing. We will be happy to act as master of ceremonies to help your event go smoothly.

Experience

With hundreds of professional performances, we have the experience to make your event a success. Please call for a free consultation, promo, demo tape, and prices.

SOLLO CELLO • STRING DUO • STRING TRIO

Alderwood Strings

1830 N.E. 13th Avenue
Portland, Oregon 97212
Contact: Dieter Ratzlaf
(503) 288-6577; Fax (503) 288-5302
E-mail: dieterratzlaf@cs.com

Types of Music

Let the Alderwood String Ensemble add elegance and sophistication to your event. We offer exquisite performances of the classics as well as charming melodies from contemporary literature. We cater to your requests.

Experience

The ensemble coordinator has won numerous musical awards and has performed extensively as soloist, recitalist and chamber musician. Alderwood musicians hold musical degrees from prestigious institutions including the San Francisco Conservatory of Music and Indiana University–Bloomington. The ensemble has enhanced dozens of weddings, banquets and special events all along the West Coast.

Cost

The Alderwood Strings are committed to affordable excellence. Cost depends on time and place of the event. Demo tape available upon request.

AMERICAN FEDERATION OF MUSICIANS

Local 99
325 N.E. 20th Avenue
Portland, Oregon 97232
(503) 235-8791

Experience

Founded in 1899, the A.F. of M. Local 99 is a nonprofit organization established by professional musicians for musicians. We represent the finest musicians from Portland to Central Oregon, the Coast and up through Southern Washington. With a membership of over 700, we can offer a wide variety of musical styles:

- Chamber groups of all sizes and styles, from a strolling violinist to a string quartet or symphony orchestra!
- Pianists, organists, harpsichordists, classical guitar, flute, harp;
- Jazz ensembles to big band, bagpipes to dulcimer;
- New Age, fusion, Latin salsa, light rock, blues, country and Top 40!

No Agency Fees...Free Referral Service

Many of our artists have tapes, song lists, and photos to make it easier for you to decide exactly what music you want and how you would like it to be presented. We will gladly put you in touch with the musicians of your choice. Local 99 charges you nothing…this is a free referral service! **Call for a free video showcasing the variety of musicians we represent.**

STRING QUARTET

BRIDGEPORT STRING QUARTET

Karen Hilley (503) 230-7116
Kim Lorati (503) 244-5208

Types of Music

Bridgeport String Quartet provides the finest quality classical and popular music for wedding ceremonies, receptions, or special events. A demo tape is available.

Experience

Members of the Bridgeport Quartet are experienced, professional musicians who have provided music for weddings, receptions, and other special events for many years. References available upon request.

Cost

Fees are determined by the duration and location of the event. A contract is provided that explains our services and requirements.

A MEMORABLE OCCASION

A representative from the quartet can help you plan special music to make your event a memorable occasion.

PIANIST AND VOCALIST

JO ANNA BURNS-MILLER

P.O. Box 20594 • Portland, Oregon 97294
(503) 254-5776, (800) 893-5776
E-mail: lilpond@internetcds.com

Types of Music

Uplifting, versatile, and professional are just a few words to describe Jo Anna Burns-Miller's music for weddings and receptions. Accomplished on vocals and piano, she will give you an occasion to remember with a variety of stylings and repertoire. Demo tape and music list available on request.

Experience and Cost

With almost 30 years of experience in the music business, Jo Anna's performances include nightclubs, resorts, churches, concerts, corporate and private functions, with over 600 weddings and receptions to her credit. Dress is color-coordinated to your colors. Her fee for most weddings is $175, and for most receptions, $250 for the first two hours (prices are negotiable for corporate and private events). She provides a sound system when necessary, and an electric piano for a cartage fee of $75, if none is available. A consultation in her home to discuss music for your event is included.

MUSIC FROM MANY ERAS

Vocals and piano include contemporary, soft pop, soft jazz, new age, semiclassical, old standards, and some originals. Jo Anna provides your prelude, postlude, processional and recessional music on piano, as well as vocal solos for your wedding ceremony.

TRADITIONAL IRISH MUSIC

CELTIC WEDDING MUSIC

by INNISFREE

Contact: Brenda or Jim (503) 282-3265

Types of Music

We specialize in heartfelt Irish/folk instrumentals and songs for wedding ceremonies, receptions and other joyful events. Our strength lies in adapting this gorgeous music to each unique ceremony, calling on our long wedding experience and drawing from the rich storehouse of airs, songs, jigs and reels in the tradition. At receptions we play sweet waltzes and great dances to encourage brides, grooms and loving fathers to step out in dances you'll always remember! Multi-instrumentalists, we perform on whistle, guitar, Irish drum, button accordion and mandolin. We can perform non-Irish standards and are happy to learn requests (songs and instrumentals) as well. And, of course, our top-quality sound system is yours to use. Please call for a demo!

UNFORGETTABLE MUSIC

We've found that couples are thrilled to use the Irish music they love, tailored to fit their own wedding. A husband-and-wife duo ourselves, we will bring all the warmth we can to your special day.

TRADITIONAL IRISH MUSIC

THE CLINTON STREET CEILI BAND

Contact: Mr. Jan DeWeese (503) 236-6752

Although the Gaelic word "ceili" now refers to any social gathering with music and dance, in the old days ceili bands played mainly for wedding parties. In addition to our quartet's extensive experience at such spirited occasions, we've been to numerous festivals, colleges and pubs—its founding members formed the first house band for Kells Irish Pub in downtown Portland—as well as to Ireland for traditional dance studies. Our instruments include fiddle, wooden flute, mandolin, cittern, guitar and bodhran (Irish drum). For the wedding service, we have a repertoire of settings from the Irish Baroque and for the reception, a wealthy reserve of traditional tunes to which the party guests can be taught dance steps. A singer of traditional and contemporary Celtic songs (including any special ones you wish to hear) is also available upon request. Please call for demo and price quote.

RENEW THE OLD WAYS

Treat your guests to a timeless form of expression that lifts the feet and moves the heart with simple means, well crafted and finely seasoned! The Irish in all of us awaits.

VIOLIN & CELLO/STRING QUARTET

Duo con Brio

7455 S.W. Alpine Drive
Beaverton, Oregon 97008
Corey Averill (503) 526-3908; Cell phone (503) 887-4448

Types of Music

Duo con Brio is a professional ensemble consisting of cellist Corey Averill and violinist George Shiolas. The duo may be augmented to a string trio or quartet. We have a large repertoire, from Baroque through Contemporary, as well as seasonal music.

Experience and Cost

Formed in 1989, the duo's members have performed with the Portland Opera, Oregon Ballet, and appeared as soloist with the Oregon Symphony and other orchestras in North America. We have also performed extensively in Europe and the Orient. Duo con Brio supplies a wide range of services, including free consultations and a demo cassette. We look forward to assisting you with your wedding, reception or other special event.

- **Duo** $275 first hour ($125 each additional hour)
- **Trio** $365 first hour ($165 each additional hour)
- **Quartet** $455 first hour ($195 each additional hour)
- **Amplification** $50

DAVID EWING
BARITONE SOLOIST

(503) 417-8047

David is a baritone soloist, and will be glad to sing unaccompanied or with your organist/piano player. He is also happy to become the second voice in a duet with your friend or family member, making the ceremony even more beautiful.

David will sing your selections if you already know what you would like, but he will help you plan—if you are like most couples, you don't really know for sure what to do about ceremony music. David specializes in classical music, romantic favorites and worship music. He will provide the right song for any of those extra-special moments in your wedding service…the processional, the welcome, giving of the bride, unity candle lighting, the marriage vows, scripture reading, exchange of rings, prayer, the pronouncement, the benediction, and the presentation of the new couple!

David is very accommodating, and welcomes suggestions from the pastor/priest/rabbi, always keeping in mind the traditions of each couple. He is also happy to include a traditional favorite hymn of parents or grandparents.

- Short notice usually not a problem
- Quick study—David will learn any song
- Songs in French, German, Italian or Latin also available
- Can cantor for Nuptial Mass
- Bachelor of Arts in Music
- Shirt sleeves to formalwear

Let David help you capture the emotion and meaning of your vows. Prices from $100.

JOHN FRESK

Contact: Nancy Anne Tice, Phone/Fax (503) 774-2511
E-mail: nwartmgt@teleport.com;
Web site: www.nwmusicpro.com

Widely known for his ability to provide music that enhances memorable occasions, John Fresk's solo style has been compared to that of Harry Connick Jr., George Winston and Jim Brickman. His technical expertise and experience playing many styles enables him to tailor his repertoire to perfectly match the mood of your special event. From jazz to popular romantic tunes to R&B, John has never failed to please his audiences. His recent CD, "Sun & Moon," is a stunning collection of elegant piano favorites and demonstrates his ability to create music that people want to listen to over and over again. Other recording projects: accompanist for Bobby McFerrin, guest appearances on three Tall Jazz CDs, two Nordstrom Holiday CDs and his own "Limelight."

John Fresk had played professionally for over 20 years in venues that include the Heathman, the Benson, the MAC and the University Club. Appearing with local favorites Mel Brown, Rebecca Kilgore, Patrick Lamb, Tall Jazz and others, John is one of the most sought-after players in town. He's been a featured pianist at Nordstrom stores throughout the area and in addition to many solo engagements, he frequently plays in his own jazz group and his popular dance band, Two Much. A polished professional, he can be found providing chic entertainment for private parties, as well as corporate events of all types. His client list includes hundreds of happy brides and grooms.

Call for a demo tape, promotional materials, references and price quotes.

Todd Gang

Singer, Guitarist, Songwriter, Recording Artist
(503) 579-3901

Type of Music

Todd Gang is one of Portland's most versatile vocalists and musicians. His talents range from straightforward jazz, to pop, soft rock, blues and Latin. Photos, demos, and promotional material are available upon request.

Experience

Todd Gang has been singing and performing professionally since he was 16. He is suited for anything from a casual party to the most formal wedding reception. Todd has appeared internationally, and on television and radio in the United States, Mexico, and the Caribbean.

Cost and Terms

Cost varies according to the number of musicians required, hours and distance traveled. He specializes in romantic love songs, and has a large repertory—he is able to mold the music to the specific desires of couples on their wedding day.

Services

Todd Gang is a singer, songwriter, guitarist and recording artist. He is available for weddings or private parties, from a solo act (guitar only), to a jazz duo, trio, quartet, or even a 12-piece Latin band. Todd writes equally well in Spanish and English. Whatever your wedding or party musical needs, Todd Gang's smooth voice and classy delivery will be the perfect complement to your special occasion.

Tom Grant

P.O. Box 25711 • Portland, Oregon 97225
(503) 244-9547

Types of Music

Tom Grant is an international recording artist who resides in his native Oregon. He has 15 albums to his credit and has toured the world playing his own special blend of pop and jazz. His records have regularly topped the charts in *Billboard* and the other major music industry publications. In Portland, he has his own show on KKJZ and his music is a staple of KKJZ and KMHD radio.

Experience and Demo

Tom has over 20 years experience as a performing musician. He is a pianist, singer, and songwriter. He regularly plays weddings and other types of private events. The cost is variable depending on whether Tom plays solo piano or provides a band. He often provides a high quality grand piano and a sound system as part of the package and his repertoire usually includes his own music as well as other favorites as per the client's wishes. Photos, demos, and press packages are available upon request.

PIANO

DARLENE HARKINS

(503) 357-9037

Types of Music

Darlene has an easy-listening style enjoyed by all ages. She performs your requests for music from all eras, including contemporary love songs, country, sacred and light classics, Broadway show tunes, New Age, and current favorites.

Experience

Darlene has studied piano from age five. She received a music scholarship to and graduated from Pacific University. An accomplished pianist, she can hear a tune and adapt it to the piano to fulfill special requests. Her personality is reflected in the warmth and charm of her playing, setting whatever mood you desire for your event. Her music will indeed calm the nerves and make the ceremony flow smoothly.

Free Consultation and Planning

Call Darlene to play for you over the phone–"a neat idea and real time saver," say many brides and grooms. She will play your choices and, if you wish, offer suggestions based on her extensive experience. In addition, a suggested list of music will be sent to you.

For your ceremony, she carefully correlates music to the proceedings, timing your selections to the entrances of candlelighters, parents, and the wedding party.

For your reception, her ability to play requests from your guests can contribute greatly to creating the happy, upbeat atmosphere for a festive celebration.

FLUTE/SAX AND GUITAR DUO

GARY HARRIS AND MATT SCHIFF

Contact: Nancy Anne Tice, Phone/Fax (503) 774-2511
E-mail: nwartmgt@teleport.com; www.nwmusicpro.com

Types of Music

Gary Harris and Matt Schiff blend a vast knowledge of musical styles ranging from classical to jazz and the popular music of the 20th century into a polished, versatile ensemble perfect for weddings, receptions and elegant celebrations of all kinds. For weddings they play all the most beloved and requested traditional pieces. For receptions, they offer lighter, more upbeat jazz and contemporary favorites played on flute as well as tenor and soprano saxophone with guitar. Call for free promotional packages, demo tape, play list, references and price quote.

Experience

Their many years of national and international touring and performing experiences enable them to create a perfect mood and sparkling atmosphere for your next special occasion. Either as a duo or with added rhythm selection, their music is appropriate for listening and dancing. They are always happy to play your requests.

Cost

Highly cost-effective, professional ensemble. All details in contract. Tuxedo, semi-formal or casual attire.

PIANO • DAVE LEE

(503) 648-1796
dave@daveleemusic.com

Your Wedding Is Special

Your wedding should be unique and special. Dave Lee can help you make it that way. Hear Dave at Nordstrom Washington Square, at the Airport Shilo, on Dave's recordings ***After the Storm, When Your Eyes Met Mine*** and ***Jukebox*** or on-line at **www.daveleemusic.com**.

Experience

Dave Lee has played keyboards for 34 years—24 in a professional capacity. Attire is coordinated to your event. A **free** consultation is offered to discuss your entertainment requirements.

Recordings

Dave Lee's recordings ***After the Storm*** (December 1995),***When Your Eyes Met Mine*** (June 1997), and ***Jukebox*** (March 1999) have been heard on the West coast from California to Alaska to here in Portland on KINK, KKJZ and KMHD.

Media Reaction

The Oregonian A&E states, "Lee is a fine pianist whose musicianship elevates the CD over many run-of-the-mill jazz artists." KKJZ says, "Your album has the melodies and hooks we look for in any release—local or national."

More Than Piano

Dave's work on piano is supplemented with electronic keyboards. The **Dave Lee Band** is available as well in various configurations.

Luminos

1035 S.W. Carson Street • Portland, Oregon 97219
Contact: Fritz or Julie Weber (503) 245-5055
E-mail: Julie@luminos.net

Experience

We've played music together since 1973, performing for numerous wedding services and receptions. Fritz plays piano, organ and electric keyboards. Julie plays flute, alto flute and various percussion instruments. Both of us are vocalists and Julie also sings in French, Spanish and Portuguese. Fritz is an experienced sound engineer and can assist with sound systems.

We can work with you or your musical friends to prepare and perform special songs. Fritz is the Director of Music at St. James Episcopal Church in Tigard. He is familiar with the special needs of services and is accustomed to working with ministers and celebrants.

Reception Music

We can also provide live music for your reception or with our band, Luminos. Take care of all your wedding music with one call.

"On your wedding day you should feel like royalty. As your Personal Music Director, I will see to it that the music ties your ceremony together as a unique celebration and a reflection of the two of you." – Fritz

Mezzanotte Strings

Quartets, Trios, Duos and Soloists

Contact: Nancy Anne Tice

Northwest Artist Management (503) 774-2511

Type of Music

Portland's premiere wedding quartet, The Mezzanotte Strings, combines musical excellence and personalized attention to create an enchanting atmosphere for your ceremony and reception.

While the group specializes in classical music, our extensive repertoire also includes romantic favorites, jazz standards, swing, ragtime, pop songs, waltzes, and Broadway hits. From Bach to The Beatles, we continuously update our repertoire in order to bring you the finest music possible.

Experience and Cost

The Mezzanotte Strings are gifted, experienced professional musicians who perform with many of Portland's finest orchestras. We have played for countless weddings, receptions, and special events in the area's most prestigious locales, and we combine our wealth of experience with a commitment to personalized service. We will be responsive to your suggestions, sensitive to your needs, and provide consultations at no extra fee.

Quotes given include musicians in formal attire, music for your entire event, and travel allowance if applicable. Call for a free demo tape, promotional package and repertoire list.

CLASSICAL GUITARIST, ALFREDO MURO

Contact: Nancy Anne Tice,

Phone/Fax (503) 774-2511

E-mail: nwartmgt@teleport.com;

Web site: www.nwmusicpro.com

Type of Music

Originally from Lima, Peru, Alfredo Muro's elegant, sensitive and polished style has been honed by many years on concert stages around the world. He has studied with masters such as Carlos Hayre and Manuel Lobez Ramos, and performed in all mediums from television to small intimate gatherings. While on tour in Italy in 1986, he played for Pope John Paul II at a Vatican "Special Audience." His repertoire includes European Classical composers such as Bach, Handel and Albeniz, Latin American Traditional Folklore, Latin Jazz, Caribbean, Bosa Nova and Samba, Andian, and Latin American Classical composers such as Villa-Lobos, Barios, Laureo and a touch of new flamenco.

Experience and Cost

A celebrated soloist, Alfredo Muro also leads small ensembles for weddings, corporate events, private parties, concerts, dances and festive celebrations of all kinds. His recent CD, "Journey Through the Strings," which includes solo as well as arrangements with violins, cello, bass, flute and percussion, was praised by Jose Feliciano as "elevating the guitar to a higher plane…moody and melodic, and richly eloquent." Call for free promotional materials, demo and quote.

THE WEDDING MUSICIANS

LOIS BACHHUBER

(503) 246-4464
E-mail: lnbach@teleport.com

Organ (strings)
String Duo/Trio/Quartet
Violin – Viola – Cello
Piano (strings)

Quality custom tailored music for your wedding ceremony and reception

---

PIANO • KEYBOARDS • VOCALS

SUSY WOLFSON

(503) 244-9607

Solo Background

Susy Wolfson is a musician of uncommon versatility. She is equally comfortable as a solo pianist or accompanying her own vocals, moving smoothly from contemporary styles, jazz standards, rock 'n' roll or rhythm & blues to classical music. Her background includes a magna cum laude performance degree from the prestigious Indiana University School of Music and performances at numerous festivals and engagements including the Spoleto Festival in Italy as well as many years as a freelance musician.

Trio/Quartet/Quintet

Using the classic format of the piano trio plus guitar (with vocals or instrumental only), these musicians are in constant demand for receptions, corporate events, country clubs and winery festivals. From black tie and smooth jazz one night to a kick-off-your shoes rock 'n' roll dance the next, this group will keep 'em dancing! Their song list ranges from Duke Ellington to Sheryl Crow to Stevie Ray Vaughn… and all points in between!

Performance Combinations

- **Solo Piano or Keyboard**
- **Trio/Quartet/Quintet** (vocals, keyboard, guitar, bass, drums—optional saxophone or flute)
- **Vocals and Piano/Keyboard**
- **Flute and Piano Duo** (vocals optional)

Demos, song lists and references for all musical combinations are available upon request.

© Edmund Keene Photographers • page 490

Traditions

Gifts to the bride's parents:

The groom would indicate how much he thought the bride was worth by giving farm animals, weapons or crops to the bride's family. The more gifts, the more valuable the bride.

HELPFUL HINTS

- **Why are photographs important?** After the cake's been eaten, the tuxes returned, the flowers wilted, and you've shaken the last grains of sand off from the honeymoon, what's left of the wedding? Those treasured glimpses captured in photographs can in a moment rekindle the joy for both of you, bring back the friends, and show the love within families.
- **Selecting a photographer:** Find a photographer whose style you feel comfortable with. Look closely at his or her sample albums, and don't be afraid to ask for references. A contract is important to reserve the date and should confirm that the estimate given will be the total cost excluding extra prints or specialty photographs ordered. Within this section you will find pages of photographers; compare the information listed and make sure they meet your needs. The prices vary from one photographer to another; make sure you understand what the "package price" is and what the extras are.
- **Consulting with your photographer:** When you finally select your photographer, sit down together so you can communicate what you imagine your pictures to be. Get specific about formal and candid photographs. Be sure you let the photographer know what you are expecting. Some provide a checklist for you to fill out.
- **Assigning a photographer's helper:** You should submit a list of photographic requests to both the photographer and helper so that your helper can guide the photographer to the right people.
- **Have formal portraits taken before the ceremony:** More brides and grooms are deciding to have formal portraits taken before the ceremony to maximize time with their guests. If you do choose to have formals done before the ceremony, make sure everyone is dressed and ready for pictures at the time designated.
- **Black and white photos:** The traditional formal wedding photos are taking on some new and exciting looks, such as the photojournalist style, which is a more candid documentation of the day. Black and whites are timeless and classic, and handpainting will make the photos an original piece of artwork.
- **View your wedding photos on computer:** This relatively new technology allows you to see your photos very quickly after the wedding. You can see photos in different sizes and shapes, and lay out your entire wedding album before making those expensive decisions on which photos to choose. Some photographers will set it up so your entire family and friends can attend the viewing and order photos.
- **Store your wedding photos on CD:** Ask your photographer if he or she can help you store your photos on CD for safe-keeping.
- **Storing your photos:** Store your wedding photos in a safe place; it is recommended to keep them in the box provided with the wedding album. If you just ordered the photos and no album, make sure to put them in an album soon after receiving them. Keep them out of a damp area.
- **Engagement photo guest book:** A fun idea is to use your engagement photo with a large matte area around it for your guest book. This way family and friends can sign around your photo with well wishes. This is a wonderful keepsake to frame and display on your wall. Rarely do you pull out your guest book and think about all who were there to celebrate your wedding day with you.

A Special Day Photography AE

(503) 639-6666

Web site: www.northwestweddings.com/aspecialday.htm

Your wedding day can be perfect! The splendor of your dress, the fragrance of your flowers, walking down the aisle to the man of your dreams, the joy of sharing your happiness with your friends and family at the reception…can all be captured in the timeless beauty of your photographs. **A SPECIAL DAY PHOTOGRAPHY AE** will be there to capture your unforgettable day in priceless photographs that you can return to again and again.

- **Two photographers at every wedding.** The husband and wife team of Daniel Bernath and Martha Wong photographs every wedding. Dan has been a TV/radio newscaster and a lawyer, *"but most of all, I like capturing special moments for a memory book that I know the bride will love forever."* Dan creates in the classical style. *"I love the pictures of Ross and myself, the misty and romantic look. It's light, romantic, warm, fuzzy…gives you a good feeling when you look at it."* **Verna S.**
  Martha is an architect and believes, *"nothing is more enjoyable than capturing the joys and emotions of people in love on their wedding day."* Martha's style is photojournalistic.
- **We bring an entire photo studio to your wedding** to create studio-quality portraits of all your family members, you and your new husband and special friends. *"When I look at my pictures I get the same feelings of the closeness of my husband and I. My mother showed my pictures and everybody came to tears because they really brought out the feelings of us and the day."* **Lisa G.** *"You definitely captured the 'romance of the day.' You made us feel comfortable enough that we both looked natural. The pictures captured our enjoyment of the day and our feelings for each other."* **Lisa M.**
- **Exclusive Panorama Montage Album.** You can put large photographs up to two feet by two feet of your wedding ceremony into the same album with tons of candid photographs. *"Looking at my panorama album, I get the same feelings I got on my wedding day, over and over again. Martha captured little moments all day long."* **Laura B.**
- **Photograph your wedding for $189.** AE can photograph your wedding for only $189. You buy only the pictures you want in the sizes you want. You won't be stuck with a "package" before you even see your wedding pictures. Print prices are as low as $11.95. Ask about our special. *Buy three pictures of a view and get five.* That's two for free and brings the price down per picture to around $7. Ask about our *48 free thank-you note photos* of you and your groom—a $288 value for free!
- **Don't hire a photographer!** Instead, invite two artists, Dan and Martha, to capture your wedding memories. *"It's not just a job or income to you. I do believe you really want to give your customers those memories for a lifetime…"* **Samantha B.**
  A craftsman creates with his eyes and hand. An artist with his heart. **A SPECIAL DAY AE** has the uncommon gift of capturing your wedding day by hand, eyes and heart.

Adams & Faith Photography

800 N.W. 6th Avenue, Suite 211
Portland Oregon 97209
Contact: Tony or Lori
(503) 227-7850;
Fax (503) 227-1863

Adams & Faith Photography is undoubtedly the Northwest's premier photography studio…

Located in the glorious (and convenient) Union Station in downtown Portland since 1976, they have made style and creativity coupled with superb professional service their hallmark.

As Tony and his wife, Lori, owners of the prestigious Adams & Faith, along with their staff go about their daily business of managing the studio, they are humbled again and again as their work gains an ever-expanding audience...a photo in *Bride's Magazine*, an image in Beverly Clark's book, "Weddings: A Celebration," one prize-winning photograph after another.

Just recently, Tony received one of the highest honors possible for a photographer. Kodak chose him for their elite International Pro Team and included his story in their book, Promise of Excellence Pro Team.

The recognition of their work has brought national attention, accolades from a state senator and acknowledgment from business leaders throughout the community, but none of that compares to the pride Tony, Lori and their photographers take in capturing wedding images for brides and grooms.

Adams & Faith offers a service that is practically unheard of in the photography business... To determine which photographer best suits their own style, brides and grooms look through the outstanding display of wedding albums and the unique photographs that surround the consultation room at Adams & Faith. There they are met by Tony, Lori or one or their knowledgeable staff who introduce them to the philosophy of Adams & Faith and the creative styles of their extraordinary photographers.

Once the bride and groom make their selection, they meet with their chosen photographer before the wedding for a "details meeting." This enables everyone to familiarize themselves with each other and go over all the necessary details, eliminating any last-minute questions and ensuring that every aspect of the day shall be captured… from the superb images that add extra meaning to your special day, to the formals, and party candids.

After the wedding, Adams & Faith puts your story together with photographs of your choosing in an exquisite album featuring the highest quality professional prints that are backed by Kodak's lifetime warranty.

Because Adams & Faith focuses on you and your story, your photographs will be simply spectacular... a tender moment, a gentle nudge, the essence of true love will be forever captured and then turned into your own Adams & Faith trademark image.

Please visit us at our Web site: www.adamsandfaith.com

Keith Aden

Photography & Video Productions

1613 SE 7th Avenue • Portland, Oregon 97214

503 230-0325

Toll Free: 877 230-0325

Web Address: www.adenphoto-video.com

www.bravowedding.com/pdx00/keithadenvideo

E-Mail: kaphoto@internetcds.com

Wedding Packages

Packages are designed to suit weddings of all sizes and start at $450. Wedding coverages from one hour to unlimited time, as needed. Brochures listing services and prices can be sent to you upon request. Call for an appointment at the studio to see samples of photography and video.

Services and Equipment

Only the finest camera equipment is used, Hasselblad ***medium-format*** cameras with backup Hasselblads, ***not*** 35mm cameras.

- We can shoot in available light or will provide light as needed
- Formals may be done either before or after the ceremony; it's your choice
- Photo requests gladly accepted—after all, it's your wedding
- Video Coverage (3-Chip S-VHS Cameras and a state of the art Digital Editing Suite)
- Wedding Invitations, Photo Christmas/Thank-You Cards, Gift Albums
- Wedding announcement photographs for the newspaper are $15 each.

Original Prints and Reprints

Original prints are available in approximately three to four weeks after the wedding. Reprint sizes are 5x5 to 40x60, and start at $10. Original photographs are included in the package price. Art Leather albums are included in all plans. No minimum order required.

Terms and Payment

Reserve our services as soon as possible or six months or more in advance of your wedding. A $100 deposit is required, with the balance due 10 days before the wedding. A full refund is given for cancellations if the date and time can be filled. Travel outside the metro area may require an additional charge. Discover,Visa or Mastercard accepted.

SENSITIVE, CREATIVE AND EXPERIENCED PHOTOGRAPHY!

It's your special wedding day, a day to be remembered for the rest of your life. Through the years, your memories will become even more special, as will your wedding album and videotape. Your choice of a photographer is an important one. Since 1968, Keith Aden has been specializing in wedding and commercial advertising photography, including video production. His 32 years of experience and knowledge of the very special art of wedding photography make him sensitive to your needs and requests. Keith is a photographer who actually cares about you and your wedding.

AJ's Photo Expressions
(360) 694-6684
www.WeLoveWeddings.com

We Love Weddings!

A wedding is a wonderful event that evokes once-in-a-lifetime memories—a time you will want to capture with sensitive, quality, professional photography. We know that you will be pleased with our coverage of your wedding. Beautiful, relaxed portraits are the result of feeling confident and comfortable with your wedding photographer. We specialize in capturing the mood, style, and fun of your special day.

AJ's Photo Expressions feature a husband and wife team whose studio is devoted exclusively to weddings. You will have two photographers regardless of the coverage you choose. This enables us to capture the details of your day with traditional color portraits and imaginative European Style black and white images.

Only AJ's—Web and Watercolors

AJ's is proud to include your own Wedding Web site in all coverage. Family and friends can now view and order portraits from your wedding online! We are also the first and only studio to offer the "Watercolor", one of many digital filters we designed, to enhance any portrait to look like a real watercolor painting. You can actually see the strokes, texture and bleeds of the watercolor. Also available: Sepia Tone, Colorization, Hand Painted B&W and MORE!

Album Creation Credit

Does it really make sense to decide the number and size of photographs you'll want before you even see them? Album creation credit allows you to choose the quantity, size, and style of photographs you want, not what a photographer has predetermined. When you book with AJ's, you need only to choose the amount of coverage you desire. No restrictive packages. No headaches. At your album consultation you select the number and style of photographs that reflect your wedding day, from which we will custom assemble your album. We offer a wide selection of albums, from traditional to the latest in coffee table boxes.

Thank you for considering us to photograph your wedding. We can make your day come alive in photographs—yours to enjoy forever. **We Love Weddings!**

ASPEN PHOTOGRAPHY & VIDEO STUDIO

14120 S.W. Stallion Drive
Beaverton, Oregon 97008
Contact Gregg & Lee Ann Childs
(503) 524-8230
Business hours: by appointment

Selecting a Professional Wedding Photographer

There are two important areas to consider: the professional abilities of the photographer and the pricing structure. At *Aspen Photography & Video*, Gregg Childs is an educated, trained and licensed professional photographer. He has been a professional studio and wedding photographer for 16 years and he uses the same lighting techniques at weddings that are used in the studio. Many of the photographs that Gregg sets up with natural lighting have won awards and honors.

With respect to pricing, *Aspen Photography* has made it very simple. First, we have a photographer's fee of $195. There is no time limit. (Aspen does only one wedding per day), and there are no add-on fees for going to a different location for the reception. We do not have packages that constrain you to purchase a certain selection and number of pictures. Instead, we offer deluxe previews and reprints at specified prices and let you select what you desire. **Price structure:** 4x5 $12; 5x7 $18; 8x10 $22.

"Thanks, Gregg, for the outstanding photographs. You're definitely one of the top three wedding photographers in the metro area." M.L. — 1993

What Makes a Professional Photographer a GREAT Photographer?

Even if you find a photographer with professional capabilities and a pricing structure that matches your budget, you will also want to make sure it is a person with whom you feel comfortable. A GREAT photographer is one who is compatible with you and your needs, and one who helps you feel at ease. After all, if you're not relaxed, it will show in your photographs. Aspen excels at making people feel comfortable and relaxed in front of our cameras.

"Thanks for making me feel so relaxed. I have always hated having my picture taken, but you make everything so natural... You're the greatest." S.L. — 1994

Why Should your *Videographer* be a Professional *Photographer*?

Videographers, traditionally, are not trained to be concerned with good lighting and composition (we know, because we have taken the same classes with other professional videographers). On the other hand, professional photographers have been trained to use good lighting techniques and see good composition.

Aspen Photography & Video is the only studio with photographers who are technically trained and expert in both photography and videography. We are professionals in both fields; we do not use outside sources for our video. The artistic lighting and composition talents we have developed as photographers transfer very well to the discipline of video. It is all very evident when you see our videos and how well they complement our still photographs. Our wedding videos are vibrant, colorful and artistically beautiful!!

"We're so happy that we decided to have you do our video also. It's a beautiful package." B.B — 1994

"Your video of our wedding has been edited in a very sensitive manner. Thanks for your artistic touch." L.Z. — 1993

Ray Bidegain Photography

17 S.E. Third Ave., Suite 403 • Portland, Oregon 97214
(503) 289-5998
Web site: www.rbstudio.com

I have been a professional photographer for 17 years and have photographed hundreds of weddings. I know from experience that each couple, each ceremony and each reception are unique. I 'd like to meet with you, show you my work and discuss your ideas and vision for your wedding day. I usually take a few formal group portraits, in combinations that you specify. However, the majority of my time is spent capturing those lyrical moments that will spark your memories of the event. I am particularly talented at catching those candid, fleeting moments and at recording the unique story of your wedding day as it unfolds. I find that my friendly, easygoing style helps the bridal couple and their guests relax so that photos truly reflect their personalities and the joy that they share, rather than looking stiff or posed.

I am very experienced in both color and black and white photography, and I especially enjoy creating fine art black & white and hand-tinted photos. I do my own darkroom work with the black and white photography to ensure flawless prints, and many couples choose to combine the timeless look of black and white prints with the traditional color prints for their wedding album. There are many wedding package options, and all can be customized to meet your specific needs. I only book one wedding per day so that I have no time constraints and am able to arrive early to record your preparations and take some group photos, and to stay at your reception until the last guest says good-bye.

Please call and set up an appointment to view my portfolio and discuss your wedding plans. I will gladly put you in touch with any of my past clients. They will tell you I am friendly, flexible and professional and that the wedding photos I created record the memories of their wedding day perfectly.

I will spend the day with you, usually about seven or eight hours, trying to tell the story of your wedding on film… I'm not there to create the day, I'm there to record it as it happens. Many of my clients have thanked me for my unobtrusive presence, always surprised at the variety of photographs. You will see happy, relaxed people in my pictures, the same happy people you saw around you at your party. The only part of the day that requires organization is the time we set aside for the formal group photographs… the rest of the day should be yours to enjoy with your family and friends.

I hear from a lot of my brides and grooms that the day was almost a blur… when they look through my photographs, they truly get to see the special details, all the lovely things that they spent so much time designing.

Plan on spending an hour or so with me… I will show you many photographs. While you look, we will talk about your wedding ideas and how you see the day unfolding. As we talk and I get a feel for what you like, I can start to tailor my working approach to suit you. I use a mix of 35mm and medium format cameras… I shoot color, black and white and infrared films. There are also some special things we can do after the fact, like Polaroid transfers and toned photographs.

After thirty two years of photography, thirteen as a professional, I feel like I can bring a lot of heart and experience to your wedding.

Please visit my Web site at www.lightdancestudio.com.

Jamie Bosworth Photographer
by appointment, please
(503) 246-5378

BILL Duff PHOTOGRAPHY

— *Your Photographer*

4206 S.E. 72nd Avenue • Portland, Oregon 97206-3448
Contact: Bill Duff
(503) 775-8589 • Fax (503) 775-2126
Business Hours: Mon–Fri 9am–5pm; please call first

Wedding Packages and Prices $595–$1,595

Various packages are available for you to choose from, depending on the services you request. Packages include photographer's time, completed photographs, and your choice of two styles of albums. The number of photographs taken will depend on the package you select. Albums, folios, and wedding portraits are available for your review. Firm bids in writing are given from a price list provided upon request. Special packages include flexible combinations and photographs for the parents. May through September weddings should be booked one year in advance. I have 29 years experience in photographing people and events. Please call for additional information on convention, corporate identity, awards, and advertising photography.

Services and Equipment

Photo-session planning, portraits and news releases, studio sessions, and album planning are all part of the services available to each bride.

- Medium-format 2 1/4″ cameras and professional lighting are used.
- A new studio and an outdoor garden setting are available for portrait shots.
- Bridal announcement pictures for the newspaper are $25 per session.
- The bride chooses when to take pictures, before or after the wedding ceremony.
- The bride's input and photo requests are greatly appreciated.

Proofs and Reprints

Single or multiple proof sets can be purchased at a discounted rate. There is no minimum order. An example of costs of reprints is an 8x10 for $19. All sizes of prints and reprints are available. Proofs are available two weeks after the wedding.

Terms and Payment

A deposit of $295 is required on booking. Visa, MasterCard and American Express are accepted, and 90-day payment plans are available. Credit is given for cancellations made 30 days in advance of the event. Within the Portland area, all travel charges are included in the package price.

Additional Services

Black and white images with color added, thank-you cards, gift albums for relatives, retouching services and more. For an evening appointment call (503) 775-8589.

BRIAN FOULKES PHOTOGRAPHY

5711 S.W. Boundary Street
Portland, Oregon 97221
Contact: Brian Foulkes (503) 245-2697
Business Hours: by appointment

Wedding Packages and Prices

Brian Foulkes Photography specializes in candid photographs of weddings and wedding-related parties like your wedding rehearsal and dinner. We focus on all the fun, candid photos of family and friends. There are no packages as such, because we just charge a flat rate for time plus film costs, then hand the film over to you so you can handle the processing and place the print order yourself. Call for an appointment to see samples of our work.

Services and Equipment

- Use medium format and 35 mm cameras
- Can shoot in available light or use studio lighting as needed
- Will work with you or a person of your choice to make sure you get the photographs you want of family and friends
- You keep the negatives

Proofs and Reprints

For most couples, after the wedding we drop off their film at the lab we recommend, in the couple's name. Those who wish can also keep the film to take to a lab of their choice. All prints and reprints are thus purchased at cost with no mark-up. Those who wish to go digital can easily have their negatives scanned onto a photo CD.

Terms and Payment

Fees are based on a flat rate of $375 to $475 and include up to six hours of on-site photography. A $25 deposit is required to hold the date, with the balance due on delivery of the film. Travel time is included in the flat rate unless the site is more than 25 miles away. Overtime is negotiable.

WONDERFUL, NATURAL PHOTOS

This service is for people who want candid photographs of their wedding and party. All of the traditional portraits are taken; however, the idea is to include pictures of the preparations, the setting, your friends, and the party. For those who are getting married at a private home or outdoors, perhaps in a small ceremony followed by a reception, here is a way of getting wonderful, natural photos that record the day. Brian Foulkes is sensitive to your wishes and will fit in comfortably with your family and guests. Charges are based on a reasonable flat rate plus the cost of film used. The exposed film then is either left with you, or we will arrange processing. Either way, you keep the negatives.

Brides' Choice

Contact: Kirby & Pam Harris
(800) 362-8796 or (360) 574-7195

Business Hours: appointments available; days and evenings
Web site: http://www.weloveweddings.com/brideschoice

Your wedding photography is too important to entrust to anyone but a professional. We have over 20 years experience photographing weddings, as well as five years teaching photography at the college level. Photography is our full-time occupation.

As a husband and wife team, we are committed to giving you superior quality photographs, creatively capturing the mood and joy of your special day. We use medium format film and equipment, and professional labs for processing and printing.

This Day Belongs To You

By maintaining a low profile, remaining flexible, and flowing with events as they occur, we do our part to make your day memorable and enjoyable. Brides consistently thank us for helping them feel relaxed and at ease.

Thorough preparation for your wedding photography is our priority. We welcome and encourage your participation in pre-planning the type of photographic services that most completely meet your needs and desires. A pre-wedding consultation is scheduled three to four weeks prior to your wedding date. In addition, we usually attend your rehearsal so that we will have the opportunity to meet your family and attendants.

Our Brides Tell It Like It Is

"...and as soon as you walked in the room, Pam, we could feel the stress drain out of us. You're a calming influence. Thank you for that." ~Sally, a bride's mother

"You were so patient and helped us to relax and enjoy the day." ~Shelly and Charlie

"...we feel that you have become part of our family." ~Gabriela and Ian

"How did you get all those great shots? We didn't even know you were taking them!" ~Pete and Debbie

Pricing Information

- Pre-selected packages are available; however, we will be glad to custom-tailor a package to meet your specific requirements and budget.
- Pre-selected wedding packages are priced from $695 to $2,795.
- Ask about our **Y2K Celebration Package.**
- Color preview originals are included in all packages. They are yours to keep.
- You are not required to make a package selection at the time you reserve your wedding date. After you receive your preview album, you can curl up on your sofa, in front of a fire, and leisurely make your selection.

Located in The Fountains Ballroom

223 S.E. 122nd Avenue • Portland, Oregon 97233

(503) 261-9424

Web site: www.fountainsballroom.com

Business Hours: Tues–Thurs 9am–9pm or by appointment

With over 20 years of wedding photography experience, C Studio has formed a way to keep your special day fun and relaxing. We keep everything simple, affordable and best of all, we capture your wedding style and creativity.

Customize Your Own Package

- **negatives**
- **proofs**
- proof albums
- custom wedding and parent albums
- beautiful enlargements
- studio portraits
- black and white; custom hand coloring
- basic to complete coverage (2–8 hours)
- newspaper photos

Packages Ranging from $895–$1,995

Our Offices Also Provide *A Complete Wedding Package Like No Other in the Entire Portland Area!*

- elegant ballroom facility—up to 300 guests
- wedding catering
- bridal flowers
- decorating
- wedding cakes
- ice carvings
- video, DJ, limousine and formal wear referrals

See page 136 under Banquet & Reception Sites.
See page 304 under Caterers & Ice Carvings.

CAMERA ART

5285 N.W. 253rd
Hillsboro, Oregon 97124
(503) 648-0851

Weddings are supposed to be one of the highlights of a couple's life, but all too often the planning—choosing a dress, selecting a florist, a bakery, or even the invitations—can become a blur.

Have you reached the frustration stage in trying to choose your photographer? Are you having trouble comparing the Gold Edition package from one photographer to the Prestige Album set from another? Or maybe three 8x10s and 40 4x5s just don't meet your needs. Well, Camera Art has a better way.

Our goal is to take all the confusion out of pricing a wedding, and at the same time, allow the bride and groom to control their own budget and what they order.

Here is How it Works

We charge a $195 camera fee to shoot your wedding. That covers the photographer's time regardless of how long it takes to cover your wedding from start to finish. We'll follow you from dressing shots beforehand until you leave your reception. The camera fee also covers all travel fees and location changes.

After you receive your proofs, you simply order what **you** want. You order what meets your needs and budget. If your order consists of three 8x10s and 40 4x5s, that's fine, but if your order is one 8x10, nine 5x7s, and 17 4x5s, that's fine, too. The cost of your "package" is simply the cost of your individual prints.

No extra fees, no hidden costs. Simple–YES. Confusing–NO, and we like it that way. So do our customers—8x10s are $22, 5x7s are $18, and 4x5s are $12.

Services and Equipment

- Professional medium-format cameras (including backup equipment) are used
- Portable studio backdrop and lighting are used at each wedding
- Special effects include soft focus
- Available-light photographs are a specialty

Terms and Payment

A $95 deposit reserves the day. The remainder of the $195 camera fee is due 30 days prior to the wedding.

NATIONAL AWARD-WINNING PHOTOGRAPHY AT SENSIBLE PRICES

by Michael Bickler, Robert Kuhn and Matt Furcron

 Please let this business know that you heard about them from the Bravo! Bridal Resource Guide.

CLASSIC PORTRAITS

in Salem
Contact: Neal White
(503) 399-1994, (800) 290-1994
Business Hours: Mon–Fri 4–9pm
E-mail: Newneal@aol.com

Classic wedding photography for over 25 years. Your wedding memories will be preserved for a lifetime for only $650

Wedding Packages

Your wedding photography coverage starts three hours prior to the ceremony. The wedding coverage begins with candid photographs in the dressing room before the formal photography. The formals will include: portraits of the bride, the groom and the entire wedding party. This very special day also includes photographs of the immediate families of the bride and groom. We will also photograph extended family members and friends.

Formal portraits may include studio-style lighting and outdoor portraiture, candlelight and natural window light portraits. We carefully blend formal portraits with special candids of the wedding and the reception to create a love story about your wedding day.

We will photograph the ceremony using ambient light. This light enhances the warmth of your wedding ceremony. These photographs include: the processional, significant parts of the ceremony, such as the vows the ring exchange, the unity candle, the first kiss and the recessional.

After the ceremony, we will travel with you to the reception site. We will capture all the festive activities of cutting the cake, toasting, bouquet and garter toss, first dance and wedding party dance.

After the wedding, you will receive approximately 80 finished 5x7 enlargements. YOU also *keep* the negatives. This gives you the flexibility for album selection and control of the negatives.

Terms and Payment

You will receive an agreement of complete wedding coverage.
A $100 deposit is required to reserve your wedding date.
Visa and MasterCard are accepted.

Please call (503) 399-1994 for a free consultation.

mark w. derry, photographer
406 nw second avenue
canby, or 97013
(503) 266-9393
Business Hours: Tues–Fri 9am–5:30pm; Sat by appointment

Wedding Packages and Prices

The most popular full-coverage package starts at $1,000, and includes four-and-one-half hours of time, prints in the sizes of your choice, lacquer finish of prints, an album, pages, engraving, and thank-you cards. The average number of wedding pictures taken ranges from 150 to 250. Please reserve your date from four months to a year in advance.

Experience, Services, and Equipment

Mark Derry graduated from Brooks Institute of Photography, one of the best-known schools for professional photographers, and is one of 20 Certified Professional Photographers in the state of Oregon. He is a past President of Professional Photographers of Oregon. Mark is trained in commercial photography and has corporate clients such as Johnson Controls, Chiquita Bananas, and Super 8 Motels. He has 17 years of experience in his full-service portrait studio and enjoys giving people a visual record of their wedding day. A list of references is available upon request. Mark works with medium-format Hasselblad cameras and can provide images up to 40x60 in size. Brides and their families may choose from a variety of styles and extra effects, including double exposures and misties. Mark will be happy to work with your preference of background, be it a formal portrait, beach location, etc. We recommend formal photos be taken before the ceremony, but scheduling is completely your choice.

Proofs and Reprints

The choice is yours regarding what portraits to print, in what quantities, and at what sizes. Prices range from $17 for a 4x5 and up.

Terms and Payment

A down payment of one half the total is required to reserve your date, with the balance due before the wedding. The reservation fee is nonrefundable, but may be credited toward other services. Overtime hours will be charged at $65 per half hour.

Additional Services

Mark offers a Complimentary Engagement Sitting for all wedding couples. Invitations, newspaper black-and-whites, wallets, folios, parents' albums, and wall-decor portraits are all available. Mark generally wears a tuxedo to the wedding.

PHOTOS CAN EXPRESS ALL YOUR LOVE AND JOY

Mark has a real gift for understanding people through the lens, and is able to capture the love and joy that make weddings so special. Above all, Mark is flexible to the needs of the bride, groom, and their families, so that final pictures reflect the spirit of the event.

DEBORAH DOMBROWSKI PHOTOGRAPHY

4631 N.E. Ainsworth Street • Portland, Oregon 97218
Contact: (503) 282-5511; E-mail: dphoto@jps.net
Business Hours: by appointment

I Take Wonderful Photographs; Come See My Portfolio!

You'll find pictures that shine with the tenderness, humor, excitement, and love that fill a wedding day. Although I am happy to take formal portraits and group pictures, I am especially skilled in making affectionate, candid portraits of you and your guests. It's important to be sensitive to the small moments that make up the day—reunions between old friends, nervous laughter, shared secrets and jokes. I'll take the photographs that your best friend would take if she had 10 years of training in art and photography. From dressing up, to cutting the cake and dancing all night, there will be pictures of the two of you that will capture the joy of your celebration. I'll consult with you before the wedding to find out what photographs are especially significant to you. Are your grandparents visiting from England? Does your sister have a new baby? We can fit these pictures into your plans for the day. Working with you, I'll create a beautiful and spontaneous record of your wedding.

Services and Proofs

I offer a flexible range of photographic services. I have recorded formal weddings in cathedrals and small family gatherings in backyards. Both black and white and color photography are available. We can design a plan together that will fit your needs and desires. You will receive from 200 to 300 proofs that are yours to keep. Proofs are available approximately six weeks after the wedding. Beautiful custom albums are available upon request, and enlargements may be ordered separately. Black and white photos are available for newspaper announcements.

Equipment

I use all Nikon equipment for candid shots, and I am equally adept at working with natural or artificial light. I use a medium format camera for detailed portraits in both black and white and color.

Cost and Terms

I'll work with you to plan the perfect coverage of your entire wedding day. I've been photographing people for 15 years, and it shows! It's a good idea to reserve your wedding date a few months in advance. I look forward to talking with you in person.

EDMUND KEENE
photographers

920 S.W. 13th Avenue
Portland, Oregon 97205
(503) 224-4410
Fax (503) 224-4429
Web site: EKeenephotographers.com

Business Hours: Mon–Fri 9:30am–5:30pm; other hours by appointment

---

Photographing Portland's important events since 1968.

Q. Why should I hire a professional photographer?

A. Photography is the only way to remember all the details of the most exciting times in your life. After nearly every wedding, we are told, "The day seemed to go by in a blur–I don't remember this. I'm so glad you got the picture." Only a trained, experienced photographer knows the difference between a "snapshot" and an image that becomes a lasting MEMORY of your most valued moments.

Q. But isn't good photography expensive?

A. Our prices are as varied as the individuals we serve. This is why we have so many options on the number of photographs and the amount of time for photography coverage. The old saying "you get what you pay for" is especially true in this instance. Our prices have always represented exceptional value. You cannot buy equivalent quality for less money anywhere.

Q. Why choose Edmund Keene Photographers?

A. Because your photographs mean as much to us as they do to you. Our aim is to make you so happy with your photographs that you'll be able to relive the day over and over again five, ten, or fifty years from now as you look through the memories kept in your wedding album.

If you're planning a **corporate event such as a holiday party, awards banquet, or seminar** that needs the careful attention and unobtrusive approach of an experienced professional ... WE CAN HANDLE THE ASSIGNMENT.

SO GIVE US A CALL. WE WOULD LOVE TO MEET YOU.
(503) 224-4410

Please visit our Web site at EKeenephotographers.com
for additional examples of our photography.

ENCORE STUDIOS

Portland, Oregon
(503) 255-8047
E-mail: encore@webcombo.net
Web site:
www.bravowedding.com/pdx00/encore-photo

With over 20 years of experience, Encore Studios offers the widest of selections of wedding packages in the Northwest, designed with *your* preferences and budget in mind. You'll meet with your photographer making sure all the details of your wedding are thoroughly discussed to ensure the photographs most important to you. On your wedding day, we take special pride in being as unobtrusive as possible, capturing traditional as well as those one-of-a-kind photographs that are most cherished.

Equipment and Services

The finest and most current cameras are utilized, including medium format and *digital* cameras. State-of-the-art digital cameras are highly advanced, and we are one of the few studios using this innovative technology for your picture perfect wedding! We are able to shoot in only available light or in studio-type light, and you are welcome to request as many photographs as you wish, indoor or out, and formals may be taken either pre or post-ceremony—it's your choice! Your photographs may be either printed and received usually within two weeks of your wedding, or you may choose to have then printed immediately on site! Most packages include a complimentary engagement portrait session in the settings of your choice, with prints you choose to keep and treasure.

Additional Services

- Black and white photography
- Newspaper photographs
- Parent and family albums
- Folios and frames
- Portraits in new studio
- Invitations
- Wallets to 40"x60" sizes
- Canvas and poster prints

Packages and Prices

With the most comprehensive package selection in the Northwest, you are welcome to choose from our many selections or customize your own package as you'd like. Individual reprints are one of the lowest, and start as low as $3.75 for 2x3 and $12 for 4x5 prints, for example. There is no minimum order required. You are welcome to *own* your negatives as well. A $100 deposit reserves your wedding date. Visa and Mastercard gladly accepted as well as financing, with no interest payments.

Consultants are available day
or evenings for appointments.

EXCEPTIONAL PHOTOGRAPHS BY

STEWART HARVEY
& Associates

2405 NW THURMAN
PORTLAND, OR 97210
(503) 274-9711

Storybook Weddings

"There's magic in the smallest things: The quiet touch of hands, or a moment of joyful abandon…" Your wedding is a statement about your personal artistic style, and your wedding photographs should be as individual and expressive as you. Whether your wedding is fancy and formal or candid and spontaneous, Stewart Harvey discovers the personal moments that are unique to your wedding day. From his studio in a charming turn-of-the-century theater building, Stewart has gathered together a small group of talented group of photographers who share his commitment to capturing each wedding story in a visual style that is the most appropriate and authentic to the occasion.

Why Choose Stewart Harvey Photography?

The reasons are many: state-of-the-art studio cameras and equipment, a commitment to medium format, the best wedding products available, and multiple service options. You may choose between A La Carte, Create-A-Story and limited or unlimited Storybook Packages. **There is also the Stewart Harvey attitude.** After 25 years of photographing some of Portland's most distinctive couples, he doesn't believe in generic weddings or generic wedding photographers. Each photographer is an individual artist chosen for their talent and personality, and you book the person whose style and vision fits with your wedding and budget.

These are many great reasons for choosing Stewart Harvey, but the most compelling reasons of all are best expressed by some of the hundreds of delighted couples who have selected Stewart Harvey and Associates as their wedding photographers:

"Adam and I wanted to thank you for the wonderful engagement photos of us at the Rhododendron Gardens. We love them! We also wanted you to know how much we loved having Shane as our wedding day photographer. We thought his professionalism, love for his job, respect for others, and low-key nature was great!" ~ Kristen and Adam

"Thanks for making our wedding special with your beautiful photographs. Your attitude and friendly personality helped make the picture taking lighthearted and fun!"
~ Frank and Alaina

"Gary and I would like to thank you for helping to make Kristin and Matt's wedding day go so smoothly. You made it so easy for us!… We are all thrilled. Your kind attentions are very much appreciated!" ~ Karen Genzer

ELEANOR GLORIOSO
photographer

Specializing in weddings
and romantic portraiture
Relaxed • Creative • Professional
Storybook style

503.590.9320

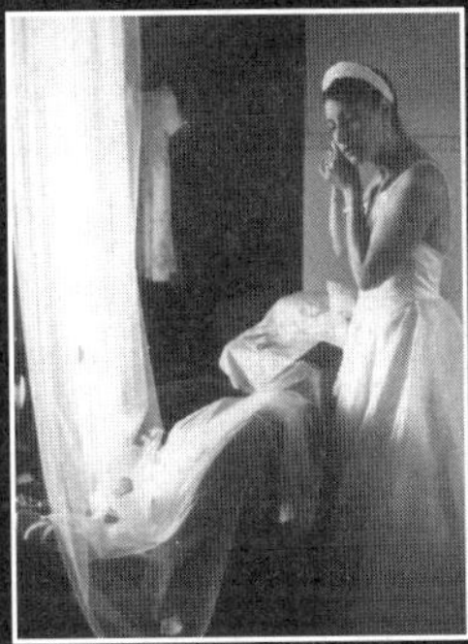

Background

Eleanor trained as a professional artist in her youth and has been a working artist for over 30 years. Her photojournalistic style reflects this with her keen sense of timing and artistic eye. Internationally published and an award-winning photographer, she has received acclaim for her creativity and flair.

Getting the Shots

I began my photographic career as a newspaper photographer, getting shots that "tell the story." Being a romantic at heart, wedding and portrait photography was an easy and natural progression for me. My passion to capture the beauty of life on film, authentic and honest, to "tell the story" is my inspiration. It keeps my work fresh, exciting and alive. As a wedding photojournalist, my goal is to photograph the real wedding story as it happens, as well as the "must get" formal group photographs in a traditional or casual style. After chronicalizing hundreds of weddings, I have learned some simple truths, every wedding is different. Every picture does tell a story, and the best things in life just happen naturally. The images you can feel are the images of the heart. These are the ones I strive to capture in film, the authentic, honest moments shared with loved ones and friends.

"Bob and I are so glad we chose you as our wedding photographer. Your work is fabulous and we are delighted to have our wedding day captured by someone with your skill and talent. The pictures really captured the spirit of the day. We really enjoyed working with you and feel we gained a friend in the process."

– Erick and Nick, Bride and Groom

"Eleanor's natural talent produced exquisite pictures of our wedding, we loved every one of them and highly recommend her!"

– Erica and Nick, Bride and Groom

"Eleanor's photography is just stunning! We loved the photographs of both our children's weddings."

– Paula, Mother of the Bride

"Ellie is a true artist. She captured the most precious moments of our wedding day."

– Heather and Mike, Bride and Groom

"Thank you so much for capturing our wedding with such beauty. We are thrilled with our albums. Thanks again, you are a photo god!"

– Kim and Gavin, Bride and Groom

Photographs of your wedding day are priceless. I will personally work with you to capture the joy, excitement and cherished moments of your special day. I invite you to view my portfolio and discuss your wedding plans. Please call to schedule an appointment **(503) 590-9320.**

V I C K I G R A Y L A N D

P H O T O G R A P H E R

phOne 5 0 3. 8 7 2. 9 7 0 0

Experience

I have worked in photojournalism for 25 years and have shown my work in galleries for seven years. I bring my passion for photographing real people and real events to wedding photography. My approach is that of fine art documentary work.

Specializing in Black and White

I specialize in black and white work that I process and print myself. Many clients choose a combination of color and black and white. I have a selection of packages, and will also work with clients to customize the work to their wishes.

I prefer to meet with couples several times: to show them my work, to finalize details a few weeks before the wedding, and to attend the rehearsal. On the day of the wedding, all parties are prepared and comfortable with each other.

On the wedding day, I like to arrive early to start photographing the preparations, then continue through the ceremony, celebration and send-off.

Some of My Clients' Comments

"I picked you because I knew you'd stay calm." – Kimberly S.

"We love our photos. And there are so many!" – Felicia H.

Please phone for an appointment.

503. 872. 9700

E-mail: Grayland@aol.com

HOLLAND STUDIOS

SPECIAL OCCASION PHOTOGRAPHY

Professional • Relaxed • Creative

134 S.E. Taylor
Portland, Oregon 97214
Contact: Eric Holen (503) 706-5763
Business Hours: By appointment
Web site: www.hollandstudios.com

Portraits that will give you goose bumps and capture a memory for a lifetime...this is what I strive to shoot for you at **Holland Studios**. The images of your special day should portray a complete story—from the engagement sitting on Cannon Beach, to the last kiss before the door closes on your honeymoon suite. My desire as a wedding photographer is to be involved from the very first phone call, to perhaps photographing your family in a few years time…

It's imperative to me that I know my clients before the wedding day—most of my packages include an engagement session, and ***all*** require a details meeting.

> ***"We are excited to work with you on our special day, especially after seeing the finished work at our engagement session."*** — Jean, bride

As you know, before booking a photographer, first meet with him or her. Discuss your ideas and visions for your wedding day; ask for references, and observe samples of their more recent work. Most importantly, see how your personalities complement one another.
I go out of my way to ensure that things are not rushed; I want you to relax and enjoy your day.

> ***"Eric is an incredibly talented photographer and also has a natural talent for putting people at ease,"*** — Carol, mother of the bride

My assistant and I will dress for the occasion. As professionals, our goal as a team is to make sure your day is a special day for everyone, especially ***you***.

I only shoot one wedding a day, allowing for unlimited time. The packages will fit everyone's budget, ranging from $695 to $2,795. Whether it's a black tie affair or an intimate gathering on the beach, I will be there to capture those special moments.

> ***"Thank you so much, each picture is better than the last."*** — Lisa, bride

I look forward to helping you create and document your wedding day. Please call me to schedule an appointment to view my portfolio, or with any questions you may have. Remember, ***you*** are unique and deserve only the best.

"This is your time.
And with a classic image from
Holland Studios,
Your time is Forever."

PMPA — Portland Metropolitan Photographers Association

Kodak — Promise of Excellence — Professional Imaging Products

IMAGES
By Floom

(in Multnomah Village)
7843 S.W. Capitol Highway
Portland, Oregon 97219
(503) 245-3676

- **Beautiful Formals**
- **Spectacular Candids**
- **Reprints starting as low as $7**
- **Superior customer service second to none**

These are just a few of the fantastic features *Images by Floom* has to offer. You've probably already heard our name. It is commonly becoming a "buzz" word among brides, wedding and church coordinators who all want the perfect photographer to capture those treasured moments, without being pushy or controlling the event. Our job is to make your special day go as smoothly as possible, without any glitches. Our highly professional and trained staff are committed to this. Our packages start as low as $395 and go up to $1,895. Reprints at $7 per 4x6 photograph are almost unheard of in the wedding business. This is fantastic for parents, friends and relatives who want extra pictures—which we all know are usually too expensive to buy.

When we photograph your wedding it does not stop there; we will photograph your first anniversary, children's pictures, and so on. In our full-service studio, conveniently located in the heart of SW Portland, we know you'll be so pleased with the quality and customer service you'll receive at your wedding that we really will be your photographers for life!

- **$150 deposit books us for your day**–make no other package decisions until one month prior to the wedding.
- **There are no hidden costs**–at our initial meeting we will go over everything so you know exactly what you are paying.
- **We have packages for every budget.**

LOOK FOR US AT EVERY BRIDAL SHOW
OR
CALL TODAY FOR AN APPOINTMENT
(503) 245-3676

"They photographed three of my children's weddings beautifully. Don't bother going anywhere else." Mrs. Pat Reser, Reser's Fine Foods

Images Forever Studio

Artistry in Portraiture

(503) 626-2738

Realizing your Dream ...

Since you were a little girl you have dreamed of the wonder of your wedding day.

Capturing the Glow ...

The magic of this day must be something to hold in your heart and share with your loved ones through your fabulous photographs.

Warming the Heart ...

with images to treasure for a lifetime. ***Images Forever*** has been creating cherished wedding storybooks for 20 years. After the day has ended your photographs will keep the memories fresh and vibrant.

About *Images Forever Studio* and *Kyle Saunders'* philosophy

Flexibility

Images Forever is committed to excellence in wedding photography...**your way!** Whether you prefer a traditional coverage or have special considerations, Kyle will cover your event as you request. Kyle is an expert at combining elegant, relaxed portraits with romantic wedding illustration and delightfully fun candids.

Romance

Images Forever takes romance seriously and strives to create images that show genuine emotion. Your photographs will bring back exquisite, tender memories and remind you of your lifelong promise to each other.

Experience

Kyle Saunders has worked for 20 years and personally photographs each wedding. Count on Kyle's expertise in planning and coordinating so that your day will flow perfectly and be relaxed and fun.

If your wedding portraits are important to you,
you need to talk with Kyle today.
For an appointment call:
(503) 626-2738

WEDDING & PORTRAIT PHOTOGRAPHERS INTERNATIONAL WPPI™

PPA Professional Photographers of America
THE WORLD'S GREAT STORYTELLERS℠

PROMISE OF Kodak Professional Imaging Products EXCELLENCE

Jak Tanenbaum PHOTOGRAPHY ASSOCIATES

P. O. Box 82758
Portland, Oregon 97282
Contact: Lynden or Jak Tanenbaum
Phone/Fax: (503) 232-1455
Available By Appointment
E-mail: info@photographyassociates.com
Web site:www.photographyassociates.com

Wedding Packages and Prices

Our unique photographic documentaries are tailored to meet the needs of all sizes and styles of weddings. Our basic coverage starts at $499 and includes up to two hours of photography time, 20 deluxe color prints bound in a quality presentation album, plus two 8x10 wall portraits. We also offer unlimited wedding coverage, reception coverage, studio portraiture and classic black and white fine art wedding portfolios. Please call for additional information, our brochure and price lists, or an appointment in our conveniently located Westmoreland-Sellwood studio.

Services and Equipment

We use medium-format Hasselblad cameras, the best portable studio-style lighting available, and never go on location without carrying backup cameras and strobelights.

Proofs and Reprints

Our photography contract includes a specific number of color photographs displayed in a quality album. Additional 5″x5″ preview photographs can be purchased for as little as $4 each. Our reprints and enlargements are reasonably priced, and with our *"Punctuality Plus"* discount you can save 15% off our published prices when ordering reprints or enlargements within 30 days of the delivery of your presentation album.

Terms and Payment

In order to guarantee our availability for your wedding date, we require a $200 deposit upon the receipt of our signed *Contract for Photography*. The balance is payable 30 days before the day of the wedding. We accept all major credit cards.

FINE ARTISTS! PROFESSIONAL TRAINING! EXPERIENCE!

For over 20 years Jak Tanenbaum PHOTOGRAPHY ASSOCIATES has been providing individuals, families, galleries, museums, publications, collectors and corporations with the finest in photographic portraiture. We tailor each job to your desires, and we listen. We offer sensitive informed advice gained from years of experience and provide a variety of unique photographic services.

Jak Tanenbaum received a B.F.A. in photography and design from the University of North Carolina and an M.F.A. in photography from the Academy of Art College in San Francisco. He has been an active exhibiting artist for 25 years. His wife and partner, Lynden Tanenbaum received her B.F.A. in photography from Humboldt State University and is also actively involved in exploring the creative, fine-art aspect of the medium. Jak and Lynden often work as a team, and when they put their minds together, amazing things can happen. WOW!

James Loomis Photography

Wedding and Event Photographer

(503) 254-1401

My aim is to provide you with personable service before, during and after the wedding day. I am here to listen to your wants and needs, so that I may provide you with exactly what you desire in your wedding album.

A Wedding Day is Filled with Moments…

I want you to relive the love, laughter and romance of your wedding day by taking a documentary approach in a style that is said to be formal and casual, serious and silly. Remember the joy, relive the day and forever savor the many moments that made it a once-in-a-lifetime experience…

Dear James

Thank you so much for the wonderful job you did at our wedding. We are really proud of the pictures you took and are very impressed. We would be more than happy to provide an excellent reference to anyone seeking your service as a photographer. You are terrific and we would love to tell people this!

~ Jennifer and Mac Brown

Dear Jim

I just wanted to thank you for your professionalism in taking our pictures, but still making it fun. You gave us all a sense of confidence. By the end of the evening we felt you were a friend. We appreciate all you did to make the day special and recording special moments as you saw them.

Thank you again,
Diane Scrutton (mother of Lisa)

For more than a decade I have been producing beautiful images with an emphasis on quality.

Let me show you what I can do for you…

(503) 254-1401

Jim's Photography

"capturing a moment of a lifetime"

9500 N.E. 21st Street • Vancouver, Washington 98664
Contact: Jim and Carolyn Tuchtenhagen (360) 253-2412
Business Hours: by appointment; Web site: www.jimsphotography.com

Personal Attention

Let us take this time to say, "Congratulations on your upcoming wedding day!" Jim's Photography appreciates that you are considering us to be a part of your once-in-a-lifetime memory. We are a husband and wife team. Jim and Carolyn's artistic skills and professionalism will create and capture those special moments on your wedding day. We'll work with the bride and groom to ease those stressful moments from the time we arrive, to the time we leave. Jim personally shows up on your rehearsal day at no charge!

Experience

Jim has over 18 years of experience, 12 years professionally in weddings and portraits. He uses only professional medium format 2 1/4" and professional 35mm camera equipment. Professionally portable lighting, umbrellas and backgrounds are available upon request. We provide a complete photo checklist for the bride and groom. We also highly encourage the bride and groom to request photos before or during the event. Jim is very flexible in photographing formal pictures. Some before, some after, or all before or all after…this is the bride and groom's day!

Proofs and Reprints

Original proofs are available approximately two to three weeks after the wedding. Discounts on large quantity reorders. Please call for brochures and price lists.

Terms and Payment

A deposit of $100 is required to secure your wedding date upon a receipt of our signed contract for photography. The balance is due in full on or before the wedding date. We accept major credit cards. Ask about our no-interest payment plan. There is no charge for travel in the Vancouver-Portland metropolitan areas.

Additional Services

- Black and white photographs
- Photojournalistic or candid for nontraditional coverage
- Large variety of albums, folios, frames and wedding attire
- Discounts on wedding announcements, invitations and thank you cards
- Engagement "love story" photo sessions, frames and signature mats (very popular)
- Hand-colored black and white photos

 Please let this business know that you heard about them from the Bravo! Bridal Resource Guide.

Joseph PHOTOGRAPHER

5500 S.W. Ames Way
Portland, Oregon 97225
(503) 246-7911
E mail: fotojo@teleport.com
Web site: www.josephoto.com
Business Hours: by appointment please

Still so much to do! Look at invitations, call the caterers, taste the cakes, listen to bands, hire the limousine, find the florist, select a photographer…Wait a minute—a photographer? That should be easy. Let's look in the yellow pages. Lots of ads…"We do babies, boudoir, and weddings," "Best price in town"…get serious!

Consider asking friends of recently married couples. Find out who they used and listen for the same name several times. If you hear about someone not getting this photographer because they waited too long, then it's time to pick up the phone. Speak directly with the photographer and ask, "Why should I choose you to take my wedding pictures?" You may be amused and amazed with the answers, but what you're really listening for is attitude. A warm, sincere, friendly attitude.

An experienced wedding specialist will blend in comfortably with your family and friends and will be sensitive to unusual situations that may arise. Enthusiasm and a light-hearted sense of humor can help too! (What you don't need is a director with an ego or an amateur anxious to practice "the shot list" from a bridal magazine.) If the chemistry is right on the phone, make an appointment to see the photographs, and bring along everyone who is involved in making the decision.

Looking at wedding pictures can be very interesting. You'll be distracted at first by flower arrangements, beautiful settings and maybe even some familiar faces. But, look at expressions! Do people look happy and relaxed? Are they enjoying themselves? And look for natural lighting effects. Window light that puts sparkle in the groom's eyes when he first sees the bride. The glow of candlelight illuminating the exchange of rings at the altar. And while everyone else watches the bride's first dance, who sees the light that softens mom's tears? The right photographer does. Great images abound, not fake, not cheesecake, but real, honest…natural!

And when the the day comes to plan your daughter's wedding, she'll get out "mom's album," and you'll realize that it wasn't about fancy camera equipment or discount deals, but it was about faces and feelings. Not a sampling of sizes, but a storybook of sweet sensations. Like a fond fragrance and a familiar refrain, the memories will come rushing back, and you'll be glad that you selected the right photographer.

Since 1970, Joseph Photographer, Raleigh Hills.

LAKE OSWEGO PHOTOGRAPHERS

15830 S.W. Upper Boones Ferry Road
Lake Oswego, Oregon 97035-4066
Contact: Dan or Teresa Poush
(503) 624-1515, (888) 269-4000
E-mail: lophoto@integrityonline.com
Call for an appointment

Dedicated to Christian Values

Making The Right Choice...

We know it is a difficult task for you to select your wedding photographer. To convince you to meet us and see our work is equally difficult, but once you do, you will understand why we have a real advantage.

It's A Gift

Our husband-and-wife team combines photographic talent with a special gift for working with people. We feel it's our most important service. All photographers in this book will most likely produce nice photographs. Our value is measured in the quality of service. Throughout your day, we try to capture all the beauty of your wedding, while at the same time making the photography a very positive and pleasant activity.

We work with you and your family to individualize your coverage while producing elegant photographs in a relaxed atmosphere.

Everything You've Always Wanted

Our service is intended to be simple. You select the package you desire, and we do the rest. All packages include our time, the selected color enlargements, and a beautiful album of your choice.

The Finest Quality

Our beautiful wedding prints are produced by the finest color lab in the Pacific Northwest. This allows our studio to "guarantee your photographs for a lifetime." So, give us a call. Our showroom is a relaxed place to view sample albums and wall prints.

Invest In Friends

Once you meet us, you will see why so many of our couples consider us friends, long after the wedding photographs are delivered.

Our Prints are LIFETIME GUARANTEED

DELIVERING A LIFETIME OF PROFESSIONAL PHOTOGRAPHY

Call early for an appointment.
Dan & Teresa Poush
(503) 624-1515 or toll free (888) 269-4000

With over 20 years experience in photography, we can also handle any celebration, party, or corporate event with ease.

LASTING MEMORIES PHOTOGRAPHY

6235 E. Burnside
Portland, Oregon 97215
Contact: Ron or Mary Price
(503) 236-0174
Business Hours:
by appointment to accommodate your schedule

At Lasting Memories Photography we realize that your wedding day is the most important day of your life. Your wedding photographs will help make the memories of your day last forever. We cater to making your wedding photography as simple and stress-free as possible. Call us today for an appointment, then come in and discuss your wedding and we can show you our many samples.

Wedding Packages

All packages start with a romantic engagement session. We start this session in our studio for some formal portraits, then after a clothes change we finish the session in a local park. You receive any eight prints in a folio to display at your wedding.

We photograph your wedding much like a photographic journal. We cover everything from last-minute touches to the bride, formal posed pictures, fun shots, wedding ceremony and all the traditional and fun events that happen at the reception. You receive all your proofs assembled in an album. You also receive a black and white photo for the newspaper.

Experience

Mary Price is a photographer with an eye for romance and a personality for fun. She has the experience and expertise to make your wedding memories all you want them to be. Working all weddings by her side is her husband, Ron, who also manages the business. They have worked hundreds of weddings together and their teamwork shows. We know that you will feel very comfortable working with Ron and Mary and that will be visible in your wedding photographs.

"Thank you so much for being our wedding photographers. You two are the Best team! Everything went so smoothly and we appreciate your professional, caring approach to taking pictures. We definitely will be referring you two to the newly engaged. Thank you for being a huge part of our special day."

Sunshine Always,
– Kim and Eric 8/15/99

"Thank you for everything you did for us on our big day (besides taking pictures)! You were both a big help and we really appreciate it. All of your help made it an even more perfect day for us and we will cherish the memories of it always. We could not have asked for better than you guys and wanted to let you know. Everyone else thought you were great, too. Thanks again—you went above and beyond. There's no way we can thank you for what you did for us."

– Beth and Mark 7/18/99

leo commercial photography

1412 S.E. Stark Street
Portland, Oregon 97214
(503) 235-7655

The saying, "A picture is worth a thousand words" is never truer than on your wedding day. Leo Commercial Photography knows this and strives to capture the memories and emotions that will be cherished by you throughout the years.

Listening to your needs is a key element in delivering what is going to be viewed by you and your family for years to come.

I smoothly blend my advertising background with the perfection of the best classic wedding photography styles. Quick fleeting moments of real life intertwined with the old world romantic…your emotions on film.

When I look through the camera, release the shutter and capture that fleeting moment, I am happy to be a part of your special day. I feel a sense of pride that you have entrusted me with the responsibility of delivering these most important memories on film.

Thank you for considering Leo Commercial Photography, where the photographs speak for themselves.

Mainlight Media, Inc.
642-1251

17900 S.W. Frances Street
Aloha, Oregon 97006
Contact: Gordy Teifel
(503) 642-1251
E-mail: teifel@pacifier.com

Event Packages and Prices

Mainlight Media album packages will fit your budget perfectly: $165 to $2,490. Our professional photography extends from appropriate films and exposure to print production and presentation. Most of all, our packages are good starting points to tailor to exactly what you want. We feature electronic previews—positive video images made from color negatives. Client may request color previews.

Photography and Video Services

The personality of the photographer is important on your special day. Gordy Teifel, our lead photographer, will easily guide you through the process of photographing your story. His assured style can be applied to creating your memories. Trust this assignment to Gordy Teifel, a veteran of hundreds of weddings. Call for an interview. **BONUS: If you sign up for both photography and video recording, we'll supply another video camera at your wedding service at no additional charge.**

Video Production Services

Relive the first day in your married life! Memories of a lifetime are captured through the imaginative direction of a video producer. Enjoy the treasured moments of getting ready, sharing your vows with each other, the rings, the cake cutting, the toasting and the expressive comments of guests and relatives.

Quality programming with the benefits of Digital Video and Hi8 industrial equipment. Audio is the foundation of successful videos. Audio sourcing includes wireless mics, a PZM and other microphone types with mixing techniques. Our cameras carry exceptionally low light capability. However, superior performance is attained with complimentary illumination. Editing with Adobe Premiere is performed on a computer loaded with video and photographic imaging tools.

Additional Benefits

Mainlight Media produces tape-slide and video programs that visually show family histories. This high-impact presentation is caringly created from old photographs. Background music is added to set the mood. The tape-slide format is excellent to share with an audience. The video version is ideal to enjoy at home. Call Mainlight Media to begin the planning of your Nostalgia Program. The Nostalgia Programs are often associated with grateful responses, heartfelt appreciation, and even inexpressible joy.

Moments In Time
MIT
Photography

Photography by Bob Welsh • Master Photog. Cr., • PPA Certified, FP
5035 N.E. Elam Young Parkway, Suite 300 • Hillsboro, Oregon 97124
(503) 648-0586; Fax (503) 640-1617
E-mail: mitp@teleport.com • Web site: www.mitstudio.com

"I Do"

...believe in love
...want to grow old with you
...want the wedding of my dreams
...want to be a princess bride

I Do...I Do...I Do...

Your Wedding...

Is an expression of Love that you have spent much time and energy to create. You have chosen the perfect dress, colors and flowers for your wedding. Everything is in place and your wedding memories will be forever captured with portraits designed by ***Moments in Time Photography.***

Exciting Pictorial Session...

This sought after session, at a favorite location of your choice, has become one of the featured elements of our relationship with couples from Seattle to San Francisco.

Artistic views showcased through black and white and architectural design make this an irreplaceable memory.

Your Search...

As you search for your photographer, take the time to visit our studio. We believe that once you visit us, your search will be over and you will feel assured your wedding portraits are photographed by wedding experts.

COMMUNICATION
DESIGN
ART

www.mitstudio.com

MOSER
FINE PHOTOGRAPHY

The Storybook Wedding

319 E. Evergreen
Vancouver, Washington
(360) 699-6221, (888) 699-6221

You Have Dreamed of This Day All of Your Life

You worked hard to make everything perfect. Preserve this day forever with the ultimate in wedding photography.

Imagine…

No rushing around, no confusion and no one to intrude on your intimate moments with your friends and loved ones. We'll create the Storybook Wedding for you. You will be pampered as we create breathtaking images that you will cherish for a lifetime.

The Storybook Wedding:

Designed to give you total control and flexibility of your wedding photography, your Storybook Wedding includes:

- European-style black and white coverage
- Pre-wedding planning session
- Unlimited coverage of the wedding and reception
- Unlimited number of locations
- Unlimited number of images created
- Album design session using our unique album designing system
- Custom designed album selections to suit your needs

Custom Designed Albums

After the honeymoon, you will be blown away when you view your images in our surround sound mini theater. You will view these high impact images on a large screen set to music. After which, our album design specialist will assist you in designing your custom album as you view the album page by page on the screen.

*"**Thank you! Thank you!** Our photos are absolutely beautiful. You captured our wedding day so perfectly. We are so glad we found you and you were able to do our wedding."*

~Tina and Damon

"Thank you so much for helping our day go so smoothly. You really helped to coordinate things and keep us relaxed and enjoying the day. Thank you again."

~Kymberly and Brian

Please give us a call and let's talk about your wedding dreams.
As this couple said, you'll be glad you did!
(888) 699-6221 • (360) 699-6221

MOUNT BURNS
PHOTOGRAPHY

503.289.4234

As a photographer, my goal is to record the spirit of your wedding day by capturing the energy and spontaneity of everyone there. To accomplish this, I devote an entire day to your wedding alone so that I am able to document the events that play such an integral part in making your wedding day special.

Over twenty years professional experience enables me to capture these fleeting moments in an artful, yet unobtrusive manner. Brides and grooms, after seeing their wedding photos often comment, "We weren't even aware of you being there," and "Every time we look at our photos we see something new."

My experience also enables me to thoughtfully compose each image so that your wedding photos have a timeless feel with a strong sense of design,whether it's candids or formal portraits, making them much more than just snapshots.

These photographs are what will tell the story of your wedding day, proving to be the most important and memorable images in the years to come.

I have a variety of packages available to meet your needs. Please call to schedule an appointment to discuss your wedding photography.

For an appointment, call:

Mount Burns Photography

(503) 289-4234
e-mail: mbphoto@teleport.com

Major credit cards accepted

Northwest Weddings... Let's Have Fun!

Portland, Oregon • (800) 736-9646
By appointment, for individual service
Web site: www.northwestweddingsinc.com

The Best Prices in Town...

Great wedding photography doesn't have to cost a fortune. With every package, **you keep all the negatives** and the previews.

Wedding Packages

Group 1: 3 hours, up to 72 previews, all negatives. . . . $675

Group 2: 4 hours, up to 90 previews, all negatives. . . . $750

Group 3: 5 hours, up to 120 previews, all negatives. . . $850

Group 4: 6 hours, up to 150 previews, all negatives. . . $950

Group 5: 7 hours, up to 200 previews, all negatives. . . $1,075

(a selection of enlargements is included in groups 2–5)
Seasonal specials! Call or visit our Web site!

Great Quality...

We photograph all your formal portraits with a medium format camera for superior resolution. By including the negatives and preview prints in every package, Northwest Weddings offers a completely unique photography service. For a small garden wedding or an evening black-tie affair, you'll select from an experienced staff of professionals.

Beautiful portraits, affordable prices...It's about time.
(800) 736-9646

Videography and DJ services are also available at equally impressive prices.

WILLIAM OCELLO PHOTOGRAPHER

(503) 698-4262

Web site:
www.bravowedding.com/pdx00/williamocello

Are You Looking For...

A photographer whose signature photojournalist style includes excellent unposed candids?

An accomplished black-and-white artist who uses black and white film?

A photographer who captures beautiful photos of people who do not think they are photogenic?

An artist who treats your families with respect, and has a great sense of humor?

An artist who wants you both to enjoy the experience?

... then call William

I'll only shoot one wedding a day, so you'll have my complete attention. This helps you to enjoy a more carefree celebration, and allows me to shoot a balanced wedding. One where you both get what you want, while I use the time to photograph your families equally. I shoot light formals before the ceremony so that traditional formals will not dominate your day. This will ensure that you'll have more time to enjoy each other at the reception. I also shoot a strong ceremony in order to record the commitment you've made. And, if you wish, I'll shoot the traditional cake cutting, toast, etc., in between the many candids at the party.

I have offered black and white in addition to color images for many years. Couples have chosen to mix both, or to have their wedding photographed entirely in the uniqueness of black and white.

If you're looking for a fun, unhurried style, then call me to set up a relaxed meeting. Please remember, I never book at the first meeting in order to give you time to compare styles.

Wedding Coverage and Prices

My coverage is designed to include most situations, and I also welcome custom coverage to suit your plans.

Location and studio shoots are always available.

Why call?
Because I'll be happy to be there.

Pearl Studios

Portland, Oregon • (503) 771-6409
Business Hours: by appointment please
E-mail: pearl.studios@cwix.com
Web site:ww.pearlstudios.com

Background

Gustav Knecht, owner of Pearl Studios, has worked in cosmopolitan cities in both Europe and North America. His pictures are fresh and original, reflecting his creativity while still capturing each couple's individual personality and style. Romantic, unique, and timeless images you will never tire of. Gus is the sole photographer, so the quality images you see are the images you will get, all captured by medium format camera in color and black and white.

> ***"The pictures are fantastic! The composition of the shots including different shapes, colors and lighting are outstanding."*** — Pat and Gary Ray

Service

At Pearl Studios, every wedding is unique and special to us, with customer service as our priority before, during and after the wedding day. With two consultations before the day, we can plan everything so you can be relaxed and therefore ***enjoy*** your wedding, which is the most important thing!

> ***"Your kind, friendly, and caring way really helped us to have a fun and relaxing day! The pictures are absolutely wonderful. They are more than we could have ever hoped for."*** — Shannon and Bret VanHorn

Quality

We will ensure that your finalized album will be of the highest quality. All photographs are studio prints with color correction, not proofs. We also offer handcrafted customized prints featuring specialized borders, textures and handtinting to enhance your album. All these are created and printed by Gus himself. He enjoys all aspects of the business, from the initial meeting to the assembly of the album. This results in a beautiful album, one that has been created especially for you by someone who takes pride in his work from start to finish.

> ***"Thanks for taking the time to make our pictures special. Our families are so impressed with them, too. We actually felt like you were enjoying photographing us."*** — Janene and Paul Tamborello

Price

Choose from our set packages or let us custom design something specific to fit your needs.

P.S. Thank-you for reading about us. We hope to work with you soon.

PHOTO MEMORIES BY HARVEY

955 S.W. 193rd Court
Aloha, Oregon 97006 • Please Call for Directions
Harvey Thomas (503) 629-5605 or (800) 743-2905
Fax (503) 690-8537; E-mail: harvey@ipinc.net
Hours: Mon–Fri 8:30am–5:30pm; Sat 9am–2pm;
evenings by appointment

Wedding Packages and Prices

My hundreds of happy customers are my best advertisement:
"We couldn't have done it without you. You knew just when to do things; never intrusive, but always getting the photo." ~Eileen & Darrel Burt

"Harvey did our daughter's wedding. We had as much fun, and Harvey did as great a job as he did 26 years ago at our wedding" ~Jan & Darrel Mattoon

I offer couples a variety of choices from one to six hours of coverage, and from 24 to 120 originals. Package prices range from $325 to $1,375. I can also tailor any package to fit your needs. Come to my studio to review my work.

Services and Equipment

- 2 1/4 ideal-format cameras; professional lighting as needed.
- Full-service studio with controlled lighting and backgrounds.
- Photo requests encouraged. I'll provide you with a checklist of photo poses so you can determine all the important photos you want before the wedding day.
- I encourage formal wedding pictures be taken before the ceremony to make sure the bride and groom are thoroughly relaxed before they go down the aisle, and so there won't be any delays between the ceremony and the reception.

Previews and Reprints

I allow you to take your previews home so that you can select the photos you want in a relaxed and familiar environment. All standard sizes of reprints are available. Proofs and reprints are deluxe, professionally processed, and finished in a lab for the best quality and color. **SPECIAL INCENTIVE: if reprint orders are received within 21 days from the date the originals are delivered, you will receive a 10% discount on the reprint order. No exceptions please.**

Terms, Payment, and Additional Services

A 50% deposit is due to reserve your wedding date, with an additional 25% due by the week of the wedding. The balance is due upon receipt of your previews—usually two to three weeks after the wedding. I try to be flexible to your needs. In case of cancellation, your deposit may be applied to a later date. Moderate charges for travel outside of the metro area. I also do portraits for individuals, couples, families, and high school seniors. Invitations and accessories available at a discount.

WEDDING MEMORIES *To the bride and groom,*

Your wedding is a special day in your life. My philosophy is to capture those memories on film. By getting to know the people involved in your wedding and putting you at ease, I am able to make your loving day become a cherished and captured memory. The all-important traditional formal poses will be recorded as well as contemporary and candid memories.

~Harvey

PHOTOGRAPHY BY

PETER PAUL RUBENS

(503) 293-0467

Visit us at: www.peterpaulrubens.com

If you pride yourself on researching carefully, consider closely Peter Paul Rubens. Discover:

- A personable, friendly, yet clearly professional approach
- An image style described by brides as, "*...fresh, innovative, and romantic*"
- National award-winning, published photography

Peter is known as the "photographer's photographer" with coverages nationwide. The Chairman of Kodak wrote: "*The price seemed a small amount to pay. It was obvious that you were not only doing fine work in the overall wedding celebration, but there was evidence of true creative approaches. I thought the photographs were absolutely outstanding. You obviously are an accomplished artist.*"

Services and Equipment

Expect imaginatively composed images, blended with fresh, candid scenes. Count on a responsive approach to the look you like whether it's casual and fun, simple and elegant or stunningly grand. The most frequently chosen coverages range between $1,895 and $3,995.

- He cares—enough to learn the names of everyone in your wedding party and family.
- Quality equipment—superb, medium-format cameras, together with sophisticated candid systems. Multiple light approach for a dimensional look, as well as natural lighting.
- Skilled—Highest award for wedding photography in Oregon, 1999.
  Masters Degree: Professional Photographers of America.
- Appropriate. Peter adapts his attire from tuxedo to jacket/tie to professionally casual.
- Special procedures to ease and clarify ordering if you or family live out of town.
- Black and White option—check it out!
- Way Fun. "*...such a character. Your sense of humor is priceless*" ~D. Nicolik
- Experienced. Professional over 15 years. Reliable.
- Not a one-man show. Responsive office staff. Fast results.
- Skilled assistants provide technical support, enabling Peter to devote full attention to you.
- Studio photographs are lifetime guaranteed by the studio's lab.

You can count on a photography session that beyond being a vivid record, is a full-on good time—a session that delights in laughter and is naturally romantic. This note arrived two years after the wedding: "*The wedding album is such an unbelievable hit with everyone who sees it! I'm embarrassed you made me look so beautiful.*" ~Angela Hart

That's Photography by Peter Paul Rubens—

Unmistakably Unforgettable

PORTLAND R•E•I•G•N PHOTOGRAPHY

10823 Parkview Drive
Wilsonville, Oregon 97070
Contact: Danny or Linda Abrego
(503) 682-0811; Fax (503) 682-4567
By appointment only

Besides those beautiful memories of your wedding date, your wedding photographs and portraits are two of the few things that will stay with you for the rest of your lives. The importance of choosing the right photographer cannot be overstated.

Professionalism

Danny started Portland Reign Photography in 1990 and has slowly built a full-service studio, specializing in "people photography." Attention to detail and superior customer service are trademarks of our studio. Using medium format equipment, professional lighting and services ensures superior results. Additionally, Linda can assist you as your wedding consultant to make your planning less stressful. We are proud, active members of Professional Photographers of America, Wedding & Portrait Photographers International, and Portland Metropolitan Photographers Association.

Creative, Artistic, Distinctive

We offer a pleasant mixture of varying styles, from traditional to photojournalistic and offering black and white for a unique touch in your display portraits. Creative posing and lighting ensures that your photographic experience will result in portraits you will treasure.

Simplified Yet Dynamic

Our goal is to avoid confusing packages to choose from. Instead, we offer a simplified wedding session of five hours but we'll work with you to tailor this session to meet your exacting needs. Your wedding session includes a beautiful leather album and a photographic credit to be used to order the exact number and size of portraits you need—all at competitive prices.

Building a Relationship

Call Danny or Linda for an appointment to meet with us and view our work. This is the first step in building confidence and a relationship that will make your wedding day easier for you and your families.

PounCey Studio

Wedding Photography & Video
Bob & Linda PounCey Photographers
Call (360) 892-1565

Linda and I have worked from our home-studio as a team for more than 20 years with couples like yourselves to capture those special moments when two people promise to share their lives together. It is our desire to capture the romance, love and joy of your wedding day with our ***unique style*** of photography. With our ***classic portraiture***, we will create timeless images you will cherish for a lifetime.

What We Represent

We're flexible. We can photograph your wedding using any one or a couple of styles, or a combination of all of them.

Storybook Line—Combination of portraits and candids

Photojournalistic—Completely unposed

Color/Black and White/Classic Portraiture—All of the pictures can be taken the day of the wedding, or bridal portraits can be taken before the wedding day. All the posed pictures can be taken before the ceremony, or pictures of the bride and groom together can be made after the ceremony.

We are looking for clients who want only the most creative and artistic photographs! We insist that you have fun at your wedding, without having to leave your guests to pose for the photographer. We'll be there when you want us, while remaining somewhat invisible in the crowd. We assure you that we will listen to your wishes and respect them.

If a photograph must be posed, the people will always appear natural, graceful and relaxed—never stiff our contrived. We will photograph your wedding the way you want it done. **We keep our promises.**

If time and conditions permit, we will set up a full portrait studio on location to create beautiful classic portraits of the bride and groom and their families. Of course we use medium format and the highest quality camera equipment.

PounCey Studio offers a variety of wedding packages suitable for every budget. However, if the packages we offer do not suit your needs, **you can create your own wedding "package" from our A'la Carte price list.** You choose only the photographs you want, in the sizes and quantities you like. Add a wedding album if you wish. **The choice is yours.** Please give us a call.

Video services available. Special prices when added to your photography.

Visit our Web site at www.WeLoveWeddings.com/pouncey
E-mail: Rpouncey@aol.com and Rpouncey@juno.com

PROTHE STUDIO

PATRICK PROTHE

503.788.1440
protheweddings.com

PHOTOGRAPHY THAT CAPTURES THE SPIRIT OF YOUR BIG DAY

Your wedding day is one of the most significant events in your life. My mission is to capture the joy, emotion, spontaneity, preparation, and celebration in a collection of creative pictures that tell the story of your event.

I prefer to spend most of the time shooting candids in black and white as well as color, while incorporating a few key formal portraits. I shoot only one wedding per day, spending the entire day with you from the moment you arrive to prepare until the reception winds down and you depart.

There are no set packages as each couple is different, and there are many options for your final presentation. I meet with you and develop a package around your wish list. You end up with a binder generally containing 200–300 proofs from which we collaborate to select the images that best cature the spirit of the event. The final prints are carefully printed and packaged in either a portfolio of individually matted prints or a custom album.

The work speaks for itself. Check out protheweddings.com to review recent images. For a fresh, unique wedding portfolio, let ProtheStudio produce a creative, visual story of your Big Day.

– Patrick Prothe

ROB POWELL PHOTOGRAPHY

since 1975

Beaverton, Oregon
(503) 646-4710
Business Hours:
by appointment
E-mail: AnselRob@aol.com

"Thanks for doing such a nice job on our photos! It was great to have a photographer who was so polite to our friends and relatives." —David and Paula Lynn Olson

"Our wedding album looks so much better than others we've seen! You really helped us relax and have fun on our special day." —Paul and Chris Vincent

Honors

- National Master of Photography degree
- Oregon Fellow of Photography degree
- Numerous prints in the international traveling loan collection

Prices

My most popular plan is three hours of time with a leather-bonded album of 120 5x5 original prints and nine separate 8x10s for a total cost of $625. Other options are available. I can send you a complete list by mail, E-mail or fax.

Reprints

Reorders are not required. If you would like additional photos, my prices are lower than most: 5x5=$8; 5x7=$10; 8x10=$15. I can make print sizes from wallets through 40x60. Complete retouching is available, including new digital techniques.

Free Studio Portrait

For any couple using three or more hours on their wedding day. Includes up to one hour of studio photography and eight 4x5 original prints, at no extra charge! Please wear your gown. If you wish, bring loved ones and relatives to be photographed with you.

Experience and Qualifications

In the last 25 years, I have personally photographed over 750 weddings. In that time I have never failed to show up as scheduled for a wedding. I have never sent out a substitute photographer in my place, and I have never ruined or lost wedding film. You can depend on me.

I Believe in Marriage

My wife Roberta and I have been joyfully married since April 12th, 1980—20 happy years! We wish the same blessing for you. The vows you take will be sacred and permanent, and I will act in a supportive and respectful manner on your wedding day. I truly enjoy seeing a man and woman in love give their lives to each other. I would be honored to join your celebration.

May God bless your engagement... *—Rob Powell, M. Photog.*

Raleigh Bennett, Master Photographer
Lois Bennett, Consultant and Photographer
Call (503) 646-4624 for additional information

Who is Raleigh ?

Raleigh and Lois Bennett, owners of Raleigh Studios, have been creating visual magic from their home-studio for more than 22 years. In that time, Raleigh has specialized in beautiful story-telling weddings and elegant portraits wall decor. Raleigh and Lois are committed to photographic excellence and superior client service. Careful planning and attention to detail are a key to client satisfaction and are some of the many differences that separate Raleigh and Lois from all the others…

Your Love Story

The two of you met, fell in love, and that love has grown to the love you now share. Your Love Story, on the beach, in the mountains, or at the park is designed with you to reflect that special time and the feelings that are a part of it. With Raleigh's sensitive and artistic approach, your romance and the feelings you share will be captured forever…

Your Wedding Story

The most beautiful and elegant Wedding Stories are illustrated by Raleigh. The love you share, the special time spent with family and friends, the traditional and creative moments, as well as those spontaneous candids, will all be captured with a unique style and elegance. Your wedding story will be ready for your "album design session" on our Album Arranger Computer within five days of your wedding. With the very latest computer technology you will design and visualize your completed wedding album. Visit our studio today and see this fantastic process…

What You Can Expect From Raleigh

…Wedding photographs with a unique style and elegance.
…Beautiful portraits of loved ones.
…Photographs created in an informal, relaxed atmosphere.
…Sensitivity to your needs and desires.
…Meticulous planning and careful attention to detail.

Member:
Weddings of Distinction
Wedding Photographers International
Professional Photographers of Oregon
Professional Photographers of America
Portland Metro Photographers Association

red door studio

(360) 699-0604

Web site: www.reddoorstudio.com

"the truth about weddings"

No, this is not your typical wedding photography. We don't feel that it's our role to orchestrate the events of your day or ask the two of you to strike silly, contrived poses to create stiff, cheesy portraits. (Besides, grooms really hate that stuff!) We believe you want something a little more honest and artistic than that. Weddings are filled with so many visual and emotional nuances that there is no need to fictionalize them. We choose instead to use our skills as photographic storytellers to simply recognize and record those genuine moments on film, quietly capturing traditions, rituals and interpersonal relationships in their purest form. It's about telling the truth. What we offer you in the end is a full album, a fine-art photographic journal, filled with moving images that tell your own unique story.

"the essence of black and white"

Black and white is the signature look that defines the journalistic story of your wedding. Bold, crisp and infinitely detailed, the black and white image beholds a timeless, classic quality that ordinary color simply cannot match. Formals are photographed on color film, at your request. Our price is not based on number of hours, prints or rolls of film. We work on an all-inclusive fee that includes two photographers, all day. Complete, meticulous coverage.

"the book"

Designed exclusively by red door studio, the wedding journal is an art piece worthy of display. Each page bears a single image, leaving you to ponder and reflect on each precious moment individually. Custom printed by the artists, every photograph exudes an exquisite tonal quality that far surpasses that of even the most respected professional labs. Available in classic black and white, or warm brown sepia, both styles are bound in an album of the richest Napa leather we could find. Simple, yet classic styling. They're heirloom quality, as we want future generations to derive as much pleasure from them as you will.

"the sophisticated bride"

You made it possible for me to express my joy naturally...each picture is filled with so much life and emotion...this was the best wedding present we could have given ourselves.

Allison and Reuben Johnson, 8/16/97

We were thinking of the future when choosing red door studio. It was money well spent... a quality journal of life that we can share with our family for generations to come.

Nancy and Jamie Anderson, 7/18/98

Each time we open our book, we relive the most perfect day of our lives.

Chris and Eric Hubbard, 7/6/96

We invite you to experience the ***red door studio*** difference.

remembrance
Photography

stephen b. hamilton, photographer

by appointment please (503) 957-7758

Artistic and Unique

I use my background in fine art to capture the moments of your day creatively. I have created both black and white sepia-toned, infrared, and color images for 15 years. I feel that the dramatic and timeless qualities of black and white bring out the couple's personality on film. Most clients ask me to combine this with color images to create a combination of images that you will love to look at over and over again in years to come. I also offer unique 3-D stereoscopic packages—remember Viewmaster?

Candid and Natural

My goal is to photograph each couple being themselves, and guests participating, laughing and enjoying the day. I believe in catching the moments as they happen, and only stepping in to pose shots when truly necessary (as in formal and group shots) to catch the real emotion and feeling of the day.

Friendly and Relaxed

The presence of a photographer should not distract your guests or interfere with the natural flow of the day. I believe in catching the events of the day in an easygoing and friendly manner, to help make the experience as non-stressed as possible.

Professional and Experienced

I have been a professional photographer for 10 years, after receiving my B.F.A. degree in photography in 1989. I use a mixture of medium format and 35mm professional cameras and studio lighting and flashes. To ensure quality and custom enlargements, I do my own darkroom work and use black and white film for all black and white photographs.

Packages

All packages include full coverage of your event and 120 proofs which you keep. My negatives are also available for purchase. A $200 deposit holds your date, and 10% of my proceeds are donated to charities.

I'd like to meet with you to discuss your photographic needs, and to show you samples of my work.

(503) 957-7758

Sharper Image
PHOTOGRAPHY

930 N.E. 75th Avenue
Portland, Oregon 97213
Contact: Gary Cornilles
(503) 539-0215
Business Hours:
By Appointment Only

Flexible Coverage

We know that not every couple wants the same thing when it comes to wedding coverage. So, we offer several unique packages that allow you flexibility to create the perfect album. For larger formal events, we offer several packages with combinations of prints, albums, wall portraits, and parent albums starting at $1,295. A private consultation is recommended to personally view our collection of sample albums and wall portraits. Consultations are available by appointment and can be arranged to fit your busy schedule.

Studio Information and Equipment

- Full-time professional photographer with 14 years of experience.
- Family-owned and -operated from comfortable home studio.
- Centrally located minutes from downtown Portland.
- All medium-format equipment/studio quality lighting.
- Computerized album design.
- Fine art custom black-and-white prints available.

Reserving your Wedding Date

Because dates fill up very quickly during the spring and summer months, we recommend booking your date as soon as you possibly can. Typically, six to nine months in advance is advised though not always necessary. Please call for availability. A deposit of $250 will reserve your exclusive date/time. All services are reserved by contract.

Capturing Memories

"On one of the most important days of your life, we want you to have it all! Let us capture these memories in a way that you will never forget! The love, the humor, the family, and all the little things are what we ***focus*** on."

www.sharperphoto.com

E-mail: garyc@teleport.com

Strong photography

www.strongphotography.com
(503) 249-7575

Don't Say "Cheese."

There's no reason to spend your wedding day doing things you "have to do" instead of celebrating with those you love. Unfortunately, many brides and grooms (and photographers) miss out on some of the best moments of a wedding day because of an emphasis on posing for (and shooting) long lists of pre-planned photos—before, during, and after the ceremony and reception. Thankfully, there is another option that is becoming increasingly sought after: journalistic-style wedding photography that incorporates a modest number of portraits, yet stresses honest and genuine (not cheesy, frozen-grin) photographs. This style—including an emphasis on dramatic black-and-white, fine art images—is the focus of Strong Photography.

"We Didn't Want Any Stiffly Posed or Phony Pictures..."

"We were looking for a photographer who could capture the mood and spirit of our wedding," says Leslie Constans. "We didn't want any stiffly posed or phony pictures—we wanted real emotion and spontaneity. That's what was appealing about Craig Strong's photojournalistic style. We never felt nervous or on the spot, as people often do around professional photographers, because Craig blended into the background. In fact, we often didn't realize he was taking photos. The result: he captured some wonderful private moments and emotions that I don't think would have been possible otherwise."

Creative. Artistic. Honest. Different.

The most joyful weddings are the ones that allow the bride and groom time and freedom to experience, savor, and celebrate. These are the days best served by a photojournalist's touch. Strong Photography is not interested in shooting every wedding in town and won't take an assignment if it's not a good match. Craig Strong is dedicated to chronicling the stories of couples who share a vision for spontaneity, honesty, art, and beauty.

If that's you, give Strong Photography a call. Check out Craig Strong's portfolio and references. You just may decide to entrust your memories to an award-winning photojournalist. Then there's nothing left to do but relax, bask in the moment, and focus on the things that truly matter to you—your marriage, your family and friends… and each other.

Visa, MasterCard, American Express, and Discover accepted.

THROUGH A LOOKING GLASS by Gayle

Contact: Gayle Hoffman-Aman (503) 524-3544
Business Hours: by appointment

...for photography that does much more than simply document your wedding; it helps you re-experience each unique moment.

It's part of wedding tradition to have a series of posed, formal photographs. But in order to remember your wedding with the warmth and spontaneity of that special day, you should have the creative touch of THROUGH A LOOKING GLASS...to remember the proud look on a father's face as he escorts his daughter down the aisle, or the gleeful smile of a child being asked to dance.

THROUGH A LOOKING GLASS provides a one-of-a-kind photographic memento of the entire wedding experience—literally from rehearsal to reception—or anything in-between. We work with the bride and groom ahead of time to make sure nothing is overlooked—neither traditional elements nor the creative, unique features you've added just for your wedding. Advance planning assures that the natural, spontaneous, personal moments you'll want to save will be captured forever.

Call THROUGH A LOOKING GLASS by Gayle to see photography that is special and unique...the kind of pictures you should have of your wedding.

Wedding Packages and Prices

Packages are tailored to fit your individual needs. Prices include consultation, photographer's time, all the processing, original proofs and negatives. *You own all the negatives and all the proofs!* You can do your own reprints and enlargements or we will gladly handle it for you. Complete packages begin at $600. If you want, additional time can be added, billed at half-hour increments. You can also add more film, charged at a flat per-roll rate which includes processing, *all your original proofs and negatives*. Travel time within the Portland/Vancouver area is included. A price list for enlargements, albums and gift folios is available upon request.

Terms and Payment

Services should be booked as far in advance as possible. A $300 deposit is required, with the balance due upon receipt of the proofs and negatives. At the time of booking you will be given a clearly written, signed agreement summarizing and guaranteeing services to be provided. Your deposit or booking fee is subtracted from the invoice and, in the case of cancellation, is fully refundable if the date and time can be rebooked.

Woodstock PHOTOGRAPHY

4416 S.E. Woodstock Boulevard
Portland, Oregon 97206
(503) 771-8171
John Bernunzio, photographer
www.woodstockphotography.com
Visa and MasterCard accepted

My responsibility to my clients on their wedding day is to devote my full attention to them. By planning carefully, paying attention to details, and offering black and white and color images in artistic, traditional and photojournalistic styles, I make sure the expectations of the bride and groom are exceeded—not just met.

Couples remember me because I work closely with them to find out what thoughts they have about their wedding photography. I am always interested in any ideas the couples may have, because I can produce my best work if I know what is important to the bride and groom. For example, sometimes I'll talk to a bride who doesn't want to be seen by the groom on her wedding day until she walks down the aisle, and she will ask me if that's okay. I respond by saying, "Sure. It's your wedding, and I'm working for you."

I am best known for my ability to capture the details and candid moments of that special day. As much as I enjoy creating the formal group photos and the portraits of the bride and groom, I love the spontaneous images of people visiting and little kids playing. After all, the wedding is a celebration shared with family and friends, and so should the memories—the history—be shared and preserved through photography.

The styles and techniques used in wedding photography have changed over the years. However, one aspect that hasn't changed is the importance a bride and groom place on the quality of the photographs taken on their wedding day.

You are encouraged to invest some time visiting with me at the studio where you can review some of my work, and we can talk about your wedding photography needs.

~ John Bernunzio

Notes

RENTAL ITEMS AND EQUIPMENT

© red door studio • page 520

AISLE RUNNER

The red carpet and white aisle runner are vestiges of the many fanciful ways that brides were kept "walking on air."

HELPFUL HINTS

- **Rental stores carry almost everything**, from candelabras to coffee makers. They feature specialty wedding items for your ceremony and reception. You'll find such things as serviceware, portable bars, arches, tents, chairs, tables and all the tableware, dishes, glassware, flatware, and much more. Many shops also carry disposable paper products, decorations, and a selection of bridal accessories.
- **Visit a rental shop while planning:** It's smart to visit a showroom for ideas and to see the types and styles of merchandise and equipment in stock. Brochures describe all the different items available for rent: style, colors, sizes and prices. Rental shops are also a terrific place to obtain decorating ideas. Meet with one of the shop's consultants and go through your wedding plans step-by-step. You'll find they will help you select just the right wedding items to suit your style and taste, as well as help you determine quantities needed.
- **Decide on formality and budget:** Keep in mind the colors and decor of the site. Pick linens or paper products and tableware that will complement the room. Prices vary depending on the formality you choose; cloth linens will be more expensive than disposable tablecloths.
- **Rental items for all occasions:** Don't forget the rental store for all your wedding-related party needs—rehearsal dinner, showers, bachelor and bachelorette parties, birthdays, anniversaries and theme parties.
- **Deposits, delivery, and setup:** Reserve your items as far in advance as possible, especially during the summer months when outdoor weddings are popular. A deposit will secure the order for your date. There are only a certain number of heart-shaped candelabras available, and every item is reserved on a first-come, first-served basis. There is a charge on most items for delivery, setup, and pickup. Make sure you ask in advance how much those charges are so you can include them in your budget. You can also make arrangements to pick up and return the items yourself.
- **Tent rental:** A tent often serves as an ideal back up location for an outdoor event, in case of unsuitable weather conditions. many tents feature transparent vinyl siding that can be raised and lowered as needed. A tent supplier can recommend sources for any portable heating or air conditioning that you might need.

  Important note: Never use canvas tents treated with mineral oil for waterproofing, they are extremely flammable.
- **Tent capacities:** The following are estimated capacities for tents of typical sizes under normal conditions:

Tent Size	*Reception*	*Accommodates Buffet w/ seating*	*Sit-down Dinner*
16′ x 16′	45	32	24
20′ x 20′	65	56	40
20′ x 30′	100	86	60
30′ x 30′	180	124	100
40′ x 40′	350	280	240

- **Choosing a tent site:** When arranging tents with a single transparent vinyl side, consider the position of the sun during your event; if the clear portion faces due west through an evening reception, the sunset may be blinding. Also, be certain that you do not pitch your tent over low or uneven ground that might accumulate water runoff. **Returning items:** If you don't arrange delivery and pickup services with the rental company, you will want to put someone in charge of picking up and returning the rented items for you. You will be responsible and may forfeit any deposit for items that are damaged, broken, lost, or late.

Custom Chair Covers

The Pacific Northwest's Original Chair Cover Rental Company

28 "U" Place N.E. • Auburn, Washington 98002
(800) 994-1055 • (253) 939-7119

AFFORDABLE ELEGANCE
for
"The Discriminating Bride"

We Can Bring Your Ideas to Life...

Let us help you bring your ideas and party theme to life with chair covers that will make your special event extraordinary, not ordinary.

- Rehearsal Dinner
- Wedding Reception
- Birthday
- Anniversary
- Holiday Party
- Special Event

With Custom Chair Covers Designed to Match Your Colors and Theme...

We work with you to coordinate all the decor with chair covers accented with flowers or decorative bows.

Accented With Festive Bows to Finish the Look...

At Custom Chair Covers, we provide you with a variety of matching or contrasting bows or sashes that will complement and enhance your wedding colors and theme. Match them to your flowers or table linens as well as the room decor.

Custom Chair Covers
Making Ordinary Chairs... Extraordinary

For Rental or Sales Information,
Please Call: (800) 994-1055

Custom Decor Wedding & Party Rentals

Reed Opera House Mall
189 Liberty N., Suite 208
Salem, Oregon 97301
Contact: Jane Huntley (503) 585-7522
Hours: Tues–Thurs 1:30pm–5:30pm;
or by appointment

Rental Items Available

We specialize in renting unique items for event decorating.

- **Specialty table linens:** excellent selection of round cloths in solid colors, florals, prints, damask, and moiré; square overlays in coordinating colors and florals; banquet cloths; lace cloths in several colors and sizes; napkins also available
- **Tabletop decor:** metal bird cages, hats, baskets, vases in all sizes, rose bowls, chimneys, candleholders, candles, wreaths, mirrored squares, etc.
- **Wedding baskets:** baskets in all shapes and sizes for floral arrangements or food service; pedestal baskets with or without silk-flower arrangements; large, antique, freestanding wicker baskets
- **Silk plants and dried flowers:** ficus and topiary trees, table arrangements, silk altar arrangements in freestanding white wicker baskets, garlands, and more
- **Other rental items** include a wonderful wrought iron bench and table and chair set perfect for the garden wedding; wicker settee, wrought iron candelabra, trellis, parasols, money trees, wall decor, pedestals, flower boxes, etc.

Bridal Accessories

We carry a selection of wedding planners, shower guides, guest books, pens, albums, garters, ring-bearer pillows, aisle runners, cake knives and servers, and toasting goblets.

Special Services

At Custom Decor Rentals we specialize in decorating for private parties, proms, class reunions, rehearsal dinners, weddings, receptions, and meetings. We can show you what to do, or do it for you! We are not limited to decorating, but can also offer individualized service in handling many of the details involved in coordinating your event.

THE PERSONAL TOUCH FOR YOUR SPECIAL OCCASION

If you have an idea, we will make it work. If you have a need, we will make it happen. We pay attention to every detail to make sure everything is just right.

A TO Z PARTY RENTAL

995 Commercial Street, S.E.
Salem, Oregon 97302
Business Hours: Mon–Sat 7:30am–5:30pm; Sun noon–4pm
(503) 585-7782; Fax (503) 362-8647

A to Z Party Rental is a full-service, special event supplier. Our large inventory of equipment and supplies will ensure a successful event.

Knowledgeable Staff

Our staff will work with you to sort out the details for your event. Years of experience are at your disposal with proven success. You can count on receiving your rentals and purchases as ordered and ready for use with no worries or hassles. Our job is to make you a guest of your own party or event.

Ordering and Delivery

Our delivery rates are determined per zone and amount of time and man-power required.

Equipment and Accessories

- Tables and chairs
- Canopies
- Candelabras and pew abras
- Fencing and panels
- Audiovisuals
- Food preparation equipment
- Barbecues and crab pots
- Silk arrangements
- China and glassware
- Cutlery
- Arches
- Party lighting
- Chafers, trays, salad bars
- Stanchions, traffic cones
- Balloon bouquets
- *Please call for complete list*

Merchandise

- Items available in 23 colors:
  Plates, cups, napkins, cutlery, tablecovers, and tablerolls
- Balloons, balloon bouquets, candles, and arches also available

**We Can Special Order Merchandise For You—
Ask For Details!**

DELIVERY SERVICE AVAILABLE

BBR

BARBUR BLVD. RENTALS, INC.

• 246·4268 •

8205 S.W. Barbur Boulevard • Portland, Oregon 97219
Fax (503) 246-9375
Business Hours: Mon–Sat 7:30am–6pm; Sun 8am–4pm

Rental Items Available

- **Wedding accessories:** brass or white candelabras in various sizes, tables candelabra, flower stands, arches, arbors, new natural wood arch, kneeling benches, gazebo, balloons and helium tanks. New! Luminaries—special occasion designs candleabra 2'–3' centerpieces in a variety of styles and colors—this is a must see!
- **Serviceware:** silverplate: trays, punch bowls, coffee and tea service, bowls, candy dishes, serving utensils, chafers, cake and knife servers, goblets, champagne buckets. Glassware: punchbowls with ladle, large trays, serving bowls, chafers
- **Tables and chairs:** round, half-round, rectangle and square tables, umbrella tables, white wood and brown folding chairs; stacking chairs; Chiavari chairs; white bistro; white samsonite, poker tables, folding picnic tables
- **Glassware:** large assortment; champagne, wine and cocktail, and crystal
- **China:** white, black and clear; ivory with gold trim
- **Flatware:** stainless and silverplate
- **Linens:** over 20 colors; table covers, napkins, lace overlays, skirting
- **Beverage service:** bar, beer taps, beverage fountains, champagne/wine cooler, coffee makers (30-100 cup); new portable bar, power taps, and margarita machines
- **Decorations:** balloons, streamers, and special luminaries

Speciality Rental Items

Champagne fountains, water display, cake fountain, gold accessories, various glass and candle centerpieces, brass wedding canopy, white pillars, two and three-tiered trays. Pipe and drape in various colors; lattice panels.

Retail Party Goods

Plastic tablecloths; large assortment of colors in round and banquet sizes; matching silverware and cups; napkins: dinner, lunch and beverage in all colors; napkin imprinting available. Balloons, streamers, and luminaries; special designs for birthdays, showers and anniversaries.

Tents and Canopies

All white canopies; all sizes (10'x10' to 60'x180'). Legcovers in white, sleeves in various colors.

Professional Assistance for 40 Years

Family-owned and operated, Barbur Blvd. Rentals takes pride in providing quality merchandise, equipment and service. Our experienced personnel are available to answer your questions, will special order upon request and share their knowledge and ideas. Let Barbur Blvd. Rentals help make your event extra special.

THE PARTY PRO'S AT FOSTER RENTALS

5100 S.E. Foster Road • Portland, Oregon 97206
(503) 774-5508; Fax (503) 774-8563

THE PARTY PRO'S

2460 N.E. Griffin Oaks Street Suite 1500 • Hillsboro, Oregon 97124
(503) 844-9798; Fax (503) 844-2902

Business Hours: Mon–Sat 9am–5:30pm
E-mail: PARTYPRO1@juno.com • Web site: www.THEPARTYPROS.com

Rental Items Available

- **Wedding accessories:** gazebo; arbors, arches, lattice screens, guestbook stands, Grecian pillars, urns, wicker flower stands, kneeling benches, brass candelabra (several styles), candlelighters, silver tabletop candelabra, a wide selection of centerpiece bowls and decorations for floating flowers or candles.
- **Tents and canopies:** many sizes to fit your needs
- **Serving pieces:** punch bowls; chafing dishes; acrylic, stainless and silver: bowls, trays, tongs, spoons and servers; silver tea service; stainless flatware
- **Glassware:** champagne, punch, coffee, rocks, wine, water, or specialty
- **China:** sophisticated ivory with gold trim, or simple clear glass
- **Tables and chairs:** banquet and round tables; Samsonite folding chairs and white wood folding chairs
- **Linens:** fine-quality linens available in many different colors; banquet, 90″ round, 120″ round, napkins and skirting
- **Beverage service:** champagne fountains, coffee makers, insulated beverage dispensers, carafes, pitchers and beer taps

Specialty Wedding Retail Items

Custom silk flower bouquets, wishing wells, decorations, centerpieces and ideas galore. Wedding invitations, imprinted napkins, matchbooks and ribbons. Mylar and latex balloons in many colors as well as curling ribbons.

Retail Paper, Plastic and Disposable Items

Paper tableware: floral and solid plates, cups and napkins. Plastic cups, cutlery, glasses, tablecloths, skirting, bowls and trays. Dripless candles in many colors. Cake tops, plume pens, guest books, unity candles. Beautiful pew and flower bows.

Full-service, On-site Decorating Service

Were you wondering how to decorate your reception site, church, house or backyard to complete the feeling for your wedding? We will meet you at your location to design the decorations to best fit the location with the ambiance you would like to create. The day of the wedding we will take care of everything from setup to cleanup. References are available on request.

Ordering and Delivery

Reservations are highly recommended to guarantee item availability for your special event. We are happy to deliver and pick up. Please call our party consultants for an estimate.

NO STANDARD IS TOO HIGH!

Our ultimate goal is total customer satisfaction during and after the hustle and bustle of your wedding or event planning. Large or small, we can make it happen for you!

INTERSTATE *Special Events*

5420 N. Interstate Avenue
Portland, Oregon 97217-4597
(503) 285-6685

Tents and Canopies

Whether rain or shine is predicted for your wedding day, our white canopies will dress up your wedding and reception. Sizes begin at 10'x10'. We have many accessories to help create an elegant and finished look for your special day. These include fabric pole sleeves, dance floor, white liner, cathedral window siding, lighting and much more.

Tables and Chairs

We offer banquet, round, half-round, umbrella, bistro, and even stylish serpentine tables. One of our experts will help you determine your size and quantity needs. Classic white wood chairs are available, as well as folding Samsonites, white patio and Bistro, and black, padded stacking chairs. And don't forget—we have one-of-a-kind wedding table linens!

Wedding Accessories

Select from different styles of floor brass candelabra, brass and white wood arches, white Grecian pillars, and white lattice panels. Some of our centerpieces include 14" hurricane lamps, glass floral bowls, and 29" five-branch candelabra. Dance floors available in oak or classic black and white.

Tableware

We offer linen tablecloths, napkins, and skirting in a wide variety of colors and sizes as well as ivory and white lace. China styles include classic white, elegant ivory with gold band, and clear glass. Glassware includes styles for any reception need. Stainless and silverplate flatware and serving accessories are available.

Serviceware

We have many silverplate items such as tea services, trays, punch bowls, chafing dishes, as well as vases and bowls in glass, stainless, acrylic, and silver.

Beverage Service

We offer porta bars, beermeisters, beverage fountains, kegtainers, coffeemakers and carafes, pitchers, and insulated dispensers.

Retail and Disposables

Over 20 solid colors to choose from in paper plates, napkins, table covers, table rolls, cups, and balloons.

Ordering and Delivery

Reservations are most definitely recommended to ensure availability and assist us in meeting your needs. A deposit and rental fee are due upon receipt of the equipment. Affordable and convenient delivery, as well as setup services, are available. Please call for a price quote.

❤ Member of Weddings of Distinction

The Party Place

A DIVISION OF PORTLAND RENT ALL

***Eastside:** 10101 S.E. Stark, Portland, Oregon (503) 252-3466*
***Westside:** 8904 S.W. Canyon Road, Portland, Oregon (503) 292-8875*

Web site: www.portlandrentall.com

TENTS AND CANOPIES

Sizes range from 10′x10′ to our new 60′x160′ New Century Tent. Styled with futuristic elegance, this beautiful tent will provide the right atmosphere to your next event. Also available: sidewall, liners, pole covers, lighting, heating, air conditioning and generators. Larger tent sizes available.

STAGING AND DANCE FLOOR

- Staging and stage skirting
- Dance floor available in wood parquet or black and white check.

TABLES AND CHAIRS

- 6′ and 8′ Banquet Tables
- Conference Tables
- 30″, 36″, 48″, 60″, 72″ Round Tables
- Card and Serpentine Tables
- Childrens Tables
- White and Black Wood Folding Chairs
- Resin Black and White Bistro Chairs
- Brown, White or Ivory Samsonite Folding Chairs
- Black Stack Chairs (padded)
- Elegant Chivari Chairs
- Childrens Chairs

LINENS AND SERVICEWARE

- 46 colors available
- Banquet Cloths (60″x120″)
- 90″, 108″, 120″ Rounds
- Card Table Cloths
- Elegant Gathered Skirting or Box Skirts (prints also available)
- Chafers in Plain Stainless, Brass Trim
- Stainless or Silver Serviceware
- Stainless and Silver Trays (variety of sizes)
- Serving Bowls in Plastic, Glass or Silver
- Other Silver Pieces and Gold Holloware
- Coffee Makers and Insulated Dispensers

CHINA, GLASSWARE AND FLATWARE

Our china styles include Clear Glass, White, Ivory with a Gold Band, White with a Silver Band and Black Octagonal. We also offer a wide variety of glassware options, such as Crystal, Cutglass or Black Stem and our standard glass barware. From Margaritas to Martinis, you'll find the glassware you're looking for. Flatware styles available are plain stainless, hammered stainless or silverplate.

WEDDING ACCESSORIES

- Kneeling Benches
- Pew Candelabras
- Guest Book Stands
- White Wishing Well
- Gazebo
- Aisle Runners
- Candle Holders
- Money Tree
- Table and Floor Candelabras
- Brass and White Wood Arbors
- Flower Bowls and Mirrors
- Columns and Flower Stands

WEDDING MERCHANDISE

- Paper Bells and Streamers
- Centerpieces
- Trays and Bowls
- Favor Ideas
- Balloons
- Invitations
- Doilies
- Wedding Organizers
- Wedding and Guest Books
- Paper Plates and Napkins
- Paper and Plastic Table Covers
- Plastic Flatware, Cups, Plates

Snead's PARTY TIME Rentals & Decorations
"ONE STOP PARTY SHOP"

141st & Tualatin Valley Highway
Beaverton, Oregon 97005
(503) 641-6778
Mon–Sat 7:30am–6pm; Sun 8am–4:30pm

Rental Items Available *(call for free brochure)*

- **Wedding accessories:** Arches, arbors, gazebos, flower stands, pillars, pedestals, and columns. Candelabra: brass in 12 styles, pew, spiral, and heart shapes (some styles in white, silver, and pewter), silver and brass table candelabra. Centerpieces: rose bowls, brandy snifters, champagne glasses for floating candles or flowers, marbles and mirrors, socialite votive holders with pastel candle rings.
- **Tableware:** Tables: banquet, round, heart, serpentine, card, and cocktail. Chairs: white folding, bistro and samsonite. China: ivory, white, and black. Flatware: stainless or silverplate. Glassware: stemware, lead crystal, black stem, and barware. Linens: 22 colors, banquet, round or cardtable. Napkins. Skirting: four styles.
- **Serviceware:** Trays, bowls, candy and nut dishes, and food servers. Chafers, food warmers, and prep. equipment, champagne or wine coolers. Cake knife and servers.
- **Beverage service:** Silver, gold, glass punch bowls, fountains, goblets, coffee and tea service. Coffee makers and servers. Bars, beer dispensers and taps.

Specialty Rental Items

- **For the wedding:** White heart-shaped arbor. Chuppa canopy. White and gray carpet aisle runners. Bride's full-length mirror. Guest-book stands. Kneeling benches. Ornate white bird cage. Silk flower church bouquets: 11 colors. Lighted ficus trees, flowering trees, ivy and floral garlands. Sound systems. Camcorders.
- **For the reception:** ***Antique*** silver table items. Deluxe white canopies in many sizes and white, silky, linen canopy liners and leg drapes. 16′ white market umbrella. Dance floors: outdoor and indoor, oak or white. Staging, lighting, and fountains. Umbrella tables and umbrellas, barbecues, and helium tanks.

Wedding Accessories, Invitations, Disposables, and Balloons

- Huge selection of **Paper Tableware**: 22 colors, wedding patterns plus florals. **Plastic Tableware**: plates, trays, tablecovers, barware and more. **Favors–Ribbons–Candles–Books**: mini champagne glasses, floral ribbon and bows, ice sculpture molds, candelabra and unity candles, guest books, toasting glasses and more. **Wedding Decorations**: garlands, streamers, bells, confetti, signs, banners and more. **Balloons**: 45 colors in 2 sizes. We rent heart and column frames with lights. **Helium**: we rent 8 sizes. We teach you how to decorate with balloons. **Invitations**: large selection. ***See invitations in this book***. **Imprinting is our specialty!** Quality imprinting in our store of your napkins, matches, ribbon etc. Assorted type styles and colors, wedding symbols, emblems. Fast service!

FOR A PERFECT WEDDING, VISIT SNEAD'S

Advance reservations and delivery available. Serving West Portland for 34 years. Our staff will make your event ours...by providing service and quality products at reasonable prices. Receive a 10% discount on ***wedding rental items*** with this book!

SPECIAL EVENTS CO.

79 S.W. Oak Street
Portland, Oregon 97204
(503) 222-1664
Fax: (503) 222-1047
Business Hours: Mon–Sat 8am–6pm
Since 1958

Tents and Canopies

- Canopies from sizes 10'x10' up to 100'x100'
- Chiffon canopy liners & pole sleeves
- Clear canopy tops
- Sidewall: clear, white & windows
- Lighting & generators
- Flooring
- Heating & air conditioning

Dance Floor/Staging

- Wood parquet dance floor
- Black & white checkered dance floor
- Stage risers
- Stage carpet & skirting

Tables and Chairs

- 4', 6' & 8' banquet tables
- 24", 30", 36", 48", 60", & 72" round tables
- Umbrella tables with umbrellas
- Bistro resin chairs: white or black
- Folding chairs: white, black or brown
- White wood folding chairs
- Black padded stack chairs
- Gold Chivari chairs, ivory cushion

Linen

- Various colors & sizes
- Banquet & round linens
- Cloth table skirting
- Table runners
- Napkins: solid & damask
- Patterns: fleur de leis, grape damask white rose damask, floral Monet
- Lace & gold lame cloths
- White linen chair covers
- Aisle runners

China, Glassware and Flatware

- China: ivory with gold rim, white, white lace & glass
- Flatware: silver & stainless
- Glassware & stemware: many styles

Serviceware

- Silver five-piece coffee service
- Champagne fountains & punch bowls
- Barware, blenders & bar accessories
- Silver serving trays & bowls
- Portable bars & beermeisters
- Coffee makers
- Silver or gold plate chargers
- Chafers: silver & stainless

Wedding Specialty Items

- Gazebos: lattice & wrought iron
- Arches: lattice & wrought iron
- Picket fencing & lattice panels
- Guest book stands
- Candelabras: floor, table, pew
- Water fountains
- Audiovisual, lighting, & sound systems
- Grecian columns
- Floral & candle stands
- Centerpieces & vases
- Ficus trees, floral garlands
- Market umbrellas
- Candle lighters & unity candles
- *and much, much more!*

Special Events Co. offers a spectacular variety of rental items. Our company is dedicated to quality service at affordable prices. We have 40 years of industry expertise and event planning to ensure a successful event. Our staff can assist you in design and implementation of your wedding needs. Delivery, pickup and decorating services are also available.

West Coast
EVENT PRODUCTIONS, INC.

1400 N.W. 15th Avenue
Portland, Oregon 97209
(503) 294-0412; Fax (503) 294-0616
Business Hours: Mon–Sat 8:30am–6pm
Appointments available any hour

Services

West Coast Event Productions is the Northwest's premier idea center for all events and special occasions. We specialize in the custom planning and design of event staging, lighting, sound, special effects, audiovisual presentations, tabletop décor, and event and theme production. We are able to tailor your event or special occasion to mirror your vision. We are here to help you make all your important event planning decisions. Please feel free to visit our newly designed showroom. Browse for ideas with our Photo Inventory Books. We have many of our specialty props, catering items and equipment displayed to aid in your event planning.

Rental Items Available

Tents and canopies: Sizes range from 10′ x 10′ to 100′ x 200′+ and vary in color from solid white to striped red, green, blue or yellow. Custom tent decorating includes elegant fabric liner, fabric tent pole covers in any color, floral garlands, ambient tent lighting and twinkle lights. French and Cathedral window sidewalls, heaters, air conditioning and flooring are also available.

Wedding accessories: Select from several styles of candelabras, brass and silver table candelabras, brass and contemporary full standing candelabras; wedding aisle and carpet runners; custom chuppah; gazebos and arches; wood, ceramic, marble finish and Grecian columns; table accessories include urns, vases, hurricanes, votives, cherubs and table lamps.

Tables and chairs: Choose from our complete selection of tables and chairs in a variety of sizes and styles: White wood garden chairs, black wood chairs, gold ballroom chairs, folding and stacking chairs. ***Ask about our new specialty chair covers.***

China, flatware, glassware and serviceware: Impressive selection of china in 14 different patterns: ivory with gold, white, black octagon and clear octagon. Solid colors in red, yellow, blue and green, formal bone china, contemporary patterns. Stainless, silverplate and goldplate flatware. Glassware for every occasion. Catering items for food service and many other items available.

Sound system, lighting and audiovisual: Complete array of sound equipment from amplifiers, microphone and mixing counsels to high-end data projectors. We offer a variety of unique lighting fixtures and special effects for outdoor receptions.

Stage and dance floor: An assortment of floors from elegant oak parquet to black and white or colored checks. Elevated foundations for ceremony, head table riser and entertainment—all attractively carpeted and skirted.

Portland now has *Skydancers! Skydancers* are 20-foot tall brightly colored tubular balloon people that dance and sway under a large turbine fan. As seen at the 1998 Super Bowl. Perfect for grand openings and high profile events. Available through West Coast Event Rental Department.

When Traveling

Newlyweds were thought to be particularly vulnerable while traveling, so tin cans, horns and other noisemakers were tied to the carriage or wagon to create such a racket that evil spirits would be scared away.

HELPFUL HINTS

- **Renting a limousine:** Everyone enjoys the experience of riding in a luxury limousine at least once in a lifetime. It can be the final touch that makes your wedding day or event complete, so be sure to include it in your budget. The bride and her parents ride to the ceremony site in a relaxed and stylish atmosphere, then the bride and groom make their grand exit as they leave for the reception.
- **Don't reserve a limousine over the phone:** Go to the limousine service and personally inspect the vehicle you are considering renting. Be sure you're dealing with an established, reputable company. These businesses will display or readily have available important information like a business license and liability insurance certificate. If you have any concerns or questions about the service, ask for references and check them out.
- **Be sure to get what you paid for:** Make sure the limousine will be cleaned and presentable when it arrives on your wedding day. Read the contract carefully before paying a deposit. Make sure the date, times, locations (addresses), and the specific limousine you want are spelled out in writing on your contract. Remember that gratuities are usually additional. If the vehicle is not presentable and the chauffeur isn't professional, you are under no obligation to pay a tip.
- **Many styles of luxury transportation:** Various styles of limousines are available: Presidential stretch, super-stretch, mega-stretch, stretch flagships, and vintage limousines (including Rolls Royces). Luxury vans for transporting wedding party members and guests are also available.
- **Transportation for wedding attendants:** The wedding attendants are usually responsible for providing their own transportation to and from the wedding and reception. Sometimes, however, arrangements are made by the bride and groom. Luxury vans are a convenient way to transport wedding attendants to the ceremony and reception sites and also ensure everyone arrives at once and on time.
- **Many uses for luxury vans:** Vans are also handy for transporting wedding gifts to their designated destination conveniently and safely. You may want to ask a responsible person to be in charge of supervising the moving of gifts to the place they will be stored until you return from your honeymoon. Other uses include carrying decorations, food, and out-of-town guests.

For more assistance with staying organized during the wedding planning process, check out the Bravo! Wedding Organizer. Detailed question worksheets double as contracts. This step-by-step system will keep every detail of your wedding organized. To order, refer to the order form on page 24 in this Guide.

PREMIERE VALET SERVICE

LLC

(503) 244-7758

Have You Thought About Parking?

Let us do the thinking for you…When planning for your wedding day, selecting the right valet service will add a great first impression, as well as smooth, convenient parking accommodations.

Consider the unparalleled level of personalized service and professionalism that Premiere Valet Service, LLC ensures. Superior guest service and responsiveness to our clients' needs are our preeminent themes. From the relaxed, comfortable initial consultation to the graciously assisted departure of your last guest, Premiere Valet Service, LLC will make the impression that you and your guests will notice and appreciate.

With our experience and knowledge, we have the ability to solve any parking problem. Insurance, claim checks, and signs are provided.

Services

- Shuttle vans
- Lot attendants
- Parking consulting services
- Fully insured and licensed

Cost and Terms

Charges start as low as $100, but do vary according to parking circumstances and time duration. Please reserve your event date as far in advance as possible to ensure availability. A deposit of 50% of the total bill is required upon booking. Balance is due the day of the event.

LET PREMIERE VALET SERVICE, LLC ENHANCE YOUR WEDDING OR EVENT

Premiere Valet Service, LLC has been giving Portland residents and restaurants quality valet service for more than six years. All valets are trained, screened and field tested to ensure that you will receive only the finest service available.

"Parking with a Personal Touch"

Clara's Limousine Service

916 S.E. 29th Ave.
Portland, Oregon 97214
(503) 234-3484; Fax (503) 234-0404
E-mail: claraswe@sprynet.com
Web site:
portlandbridalshow.com/clarasweddingest/

Every Bride Deserves The Best!
We Are Portland's Wedding Limousine Specialists.

Clara's Limousine Service is a division of Clara's Wedding Establishment Ltd. We specialize in providing the best service possible for your wedding day. All of our cars are white stretch Lincoln limousines. We cater to your every need for that special day with:

- Immaculate stretch limousines
- Professional, formally attired drivers
- Complimentary soft drinks
- All of the amenities necessary
- No minimum hours required for weddings

Our Customers Say

- "The end to a perfect wedding!"
- "The service was outstanding… we will recommend you to everyone."
- "The driver went out of her way to give us special treatment."
- "Just perfect."

Make an appointment today
to see one of our limousines!

Call **(503) 234-3484** to reserve a
limousine for your wedding day.

LET CLARA'S LIMOUSINE SERVICE PROVIDE YOUR CHARIOT FOR YOUR DREAM WEDDING!

See page 238 under Bridal Accessories & Attire.
See page 453 under Disc Jockeys.

PORTLAND LIMOUSINE COMPANY

730 N.E. Twenty-First Avenue
Portland, Oregon 97232
(503) 235-2221, (800) 826-1431;
Fax (503) 235-2821
Office Hours:
Mon–Fri 8am–7pm; Sat 10am–3pm

PORTLAND LIMOUSINE COMPANY: YOUR COMPLETE GROUND TRANSPORTATION COMPANY

Portland Limousine Company has

- Sedans
- Limousines (six, eight and ten passenger)
- Fifteen passenger vans
- Nineteen passenger buses
- 1961 Bentley S2

All of the vehicles from Portland Limousine Company are driven by professionally trained, uniformed chauffeurs. Our limousines have all the amenities including televisions, stereos, CD players, halo lighting, VCRs, cellular phones, moon roofs, champagne flutes, crystal glasses, and are stocked with ice. Our limousines and buses will accommodate from one to 19 people depending on vehicle type.

Cost and Terms

Some vehicles have a minimum of only one hour of service. Chargeable time in the Portland tri-county area begins upon arrival and ends at final destination. Various special wedding packages and tours are available. Please call for details.

Additional Information

Portland Limousine Company has provided the finest limousine service since 1983. We pride ourselves on efficient, professional, courteous service. Our trained staff and concierge are available to help plan your wedding event and will help you find those little extras that will make your special day "perfect."

SPECIAL ATTENTION

Portland Limousine Company has the largest fleet of limousines in the area. We have provided special-occasion service since 1983. We pride ourselves on efficient, professional, courteous service.

CALL PORTLAND LIMOUSINE COMPANY FOR
OREGON'S FINEST CHAUFFEURED VEHICLES
(503) 235-2221 OR (800) 826-1431
Web site: http://www.portlandlimousine.com
E-mail: Portlandlimo@juno.com

GOLDEN TIMES CARRIAGE SERVICE

Contact: Duane or Roberta Ogle
(503) 666-4647

Types of Horse-drawn Carriages

- **Vis-à-vis carriage:** single horse; driver; midnight blue; holds four people
- **Enclosed Cinderella coach:** white; team of horses; driver and doorman; holds up to six people; completely upholstered inside the coach

Service Fee

Fees are based on time. Carriage: $200 for up to one and a half hours, $100 for each additional hour. Coach: $300 for up to one and a half hours, $150 for each extra hour. There is an additional charge for transporting carriage/coach if location is outside of Portland area. Gratuities are extra and much appreciated.

Reservations

The carriage or coach should be reserved as soon as possible, especially during the summer months. A deposit is required on both the carriage and coach; $75 and $100 respectively. The deposit is applied to the total charge for the carriage or coach. In case of cancellation the deposit is nonrefundable. Prices are subject to change without notice.

Decorations

The carriage and coach may be decorated, but please, nothing that will damage the finish.

Portland's Oldest Carriage Service

Golden Times Carriage Service has been providing brides and grooms with the most professional and courteous service available for over 15 years.

AN AFFORDABLE REMEMBRANCE

Golden Times Carriage Service—carriage for hire. This is a special form of transportation on a day you will always cherish, an affordable remembrance for any occasion: weddings, birthdays, anniversaries, proms, and special events to make a grand entrance or departure.

MONARCH CARRIAGE CO.

(Formerly The Palmer House Carriage Co.)
P.O. Box 2633
Portland, Oregon 97208
Contact: Mary
(503) 284-5893, (800) 518-5893
E-mail: zoe@1228@teleport.com
Web site: monarchcarriage.uswestdex.com

Weddings, Proms, Proposals, Anniversaries, Special Events, Historic City Tours of Portland and Vancouver

No matter what you are celebrating, the Monarch Carriage Co. has carriages to cover your needs, rain or shine. Our Coachmen and Footmen are dressed in immaculate and appropriate attire and our horses come in single and pairs to suit you and the carriage.

From our new black vis-a-vis, to our antique 1885 Phaeton, we have carriages to delight you. Our collector's scries have carried royalty in Great Britain; Teddy Roosevelt in Chicago; Shirley Temple, Shirley Boothe, Judy Garland and Sir Laurence Oliver as passengers in major Hollywood films—as well as our very special Portland Brides.

Fees

Wedding carriages start at $205 for the first hour. This includes gratuity. City tours start at $75 per hour. Additional charges are based on distance and on the specific requirements necessary to provide both a safe and memorable ride.

Reservations

To avoid disappointment, we suggest that reservations be made as soon as your date is set. Weddings require a nonrefundable deposit to hold the date.

DISTINCTIVE CARRIAGES FOR THE DISCRIMINATING CLIENT

Owners Mary and Richard Sauter love horses, carriages and weddings, which is why after 13 years in the carriage business, they decided to specialize in weddings. While only three carriages are on the street at any given time, their fleet expands yearly to provide choices to fit different tastes and budgets. The greatest joy, they say, is being able to provide a remarkable carriage with beautiful horses and appropriately-attired driver and footman for a truly unforgettable event.

Flyer, photos and "How to Shop for a Wedding Carriage" available upon request.

Notes

VIDEO SERVICES

© red door studio • page 520

The Marriage Sacrament

In many parts of Sicily, Italy, the bride and groom did not take the marriage sacrament until the death of one of them. The reason for this is that until they had lived a life together they were not spiritually bound by the marriage tie.

HELPFUL HINTS

- **Why videotape?** Videotaping your wedding or event is a wonderful way to bring the event to life. Extra copies of the wedding or special event make great gifts.
- **A good recommendation:** Store one copy of your video in a safe place. Many times the video is watched so much that it gets worn out or lost in a move. In years to come you will want to share your wedding day with your children.
- **Why hire a professional?** There are many reasons why it is important to hire a professional. They have the technical equipment and skills such as editing and sound variations to create a professional video. Ask what kind of equipment they have. Take the time to view video samples from other events they have done; it will be worth your time. Check the background of the company or individual; have they been professionally trained or are they self-taught?

  Don't take the chance of letting an amateur practice his or her video skills at your event. Your video might be out of focus, the shots will be all wrong, or it will be too dark. This is not to say that you can't have a friend or family member videotape, but just remember—there's only one chance to get it right.
- **Research the different packages:** Packages that offer two video cameras provide different perspectives. With only one camera, you can't tape the processional and get to the altar in time to set up and catch those special close-up shots. Two camera locations offer different views of the wedding that can be edited down using only the best shots. Many brides and grooms comment after the wedding is over, "the day went so fast, it was just a blur." A videotape can put the whole day back into focus. **NOTE:** You'll also want to coordinate their needs with those of your photographer to avoid confusion or bad feelings on the wedding day.
- **Traditions first, then have fun!:** After the meal, go right to the cake cutting, then immediately to the first dance, followed by throwing the bouquet and garter, etc. If these events are moved through one after another, then all the traditional duties will be done and the fun can begin. This way you will only need your photographer and video person for one to two hours at the reception instead of three to four.
- **Pay by the hour or the special package:** Figure out the prices for both hourly and special package rates. You may pay just as much with a package, and with hourly you might be able to custom design a package that better suits your needs.
- **What you ask is what you get:** Be sure to communicate with your video person what you expect your video to be like. Sentimental, glittery, romantic, story, interview style. Ask to view some different styles of videos he/she has done.
- **Interviewing guests:** A fun suggestion is to interview guests at the event or reception. It's enjoyable to hear what people have to say, and provides entertainment for the guests as well.
- **Low lighting:** The low light level of a candlelight ceremony makes it difficult for your videographer to work. He or she may need to bring in extra lights that could cancel out the candlelight atmosphere you were seeking. Be sure you discuss the lighting needs well in advance so everything meets your satisfaction.

For more assistance with staying organized during the wedding planning process, check out the Bravo! Wedding Organizer. Detailed question worksheets double as contracts. This step-by-step system will keep every detail of your wedding organized. To order, refer to the order form on page 24 in this Guide.

A VIDEO REFLECTION

P.O. Box 1478
Oregon City, Oregon 97045
Contact: John or Kris Gardner
(503) 631-7054
Web site: www.avideoreflection.com

Call Now for a Free Wedding Demo and Information

When you call A Video Reflection, you will not listen to a big sales pitch or be told you have to come in to see samples of our work. The only thing we will ask for is your name and address so we can send our free wedding demo, saving specials, price sheet and information about A Video Reflection. We want you to view our 3-chip digital camera quality on your own television set. Isn't the sight, sound, and most of all, the person shooting the event's camera work what you're really shopping for—not just sales talk?

After watching cuts from many different weddings, you then can compare our quality with the rest from your own home. Being in the business eight years, we know how to create on digital tape one the most important days of your life. Call now so we can send you our saving specials, price sheet, over an hour of wedding demo, with lots of wonderful ideas you can use for your own wedding day.

All Packages Include

- Pure digital, state-of-the-art, 3 chip digital cameras
- FireWire editing for incredible quality and resolution
- Two to three camera ceremony coverage
- Pro-diversity lapel mic on groom
- Post-production editing in our studio, using slow motion computer graphics and special effects to polish off your wedding video
- Also, we try to attend every rehearsal

Five Wedding Packages and Prices to Choose From

Corsage Package I: Two camera ceremony coverage plus your reception. Four hour, one videographer package. **$799**

Bouquet Package II: Pre-activity highlights, two camera ceremony coverage, plus your reception. A six hour, one videographer package. **$999**

Bridal Gown Package III: Two videographers covering ceremony for incredible close-up shots that only two videographers could capture plus your pre-dressing and reception activities. **$1,199**

Black Tie Package IV: Two videographers, three camera ceremony coverage, for those unforgettable close-ups, also pre-activities, and of course your reception party. Seven huge hours! **$1,399**

The Ultimate Wedding Day Package V: All day—eight hours with two videographers and all of the Black Tie Package IV. Plus, taping your photo shoot, and showing a montage from baby to engagement pictures at your reception. Your guests will love it! **$1,799**

Keith Aden

Photography & Video Productions

1613 SE 7th Avenue • Portland, Oregon 97214

503 230-0325

Toll Free: 877 230-0325
Web Address: www.adenphoto-video.com
www.bravowedding.com/pdx00/keithadenvideo
E-Mail: kaphoto@internetcds.com

Since 1968, Keith Aden Photography has been specializing in wedding photography. Our professional and unobtrusive style bends perfectly with even the most elegant of weddings. We feel that you are the most important part of the wedding and therefore we listen very carefully to your wants and needs. Every wedding is unique and must be recorded in a way that reflects your personality, not ours!

Equipment

We use professional 3-chip SVHS stereo Hi-Fi cameras with 700 lines of resolution for quality that surpasses most home video playback equipment, at 240 lines of resolution, even after editing and duplication. Also, we use broadcast quality wireless remote microphones for superb sound. In one plan we offer two-camera coverage of the ceremony and digital non-linear studio editing with special effects. In the edited versions we can, depending on the plan chosen, include childhood, engagement, wedding and honeymoon photographs, titles, music and interviews with family and friends.

Personalized Wedding Coverage

Many plans designed for different needs are available to choose from. Basic Coverage starts at $450 for a four hour coverage. Ask about our extra bonus gift to you for also booking Photography Coverage.

Reservations and Overtime

You should make your reservation right away. Six months or more in advance would be wise during the peak summer season. A deposit of $100 will hold your date and the balance is due 10 days before the wedding. Duplicate VHS tapes are $25. Additional coverage time is $75 per hour. Corporate events, conventions, industrial, business, educational, and other special events by quotation, based on your specific needs. Discover,Visa or Mastercard accepted.

SOMEONE WHO CARES

It's your special wedding day, a day to be remembered for the rest of your life. Through the years, your memories will become even more special, as will your wedding album and videotape. Your choice of a photo or video professional is an important one. Since 1968, Keith Aden has been specializing in wedding and commercial advertising photography, including video production. His 32 years of experience and knowledge of the very special art of wedding photography and video make him sensitive to your needs and requests. Keith is a photographer who actually cares about you and your wedding.

ASPEN PHOTOGRAPHY & VIDEO STUDIO

14120 S.W. Stallion Drive
Beaverton, Oregon 97008
Contact: Gregg and Lee Ann Childs
(503) 524-8230
Business Hours: by appointment

Selecting a Professional Wedding Videographer

Selecting a professional videographer for your wedding is a very difficult adventure. There are several factors to consider: 1) you want a professional that is an artist and enjoys what he/she is doing; 2) you want someone who is very personable, someone that can blend in with you and your guests; 3) yet you want someone who will be discreet and not attract attention; 4) you want a studio that uses top-of-the-line equipment; and 5) you want an editor that is sensitive and artistic.

Exceeding Your Expectations

Many brides and grooms, their families, and their friends have told us that Aspen Video & Photography meets and exceeds all these factors. We are professional videographers by trade and by training. And we go one big step further than all other video studios: we are also professional photographers. We have been professional wedding photographers and videographers in the Portland area for over 15 years. In fact, we are the only professional photographers who are also professional videographers in the metro area. The artistic lighting and composition talents we have developed as photographers transfer very well to the medium of video.

Experience

We are experienced with the needs and desires of brides and grooms, of families, and of friends. The experiences gained at over 600 weddings make us one of the best wedding service providers in the area.

Wedding Package

Our wedding package is awesome: edited highlights of wedding/reception, growing-up pictures with music, two-camera coverage at wedding and reception, honeymoon pictures, all with sensitive and artistic editing. Price: $795.

Please come and meet us, see our portfolios, and ask for references. We love working weddings, and our results show it.

"Your video of our wedding has been edited in a very sensitive manner. Thanks for your artistic touch." L.Z. — 1993

CINEMAGIC STUDIOS

Since 1980, Portland's Finest Wedding Videographer

2316 N.E. Glisan • Portland, Oregon 97232

Contact: Joe Wash or Rick Hines (503) 233-2141

We Use Broadcast-Quality Equipment

You have most likely dreamed about and planned for your wedding day for a long time now and that day is soon approaching. Naturally, we want everything to be just right for you. Because this day is so important, we use only our broadcast-quality cameras and high-end digital video formats to give you clear and lasting, picture-perfect memories. To ensure this quality, we provide at least two people to videotape your wedding and reception to create a stunning recreation of one of the most memorable days of your life.

We Offer Multiple-Camera Packages

Our multiple-camera packages give you the benefit of capturing the whole range of emotion of all who attend your ceremony. We also provide you with a Director of Videography who monitors the ceremony behind the scenes and directs every move each camera person makes. The result is simply a classy, professional wedding video that you can view and share with everyone forever.

We Attend Your Rehearsal

We value your wedding as one that you have put your personal touches on and have thoughtfully planned, to ensure we are completely prepared for your day, we attend the rehearsal, confirming camera placements, establishing audio locations, and familiarizing ourselves with the succession of events of your ceremony and reception, and listening to any additional ideas you want to share with us.

DVD

In keeping up with the latest technology trends, Cinemagic Studios has become the only Portland studio to offer your wedding video on DVD. Enjoy the highest picture and audio quality possible with complete random access on your computer or television.

The Final, Edited Video

To fully recreate the joys of all those moments when you first shared your lives together, we include a photo montage of both of your individual childhoods through the time you met. We also recreate your wedding invitation as part of your video's introduction, the names of those involved, and a highlight montage for your video's conclusion.

Plese call for an appointment (503) 233-2141

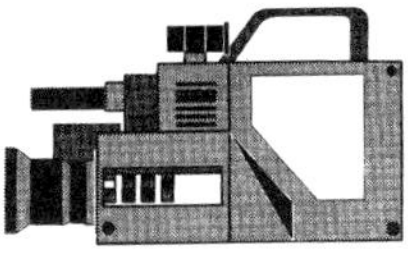

Creative Video Productions

8375 S.W. Beaverton-Hillsdale Hwy.
Beaverton, Oregon 97225
Contact: Randy Stumman (503) 524-1780
Web site: www.cvpvideo.com

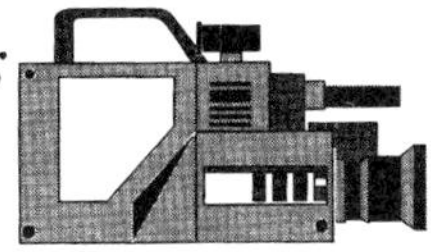

Premier Video Production Company

Creative Video Productions is a premier video production company. We will produce for you a grand and elegant wedding video that will amaze and astound you and your family. Our wedding productions rival the high standards and extreme perfection of broadcast television. We will bring our television commercial expertise and broadcast level equipment department on location to your ceremony and reception locations thus bringing to you the very finest in wedding picture quality and special effects. And doing all this in a way that our clients find incredibly unobtrusive. Then back in the studio, our editing department—utilizing only frame accurate computerized editing equipment complete with computer graphics, 3D motion titles and television graphic composer titling—will develop a wedding production that will leave you wanting to watch your wedding over and over again.

Production Tools

Ceremony: *Creative Video Productions* will use only industrial broadcast digital 3 Chip cameras producing over 750 lines of resolutions, multiple tru-diversity wireless microphones to capture all the audio, completely manned cameras with professional tripods for stability, broadcast quality videotape, 4 point star filters and composed videotaping for truly professional results.

Studio: *Creative Video Productions* utilizes computer editing, computer graphic programs, computer 3D animation, television graphics composers, computer digital non-linear editing, frame accurate editing, music composition capabilities, only Betacam SP mastering, digital transitions and Hollywood type special effects.

Production Prices–*Plus Three More Complete Productions Starting at $350*

Bridal Production: ceremony and reception coverage, up to 4 hours—1 camera, 3D motion titling, slo-motion effects, interviews of guests and 2 copies **$675**

Ceremonial Production: complete coverage using up to 5 hours—2 cameras, all of the above plus photo montage, digital transitions, 4 point star filter, split screen effects, , 6—3D motion titles and more **$985**

Grand Elegance Production: wedding coverage up to 6 hours—2 cameras, includes all of the effects and editing from the first two productions, plus picture in picture effects, 60% digital transitional effects, 9—3D motion titles, highly composed videotaping techniques and much more **$1,175**

Supreme Royale Production: all-day coverage, 2 cameras, includes all the effects and editing from the first three productions, plus TV graphics titling, unlimited music selections, leather type cassette case, special cleaning process of photos, non-linear editing, custom 3D titling using your names, engagement re-enactment, video analyzed and adjusted with vectorscope and waveform monitor, 3 tape copies all in custom cases, 80% digital transitional effects, 2 stage morphing, 15 minute highlite tape, complete animated titling of all events and more **$1,895**

Creative Video Productions will help guide you through the video production process to ensure you acquire the highest quality wedding video on the market today. We have a price for all budgets but only 1 high level of quality. Call today for an appointment and then stop by for our free demo copy and a "no-hassle" exploration to see how ***Creative Video Productions*** can turn the most important day of your life into a loving and lasting memory.

VISA — MASTERCARD — WEVA MEMBER

DAVIDEO

6587 River Springs Drive S.
Salem, Oregon 97306
(503) 375-7363; E-mail: davideo@juno.com

Can you spot the videographer in this photo?

No? That's because they hired Davideo!

Our Mission Statement: Reaching People One Video At A Time.

Why is Davideo Unique?

As a photojournalist, my philosophy is to capture events as they unfold around me. That means I keep a low profile to ensure a natural environment as I videotape people's authentic reactions.

How Do I Capture the Excitement?

I use digital 3-chip cameras. Often I place two or three cameras in strategic places that are out of sight, but positioned for dramatic shots. I also use wireless lapel mics, and instruct the person wearing the mic to avoid using the lavatory at all cost.

What Do Davideo Packages Include?

A Love Story: A personal interview with the bride and groom captured on video as they tell their story: how they met, fell in love, and got engaged; shot at a romantic location of their choice.

The Photo Story: A five-minute video slide show featuring the bride and groom from childhood to the present; includes 60 photos and a musical background of their choice.

The Flashback: An interview of the bride and groom at the close of the wedding day to capture their thoughts and feelings about the magical day they just experienced, illustrated with video clips.

The Grand Finale: A three-minute overview of the entire day, edited in a dramatic fashion that leaves the bride and groom wondering why they didn't charge their friends admission to watch the wedding video.

What Are the Davideo Packages and Prices?

The Da'Light Package: The Photo Story; The Wedding Ceremony; The Reception. $800

The Da'Signer Package: The Photo Story; The Wedding Ceremony; The Reception; The Flashback. $1,000

The Da'Lux Package: The Love Story; The Photo Story; The Wedding Ceremony; The Reception; The Flashback; The Grande Finale. $1,500

All packages are interchangeable with price adjustments.

What Are People Saying About Davideo?

"Thanks for doing such a nice tape and so promptly too! We will be pleased to recommend you to all our friends" – Nancy

"You were able to capture so many thoughtful moments that we would have missed but now we are able to treasure!" – Don and Linda

"When we sat down to watch (the video) we were amazed at how beautiful it was. You did a magnificent job of telling the story of such a special day." – Mike and Kristy

"He's the best videographer in the world!" – My Mom

ENCORE STUDIOS

Portland, Oregon
(503) 255-8047
E-mail: encore@webcombo.net
Web site:
www.bravowedding.com/pdx00/encore-video

Let our professional videographers help you create those precious moments to be cherished forever! You are welcome to choose a package to suit your special needs and budget or customize your own package according to your preferences.

Videography packages and prices

Videos begin at $495 with the average package of 4 hours. Options available include:

- History of bride and groom
- Pre-ceremony events
- Entire reception
- Cordless microphones
- Montages and music
- Getting ready at your home(s)
- Entire ceremony
- Personal messages
- Special digital effects
- Customized keepsake video cases

Special Video Services

- Engagement scenic video
- Engagement party video
- Rehearsal dinner video
- Multiple camera angles
- Multiple locations
- Tape duplication

Description of Service and Equipment

We utilize the newest *digital* formats available for ultimate picture quality; our equipment enables us to shoot even candlelight ceremonies without lighting. We also use wireless remote microphones for superior sound quality, especially during your ceremony. Our edit suite features complete editing services with music selections from all styles and eras, according to your taste. Special effects including digital as well as studio audio dubbing and mixing are included. We welcome you to include photographs, invitations, programs, and other keepsakes for your wedding video.

Reservations

A deposit of $100 reserves your wedding date. Visa and Mastercard gladly accepted as well as financing, with no interest payments.

Consultants are available for day or evening appointments.

Hybrid Moon

ITVA International Television Association.
Member WEVA International
VISA
MasterCard

VIDEO PRODUCTIONS

2580 N.W. Upshur Street
Portland, Oregon 97210
Contact: Eric Newland
(503) 295-1991 or (360) 993-1991
Web site: http://www.hybridmoon.com

What is so Different about Hybrid Moon?

We are the experts in helping you tell the story of the most important day of your life. We work with you to create a customized video production you will cherish forever. Our equipment is top-notch and our production team is second-to-none. Hybrid Moon was recently awarded a coveted **1998 and 1999 Videographers Award of Excellence.** But to us, every wedding video we produce is an award-winner. Our demo reel speaks for itself.

Program Features...

Our wedding video programs include coverage of the ceremony and reception with up to three video cameras. We will capture every special moment of your wedding day from the pre-ceremony activities to the bon voyage send off.

Hybrid Moon Video also features unique video services to help you tell your special story.

- **Photos-n-Motion:** a creative combination of your memorable photos and music.
- **Engagement Sitting:** an ensemble of special moments to create a living portfolio of your special relationship together.
- **Ceremony Switched Live:** when it comes to recording every thrilling moment of the ceremony, we don't miss a beat!
- **Male/Female Camera Crews:** we capture all the excitement and anticipation leading up to the main event!
- **Candid Interview:** a personalized interview that you will never forget.
- **Reception Projection:** a heart-warming production of your love story presented on a big screen during your reception.
- **Full Production Package:** we combine your wedding video with sound, music, graphics, titles, and EFX to create a finished product you will enjoy watching for years to come!

Hybrid Moon Video allows you to tell your own unique story in a way that will perfectly describe the excitement and rush of emotions during this once in a lifetime event. Catering to individual needs and styles is what we do best! Call us today and let us help you design your special video. When you see what we can do, you'll agree: *there's nothing like Hybrid Moon!*

Discover the Hybrid Moon advantage
(360) 993-1991 or (503) 295-1991

KTVA Productions

P.O. Box 22911
Milwaukie, Oregon 97269
(503) 659-4417, (800) 282-KTVA
Fax (503) 659-4438
Web site: www.ktvavideo.com
E-mail: mail@ktvavideo.com

The Finest in Professional Wedding Videography since 1987

We continually marvel at the energy and emotion that are a part of each of the hundreds of wedding celebrations we have witnessed and recorded. We respect the importance of each and every one of these events and specialize in discreetly capturing wedding day memories with award-winning service. We will not intrude upon the sanctity of your wedding with a grand production or inappropriate unprofessional behavior.

Your beautifully edited videotape will include special moments before the ceremony. Unobtrusive one, two or three-camera coverage and multiple microphones will guard the majesty of your ceremony. Romantically documented, our detail oriented, journalistic style will capture the fun of your reception forever. Technology makes this safekeeping possible; experience assures worry-free performance; artistry creates a timeless classic that you and future generations will enjoy again and again.

Wedding Memories Premium Package. Up to eight hours of coverage by two formally attired wedding videographers, three-camera ceremony coverage, Love Story opening, wedding vow reminiscence, slow motion effects, and four videotapes in elegant padded cases…$1,999.

Wedding Memories Classic Package. Up to six hours of coverage by an experienced, formally attired wedding videographer, two cameras for your ceremony, Love Story opening, wedding vow reminiscence, slow motion effects, and three videotapes in elegant padded cases…$1,049.

Wedding Memories Standard Package. Up to six hours of coverage by a professional wedding videographer, individually crafted editing, and two videotapes in elegant padded cases…$749.

Screening Party. Enjoy the premiere of your wedding day videotape in theater-style, surrounded by loved ones. This turn-key event at the classically romantic Mallory Hotel, near downtown Portland, includes food and beverages for twenty people…$599.

Bridal Gift Registry. This traditional service, offered free of charge, provides friends and family an opportunity to easily take part in the preservation and enjoyment of your special day, the perfect gift!

Conventional or Digital Services. We use high-quality, well-maintained industrial equipment, providing proven performance, yet modestly priced. We are pleased to offer you the opportunity of upgrading to our new state-of-the-art, digital broadcast-quality equipment, capturing beautiful images in soft light, combined with computerized editing of sound and imagery for seamless movement form scene to scene…$300.

A reservation fee of $100 holds your date. Our overtime rate is $100 per hour. We are one of the very few full-time video production companies in the Portland/Vancouver area that specialize in this important work. We are proud to be members of the Portland Oregon Visitors Association, the Wedding and Event Videographers Association and the Association of Catering and Event Professionals. We are on the board of directors for the Portland chapter of the International Television Association and the Gala Events Group, Inc. We are very serious about our commitment to you and our industry, but we still have fun.

Please call us, we love our work and so will you!

Masterpiece Video Productions

Ron W. Miller (503) 254-7149
10250 N.E. Morris Court • Portland, Oregon 97220
E-mail: ron@masterpiece-video.com

Description of Video Service

We will be there from start to finish. Over 600 weddings and 10 years experience in the Portland area. We pride ourselves on providing you with the highest quality wedding services available. Knowing where to be at the right time and having the creativity to make it special are where we excel. We are well versed in wedding etiquette and will create a video you will cherish.

Options and Techniques

- **NEW DIGITAL FORMAT** (All packages)
- **Wireless microphones:** to hear the vows
- **Studio editing special effects:** slow motion, titling audio dub. Montage video available incorporating childhood, couple, and honeymoon shots.
- **Summary tape:** 15 minute tape capturing emotional highlights of your wedding day
- **Multiple cameras:** fading between different angles for that smooth professional touch

Packages and Price Range

All editing is free and included in the package price!

- **Silver $950**: 4 hour coverage, ceremony and reception; single camera, Master Digital edited tape, one VHS copy
- **Gold $1,250** 6–8 hour coverage, ceremony, reception, three cameras, Master Digital edited tape, one VHS copy, childhood and honeymoon montage video
- **Platinum $2,000** Unlimited Hours; ceremony, reception, three cameras, Master Digital edited tape, 6VHS copies, childhood and honeymoon montage video, summary video, engagement video, rehearsal dinner video
- **Edited Copies:** $25
- Summary Video: $125
- **Deposit:** $200 required at the time of booking

Best of Show

Grand Prize Winner of the 1995 Wedding Video Competition at the MBA National Wedding Videographers Convention, held at the MGM Grand Hotel in Las Vegas, Nevada.

Lisa Sherman—15 years experience
Web site: www.mediafxvideo.com

Your wedding day happens only once in a lifetime, and your photographer will take a few hundred photos. We will take a few hundred thousand, complete with voices, music and live action. We care and will give you only the best. For a spectacular wedding video give us a call for a free sample tape.

"The whole video is so wonderful, but your special little touches are what really made it great...You've truly captured the special feelings of that day...thanks again for all the time and energy you put into our video." **—Lisa and Norbert Loske, March 1999**

"We loved it. I can't believe how much we had forgotten until we saw the video. We've shown it to all our friends and watched it over and over."
—Erin and Greg Moyer, September 1997

"It's like starring in your own movie. I just loved it."
—Trish and Henry Wiggen, August 1998

We are an ALL DIGITAL VIDEO production facility. We use state-of-the-art 3-chip digital video cameras, UHF wireless mics, and the best editing—Nonlinear. We master your video to a digital video cassette, so the image looks fantastic!

All of our Packages Include:
Thirty extra minutes of setup time • Videographers operating each camera • Your photos converted to video with your favorite music • Pre-wedding and reception highlights, slow motion, tasteful effects, and animations • We attend your rehearsal • Three deluxe copies and a digital video master

- ✦ **Carnation Package ($699):** One videographer, 4 hours, one camera at ceremony and reception, 20 photos to video, bride preparing sequence
- ✦ **Rose Package ($1059):** Two videographers, 6 hours, two cameras at ceremony, one at reception, bride and groom preparing, 40 photos to video
- ✦ **Stargazer Lilly Package ($1399):** Two videographers, one sound engineer, 7 hours, two cameras at ceremony and reception, bride and groom preparing, taping photo shoot, 60 photos to video, and wedding highlights sequence
- ✦ **Orchid Bouquet Package ($1799):** Three videographers, one sound engineer. Same features as the Stargazer package with 8 hours, three cameras at ceremony, two at reception, 80 photos to video.

Moments In Time Video Productions

P.O. Box 22463 • Milwaukie, Oregon 97269
(503) 653-7922

Description of Video Services

Moments In Time Video Productions will professionally videotape your ceremony and reception—skillfully and unobtrusively. We can add titles, music of your choice, and pre-recorded thoughts of the bride and groom, then create a superior-quality edited tape. For friends and relatives unable to attend, we make high-quality, affordable duplicate tapes.

Equipment, Options and Techniques

We are a professional video company and use "industrial" equipment, as opposed to consumer-level equipment. This includes cameras, recorders, tri-pods, and editing/duplicating systems. We use low-light professional cameras without video lamps, which can be distracting. Moments In Time Video Productions utilizes two broadcast-quality, wireless microphones, generally worn by the officiate and groom. These provide excellent clarity.

Wedding Packages

Packages A and B Include:

- Consultation to discuss with you various options for taping the ceremony and reception.
- Attendance at your rehearsal to plan camera and microphone locations.
- Post-production including: introductory titles, editing to create a polished, professional tape and personal touches such as still photos (limit 20) and favorite music.
- Two high-quality copies are included in all packages.

Package A: $595; includes four hours of coverage, one videographer, two-camera ceremony coverage, and coverage of your reception.

Package B: $995; includes eight hours (all day) wedding coverage, two videographers, two-camera ceremony coverage, and coverage at your reception.

Package C: $235

Moments In Time Video Productions can also compose a video show presentation for you to show at your reception or rehearsal dinner. We will create a lasting and unforgettable memory of 40 pictures of the two of you growing up and together, set to your favorite music. The presentation is shown live at your reception.

Also Available:

- Videotaping the rehearsal and rehearsal dinner (two hours of coverage)…$195
- Additional still photos…$3 each
- High-quality video tape copies…$25 each

PRESERVE THE JOY OF YOUR DAY FOREVER

Videotape is the ideal way to capture all the treasured moments on this once-in-a-lifetime day of celebration…emotions…reflections…the exchange of vows…candid comments of relatives and friends…the celebration. All these fleeting sounds and images can be part of a living record of your wedding day.

PRO 2000
VIDEO PRODUCTIONS

Boring, Oregon
Phone/Fax (503) 668-5140

E-mail: pro2000videopro@webtv.net

VISA
MasterCard

PRO 2000 Video Productions

Your Wedding Video
Let Us Capture The Magic

A Bride's Dream Come True
We bring over 25 years of wedding experience to your special day… we are a husband and wife team who worked together for 20 years as wedding photographers and, since 1993, as wedding videographers. Weddings are our life! We will see your wedding through an artist's eye and the heart of a romanticist. The result is a masterpiece to be treasured the rest of your life. We are often told, by brides of yesteryear, that the emotions we captured, continue to touch their heart.

Equipment
We bring professional Super VHS and Digital cameras to record your special day. Very importantly, we also bring backup components and equipment to cover equipment failure. We use wireless remote microphones to record every word in superb high-quality audio. Our professional cameras allow us to record your ceremony without adding glaring bright lights.

Post-Production
Our total attention is given to editing your wedding video in the days following your special day. The emotion of the day is still with us as we plan the editing and share our ideas for a personalized and unique wedding story. We include computer graphics, special effects, wipes, swipes, dissolves, scrolling, wedding and reception invitations, wedding program, reception scroll and any other special printed wedding or reception material.

Price
Full coverage: $725. No extra charges. Reserve your wedding date with a nonrefundable deposit of $350. Balance is due by your wedding date.

Optional Features
Duplicate video copies ordered and paid prior to wedding: $25 each. Copies ordered after delivery of edited videos: $30 each. Rehearsal coverage: $50. Rehearsal dinner coverage: $50.

"Pathways to A Love Story"
A 20-minute photo video for presentation at the rehearsal dinner, wedding ceremony or reception. Comprised of childhood photos, courtship and engagement photos, complete with computer graphics, special effects and music: $175.

Other Services
Bar/Bat Mitzvahs, anniversary receptions, family reunions, birthday celebrations, awards banquets… other special occasions.

"Through the music of our marriage, we will, together, wander through time."

ROYAL VIDEO AND ELECTRONICS

Specializing in Special Event Videography

224 Northridge Court, N. • Keizer, Oregon 97303
Contact: Wes Jensen
(503) 390-4220 or (800) 290-6584 (PIN #4602)
E-mail: wesj@mail2ncn.com; Web site: www2.ncn.com/~wesj
Business Hours: by appointment

Description of Video Service

Video for all special occasions; specializing in wedding photography, editing and copying service. Providing service since 1987.

Options and Techniques

- **We've gone digital!!!** Digital format for best picture quality
- **Non-Linear Editing** with dazzling **3-D Transitions** and **Digital Effects**
- True Diversity **Wireless Mic** available; direct connect to sound system when possible
- Studio editing providing **Special Effects** (as appropriate) such as mosaics, slow motion, dissolves, paint, titles, and inclusion of still photographs
- Studio audio mixing to add **Music** for viewing pleasure
- Tape copies available on VHS, or 8mm, S-VHS, or Hi-8 on request

Packages and Prices for 2000—*Full Coverage!*

- **"Basic" Package $550: One camera;** includes titles (scrolling names of everyone in the wedding party), pre-ceremony family group pictures, ceremony and reception. Still pictures such as engagement or baby pictures can be incorporated into your video. Music can be added in the studio for your viewing pleasure. Price includes three copies. The "edit master" is kept in my library for making additional copies on request, but can be purchased for $25. Additional copies may be purchased for $15 each. A video "highlights" (5–10 minute short of entire video) as part of the finished video is standard.
- **"Basic+" Package $650:** All the features of our "Basic" package, including one cameraman, plus a second camera for the ceremony.
- **"Royal" Package $750:** All the features of our "Basic" package, but with **two cameras** and two camera operators, providing two angles for better coverage. We are a husband and wife team.

Typical coverage begins around two hours before the ceremony, while the photographer is taking the formal pictures, and continues through the reception—often around two hours into the reception, allowing for cake cutting, toast, dance, bouquet and garter toss. Up to six hours of coverage—no extra charges.

Reservations

Many weddings are booked months in advance. Book early to reserve your date.

Deposit

A 50% deposit is required at the time of booking, with the balance due on your wedding day.

Relive the Sights and Sounds of Your Wedding Day!

Sit back and relax with friends and relatives, and watch the beauty and excitement of your wedding unfold. See pictures and hear comments from your friends and relatives wishing you a life of happiness together.

What some of them are saying . . .

"We watch the tape every couple of weeks. It brings back so many fond memories."

"We watched the tape on our anniversary, and cried as we relived our day."

"Very professional . . ."

© Oregon Zoo • page 176

Tradition

To symbolize family unity, three candles are lit: first the bride's parents light the candle on the right, then the groom's parents light the candle on the left, and finally, the bride and groom light the third candle, called the unity candle, from the flames of the other two candles.

PORTLAND AREA CEREMONY SITE LISTINGS

ADDRESS	CAPACITY	CONTACT
Agnes Flanagan Chapel Lewis & Clark College 0615 S.W. Palatine Hill Rd. Portland, OR 97219-7899	Indoor: Up to 600 W/	Emi Jean Sakamoto (503) 768-7085 Fax (503) 768-7084
Atkinson Memorial 710 Sixth St. Oregon City, OR 97045	Ceremony: Up to 225 Reception: Up to 180 W/R/	Church Secretary (503) 656-7296
Baker Cabin Pioneer Church Corner Hattan & Gronlund Rd. Oregon City, OR 97045	Up to 90 W/R/ (outdoor)	Reservations Secretary (503) 631-8274
Beaverton Christian Church 13600 S.W. Allen Blvd. Beaverton, OR 97005	Chapel: 185 Worship Center: 1,400 W/R/	Rose (503) 646-2151 Fax (503) 627-0780
Canby Pioneer Chapel N.W. Third & Elm Canby, OR 97013 *See page 327*	Up to 120 W/	Darlene Key (503) 263-6126
Canterbury Falls & English Gardens P.O. Box 156 Molalla, OR 97038 *See page 109*	Outdoor: Up to 400 W/R/B/M/P/	Judy Hall (503) 829-8821
The Carus House Wedding Chapel 23200 S. Highway 213 Oregon City, OR 97045 *See page 328*	Sit-down: Up to 145 W/R/B/	Wedding Coordinator (503) 631-7078
Christian Life Church 9215 S.E. Church St. Clackamas, OR 97015 *See page 328*	Up to 120 W/R/	Wedding Coordinator (503) 655-1224
Crystal Springs Rhododendron Garden S.E. 28th/North of Woodstock Portland, OR 97215 *See page 325*	Indoor: Up to 125 Outdoor: Up to 300 W/R/P/	Event Coordinator (503) 256-2483
First Christian Church 1315 S.W. Broadway Portland, OR 97201	Up to 300 W/R/	Dorothy Pearce (503) 228-9211 Fax (503) 222-1313
First Congregational Church 1126 S.W. Park Ave. Portland, OR 97205 *See page 329*	Ceremony: 40-850 W/	Church Office (503) 228-7219
First Pentacostal Church of God 6030 S.E. 136th Ave. Portland, OR 97236	Up to 175 W/R/S/M/	Rev. Lawrence Haddock (503) 761-1491

W=Wedding Ceremony R=Reception B=Banquet S=Seminar M=Meeting P=Picnic

PORTLAND AREA
CEREMONY SITE LISTINGS

ADDRESS	CAPACITY	CONTACT
The Grotto Catholic Church Sandy at N.E. 85th Portland, OR 97294	Indoor: up to 450 Outdoor: up to 700 *bride or groom must be a practicing Catholic and registered in a parish W/	Sr. Ruth Arnott (503) 254-7371
The Grove at Oaks Amusement Park Portland, OR 97202 *See page 330*	Up to 450 W/R/P/	Volanne Stephens (503) 233-5777
Hillsdale Community Church 6948 S.W. Capitol Hwy. Portland, OR 97219	Ceremony: Up to 325 Reception: Up to 325 W/R/B/	Secretary Day (503) 246-5474 Evening (503) 245-2960
McLean House 5350 River St. West Linn, Oregon 97068 *See page 330*	Indoor/Outdoor: Up to 100 W/R/B/S/M/P/	(503) 655-4268
Meridian United Church of Christ 6750 S.W. Boeckman Rd. Wilsonville, OR 97070	Up to 100 W/R/	Joyce Liden (503) 682-0339 Fax (503) 682-0339
New Hope Community Church 11731 S.E. Stevens Rd. Portland, OR 97226	Ceremony: Up to 2,500 Reception: Up to 500 W/R/B/S/M/	Gloria Leslie (503) 698-5095 or (503) 659-5683
Oaks Pioneer Church 455 S.E. Spokane St. Portland, OR 97202 *See page 331*	Up to 75 W/	Manager (503) 233-1497
The Old Church 1422 S.W. 11th Ave. Portland, OR 97201 *See page 331*	Ceremony: 300 Reception: 200 W/R/	Wedding Coordinator (503) 222-2031
Old Laurelhurst Church 3212 S.E. Ankeny Portland, OR 97214 *See page 326*	Ceremony: Up to 650 W/R/M/	Deborra Buckler (503) 231-0462
Open Bible Church 3223 S.E. 92nd Portland, OR 97266	Up to 300 W/R/	Wedding Coordinator (503) 775-1565
Rivercrest Community Church 3201 N.E. 148th Portland, OR 97230	Ceremony: 300 Reception: 200 W/R/	Office (503) 254-4400 or (503) 661-3767
Scottish Rite Center 709 S.W. 15th Ave. Portland, OR 97205 *See page 191*	Ceremony: Up to 580 Reception: Up to 400 W/R/B/S/M/	Bill Stanger (503) 226-7827

W=Wedding Ceremony R=Reception B=Banquet S=Seminar M=Meeting P=Picnic

PORTLAND AREA CEREMONY SITE LISTINGS

ADDRESS	CAPACITY	CONTACT
St. James Lutheran 1315 S.W. Park Portland, OR 97201	Up to 350 Small receptions W/	Pastor Smith (503) 227-2439
St. Mark Presbyterian 9750 S.W. Terwilliger Blvd. Portland, OR 97219	Up to 150 W/	Rev. David Lee (503) 244-8177
Sunnyside Centenary United Methodist Church 3520 S.E. Yamhill Portland, OR 97213	Up to 350 W/R/	(503) 235-8726
Tallina's Gardens & Conservatory 15791 S.E. Hwy 224 Clackamas, OR 97015 *See page 200*	Rose Garden: Up to 200 Conservatory: Up to 160 W/R/B/M/P/	Tallina or Tina (503) 658-6148
Tigard United Methodist 9845 S.W. Walnut Pl. Tigard, OR 97223 *See page 332*	Ceremony: Up to 500 seated Reception: Up to 400 R/B/M/	Pastor Wesley Taylor (503) 639-3181
Thunder Island at Cascade Locks Cascade Locks Marine Park Cascade Locks, OR 97014	Outdoor: Up to 4,000 Covered: Up to 400 W/R/B/M/P/	Cascade Sternwheelers (503) 223-3928 Fax (503) 223-4013
Unity of Beaverton 12650 S.W. Fifth St. Beaverton, OR 97005	Up to 140 W/	Wedding Coordinator (503) 646-3364
The Wedding House 2715 S.E. 39th Ave. Portland, OR 97202 *See page 205*	Ceremony: Up to 100 Reception: Up to 150 W/R/B/S/M/	Owner (503) 236-7353
West Hills Unitarian 8470 S.W. Oleson Rd. Portland, OR 97223 *See page 332*	Ceremony: Up to 175 W/	(503) 293-3161
YWCA 8010 N. Charlston St. Portland, OR 97203	Fireplace Rm: Up to 50 Auditorium: Up to 200 W/R/B/M/	Outreach Coordinator (503) 721-6777

W=Wedding Ceremony R=Reception B=Banquet S=Seminar M=Meeting P=Picnic

PORTLAND AREA
BANQUET SITE LISTINGS

ADDRESS	CAPACITY	GUEST ROOMS	CONTACT
ALOHA			
Aloha Odd Fellows Hall 3670 S.W. 185th Ave. Aloha, OR 97007	Up to 100 W/R/B/S/M/		Rental Manager (503) 292-3988
The Reserve Vineyard & Golf Club 4805 S.W. 229th Ave. Aloha, OR 97007	Up to 175 W/R/B/M/		Nancy Marshall (503) 649-2345
AURORA			
Aurora Colony Historical Society 2nd & Liberty Aurora, OR 97002	Indoor/Outdoor: Up to 150 W/R/B/P/		Dan McElhinny (503) 678-5754
Heritage House Farm & Gardens Aurora, OR 97002 *See page 148*	Outdoor: Up to 300 W/R/B/S/M/		Derolyn Johnson (503) 678-5704 (888) 479-3500
Willamette Gables 10323 Schuler Rd. Aurora, OR 97002 *See page 209*	Outdoor: Up to 200 W/R/B/P/		Laurel Cookman (503) 678-2195
BEAVERTON			
Beaverton Community Center 12350 S.W. Fifth St. Beaverton, OR 97006	Small room: Up to 35 Large room: Up to 140 R/B/M/S/P/		(503) 526-2648
Elsie J. Stuhr Adult Leisure Center 5550 S.W. Hall Blvd. Beaverton, OR 97005	Sit-down: Up to 150 Reception: Up to 200 *No alcohol W/R/B/S/M/		Center Supervisor (503) 643-9434
The Greenwood Inn 10700 S.W. Allen Blvd. Beaverton, OR 97005 *See page 144*	Up to 500 W/R/B/S/M/	250	Catering Office (503) 643-7444 Ext. 726 or 727
Griffith Park Athletic Club 4925 S.W. Griffith Dr. Beaverton, OR 97005	Reception: Up to 300 R/		Manager (503) 644-3900
Hall Street Grill 3775 S.W. Hall Blvd. Beaverton, OR 97005 *See page 76*	Up to 100 W/B/M/		(503) 641-6161
Hilton Garden Inn 15520 N.W. Gateway Ct. Beaverton, OR 97006 *See page 149*	Up to 100 W/R/B/S/M/	150	Lisa Brown (503) 466-2604 Fax (503) 439-1818

W=Wedding Ceremony R=Reception B=Banquet S=Seminar M=Meeting P=Picnic

Please let these businesses know that you heard about them from the Bravo! Bridal Resource Guide.

PORTLAND AREA BANQUET SITE LISTINGS

ADDRESS	CAPACITY	GUEST ROOMS	CONTACT
McCormick & Schmick's Fishhouse & Bar 9945 S.W. Beaverton-Hillsdale Hwy. Beaverton, OR 97005	Up to 35 W/R/B/S/M/		General Manager (503) 643-1322
McMenamins—Cedar Hills 2927 S.W. Cedar Hills Blvd. Beaverton, OR 97005	Sit-down: Up to 64 Patio: Up to 48 R/B/M/		Management Team (503) 641-0151
New Seoul Yakiniku Korean Restaurant 10860 S.W. Beav-Hills Hwy. Beaverton, OR 97005 *See page 168*	Up to 180 R/B/S/M/		Paul Rouse (503) 643-8818 Fax (503) 256-8800
Red Robin 4105 S.W. 117th Beaverton, OR 97005	Up to 75 R/B/M/		Manager (503) 641-3784 Fax (503) 626-1899
Sayler's Old Country Kitchen 4655 S.W. Griffith Dr. Beaverton, OR 97005 *See page 83*	Up to 300 R/B/M/		Sally Kanan (503) 644-1492 or (503) 252-4171
Stockpot Restaurant & Catering Co. 8200 S.W. Scholls Ferry Rd. Beaverton, OR 97005 *See page 198*	Indoor: Up to 350 Outdoor: Up to 600 W/R/B/S/M/P/		Gary (503) 643-5451 Fax (503) 641-3265
BRIDAL VEIL/CORBETT			
Bridal Veil Lakes P.O. Box 5 Bridal Veil, OR 97010 *See page 107*	Indoor: Up to 150 Outdoor: Up to 1,000 W/R/B/M/S/		Jennifer Miller (503) 981-3695
CLACKAMAS			
Clackamas Armory 10101 S.E. Clackamas Rd. Clackamas, OR 97015	Sit-down: Up to 450 Reception: Up to 750 W/R/S/M/B/		Facility Manager (503) 557-5368
Clackamas Community Club Dow Center 15711 S.E. 90th Ave. Clackamas, OR 97015	Sit-down: Up to 110 Reception: Up to 150 W/R/B/S/M/		Director (503) 653-7432
Clackamas County Fair & Event Center 694 N.E. Fourth Ave. Canby, OR 97013	Sit-down: Up to 450 Reception: Up to 500 R/B/P/S/M/		Events Coordinator (503) 266-1136 Fax (503) 266-2833

W=Wedding Ceremony R=Reception B=Banquet S=Seminar M=Meeting P=Picnic

 Please let these businesses know that you heard about them from the Bravo! Bridal Resource Guide.

ADDRESS	CAPACITY	GUEST ROOMS	CONTACT
The Old Spaghetti Factory 12725 S.E. 93rd Ave. Clackamas, OR 97015	Sit-down: Up to 75–150 R/B/S/M/		Banquet Manager (503) 653-7949
Tallina's Gardens & Conservatory 15791 S.E. Hwy. 224 Clackamas, OR 97015 *See page 200*	Indoor: 160 Outdoor: 300 W/R/B/M/P/		Tallina or Tina (503) 658-6148
COLUMBIA GORGE/HOOD RIVER			
Big Horse Brewery & Pub 115 State St. Hood River, OR 97031	Sit-down: Up to 40 R/B/		Randy Orzeck (541) 386-4411
Charburger Restaurant 4100 Westcliff Dr. Hood River, OR 97031	Sit-down: Up to 95 R/B/		Steve or Blanch (541) 386-3101
Cherry Hill Bed & Breakfast 1550 Carroll Rd. Mosier, OR 97040 *See page 116*	Indoor: Up to 80 Garden: Up to 200 W/R/B/S/M/P/	3	Elizabeth Toscano (541) 478-4455 Fax (541) 478-4457
Columbia Gorge Hotel 4000 Westcliff Dr. Hood River, OR 97031 *See page 119*	Up to 200 W/R/B/S/M/	41	Wedding Consultant (541) 387-5403 (800) 345-0931
Hood River Hotel & Pasquale's Ristorante 102 Oak Ave. Hood River, OR 97031 *See page 153*	Up to 250 W/R/B/S/M/	41	Reservations (800) 386-1859 Sales Office (541) 386-1900
Hood River Inn 1108 E. Marina Way Hood River, OR 97031	Sit-down: Up to 225 Reception: Up to 300 W/R/B/S/M/	149	Sales & Catering (541) 386-2200 (800) 828-7873
Maryhill Museum of Art 35 Maryhill Museum Dr. Goldendale, WA 98620	Indoor: Up to 175 Outdoor: Up to 1,500 W/R/B/S/M/P/		Elizabeth Toscano at Cherry Hill (541) 478-4455
Mt. Hood Bed & Breakfast 8885 Cooper Spur Rd. Parkdale, OR 97041 *See page 167*	Indoor/Outdoor: Up to 200+ W/R/B/P/	4	Jackie Rice (541) 352-6885
Oregon Nat. Guard Armory 1590 12th St. Hood River, OR 97031	Reception: Up to 450 R/B/		David Arnold (541) 386-3161
CORNELIUS			
Pumpkin Ridge Golf Course 12930 Old Pumpkin Ridge Rd. Cornelius, OR 97113-6147 *See page 184*	Up to 250 W/R/B/S/M/		Catering Director (503) 647-4747

W=Wedding Ceremony R=Reception B=Banquet S=Seminar M=Meeting P=Picnic

PORTLAND AREA
BANQUET SITE LISTINGS

ADDRESS	CAPACITY	GUEST ROOMS	CONTACT
CORVALLIS/ALBANY			
Bell Fountain Cellars 25041 Llewellyn Rd. Corvallis, OR 97333	Indoor: Up to 50 Outdoor: Up to 100 R/B/S/M/		Jeanne Mommsen (541) 929-3162
Benton County Fairgrounds 110 S.W. 53rd Corvallis, OR 97330	Indoor: Up to 400 Outdoor: Up to 1,500 R/B/S/M/		(541) 757-1521
CH2M Hill Alumni Center at OSU 204 CH2M Hill Alumni Center Corvallis, OR 97330	Up to 1,000 R/B/S/M/		Lisa Templeton (541) 737-2351 Fax (541) 737-3481
Salbasgeon Suites 1730 N.W. Ninth St. Corvallis, OR 97330	Up to 150 M/B/R/S/	105	Virginia Gillespie (800) 965-8808
Willamette Queen located at Riverfront Park Salem, OR 97330 *See page 92*	Up to 107 R/B/S/M/		Irene Salomon (541) 928-4090
Willamette Events Center at the Linn County Fair & Expo 3700 Knox Butte Rd. Albany, OR 97321 *See page 207*	Up to 6,000 B/R/M/		Jill Henderson (541) 926-4314 (800) 858-2005
DUNDEE			
Alfie's Wayside Country Inn 1111 Hwy. 99 W. Dundee, OR 97115 *See page 99*	Up to 400 W/R/B/		(503) 538-9407
FOREST GROVE			
Elk Cove Vineyards 27751 N.W. Olson Rd. Gaston, OR 97119	Up to 200 W/R/B/S/M/P/		Brett Butler (503) 985-7760
Laurel Ridge Winery 46350 N.W. David Hill Rd. Forest Grove, OR 97116	Sit-down: Up to 65 Reception: Up to 200 W/R/B/S/M/P/		David Teppola (503) 359-5436
Masonic Lodge 2019 Main St. Forest Grove, OR 97116	Reception: Up to 120 R/B/P/S/M/ *No alcohol		Harold Johnson (503) 357-6979
Oregon Nat'l Guard Armory 2950 Taylor Way Forest Grove, OR 97116	Reception: Up to 450 R/B/		Frank Wallace (503) 359-4632
Pacific University University Center 2043 College Way Forest Grove, OR 97116	Up to 50 R/B/S/M/W/		Director of Conferences (503) 359-2133

W=Wedding Ceremony R=Reception B=Banquet S=Seminar M=Meeting P=Picnic

 Please let these businesses know that you heard about them from the Bravo! Bridal Resource Guide.

ADDRESS	CAPACITY	GUEST ROOMS	CONTACT
GRESHAM/BORING			
Briarwood Inn 2752 N.E. Hogan Rd. Gresham, OR 97030 *See page 106*	Up to 300	169	(503) 665-3894 (360) 253-8326 Fax (503) 492-2638
Club Paesano 3800 W. Powell Loop Gresham, OR 97030	Up to 500 W/R/B/S/M/P/		Rose Sisson (503) 666-7636
East Fork Country Estate 9957 S.E. 222nd Gresham, OR 97080 *See page 130*	Indoor/Outdoor: Up to 250 W/R/B/S/M/P/		Karen Reed (503) 667-7069
Garden View Estates Gresham, OR *See page 137*	Up to 500 W/R/B/M/		Kristina McMorris (503) 666-4725
Gresham Armory 500 N.E. Division St. Gresham, OR 97030	Up to 379 W/R/B/S/M/		State Employee (503) 665-2511
Mt. Hood Community College 26000 S.E. Stark St. Gresham, OR 97030	Indoor: Up to 371 Outdoor: Up to 500 W/R/B/M/		Dee Ann Melland (503) 491-7449 Fax (503) 491-6011
Persimmon Country Club 500 S.E. Butler Rd. Gresham, OR 97080 *See page 180*	Sit-down: Up to 300 Reception: Up to 500 W/R/B/S/M/		Event Coordinator (503) 667-7500
HILLSBORO			
Cavanaughs Hillsboro Hotel 3500 N.E. Cornell Rd. Hillsboro, OR 97124 *See page 111*	Sit-down: Up to 150 Reception: Up to 170 W/R/B/S/M/	124	Catering Office (503) 648-3500 (800) 325-4000
McMenamins—Cornelius Pass Roadhouse 4045 N.W. Cornelius Pass Rd. Hillsboro, OR 97214	Indoor: Up to 65 R/B/S/M/		Management Team (503) 640-6174 or (503) 492-2777
Meriwether National Golf Course 5200 S.W. Rood Bridge Hillsboro, OR 97123	Up to 300 R/B/S/M/		John Derr (503) 693-8707
Tuality Health Education Center 334 S.E. Eighth Ave. Hillsboro, OR 97123 *See page 204*	Sit-down: Up to 250 Reception: Up to 400 R/B/S/M/		(503) 681-1700

W=Wedding Ceremony R=Reception B=Banquet S=Seminar M=Meeting P=Picnic

PORTLAND AREA
BANQUET SITE LISTINGS

ADDRESS	CAPACITY	GUEST ROOMS	CONTACT
Washington County Fair Complex 873 N.E. 28th St. Hillsboro, OR 97124	40 to 2,500 W/R/B/S/M/P/		Margaret Garza (503) 648-1416 Fax (503) 648-7208
JUNCTION CITY			
Shadow Hills Country Club 92512 River Rd. Junction City, OR 97448	Up to 250 W/R/B/S/M/		Jennifer Brandt (541) 998-2365 Fax (541) 998-6779
LAKE OSWEGO			
A Touch of Romance Ltd. 530 First St. Lake Oswego, OR 97034	Up to 25 B/Showers		Stephanie (503) 636-0179
Amadeus 148 B. Ave. Lake Oswego, OR 97034	Up to 100 R/B/M/		General Manager (503) 636-7500
Celebrate! Catering & Reception Facility 15555 S.W. Bangy Rd. Lake Oswego, OR 97035 *See page 113*	Sit-down: Up to 200 Reception: Up to 300 W/R/B/S/M/		Barb Chirgwin (503) 684-1880
Crowne Plaza 14811 Kruse Oaks Blvd. Lake Oswego, OR 97035 *See page 123*	Up to 300 W/R/B/S/M/	161	Crystal Harrell (503) 624-8400 ext.253
Fuddruckers 17815 S.W. 65th Ave. Lake Oswego, OR 97035	Up to 75		Manager (503) 620-5119 (Fax) 639-1787
Hunan Pearl 15160 S.W. Bangy Rd. Lake Oswego, OR 97035	Sit-down: Up to 30 R/B/		Miles Shu (503) 968-6868
Lacey's in Lake Oswego 500 S.W. First St. Lake Oswego, OR 97034	Sit-down: Up to 60 Reception: Up to 100 R/B/P		Ed Lacey (503) 636-2024
Lakewood Center for the Arts 368 S. State St. Lake Oswego, OR 97034 *See page 159*	Sit-down: Up to 150 Reception: Up to 225 Theater: 200 W/R/B/S/M/		Executive Director (503) 635-6338
Ram Restaurant & Big Horn Brewery Co. 320 Oswego Point Blvd. Lake Oswego, OR 97034	Up to 70 W/R/B/S/M/		(503) 697-8818
Sherwood Inn/Best Western 15700 S.W. Upper Boones Ferry Rd. Lake Oswego, OR 97035	Sit-down: Up to 80 Reception: Up to 100 W/R/B/S/M/	101	General Manager (503) 620-2980 Fax (503) 639-9010

W=Wedding Ceremony R=Reception B=Banquet S=Seminar M=Meeting P=Picnic

 Please let these businesses know that you heard about them from the Bravo! Bridal Resource Guide.

ADDRESS	CAPACITY	GUEST ROOMS	CONTACT
A Taste of China 15450 Boones Ferry Rd. Lake Oswego, OR 97035	Up to 50 W/R/B/S/M/		Owner/Manager (503) 699-5056 Fax (503) 699-0319
MCMINNVILLE			
Golden Valley Brewery & Pub 980 E. Fourth McMinnville, OR 97128	Sit-down: Up to 65 Reception: Up to 100 (Private room) R/B/S/M/		Banquet Manager (503) 472-2739 Fax (503) 434-8523
McMenamins Hotel Oregon 310 N.E. Evens St. McMinnville, OR 97128	Up to 80 R/B/S/M/	42	(503) 492-2777 or (877) 492-2777
Youngberg Hill Vineyard 10660 Youngberg Hill Rd. McMinnville, OR 97128	Indoor: Up to 20 Outdoor: Up to 150 W/R/B/S/M/P/	6	Tasha and Kevin Byrd (503) 472-2727 (888) 657-8668
MILWAUKIE			
Amadeus at the Fernwood 2122 S.E. Sparrow Milwaukie, OR 97222 *See page 100*	Up to 300 W/R/B/S/M/		Kristina Poppmeier (503) 659-1735
Historic Broetje House 3101 S.E. Courtney Milwaukie, OR 97222 *See page 108*	Indoor/Outdoor: Up to 150 W/R/B/S/M/P/	3	Lorraine or Lois (503) 659-8860
Gray Gables Estate 3009 S.E. Chestnut Milwaukie, OR 97267 *See page 142*	Indoor/Outdoor: Up to 290 W/R/B/S/M/P/	7	(503) 654-0470 (877) 500-4729
Milwaukie Center (in North Clackamas Park) 5440 S.E. Kellogg Creek Dr. Milwaukie, OR 97222 *See page 165*	Sit-down: Up to 350 Reception: Up to 600 Two rooms W/R/B/S/M/P/		Community Use Scheduler (503) 653-8100
The Milwaukie Grange P.O. Box 220071 Milwaukie, OR 97269	Up to 150 W/R/B/S/M/		(503) 654-8771
MOLALLA			
Canterbury Falls & English Gardens P.O. Box 156 Molalla, OR 97038 *See page 109*	Outdoor: Up to 400 W/R/B/M/P/S/		Judy Hall (503) 829-8821

W=Wedding Ceremony R=Reception B=Banquet S=Seminar M=Meeting P=Picnic

PORTLAND AREA
BANQUET SITE LISTINGS

ADDRESS	CAPACITY	GUEST ROOMS	CONTACT
MOUNT HOOD/SANDY			
Best Western Sandy Inn 37465 Hwy 26 Sandy, OR 97055	Sit-down: Up to 50 B/R/P/	45	Kevin Ryan (503) 668-7100
Cedar Springs Country Estate 12353 S.E. Lusted Rd. Sandy, OR 97055 *See page 112*	Up to 200 W/R/B/		Keri or Tammy (503) 663-0772 Fax (503) 663-0772
Mt. Hood Bed & Breakfast 8885 Cooper Spur Rd. Parkdale, OR 97041 *See page 167*	Indoor/Outdoor Up to 200+ W/R/B/P/	4	Jackie Rice (541) 352-6885
Mt. Hood Meadows Ski Resort 1975 S.W. First Ave., Suite M Portland, OR 97201	Up to 400 W/R/B/S/M/P/		Marketing & Sales Office (503) 287-5438
Mt. Hood Village 65000 E. Hwy 26 Welches, OR 97067	Indoor: Up to 340 Outdoor: Up to 400+		Marilyn Peterson (503) 622-4011 ext. 215 Fax (503) 622-4881
Timberline Lodge Mount Hood, OR 97028 *See page 202*	Sit-down: Up to 200 Reception: Up to 400 W/R/B/S/M/P/	70	Catering (503) 622-0722 Fax (503) 272-3708
NEWBERG			
Chehalem Armory 620 N. Morton St. Newberg, OR 97132	Reception: Up to 350 W/R/B/S/M/		Anna (503) 538-7454
Chehalem Community Center 502 E. Second St. Newberg, OR 97132	Up to 350 R/B/		Anna (503) 538-7454
Chehalem Community Senior Center 501 Foothills Dr. Newberg, OR 97132	Up to 225 W/R/B/S/M *No alcohol		Anna (503) 538-7454
Shilo Inn 501 Sitka Ave. Newberg, OR 97132	Up to 50 R/B/		Manager (503) 537-0303
OREGON CITY			
Captain Ainsworth House Bed & Breakfast 19130 Lot Whitcomb Dr. Oregon City, OR 97045 *See page 110*	Sit-down: Up to 70 Reception: Up to 100 W/R/B/S/M/P/	4	(503) 655-5172

W=Wedding Ceremony R=Reception B=Banquet S=Seminar M=Meeting P=Picnic

 Please let these businesses know that you heard about them from the Bravo! Bridal Resource Guide.

PORTLAND AREA
BANQUET SITE LISTINGS

ADDRESS	CAPACITY	GUEST ROOMS	CONTACT
Carpenter Hall 276 Warner Milne Rd. Oregon City, OR 97045	Up to 200 W/R/B/S/M/		Manager (503) 656-7716 Fax (503) 650-8051
The Carus House Wedding Chapel 23200 S. Highway 213 Oregon City, OR 97045 *See page 328*	Sit-down: Up to 145 W/R/B/		Wedding Coordinator (503) 631-7078
Edgewater Inn 1900 Clackamette Dr. Oregon City, OR 97045	Up to 125 R/B/S/M/		Banquet Coordinator (503) 655-5155
Environmental Learning Center (Clackamas Community College) 19600 S. Molalla Ave. Oregon City, OR 97045	Up to 110 P/R/B *No alcoholic beverages		(503) 657-6958 ext. 2351 Fax (503) 650-6669
Grand Oregon Lodge 604 Seventh St. Oregon City, OR 97045 *See page 141*	Up to 299 W/R/B/S/M/		(503) 722-4190
Oregon City Golf Club 20124 S. Beavercreek Rd. Oregon City, OR 97045 *See page 174*	Sit-down: Up to 125 Reception: Up to 160 W/R/B/M/S/		Event Coordinator (503) 656-2846 (503) 656-0038
Pioneer Community Center 615 Fifth St. Oregon City, OR 97045	Up to 400		(503) 657-8287 Fax (503) 657-9851
DOWNTOWN PORTLAND			
The Adrianna Hill Grand Ballroom 918 S.W. Yamhill, 2nd Floor Portland, OR 97205 *See page 95*	Up to 300 W/R/B/S/M/		Philip Sword (503) 227-6285
Arlene Schnitzer Concert Hall 1111 S.W. Broadway at Main Portland, OR 97205	Sit-down: Up to 200 Reception: Up to 400 Theatre: Up to 2,776 W/R/B/S/M/		Booking & Sales (503) 248-4335 (503) 274-7490
The Atrium 100 S.W. Market St. Portland, OR 97201 *See page 102*	Reception: Up to 300 W/R/B/S/M/		Catering Director (503) 220-3929
Atwater's Restaurant & Bar 111 S.W. Fifth Ave., 30th Floor Portland, OR 97204 *See page 71*	Up to 300 W/R/B/S/M/		Hollie Stafford (503) 275-3662

W=Wedding Ceremony R=Reception B=Banquet S=Seminar M=Meeting P=Picnic

PORTLAND AREA BANQUET SITE LISTINGS

ADDRESS	CAPACITY	GUEST ROOMS	CONTACT
The Benson Hotel 309 S.W. Broadway at Oak Portland, OR 97205 *See page 104*	Sit-down: Up to 400 Reception: Up to 500 W/R/B/S/M/	286	Sales (503) 295-4140
British Tea Garden 725 S.W. 10th Ave. Portland, OR 97205	Sit-down: Up to 60 Bridal teas, showers, luncheons		Judith (503) 221-7817
Cassidy's Restaurant 1331 S.W. Washington Portland, OR 97205 *See page 73*	Sit-down: Up to 70 Reception: Up to 300 W/R/B/S/M/		Christine, Bob or Mercedes (503) 223-0054
Central Library 801 S.W. 10th Ave. Portland, OR 97205 *See page 114*	Reception: Up to 1,200 Sit-down: Up to 300 W/R/B/M/		Events Coordinator (503) 306-5578
City Hall 1221 S.W. Fourth Ave. Portland, OR 97204 *See page 118*	Reception: Up to 4,000 W/R/B/S/M/		Faye Musselman (503) 823-6947 Fax (503) 823-6924
The Crown Ballroom & Garden Court 918 S.W. Yamhill, 5th Floor Portland, OR 97205 *See page 121*	Sit-down: Up to 275 Reception: Up to 400 W/R/M/S/B/		Manager (503) 227-8440
Crystal Ballroom 1332 W. Burnside Portland, OR 97209 *See page 124*	Sit-down: Up to 350 W/R/B/S/M/		Mary Hendrickx (503) 492-2777
Days Inn City Center 1414 S.W. Sixth Ave. Portland, OR 97201 *See page 125*	Up to 200 W/R/B/S/M/	173	Catering Sales Manager (503) 221-1611 (800) 899-0248 Fax (503) 226-0447
Demetri's Mediterranean Restaurant 1650 W. Burnside Portland, OR 97209	Up to 150 W/R/B/S/M/		Owner (503) 222-1507
DoubleTree Hotel Downtown 310 S.W. Lincoln Portland, OR 97201 *See page 127*	Up to 250 W/R/B/S/M/	235	Sales Office (503) 221-0450
Embassy Suites—Portland Downtown 319 S.W. Pine St. Portland, OR 97204 *See pages 132*	Sit-down: Up to 220 Reception: Up to 300 R/B/S/M/	276	Catering (503) 279-9000 Fax (503) 497-9051

W=Wedding Ceremony R=Reception B=Banquet S=Seminar M=Meeting P=Picnic

 Please let these businesses know that you heard about them from the Bravo! Bridal Resource Guide.

PORTLAND AREA
BANQUET SITE LISTINGS

ADDRESS	CAPACITY	GUEST ROOMS	CONTACT
Fifth Avenue Suites Hotel/ Red Star Tavern & Roast House 506 S.W. Washington Portland, OR 97204 *See page 135*	Reception: Up to 200 R/B/S/M/C/	221	Director of Catering (503) 417-3377
Four Points Hotel Sheraton 50 S.W. Morrison St. Portland, OR 97204	Sit-down: Up to 40 Reception: Up to 50 R/B/S/M/	140	Karol Norris (503) 221-0711 Fax (503) 274-0312
First Christian Church 1315 S.W. Broadway Portland, OR 97201	Up to 300 W/R/		Dorothy Pearce (503) 228-9211 Fax (503) 222-1313
First Congregational Church 1126 S.W. Park Ave. Portland, OR 97205 *See page 329*	Ceremony: 40 to 850 Reception: Up to 175 W/R/		Church Office (503) 228-7219
The Georgian Restaurant at Meier & Frank Downtown 621 S.W. Fifth Ave., 10th Fl Portland, OR 97204 *See page 139*	Sit-down: Up to 175 Reception: Up to 250 R/B/M/S/		Special Events (503) 241-5162
Jake's Catering at The Governor Hotel 611 S.W. 10th St. Portland, OR 97205 *See page 140*	Sit-down: Up to 450 Reception: Up to 600 W/R/B/S/M/	100	Catering Sales (503) 241-2125 Fax (503) 220-1849
Greek Cusina Minoan Room 404 S.W. Washington Portland, OR 97204 *See page 143*	Up to 500 W/R/B/S/M/		Ted Papas (503) 224-2288
Harborside Restaurant 0309 S.W. Montgomery Portland, OR 97201	Sit-down: Up to 70 W/R/B/S/M/		Banquet Manager (503) 220-1865
The Heathman Hotel 1001 S.W. Broadway at Salmon St. Portland, OR 97205 *See page 146*	Sit-down: Up to 120 Reception: Up to 200 W/R/B/S/M/	75	Catering Manager (503) 790-7126
Hilton Portland 921 S.W. Sixth Ave. Portland, OR 97204 *See page 150*	Up to 1,200 W/R/B/S/M/	461	Catering (503) 220-2552 Fax (503) 220-2293
Huber's 411 S.W. Third Portland, OR 97204	Sit-down: Up to 164 Reception: Up to 164 R/B/		James or David Louie (503) 228-5686 Fax (503) 227-3922

W=Wedding Ceremony R=Reception B=Banquet S=Seminar M=Meeting P=Picnic

PORTLAND AREA BANQUET SITE LISTINGS

ADDRESS	CAPACITY	GUEST ROOMS	CONTACT
Typhoon! at the Imperial Hotel 400 S.W. Broadway Portland, OR 97205	Sit-down: Up to 150 Reception: Up to 174 R/B/S/M/	136	(503) 224-8285
Jake's Grill 611 S.W. 10th Portland, OR 97205	Up to 500 R/B/S/M		Dorcas Popp (503) 241-2125
Jasmine Tree 401 S.W. Harrison Portland, OR 97201	Up to 150 W/R/B/S/M/		Manager (503) 223-7956
Kells—Portland's Irish Restaurant & Pub 112 S.W. Second Ave. Portland, OR 97204 *See page 157*	Sit-down: Up to 150 Reception: Up to 300 W/R/B/S/M/		Banquet Manager (503) 227-4057 Fax (503) 227-5931
The Mallory Hotel 729 S.W. 15th Ave. Portland, OR 97205 *See page 160*	Sit-down: Up to 90 Reception: Up to 125 W/R/B/S/M/	150	Catering Department (503) 223-6311
Mandarin Cove Chinese Restaurant 111 S.W. Columbia Portland, OR 97201	Sit-down: Up to 250 Reception: Up to 250 W/R/B/S/M/		Jen Tsui (503) 222-0006
Portland Marriott City Center 520 S.W. Broadway Portland, OR 97205	Up to 120 R/B/S/M/	249	(503) 226-6300 Fax (503) 227-7515
Marriott Hotel—Portland 1401 S.W. Naito Parkway Portland, OR 97201 *See page 161*	Up to 1,000 W/R/B/S/M/	503	Catering (503) 499-6360
McCormick & Schmick's Seafood Restaurant 235 S.W. First Ave. Portland, OR 97201	Up to 40 R/B/S/M/		General Manager (503) 224-7522 Fax (503) 220-1881
Morton's Steakhouse 213 S.W. Clay St. Portland, OR 97201	Up to 80 R/B/S/M/		T. Angelique Leonard (503) 238-2100 Fax (503) 248-2005
New Theatre Building at the Portland Center for the Performing Arts 1111 S.W. Broadway Portland, OR 97205	Sit-down: Up to 400 Reception: Up to 1,000 W/R/B/S/M/		Booking & Sales (503) 248-4335 (503) 274-7490
The Old Church 1422 S.W. 11th Ave. Portland, OR 97201 *See page 331*	Ceremony: Up to 200 Reception: Up to 200 W/R/B/S/M/		Trish Augustin (503) 222-2031 Fax (503) 222-2981

W=Wedding Ceremony R=Reception B=Banquet S=Seminar M=Meeting P=Picnic

 Please let these businesses know that you heard about them from the Bravo! Bridal Resource Guide.

PORTLAND AREA BANQUET SITE LISTINGS

ADDRESS	CAPACITY	GUEST ROOMS	CONTACT
Oregon Sports Hall of Fame & Museum 321 S.W. Salmon St. Portland, OR 97204	Sit-down: Up to 150 Reception: Up to 300 R/B/S/M/C/P		Operations Director (503) 227-7466 Fax (503) 227-6925
Pazzo Ristorante Hotel Vintage Plaza 422 S.W. Broadway Portland, OR 97205 *See page 179*	Sit-down: Up to 120 Reception: Up to 140 W/R/B/S/M/	107	Catering (503) 412-6316
Portland Art Museum North Wing 1119 S.W. Park Ave. Portland, OR 97205 *See page 181*	Up to 1,500 W/R/B/S/M/		Food & Beverage Manager (503) 226-2811 ext. 4291
RiverPlace Hotel 1510 S.W. Harbor Way Portland, OR 97201 *See page 189*	Sit-down: Up to 200 Reception: Up to 400 W/R/B/S/M/	84	Sales & Catering (503) 423-3112
Scottish Rite Temple 701 S.W. 15th Portland, OR 97205 *See page 191*	Up to 400 W/R/B/S/M/		Bill Stanger (503) 226-7827
Tiffany Center 1410 S.W. Morrison Portland, OR 97205 *See page 201*	Up to 1,200 Theatre: Up to 975 W/R/B/S/M/		Events Manager (503) 222-0703 or (503) 248-9305
The Westin Portland 750 S.W. Alder Portland, OR 97205	Up to 120 R/B/S/M		Aaron Babbie (503) 294-9000 Fax (503) 241-9565
Wilf's Restaurant & Piano Bar N.W. Sixth & Irving Portland, OR 97209	Sit-down: Up to 150 Reception: Up to 160 R/B/S/M/		Manager (503) 223-0070 Fax (503) 223-1386
World Trade Center Two World Trade Center 25 S.W. Salmon St. Portland, OR 97204 *See page 214*	Sit-down: Up to 300 Reception: Up to 400 Outdoor: Sit-down: Up to 500 Reception: Up to 800 W/R/B/S/M/		Reservations (503) 464-8688
NORTH PORTLAND			
Courtyard Marriott—Portland North Harbour 1231 N. Anchor Way Portland, OR 97217 *See page 120*	Indoor: Up to 100 Outdoor: Up to 350 R/B/S/M/	132	Christine Skarphol (503) 735-1818 Fax (503) 735-0888
Cucina! Cucina! Italian Cafe One Center Court Portland, OR 97227	Up to 200 R/B/S/M/		Doreen Lowndes (503) 238-9800 Fax (206) 238-9749

W=Wedding Ceremony R=Reception B=Banquet S=Seminar M=Meeting P=Picnic

PORTLAND AREA BANQUET SITE LISTINGS

ADDRESS	CAPACITY	GUEST ROOMS	CONTACT
DoubleTree Hotel—Columbia River 1401 N. Hayden Island Dr Portland, OR 97217 *See page 126*	Up to 1,200 W/R/B/S/M/	351	Sales Office (503) 283-2111
DoubleTree Hotel—Jantzen Beach 909 N. Hayden Island Dr. Portland, OR 97217 *See page 128*	Up to 1,400 W/R/B/S/M/	320	Sales Office (503) 283-4466
Historic Kenton Firehouse Community Center 8105 N. Brandon Portland, OR 97217	Upstairs: Up to 20 Downstairs: Up to 100 R/M/S/B/W/		Coordinator (503) 285-7843
Interstate Firehouse Cultural Center 5340 N. Interstate Ave. Portland, OR 97217	Up to 400 Theater: Up to 110 R/S/M/W/		Rental Coordinator (503) 823-2000 Fax (503) 823-2061
The John Palmer House 4314 N. Mississippi Ave. Portland, OR 97217	Indoor: Up to 50 Outdoor: Up to 200 W/R/B/S/M/P/	3	Marketing Representative (503) 284-5893 (503) 284-1239
McMenamins St. Johns Pub 8203 N. Ivanhoe Portland, OR 97203	Sit-down: Up to 100 Reception: Up to 200 Entire facility: Up to 300 *Includes bar W/R/B/S/M/		Jeff Bryant (503) 669-8610 Fax (503) 283-8609
North Star Ballroom 635 N. Killingsworth Court Portland, OR 97217 *See page 169*	Sit-down: Up to 300 Reception: Up to 375 R/B/S/M/		Harriet Fasenfest (503) 240-6088
The Overlook House 3839 N. Melrose Dr. Portland, OR 97227 *See page 177*	Indoor: Up to 75 Outdoor: Up to 150 W/R/S/M/P/		Building Coordinator (503) 823-3188
Oxford Suites Hotel 12226 N. Jantzen Dr. Portland, OR 97217	Up to 120 R/S/M/	203 Suites	Sales (503) 283-3030 (503) 735-1661
Queen Anne Victorian Mansion 1441 N. McClellan Portland, OR 97217 *See page 185*	Sit-down: Up to 200 Reception: Up to 300 W/R/B/S/M/		Bridal Coordinator (503) 283-3224 Fax (503) 283-5605
Red Lion Inn—Coliseum 1225 N. Thunderbird Way Portland, OR 97227	Sit-down: Up to 150 Reception: Up to 300 W/R/B/S/M/	212	Catering Office (503) 235-8311

W=Wedding Ceremony R=Reception B=Banquet S=Seminar M=Meeting P=Picnic

PORTLAND AREA
BANQUET SITE LISTINGS

ADDRESS	CAPACITY	GUEST ROOMS	CONTACT
Shenanigans' on the Willamette 4575 N. Channel Portland, OR 97217 *See page 194*	Sit-down: Up to 560 Reception: Up to 800 W/R/B/S/M/		Michael Baker (503) 289-1597
University of Portland Chiles Center 5000 N. Willamette Blvd. Portland, OR 97203	Up to 5,000 R/B/S/M/		Director University Events (503) 283-7523 Fax (503) 283-7451
University of Portland Commons/Main Dining Rm 5000 N. Willamette Blvd. Portland, OR 97203	Up to 600 R/B/S/M/ *Dining room available summer breaks only		Director University Events (503) 283-7330 Fax (503) 283-7544
Widmer Gasthaus 955 N. Russel Portland, OR 97227 *See page 86*	Up to 75 B/P/M/S/		Manager (503) 281-3333 Fax (503) 331-7242
YMCA—St. Johns Center 8010 N. Charleston Portland, Oregon 97203	Large hall: Up to 100 Meeting room: Up to 30 W/R/M/S/B		Rental Coordinator (503) 721-6777 Fax (503) 721-6751
NORTHEAST PORTLAND			
The Alberta Station Ballroom 1829 N.E. Alberta Portland, OR 97211 *See page 97*	Up to 570 (open floor) W/R/B/M/		Pat Goebel (503) 282-6070
Albertina's Restaurant at The Old Kerr Nursery 424 N.E. 22nd Ave. Portland, OR 97232 *See page 98*	Up to 250 W/R/B/		Catering Coordinator (503) 231-3909
Amalfi's 4703 N.E. Fremont Portland, OR 97213	Up to 40 W/R/B/S/M/		Manager (503) 284-6747
Capers Cafe & Catering 12003 N.E. Ainsworth Circle, Suite A Portland, OR 97220 *See page 303*	Up to 150 R/B/S/M/		Christian or Annette Joly (503) 252-1718 Fax (503) 252-0178
Colwood National Golf Course 7313 N.E. Columbia Blvd. Portland, OR 97218	Up to 200 R/B/S/M/		Club Manager (503) 254-2567 Fax (503) 255-0504
Courtyard by Marriot—Lloyd Center 435 N.E. Wasco St. Portland, OR 97232	Up to 40 S/M/	202	Kathy Bayerkohler (503) 234-3200

W=Wedding Ceremony R=Reception B=Banquet S=Seminar M=Meeting P=Picnic

PORTLAND AREA BANQUET SITE LISTINGS

ADDRESS	CAPACITY	GUEST ROOMS	CONTACT
Courtyard by Marriott—Portland Airport 11550 N.E. Airport Way Portland, OR 97220	Up to 125 R/B/S/M/	150	Dawna Anderson (503) 252-3200 Fax (503) 252-8921
DoubleTree Hotel—Lloyd Center 1000 N.E. Multnomah Portland, OR 97232 *See page 129*	Up to 1,100 W/R/B/S/M/	476	Catering Office (503) 249-3130
Embassy Suites—Portland Airport 9700 N.E. 82nd Ave. Portland, OR 97220	Sit-down: Up to 563 Reception: Up to 1,127 W/R/B/S/M/	251	Sales & Catering (503) 460-3000
Hilton Garden—Airport 12048 N.E. Airport Way Portland, OR 97220	Up to 100 B/S/M/		Liz Charbonneau (503) 255-8600 Fax (503) 255-8998
Holiday Inn—Airport 8439 N.E. Columbia Blvd. Portland, OR 97220 *See page 151*	Up to 1,200 W/R/B/S/M/	286	Sales & Catering (503) 256-5000
Irvington Club 2131 N.E. Thompson Portland, OR 97212	Up to 175 W/R/B/S/M/		Rental Manager (503) 287-8749 Fax (503) 284-5308
McMenamins Kennedy School 5736 N.E. 33rd Ave. Portland, OR 97211	Reception: Up to 250 Sit-down: Up to 125 Theater: Up to 250 R/B/S/M/	35	(503) 2288-3286
O'Callahan's at the Ramada Inn 6221 N.E. 82nd Ave. Portland, OR 97220 *See page 170*	Sit-down: Up to 300 Reception: Up to 500 W/R/B/S/M/	202	Ann Conger (503) 253-2400 Fax (503) 253-1635
Oregon Convention Center 777 N.E. Martin Luther King, Jr. Blvd. Portland, OR 97232	Up to 1,200 W/R/B/S/M/		(503) 731-7851
Portland Conference Center 300 N.E. Multnomah St. Portland, OR 97232 *See page 182*	Sit-down: Up to 400 Reception: Up to 700 12 rooms W/R/B/S/M/		Event Coordinator (503) 239-9921
Radisson Hotel — Portland 1441 N.E. Second Ave. Portland, OR 97232 *See page 186*	Up to 200 R/B/S/M/	238	Director of Catering (503) 233-2401 Fax (503) 238-7016
The Refectory Restaurant 1618 N.E. 122nd Ave. Portland, OR 97230 *See page 188*	Indoor: Up to 280 R/B/S/M/		Catering Director (503) 255-8545 Fax (503) 255-8230

W=Wedding Ceremony R=Reception B=Banquet S=Seminar M=Meeting P=Picnic

 Please let these businesses know that you heard about them from the Bravo! Bridal Resource Guide.

PORTLAND AREA
BANQUET SITE LISTINGS

ADDRESS	CAPACITY	GUEST ROOMS	CONTACT
Rheinlander 5035 N.E. Sandy Blvd. Portland, OR 97213 *See page 81*	Sit-down: Up to 85 Reception: Up to 100 W/R/B/S/M/		Banquet Manager (503) 288-8410
The Ringside 14021 N.E. Glisan Portland, OR 97230	Up to 65 *Not weekends B/S/M/		Cathy/John/Michelle (503) 255-0750
Salty's on the Columbia 3839 N.E. Marine Dr. Portland, OR 97211 *See page 82*	Sit-down: Up to 80 Reception: Up to 200 W/R/B/S/M/		Dorothy Lane (503) 288-4444
Sheraton Portland Airport Hotel 8235 N.E. Airport Way Portland, OR 97220-1398 *See page 195*	Sit-down: Up to 450 Reception: Up to 750 W/R/B/S/M/	215	Catering Department (503) 249-7642 Fax (503) 249-7624
Shilo Inn Suites Hotel & Convention Center—Portland Airport/I-205 11707 N.E. Airport Way Portland, OR 97220-1075 *See page 196*	Sit-down: Up to 350 Reception: Up to 500 W/R/B/S/M/	200	Catering Office (503) 252-7500 ext. 270
Sylvia's Italian Restaurant 5115 N.E. Sandy Blvd. Portland, OR 97213 *See page 85*	Up to 80 Theatre: Up to 100 W/R/B/S/M/		Banquet Manager (503) 288-6828
Windows Sky Room & Terrace at Holiday Inn 1021 N.E. Grand Ave Portland, OR 97232 *See page 211*	Up to 250 W/R/B/S/M/	160	Sales & Catering (503) 820-4160 Fax (503) 235-0396
YWCA—N.E. Center 5630 N.E. MLK Blvd. Portland, OR 97211	Meeting Room 1: Up to 12 Meeting Room 2: Up to 25 M/S/		Rental Coordinator (503) 721-1750 Fax (503) 721-1751
NORTHWEST PORTLAND			
BridgePort Brewery 1313 N.W. Marshall Portland, OR 97209	Sit-down: Up to 250 R/B/S/M/ *Non-smoking		Event Coordinator (503) 241-7179 Fax (503) 241-0625
Couch Street Fish House 105 N.W. Third Ave. Portland, OR 97209	Sit-down: Up to 20 R/B/M/		Manager (503) 223-6173 (503) 721-0802
Crown Vista Events 19875 N.W. Logie Trail Portland, OR 97231 *See page 122*	Indoor: Up to 150 Outdoor: Up to 350 W/R/B/S/M/		Wendy Daniels (503) 240-6057

W=Wedding Ceremony R=Reception B=Banquet S=Seminar M=Meeting P=Picnic

PORTLAND AREA BANQUET SITE LISTINGS

ADDRESS	CAPACITY	GUEST ROOMS	CONTACT
Friendly House 1737 N.W. 26th Portland, OR 97210	Up to 300 R/B/S/M/P/		Facility Manager (503) 228-4391 Fax (503) 228-0085
The Gatelodge at Pittock Mansion 3229 N.W. Pittock Dr. Portland, OR 97210	Sit-down: Up to 50 B/M/P/S/		Lisette Hollis (503) 823-3627
Il Fornaio 115 N.W. 22nd Ave. Portland, OR 97210 *See page 78*	Up to 150 R/B/S/M/		Faith Chhim (503) 248-9400 or (503) 248-4324
Montgomery Park 2701 N.W. Vaughn St. Portland, OR 97210 *See page 166*	Sit-down: Up to 400 Reception: Up to 1,200 W/R/B/S/M/		Event Coordinator (503) 228-7275
Northwest Neighborhood Cultural Center 1819 N.W. Everett St. Portland, OR 97209	Sit-down: Up to 200 Reception: Up to 200 W/R/B/S/M/		Scheduling Coordinator (503) 228-6972 Fax (503) 228-8368
Paragon Restaurant & Bar 1309 N.W. Hoyt Portland, OR 97209 *See page 80*	Up to 150 R/B/S/M/		Joseph Moreau (503) 833-5060
Rock Creek Country Club Clubhouse 5100 N.W. Neakahnie Ave. Portland, OR 97229-1964	Indoor: Up to 250 Outdoor: no limit R/B/S/M/W/P/		Manager (503) 690-4826
The Screening Room 925 N.W. 19th Portland, OR 97209	Up to 120 R/M/S/		(503) 294-7153
The Uptown Billiard Club 120 N.W. 23rd Ave. Portland, OR 97210	Sit-down: Up to 80 Reception: Up to 200 R/B/M/		(503) 226-6909 or (503) 226-8980
SOUTHEAST PORTLAND			
Arnegards 1510 S.E. Ninth Portland, OR 97214 *See page 101*	Up to 450 R/B/S/M/		Robin Andersen (503) 236-2759
British Tea Garden/Tea Time 3439 S.E. Hawthorne Blvd. Portland, OR 97214	Indoor: Up to 50 Outdoor: Up to 60 W/R/B/S/M/		Sarah (503) 231-7750
Brentwood/Darlington Center 7211 S.E. 62nd Ave. Portland, OR 97206 *See page 105*	Up to 130 P/R/B/S/M/		Mary Davis (503) 306-5961 ext. 223

W=Wedding Ceremony R=Reception B=Banquet S=Seminar M=Meeting P=Picnic

 Please let these businesses know that you heard about them from the Bravo! Bridal Resource Guide.

PORTLAND AREA BANQUET SITE LISTINGS

ADDRESS	CAPACITY	GUEST ROOMS	CONTACT
Chez Grill 2229 S.E. Hawthorne Portland, OR 97214	Private room: Up to 40 Restaurant: Up to 120		Charlie Slate (503) 239-4002
Chief Obie Lodge 11300 S.E. 147th Ave. Portland, OR 97236 *See page 117*	Up to 250 *No alcohol W/R/B/S/M/P/	75	Sales Office (503) 225-5759
Crystal Springs Rhododendron Garden S.E. 28th N. of Woodstock Portland, OR 97202 *See page 325*	Indoor: Up to 125 Outdoor: Up to 300 W/R/P/B/S/M/		Event Coordinator (503) 256-2483
Eastmoreland Grill at the Eastmoreland Golf Course 2425 S.E. Bybee Blvd. Portland, OR 97202 *See page 131*	Sit-down: Up to 125 Reception: Up to 250 R/B/S/M/		Jerilyn Walker (503) 775-5910
The Fountains Ballroom 223 S.E. 122nd Ave. Portland, OR 97233 *See page 136*	Up to 300 W/R/B/S/M/		Denise or Becky (503) 261-9424 Fax (503) 261-2989
Lakeside Gardens 16211 S.E. Foster Rd. Portland, OR 97236 *See page 158*	Indoor: Up to 180 Indoor/Outdoor: Up to 300 W/R/B/S/M/P/		Consultant (503) 760-6044
The Melody Ballroom 615 S.E. Alder St. Portland, OR 97214 *See page 164*	Up to 1,100 W/R/B/S/M/		Kathleen Kaad (503) 232-2759
Oaks Park Historic Dance Pavilion At Oaks Park (Sellwood) Portland, OR 97202 *See page 171*	Indoor: Up to 500 Sit-down: Up to 275 Outdoor: Up to 1,000 W/R/B/S/M/P/		Volanne Stephens (503) 233-5777
Old Laurelhurst Church 3212 S.E. Ankeny Portland, OR 97214 *See page 172*	Up to 200 W/R/B/		Deborra (503) 231-0462
OMSI 1945 S.E. Water Ave. Portland, OR 97214 *See page 173*	Up to 4,000 R/B/S/		Event Sales (503) 797-4671
NCP Pantheon Banquet Hall 5942 S.E. 92nd Ave. Portland, OR 97266 *See page 178*	Up to 500 W/R/B/S/M/		Banquet Coordinator (503) 775-7431 Fax (503) 775-3068

W=Wedding Ceremony R=Reception B=Banquet S=Seminar M=Meeting P=Picnic

PORTLAND AREA
BANQUET SITE LISTINGS

ADDRESS	CAPACITY	GUEST ROOMS	CONTACT
Persimmon Country Club 500 S.E. Butler Rd. Gresham, OR 97080 *See page 180*	Sit-down: Up to 300 Reception: 300+ R/B/S/M/		Event Coordinator (503) 667-7500 Fax (503) 667-3885
Reed College 3203 S.E. Woodstock Blvd. Portland, OR 97202	Gray Center Lounge: 75 Auditorium: 760 Chapel: Up to 240 Banquet: Up to 400 W/R/B/S/M/P *Nondenominational		Conference/Event Planner (503) 777-7289 Fax (503) 788-6688
Sayler's Old Country Kitchen 10519 S.E. Stark Portland, OR 97216 *See page 83*	Sit-down: Up to 300 R/B/S/M/		Sally Kanan (503) 252-4171 or (503) 644-1492
Scandia Hall 1125 S.E. Madison Portland, OR 97214	Up to 299 R/B/W/S/M/		Manager (503) 232-8262
Sellwood Community Center 1436 S.E. Spokane St. Portland, OR 97202	Sit-down: Up to 75 W/R/B/S/M/		Portland Parks & Rec. Building Director (503) 823-3195 Fax (503) 823-3139
The S.M.I.L.E. Station 8210 S.E. 13th Ave. Portland, OR 97202	Sit-down: Up to 80 Reception: Up to 100 W/R/B/S/M/		Booking Director (503) 234-3570
The Wedding House 2715 S.E. 39th St. Portland, OR 97202 *See page 205*	Sit-down: Up to 100 Reception: Up to 150 W/R/B/S/M/		Owner (503) 236-7353
SOUTHWEST PORTLAND			
Buffalo Gap Saloon & Eatery 6835 S.W. Macadam Ave. Portland, OR 97219 *See page 72*	Up to 50 W/R/B/S/M/		Event Coordinator (503) 244-7111 Fax (503) 246-8848
Chart House 5700 S.W. Terwilliger Blvd. Portland, OR 97201 *See page 74*	Up to 200 W/R/B/S/M/		Banquet Manager (503) 246-6963
Ernesto's Italian Restaurant 8544 S.W. Apple Way Portland, OR 97225 *See page 75*	Sit-down: Up to 150 R/B/S/M/		Gwen Tiemeyer (503) 292-0119
Fuddruckers 10100 S.W. Washington Square Rd. Portland, OR 97223	Up to 75 R/B/S/M/		Manager (503) 620-1819

W=Wedding Ceremony R=Reception B=Banquet S=Seminar M=Meeting P=Picnic

PORTLAND AREA
BANQUET SITE LISTINGS

ADDRESS	CAPACITY	GUEST ROOMS	CONTACT
Henry Ford's Restaurant 9589 S.W. Barbur Blvd. Portland, OR 97219	Up to 300 W/R/B/S/M/		General Manager (503) 245-2434 Fax (503) 246-9901
The Multnomah Center 7688 S.W. Capitol Hwy. Portland, OR 97219	Sit-down: Up to 200 Reception: Up to 450 W/R/B/S/M/		Rental Coordinator (503) 823-2787 Fax (503) 823-3161
The Old Spaghetti Factory 0715 S.W. Bancroft Portland, OR 97201	Sit-down: 75–150 R/B/S/M/		Banquet Manager (503) 222-5375
Oregon Zoo 4001 S.W. Canyon Rd. Portland, OR 97221 *See page 176*	Indoor: Up to 800 Outdoor: Up to 6,000 W/R/B/S/M/P/		Gary Wilson or Lisa Schur (503) 220-2789 Fax (503) 220-3689
Raccoon Lodge & Brew Pub 7424 S.W. Beaverton- Hillsdale Hwy. Portland, OR 97225	Sit-down: Up to 100 Reception: Up to 150 B/M/S/R/		Banquet Manager (503) 296-0110
Shilo Inns— **Portland/Beaverton** 9900 S.W. Canyon Rd. Portland, OR 97225	Up to 160 W/R/B/S/M/	142	Catering Office (503) 297-1214 (800) 222-2244
The Sweetbrier Inn 7125 S.W. Nyberg Rd. Tualatin, OR 97062 *See page 199*	Sit-down: Up to 250 Reception: Up to 300 R/B/S/M/	131	Catering Office (503) 692-5800 Fax (503) 691-2894
Willamette Cafe **(Willamette Athletic Club)** 4949 S.W. Landing Dr. Portland, OR 97201 *See page 208*	Sit-down: Up to 100 Reception: Up to 250 R/B/S/M/		Catering Coordinator (503) 225-1068
World Forestry Center 4033 S.W. Canyon Rd. Portland, OR 97221	Sit-down: Up to 300 Reception: Up to 400 W/R/B/S/M/P/		(503) 228-1367 ext. 101
SOUTHWEST SUBURBAN			
Alfie's Wayside Country Inn 1111 Hwy 99 W. Dundee, OR 97115 *See page 99*	Up to 400 W/R/B/		Alfie (503) 538-9407
SHERWOOD			
Marjorie Stewart Senior Community Center 855 N. Sherwood Blvd. Sherwood, OR 97140	Sit-down: Up to 225 W/R/B/		Peggy Federspiel (503) 625-5644

W=Wedding Ceremony R=Reception B=Banquet S=Seminar M=Meeting P=Picnic

Please let these businesses know that you heard about them from the Bravo! Bridal Resource Guide.

PORTLAND AREA BANQUET SITE LISTINGS

ADDRESS	CAPACITY	GUEST ROOMS	CONTACT
SILVERTON			
Oregon Gardens 879 W. Main St. Silverton, OR 97381	Indoor: Up to 1,200 Outdoor: Up to 2,000 R/B/S/M/		Tamara Muldoon (503) 874-8100 Fax (503) 874-8200
TIGARD/TUALATIN			
Cucina! Cucina! Italian Cafe 10205 S.W. Washington Sq. Rd. Tigard, OR 97223	Up to 30 R/B/S/M/		Banquet Manager (503) 968-2000 Fax (503) 968-2079
Embassy Suites Hotel—Washington Square 9000 S.W. Washington Sq. Rd. Tigard, OR 97223 *See page 133*	Up to 1,200 W/R/B/S/M/	354	(503) 644-4000
Rich's Restaurant 18810 S.W. Boones Ferry Rd. Tualatin, OR 97062	Up to 50 R/B/S/M/		Banquet Manager (503) 692-1460
The Sweetbrier Inn 7125 S.W. Nyberg Rd. Tualatin, OR 97062 *See page 199*	Sit-down: Up to 250 Reception: Up to 300 R/B/S/M/	132	Catering Office (503) 692-5800 (800) 551-9167 Fax (503) 691-2894
Tualatin/Durham Senior Ctr. 8513 S.W. Tualatin Rd. Tualatin, OR 97062	Sit-down: Up to 160 W/R/B/S/M/P		Parks Department (503) 692-2000
TROUTDALE			
The Lake House at Blue Lake 21160 N.E. Blue Lake Rd. Troutdale, OR 97060	Indoor: Up to 175 Outdoor: Up to 400 W/R/B/S/M/P/		Facility Manager (503) 667-3483
McMenamins Edgefield 2126 S.W. Halsey Troutdale, OR 97060 *See page 163*	Sit-down: Up to 200 Reception: Up to 250 Theater: Up to 125 W/R/B/S/M/P/	103	Sales Office (503) 492-2777
WEST LINN			
McLean House & Park 5350 River St. West Linn, OR 97068 *See page 330*	Indoor/Outdoor: Up to 100 W/R/B/S/M/P/		(503) 655-4268
The Oregon Golf Club 25700 S.W. Pete's Mountain Rd. West Linn, OR 97068 *See page 175*	Up to 500 W/R/B/S/M/P/		Sales & Catering Office (503) 650-6900

W=Wedding Ceremony R=Reception B=Banquet S=Seminar M=Meeting P=Picnic

PORTLAND AREA BANQUET SITE LISTINGS

ADDRESS	CAPACITY	GUEST ROOMS	CONTACT
WILSONVILLE			
Charboneau On The Green 32050 S.W. Charbonneau Dr. Wilsonville, OR 97070 *See page 115*	Up to 200 W/R/B/S/M/		Bob Russell (503) 694-5234 Fax (503) 694-6385
Hunter Creek Farm 14441 S.W. Wilsonville Rd. Wilsonville, OR 97070 *See page 155*	Indoor: Up to 80 Outdoor: 400+		Angela or Marilyn (503) 625-3424
Holiday Inn Select 25425 S.W. 95th Ave. Wilsonville, OR 97070 *See page 152*	Sit-down: Up to 600 Reception: Up to 900 R/B/S/M/W	170	Catering Department (503) 682-2211
YAMHILL			
Flying M Ranch 23029 N.W. Flying M Rd. Yamhill, OR 97148	Indoor: Up to 200 Outdoor: Up to 1,500 W/R/B/S/M/P/	36	Kristen (503) 662-3222 Fax (503) 662-3202

W=Wedding Ceremony R=Reception B=Banquet S=Seminar M=Meeting P=Picnic

Notes

PORTLAND AREA
BOATS, CHARTERS & TRAINS LISTINGS

ADDRESS	CAPACITY	CONTACT
BOATS & YACHTS		
Sternwheeler "Columbia Gorge" P.O. Box 307 Cascade Locks, OR 97014 *See page 89*	Sit-down: Up to 200 Reception: Up to 350 W/R/B/S/M/P/	Sales Department (503) 223-3928
Portland Spirit 110 S.E. Caruthers Portland, OR 97204 *See page 90*	Sit-down: Up to 350 Reception: Up to 540 W/R/B/S/M/	Sales Office (503) 224-3900 (800) 224-3901 Fax (503) 286-7673
The Sternwheeler Rose 6211 N. Ensign Portland, OR 97217 *See page 91*	Up to 130 W/R/B/S/M/P/	Judy (503) 286-7673
Willamette Queen Riverfront Park Salem, OR *See page 92*	Up to 107 W/R/B/S/M/	Irene Salomon (541) 928-4090
Willamette Star 110 S.E. Caruthers Portland, OR 97204 *See page 90*	Sit-down: Up to 80 Reception: Up to 120 W/R/B/S/M/	Sales Office (503) 224-3900 (800) 224-3901 Fax (503) 286-7673
Yachts-O-Fun Cruises, Inc. Foot of S.E. Marion St. Portland, OR 97202	Sit-down: Up to 48 W/R/B/P/	Vikki Collie (503) 234-6665
TRAINS		
Mt. Hood Railroad 110 Railroad Ave. Hood River, OR 97031	Up to 330 W/R/S/M/	Passenger Service (541) 386-3556 (800) 872-4661 Fax (541) 386-2140
Vintage Trolley 115 N.W. First, Suite 200 Portland, OR 97209	Up to 70 W/R/M	Sarah Fuller (503) 323-7363

W=Wedding Ceremony R=Reception B=Banquet S=Seminar M=Meeting P=Picnic

Please let these businesses know that you heard about them from the Bravo! Bridal Resource Guide.

PORTLAND AREA
PARK SITE LISTINGS

ADDRESS	CAPACITY	CONTACT
CASCADE LOCKS		
Marine Park **& Thunder Island** Port of Cascade Locks Cascade Locks, OR 97014	Outdoor: Up to 4,000 Covered: Up to 175 W/R/B/P/	Cascade Sternwheelers (503) 223-3928
ESTACADA		
McIver State Park 24101 S. Entrance Rd. Estacada, OR 97023	Up to 1,000 W/R/S/M/	Reservations Tryon Creek State Park (503) 630-7150 or (503) 636-9886
GRESHAM		
Oxbow Park 3010 S.E. Oxbow Park Way Gresham, OR 97080	Outdoor shelter (4): Up to 350 W/R/S/M/P/B	Metro Regional Parks (503) 797-1834
MILWAUKIE		
North Clackamas Park **The Milwaukie Center** 5440 S.E. Kellogg Creek Milwaukie, OR 97222	Indoor: Up to 600 Outdoor (shelter): Up to1,200 W/R/S/M/P/	(503) 653-8100
PORTLAND		
Blue Lake Park 205000 N.E. Marine Drive Fairview, OR 97024	Outdoor: Up to 7,000 Covered (10): 50 to 125 Lake House: Up to 175 W/R/P/B/S/M/	Metro Regional Parks (503) 797-1834
Council Crest Park S.W. Council Crest Dr. Portland, OR 97201	Outdoor (no shelter): Up to 150 W/R/	Parks Permit Center (503) 823-2525
Crystal Springs **Rhododendron Garden** S.E. 28th/North of Woodstock Portland, OR 97215 *See page 325*	Indoor: (shelter) Up to 150 Outdoor: 3 sites Up to 200 W/R/P/M/S/	Rita Knapp (503) 256-2483
Howell Territorial Park 13901 N.W. Howell Rd. Sauvie Island, OR	Outdoor : Up to 300 W/R/B/P/S/M/	James Metro Parks & Greenspaces (503) 797-1834
Hoyt Arboretum 4000 S.W. Fairview Blvd. Portland, OR 97221	Outdoor (shelter): Up to 140 W/R/P/	Parks Permit Center (503) 823-2514
Hoyt Wedding Meadow 4000 S.W. Fairview Blvd. Portland, OR 97221	Outdoor (no shelter): Up to 100 W/R/P/	Parks Permit Center (503) 823-2525

W=Wedding Ceremony R=Reception B=Banquet S=Seminar M=Meeting P=Picnic

PORTLAND AREA
PARK SITE LISTINGS

ADDRESS	CAPACITY	CONTACT
Laurelhurst Park S.E. 39th & Oak Portland, OR 97214	Outdoor (no shelter): 100+ W/R/P/	Parks Permit Center (503) 823-2525
Leach Botanical Gardens 6704 S.E. 122nd Ave. Portland, OR 97236	Indoor: Up to 70 Outdoor: Up to 85 W/R/B/S/M/P/	Rental Coordinator (503) 761-9503
Mt. Tabor Park S.E. 60th & Salmon Portland, OR 97214	Outdoor (shelter): 100+ W/R/P/	Parks Permit Center (503) 823-2525
Oaks Park S.E. Portland (Sellwood area) Portland, OR 97202 *See page 171*	Up to 1,000 P/R/B/S/	(503) 233-5777
The Overlook House 3839 N. Melrose Dr. Portland, OR 97227 *See page 177*	Indoor: Up to 75 Outdoor: Up to 150 W/R/S/M/P/	Building Coordinator (503) 823-3188
Peninsula Park **Rose Garden** N. Albina & Portland Blvd. Portland, OR 97217	Outdoor: Up to 70 (shelter) W/R/P/	Parks Permit Center (503) 823-2525
Pier Park N. Seneca & St. John's Portland, OR 97203	Outdoor (shelter): 200+ W/R/P	Parks Permit Center (503) 823-2525
Pioneer Courthouse **Square** 701 S.W. Sixth Ave. Portland, OR 97204	Outdoor: Up to 15,000 W/R/B/M/P/	Program Director (503) 223-1613 Fax (503) 222-7425
Washington Park **Rose Garden Amphitheater** 400 S.W. Kingston Blvd. Portland, OR 97201	Outdoor: Up to 3,000 W/R/P/	Parks Permit Center (503) 823-2525
ST. PAUL		
Champoeg Park 8239 Champoeg Rd., N.E. St. Paul, OR 97060	Indoor: Up to 49 Outdoor: Up to 200 W/R/P/	Reservation Information (503) 678-1251 (800) 452-5687
TROUTDALE		
Glenn Otto Comm Park **& Sam Cox Bldg.** 1120 E. Historic Columbia River Hwy. Troutdale, OR 97060	Indoor: Up to 250 Outdoor: Up to 1,000 W/R/B/S/M/P/	Samantha (503) 665-5175 ext. 254 Fax (503) 665-1137
WASHINGTON COUNTY		
Cedar Hills Park Cedar Hills Blvd. & Walker Rd. Beaverton, OR 97005	Outdoor only: Up to 100 W/R/P/	Tualatin Hills Park & Rec. (503) 645-3539 Fax (503) 614-9514

W=Wedding Ceremony   R=Reception   B=Banquet   S=Seminar   M=Meeting   P=Picnic

PORTLAND AREA
PARK SITE LISTINGS

ADDRESS	CAPACITY	CONTACT
Jenkins Estate Grabhorn Rd. at S.W. 209th & Farmington Aloha, OR 97006	Indoor: Up to 125 Outdoor: Up to 175 Stable: Up to 250 W/R/B/S/M/P/	Program Supervisor (503) 642-3855 Fax (503) 591-1028
Metzger Park Hall 8400 S.W. Hemlock St. Portland, OR 97223	Indoor Facility Ceremony: Up to 100 Reception: Up to 200 W/R/B/S/M/P/	Administrative Assistant (503) 246-0998
Raleigh Park 3500 S.W. 78th Ave. Portland, OR 97225	Outdoor Only: Up to 100 W/R/P/	Tualatin Hills Park & Rec. (503) 645-3539 Fax (503) 614-9514
Scoggins Valley Park/ **Henry Hagg Lake** 111 S.E. Washington Hillsboro, OR 97124	"C" Ramp Pavilion: Up to 700 Sain Pavilion: Up to 300 2 additional sites: Up to 80 W/R/P/	Administrative Asst. (503) 648-8715
WEST LINN		
McLean House & Park 5350 River St. West Linn, OR 97068 *See page 330*	Indoor/Outdoor: Up to 100 W/R/B/S/M/P/	(503) 655-4268
Willamette Park 12th & Volpp St. West Linn, OR 97068	Gazebo: Up to 35 Willamette Shelter: Up to 64 Entire Park Area: Up to 200	Parks Department (503) 557-4700 Fax (503) 657-3237

W=Wedding Ceremony R=Reception B=Banquet S=Seminar M=Meeting P=Picnic

OREGON WINERY SITE LISTINGS

ADDRESS	CAPACITY	CONTACT
Airlie Winery 15305 Dunn Forest Rd. Monmouth, OR 97361	Outdoor: Up to 200 W/R/B/P/	Owner (503) 838-6013
BeckenRidge Vineyard 300 Reuben-Boise Rd. Dallas, OR 97338 *See page 103*	Up to 120 W/R/B/S/M/	Becky Jacroux (503) 831-3652
Champoeg Wine Cellars 10375 Champoeg Rd. N.E. Aurora, OR 97002	Indoor: Up to 20 Outdoor: Up to 100 W/R/B/P	Manager (503) 678-2144
Chateau Bianca Winery 17485 Hwy 22 Dallas, OR 97338	Indoor: Up to 50 Outdoor: Up to 250 W/R/B/S/M/P/	Bianca Wetzel (503) 623-6181
Chateau Lorane 27415 Siuslaw River Rd. Lorane, OR 97451	Indoor: Up to 80 Outdoor: Up to 300 W/R/B/P/	Special Events Coord. (541) 942-8028 (541) 942-5830
Elk Cove Vineyards 27751 N.W. Olson Rd. Gaston, OR 97119	Indoor: Up to 200 Outdoor: limited W/R/B/S/M/P/	Hospitality Director (503) 985-7760
Eola Hills Wine Cellars 501 S. Pacific Hwy. W. Rickreall, OR 97371	Indoors: Up to 250 Outdoors: Up to 250+ W/R/B/S/M/P/	Special Events Coord. (503) 623-2405 Fax (503) 623-0350
Erath Vineyards 9009 N.E. Worden Hill Rd. Dundee, OR 97115	Indoor: Up to 25 Outdoor: Up to 50 P/M/S/	Sherri Rouman (800) 539-9463
Flerchinger Vineyards 4200 Post Canyon Dr. Hood River, OR 97301	Indoor: Up to 30 Outdoor: Up to 100 W/R/B/S/M/P/	Manager (800) 516-8710
Honeywood Winery 1350 Hines St. S.E. Salem, OR 97302	Indoor: Up to 150 W/R/B/S/M/P/	Special Events Coord. (503) 362-4111 Fax (503) 362-4112
Kramer Vineyards 26830 N.W. Olson Rd. Gaston, OR 97119	Indoor: Up to 30 Outdoor: Upt to 100 W/R/S/M/P/	Trudy Kramer (503) 662-4545
Laurel Ridge Winery 46350 N.W. David Hill Rd. P.O. Box 456 Forest Grove, OR 97116	Indoor: Up to 65 W/R/B/S/M/P/	Special Events Coord. (503) 359-5436
Marquam Hill Vineyards 35803 S. Hwy. 213 Molalla, OR 97038	Indoor: Up to 20 Outdoor: Up to 2,000 W/R/M/P/	Marylee or Joe Dobbes (503) 829-6677
Rex Hill Winery 30835 N. Hwy 99W Newberg, OR 97132	Indoor: Up to 150 Outdoor: Up to 200 Amphitheater: Up to 300	(503) 538-0666
Stangeland Vineyards & Winery 8500 Hopewell Rd. N.W. Salem, OR 97304	Indoor: Up to 50 Outdoor: Up to 200 W/R/B/S/M/P/	Special Events Coord. (503) 581-0355

W=Wedding Ceremony R=Reception B=Banquet S=Seminar M=Meeting P=Picnic

Please let these businesses know that you heard about them from the Bravo! Bridal Resource Guide.

OREGON
WINERY SITE LISTINGS

ADDRESS	CAPACITY	CONTACT
St. Josef's Wine Cellars 28836 S. Barlow Rd. Canby, OR 97013	Indoor: Up to 125 Indoor/Outdoor: Up to 250 W/R/B/S/M/P/	Lilly Fleischmann (503) 651-3190
Willamette Valley Vineyards 8800 Enchanted Way S.E. Turner, OR 97392 *See page 210*	Indoor/Outdoor: Up to 600 W/R/B/S/M/P/	Hospitality Coordinator (503) 588-4024 (800) 344-9463
Wine Country Farm 6855 Breyman Orchards Rd. Dayton, OR 97114 *See page 212*	Indoor: Up to 80 Outdoor: Up to 300 W/R/B/P/S/M	Joan Davenport (503) 864-3446
Youngberg Hill Vineyard 10660 S.W. Youngberg Hill McMinnville, OR 97128	Indoor: Up to 20 Outdoor: Up to 120 W/R/B/P/M/	Kevin & Tasha Byrd (503) 472-2727 (888) 657-8668

W=Wedding Ceremony R=Reception B=Banquet S=Seminar M=Meeting P=Picnic

© Hostess House Chapel and Reception Center • page 154

THE WEDDING SLIP

A law was passed in 1547 stating that if a woman wore only a slip at her wedding, it would be considered a public announcement that any debts she or a previous husband may have incurred were not her new husband's responsibility.

VANCOUVER AREA
CEREMONY & BANQUET SITE LISTINGS

ADDRESS	CAPACITY	GUEST ROOMS	CONTACT
BATTLE GROUND			
Battle Ground Senior Center 116 N.E. Third Ave. Battle Ground, WA 98604	Up to 100 *No alcohol		Battle Ground City Hall (360) 687-7131
The Burdoin Mansion 18609 N.E. Cramer Rd. Battle Ground, WA 98604 *See page 327*	Indoor: Up to 100 Outdoor: Up to 200 R/B/S/M/P/		Rob and Becky Neuschwander (360) 666-4828
BRUSH PRAIRIE			
The Cedars Golf Club 15001 N.E. 181st St. Brush Prairie, WA 98606	Sit-down: Up to 175 Reception: Up to 250 R/B/S/M/		Vickie Hernandez (360) 687-6092 (503) 285-7548
CAMAS			
Camas Community Center 1718 S.E. Seventh Camas, WA 98607	Up to 300 R/B/S/M		Parks & Recreation Dept. (360) 834-7092
Crown Park N.E. 15th Ave. & Everett St. Camas, WA 98607	20′ x 20′ Picnic Shelter *No alcohol P/		Parks & Recreation Dept. (360) 834-7092
The Fairgate Inn **Bed & Breakfast** 2313 N.W. 23rd Ave. Camas, WA 98607 *See page 134*	Up to 200 W/R/B/S/M/		Chris Foyt (360) 834-0861
GOLDENDALE			
Maryhill Museum of Art 35 Maryhill Museum Dr. Goldendale, WA 98620	Indoor: Up to 75 Outdoor: Up to 1,500 W/R/B/S/M/P/		Elizabeth Toscano at Cherry Hill (541) 478-4455
RIDGEFIELD			
Clark County **Fair Association** 17402 N.E. Delfel Rd. Ridgefield, WA 98642	Indoor: Up to 200 Outdoor: 100+ Grandstand: Up to 7,200 W/R/B/S/M/P/		Tomi Mosby Events Coordinator (360) 737-6180
VANCOUVER			
A Night In Shining Amour **Regal Hall Ballroom** 115 W. Ninth St. Vancouver, WA 98660 *See page 93*	Ceremony: Up to 125 Reception: Up to 175 R/B/S/M/		Pam and Joe Thielman (360) 750-7891

W=Wedding Ceremony R=Reception B=Banquet S=Seminar M=Meeting P=Picnic

Please let these businesses know that you heard about them from the Bravo! Bridal Resource Guide.

VANCOUVER AREA CEREMONY & BANQUET SITE LISTINGS

ADDRESS	CAPACITY	GUEST ROOMS	CONTACT
The Academy Chapel & Ballroom 400 E. Evergreen Blvd. Vancouver, WA 98660 *See page 94*	Ceremony: 225 Reception: Up to 300 Sit-down: Up to 225 W/R/B/S/M/		Windsor Consultants (360) 696-4884
Aero Club 9901 N.E. Seventh Ave. Vancouver, WA 98685 *See page 96*	Up to 150 W/R/B/S/M/		Cheryl Taylor (360) 574-7124 Fax (360) 574-2936
American Legion/Post 14 710 Esther St. Vancouver, WA 98660	Up to 350 R/B/S/M/		Les Scott (360) 696-2579
American Legion/Post 176 14011 N.E. 20th Ave. Vancouver, WA 98686	Up to 200 R/B/S/M/ W/R/S/M/		Karen (360) 573-2331 Fax (360) 573-1475
Bagley Center 4100 Plomondon Vancouver, WA 98661	Reception: Up to 350 Sit-down: Up to 300 W/R/B/S/M/ *No alcohol		Facilities Coordinator (360) 696-8219
Best Western Ferryman's Inn 7901 N.E. Sixth Ave. Vancouver, WA 98665	Up to 200 R/B/S/M/	134	Manager (360) 574-2151
Chart House 101 E. Columbia Wy. Vancouver, WA 98661	Up to 200 W/R/B/S/M/		General Manager (360) 693-9211
City Grill—Northeast 605 N.E. 78th St. Vancouver, WA 98605	Up to 125 W/R/B/S/M/		Banquet Manager (360) 574-2270
City Grill—Southeast 916 S.E. 164th Ave. Vancouver, WA 98683	Up to 125 W/R/B/S/M/		Banquet Manager (360) 253-5399
Clark County Saddle Club 10505 N.E. 117th Ave. Vancouver, WA 98662	Up to 150 R/B/S/M/		Rental Coordinator (360) 260-1408
Clark County Square Dance Center 10713 N.E. 117th Ave. Vancouver, WA 98662	Up to 500 W/R/B/S/M/		Rental Coordinator (360) 256-5049
Club Green Meadows 7703 N.E. 72nd Ave. Vancouver, WA 98661	Indoor: Up to 275 W/R/B/S/M/		Banquet Manager (360) 256-1510
Covington House 4201 Main St. Vancouver, WA 98660	Up to 75 W/R/B/S/M/		Owner (360) 695-6750
The Crossing Restaurant 900 W. Seventh St. Vancouver, WA 98660	Sit-down: Up to 100 W/R/B/S/M/		Catering Manager (360) 695-8220 Fax (360) 695-8626

W=Wedding Ceremony R=Reception B=Banquet S=Seminar M=Meeting P=Picnic

VANCOUVER AREA
CEREMONY & BANQUET SITE LISTINGS

ADDRESS	CAPACITY	GUEST ROOMS	CONTACT
First Evangelical Church 4120 N.E. St. Johns Rd. Vancouver, WA 98661	Auditorium: Up to 300 Reception: Up to 200 W/R/S/M/		(360) 694-2525
Fruit Valley Community Center 3203 Unander St. Vancouver, WA 98660	Up to 100 *No alcohol W/R/		Irene Ells (360) 694-5450
The Heathman Lodge 7801 N.E. Greenwood Dr. Vancouver, WA 98662 *See page 147*	Indoor: Up to 300 R/B/M/S/	143	Catering Office (360) 254-3100 or (888) 475-3100
Hostess House Chapel & Reception Center 10017 N.E. Sixth Ave. Vancouver, WA 98685 *See page 154*	Ceremony: Up to 200 Reception: Up to 300 Sit-down: Up to 175 W/R/B/S/M/		(360) 574-3284
Leverich Park 39th & Main St. Vancouver, WA	Sit-down: Up to 100 W/R/B/S/M/P/		Facilities Coordinator Bagley Center (360) 696-8236
Life Center Church 10709 S.E. 10th St. Vancouver, WA 98664	Reception: Up to 150 (only if using chapel) *Kitchen available		Rev. Thurston (360) 892-6020
Luepke Senior Center 1009 E. McLoughlin Blvd. Vancouver, WA 98663	Up to 300 *No alcohol W/R/B/S/M/		Facilities Coordinator (360) 696-8219
Magnolia Gardens 9113 N.E. 117th Ave. Vancouver, WA 98662	Outdoor: Up to 175 *No alcohol W/D/R/B/		Kel Crafton (360) 256-4753
Marshall Center 1009 E. McLoughlin Blvd. Vancouver, WA 98663	Up to 125 R/B/S/M/ *No alcohol		Facility Coordinator (360) 696-8219
The Marshall House 1301 Officers' Row Vancouver, WA 98661 *See page 162*	Indoor: Up to 225 W/R/S/M/		Frances Anderson (360) 693-3103
My Sister & I 116 E. Evergreen Blvd. Vancouver, WA 98660	Up to 50 W/R/B/S/M/		Owner (360) 695-2164
Pearson Air Museum 1115 E. Fifth St. Vancouver, WA 98661	Up to 500 W/R/B/		John Nold (360) 694-7026
Red Lion Hotel at the Quay 100 Columbia St. Vancouver, WA 98660 *See page 187*	Up to 600 W/R/B/S/M/	160	Director of Catering (360) 694-8341

W=Wedding Ceremony R=Reception B=Banquet S=Seminar M=Meeting P=Picnic

 Please let these businesses know that you heard about them from the Bravo! Bridal Resource Guide.

ADDRESS	CAPACITY	GUEST ROOMS	CONTACT
Sheldon's Cafe at the Grant House 1101 Officers' Row Vancouver, WA 98661 *See page 193*	Up to 100+ (3 rooms) W/D/R/B/		Gary or Barbara Sheldon (360) 699-1213
Shilo Inn—Vancouver 401 E. 13th St. Vancouver, WA 98660	Up to 25 W/R/B/S/M/	120	Manager (360) 696-0411
Touch of Elegance 205 E. 16th St. Vancouver, WA 98663 *See page 203*	Up to 125		Cindy Hammond (360) 694-3608
Water Works Park on Reserve behind Clark College Vancouver, WA	No maximum Outdoor amphitheater W/R/P/		Facilities Coordinator (360) 696-8219
The Wedding Place 908 Esther St. Vancouver, WA 98660	Indoor: Up to 50 W/R/B/S/M/		(360) 693-1798
Who-Song & Larry's 111 E. Columbia River Wy. Vancouver, WA 98661	Up to 70 W/R/B/S/M/		Manager (360) 695-1198
WASHOUGAL			
Hathaway Park G St. & 24th Washougal, WA 98671	Outdoor (shelter): Up to 50 W/R/B/P/		Brenda Snell (360) 835-8501
Washougal Community Ctr. 1681 C St. Washougal, WA 98671	Indoor: Up to 108 Auditorium: 120 R/B/S/M/		City of Washougal (360) 835-8501

W=Wedding Ceremony R=Reception B=Banquet S=Seminar M=Meeting P=Picnic

Notes

© Settlemier House • page 192

TRADITION

In Medieval times,

as part of the bride's dowry,

a shoe was given to the groom, who nailed it on the wall

over the wedding bed to symbolize the transfer of

authority of the bride to her new husband.

SALEM AREA CEREMONY SITE LISTINGS

ADDRESS	CAPACITY	GUEST ROOMS	CONTACT
Brooks Assembly of God P.O. Box 9099 9165 Portland Rd. N.E Brooks, OR 97305	Ceremony: Up to 425 W/R/		Wedding Coordinator (503) 393-2155 Fax (503) 393-0778
Calvary Baptist Church 1230 Liberty Rd. S.E. Salem, OR 97302	Up to 350 W/R/		Wedding Coordinator (503) 363-9246
Englewood United Methodist Church 1110 17th N.E. Salem, OR 97301	Up to 150 W/R/		Administrative Assistant (503) 364-4555
First United Methodist 600 State St. Salem, OR 97301	Ceremony: Up to 450 Reception: Up to 250 W/R/		Kay Kemper (503) 364-6709
Lancaster Assembly of God 491 Lancaster Dr. NE Salem, OR 97301	Up to 300 W/		Wedding Coordinator (503) 363-3303 or (503) 393-5530
Micah Ballroom 680 State St. Salem, OR 97301	Sit-down: Up to 530 *Non-smoking *No alcohol R/B/P/M/S/W/		Wedding Coordinator (503) 315-7990
Monmouth Christian Church 189 S. Monmouth Monmouth, OR 97361	Up to 250 W/R/		Church Office (503) 838-1145 Fax (503) 838-3453
Scottish Rite Masonic Center 4090 Commercial St. S.E. Salem, OR 97302	Sit-down: Up to 250 Reception: Up to 500 W/R/B/S/M/ *No alcohol		Building Manager (503) 363-9240 Fax (503) 363-2018
St. Joseph Catholic 721 Chemeketa Salem, OR 97301	Ceremony: Up to 600 W/		Wedding Coordinator (503) 581-1623
Woodland Chapel 582 High St. S.E. Salem, OR 97301 *See page 332*	Ceremony: Up to 125 W/R/M/		Office Administrator (503) 362-4139

W=Wedding Ceremony R=Reception B=Banquet S=Seminar M=Meeting P=Picnic

SALEM AREA
BANQUET SITE LISTINGS

ADDRESS	CAPACITY	GUEST ROOMS	CONTACT
DOWNTOWN SALEM			
Micah Ballroom 680 State St. Salem, OR 97301	Sit-down: Up to 530 *Non-smoking *No alcohol R/B/P/M/S/W/		Wedding Coordinator (503) 315-7990
NORTHEAST SALEM			
Best Western Pacific Highway Inn 4646 Portland Rd. N.E. Salem, OR 97305	Two banquet rooms: Up to 65 M/S		Sales Office (503) 390-3200 Fax (503) 393-7989
O'Callahans Restaurant & Catering at the Quality Inn Hotel & Convention Center 3301 Market St. N.E. Salem, OR 97301	Up to 450 W/R/B/S/M/P/	150	Sales & Catering (503) 370-7835 or (503) 370-7997
Canton Garden Restaurant 3225 Market St. N.E. Salem, OR 97301	Up to 120 R/B/S/M/		Mary or Simon (503) 588-1125
Heritage Tree Restaurant 574 Cottage N.E. Salem, OR 97301	Up to 90 W/R/B/S/M/		Owner (503) 399-7075
Izzy's Pizza Restaurant 2205 Lancaster Dr. N.E. Salem, OR 97305	Up to 35 R/B/S/M/		Manager (503) 399-0915
Oregon State Fair & Expo Center 2330 17th St. NE Salem, OR 97310	50 to 4,000+ W/R/B/S/M/P/		Events Manager (503) 378-3247 Fax (503) 373-1788
Quality Inn Hotel & Convention Center 3301 Market St. N.E. Salem, OR 97301	Up to 450 W/R/B/S/M/	150	Catering (503) 370-7835 or (800) 248-6273
Reed Opera House 189 Liberty St. N.E. Salem, OR 97301	Up to 300 W/R/B/S/M/		Events Coordinator (503) 391-4481
Salem Inn 1775 Freeway Ct. N.E. Salem, OR 97303 *See page 190*	Up to 50 R/M/S/	64	John and Dora Anderson (503) 588-0515 (888) 305-0515
Salem Senior Center 1055 Erixon St. N.E. Salem, OR 97303	Up to 300 W/R/S/M/		Center Secretary (503) 588-6303 Fax (503) 588-6377

W=Wedding Ceremony R=Reception B=Banquet S=Seminar M=Meeting P=Picnic

Please let these businesses know that you heard about them from the Bravo! Bridal Resource Guide.

SALEM AREA
BANQUET SITE LISTINGS

ADDRESS	CAPACITY	GUEST ROOMS	CONTACT
NORTHWEST SALEM			
Eola Inn 4250 Salem Hwy. Salem, OR 97304	50-150 R/B/S/M/		Owner (503) 378-7521
La Estrellita 1111 Edgewater St. N.W. Salem, OR 97304	Up to 80 R/B/S/M/		Manager (503) 362-0522
McGrath's Public Fish House 350 Chemeketa St. N.W. Salem, OR 97301	Up to 30 B/M/R/		Manager (503) 362-0736
Roth's Hospitality Meeting Center 1130 Wallace Rd. N.W. Salem, OR 97304	5 Banquet rooms: Up to 150 W/R/B/P/M/S/		Catering Dept. (503) 370-3790 Fax (503) 581-4762
SOUTH SALEM			
Phoenix Inn—South Salem 4370 Commercial St. S. Salem, OR 97302	2 Banquet rooms Up to 50 D/R/B		Sales Dept. (503) 588-9220 Fax (503) 585-3616
Rudy's at Salem Golf Club 2025 Golf Course Rd. S. Salem, OR 97302	Sit-down: Up to 150 W/R/B/S/M/		Owner (503) 399-0449
SOUTHEAST SALEM			
Alessandro's Plaza Restaurant 325 High St. S.E. Salem, OR 97301	Sit-down: Up to 300 R/B/S/M/		Chris (503) 370-9951
Big Horn Brewing Co. 515 12th St. S.E. Salem, OR 97302	Sit-down: Up to 40 Reception: Up to 75 R/B/		Banquet Manager (503) 363-1904 Fax (503) 375-9327
Chelsea's Restaurant 4053 Commercial St. S.E Salem, OR 97302	Up to 45 R/B/S/M/		Manager (503) 585-1175
Creekside Golf Club 6250 Clubhouse Dr. S.E. Salem, OR 97306	Up to 220 W/R/B/S/M/P/		Banquet Manager (503) 363-4653
Historic Deepwood Estate 1116 Mission St. S.E. Salem, OR 97302	Indoor: Up to 57 Outdoor: Up to 150 W/R/B/S/M/		Staff Director (503) 363-1825
Historic Elsinore Theatre 170 High St. S.E. Salem, OR 97301	Reception: Up to 200 R/B/W/S/M/		Manager (503) 375-3574 Fax (503) 375-0284
Izzy's Pizza Restaurant 2990 Commercial St. S.E. Salem, OR 97302	Up to 50 R/B/		Manager (503) 581-9831 Fax (503) 316-3909

W=Wedding Ceremony   R=Reception   B=Banquet   S=Seminar   M=Meeting   P=Picnic

SALEM AREA
BANQUET SITE LISTINGS

ADDRESS	CAPACITY	GUEST ROOMS	CONTACT
Mill Creek Inn—Best Western 3125 Ryan Dr. S.E. Salem, OR 97301	Up to 200 W/R/B/S/M/C/		Manager (503) 585-3332
Mission Mill Village 1313 Mill St. S.E. Salem, OR 97301	Ceremony: Up to 100 Reception: Up to 450 W/R/S/M/P/B/		Tracy Stroud (503) 585-7012
Rangler's Ranch House 3743 Commercial St. S.E. Salem, OR 97302	Up to 60 R/B/S/M/		Nancy Williams (503) 378-1738
Scottish Rite Masonic Center 4090 Commercial St. S.E. Salem, OR 97302	Sit-down: Up to 250 Reception: Up to 500 *No alcohol W/R/B/S/M/		Building Manager (503) 363-9240 Fax (503) 363-2018
DALLAS/RICKREALL			
Eola Hills Wine Cellars 501 S. Pacific Hwy. 99W Rickreall, OR 97371	Indoor: Up to 250 Outdoor: Up to 250+ P/R/B/S/M/		Special Events Coord. (503) 623-2405
Polk County Fairgrounds 520 S. Pacific Hwy. W. Rickreall, OR 97371	Up to 1,000 W/R/B/S/M/P/ *Multiple bldgs. available		Manager (503) 623-3048 or (503) 745-7256
EUGENE/SPRINGFIELD			
DoubleTree Hotel 3280 Gateway Rd. Springfield, OR 97477	Up to 2,000 R/B/S/M		Kim Barbisan (541) 988-4019
Valley River Inn 1000 Valley River Way Eugene, OR 97401	Up to 800 R/B/S/M/	257	Donna Earley-Thiel (541) 341-3461 Fax (541) 689-0289
INDEPENDENCE			
Inn at Oak Knoll 6345 Salem-Dallas Hwy. Independence, OR 97351	Up to 93 R/B/M/		Manager (503) 378-0102 Fax (503) 399-0348
KEIZER			
Collett's Restaurant & Bar 165 McNary Estate Dr., N. Keizer, OR 97303	Up to 200 W/R/B/S/M/		Banquet Coordinator (503) 393-4111
Keizer Lions Auditorium 4100 Cherry Ave. N.E. Keizer, OR 97303	Up to 180 W/R/B/M/		Rental Committee Chairperson (503) 390-1172
Wittenberg Inn 5188 Wittenberg Lane Keizer, OR 97303 *See page 213*	Up to 450 R/B/S/M/	86	Richard Andres (503) 390-4733

W=Wedding Ceremony R=Reception B=Banquet S=Seminar M=Meeting P=Picnic

SALEM AREA
BANQUET SITE LISTINGS

ADDRESS	CAPACITY	GUEST ROOMS	CONTACT
MONMOUTH			
Gentle House 855 N. Monmouth Ave. Monmouth, OR 97361 *See page 138*	Indoor: Up to 200 Outdoor: Up to 500 W/R/B/S/M/P/		Program Coordinator (503) 838-8673 Fax (503) 838-8289
SUBLIMITY			
Silver Falls Conference Center 20022 Silver Falls Hwy. S.E. Sublimity, OR 97385	Indoor: Up to 86 W/R/B/S/M/P/		Dayna Rich (503) 873-8875 Fax (503) 873-2937
Silver Falls Vineyards 4972 Cascade Hwy S.E. Sublimity, OR 97385 *See page 197*	Indoor/Outdoor: Up to 300 W/R/M/B/		Duane Defrees (503) 769-5056
TURNER			
Willamette Valley Vineyards 8800 Enchanted Way S.E. Turner, OR 97392 *See page 210*	Indoor/Outdoor: Up to 600 R/B/S/M/C/		Hospitality Coordinator (503) 588-4024 (800) 344-9463
WOODBURN			
Settlemier House 355 N. Settlemier Ave. Woodburn, OR 97071 *See page 192*	Indoor: Up to 85 Oudoor: 300+ W/R/B/M/		(503) 982-1897
SALEM			
Bush Pasture Park Rose Garden 600 Mission St. S.E. Salem, OR 97301	Outdoor: Up to 100 *No tables or chairs W/P/R/		Bruce Bolton (503) 588-6261
Cascade Gateway Park 2100 Turner Rd. S.E. Salem, OR 97302	Covered: Up to 300 2 uncovered: Up to 150		Bruce Bolton (503) 588-6261
Minto Brown Island 2200 Minto Island Rd. (Off S. River Rd.) Salem, OR 97302	Outdoor (shelter): Up to 150 W/R/M/P/		Bruce Bolton (503) 588-6261
Spongs Landing Marion County Parks 2500 Niagra St., N. Salem, OR 97303	Up to 300 2 shelter areas W/R/P/M		Denise Clark (503) 588-5036 Fax (503) 588-7970
Willamette Mission State Park 10991 Wheatland Rd., N.E. Gervais, OR 97026	Up to 2,000 W/R/B/P/		(503) 393-1172 ext. 23 (800) 452-5687

W=Wedding Ceremony R=Reception B=Banquet S=Seminar M=Meeting P=Picnic

 Please let these businesses know that you heard about them from the Bravo! Bridal Resource Guide.

© The Inn at Outer Crest • page 156

COASTAL, CENTRAL AND SOUTHERN OREGON SITES

TRADITION

In Medieval times,

as part of the bride's dowry,

a shoe was given to the groom, who nailed it on the wall

over the wedding bed to symbolize the transfer of

authority of the bride to her new husband.

COASTAL AREA
BANQUET AND EVENT SITE LISTINGS

ADDRESS	CAPACITY	GUEST ROOMS	CONTACT
The Adobe Resort 1555 Hwy 101 N. Yachats, OR 97498	Up to 100 R/B/S/M/	97 10 suites	Deana or Gary (800) 522-3623
Best Western Oceanview Resort 414 N. Prom Seaside, OR 97138	Up to 300 R/B/S/M/	104	Leslie Peterson (800) 234-8439 Fax (503) 738-3264
Chinook Winds Convention Center 1777 N.W. 44th St. Lincoln City, OR 97367	Indoor: Up to 1,500 R/B/M/S/		Sales Staff (888) CHINOOK
Driftwood Shores 88416 First Ave. Florence, OR 97439	Up to 150 R/B/S/M/	136	Jennifer Fox (800) 422-5091
Embarcadero Resort Hotel 1000 S.E. Bay Blvd. Newport, OR 97365	Up to 150 R/B/S/M/	75	(541) 265-8521 (800) 547-4779
Florence Events Center 715 Quince Florence, OR 97439	Up to 500 R/B/S/M/		Barbara Gulias (541) 997-1994 Fax (541) 902-0991
Hallmark Inns & Resorts—Cannon Beach 1400 S. Hemlock Cannon Beach, OR 97110 *See page 145*	Up to 150 W/R/B/M/	128	Sales Department (888) 448-4449
Hallmark Inns & Resorts—Newport 744 S.W. Elizabeth Newport, OR 97365 *See page 145*	Up to 200 R/B/S/M/	158	Sales Department (888) 448-4449
Holiday Inn Newport at Agate Beach 3019 N. Coast Hwy. Newport, OR 97365	Up to 500 R/B/S/M/	146	Sales Office (800) 546-5010
The Inn at Otter Crest 301 Otter Crest Lp. Otter Rock, OR 97369 *See page 156*	Up to 300 4 rooms R/B/S/M/	120	Marilyn Ebe (800) 326-5806
Inn at Spanish Head 4009 S.W. Hwy 101 Lincoln City, OR 97367	Reception: Up to 200 Sit-down: Up to 150 R/B/S/M/	120	Jeanne Schneider (541) 996-2161 (800) 452-8127 Fax (541) 996-4089
Oregon Coast Aquarium 2820 S.E. Ferry Slip Rd. Newport, OR 97365	Sit-down: Up to 100 Reception: Up to 500 R/B/S/M/		Events Office: (541) 867-3474 ext.5221 Fax (541) 867-6846

W=Wedding Ceremony R=Reception B=Banquet S=Seminar M=Meeting P=Picnic

COASTAL AREA
BANQUET AND EVENT SITE LISTINGS

ADDRESS	CAPACITY	GUEST ROOMS	CONTACT
Seaside Civic & Convention Center 415 First Ave. Seaside, OR 97138	Up to 2,500 R/B/S/M/		Gretchen Darnell (503) 738-8585 (800) 394-3303 Fax (503) 738-0198
Shilo Inn—Lincoln City 1501 N.W. 40th St. Lincoln City, OR 97367	Sit-down: Up to 500 Reception: Up to 642 R/B/S/M/	247	Group Sales (541) 994-6275 (800) 222-2244
Shilo Inn—Newport 536 S.W. Elizabeth St. Newport, OR 97365	Sit-down: Up to 350 Reception: Up to 600 R/B/S/M/	179	Group Sales (541) 265-7701 (800) 222-2244
Shilo Inn—Seaside 30 N. Prom Seaside, OR 97138	Up to 400 R/B/S/M/	112	Group Sales (503) 738-9571 (800) 222-2244
Stephanie Inn P.O. Box 219 Cannon Beach, OR 97110	Up to 15 R/B/S/M/	46	Group Sales (800) 797-4666
Surfsand Resort P.O. Box 219 Cannon Beach, OR 97110	Up to 50 Outdoor: Unlimited R/B/S/M/	82	Jesse Remer Henderson (800) 797-4666 Fax (503) 436-9116
The Westin Salishan Lodge & Golf Resort Hwy 101 Gleneden Beach, OR 97388 *See page 206*	Up to 500 R/B/S/M/	205	Group Sales (800) 890-9316 Fax (503) 764-3510

W=Wedding Ceremony R=Reception B=Banquet S=Seminar M=Meeting P=Picnic

CENTRAL & SOUTHERN OREGON AREA BANQUET AND EVENT SITE LISTINGS

ADDRESS	CAPACITY	GUEST ROOMS	CONTACT
CENTRAL OREGON			
Big K Guest Ranch & Conference Center 20029 Hwy 138 W. Elkton, OR 97436	P/R/B/S/M/	80	Kathie Williamson (800) 390-2445
Black Butte Ranch P.O. Box 8000 Black Butte Ranch, OR 97759	Indoor: Up to 40 Outdoor: Up to 300 R/B/M/		Reservations (800) 452-7455
Eagle Crest Resort 1522 Cline Falls Rd. Redmond, OR 97756	Indoor: Up to 350 R/B/S/M/	100	Sales Department (541) 923-2453 (800) 682-4786
Kah-Nee-Ta Resort P. O. Box K Warm Springs, OR 97761	Indoor: Up to 700 P/R/B/S/M/	170	Sales Department (503) 768-9830
Shilo Inn Bend 3105 O.B. Riley Rd. Bend, OR 97701	Up to 250 R/B/S/M/	151	(800) 222-2244
Mount Bachelor Village 19717 Mt. Bachelor Drive Bend, Oregon 97702	Up to 150 R/B/S/M/	130	Sales Department (800) 452-9846 Fax (541) 388-7820
Rock Springs Guest Ranch & Conference Center 64201 Tyler Rd. Bend, OR 97701	Up to 70 R/B/S/M/	20–50 people	Carole Springer or John Gill (800) 225-3833 Fax (541) 382-7774
Sunriver Resort P.O. Box 3609 Sunriver, OR 97707	Up to 500 R/B/S/M/		Catering Office (541) 593-4605 Fax (541) 593-2742
SOUTHERN OREGON			
The Running Y Ranch Resort 5115 Running Y Rd. Running Y, OR 97601	R/B/S/M/	83	(888) 850-0275
Seven Feathers Casino 146 Chief Milwaleta Lane Canyonville, OR 97417	Up to 1,500 R/B/S/M/	147	Sales & Catering Department (800) 548-8461 Fax (541) 839-4222
Windmill Inn of Ashland 2525 Ashland St. Ashland, OR 97520	Sit-down: Up to 750 R/B/S/M/	230	(541) 482-3010 (800) 333-8310

W=Wedding Ceremony R=Reception B=Banquet S=Seminar M=Meeting P=Picnic

INDEX BY NAME & SUBJECT

A

B

C

G

H

I

J

K

L

M

N

O

P

Q

R

S